AUTOMOTIVE ELECTRICITY AND ELECTRONICS

AUTOMOTIVE ELECTRICITY AND ELECTRONICS

SIXTH EDITION

James D. Halderman

Director of Product Management: Linea Rowe
Product Manager, Trades, Hospitality, & Careers: Derril Trakalo
Senior Analyst, HE Global Content, Trades & Hospitality: Tara Warrens
Analyst, HE Global Content, Careers & Professional: Bridget Daly
Manager Content HE, Careers & Professional: Jenifer Niles
Director, Digital Studio & Content Production: Brian Hyland
Managing Content Producer: Jennifer Sargunar
Managing Producer, Teacher Education & Careers: Autumn Benson
Content Producer (Team Lead): Faraz Sharique Ali
Permissions Editor: Jenell Forschler
Cover Design: Carie Keller, SPi
Cover Credit: Courtesy of ASE; Henrik5000/E+/Getty images
Full-Service Management and Composition: Integra Software Service Pvt. Ltd.
Printer/Binder: LSC Communications, Inc.
Cover Printer: LSC Communications, Inc.
Text Font: Helvetica Neue LT W1G

Library of Congress Cataloging-in-Publication Data

Names: Halderman, James D., author.
Title: Automotive electricity and electronics / James D.
  Halderman.
Description: Sixth edition. | Hoboken, New Jersey : Pearson, 2020. |
  Includes index.
Identifiers: LCCN 2019033309 | ISBN 9780135764428 (paperback) | ISBN 9780135764626 (epub)
Subjects: LCSH: Automobiles—Electric equipment. | Automobiles—Electronic
  equipment. | Automobiles—Electric equipment.—Maintenance and repair. |
  Automobiles—Electronic equipment—Maintenance and repair.
Classification: LCC TL272 .H22256 2020 | DDC 629.25/4—dc23
  LC record available at https://lccn.loc.gov/2019033309

1 2019

ISBN-10:   0-13-576442-4
ISBN-13: 978-0-13-576442-8

BRIEF CONTENTS

chapter 1   Service Information, Work Orders, and Vehicle Identification   1

chapter 2   Tools and Safety   9

chapter 3   Environmental and Hazardous Materials   42

chapter 4   Electrical Fundamentals   53

chapter 5   Electrical Circuits and Ohm's Law   64

chapter 6   Series Circuits   72

chapter 7   Parallel Circuits   79

chapter 8   Series–Parallel Circuits   86

chapter 9   Circuit Testers and Digital Meters   93

chapter 10   Oscilloscopes and Graphing Multimeters   111

chapter 11   Automotive Wiring and Wire Repair   119

chapter 12   Wiring Schematics and Circuit Testing   134

chapter 13   Capacitance and Capacitors   152

chapter 14   Magnetism and Electromagnetism   158

chapter 15   Electronic Fundamentals   171

chapter 16   Computer Fundamentals   189

chapter 17   CAN and Network Communications   197

chapter 18   Batteries   214

chapter 19   Battery Testing and Service   223

chapter 20   Cranking System   238

chapter 21   Cranking System Diagnosis and Service   251

chapter 22   Charging System   266

chapter 23   Charging System Diagnosis and Service   279

chapter 24   Lighting and Signaling Circuits   301

chapter 25   Driver Information and Navigation Systems   321

chapter 26   Security and Anti-Theft Systems   338

chapter 27   Airbag and Pretensioner Circuits   347

chapter 28 Body Electrical Accessories 362

chapter 29 Advanced Driver Assist Systems (ADAS) 392

chapter 30 Audio System Operation and Diagnosis 404

APPENDIX 1
SAMPLE ELECTRICAL (A6) ASE-TYPE CERTIFICATION TEST
WITH ANSWERS 419

APPENDIX 2
2017 ASE CORRELATION CHART 423

GLOSSARY 426

INDEX 438

CONTENTS

chapter 1

SERVICE INFORMATION, WORK ORDERS, AND VEHICLE IDENTIFICATION   1

- Learning Objectives   1
- Key Terms   1
- Owner's Manuals   1
- Service Information   2
- Technical Service Bulletins   2
- Recalls and Campaigns   2
- Work Order   3
- Service Records   3
- Additional Information   5
- Parts of a Vehicle   5
- Front-Wheel Drive Versus Rear-Wheel Drive   5
- Vehicle Identification   5
- Vehicle Safety Certification Label   7
- VECI Label   7

SUMMARY   7
REVIEW QUESTIONS   8
CHAPTER QUIZ   8

chapter 2

TOOLS AND SAFETY   9

- Learning Objectives   9
- Key Terms   9
- Threaded Fasteners   9
- Hand Tools   13
- Screwdrivers   16
- Torx   17
- Pliers   19
- Basic Hand Tool List   22
- Tool Sets and Accessories   23
- Electrical Hand Tools   23
- Hand Tool Maintenance   25
- Trouble Lights   25
- Air and Electrically Operated Tools   25
- Personal Protective Equipment   27
- Safety Precautions   28
- Vehicle Protection   29
- Safety Lifting (Hoisting) a Vehicle   29
- Jacks and Safety Stands   31
- Drive-on Ramps   31
- Electrical Cord Safety   32
- Jump Starting and Battery Safety   32
- Fire Extinguishers   33
- Fire Blankets   34
- First Aid and Eye Wash Stations   34
- Hybrid Electric Vehicle Safety Issues   35

SUMMARY   40
REVIEW QUESTIONS   40
CHAPTER QUIZ   40

chapter 3

ENVIRONMENTAL AND HAZARDOUS MATERIALS   42

- Learning Objectives   42
- Key Terms   42
- Hazardous Waste   42
- Federal and State Laws   42
- Asbestos Hazards   44
- Used Brake Fluid   45
- Used Oil   45
- Solvents   46
- Coolant Disposal   47
- Lead-Acid Battery Waste   48
- Fuel Safety and Storage   48
- Airbag Handling   49
- Used Tire Disposal   49
- Air-Conditioning Refrigerant Oil Disposal   50

SUMMARY   52
REVIEW QUESTIONS   52
CHAPTER QUIZ   52

chapter 4

ELECTRICAL FUNDAMENTALS   53

- Learning Objectives   53
- Key Terms   53
- Introduction   53
- Electricity   53
- How Electrons Move Through a Conductor   56
- Units of Electricity   57
- Sources of Electricity   59
- Conductors and Resistance   60
- Resistors   61

SUMMARY   62
REVIEW QUESTIONS   62
CHAPTER QUIZ   63

chapter 5
ELECTRICAL CIRCUITS AND OHM'S LAW 64

- Learning Objectives 64
- Key Terms 64
- Circuits 64
- Circuit Fault Types 65
- Ohm's Law 67
- Watt's Law 69

SUMMARY 70
REVIEW QUESTIONS 70
CHAPTER QUIZ 71

chapter 6
SERIES CIRCUITS 72

- Learning Objectives 72
- Key Terms 72
- Series Circuits 72
- Ohm's Law and Series Circuits 72
- Kirchhoff's Voltage Law 73
- Voltage Drops 74
- Series Circuit Laws 75
- Series Circuit Examples 76

SUMMARY 77
REVIEW QUESTIONS 77
CHAPTER QUIZ 78

chapter 7
PARALLEL CIRCUITS 79

- Learning Objectives 79
- Key Terms 79
- Parallel Circuits 79
- Kirchhoff's Current Law 79
- Parallel Circuit Laws 80
- Determining Total Resistance in a Parallel Circuit 80
- Parallel Circuit Calculation Examples 83

SUMMARY 84
REVIEW QUESTIONS 84
CHAPTER QUIZ 85

chapter 8
SERIES–PARALLEL CIRCUITS 86

- Learning Objectives 86
- Key Terms 86
- Series–Parallel Circuits 86
- Solving Series–Parallel Circuit Calculation Problems 87
- Series–Parallel Circuit Calculation Examples 87

SUMMARY 89
REVIEW QUESTIONS 89
CHAPTER QUIZ 89

chapter 9
CIRCUIT TESTERS AND DIGITAL METERS 93

- Learning Objectives 93
- Key Terms 93
- Fused Jumper Wire 93
- Test Lights 94
- Logic Probe 95
- Digital Multimeters 95
- Inductive Ammeters 99
- Diode Check, Duty Cycle, and Frequency 100
- Electrical Unit Prefixes 101
- How to Read Digital Meters 102

SUMMARY 110
REVIEW QUESTIONS 110
CHAPTER QUIZ 110

chapter 10
OSCILLOSCOPES AND GRAPHING MULTIMETERS 111

- Learning Objectives 111
- Key Terms 111
- Types of Oscilloscopes 111
- Scope Setup and Adjustments 112
- AC Voltage 113
- DC and AC Coupling 113
- Pulse Trains 114
- Number of Channels 114
- Triggers 114
- Using a Scope 115
- Graphing Multimeter 117
- Graphing Scan Tools 117

SUMMARY 118
REVIEW QUESTIONS 118
CHAPTER QUIZ 118

chapter 11
AUTOMOTIVE WIRING AND WIRE REPAIR 119

- Learning Objectives 119
- Key Terms 119
- Automotive Wiring 119
- Ground Wires 121
- Battery Cables 121
- Jumper Cables 122

- Fuses and Circuit Protection Devices   122
- Terminals and Connectors   128
- Wire Repair   129
- Electrical Conduit   131

SUMMARY   132
REVIEW QUESTIONS   133
CHAPTER QUIZ   133

chapter 12
WIRING SCHEMATICS AND CIRCUIT TESTING   134

- Learning Objectives   134
- Key Terms   134
- Wiring Schematics and Symbols   134
- Schematic Symbols   135
- Relay Terminal Identification   140
- Locating an Open Circuit   143
- Common Power or Ground   144
- Circuit Troubleshooting Procedure   145
- Locating a Short Circuit   145
- Electrical Troubleshooting Guide   148
- Step-by-Step Troubleshooting Procedure   149

SUMMARY   150
REVIEW QUESTIONS   150
CHAPTER QUIZ   150

chapter 13
CAPACITANCE AND CAPACITORS   152

- Learning Objectives   152
- Key Terms   152
- Capacitance   152
- Capacitor Construction and Operation   152
- Factors of Capacitance   155
- Uses for Capacitors   155
- Capacitors in Circuits   156

SUMMARY   157
REVIEW QUESTIONS   157
CHAPTER QUIZ   157

chapter 14
MAGNETISM AND ELECTROMAGNETISM   158

- Learning Objectives   158
- Key Terms   158
- Fundamentals of Magnetism   158
- Electromagnetism   160
- Uses of Electromagnetism   162

- Electromagnetic Induction   165
- Ignition Coils   166
- Electromagnetic Interference   168

SUMMARY   169
REVIEW QUESTIONS   169
CHAPTER QUIZ   169

chapter 15
ELECTRONIC FUNDAMENTALS   171

- Learning Objectives   171
- Key Terms   171
- Semiconductors   171
- Summary of Semiconductors   172
- Diodes   173
- Zener Diodes   174
- High-Voltage Spike Protection   174
- Diode Ratings   176
- Light-Emitting Diodes   176
- Photodiodes   177
- Photoresistors   177
- Silicon-Controlled Rectifiers   178
- Thermistors   178
- Rectifier Bridges   178
- Transistors   179
- Field-Effect Transistors   180
- Phototransistors   181
- Integrated Circuits   181
- Transistor Gates   182
- Operational Amplifiers   182
- Electronic Component Failure Causes   183
- How to Test Diodes and Transistors   184
- Converters and Inverters   185
- Electrostatic Discharge   186

SUMMARY   187
REVIEW QUESTIONS   187
CHAPTER QUIZ   187

chapter 16
COMPUTER FUNDAMENTALS   189

- Learning Objectives   189
- Key Terms   189
- Computer Fundamentals   189
- Computer Functions   189
- Digital Computers   191
- Computer Input Sensors   193
- Computer Outputs   193

SUMMARY   195
REVIEW QUESTIONS   196
CHAPTER QUIZ   196

chapter 17

CAN AND NETWORK COMMUNICATIONS   197

- Learning Objectives   197
- Key Terms   197
- Module Communications and Networks   197
- Network Fundamentals   197
- Module Communications Configuration   199
- Network Communications Classifications   199
- General Motors Communications Protocols   200
- Ford Network Communications Protocols   203
- Chrysler Communications Protocols   203
- Controller Area Network   205
- Honda/Toyota Communications   206
- European Bus Communications   207
- Network Communications Diagnosis   208
- OBD-II Data Link Connector   211

SUMMARY   212
REVIEW QUESTIONS   212
CHAPTER QUIZ   213

chapter 18

BATTERIES   214

- Learning Objectives   214
- Key Terms   214
- Introduction   214
- Battery Construction   214
- How a Battery Works   217
- Specific Gravity   217
- Battery Construction Types   218
- Causes and Types of Battery Failure   219
- Battery Ratings   220
- Battery Sizes   221

SUMMARY   221
REVIEW QUESTIONS   222
CHAPTER QUIZ   222

chapter 19

BATTERY TESTING AND SERVICE   223

- Learning Objectives   223
- Key Terms   223
- Battery Service Safety Considerations   223
- Symptoms of a Weak or Defective battery   223
- Battery Maintenance   224
- Battery Voltage Test   225
- Hydrometer Testing   226
- Battery Load Testing   226
- Electronic Conductance Testing   227
- Battery Charging   228

- Battery Charge Time   230
- Float-Type Battery Chargers   230
- Jump Starting   231
- Battery Electrical Drain Test   231
- Maintaining Electronic Memory Functions   233
- Battery Symptom Guide   235

SUMMARY   236
REVIEW QUESTIONS   236
CHAPTER QUIZ   236

chapter 20

CRANKING SYSTEM   238

- Learning Objectives   238
- Key Terms   238
- Cranking Circuit   238
- Computer-Controlled Starting   239
- Starter Motor Operation   240
- How the Starter Motor Works   242
- Gear-Reduction Starters   245
- Starter Drives   245
- Starter Solenoids   247
- Stop-Start Systems   248

SUMMARY   249
REVIEW QUESTIONS   249
CHAPTER QUIZ   250

chapter 21

CRANKING SYSTEM DIAGNOSIS AND SERVICE   251

- Learning Objectives   251
- Key Terms   251
- Starting System Troubleshooting Procedure   251
- Voltage Drop Testing   252
- Control Circuit Testing   254
- Starter Amperage Test   254
- Starter Removal   255
- Starter Motor Service   255
- Bench Testing   257
- Starter Installation   257
- Starter Drive-to-Flywheel Clearance   257
- Starting System Symptom Guide   259

SUMMARY   264
REVIEW QUESTIONS   264
CHAPTER QUIZ   264

chapter 22

CHARGING SYSTEM   266

- Learning Objectives   266
- Key Terms   266

- Principle of Alternator Operation   266
- Alternator Construction   266
- Alternator Overrunning Pulleys   267
- Alternator Components and Operation   269
- How an Alternator Works   271
- Alternator Output Factors   272
- Alternator Voltage Regulation   273
- Alternator Cooling   274
- Computer-Controlled Charging Systems   275

SUMMARY   277
REVIEW QUESTIONS   277
CHAPTER QUIZ   277

chapter 23
CHARGING SYSTEM DIAGNOSIS AND SERVICE   279

- Learning Objectives   279
- Key Terms   279
- Charging System Testing and Service   279
- Drive Belt Inspection and Adjustment   281
- AC Ripple Voltage Check   282
- Testing AC Ripple Current   284
- Charging System Voltage Drop Testing   285
- Alternator Output Test   286
- Minimum Required Alternator Output   286
- Alternator Removal   287
- Alternator Disassembly   288
- Testing the Rectifier   290
- Reassembling the Alternator   290
- Remanufactured Alternators   291
- Alternator Installation   291

SUMMARY   299
REVIEW QUESTIONS   299
CHAPTER QUIZ   299

chapter 24
LIGHTING AND SIGNALING CIRCUITS   301

- Learning Objectives   301
- Key Terms   301
- Lighting Systems   301
- LED Lighting   302
- Bulb Numbers   304
- Brake Lights   305
- Turn Signals   305
- Daytime Running Lights   308
- Headlights   308
- High-Intensity Discharge Headlights   309

- LED Headlights   312
- Adaptive Front Lighting System   312
- Automatic Headlights   313
- Headlight High/Low Beam Switch   314
- Auto Dimming Headlights   314
- Headlight Aiming   314
- Fog and Driving Lights   314
- Automatic Dimming Mirrors   314
- Courtesy Lights   316
- Illuminated Entry   316
- Headlight System Diagnosis   317
- Lighting System Diagnosis   317
- Lighting System Symptom Guide   318

SUMMARY   320
REVIEW QUESTIONS   320
CHAPTER QUIZ   320

chapter 25
DRIVER INFORMATION AND NAVIGATION SYSTEMS   321

- Learning Objectives   321
- Key Terms   321
- Dash Warning Symbols   321
- Steering Wheel Controls   322
- Voice Activation   322
- Maintenance Indicators   323
- Analog and Digital Displays   323
- Head-up Display   324
- Night Vision   325
- Electronic Displays   326
- Virtual Display   327
- Touch Screens   327
- Speedometers/Odometers   328
- Dash Gauges   330
- Navigation and GPS   331
- Telematics   333
- Backup Camera   335

SUMMARY   336
REVIEW QUESTIONS   336
CHAPTER QUIZ   336

chapter 26
SECURITY AND ANTI-THEFT SYSTEMS   338

- Learning Objectives   338
- Key Terms   338
- Vehicle Security Systems   338
- Immobilizer Systems   339
- Chrysler Immobilizer System   341

- Ford PATS System   341
- General Motors Antitheft System   342
- Testing Immobilizer Systems   343

SUMMARY   345
REVIEW QUESTIONS   345
CHAPTER QUIZ   345

chapter 27
AIRBAG AND PRETENSIONER CIRCUITS   347
- Learning Objectives   347
- Key Terms   347
- Safety Belts and Retractors   347
- Front Airbags   349
- Airbag Diagnosis Tools and Equipment   353
- Airbag System Service   355
- Driver Side Airbag Module Replacement   356
- Safety When Manually Deploying Airbags   356
- Occupant Detection Systems   357
- Seat and Side Curtain Airbags   359
- Event Data Recorders   359

SUMMARY   360
REVIEW QUESTIONS   360
CHAPTER QUIZ   360

chapter 28
BODY ELECTRICAL ACCESSORIES   362
- Learning Objectives   362
- Key Terms   362
- Horns   362
- Horn Diagnosis   363
- Windshield Wipers   364
- Windshield Washers   366
- Rain-Sense Wipers   369
- Blower Motor   370
- Cruise Control   372
- Heated Rear Window Defoggers   373
- Power Windows   375
- Electric Power Door Locks   377
- Trunk/Lift Gate Locks   380
- Power Sun Roof/Moon Roof   380
- Sun Shades   380
- Power Seats   381
- Electrically Heated Seats   383
- Heated and Cooled Seats   383
- Heated Steering Wheel   384
- Heated Mirrors   385
- Adjustable Pedals   385
- Folding Outside Mirrors   386
- Keyless Entry   386
- Garage Door Opener   388
- Remote Start   389

SUMMARY   390
REVIEW QUESTIONS   390
CHAPTER QUIZ   390

Chapter 29
ADVANCED DRIVER ASSIST SYSTEMS (ADAS)   392
- Learning Objectives   392
- Key Terms   392
- Advanced Driver Assist Systems   392
- Blind Spot Monitor   393
- Parking-Assist Systems   394
- Lane Departure Warning   395
- Lane Keep Assist   395
- Adaptive Cruise Control   396
- Rear Cross-Traffic Warning (RCTW)   398
- Automatic Emergency Braking   398
- Pre-Collision System   399
- Hill Start Assist   399
- ADAS Diagnosis   400
- Camera and Radar Sensor Calibration   400

SUMMARY   402
REVIEW QUESTIONS   403
CHAPTER QUIZ   403

chapter 30
AUDIO SYSTEM OPERATION AND DIAGNOSIS   404
- Learning Objectives   404
- Key Terms   404
- Audio Fundamentals   404
- Radios and Receivers   406
- Antennas   406
- Antenna Diagnosis   407
- Speakers   408
- Speaker Types   410
- Sound Levels   410
- Crossovers   411
- Aftermarket Sound System Upgrade   411
- Voice Recognition   413
- Bluetooth   413
- Satellite Radio   414
- Radio Interference   415

SUMMARY 418
REVIEW QUESTIONS 418
CHAPTER QUIZ 418

appendix 1
Sample Electrical (A6) ASE-Type Certification Test with
Answers 419

appendix 2
2017 ASE Correlation Chart 423

GLOSSARY 426

INDEX 438

PREFACE

NEW TO THIS EDITION. Based on the suggestions and recommendations from automotive instructors and reviewers, the following changes have been made to the sixth edition:

1. The number of chapters has been increased from 28 to 30 making it easier to select the exact content to study or teach.
2. The content in each chapter has been updated and expanded with over 40 new full color photos and line drawings to make the subject come alive.
3. The beginning chapters are more concisely organized making learning electrical systems easier. For example, the first chapter has been expanded and then divided into two shorter chapters:

   - **Chapter 1**—Service Information, Work Orders, and Vehicle Identification
   - **Chapter 2**—Tools and Safety

4. All of the electrical accessory circuits have been expanded so that it meets all of the latest ASE tasks and then divided into three chapters including:

   - **Chapter 26**—Security and Anti-Theft Systems
   - **Chapter 28**—Body Electrical Accessories
   - **Chapter 29**—Advanced Driver Assist Systems

5. New Case Studies included in this edition covering the "three Cs" (Complaint, Cause, and Correction).
6. New OSHA hazardous chemical labeling requirements added to Chapter 3 (Environmental and Hazardous Materials).
7. Static electricity and lightning information added to Chapter 4 (Electrical Fundamentals)
8. New content on three-legged and low-profile fuses, plus smart junction boxes, added to Chapter 11 (Automotive Wiring and Wire Repair).
9. Enhanced lead–acid batteries (ELA) information added to Chapter 18 (Batteries).

10. New content on float-type battery charges and memory saver tool that uses a 12-volt battery to connect to the power (terminal 16) and ground (terminals 4 and 5) of the DLC added to chapter 19 (Battery Testing and Service).
11. Stop-start and push-button start system added to Chapter 20 (Cranking Systems).
12. Cloudy headlight restoration information added to Chapter 24 (Lighting and Signaling Circuits).
13. Dash warning symbols (122 of them) added to Chapter 25 (Driver Information and Navigation Systems).
14. Airbag inflator sequences of inflation added to Chapter 27 (Airbags and Pretensioners).

ASE CORRELATED ASE-certified programs need to demonstrate that they use course material that covers ASE tasks. All *Professional Technician* textbooks have been correlated to the appropriate ASE task lists.

A COMPLETE INSTRUCTOR AND STUDENT SUPPLEMENTS PACKAGE All *Professional Technician* textbooks are accompanied by a full set of instructor and student supplements. Please see page xvi for a detailed list of supplements.

A FOCUS ON DIAGNOSIS AND PROBLEM SOLVING The Professional Technician Series has been developed to satisfy the need for a greater emphasis on problem diagnosis. Automotive instructors and service managers agree that students and beginning technicians need more training in diagnostic procedures and skill development. To meet this need and demonstrate how real-world problems are solved, the Case Study features are included throughout and highlight how real-life problems are diagnosed and repaired.

The following pages highlight the unique core features that set the Professional Technician Series book apart from other automotive textbooks.

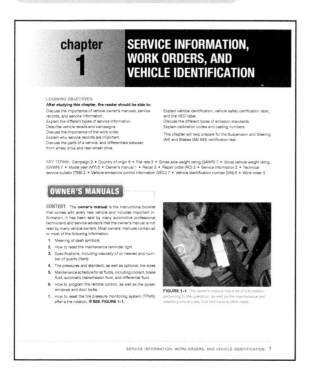

LEARNING OBJECTIVES AND KEY TERMS appear at the beginning of each chapter to help students and instructors focus on the most important material in each chapter. The chapter objectives are based on specific ASE and NATEF tasks.

Safety Tip

Shop Cloth Disposal

Always dispose of oily shop cloths in an enclosed container to prevent a fire. ● **SEE FIGURE 1–69.** Whenever oily cloths are thrown together on the floor or workbench, a chemical reaction can occur, which can ignite the cloth even without an open flame. This process of ignition without an open flame is called **spontaneous combustion.**

SAFETY TIPS alert students to possible hazards on the job and how to avoid them.

TECH TIP

It Just Takes a Second

Whenever removing any automotive component, it is wise to screw the bolts back into the holes a couple of threads by hand. This ensures that the right bolt will be used in its original location when the component or part is put back on the vehicle.

TECH TIPS feature real world advice and "tricks of the trade" from ASE-certified master technicians.

CASE STUDY

Lightning Damage

A radio failed to work in a vehicle that was outside during a thunderstorm. The technician checked the fuses and verified that power was reaching the radio. Both the radio and the antenna were replaced to correct the problem. ● **SEE FIGURE 28–26.**

Summary:

- **Complaint**—Customer stated that the radio did not work.
- **Cause**—Visual inspection showed an antenna that had been stuck by lightning.
- **Correction**—Replacing the radio and the antenna restored proper operation.

CASE STUDY present students with actual automotive scenarios and show how these common (and sometimes uncommon) problems were diagnosed and repaired.

? FREQUENTLY ASKED QUESTION

How Many Types of Screw Heads Are Used in Automotive Applications?

There are many, including Torx, hex (also called Allen), plus many others used in custom vans and motor homes. ● SEE FIGURE 1–9.

FREQUENTLY ASKED QUESTIONS are based on the author's own experience and provide answers to many of the most common questions asked by students and beginning service technicians.

Note: Claw hammer has a claw used to remove nails; therefore, it is not for automotive service.

NOTES provide students with additional technical information to give them a greater understanding of a specific task or procedure.

CAUTION: Do not use a screwdriver as a pry tool or chisel. Screwdrivers use hardened steel only at the tip and are not designed to be pounded on or used for prying because they could bend easily. Always use the proper tool for each application.

CAUTIONS alert students about potential damage to the vehicle that can occur during a specific task or service procedure.

 WARNING

Do not use incandescent trouble lights around gasoline or other flammable liquids. The liquids can cause the bulb to break and the hot filament can ignite the flammable liquid, which can cause personal injury or even death.

WARNINGS alert students about potential dangers to themselves during a specific task or service procedure.

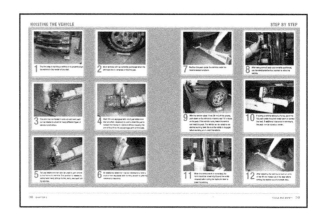

STEP-BY-STEP photo sequences show in detail the steps involved in performing a specific task or service procedure.

SUMMARY

1. Bolts, studs, and nuts are commonly used as fasteners in the chassis. The sizes for fractional and metric threads are different and are not interchangeable. The grade is the rating of the strength of a fastener.
2. Whenever a vehicle is raised above the ground, it must be supported at a substantial section of the body or frame.
3. Wrenches are available in open end, box end, and combination open and box end.
4. An adjustable wrench should only be used where the proper size is not available.
5. Line wrenches are also called flare-nut wrenches, fitting wrenches, or tube-nut wrenches and are used to remove fuel or refrigerant lines.
6. Sockets are rotated by a ratchet or breaker bar, also called a flex handle.
7. Torque wrenches measure the amount of torque applied to a fastener.
8. Screwdriver types include straight blade (flat tip) and Phillips.
9. Hammers and mallets come in a variety of sizes and weights.
10. Pliers are a useful tool and are available in many different types, including slip-joint, multigroove, linesman's, diagonal, needle-nose, and locking pliers.
11. Other common hand tools include snap-ring pliers, files, cutters, punches, chisels, and hacksaws.
12. Hybrid electric vehicles should be de-powered if any of the high-voltage components are going to be serviced.

REVIEW QUESTIONS

1. Why are wrenches offset 15 degrees?
2. What are the other names for a line wrench?
3. What are the standard automotive drive sizes for sockets?
4. Which type of screwdriver requires the use of a hammer or mallet?
5. What is inside a dead-blow hammer?

CHAPTER QUIZ

1. The correct location for the pads when hoisting or jacking the vehicle can often be found in the _____.
   a. service manual
   b. shop manual
   c. owner's manual
   d. all of the above
2. For the best working position, the work should be _____.
   a. at neck or head level
   b. at knee or ankle level
   c. overhead by about 1 foot
   d. at chest or elbow level
3. A high-strength bolt is identified by _____.
   a. a UNC symbol
   b. lines on the head
   c. strength letter codes
   d. the coarse threads
4. A fastener that uses threads on both ends is called a _____.
   a. cap screw
   b. stud
   c. machine screw
   d. crest fastener
5. Wrenches are made from _____.
   a. cast from nickel steel
   b. forged alloy steel
   c. machined from billet steel
   d. cast from chrome steel
6. The proper term for Channel Locks is _____.
   a. Vise Grips
   b. crescent wrench
   c. locking pliers
   d. multigroove adjustable pliers
7. The proper term for Vise Grips is _____.
   a. locking pliers
   b. slip-joint pliers
   c. side cuts
   d. multigroove adjustable pliers

THE SUMMARY, REVIEW QUESTIONS, AND CHAPTER QUIZ at the end of each chapter help students review the material presented in the chapter and test themselves to see how much they've learned.

SUPPLEMENTS

RESOURCES IN PRINT AND ONLINE
Automotive Electricity and Electronics

NAME OF SUPPLEMENT	PRINT	ONLINE	AUDIENCE	DESCRIPTION
Instructor Resource Manual 0135764394		✔	Instructors	NEW! The Ultimate teaching aid: Chapter summaries, key terms, chapter learning objectives, lecture resources, discuss/demonstrate classroom activities, and answers to the in-text review and quiz questions.
TestGen 0135764580		✔	Instructors	Test generation software and test bank for the text.
PowerPoint Presentation 0135764475		✔	Instructors	Slides include chapter learning objectives, lecture outline of the text, and graphics from the book.
Image Bank 0135764467		✔	Instructors	All of the images and graphs from the textbook to create customized lecture slides.
ASE Correlated Task Sheets—for Instructors 0135764602		✔	Instructors	Downloadable ASE task sheets for easy customization and development of unique task sheets.
ASE Correlated Task Sheets—for Students 0135764564	✔		Students	Study activity manual that correlates ASE Automobile Standards to chapters and pages numbers in the text. Available to students at a discounted price when packaged with the text.
VitalSource eText 0134074890		✔	Students	An alternative to purchasing the print textbook, students can subscribe to the same content online and save up to 50% off the suggested list price of the print text. Visit **www.vitalsource.com**

All online resources can be downloaded from the Instructor's Resource Center: **www.pearsonhighered.com/irc**

ACKNOWLEDGMENTS

A large number of people and organizations have cooperated in providing the reference material and technical information used in this text. The author wishes to express sincere thanks to the following for their special contributions:

ASE
Automotion, Inc.
Automotive Parts Rebuilders Association (APRA)
Dr. John Kershaw, Criterion Technical Education
  Consultants
Dave Scaler, Mechanics Education Association
Graphic Home
Jeff Trick, Wright State University
John Thornton, Autotrain Inc.
Mark Warren, Society of Automotive Engineers (SAE)
Tom Birch, Toyota Motor Sales, USA, Inc.
Wurth USA, Inc.

TECHNICAL AND CONTENT REVIEWERS The following people reviewed the past and current edition's manuscripts before production and checked them for technical accuracy and clarity of presentation. Their suggestions and recommendations were included in the final draft of the manuscript. Their input helped make this textbook clear and technically accurate while maintaining the easy-to-read style that has made other books from the same author so popular.

Jim Anderson
Greenville High School
Brett Baird
Salt Lake Community College
Tyler Boyles
Illinois Eastern Community College
Victor Bridges
Umpqua Community College
Dr. Roger Donovan
Illinois Central College
C. Durdin
Moraine Park Technical College
Gerry Egan
Wake Tech Community College
Al Engledahl
College of Dupage
Aaron Gregory
Merced College
Larry Hagelberger
Upper Valley Joint Vocational School
Oldrick Hajzler
Red River College

Paul Hidy
Solano Community College
Betsy Hoffman
Vermont Technical College
Richard Krieger
Michigan Institute of Technology
Steven T. Lee
Lincoln Technical Institute
Carlton H. Mabe, Sr.
Virginia Western Community College
Roy Marks
Owens Community College
Tony Martin
University of Alaska Southeast
Kerry Meier
San Juan College
Jim Morton
Automotive Training Center (ATC)
Fritz Peacock
Indiana Vocational Technical College
Greg Pfahl
Miami-Jacobs Career College
Dennis Peter
NAIT (Canada)
Kenneth Redick
Hudson Valley Community College
Douglas Redman
College of the Desert
Jeff Rehkopf
Florida State College
Steve Scheuler
State Technical College of Missouri
John Skupien
Rock Valley College
Mark Spisak
Central Piedmont Community College
Mitchell Walker
St. Louis Community College at Forest Park
Jennifer Wise
Sinclair Community College

Special thanks to instructional designer Alexis I. Skriloff James.

The author wishes to thank Chuck Taylor of Sinclair Community College in Dayton, Ohio, and Jeff Trick, who helped with many of the photos. A special thanks to Carl Borsani for his help with many of the new figures used in this edition. Most of all, I wish to thank Michelle Halderman for her assistance in all phases of manuscript preparation.

—James D. Halderman

ABOUT THE AUTHOR

JIM HALDERMAN brings a world of experience, knowledge, and talent to his work. His automotive service experience includes working as a flat-rate technician, a business owner, and a professor of automotive technology at a leading U.S. community college for more than 20 years.

He has a Bachelor of Science Degree from Ohio Northern University and a Masters Degree in Education from Miami University in Oxford, Ohio. Jim also holds a U.S. Patent for an electronic transmission control device. He is an ASE-certified Master Automotive Technician (A1–A8), plus A9, F1, G1, L1 and L3).

Jim is the author of many automotive textbooks, all published by Pearson Education.

He has presented numerous technical seminars to national audiences including the California Automotive Teachers (CAT) and the Illinois College Automotive Instructor Association (ICAIA). He is also a member and presenter at the North American Council of Automotive Teachers (NACAT). Jim was also named Regional Teacher of the Year by General Motors Corporation and a member of the advisory committee for the department of technology at Ohio Northern University and named MVP at the North American Council of Automotive Teachers (NACAT) conference in 2013.

Jim and his wife, Michelle, live in Dayton, Ohio. They have two children. You can reach Jim at

jim@jameshalderman.com

AUTOMOTIVE ELECTRICITY AND ELECTRONICS

chapter 1

SERVICE INFORMATION, WORK ORDERS, AND VEHICLE IDENTIFICATION

LEARNING OBJECTIVES:

After studying this chapter, the reader should be able to:

Discuss the importance of vehicle owner's manuals, service records, and service information.

Explain the different types of service information.

Describe vehicle recalls and campaigns.

Discuss the importance of the work order.

Explain why service records are important.

Discuss the parts of a vehicle, and differentiate between front-wheel drive and rear-wheel drive.

Explain vehicle identification, vehicle safety certification label, and the VECI label.

This chapter will help prepare for the Suspension and Steering (A4) and Brakes (A5) ASE certification test.

KEY TERMS: Campaign 2 • Country of origin 6 • Flat rate 3 • Gross axle weight rating (GAWR) 7 • Gross vehicle weight rating (GVWR) 7 • Model year (MY) 6 • Owner's manual 1 • Recall 2 • Repair order (RO) 3 • Service information 2 • Technical service bulletin (TSB) 2 • Vehicle emissions control information (VECI) 7 • Vehicle identification number (VIN) 6 • Work order 3

OWNER'S MANUALS

CONTENT The **owner's manual** is the instructional booklet that comes with every new vehicle and includes important information. It has been said by many automotive professional technicians and service advisors that the owner's manual is not read by many vehicle owners. Most owners' manuals contain all or most of the following information.

1. Meaning of dash symbols
2. How to reset the maintenance reminder light
3. Specifications, including viscosity of oil needed and number of quarts (liters)
4. Tire pressures and standard, as well as optional, tire sizes
5. Maintenance schedule for all fluids, including coolant, brake fluid, automatic transmission fluid, and differential fluid
6. How to program the remote control, as well as the power windows and door locks
7. How to reset the tire pressure monitoring system (TPMS) after a tire rotation. ● **SEE FIGURE 1–1.**

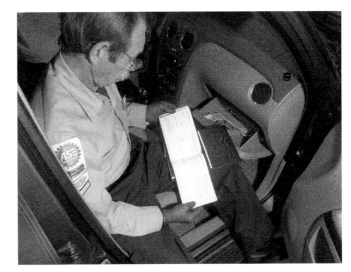

FIGURE 1–1 The owner's manual has a lot of information pertaining to the operation, as well as the maintenance and resetting procedures, that technicians often need.

SERVICE INFORMATION

PURPOSE OF SERVICE INFORMATION **Service information** is needed to correctly service or repair vehicles because it contains all of the specifications, as well as the specified procedures to follow when servicing or repairing a vehicle.

FACTORY SERVICE INFORMATION Until the 1990s, most service information was found in paper manuals called *service manuals* or *shop manuals*. More recently, the manufacturer provides this information in a digital format. The most comprehensive and accurate service information is the service information from the vehicle manufacturer. This information is available for most, if not all, vehicles and can be purchased from their website. For the exact location for purchasing factory service information, visit National Automotive Service Task Force (NASTF) website for the websites for all vehicle manufacturers' service information and cost: www.NASTF.org.

AFTERMARKET SERVICE INFORMATION While factory service manuals cover just one year and one or more models of the same vehicle, most aftermarket service manuals cover multiple years and/or models in one manual. Originally, aftermarket service information was available in only paper manuals. Paper service manuals had the following disadvantages:

1. Required a lot of storage space
2. The pages would become dirty from handling
3. Difficult to use at the vehicle or to make copies from the thick manuals

Paper service manuals were replaced with electronic service information that came on CDs and then DVDs, before becoming available on the Internet. Most electronic service information has technical service bulletins (TSBs), wiring diagrams, and a main menu that includes the major components of the vehicle as a starting point. ALLDATA and Mitchell On-Demand are examples of commonly used subscription services that include service information for many vehicles. ● **SEE FIGURE 1–2.**

 **TECH TIP**

Print It Out

It is often a benefit to have the written instructions or schematics (wiring diagrams) at the vehicle while diagnosing or performing a repair. The advantage of electronic service information is that the material can be printed out and taken to the vehicle for easy access. This also allows the service technician to write or draw on the printed copy, which can be a big help when performing tests, such as electrical system measurements. The schematic can be color-coded to show where there should be voltage and where a ground should be detected. These notes can then be used to document the test results on the work order.

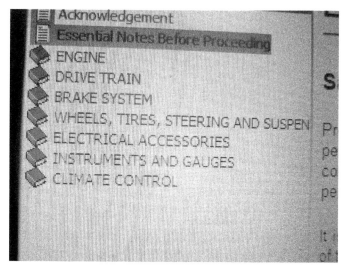

FIGURE 1–2 A main menu showing the major systems of the vehicle. Clicking on one of these major topics opens up another menu showing more detailed information.

TECHNICAL SERVICE BULLETINS

A **technical service bulletin (TSB)** is issued by the vehicle manufacturer to notify service technicians of a potential problem or other critical information. The TSB may include diagnostic procedures and the necessary corrective action. TSBs are not an authorization for repair or a guarantee to correct a concern. TSBs are designed for dealership technicians, but are republished by aftermarket companies and made available along with other service information to shops and vehicle repair facilities.

RECALLS AND CAMPAIGNS

A **campaign** is typically issued when a manufacturer wants to improve a product's performance or increase the customer's satisfaction. If the campaign involves a safety or emissions concern, it is considered a recall. A **recall** can occur when either the manufacturer or the National Highway Traffic Safety Administration (NHTSA) determines there is a concern. A recall or campaign is issued by a vehicle manufacturer and a notice is sent to all owners of record. While these faults may be repaired by independent shops, it is generally handled by a local dealer and treated as a warranty repair. Items that have created recalls in the past have included potential fuel system leakage problems, exhaust leakage, or electrical malfunctions that could cause a possible fire or the engine to stall. Unlike TSBs, whose cost is only covered when the vehicle is within the warranty period, a recall or campaign is always done at no cost to the vehicle owner regardless of the age or mileage on the vehicle. To check if a vehicle is subject to a recall, visit www.nhtsa.gov/recalls.

The site is free and requires that the vehicle identification number (VIN) be entered to get access to the data base.

WORK ORDER

SERVICE ADVISOR DOCUMENTATION The **work order**, also called a **repair order (RO)**, is a legal document that is signed by the vehicle owner or his/her representative. Historically, the RO has been a paper document. However, more recently, many repair facilities have switched to using an electronic RO. The service advisor or the person designated to complete the work order has to include the following information:

- Make, model, and year and other identifying information, such as color and vehicle identification number (VIN)
- Name and address of the owner with contact information, such as the cell phone number and email address
- Date of service and the name of the person who wrote the service invoice
- The miles shown on the odometer
- Estimate amount and list of requested work

All professional service facilities and shops use a form that is designed for their purposes and include all of the required information, as specified by the local area and state. The work order is a legal document because it is basically a contract between the owner of the vehicle and the shop. If the invoice is not paid, a lien can be placed on the vehicle and it will not be released to the owner until the bill is paid. If the bill is not paid, the ownership of the vehicle can be transferred to the shop. Because this document is so important, all work performed on the vehicle should be clearly stated, including any measured values along with the specified values from service information. Also listed on the service invoice (work or repair order) are the parts used and their costs.

SERVICE TECHNICIAN DOCUMENTATION The role of the service technician is to not only perform the services and repairs as requested by the vehicle owner, but also to document the work order so that an accurate record of what was performed and the parts used on the work order. The service technician is usually identified by a technician number and the number is included under each operation that was performed by the shop. For example, there may be more than one technician assigned to one vehicle and the number of the technician who performed each operation is documented. This is commonly used where the oil change is performed by the lube technician, while the electrical diagnosis and repair was performed by another service technician. The technician should document the work order by stating not only what was done, but what service tools were used such as:

1. Verified the customer concern of a rough running engine and the "check engine light" was on by visual inspection.
2. Looked for stored diagnostic trouble codes using a factory scan tool and noted that a P0300 (random misfire detected) was set.

3. Performed a visual inspection of the secondary ignition system components.
4. Found evidence of a coil boot that arced to the cylinder head on cylinders 2 and 3. Recommended the replacement of the coils and boots for cylinders 2 and 3. The technician also stated on the work order that the coils and the boots on the other cylinder may need to be replaced too, because they are all operating under the same operating conditions. ● **SEE FIGURE 1–3.**

PARTS DOCUMENTATION Parts are those items used to repair a vehicle or to restore it to useful service. The part number(s) and the costs are usually documented on the work order by the parts department personnel in larger shops, or the shop owner or service manager in smaller shops. The service technician orders and installs parts. The service technician should provide all of the necessary information as may be required, including the VIN so that the correct part can be ordered or pulled from stock.

LABOR TIME DOCUMENTATION The labor time, called **flat rate**, is found in labor guides, and lists vehicle service procedures and the time it should take an average technician to complete the task. This flat-rate time is the basis for estimates and the pay for the technicians. The flat rate is not determined by the technician in most cases, but is determined by the designated warranty person or the shop owner in small shops. All times are expressed in tenths of an hour with each tenth representing six minutes. ● **SEE CHART 1–1.**

Some TSBs include the time needed to accomplish the task. ● **SEE FIGURE 1–4.**

SERVICE RECORDS

PURPOSE The purpose of service records is to provide a history of the service work that has been performed on the vehicle in the past. Whenever service work is performed, a record of what was done is usually kept on file or stored electronically on a network or online server for a number of years. The wise service technician will check the vehicle service history if working on a vehicle with an unusual problem. Often, a previous repair may indicate the reason for the current problem or it could be related to the same circuit or components.

- **Example #1**—A collision could have caused hidden damage that can affect the operation of the vehicle. Knowing that a collision had been recently repaired may be helpful to the technician. An accident could cause faults due to hidden damage and some faults could be related to a previous repair.
- **Example #2**—If the current issue is an error code for an engine misfire and the history of the service work on the vehicle does not show an oil change for several years, this might help the technician to find the root cause.

Work Order (Figure 1-3)

Customer's Description of Problem/Repair:

This accurately describes the problem or symptom I am experiencing with my motor vehicle. Customer's Initials_____

HOME TOWN CHEVROLET
100 N. MAIN ST.

8993

COST	QUAN.	PART NUMBER / DESCRIPTION	PRICE	
	1	Battery Interstate 60 Month Battery	74	00
	1	Oil filter	11	25
	1	Air filter	36	59
	1	Seal Ring		25
	1	Ant Mast	67	97
			190	06

SUBLET REPAIRS

NAME: MR CUSTOMER
ADDRESS: 444 W. 3rd St.
CITY / STATE / ZIP
VIN: 1G2NW51AAFS6201 ENGINE NO: 1.8 L MAKE: CHEVY
TYPE OR MODEL: Cruze YEAR: 2015 LICENSE NUMBER: BQU449
TERMS / ORDER ACCEPTED BY / PHONE

DATE RECEIVED: 1/25/19
COMPLETION DATE
MILEAGE IN: 50,340
MILEAGE OUT
PHONE WHEN READY: YES ☐ NO ☐

OPER. NO.	INSTRUCTIONS:		
1.0	50 K Service	450	00
.6	Check Battery Replace	22	50
.5	Ant Mast	22	50
.5	Check left front Headlight	22	50

TECH ID # / INIT. | LABOR CHARGE

☐ CHANGE OIL
☐ CHANGE OIL FILTER CART
☐ CHANGE TRANS OIL
☐ CHANGE DIFF OIL
☐ LUBRICATE
☐ PACK FRONT WHEEL BRGS
X TIRES ☐
☐ ADJUST BRAKES
☐ WASH
☐ SAFETY INSPECTION

ESTIMATE
(UNDER OHIO LAW) YOU HAVE THE RIGHT TO AN ESTIMATE IF THE EXPECTED COST OF REPAIRS OR SEVENTY-FIVE DOLLARS. INITIAL YOUR CHOICE.
____ WRITTEN   ____ ORAL
____ ESTIMATE   ____ ESTIMATE
____ I DO NOT REQUEST
____ AN ESTIMATE

WARRANTY STATEMENT AND DISCLAIMER: THE DEALER HEREBY DISCLAIMS ALL WARRANTIES EXPRESS OR IMPLIED, INCLUDING ANY IMPLIED WARRANTIES OF MERCHANTABILITY OR FITNESS FOR A PARTICULAR PURPOSE, AND NEITHER ASSUMES NOR AUTHORIZES ANY OTHER PERSON TO ASSUME FOR IT ANY LIABILITY IN CONNECTION WITH THE SALE OF SAID PARTS OR THIS REPAIR. THIS DISCLAIMER IN NO WAY AFFECTS THE PROVISIONS OF ANY MANUFACTURER OR OTHER SUPPLIER WARRANTIES. IF DEALER PROVIDES A WRITTEN WARRANTY, ANY IMPLIED WARRANTIES ARE EXPRESSLY LIMITED TO THE TERM OF THE WRITTEN WARRANTY.

ORIGINAL ESTIMATE $_____
AUTHORIZED ADDITIONS
$_____

CUSTOMERS ACCEPTANCE
INITIAL HERE_____
DATE_____
TIME_____
BY_____

In the event that you, the customer, authorize commencement but do not authorize completion of a repair or service, a charge will be imposed for disassembly, reassembly or partially completed work. Such charge will be directly related to the actual amount of labor or parts involved in the inspection, repair or service.

ALL PARTS ARE NEW UNLESS SPECIFIED OTHERWISE.

This Facility charges _____ % of the Total _____ Charges, up to a Maximum of $_____ , for Shop Materials.

WE WILL OFFER TO RETURN TO YOU ALL REPLACED PARTS, AS REQUIRED BY LAW, UNLESS THEY ARE TO BE REBUILT, SOLD, OR RETURNED TO THE MANUFACTURER.

I hereby authorize the repair work herein set forth to be done by you, together with the furnishing by you of the necessary parts and other material for such repair, and agree: that you are not responsible for any delays caused by unavailability or delayed availability of parts or material for any reason; that you neither assume nor authorize any other person to assume for you any liability in connection with such repair; that you shall not be responsible for loss of or damage to the above vehicle, or articles left therein, in case of fire, theft or other cause beyond your control; that an express mechanic's lien is hereby acknowledged on the above vehicle to secure the amount of repairs thereto; that your employees may operate the above vehicle on streets, highways or elsewhere for the purpose of testing and/or inspecting such vehicle.
I HEREBY ACKNOWLEDGE RECEIPT OF A COPY HEREOF.

X _____

	SALE	
TOTAL LABOR	517	50
TOTAL PARTS	190	06
GAS, OIL & GREASE	18	75
SUBLET REPAIRS		
	726	31
TAX 6.5%	47	21
TOTAL	773	52

FIGURE 1–3 A typical work order showing the customer concern and what was done to correct the issue. Electronic work orders include all of the same required information. This included a stored diagnostic trouble code and what was found to be wrong and what was done to complete the repair.

TENTHS OF AN HOUR	NUMBER OF MINUTES
0.1	6 minutes
0.2	12 minutes
0.3	18 minutes
0.4	24 minutes
0.5	30 minutes
0.6	36 minutes
0.7	42 minutes
0.8	48 minutes
0.9	54 minutes
1.0	60 minutes

CHART 1–1

The time that is published for repair and service operations are expressed in tenths of an hour.

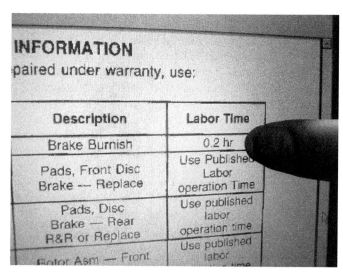

INFORMATION
...paired under warranty, use:

Description	Labor Time
Brake Burnish	0.2 hr
Pads, Front Disc Brake — Replace	Use Published Labor operation Time
Pads, Disc Brake — Rear R&R or Replace	Use published labor operation time
Rotor Asm — Front	Use published labor time

FIGURE 1–4 Some technical service bulletins also include the designated flat-rate time when specifying a repair procedure.

ADDITIONAL INFORMATION

FROM THE CUSTOMER The service advisor or shop owner records the following information from the customer and about the vehicle:

1. Record the vehicle identification number (VIN) of the vehicle on the work order
2. Record the make, model, year, and mileage on the work order
3. Record what the customer's complaint (concern) is so that the service technician can verify the complaint and make the proper repair
4. Review the customer's vehicle history file and identify additional required service

CHECK THE VEHICLE BEFORE WORK IS STARTED As part of the work order writing process, the service advisor should look over the vehicle and make a written note of any vehicle damage that may already exist. If any damage is noted, it should be mentioned to the customer and noted on the work order. Often the customer is not aware of any damage, especially on the passenger side, and thus would blame the shop for the damage after the service work was performed.

SPECIAL SERVICE TOOLS (SSTs) Automotive dealerships have tool rooms that are supposed to have all the SSTs that are recommended by the factory. These tool rooms are for the use of the dealership technicians so that they have access to the tools needed to work on the vehicle being serviced. The tools are often sorted by content area and are identified by a tool number. SSTs are made primarily by a small group of manufacturers. They make the following SSTs:

- Miller Special Tools (Chrysler)
- Rotunda Tools (Ford, Mazda, Jaguar, Land Rover)
- Kent-Moore Tools (Detroit Diesel, General Motors, Hyundai, Lexus, Mitsubishi, Nissan, Saab, Subaru, Volvo, Kia, Toyota, Isuzu). ● SEE FIGURE 1–5.

Other Manufacturers of SSTs include:

- Sir Tools
- Assenmacher
- Baum Tools

PARTS OF A VEHICLE

The names of the parts of a vehicle are based on the location and purpose of the component.

LEFT SIDE OF THE VEHICLE—RIGHT SIDE OF THE VEHICLE Both of these terms refer to the left and right as if the driver is sitting behind the steering wheel.

FIGURE 1–5 The special tool number is printed or stamped on the tool for easy identification. The Kent-Moore part number J-44217 indicates a tool used to hold a timing chain.

FRONT AND REAR The proper term for the back portion of any vehicle is rear (e.g., left rear tire).

FRONT-WHEEL DRIVE VERSUS REAR-WHEEL DRIVE

Front-wheel drive (FWD) means that the front wheels are being driven by the engine, as well as turned by the steering wheel. Rear-wheel drive (RWD) means that the rear wheels are driven by the engine. If the engine is in the front, it can be either front- or rear-wheel drive. In many cases, a front engine vehicle can also drive all four wheels, called four-wheel drive (4WD) or all-wheel drive (AWD). If the engine is located at the rear of the vehicle, it can be rear-wheel drive or four-wheel drive.

VEHICLE IDENTIFICATION

All service work requires that the vehicle, including the engine and accessories, be properly identified. The most common identification is the make, model, and year of the vehicle.

Make: e.g., Chevrolet

Model: e.g., Traverse

Year: e.g., 2018

The year of the vehicle is often difficult to determine exactly. A model may be introduced as the next year's model as soon as January of the previous year. Typically, a new **model year** (abbreviated **MY**) starts in September or October of the year prior to the actual new year, but not always. This is why the **vehicle identification number**, usually abbreviated **VIN**, is so important. ● **SEE FIGURE 1–6.**

Since 1981, all vehicle manufacturers have used a VIN that is 17 characters long. ● **SEE FIGURE 1–7.** Although every vehicle manufacturer assigns various letters or numbers within these 17 characters, there are some constants, including:

- The first number or letter designates the **country of origin**. ● **SEE CHART 1–2.**
- The model of the vehicle is commonly the fourth and/or fifth character.
- The eighth character is often the engine code. (Some engines cannot be determined by the VIN.)
- The tenth character represents the model year (MY) on all vehicles. ● **SEE CHART 1–3.**

1 = United States	J = Japan	T = Czechoslovakia
2 = Canada	K = Korea	U = Romania
3 = Mexico	L = China	V = France
4 = United States	M = India	W = Germany
5 = United States	N = Turkey	X = Russia
6 = Australia	P = Philippines	Y = Sweden
8 = Argentina	R = Taiwan	Z = Italy
9 = Brazil	S = England	

CHART 1–2

The first number or letter designates the country of origin.

A = 1980/2010	L = 1990/2020	Y = 2000/2030
B = 1981/2011	M = 1991/2021	1 = 2001/2031
C = 1982/2012	N = 1992/2022	2 = 2002/2032
D = 1983/2013	P = 1993/2023	3 = 2003/2033
E = 1984/2014	R = 1994/2024	4 = 2004/2034
F = 1985/2015	S = 1995/2025	5 = 2005/2035
G = 1986/2016	T = 1996/2026	6 = 2006/2036
H = 1987/2017	V = 1997/2027	7 = 2007/2037
J = 1988/2018	W = 1998/2028	8 = 2008/2038
K = 1989/2019	X = 1999/2029	9 = 2009/2039

CHART 1–3

VIN year chart. (The pattern repeats every 30 years.)

🔧 TECH TIP

Use a VIN Decoder

Perform a search for "VIN decoder" and many will be found, including the free one posted on the National Highway Traffic Safety Administration website (www.nhtsa.gov). A VIN decoder is useful to find what equipment and accessories the vehicle has.

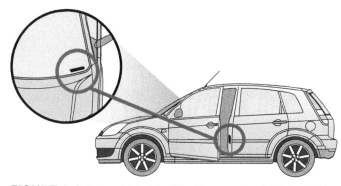

FIGURE 1–6 The vehicle identification number (VIN) is visible through the base of the windshield and on a decal inside the driver's door.

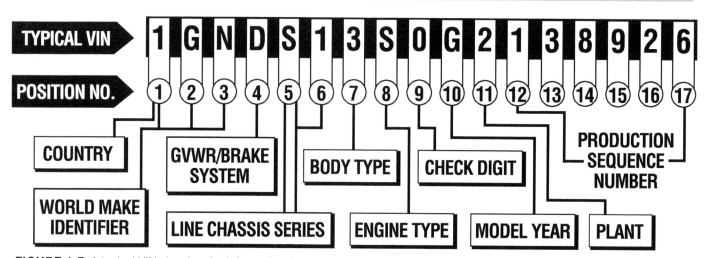

FIGURE 1-7 A typical VIN showing the information that is represented.

VEHICLE SAFETY CERTIFICATION LABEL

A vehicle safety certification label is attached to the left side pillar post on the rearward-facing section of the left front door. This label indicates the month and year of manufacture, the (VIN), as well as the GVWR and GAWR.

Gross vehicle weight rating (GVWR)—The maximum (upper limit) weight of a vehicle as specified by the vehicle manufacturer. This is important to know if hauling a heavy load, such as in a truck or SUV.

Gross axle weight rating (GAWR)—The maximum weight that an axle can support is usually followed by "FR" for front axle and "RR" for rear axle. ● **SEE FIGURE 1–8.**

VECI LABEL

The **vehicle emissions control information (VECI)** label under the hood of the vehicle shows informative settings and emission hose routing information. ● **SEE FIGURE 1–9.**

■ The VECI label (sticker) can be located on the bottom side of the hood, the radiator fan shroud, the radiator core support, or the strut towers.

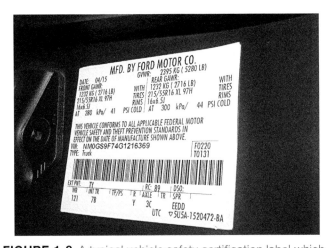

FIGURE 1-8 A typical vehicle safety certification label which shows the gross vehicle weight, gross axles weight rating, as well as the size and inflation pressure of the tires.

FIGURE 1-9 This vehicle emission control information (VECI) decal indicates this vehicle meets both national EPA Tier 2, Bin 5 (T2B5), and California (ULEV II) emission standards.

SUMMARY

1. Service information is needed to correctly service or repair vehicles because it contains all of the specifications, as well as the specified procedures to follow when servicing or repairing a vehicle.

2. A technical service bulletin (TSB) is issued by the vehicle manufacturer to notify service technicians of a potential problem or other critical information.

3. A campaign is typically issued when a manufacturer wants to improve a product's performance or increase the customer's satisfaction. If the campaign involves a safety or emissions concern, it is considered a recall. A recall can occur when either the manufacturer or the National Highway Safety Administration (NHTSA) determines there is a concern.

4. The work order, also called a repair order (RO), is a legal document that is signed by the vehicle owner or his/her representative.

5. The purpose of service records is to provide a history of the service work that has been performed on the vehicle in the past.

6. The new model year (MY) starts in September or October of the year prior to the actual new year, but not always. This is why the vehicle identification number (VIN) is so important.

7. The vehicle emissions control information (VECI) label under the hood of the vehicle shows informative settings and emission hose routing information

1. What is included in the vehicle owner's manual that could be helpful for a service technician?

2. Why is factory service information the most detailed of all service information?

3. What customer information needs to be included on a repair order (RO)?

4. What should the service technician include on the work order?

5. What are the major pieces of information that are included in the vehicle identification number (VIN)?

CHAPTER QUIZ

1. What type of information is commonly included in the owner's manual that would be a benefit to service technicians?
   a. Maintenance reminder light reset procedures
   b. Tire pressure monitoring system reset procedures
   c. Maintenance items specifications
   d. All of the above

2. Two technicians are discussing the need for the history of the vehicle. Technician A says that an accident could cause faults due to hidden damage. Technician B says that some faults could be related to a previous repair. Which technician is correct?
   a. Technician A only
   b. Technician B only
   c. Both Technicians A and B
   d. Neither Technician A nor B

3. A campaign (recall) is mailed to the owner of a vehicle from the _____.
   a. vehicle manufacturer
   b. local dealer
   c. federal government
   d. state or local government

4. Technical service bulletins (TSBs) are issued by the _____
   a. vehicle manufacturer
   b. local dealer
   c. federal government
   d. state or local government

5. Four tenths of an hour is how many minutes?
   a. 14   c. 34
   b. 24   d. 44

6. What should the service technician document on the work order?
   a. The results of any inspections and tests
   b. What was replaced or serviced
   c. The dimensions of the related component and comparison to factory specifications
   d. Any of the above

7. The labor rate for each operation is included on the work order and is added by the _____.
   a. service technician
   b. service advisor
   c. shop owner or designated warranty person
   d. Any of the above

8. Which of the following are performed at no cost to the vehicle owner?
   a. TSBs   c. Either a or b
   b. Campaigns (recalls)   d. Neither a nor b

9. The first character of the vehicle identification number is the country of origin. Where was the vehicle built that has a "5" as the first character?
   a. United States   c. Mexico
   b. Canada   d. Japan

10. The VECI label includes all *except* _____.
    a. engine identification
    b. horsepower and torque rating of the engine
    c. California emission standard
    d. Federal (EPA) emission standard

chapter 2

TOOLS AND SAFETY

LEARNING OBJECTIVES:

After studying this chapter, the reader will be able to:

Identify the strength ratings of threaded fasteners.

Explain the difference between the brand name (trade name) and the proper name for tools.

Describe what tool is the best to use for each job.

Explain how to maintain hand tools.

Identify the personal protective equipment (PPE) that all service technicians should wear.

Discuss how to safely use hand tools.

Describe how to safely hoist a vehicle.

This chapter will help you understand the ASE content knowledge for vehicle identification and the proper use of tools and shop equipment.

KEY TERMS: Bench grinder 26 • Bolts 9 • Breaker bar 14 • Bump cap 27 • Cheater bar 18 • Chisels 22 • Drive sizes 14 • Extensions 14 • Eye wash station 35 • Files 20 • Fire blanket 34 • Fire extinguisher classes 33 • Grade 10 • Hacksaws 22 • Hammers 18 • HEV 35 • LED 25 • Metric bolts 10 • Nuts 11 • PPE 27 • Pinch weld seam 30 • Pitch 9 • Pliers 19 • Punches 22 • Ratchet 14 • Screwdrivers 16 • Snips 20 • Socket 14 • Socket adapter 18 • Spontaneous combustion 29 • SST 25 • Stud 9 • Tensile strength 11 • Trouble light 25 • UNC 9 • UNF 9 • Universal joint 14 • Washers 12 • Wrenches 13

THREADED FASTENERS

BOLTS AND THREADS Most of the threaded fasteners used on vehicles are **bolts**. Bolts are called *cap screws* when they are threaded into a casting. Automotive service technicians usually refer to these fasteners as *bolts*, regardless of how they are used. In this chapter, they are called bolts. Sometimes, studs are used for threaded fasteners. A **stud** is a short rod with threads on both ends. Often, a stud will have coarse threads on one end and fine threads on the other end. The end of the stud with coarse threads is screwed into the casting. A nut is used on the opposite end to hold the parts together.

The fastener threads *must* match the threads in the casting or nut. The threads may be measured either in fractions of an inch (called fractional) or in metric units. The size is measured across the outside of the threads, called the *crest* of the thread. ● **SEE FIGURE 2–1.**

FRACTIONAL BOLTS Fractional threads are either coarse or fine. The coarse threads are called **unified national coarse** (**UNC**), and the fine threads are called **unified national fine** (**UNF**). Standard combinations of sizes and number of threads per inch (called **pitch**) are used. Pitch can be measured with a thread pitch gauge as shown in ● **SEE FIGURE 2–2.** Bolts are

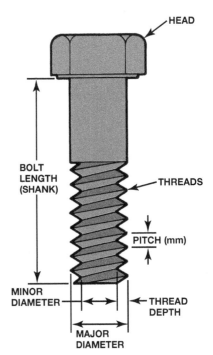

FIGURE 2–1 The dimensions of a typical bolt showing where sizes are measured.

FIGURE 2–2 Thread pitch gauge used to measure the pitch of the thread. This bolt has 13 threads to the inch.

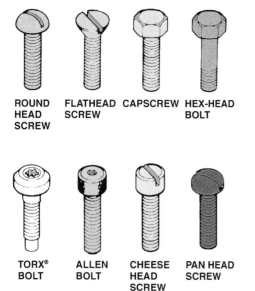

| ROUND HEAD SCREW | FLATHEAD SCREW | CAPSCREW | HEX-HEAD BOLT |

| TORX® BOLT | ALLEN BOLT | CHEESE HEAD SCREW | PAN HEAD SCREW |

FIGURE 2–3 Bolts and screws have many different heads which determine what tool is needed.

SIZE	THREADS PER INCH		OUTSIDE DIAMETER INCHES
	NC UNC	NF UNF	
0	..	80	0.0600
1	64	..	0.0730
1	..	72	0.0730
2	56	..	0.0860
2	..	64	0.0860
3	48	..	0.0990
3	..	56	0.0990
4	40	..	0.1120
4	..	48	0.1120
5	40	..	0.1250
5	..	44	0.1250
6	32	..	0.1380
6	..	40	0.1380
8	32	..	0.1640
8	..	36	0.1640
10	24	..	0.1900
10	..	32	0.1900
12	24	..	0.2160
12	..	28	0.2160
1/4	20	..	0.2500
1/4	..	28	0.2500
5/16	18	..	0.3125
5/16	..	24	0.3125
3/8	16	..	0.3750
3/8	..	24	0.3750
7/16	14	..	0.4375
7/16	..	20	0.4375
1/2	13	..	0.5000
1/2	..	20	0.5000

CHART 2–1

American standard is one method of sizing fasteners.

identified by their diameter and length as measured from below the head, and not by the size of the head or the size of the wrench used to remove or install the bolt.

Fractional thread sizes are specified by the diameter in fractions of an inch and the number of threads per inch. Typical UNC thread sizes would be 5/16–18 and 1/2–13. Similar UNF thread sizes would be 5/16–24 and 1/2–20. ● **SEE CHART 2–1.**

METRIC BOLTS The size of a **metric bolt** is specified by the letter *M* followed by the diameter in millimeters (mm) across the outside (crest) of the threads. Typical metric sizes would be M8 and M12. Metric threads are specified by the thread diameter followed by X and the distance between the threads measured in millimeters (M8 X 1.5). ● **SEE FIGURE 2–4.**

GRADES OF BOLTS Bolts are made from many different types of steel, and for this reason some are stronger than others. The strength or classification of a bolt is called the **grade**. The bolt heads are marked to indicate their grade strength.

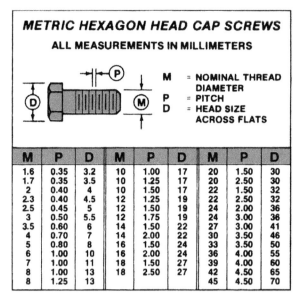

METRIC HEXAGON HEAD CAP SCREWS

ALL MEASUREMENTS IN MILLIMETERS

M = NOMINAL THREAD DIAMETER
P = PITCH
D = HEAD SIZE ACROSS FLATS

M	P	D	M	P	D	M	P	D
1.6	0.35	3.2	10	1.00	17	20	1.50	30
1.7	0.35	3.5	10	1.25	17	20	2.50	30
2	0.40	4	10	1.50	17	22	1.50	32
2.3	0.40	4.5	12	1.25	19	22	2.50	32
2.5	0.45	5	12	1.50	19	24	2.00	36
3	0.50	5.5	12	1.75	19	24	3.00	36
3.5	0.60	6	14	1.50	22	27	3.00	41
4	0.70	7	14	2.00	22	30	3.50	46
5	0.80	8	16	1.50	24	33	3.50	50
6	1.00	10	16	2.00	24	36	4.00	55
7	1.00	11	18	1.50	27	39	4.00	60
8	1.00	13	18	2.50	27	42	4.50	65
8	1.25	13				45	4.50	70

FIGURE 2–4 The metric system specifies fasteners by diameter, length, and pitch.

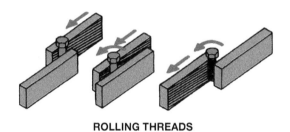

ROLLING THREADS

FIGURE 2–5 Stronger threads are created by cold-rolling a heat-treated bolt blank instead of cutting the threads, using a die.

The actual grade of bolts is two more than the number of lines on the bolt head. Metric bolts have a decimal number to indicate the grade. More lines or a higher grade number indicate a stronger bolt. In some cases, nuts and machine screws have similar grade markings. Higher grade bolts usually have threads that are rolled rather than cut, which also makes them stronger. ● SEE FIGURE 2–5.

CAUTION: *Never use hardware store (nongraded) bolts, studs, or nuts on any vehicle steering, suspension, or brake component. Always use the exact size and grade of hardware that is specified and used by the vehicle manufacturer.*

TENSILE STRENGTH OF FASTENERS Graded fasteners have a higher tensile strength than nongraded fasteners. **Tensile strength** is the maximum stress used under tension (lengthwise force) without causing failure of the fastener. Tensile strength is specified in pounds per square inch (PSI).

The strength and type of steel used in a bolt is supposed to be indicated by a raised mark on the head of the bolt. The type of mark depends on the standard to which the bolt was manufactured. Most often, bolts used in machinery are made to SAE Standard J429. ● **SEE CHART 2–2** that shows the grade and specified tensile strength.

Metric bolt tensile strength property class is shown on the head of the bolt as a number, such as 4.6, 8.8, 9.8, and 10.9; the higher the number, the stronger the bolt. ● **SEE FIGURE 2–6.**

NUTS **Nuts** are the female part of a threaded fastener. Most nuts used on cap screws have the same hex size as the cap screw head. Some inexpensive nuts use a hex size larger than the cap screw head. Metric nuts are often marked with dimples to show their strength. More dimples indicate stronger nuts. Some nuts and cap screws use interference fit threads to keep them from accidentally loosening. This means that the shape of the nut is slightly distorted or that a section of the threads is deformed. Nuts can also be kept from loosening with a nylon washer fastened in the nut or with a nylon patch or strip on the threads. ● **SEE FIGURE 2–7.**

NOTE: Most of these "locking nuts" are grouped together and are commonly referred to as *prevailing torque nuts.* This means that the nut will hold its tightness or torque and not loosen with movement or vibration. Most prevailing torque nuts should be replaced whenever removed to ensure that the nut will not loosen during service. Always follow the manufacturer's recommendations. Anaerobic sealers, such as Loctite, are used on the threads where the nut or cap screw must be both locked and sealed.

TECH TIP

A 1/2 Inch Wrench Does Not Fit a 1/2 Inch Bolt

A common mistake made by persons new to the automotive field is to think that the size of a bolt or nut is the size of the head. The size of the bolt or nut (outside diameter of the threads) is usually smaller than the size of the wrench or socket that fits the head of the bolt or nut. Examples are given in the following table:

Wrench Size	Thread Size
7/16 inch	1/4 inch
1/2 inch	5/16 inch
9/16 inch	3/8 inch
5/8 inch	7/16 inch
3/4 inch	1/2 inch
10 mm	6 mm
12 or 13 mm*	8 mm
14 or 17 mm*	10 mm

* European (Système International d'Unités-SI) metric.

SAE BOLT DESIGNATIONS

SAE GRADE NO.	SIZE RANGE	TENSILE STRENGTH, PSI	MATERIAL	HEAD MARKING
1	1/4 through 1 1/2	60,000	Low or medium carbon steel	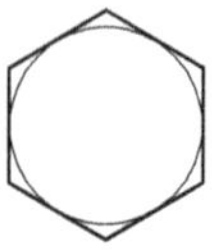
2	1/4 through 3/4	74,000		
	7/8 through 1 1/2	60,000		
5	1/4 through 1	120,000	Medium carbon steel, quenched and tempered	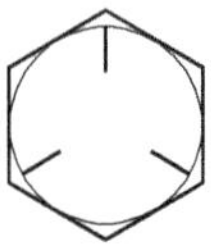
	1 1/8 through 1 1/2	105,000		
5.2	1/4 through 1	120,000	Low carbon martensite steel,* quenched and tempered	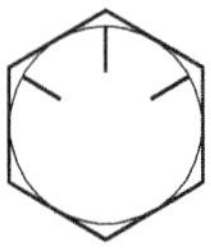
7	1/4 through 1 1/2	133,000	Medium carbon alloy steel, quenched and tempered	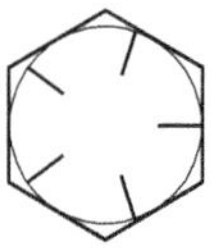
8	1/4 through 1 1/2	150,000	Medium carbon alloy steel, quenched and tempered	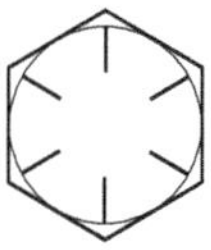
8.2	1/4 through 1	150,000	Low carbon martensite steel,* quenched and tempered	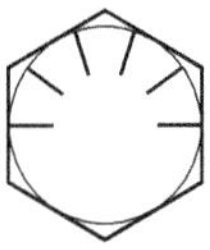

CHART 2–2

The tensile strength rating system as specified by the Society of Automotive Engineers (SAE).

*Martensite steel is a specific type of steel that can be cooled rapidly, thereby increasing its hardness. It is named after a German metallurgist, Adolf Martens.

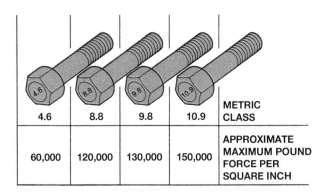

METRIC CLASS	4.6	8.8	9.8	10.9
APPROXIMATE MAXIMUM POUND FORCE PER SQUARE INCH	60,000	120,000	130,000	150,000

FIGURE 2–6 Metric bolt (cap screw) grade markings and approximate tensile strength.

HEX NUT **JAM NUT** **NYLON LOCK NUT** **CASTLE NUT** **ACORN NUT**

FIGURE 2–7 Nuts come in a variety of styles, including locking (prevailing torque) types, such as the distorted thread and nylon insert type.

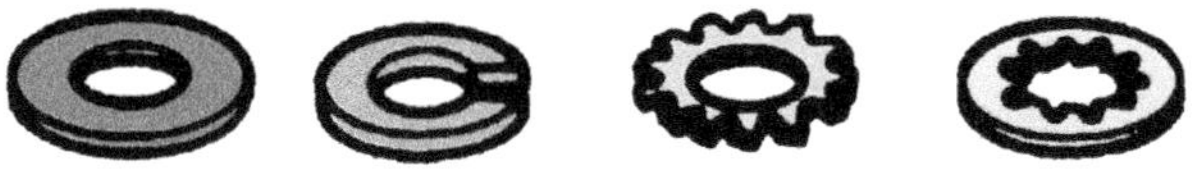

FLAT WASHER **LOCK WASHER** **STAR WASHER** **STAR WASHER**

FIGURE 2–8 Washers come in a variety of styles, including flat and serrated used to help prevent a fastener from loosening.

WASHERS **Washers** are often used under cap screw heads and under nuts. ● **SEE FIGURE 2–8.** Plain flat washers are used to provide an even clamping load around the fastener. Lock washers are added to prevent accidental loosening. In some accessories, the washers are locked onto the nut to provide easy assembly.

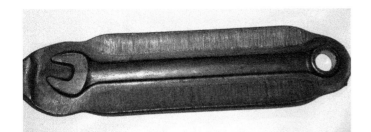

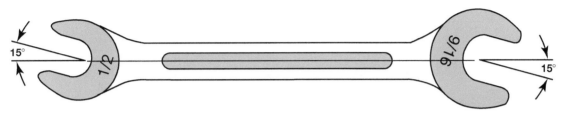

FIGURE 2–9 A wrench after it has been forged but before the flashing, extra material around the wrench, has been removed.

FIGURE 2–10 A typical open-end wrench. The size is different on each end; notice that the head is angled 15 degrees at the end.

HAND TOOLS

WRENCHES Wrenches are the most used hand tool by service technicians. **Wrenches** are used to grasp and rotate threaded fasteners. Most wrenches are constructed of forged alloy steel, usually chrome-vanadium steel. ● **SEE FIGURE 2–9.**

After the wrench is formed, it is hardened, and then tempered to reduce brittleness, and then chrome plated. There are several types of wrenches.

OPEN-END WRENCH. An open-end wrench is usually used to loosen or tighten bolts or nuts that do not require a lot of torque. Because of the *open* end, this type of wrench can be easily placed on a bolt or nut with an angle of 15 degrees, which allows the wrench to be flipped over and used again to continue to rotate the fastener. The major disadvantage of an open-end wrench is the lack of torque that can be applied due to the fact that the open jaws of the wrench only contact two flat surfaces of the fastener. An open-end wrench has two different sizes, one at each end. ● **SEE FIGURE 2–10.**

BOX-END WRENCH. A *box-end wrench*, also called a *closed-end wrench*, is placed over the top of the fastener and grips the points of the fastener. A box-end wrench is angled 15 degrees to allow it to clear nearby objects.

Therefore, a box-end wrench should be used to loosen or to tighten fasteners because it grasps around the entire head of the fastener. A box-end wrench has two different sizes, one at each end. ● **SEE FIGURE 2–11.**

Most service technicians purchase *combination wrenches*, which have the open end at one end and the same size box end on the other end. ● **SEE FIGURE 2–12.**

 **TECH TIP**

It Just Takes a Second

Whenever removing any automotive component, it is wise to screw the bolts back into the holes a couple of threads by hand. This ensures that the right bolt will be used in its original location when the component or part is put back on the vehicle. Often, the same diameter of fastener is used on a component, but the length of the bolt may vary. Spending just a couple of seconds to put the bolts and nuts back where they belong when the part is removed can save a lot of time when the part is being reinstalled. Besides making certain that the right fastener is being installed in the right place, this method helps prevent bolts and nuts from getting lost or kicked away. How much time have you wasted looking for that lost bolt or nut?

A combination wrench allows the technician to loosen or tighten a fastener using the box end of the wrench, turn it around, and use the open end to increase the speed of rotating the fastener.

ADJUSTABLE WRENCH. An *adjustable wrench* is often used where the exact size wrench is not available or when a large nut, such as a wheel spindle nut, needs to be rotated but not tightened. An adjustable wrench should not be used to loosen or tighten fasteners because the torque applied to the wrench can cause the movable jaws to loosen their grip on the fastener, causing it to become rounded. ● **SEE FIGURE 2–13.**

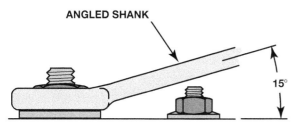

FIGURE 2–11 The end of a box-end wrench is angled 15 degrees to allow clearance for nearby objects or other fasteners.

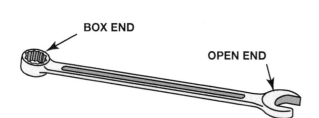

FIGURE 2–12 A combination wrench has an open end at one end and a box end at the other end.

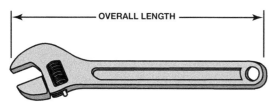

FIGURE 2–13 An adjustable wrench. Adjustable wrenches are sized by the overall length of the wrench and not by how far the jaws open. Common sizes of adjustable wrenches include 8, 10, and 12 inches.

LINE WRENCHES. Line wrenches are also called *flare-nut wrenches*, *fitting wrenches,* or *tube-nut wrenches* and are designed to grip almost all the way around a nut used to retain a fuel or refrigerant line, and yet, be able to be installed over the line. ● **SEE FIGURE 2–14.**

SAFE USE OF WRENCHES Wrenches should be inspected before use to be sure they are not cracked, bent, or damaged. All wrenches should be cleaned after use before being returned to the tool box. Always use the correct size of wrench for the fastener being loosened or tightened to help prevent the rounding of the flats of the fastener. When attempting to loosen a fastener, pull a wrench—do not push a wrench. If a wrench is pushed, your knuckles can be hurt when forced into another object if the fastener breaks loose or if the wrench slips. Always keep wrenches and all hand tools clean to help prevent rust and to allow for a better, firmer grip. Never expose any tool to excessive heat. High temperatures can reduce the strength ("draw the temper") of metal tools.

FIGURE 2–14 The end of a typical line wrench, which shows that it is capable of grasping most of the head of the fitting.

 **TECH TIP**

Hide Those from the Boss

An apprentice technician started working for a shop and put his top tool box on a workbench. Another technician observed that, along with a complete set of good-quality tools, the box contained several adjustable wrenches. The more experienced technician said, "Hide those from the boss." The boss does not want any service technician to use adjustable wrenches. If any adjustable wrench is used on a bolt or nut, the movable jaw often moves or loosens and starts to round the head of the fastener. If the head of the bolt or nut becomes rounded, it becomes that much more difficult to remove.

Never use a hammer on any wrench unless you are using a special "staking face" wrench designed to be used with a hammer. Replace any tools that are damaged or worn.

RATCHETS, SOCKETS, AND EXTENSIONS   A **socket** fits over the fastener and grips the points and/or flats of the bolt or nut. The socket is rotated (driven) using either a long bar called a **breaker bar** (flex handle) or a ratchet. ● **SEE FIGURES 2–15 AND 2–16.**

A **ratchet** is a tool that turns the socket in only one direction and allows the rotating of the ratchet handle back and forth in a narrow space. Socket **extensions** and **universal joints** are also used with sockets to allow access to fasteners in restricted locations.

DRIVE SIZE. Sockets are available in various **drive sizes**, including 1/4, 3/8, and 1/2 inch sizes for most automotive use. ● **SEE FIGURES 2–17 AND 2–18.**

Many heavy-duty truck and/or industrial applications use 3/4 and 1 inch sizes. The drive size is the distance of each side of the square drive. Sockets and ratchets of the same size are designed to work together.

REGULAR AND DEEP WELL.   Sockets are available in regular length for use in most applications or in a deep well design that

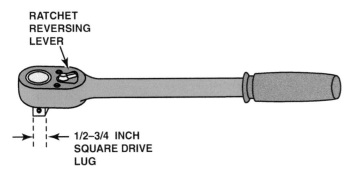

FIGURE 2–15 A typical ratchet used to rotate a socket. A ratchet makes a ratcheting noise when it is being rotated in the opposite direction from loosening or tightening. A knob or lever on the ratchet allows the user to switch directions.

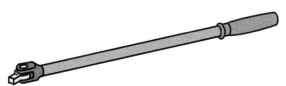

FIGURE 2–16 A typical flex handle used to rotate a socket, also called a breaker bar because it usually has a longer handle than a ratchet and, therefore, can be used to apply more torque to a fastener than a ratchet.

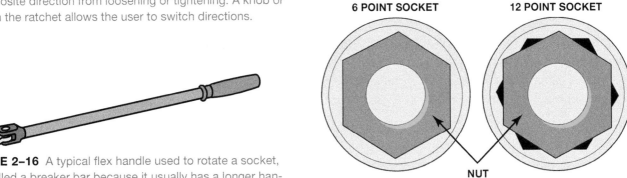

FIGURE 2–17 The most commonly used socket drive sizes include 1/4, 3/8, and 1/2 inch drive.

FIGURE 2–18 A 6 point socket fits the head of a bolt or nut on all sides. A 12 point socket can round off the head of a bolt or nut if a lot of force is applied.

TECH TIP

Right to Tighten

It is sometimes confusing which way to rotate a wrench or screwdriver, especially when the head of the fastener is pointing away from you. To help visualize while looking at the fastener, say "righty tighty, lefty loosey."

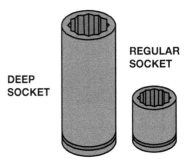

FIGURE 2–19 Allows access to the nut that has a stud plus other locations needing great depth, such as spark plugs.

allows for access to a fastener that uses a long stud or other similar conditions. ● **SEE FIGURE 2–19.**

TORQUE WRENCHES Torque wrenches are socket turning handles that are designed to apply a known amount of force to the fastener. There are two basic types of torque wrenches:

1. **Clicker type.** This type of torque wrench is first set to the specified torque and then it "clicks" when the set torque value has been reached. When force is removed from the torque wrench handle, another click is heard. The setting on a clicker-type torque wrench should be set back to zero after use and checked for proper calibration regularly. ● **SEE FIGURE 2–20.**

2. **Beam-type.** This type of torque wrench is used to measure torque, but instead of presenting the value, the actual torque is displayed on the dial of the wrench as the fastener is being tightened. Beam-type torque wrenches are available in 1/4, 3/8, and 1/2 inch drives and both English and metric units. ● **SEE FIGURE 2–21.**

SAFE USE OF SOCKETS AND RATCHETS Always use the proper size socket that correctly fits the bolt or nut. All sockets and ratchets should be cleaned after use before being placed back into the tool box. Sockets are available in short and deep well designs. Never expose any tool to excessive

FIGURE 2-20 Using a clicker-type torque wrench to tighten connecting rod nuts on an engine.

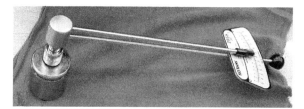

FIGURE 2-21 A beam-type torque wrench that displays the torque reading on the face of the dial. The beam display is read as the beam deflects, which is in proportion to the amount of torque applied to the fastener.

FIGURE 2-22 Torque wrench calibration checker.

heat. High temperatures can reduce the strength ("draw the temper") of metal tools.

Never use a hammer on a socket handle unless you are using a special "staking face" wrench designed to be used with a hammer. Replace any tools that are damaged or worn.

Also select the appropriate drive size. For example, for small work, such as on the dash, select a 1/4 inch drive. For most general service work, use a 3/8 inch drive and for suspension and steering and other large fasteners, select a 1/2 inch drive. When loosening a fastener, always pull the ratchet toward you rather than push it outward.

SCREWDRIVERS

STRAIGHT-BLADE SCREWDRIVER Many smaller fasteners are removed and installed by using a **screwdriver**. Screwdrivers are available in many sizes and tip shapes. The most commonly used screwdriver is called a *straight blade* or *flat tip*.

TECH TIP

Check Torque Wrench Calibration Regularly

Torque wrenches should be checked regularly. For example, Honda has a torque wrench calibration setup at each of its training centers. It is expected that a torque wrench be checked for accuracy before every use. Most experts recommend that torque wrenches be checked and adjusted as needed at least every year and more often if possible. ● SEE FIGURE 2-22.

Flat-tip screwdrivers are sized by the width of the blade and this width should match the width of the slot in the screw. ● **SEE FIGURE 2-23.**

CAUTION: Do not use a screwdriver as a pry tool or as a chisel. Screwdrivers are hardened steel only at the tip and are not designed to be pounded on or used for prying because they could bend easily. Always use the proper tool for each application.

PHILLIPS SCREWDRIVER Another type of commonly used screwdriver is called a Phillips screwdriver, named for Henry F. Phillips, who invented the crosshead screw in 1934. Due to the shape of the crosshead screw and screwdriver, a Phillips screw can be driven with more torque than can be achieved with a slotted screw.

A Phillips head screwdriver is specified by the length of the handle and the size of the point at the tip. A #1 tip has a

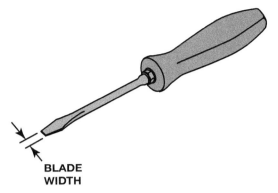

FIGURE 2–23 A flat-tip (straight-blade) screwdriver. The width of the blade should match the width of the slot in the fastener being loosened or tightened.

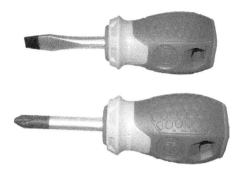

FIGURE 2–24 Two stubby screwdrivers that are used to access screws that have limited space above. A straight blade is on top and a #2 Phillips screwdriver is on the bottom.

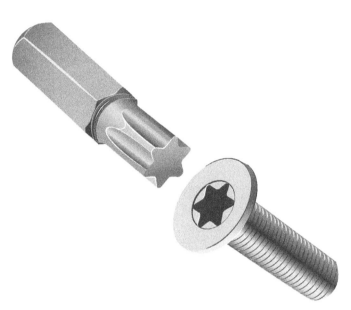

FIGURE 2–25 A Torx bit and fastener.

FIGURE 2–26 An impact screwdriver used to remove slotted or Phillips head fasteners that cannot be broken loose using a standard screwdriver.

sharp point, a #2 tip is the most commonly used, and a #3 tip is blunt and is only used for larger sizes of Phillips head fasteners. For example, a #2 × 3 inch Phillips screwdriver would typically measure 6 inch from the tip of the blade to the end of the handle (3 inch long handle and 3 inch long blade) with a #2 tip.

Both straight-blade and Phillips screwdrivers are available with a short blade and handle for access to fasteners with limited room. ● SEE FIGURE 2–24.

A Torx is a six-pointed star shaped tip that was developed by Camcar (formerly Textron) to offer higher loosening and tightening torque than is possible with a straight (flat tip) or Phillips. Torx is very commonly used in the automotive field for many components. Commonly used Torx sizes from small to large include: T15, T20, T25, and T30. ● SEE FIGURE 2–25.

Some Torx fasteners include a round projection in the center requiring that a special version of a Torx bit be used. These are called security Torx bits that have a hole in the center to be used on these fasteners. External Torx fasteners are also used mostly as engine fasteners and are labeled E instead of T plus the size, such as E45.

OFFSET SCREWDRIVERS   Offset screwdrivers are used in places where a conventional screwdriver cannot fit. An offset screwdriver is bent at the ends and is used similar to a wrench. Most offset screwdrivers have a straight blade at one end and a Phillips end at the opposite end.

IMPACT SCREWDRIVER   An *impact screwdriver* is used to break loose or tighten a screw. A hammer is used to strike the end after the screwdriver holder is placed in the head of the screw and rotated in the desired direction. The force from the hammer blow does two things: It applies a force downward holding the tip of the screwdriver in the slot and then applies a twisting force to loosen (or tighten) the screw. ● SEE FIGURE 2–26.

FIGURE 2–27 A typical ball-peen hammer.

FIGURE 2–28 A rubber mallet used to deliver a force to an object without harming the surface.

FIGURE 2–29 A dead-blow hammer that was left outside in freezing weather. The plastic covering was damaged, which destroyed this hammer. The lead shot is encased in the metal housing and then covered.

SAFE USE OF SCREWDRIVERS   Always use the proper type and size screwdriver that matches the fastener. Try to avoid pressing down on a screwdriver because if it slips, the screwdriver tip could go into your hand, causing serious personal injury. All screwdrivers should be cleaned after use. Do not use a screwdriver as a prybar; always use the correct tool for the job.

HAMMERS AND MALLETS   **Hammers** and mallets are used to force objects together or apart. The shape of the back part of the hammer head (called the *peen*) usually determines the name. For example, a ball-peen hammer has a rounded end like a ball and it is used to straighten oil pans and valve covers, using the hammer head, and for shaping metal, using the ball peen. ● **SEE FIGURE 2–27.**

NOTE: A claw hammer has a claw used to remove nails and is not used for automotive service.

A hammer is usually sized by the weight of the head of the hammer and the length of the handle. For example, a commonly used ball-peen hammer has an 8 ounce head with an 11 inch handle.

MALLETS.   *Mallets* are a type of hammer with a large striking surface, which allows the technician to exert force over a larger area than a hammer, so as not to harm the part or component. Mallets are made from a variety of materials including rubber, plastic, or wood. ● **SEE FIGURE 2–28.**

DEAD-BLOW HAMMER.   A shot-filled plastic hammer is called a *dead-blow hammer*. The small lead balls (shot) inside a plastic head prevent the hammer from bouncing off of the object when struck. ● **SEE FIGURE 2–29.**

SAFE USE OF HAMMERS AND MALLETS All mallets and hammers should be cleaned after use and not exposed to extreme temperatures. Never use a hammer or mallet that is damaged in any way and always use caution to avoid doing damage to the components and the surrounding area. Always follow the hammer manufacturer's recommended procedures and practices.

PLIERS

SLIP-JOINT PLIERS **Pliers** are capable of holding, twisting, bending, and cutting objects and is an extremely useful classification of tools. The common household type of pliers is called the *slip-joint pliers.* There are two different positions where the junction of the handles meets to achieve a wide range of sizes of objects that can be gripped. ● **SEE FIGURE 2–30.**

MULTIGROOVE ADJUSTABLE PLIERS For gripping larger objects, a set of *multigroove adjustable pliers* are a commonly used tool of choice by many service technicians. Originally designed to remove the various size nuts holding rope seals used in water pumps, the name *water pump pliers* is also used. These types of pliers are commonly called by their trade name *Channel Locks*®. ● **SEE FIGURE 2–31.**

LINESMAN'S PLIERS *Linesman's pliers* are a hand tool specifically designed for cutting, bending, and twisting wire. While commonly used by construction workers and electricians, linesman's pliers are very useful tool for the service technician who deals with wiring. The center parts of the jaws are designed to grasp round objects such as pipe or tubing without slipping. ● **SEE FIGURE 2–32.**

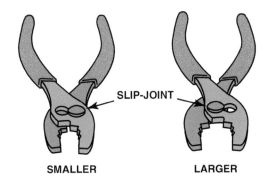

SMALLER   LARGER

FIGURE 2–30 Typical slip-joint pliers is a common household pliers. The slip joint allows the jaws to be opened to two different settings.

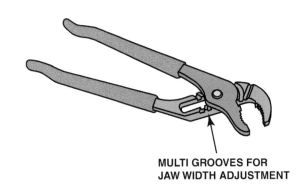

MULTI GROOVES FOR JAW WIDTH ADJUSTMENT

FIGURE 2–31 Multigroove adjustable pliers are known by many names, including the trade name "Channel Locks®."

DIAGONAL PLIERS *Diagonal pliers* are designed to cut only. The cutting jaws are set at an angle to make it easier to cut wires. Diagonal pliers are also called *side cuts* or *dikes*. These pliers are constructed of hardened steel and they are used mostly for cutting wire. ● **SEE FIGURE 2–33.**

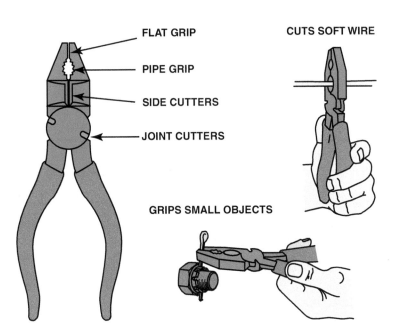

FLAT GRIP

PIPE GRIP

SIDE CUTTERS

JOINT CUTTERS

CUTS SOFT WIRE

GRIPS SMALL OBJECTS

FIGURE 2–32 Linesman's pliers are very useful because it can help perform many automotive service jobs.

CUTTING WIRES CLOSE TO TERMINALS

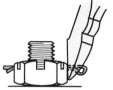

PULLING OUT AND SPREADING COTTER PIN

FIGURE 2–33 Diagonal-cut pliers are another common tool that has many names.

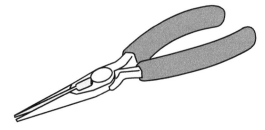

FIGURE 2–34 Needle-nose pliers are used where there is limited access to a wire or pin that needs to be installed or removed.

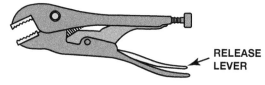

RELEASE LEVER

FIGURE 2–35 Locking pliers are best known by their trade name Vise Grips®.

TECH TIP

Pound with Something Softer

If you must pound on something, be sure to use a tool that is softer than what you are about to pound on to avoid damage. Examples are given in the following table.

The Material Being Pounded	What to Pound with
Steel or cast iron	Brass or aluminum hammer or punch
Aluminum	Plastic or rawhide mallet or plastic-covered dead-blow hammer
Plastic	Rawhide mallet or plastic dead-blow hammer

NEEDLE-NOSE PLIERS   *Needle-nose pliers* are designed to grip small objects or objects in tight locations. Needle-nose pliers have long, pointed jaws, which allow the tips to reach into narrow openings or groups of small objects. ● SEE FIGURE 2–34.

Most needle-nose pliers have a wire cutter located at the base of the jaws near the pivot. There are several variations of needle nose pliers, including right angle jaws or slightly angled to allow access to certain cramped areas.

LOCKING PLIERS   *Locking pliers* are adjustable pliers that can be locked to hold objects from moving. Most locking pliers also have wire cutters built into the jaws near the pivot point. Locking pliers come in a variety of styles and sizes and are commonly referred to by the trade name *Vise Grips®.* The size is the length of the pliers, not how far the jaws open. ● SEE FIGURE 2–35.

SNAP-RING PLIERS   *Snap-ring pliers* are used to remove and install snap rings. Many snap-ring pliers are designed to be able to remove and install both inward, as well as outward, expanding snap rings. Some snap-ring pliers can be equipped with serrated-tipped jaws for grasping the opening in the snap ring, while others are equipped with points, which are inserted into the holes in the snap ring. ● SEE FIGURE 2–36.

SAFE USE OF PLIERS   Pliers should not be used to remove any bolt or other fastener. Pliers should only be used when specified for use by the vehicle manufacturer.

FILES   **Files** are used to smooth metal and are constructed of hardened steel with diagonal rows of teeth. Files are available with a single row of teeth called a *single cut file*, as well as two rows of teeth cut at an opposite angle called a *double cut file*. Files are available in a variety of shapes and sizes from small flat files, half-round files, and triangular files. ● SEE FIGURE 2–37.

SAFE USE OF FILES   Always use a file with a handle. Because files only cut when moved forward, a handle must be attached to prevent possible personal injury. After making a forward strike, lift the file and return the file to the starting position; avoid dragging the file backward.

SNIPS   Service technicians are often asked to fabricate sheet metal brackets or heat shields and need to use one or more types of cutters available called **snips**. *Tin snips* are the simplest and are designed to make straight cuts in a variety of materials, such as sheet steel, aluminum, or even fabric. A variation of the tin snips is called *aviation tin snips*. There are three designs of aviation snips including one

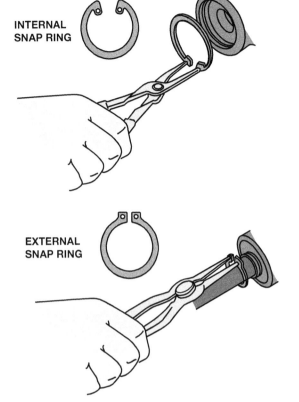

INTERNAL SNAP RING

EXTERNAL SNAP RING

FIGURE 2–36 Snap-ring pliers are also called lock-ring pliers and most are designed to remove internal and external snap rings (lock rings).

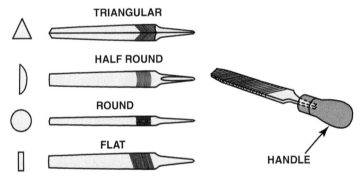

TRIANGULAR

HALF ROUND

ROUND

FLAT

HANDLE

FIGURE 2–37 Files come in many different shapes and sizes. Never use a file without a handle.

designed to cut straight (called a *straight cut aviation snip*), one designed to cut left (called an *offset left aviation snip*), and one designed to cut right (called an *offset right aviation snip*). ● **SEE FIGURE 2–38.**

UTILITY KNIFE A *utility knife* uses a replaceable blade and is used to cut a variety of materials such as carpet, plastic, wood, and paper products, such as cardboard. ● **SEE FIGURE 2–39.**

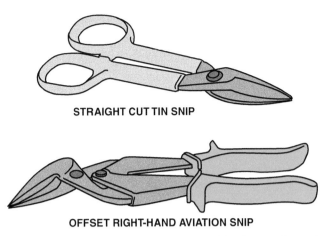

STRAIGHT CUT TIN SNIP

OFFSET RIGHT-HAND AVIATION SNIP

FIGURE 2–38 Tin snips are used to cut thin sheets of metal or carpet.

FIGURE 2–39 A utility knife uses replaceable blades and is used to cut carpet and other materials.

 **TECH TIP**

Brand Name Versus Proper Term

Technicians often use slang or brand names of tools rather than the proper term. This results in some confusion for new technicians. Some examples are given in the following table.

Brand Name	Proper Term	Slang Name
Crescent wrench®	Adjustable wrench	Monkey wrench
Vise Grips®	Locking pliers	
Channel Locks®	Water pump pliers or multigroove adjustable pliers	Pump pliers
	Diagonal cutting pliers	Dikes or side cuts

FIGURE 2–40 A punch used to drive pins from assembled components. This type of punch is also called a pin punch.

FIGURE 2–41 Warning stamped on the side of a punch warning that goggles should be worn when using this tool. Always follow safety warnings.

SAFE USE OF CUTTERS Whenever using cutters, always wear eye protection or a face shield to guard against the possibility of metal pieces being ejected during the cut. Always follow recommended procedures.

PUNCHES A **punch** is a small diameter steel rod that has a smaller diameter ground at one end. A punch is used to drive a pin out that is used to retain two components. Punches come in a variety of sizes, which are measured across the diameter of the machined end. Sizes include 1/16, 1/8, 3/16, and 1/4 inch.
● **SEE FIGURE 2–40.**

CHISELS A **chisel** has a straight, sharp cutting end that is used for cutting off rivets or to separate two pieces of an assembly. The most common design of chisel used for automotive service work is called a *cold chisel*.

SAFE USE OF PUNCHES AND CHISELS Always wear eye protection when using a punch or a chisel because the hardened steel is brittle and parts of the punch could fly off and cause serious personal injury. See the warning stamped on the side of this automotive punch in ● **FIGURE 2–41.**

The tops of punches and chisels can become rounded off from use, which is called "mushroomed." This material must

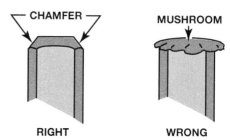

FIGURE 2–42 Use a grinder or a file to remove the mushroom material on the end of a punch or chisel.

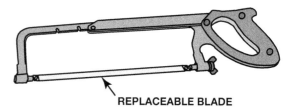

FIGURE 2–43 A typical hacksaw that is used to cut metal. If cutting sheet metal or thin objects, a blade with more teeth should be used.

be ground off to help avoid the possibility of the overhanging material being loosened and becoming airborne during use.
● **SEE FIGURE 2–42.**

HACKSAWS A **hacksaw** is used to cut metals, such as steel, aluminum, brass, or copper. The cutting blade of a hacksaw is replaceable and the sharpness and number of teeth can be varied to meet the needs of the job. Use 14 or 18 teeth per inch (TPI) for cutting plaster or soft metals, such as aluminum and copper. Use 24 or 32 teeth per inch for steel or pipe. Hacksaw blades should be installed with the teeth pointing away from the handle. This means that a hacksaw only cuts while the blade is pushed in the forward direction.
● **SEE FIGURE 2–43.**

SAFE USE OF HACKSAWS Check that the hacksaw is equipped with the correct blade for the job and that the teeth are pointed away from the handle. When using a hacksaw, move the hacksaw slowly away from you, then lift slightly and return for another cut.

BASIC HAND TOOL LIST

The following is a typical list of hand tools every automotive technician should possess. Specialty tools are not included.

    Safety glasses

    Tool chest

    1/4 inch drive socket set (1/4 to 9/16 inch standard and
        deep sockets; 6 to 15 mm standard and deep sockets)

1/4 inch drive ratchet

1/4 inch drive 2 inch extension

1/4 inch drive 6 inch extension

1/4 inch drive handle

3/8 inch drive socket set (3/8 to 7/8 inch standard and deep sockets; 10 to 19 mm standard and deep sockets)

3/8 inch drive Torx set (T40, T45, T50, and T55)

3/8 inch drive 13/16 inch plug socket

3/8 inch drive 5/8 inch plug socket

3/8 inch drive ratchet

3/8 inch drive 1 1/2 inch extension

3/8 inch drive 3 inch extension

3/8 inch drive 6 inch extension

3/8 inch drive 18 inch extension

3/8 inch drive universal

1/2 inch drive socket set (1/2 to 1 inch standard and deep sockets)

1/2 inch drive ratchet

1/2 inch drive breaker bar

1/2 inch drive 5 inch extension

1/2 inch drive 10 inch extension

3/8 to 1/4 inch adapter

1/2 to 3/8 inch adapter

3/8 to 1/2 inch adapter

3/8 and 1/2 inch torque wrench

Torque angle gauge

Crowfoot set (fractional inch)

Crowfoot set (metric)

3/8 through 1 inch combination wrench set

10 through 19 mm combination wrench set

1/16 through 1/4 inch hex wrench set

2 through 12 mm hex wrench set

3/8 inch hex socket

13 to 14 mm flare-nut wrench

15 to 17 mm flare-nut wrench

5/16 to 3/8 inch flare-nut wrench

7/16 to 1/2 inch flare-nut wrench

1/2 to 9/16 inch flare-nut wrench

Diagonal pliers

Needle pliers

Adjustable-jaw pliers

Locking pliers

Snap-ring pliers

Stripping or crimping pliers

Ball-peen hammer

Rubber hammer

Dead-blow hammer

Five-piece standard screwdriver set

Four-piece Phillips screwdriver set

#15 Torx screwdriver

#20 Torx screwdriver

Center punch

Pin punches (assorted sizes)

Chisel

Utility knife

Valve core tool

Filter wrench (large filters)

Filter wrench (smaller filters)

Test light

Feeler gauge

Scraper

Pinch bar

Magnet

 TECH TIP

Need to Borrow a Tool More Than Twice? Buy It!
Most service technicians agree that it is okay for a beginning technician to borrow a tool occasionally. However, if a tool has to be borrowed more than twice, then be sure to purchase it as soon as possible. Also, whenever a tool is borrowed, be sure that you clean the tool and let the technician you borrowed the tool from know that you are returning the tool. These actions will help in any future dealings with other technicians.

TOOL SETS AND ACCESSORIES

A beginning service technician may wish to start with a small set of tools before purchasing an expensive tool set. ● **SEE FIGURES 2–44 AND 2–45.**

ELECTRICAL HAND TOOLS

TEST LIGHT A test light is used to test for electricity. A typical automotive test light consists of a clear plastic screwdriver-like handle that contains a lightbulb. A wire is attached to one terminal of the bulb, which the technician connects to a clean metal part of the vehicle. The other end of the bulb is attached to a point that can be used to test for electricity at a connector or wire. When there is power at the

FIGURE 2–44 A typical beginning technician tool set that includes the basic tools to get started.

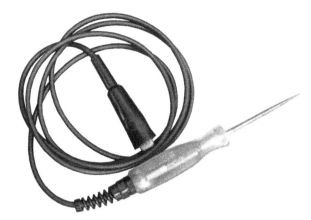
FIGURE 2–46 A typical 12 volt test light.

FIGURE 2–45 A typical 40 inch wide top and bottom professional tool box.

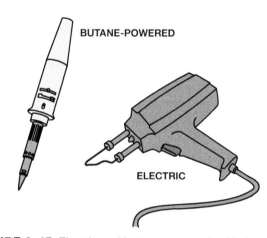
FIGURE 2–47 Electric and butane-powered soldering guns used to make electrical repairs. Soldering guns are sold by the wattage rating. The higher the wattage, the greater the amount of heat created. Most solder guns used for automotive electrical work usually fall within the 60 to 160 watt range.

point and a good connection at the other end, the lightbulb lights. ● SEE FIGURE 2–46.

SOLDERING GUNS

ELECTRIC SOLDERING GUN. This type of soldering gun is usually powered by 110-volt AC and often has two power settings expressed in watts. A typical electric soldering gun will produce from 85 to 300 watts of heat at the tip, which is more than adequate for soldering.

ELECTRIC SOLDERING PENCIL. This type of soldering iron is less expensive and creates less heat than an electric soldering gun. A typical electric soldering pencil (iron) creates 30 to 60 watts of heat and is suitable for soldering smaller wires and connections.

BUTANE-POWERED SOLDERING IRON. A butane-powered soldering iron is portable and very useful for automotive service work because an electrical cord is not needed. Most butane-powered soldering irons produce about 60 watts of heat, which is enough for most automotive soldering. ● SEE FIGURE 2–47.

ELECTRICAL WORK HAND TOOLS In addition to a soldering iron, most service technicians who do electrical-related work should have the following:

- Wire cutters
- Wire strippers
- Wire crimpers
- Heat gun for heat shrink tubing

DIGITAL METER A digital meter is a necessary tool for any electrical diagnosis and troubleshooting. A digital

What Is an "SST"?

Vehicle manufacturers often specify a **special service tool (SST)** to properly disassemble and assemble components, such as transmissions and other components. These tools are also called special tools and are available from the vehicle manufacturer or their tool supplier, such as Kent-Moore and Miller tools. Many service technicians do not have access to special service tools so they use generic versions that are available from aftermarket sources.

multimeter, abbreviated DMM, is usually capable of measuring the following units of electricity:

- DC volts
- AC volts
- Ohms
- Amperes

HAND TOOL MAINTENANCE

Most hand tools are constructed of rust-resistant metals but they can still rust or corrode if not properly maintained. For best results and long tool life, the following steps should be taken:

- Clean each tool before placing it back into the tool box.
- Keep tools separated. Moisture on metal tools will start to rust more readily if the tools are in contact with another metal tool.
- Line the drawers of the tool box with a material that will prevent the tools from moving as the drawers are opened and closed. This helps to quickly locate the proper tool and size.
- Release the tension on all "clicker-type" torque wrenches.
- Keep the tool box secure.

TROUBLE LIGHTS

INCANDESCENT   *Incandescent lights* use a filament that produces light when electric current flows through the bulb. This was the standard **trouble light**, also called a *work light* for many years until safety issues caused most shops to switch to safer fluorescent or LED lights. If incandescent lightbulbs are used, try to locate bulbs that are rated "rough service,"

which is designed to withstand shock and vibration more than conventional lightbulbs.

FLUORESCENT   A trouble light is an essential piece of shop equipment, and for safety, should be fluorescent rather than incandescent. Incandescent lightbulbs can scatter or break if gasoline were to be splashed onto the bulb creating a serious fire hazard. Fluorescent light tubes are not as likely to be broken and are usually protected by a clear plastic enclosure. Trouble lights are usually attached to a retractor, which can hold 20 to 50 feet of electrical cord.

LED TROUBLE LIGHT   Light-emitting diode (LED) trouble lights are excellent to use because they are shock resistant, are long lasting, and do not represent a fire hazard. Some trouble lights are battery powered, and therefore, can be used in places where an attached electrical cord could present problems. ● **SEE FIGURE 2–48.**

AIR AND ELECTRICALLY OPERATED TOOLS

IMPACT WRENCH   An impact wrench, either air or electrically powered, is a tool that is used to remove and install fasteners. The air-operated 1/2 inch drive impact wrench is the most commonly used unit. ● **SEE FIGURE 2–49.**

Electrically powered impact wrenches commonly include:

- Battery-powered units. ● **SEE FIGURE 2–50.**
- 110-volt AC-powered units. This type of impact is very useful, especially if compressed air is not readily available.

AIR RATCHET   An air ratchet is used to remove and install fasteners that would normally be removed or installed using a ratchet and a socket. ● **SEE FIGURE 2–52.**

DIE GRINDER   A die grinder is a commonly used air-powered tool which can also be used to sand or remove gaskets and rust. ● **SEE FIGURE 2–53.**

FIGURE 2–48 A battery-powered LED trouble light.

FIGURE 2–50 A typical battery-powered 1/2 inch drive impact wrench.

FIGURE 2–49 A typical 1/2 inch drive air impact wrench. The direction of rotation can be changed to loosen or tighten a fastener.

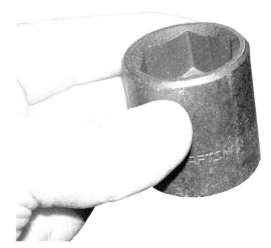

FIGURE 2–51 A black impact socket. Always use an impact-type socket whenever using an impact wrench to avoid the possibility of shattering the socket, which could cause personal injury. If a socket is chrome plated, it is not to be used with an impact wrench.

BENCH OR PEDESTAL-MOUNTED GRINDER These high-powered grinders can be equipped with a wire brush wheel and/or a stone wheel.

- **Wire brush wheel**—This type is used to clean threads of bolts as well as to remove gaskets from sheet metal engine parts.
- **Stone wheel**—This type is used to grind metal or to remove the mushroom from the top of punches or chisels. ● **SEE FIGURE 2–54.**

Most **bench grinders** are equipped with a grinder wheel (stone) on one end and a wire brush wheel on the other end. A bench grinder is a very useful piece of shop equipment and the wire wheel end can be used for the following:

- Cleaning threads of bolts
- Cleaning gaskets from sheet metal parts, such as steel valve covers

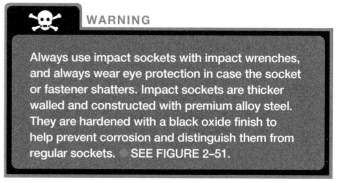

WARNING

Always use impact sockets with impact wrenches, and always wear eye protection in case the socket or fastener shatters. Impact sockets are thicker walled and constructed with premium alloy steel. They are hardened with a black oxide finish to help prevent corrosion and distinguish them from regular sockets. ● SEE FIGURE 2–51.

CAUTION: Only use a steel wire brush on steel or iron components. If a steel wire brush is used on aluminum or copper-based metal parts, it can remove metal from the part.

FIGURE 2–52 An air ratchet is a very useful tool that allows fast removal and installation of fasteners, especially in areas that are difficult to reach or do not have room enough to move a hand ratchet or wrench.

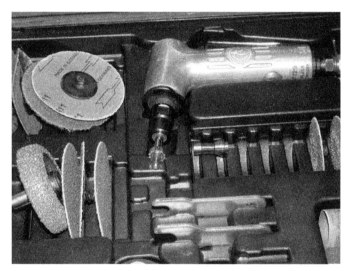

FIGURE 2–53 This typical die grinder surface preparation kit includes the air-operated die grinder as well as a variety of sanding disks for smoothing surfaces or removing rust.

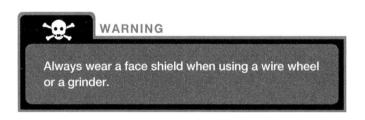

☠ **WARNING**

Always wear a face shield when using a wire wheel or a grinder.

The grinding stone end of the bench grinder can be used for the following:

- Sharpening blades and drill bits
- Grinding off the heads of rivets or parts
- Sharpening sheet metal parts for custom fitting

FIGURE 2–54 A typical pedestal grinder with a wire wheel on the left side and a stone wheel on the right side. Even though this machine is equipped with guards, safety glasses or a face shield should always be worn whenever using a grinder or wire wheel.

PERSONAL PROTECTIVE EQUIPMENT

Service technicians should wear **personal protective equipment (PPE)** to prevent personal injury. The personal protection devices include the following:

SAFETY GLASSES Wear safety glasses at all times while servicing any vehicle and be sure that they meet standard ANSI Z87.1. ● **SEE FIGURE 2–55.**

STEEL-TOED SAFETY SHOES ● **SEE FIGURE 2–56.** If steel-toed safety shoes are not available, then leather-topped shoes offer more protection than canvas or cloth covered shoes.

BUMP CAP Service technicians working under a vehicle should wear a **bump cap** to protect the head against under-vehicle objects and the pads of the lift. ● **SEE FIGURE 2–57.**

HEARING PROTECTION Hearing protection should be worn if the sound around you requires that you raise your voice (sound level higher than 90 dB). For example, a typical lawnmower produces noise at a level of about 110 dB. This means that everyone who uses a lawnmower or other lawn or garden equipment should wear ear protection.

GLOVES Many technicians wear gloves not only to help keep their hands clean but also to help protect their skin from the effects of dirty engine oil and other possibly hazardous materials.

Several types of gloves and their characteristics include:

- **Latex surgical gloves.** These gloves are relatively inexpensive, but tend to stretch, swell, and weaken when exposed to gas, oil, or solvents.

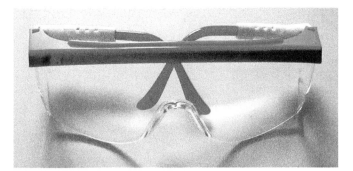

FIGURE 2–55 Safety glasses should be worn at all times when working on or around any vehicle or servicing any components.

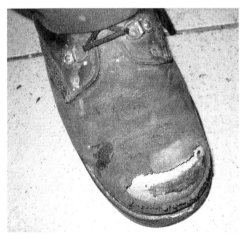

FIGURE 2–56 Steel-toed shoes are a worthwhile investment to help prevent foot injury due to falling objects. Even these well-worn shoes can protect the feet of this service technician.

FIGURE 2–57 One version of a bump cap is a molded plastic insert that is worn inside a regular cloth cap.

- **Vinyl gloves.** These gloves are also inexpensive and are not affected by gas, oil, or solvents.
- **Polyurethane gloves.** These gloves are more expensive, yet very strong. Even though these gloves are also not affected by gas, oil, or solvents, they do tend to be slippery.

FIGURE 2–58 Protective gloves are available in several sizes and materials.

- **Nitrile gloves.** These gloves are exactly like latex gloves, but are not affected by gas, oil, or solvents, yet they tend to be expensive.
- **Mechanic's gloves.** These gloves are usually made of synthetic leather and spandex and provide thermo protection, as well as protection from dirt and grime.
  ● **SEE FIGURE 2–58.**

SAFETY PRECAUTIONS

Besides wearing personal safety equipment, there are also many actions that should be performed to keep safe in the shop. These actions include the following:

- Remove jewelry that may get caught on something or act as a conductor to an exposed electrical circuit.
  ● **SEE FIGURE 2–59.**
- Take care of your hands. Keep your hands clean by washing with soap and hot water that is at least 110°F (43°C).
- Avoid loose or dangling clothing.
- When lifting any object, get a secure grip with solid footing. Keep the load close to your body to minimize the strain. Lift with your legs and arms, not your back.
- Do not twist your body when carrying a load. Instead, pivot your feet to help prevent strain on the spine.
- Ask for help when moving or lifting heavy objects.
- Push a heavy object rather than pull it. (This is opposite to the way you should work with tools—never push a wrench! If you do and a bolt or nut loosens, your entire weight is used to propel your hand(s) forward. This usually results in cuts, bruises, or other painful injury.)

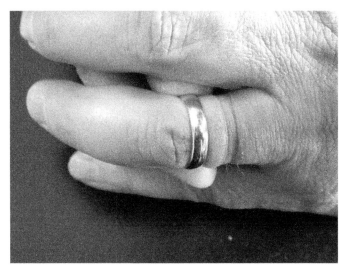

FIGURE 2–59 Remove all jewelry before performing service work on any vehicle.

FIGURE 2–60 Always connect an exhaust hose to the tailpipe of a vehicle to be run inside a building.

- Always connect an exhaust hose to the tailpipe of any running vehicle to help prevent the buildup of carbon monoxide inside a closed garage space. ● **SEE FIGURE 2–60.**
- When standing, keep objects, parts, and tools with which you are working between chest height and waist height. If seated, work at tasks that are at elbow height.
- Always be sure the hood is securely held open.

VEHICLE PROTECTION

FENDER COVERS Whenever working under the hood of any vehicle, be sure to use fender covers. They not only help protect the vehicle from possible damage but they also provide a clean surface to place parts and tools. The major problem

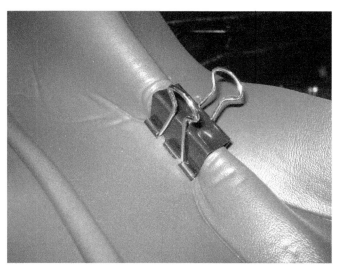

FIGURE 2–61 A binder clip being used to keep a fender cover from falling off.

with using fender covers is that they tend to move and often fall off the vehicle. To help prevent the fender covers from falling off, secure them to a lip of the fender using a *binder clip* available at most office supply stores. ● **SEE FIGURE 2–61.**

INTERIOR PROTECTION Always protect the interior of the vehicle from accidental damage or dirt and grease by covering the seat, steering wheel, and floor with a protective covering. ● **SEE FIGURE 2–62.**

SAFETY LIFTING (HOISTING) A VEHICLE

Many chassis and underbody service procedures require that the vehicle be hoisted or lifted off the ground. The simplest methods involve the use of drive-on ramps or a floor jack and safety (jack) stands, whereas in-ground or surface-mounted lifts provide greater access.

 SAFETY TIP

Shop Cloth Disposal

Always dispose of oily shop cloths in an enclosed container to prevent a fire. ● **SEE FIGURE 2–63.** Whenever oily cloths are thrown together on the floor or workbench, a chemical reaction can occur, which can ignite the cloth even without an open flame. This process of ignition without an open flame is called **spontaneous combustion**.

FIGURE 2–62 Covering the interior as soon as the vehicle comes in for service helps improve customer satisfaction.

FIGURE 2–63 All oily shop cloths should be stored in a metal container equipped with a lid to help prevent spontaneous combustion.

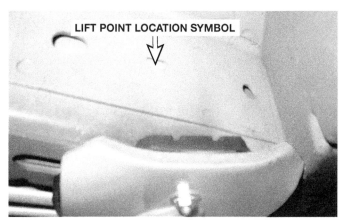

LIFT POINT LOCATION SYMBOL

FIGURE 2–64 Most newer vehicles have a triangle symbol indicating the recommended hoisting lift location.

Setting the pads is a critical part of this hoisting procedure. All vehicle service information, including service, shop, and owner's manuals, include recommended locations to be used when hoisting (lifting) a vehicle. Newer vehicles have a triangle decal on the driver's door indicating the recommended lift points. The recommended standards for the lift points and lifting procedures are found in SAE Standard JRP-2184. ● **SEE FIGURE 2–64.**

These recommendations typically include the following points:

1. The vehicle should be centered on the lift or hoist so as not to overload one side or put too much force either forward or rearward. ● **SEE FIGURE 2–65.**
2. The pads of the lift should be spread as far apart as possible to provide a stable platform.
3. Each pad should be placed under a portion of the vehicle that is strong and capable of supporting the weight of the vehicle.
   a. Pinch welds at the bottom edge of the body are generally considered to be strong.

CAUTION: Even though pinch weld seams are the recommended location for hoisting many vehicles with unitized bodies (unit-body), care should be taken not to place the pad(s) too far forward or rearward. Incorrect placement of the vehicle on the lift could cause the vehicle to be imbalanced, and the vehicle could fall. This is exactly what happened to the vehicle in ● FIGURE 2–66.

   b. Boxed areas of the body are the best places to position the pads on a vehicle without a frame. Be careful to note whether the arms of the lift might come into contact with other parts of the vehicle before the pad touches the intended location. Commonly damaged areas include the following:
      (1) Rocker panel moldings
      (2) Exhaust system (including catalytic converter)
      (3) Tires or body panels (● **SEE FIGURES 2–67 AND 2–68.**)
4. The vehicle should be raised about a foot (30 cm) off the floor, then stopped and shaken to check for stability. If the vehicle seems to be stable when checked at a short distance from the floor, continue raising the vehicle and continue to view the vehicle until it has reached the desired height. The hoist should be lowered onto the mechanical locks, and then raised off of the locks before lowering.

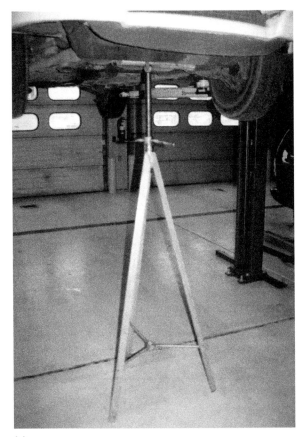

(a)

(b)

FIGURE 2–65 (a) Tall safety stands can be used to provide additional support for the vehicle while on the hoist. (b) A block of wood should be used to avoid the possibility of doing damage to components supported by the stand.

CAUTION: Do not look away from the vehicle while it is being raised (or lowered) on a hoist. Often one side or one end of the hoist can stop or fail, resulting in the vehicle being slanted enough to slip or fall, creating physical damage not only to the vehicle and/or hoist but also to the technician or others who may be nearby.

HINT: Most hoists can be safely placed at any desired height. For ease while working, the area in which you are working should be at chest level. When working on

FIGURE 2–66 This training vehicle fell from the hoist because the pads were not set correctly. No one was hurt but the vehicle was damaged.

brakes or suspension components, it is not necessary to work on them down near the floor or over your head. Raise the hoist so that the components are at chest level.

5. Before lowering the hoist, the safety latch(es) must be released and the direction of the controls reversed. The speed downward is often adjusted to be as slow as possible for additional safety.

JACKS AND SAFETY STANDS

Floor jacks properly rated for the weight of the vehicle being raised are a common vehicle lifting tool. Floor jacks are portable and relatively inexpensive and must be used with safety (jack) stands. The floor jack is used to raise the vehicle off the ground and safety stands should be placed under the frame on the body of the vehicle. The weight of the vehicle should never be kept on the hydraulic floor jack because a failure of the jack could cause the vehicle to fall. ● **SEE FIGURE 2–69.** The jack is then slowly released to allow the vehicle weight to be supported on the safety stands. If the front or rear of the vehicle is being raised, the opposite end of the vehicle must be blocked.

CAUTION: Safety stands should be rated higher than the weight they support.

DRIVE-ON RAMPS

Ramps are an inexpensive way to raise the front or rear of a vehicle. ● **SEE FIGURE 2–70.** Ramps are easy to store, but they can be dangerous because they can "kick out" when driving the vehicle onto the ramps.

(a)

(b)

FIGURE 2–67 (a) An assortment of hoist pad adapters that are often needed to safely hoist many pickup trucks, vans, and sport utility vehicles (SUVs). (b) A view from underneath a Chevrolet pickup truck showing how the pad extensions are used to attach the hoist lifting pad to contact the frame.

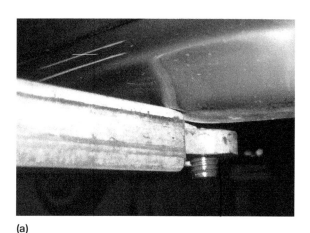

(a)

(b)

FIGURE 2–68 (a) The pad arm is just contacting the rocker panel of the vehicle. (b) The pad arm has dented the rocker panel on this vehicle because the pad was set too far inward underneath the vehicle.

CAUTION: Professional repair shops do not use ramps because they are dangerous to use. Use only with extreme care.

ELECTRICAL CORD SAFETY

Use correctly grounded three-prong sockets and extension cords to operate power tools. Some tools use only two-prong plugs. Make sure these are double insulated and repair or replace any electrical cords that are cut or damaged to prevent the possibility of an electrical shock. When not in use, keep electrical cords off the floor to prevent tripping over them. Tape the cords down if they are placed in high foot traffic areas.

JUMP STARTING AND BATTERY SAFETY

To jump-start another vehicle with a dead battery, connect good-quality copper jumper cables as indicated in ● **FIGURE 2–71** or a jump box. The last connection made should always be on the engine block or an engine bracket as far from the battery as possible. It is normal for a spark to be created when the jumper cables finally complete the jumper cable connections, and this spark could cause an explosion of the gases around the battery. Many newer vehicles have special ground connections built away from the battery just for the purpose of jump starting. Check the owner's manual or service information for the exact location.

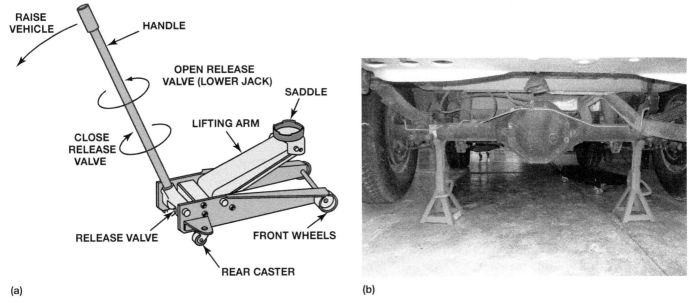

(a)

(b)

FIGURE 2–69 (a) A hydraulic hand-operated floor jack. (b) Whenever a vehicle is raised off the ground, a safety stand should be placed under the frame, axle, or body to support the weight of the vehicle.

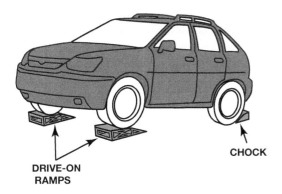

FIGURE 2–70 Drive-on-type ramps are dangerous to use. The wheels on the ground level must be chocked (blocked) to prevent accidental movement down the ramp.

Batteries contain acid and should be handled with care to avoid tipping them greater than a 45-degree angle. Always remove jewelry when working around a battery to avoid the possibility of electrical shock or burns, which can occur when the metal comes in contact with a 12-volt circuit and ground, such as the body of the vehicle.

SAFETY TIP

Air Hose Safety

Improper use of an air nozzle can cause blindness or deafness. Compressed air must be reduced to less than 30 PSI (206 kPa). ● **SEE FIGURE 2–72.** If an air nozzle is used to dry and clean parts, make sure the airstream is directed away from anyone else in the immediate area. Coil and store air hoses when they are not in use.

FIRE EXTINGUISHERS

There are four **fire extinguisher classes**. Each class should be used on specific fires only:

- Class A is designed for use on general combustibles, such as cloth, paper, and wood.

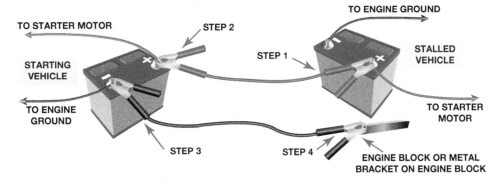

FIGURE 2–71 Jumper cable usage guide. Follow the same connections if using a portable jump box.

FIGURE 2–72 The air pressure going to the nozzle should be reduced to 30 PSI or less to help prevent personal injury.

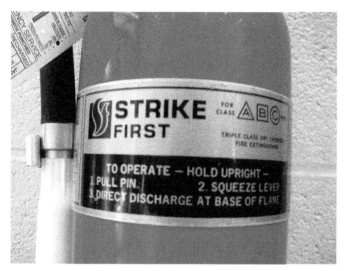

FIGURE 2–73 A typical fire extinguisher designed to be used on type A, B, or C fires.

- Class B is designed for use on flammable liquids and greases, including gasoline, oil, thinners, and solvents.
- Class C is used only on electrical fires.
- Class D is effective only on combustible metals such as powdered aluminum, sodium, or magnesium.

The class rating is clearly marked on the side of every fire extinguisher. Many extinguishers are good for multiple types of fires. ● **SEE FIGURE 2–73.**

When using a fire extinguisher, remember the word "PASS."

P = Pull the safety pin.

A = Aim the nozzle of the extinguisher at the base of the fire.

S = Squeeze the lever to actuate the extinguisher.

S = Sweep the nozzle from side to side.

● **SEE FIGURE 2–74.**

FIGURE 2–74 A CO_2 fire extinguisher being used on a fire set in an open drum during a demonstration at a fire training center.

TYPES OF FIRE EXTINGUISHERS Types of fire extinguishers include the following:

- **Water.** A water fire extinguisher, usually in a pressurized container, is good to use on Class A fires by reducing the temperature to the point where a fire cannot be sustained.
- **Carbon dioxide (CO_2).** A carbon dioxide fire extinguisher is good for almost any type of fire, especially Class B and Class C materials. A CO_2 fire extinguisher works by removing the oxygen from the fire and the cold CO_2 also helps reduce the temperature of the fire.
- **Dry chemical (yellow).** A dry chemical fire extinguisher is good for Class A, B, and C fires. It acts by coating the flammable materials, which eliminates the oxygen from the fire. A dry chemical fire extinguisher tends to be very corrosive and will cause damage to electronic devices.

FIRE BLANKETS

Fire blankets are required to be available in the shop areas. If a person is on fire, a fire blanket should be removed from its storage bag and thrown over and around the victim to smother the fire. ● **SEE FIGURE 2–75** showing a typical fire blanket.

FIRST AID AND EYE WASH STATIONS

All shop areas must be equipped with a first aid kit and an eye wash station centrally located and kept stocked with emergency supplies. ● **SEE FIGURE 2–76.**

FIGURE 2–75 A treated wool blanket is kept in an easy-to-open wall-mounted holder and should be placed in a central location in the shop.

FIGURE 2–76 A first aid box should be centrally located in the shop and kept stocked with the recommended supplies.

FIRST AID KIT   A first aid kit should include:

- Bandages (variety)
- Gauze pads
- Roll gauze
- Iodine swab sticks
- Antibiotic ointment
- Hydrocortisone cream
- Burn gel packets
- Eye wash solution
- Scissors
- Tweezers

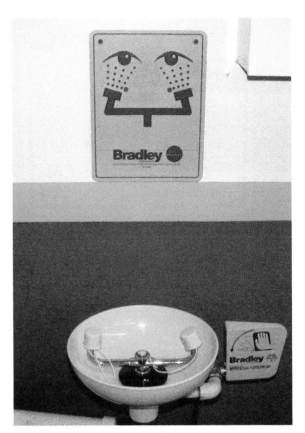

FIGURE 2–77 A typical eye wash station. Often a thorough flushing of the eyes with water is the first and often the best treatment in the event of eye contamination.

- Gloves
- First aid guide

Every shop should have a person trained in first aid. If there is an accident, call for help immediately.

EYE WASH STATION   An **eye wash station** should be centrally located and used whenever any liquid or chemical gets into the eyes. If such an emergency does occur, keep eyes in a constant stream of water and call for professional assistance. ● **SEE FIGURE 2–77.**

HYBRID ELECTRIC VEHICLE SAFETY ISSUES

Hybrid electric vehicles (HEVs) use a high-voltage battery pack and an electric motor(s) to help propel the vehicle. ● **SEE FIGURE 2–78** for an example of a typical warning label on a hybrid electric vehicle. The gasoline or diesel engine also is equipped with a generator or a combination starter and an integrated starter generator (ISG) or integrated starter alternator (ISA). To safely work

FIGURE 2–78 A warning label on a Honda hybrid warns that a person can be killed due to the high-voltage circuits under the cover.

FIGURE 2–79 The high-voltage disconnect switch is in the trunk area on a Toyota Prius. Insulated rubber lineman's gloves should be worn when removing this plug.

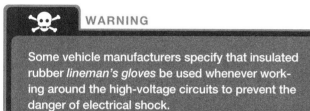
WARNING

Some vehicle manufacturers specify that insulated rubber *lineman's gloves* be used whenever working around the high-voltage circuits to prevent the danger of electrical shock.

around a hybrid electric vehicle, the high-voltage (HV) battery and circuits should be shut off following these steps:

STEP 1 Turn off the ignition key (if equipped) and remove the key from the ignition switch. (This will shut off all high-voltage circuits if the relay[s] is[are] working correctly.)

STEP 2 Disconnect the high-voltage circuits.

TOYOTA PRIUS The cutoff switch is located in the trunk. To gain access, remove three clips holding the upper left portion of the trunk side cover. To disconnect the high-voltage system, pull the orange handled plug while wearing insulated rubber lineman's gloves. ● **SEE FIGURE 2–79.**

FORD ESCAPE/MERCURY MARINER Ford and Mercury specify that the following steps should be included when working with the high-voltage (HV) systems of a hybrid vehicle:

■ Four orange cones are to be placed at the four corners of the vehicle to create a buffer zone.

■ High-voltage insulated gloves are to be worn with an outer leather glove to protect the inner rubber glove from possible damage.

SAFETY TIP

Infection Control Precautions

Working on a vehicle can result in personal injury including the possibility of being cut or hurt enough to cause bleeding. Some infections such as hepatitis B, HIV (which can cause acquired immunodeficiency syndrome, or AIDS), and hepatitis C virus are transmitted through blood. These infections are commonly called blood-borne pathogens. Report any injury that involves blood to your supervisor and take the necessary precautions to avoid coming in contact with blood from another person.

■ The service technician should also wear a face shield and a fiberglass hook should be in the area and used to move a technician in the event of electrocution.

The high-voltage shut-off switch is located in the rear of the vehicle under the right side carpet. ● **SEE FIGURE 2–80.** Rotate the handle to the "service shipping" position, lift it out to disable the high-voltage circuit, and wait five minutes before removing high-voltage cables.

HONDA CIVIC To totally disable the high-voltage system on a Honda Civic, remove the main fuse (labeled number 1) from the driver's side underhood fuse panel. This should be all that is necessary to shut off the high-voltage circuit. If this is not possible, then remove the rear seat cushion and seat back. Remove the metal switch cover labeled "up" and remove the red locking cover. Move the "battery module switch" down to disable the high-voltage system.

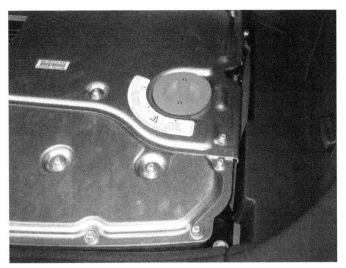

FIGURE 2–80 The high-voltage shut-off switch on a Ford Escape hybrid. The switch is located under the carpet at the rear of the vehicle.

FIGURE 2–81 The shut-off switch on a GM parallel hybrid truck is green because this system uses 42 volts instead of higher, and possibly fatal, voltages used in other hybrid vehicles.

 **WARNING**

Do not touch any orange wiring or component without following the vehicle manufacturer's procedures and wearing the specified personal protective equipment.

CHEVROLET SILVERADO/GMC SIERRA PICKUP TRUCK The high-voltage shut-off switch is located under the rear passenger seat. Remove the cover marked "energy storage box" and turn the green service disconnect switch to the horizontal position to turn off the high-voltage circuits.
● **SEE FIGURE 2–81.**

HOISTING THE VEHICLE

1 The first step in hoisting a vehicle is to properly align the vehicle in the center of the stall.

2 Most vehicles will be correctly positioned when the left front tire is centered on the tire pad.

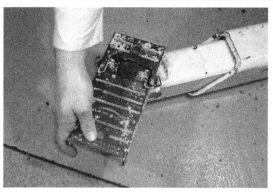

3 The arms can be moved in and out and most pads can be rotated to allow for many different types of vehicle construction.

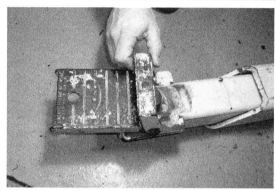

4 Most lifts are equipped with short pad extensions that are often necessary to use to allow the pad to contact the frame of a vehicle without causing the arm of the lift to hit and damage parts of the body.

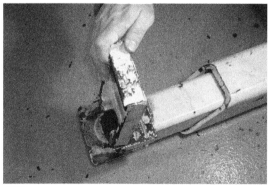

5 Tall pad extensions can also be used to gain access to the frame of a vehicle. This position is needed to safely hoist many pickup trucks, vans, and sport utility vehicles.

6 An additional extension may be necessary to hoist a truck or van equipped with running boards to give the necessary clearance.

7 Position the pads under the vehicle under the recommended locations.

8 After being sure all pads are correctly positioned, use the electromechanical controls to raise the vehicle.

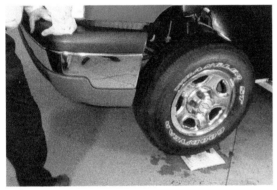

9 With the vehicle raised 1 foot (30 cm) off the ground, push down on the vehicle to check to see if it is stable on the pads. If the vehicle rocks, lower the vehicle and reset the pads. The vehicle can be raised to any desired working level. Be sure the safety is engaged before working on or under the vehicle.

10 If raising a vehicle without a frame, place the flat pads under the pinch weld seam to spread the load. If additional clearance is necessary, the pads can be raised as shown.

11 When the service work is completed, the hoist should be raised slightly and the safety released before using the hydraulic lever to lower the vehicle.

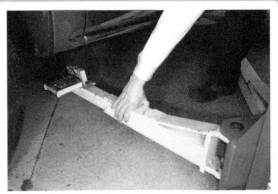

12 After lowering the vehicle, be sure all arms of the lift are moved out of the way before driving the vehicle out of the work stall.

SUMMARY

1. Bolts, studs, and nuts are commonly used as fasteners in the chassis. The sizes for fractional and metric threads are different and are not interchangeable. The grade is the rating of the strength of a fastener.

2. Whenever a vehicle is raised above the ground, it must be supported at a substantial section of the body or frame.

3. Wrenches are available in open end, box end, and combination open and box end.

4. An adjustable wrench should only be used where the proper size is not available.

5. Line wrenches are also called flare-nut wrenches, fitting wrenches, or tube-nut wrenches and are used to remove fuel or refrigerant lines.

6. Sockets are rotated by a ratchet or breaker bar, also called a flex handle.

7. Torque wrenches measure the amount of torque applied to a fastener.

8. Screwdriver types include straight blade (flat tip) and Phillips.

9. Hammers and mallets come in a variety of sizes and weights.

10. Pliers are a useful tool and are available in many different types, including slip-joint, multigroove, linesman's, diagonal, needle-nose, and locking pliers.

11. Other common hand tools include snap-ring pliers, files, cutters, punches, chisels, and hacksaws.

12. Hybrid electric vehicles should be de-powered if any of the high-voltage components are going to be serviced.

REVIEW QUESTIONS

1. Why are wrenches offset 15 degrees?
2. What are the other names for a line wrench?
3. What are the standard automotive drive sizes for sockets?
4. Which type of screwdriver requires the use of a hammer or mallet?
5. What is inside a dead-blow hammer?

CHAPTER QUIZ

1. The correct location for the pads when hoisting or jacking the vehicle can often be found in the _____.
   a. service manual
   b. shop manual
   c. owner's manual
   d. all of the above

2. For the best working position, the work should be _____.
   a. at neck or head level
   b. at knee or ankle level
   c. overhead by about 1 foot
   d. at chest or elbow level

3. A high-strength bolt is identified by _____.
   a. a UNC symbol
   b. lines on the head
   c. strength letter codes
   d. the coarse threads

4. A fastener that uses threads on both ends is called a _____.
   a. cap screw
   b. stud
   c. machine screw
   d. crest fastener

5. Wrenches are made from _____.
   a. cast from nickel steel
   b. forged alloy steel
   c. machined from billet steel
   d. cast from chrome steel

6. The proper term for Channel Locks is _____.
   a. Vise Grips
   b. crescent wrench
   c. locking pliers
   d. multigroove adjustable pliers

7. The proper term for Vise Grips is _____.
   a. locking pliers
   b. slip-joint pliers
   c. side cuts
   d. multigroove adjustable pliers

8. Two technicians are discussing torque wrenches. Technician A says that a torque wrench is capable of tightening a fastener with more torque than a conventional breaker bar or ratchet. Technician B says that a torque wrench should be calibrated regularly for the most accurate results. Which technician is correct?
   a. Technician A only
   b. Technician B only
   c. Both Technicians A and B
   d. Neither Technician A nor B

9. A yellow-handle snip is designed for _____.
   a. straight cuts
   b. left cuts
   c. right cuts
   d. cutting plastic only

10. What type of hammer is plastic coated, has a metal casing inside, and is filled with small lead balls?
   a. Dead-blow hammer
   b. Soft-blow hammer
   c. Sledgehammer
   d. Plastic hammer

chapter 3

ENVIRONMENTAL AND HAZARDOUS MATERIALS

LEARNING OBJECTIVES:

After studying this chapter, the reader will be able to:

Identify hazardous waste materials in accordance with state and federal regulations, and follow proper safety precautions while handling hazardous materials.

Define the Occupational Safety and Health Act (OSHA).

Explain the term "safety data sheets (SDS)."

Define the steps required to safely handle and store automotive chemicals and waste.

This chapter will help prepare for the ASE assumed knowledge content required by all service technicians to adhere to environmentally appropriate actions and behavior.

KEY TERMS: Aboveground storage tank (AGST) 46 • Asbestosis 44 • BCI 48 • CAA 44 • CFR 42 • EPA 42 • Hazardous waste material 42 • HEPA vacuum 44 • Mercury 51 • OSHA 42 • RCRA 43 • Right-to-know laws 43 • SDS 43 • Solvent 45 • Underground storage tank (UST) 46 • Used oil 45 • WHMIS 43

HAZARDOUS WASTE

DEFINITION OF HAZARDOUS WASTE **Hazardous waste materials** are chemicals, or components, that the shop no longer needs and that pose a danger to the environment and people if they are disposed of in ordinary garbage cans or sewers. However, no material is considered hazardous waste until the shop has finished using it and is ready to dispose of it.

PERSONAL PROTECTIVE EQUIPMENT (PPE) When handling hazardous waste material, always wear the proper protective clothing and equipment detailed in the right-to-know laws. This includes respirator equipment. All recommended procedures must be followed accurately. Personal injury may result from improper clothing, equipment, and procedures when handling hazardous materials.

FEDERAL AND STATE LAWS

OCCUPATIONAL SAFETY AND HEALTH ACT The U.S. Congress passed the **Occupational Safety and Health Act (OSHA)** in 1970. This legislation was designed to assist and encourage the citizens of the United States in their efforts to assure the following:

- Safe and healthful working conditions by providing research, information, education, and training in the field of occupational safety and health.
- Safe and healthful working conditions by authorizing enforcement of the standards developed under the act.

Because about 25% of workers are exposed to health and safety hazards on the job, OSHA standards are necessary to monitor, control, and educate workers regarding health and safety in the workplace.

EPA The **Environmental Protection Agency (EPA)** publishes a list of hazardous materials that is included in the **Code of Federal Regulations (CFR)**. The EPA considers waste hazardous if it is included on the EPA list of hazardous materials, or it has one or more of the following characteristics:

- **Reactive**—Any material that reacts violently with water or other chemicals is considered hazardous.
- **Corrosive**—If a material burns the skin, or dissolves metals and other materials, a technician should consider it hazardous. A pH scale is used, with number 7 indicating neutral. Pure water has a pH of 7. Lower numbers indicate an acidic solution and higher numbers indicates an alkaline (caustic) solution. If a material releases cyanide gas, hydrogen sulfide gas, or similar gases when exposed to low pH acid solutions, it is considered hazardous.

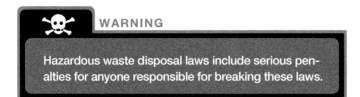

- **Toxic**—Materials are hazardous if they leak one or more of eight different heavy metals in concentrations greater than 100 times the primary drinking water standard.

- **Ignitable**—A liquid is hazardous if it has a flash point below 140°F (60°C), and a solid is hazardous if it ignites spontaneously.

- **Radioactive**—Any substance that emits measurable levels of radiation is radioactive. When individuals bring containers of a highly radioactive substance into the shop environment, qualified personnel with the appropriate equipment must test them.

RIGHT-TO-KNOW LAWS   The **right-to-know laws** state that employees have a right to know when the materials they use at work are hazardous. The right-to-know laws started with the Hazard Communication Standard published by the Occupational Safety and Health Administration (OSHA) in 1983. Originally, this document was intended for chemical companies and manufacturers that required employees to handle hazardous materials in their work situation but the federal courts have decided to apply these laws to all companies, including automotive service shops. Under the right-to-know laws, the employer has responsibilities regarding the handling of hazardous materials by their employees. All employees must be trained about the types of hazardous materials they will encounter in the workplace. The employees must be informed about their rights under legislation regarding the handling of hazardous materials.

SAFETY DATA SHEETS (SDS).   All hazardous materials must be properly labeled, and information about each hazardous material must be posted on **safety data sheets (SDS)**, formally called *material safety data sheets* (MSDS), available from the manufacturer. In Canada, MSDS information is called **Workplace Hazardous Materials Information Systems (WHMIS)**.

The employer has a responsibility to place MSDS information where it is easily accessible by all employees. The data sheets provide the following information about the hazardous material: chemical name, physical characteristics, protective handling equipment, explosion/fire hazards, incompatible materials, health hazards, medical conditions aggravated by exposure, emergency and first aid procedures, safe handling, and spill/leak procedures.

The employer also has a responsibility to make sure that all hazardous materials are properly labeled. The label information must include health, fire, and reactivity hazards posed by the material, as well as the protective equipment necessary to handle the material. The manufacturer must supply all warning and precautionary information about hazardous materials. This information must be read and understood by the employee before handling the material. ● **SEE FIGURE 3–1.**

RESOURCE CONSERVATION AND RECOVERY ACT

Federal and state laws control the disposal of hazardous waste materials and every shop employee must be familiar with these laws. Hazardous waste disposal laws include the **Resource Conservation and Recovery Act (RCRA)**. This law states that hazardous material users are responsible for hazardous materials from the time they become a waste until the proper disposal is completed. Many shops hire an independent hazardous waste hauler to dispose of hazardous waste material. The shop owner, or manager, should have a written contract with the hazardous waste hauler. Rather than have hazardous waste material hauled to an approved hazardous waste disposal site, a shop may choose to recycle the material in the shop. Therefore, the user must store hazardous waste material properly and safely, and be responsible for the transportation of this material until it arrives at an approved hazardous waste disposal site, where it can be processed according to the law. The RCRA controls the following types of automotive waste:

- Paint and body repair products waste
- Solvents for parts and equipment cleaning
- Batteries and battery acid
- Mild acids used for metal cleaning and preparation
- Waste oil and engine coolants or antifreeze
- Air-conditioning refrigerants and oils
- Engine oil filters

FIGURE 3–1 Safety data sheets (SDS), formerly known as material safety data sheets (MSDS), should be readily available for use by anyone in the area who may come into contact with hazardous materials.

FIGURE 3–2 Tag that identifies the electrical power has been removed and service work is being done.

LOCKOUT/TAGOUT According to OSHA Title 29, Code of Federal Regulations (CPR), part 1910.147, machinery must be locked out to prevent injury to employees when maintenance or repair work is being performed. Any piece of equipment that should not be used must be tagged and the electrical power disconnected to prevent it from being used. Always read, understand, and follow all safety warning tags. ● **SEE FIGURE 3–2.**

CLEAN AIR ACT Air-conditioning (A/C) systems and refrigerant are regulated by the **Clean Air Act (CAA)**, Title VI, Section 609. Technician certification and service equipment is also regulated. Any technician working on automotive A/C systems must be certified. A/C refrigerants must not be released or vented into the atmosphere, and used refrigerants must be recovered.

ASBESTOS HAZARDS

Friction materials, such as brake and clutch linings, often contain asbestos. While asbestos has been eliminated from most original equipment friction materials, the automotive service technician cannot know whether or not the vehicle being serviced is or is not equipped with friction materials containing asbestos. It is important that all friction materials be handled as if they do contain asbestos.

Asbestos exposure can cause scar tissue to form in the lungs. This condition is called **asbestosis**. It gradually causes increasing shortness of breath, and scarring to the lungs is permanent.

Even low exposures to asbestos can cause *mesothelioma*, a type of fatal cancer of the lining of the chest or abdominal cavity. Asbestos exposure can also increase the risk of *lung cancer*, as well as, cancer of the voice box, stomach, and large intestine. It usually takes 15 to 30 years or more for cancer or asbestos lung scarring to show up after exposure. Scientists call this the *latency period*.

Government agencies recommend that asbestos exposure should be eliminated or controlled to the lowest level possible. These agencies have developed recommendations and standards that the automotive service technician and equipment manufacturer should follow. These U.S. federal agencies include the National Institute for Occupational Safety and Health (NIOSH), Occupational Safety and Health Administration (OSHA), and Environmental Protection Agency (EPA).

ASBESTOS OSHA STANDARDS The Occupational Safety and Health Administration has established three levels of asbestos exposure. Any vehicle service establishment that does either brake or clutch work must limit employee exposure to asbestos to less than 0.2 fibers per cubic centimeter (cc) as determined by an air sample.

If the level of exposure to employees is greater than specified, corrective measures must be performed and a large fine may be imposed.

NOTE: Research has found that worn asbestos fibers, such as those from automotive brakes or clutches, may not be as hazardous as first believed. Worn asbestos fibers do not have sharp flared ends that can latch onto tissue, but rather are worn down to a dust form that resembles talc. Grinding or sawing operations on unworn brake shoes or clutch discs *will* contain *harmful* asbestos fibers. To limit health damage, always use proper handling procedures while working around any component that may contain asbestos.

ASBESTOS EPA REGULATIONS The federal Environmental Protection Agency has established procedures for the removal and disposal of asbestos. The EPA procedures require that products containing asbestos be "wetted" to prevent the asbestos fibers from becoming airborne. According to the EPA, asbestos-containing materials can be disposed of as regular waste. Only when asbestos becomes airborne, it is considered to be hazardous.

ASBESTOS HANDLING GUIDELINES The air in the shop area can be tested by a testing laboratory, but this can be expensive. Tests have determined that asbestos levels can easily be kept below the recommended levels by using a liquid, like water, or a special vacuum.

NOTE: Even though asbestos is being removed from brake and clutch lining materials, the service technician cannot tell whether or not the old brake pads, shoes, or clutch discs contain asbestos. Therefore, to be safe, the technician should assume that all brake pads, shoes, or clutch discs contain asbestos.

HEPA VACUUM. A special **high-efficiency particulate air (HEPA) vacuum** system has been proven to be effective in keeping asbestos exposure levels below 0.1 fibers per cubic centimeter.

SOLVENT SPRAY. Many technicians use an aerosol can of brake cleaning solvent to wet the brake dust and prevent it

from becoming airborne. A **solvent** is a liquid that is used to dissolve dirt, grime, or solid particles. Commercial brake cleaners are available that use a concentrated cleaner that is mixed with water. ● **SEE FIGURE 3–3.** The waste liquid is filtered, and when dry, the filter can be disposed of as solid waste.

DISPOSAL OF BRAKE DUST AND BRAKE SHOES.   The hazard of asbestos occurs when asbestos fibers are airborne. Once the asbestos has been wetted down, it is then considered to be solid waste, rather than hazardous waste. Old brake shoes and pads should be enclosed, preferably in a plastic bag, to help prevent any of the brake material from becoming airborne. *Always follow current federal and local laws concerning disposal of all waste.*

USED BRAKE FLUID

Most brake fluid is made from polyglycol, is water soluble, and can be considered hazardous if it has absorbed metals from the brake system.

STORAGE AND DISPOSAL OF BRAKE FLUID

- Collect brake fluid in a container clearly marked to indicate that it is designated for that purpose.

FIGURE 3–3 All brakes should be moistened with water or solvent to help prevent brake dust from becoming airborne.

- If the waste brake fluid is hazardous, be sure to manage it appropriately and use only an authorized waste receiver for its disposal.
- If the waste brake fluid is nonhazardous (such as old, but unused), determine from your local solid waste collection provider what should be done for its proper disposal.
- Do not mix brake fluid with used engine oil.
- Do not pour brake fluid down drains or onto the ground.
- Recycle brake fluid through a registered recycler.

USED OIL

Used oil is any petroleum-based or synthetic oil that has been used. During normal use, impurities such as dirt, metal scrapings, water, or chemicals can get mixed in with the oil. Eventually, this used oil must be replaced with virgin or re-refined oil. The EPA's used oil management standards include a three-pronged approach to determine if a substance meets the definition of *used oil*. To meet the EPA's definition of used oil, a substance must meet each of the following three criteria:

- **Origin.** The first criterion for identifying used oil is based on the oil's origin. Used oil must have been refined from crude oil or made from synthetic materials. Animal and vegetable oils are excluded from the EPA's definition of used oil.
- **Use.** The second criterion is based on whether and how the oil is used. Oils used as lubricants, hydraulic fluids, heat transfer fluids, and for other similar purposes are considered used oil. The EPA's definition also excludes products used as cleaning agents, as well as certain petroleum-derived products like antifreeze and kerosene.
- **Contaminants.** The third criterion is based on whether or not the oil is contaminated with either physical or chemical impurities. In other words, to meet the EPA's definition, used oil must become contaminated as a result of being used. This aspect of the EPA's definition includes residues and contaminants generated from handling, storing, and processing used oil.

NOTE: The release of only one gallon of used oil (a typical oil change) can make a million gallons of fresh water undrinkable.

If used oil is dumped down the drain and enters a sewage treatment plant, concentrations as small as 50 to 100 PPM (parts per million) in the waste water can foul sewage treatment processes. Never mix a listed hazardous waste, gasoline, waste water, halogenated solvent, antifreeze, or an unknown waste material with used oil. Adding any of these substances will cause the used oil to become contaminated, which classifies it as hazardous waste.

STORAGE AND DISPOSAL OF USED OIL   Once oil has been used, it can be collected, recycled, and used over and over again. An estimated 380 million gallons of used oil are recycled

each year. Recycled used oil can sometimes be used again for the same job or can take on a completely different task. For example, used engine oil can be re-refined and sold at some discount stores as engine oil or processed for furnace fuel oil. After collecting used oil in an appropriate container such as a 55 gallon steel drum, the material must be disposed of in one of two ways:

■ Shipped offsite for recycling

■ Burned in an onsite or offsite EPA-approved heater for energy recovery

Used (waste) oil must be stored in compliance with an existing **underground storage tank (UST)** or an **aboveground storage tank (AGST)** standard, or kept in separate containers. ● **SEE FIGURE 3–4.** Containers are portable receptacles, such as a 55 gallon steel drum.

KEEP USED OIL STORAGE DRUMS IN GOOD CONDITION. This means that they should be covered, secured from vandals, properly labeled, and maintained in compliance with local fire codes. Frequent inspections for leaks, corrosion, and spillage are an essential part of container maintenance.

NEVER STORE USED OIL IN ANYTHING OTHER THAN TANKS AND STORAGE CONTAINERS. Used oil may also be stored in units that are permitted to store regulated hazardous waste.

USED OIL FILTER DISPOSAL REGULATIONS. Used oil filters contain used engine oil that may be hazardous. Before an oil filter is placed into the trash or sent to be recycled, it must be drained using one of the following hot-draining methods approved by the EPA :

■ Puncture the filter antidrainback valve or filter dome end and hot-drain for at least 12 hours

■ Hot-drain and crushing

■ Dismantling and hot-draining

■ Any other hot-draining method, which will remove all the used oil from the filter

FIGURE 3–4 A typical aboveground oil storage tank.

After the oil has been drained from the oil filter, the filter housing can be disposed of in any of the following ways:

■ Sent for recycling

■ Picked up by a service contract company

■ Disposed of in regular trash

SOLVENTS

The major sources of chemical danger are liquid and aerosol brake cleaning fluids that contain chlorinated hydrocarbon solvents. Several other chemicals that do not deplete the ozone, such as heptane, hexane, and xylene, are now being used in nonchlorinated brake cleaning solvents. Some manufacturers are also producing solvents they describe as environmentally responsible, which are biodegradable and noncarcinogenic (non-cancer-causing).

There is no specific standard for physical contact with chlorinated hydrocarbon solvents or the chemicals replacing them. All contact should be avoided whenever possible. The law requires an employer to provide appropriate protective equipment and ensure proper work practices by an employee handling these chemicals.

EFFECTS OF CHEMICAL POISONING The effects of exposure to chlorinated hydrocarbon and other types of solvents can take many forms. Short-term exposure at low levels can cause symptoms, such as the following:

■ Headache

■ Nausea

■ Drowsiness

■ Dizziness

■ Lack of coordination

■ Unconsciousness

It may also cause irritation of the eyes, nose, and throat, and flushing of the face and neck. Short-term exposure to higher concentrations can cause liver damage with symptoms such as yellow jaundice or dark urine. Liver damage may not become evident until several weeks after the exposure.

 SAFETY TIP

Hand Safety

Service technicians should wash their hands with soap and water after handling engine oil, differential oil, or transmission fluids or wear protective rubber gloves. Another safety tip is that the service technician should not wear watches, rings, or other jewelry that could come in contact with electrical or moving parts of a vehicle. ● **SEE FIGURE 3–5.**

FIGURE 3–5 Washing hands and removing jewelry are two important safety habits all service technicians should practice.

FIGURE 3–6 Typical fireproof flammable storage cabinet.

 FREQUENTLY ASKED QUESTION

How Can You Tell If a Solvent Is Hazardous?
If a solvent or any of the ingredients of a product contains "fluor" or "chlor," it is likely to be hazardous. Check the instructions on the label for proper use and disposal procedures.

HAZARDOUS SOLVENTS AND REGULATORY STATUS

Most solvents are classified as hazardous wastes. Other characteristics of solvents include the following:

- Solvents with flash points above 140°F (60°C) are considered flammable and, like gasoline, are federally regulated by the Department of Transportation (DOT).
- Solvents and oils with flash points above 140°F (60°C) are considered combustible and, like engine oil, are also regulated by the DOT. All flammable items must be stored in a fireproof container. ● **SEE FIGURE 3–6.**

It is the responsibility of the repair shop to determine if spent solvent is hazardous waste. Solvent reclaimers are available that clean and restore the solvent so it lasts indefinitely.

USED SOLVENTS Used or spent solvents are liquid materials that have been generated as waste and may contain xylene, methanol, ethyl ether, and methyl isobutyl ketone (MIBK). These materials must be stored in OSHA-approved safety containers with the lids or caps closed tightly. Additional requirements include the following:

- Containers should be clearly labeled "Hazardous Waste" and the date the material was first placed into the storage receptacle should be noted.

- Labeling is not required for solvents being used in a parts washer.
- Used solvents will not be counted toward a facility's monthly output of hazardous waste if the vendor under contract removes the material.
- Used solvents may be disposed of by recycling with a local vendor, like SafetyKleen®, to have the used solvent removed according to specific terms in the vendor agreement.
- Use aqueous-based (nonsolvent) cleaning systems to help avoid the problems associated with chemical solvents. ● **SEE FIGURE 3–7.**

COOLANT DISPOSAL

Coolant is a mixture of antifreeze and water. New antifreeze is not considered to be hazardous even though it can cause death if ingested. Used antifreeze may be hazardous due to dissolved metals from the engine and other components of the cooling system. These metals can include iron, steel, aluminum, copper, brass, and lead (from older radiators and heater cores). Coolant should be disposed of in one of the following ways:

- Coolant should be recycled either onsite or offsite.
- Used coolant should be stored in a sealed and labeled container. ● **SEE FIGURE 3–8.**
- Used coolant can often be disposed of into municipal sewers with a permit. Check with local authorities and obtain a permit before discharging used coolant into sanitary sewers.

FIGURE 3–7 Using a water-based cleaning system helps reduce the hazards from using strong chemicals.

FIGURE 3–8 Used antifreeze coolant should be kept separate and stored in a leakproof container until it can be recycled or disposed of according to federal, state, and local laws. Note that the storage barrel is placed inside another container to catch any coolant that may spill out of the inside barrel.

LEAD-ACID BATTERY WASTE

About 70 million spent lead-acid batteries are generated each year in the United States alone. Lead is classified as a toxic metal, and the acid used in lead-acid batteries is highly corrosive. The vast majority (95% to 98%) of these batteries are recycled through lead reclamation operations and secondary lead smelters for use in the manufacture of new batteries.

BATTERY DISPOSAL Used lead–acid batteries must be reclaimed or recycled in order to be exempt from hazardous waste regulations. Leaking batteries must be stored and transported as hazardous waste. Some states have more strict regulations, which require special handling procedures and transportation. According to the **Battery Council International (BCI)**, battery laws usually include the following rules:

1. Lead–acid battery disposal is prohibited in landfills or incinerators. Batteries are required to be delivered to a battery retailer, wholesaler, recycling center, or lead smelter.

2. All retailers of automotive batteries are required to post a sign that displays the universal recycling symbol and indicates the retailer's specific requirements for accepting used batteries.

3. Battery electrolyte contains sulfuric acid, which is a very corrosive substance capable of causing serious personal injury, such as skin burns and eye damage. In addition, the battery plates contain lead, which is highly poisonous. For this reason, disposing of batteries improperly can cause environmental contamination and lead to severe health problems.

BATTERY HANDLING AND STORAGE Batteries, whether new or used, should be kept indoors if possible. The storage location should be an area specifically designated for battery storage and must be well ventilated (to the outside). If outdoor storage is the only alternative, a sheltered and secured area with acid-resistant secondary containment is strongly recommended. It is also advisable that acid-resistant secondary containment be used for indoor storage. In addition, batteries should be placed on acid-resistant pallets and never stacked.

FUEL SAFETY AND STORAGE

Gasoline is a very explosive liquid. The expanding vapors that come from gasoline are extremely dangerous. These vapors are present even in cold temperatures. Vapors formed in gasoline tanks on many vehicles are controlled, but vapors from gasoline storage may escape from the can, resulting in a hazardous situation. Therefore, place gasoline storage containers in a well-ventilated space. Although diesel fuel is not as volatile as gasoline, the same basic rules apply to diesel fuel and gasoline storage. These rules include the following:

1. Use storage cans that have a flash-arresting screen at the outlet. These screens prevent external ignition sources from igniting the gasoline within the can when pouring the gasoline the gasoline or diesel fuel.

FIGURE 3-9 This red gasoline container holds about 30 gallons of gasoline and is used to fill vehicles used for training.

2. Use only a red approved gasoline container to allow for proper hazardous substance identification. ● **SEE FIGURE 3-9.**

3. Do not fill gasoline containers completely full. Always leave the level of gasoline at least 1 inch from the top of the container. This action allows expansion of the gasoline at higher temperatures. If gasoline containers are completely full, the gasoline will expand when the temperature increases. This expansion forces gasoline from the can and creates a dangerous spill. If gasoline or diesel fuel containers must be stored, place them in a designated storage locker or facility.

4. Never leave gasoline containers open, except while filling or pouring gasoline from the container.

5. Never use gasoline as a cleaning agent.

6. Always connect a ground strap to containers when filling or transferring fuel or other flammable products from one container to another to prevent static electricity that could result in explosion and fire. These ground wires prevent the buildup of a static electric charge, which could result in a spark and disastrous explosion.

AIRBAG HANDLING

Airbag modules are pyrotechnic devices that can be ignited if exposed to an electrical charge or if the body of the vehicle is subjected to a shock. Airbag safety should include the following precautions:

1. Disarm the airbag(s) if you will be working in the area where a discharged bag could make contact with any part of your body. Consult service information for the exact procedure to follow for the vehicle being serviced. The usual procedure is to deploy the airbag using a 12-volt power supply, such as a jump start box, using long wires to connect to the module to ensure a safe deployment.

2. Do not expose an airbag to extreme heat or fire.

3. Always carry an airbag pointing away from your body.

4. Place an airbag module facing upward.

5. Always follow the manufacturer's recommended procedure for airbag disposal or recycling, including the proper packaging to use during shipment.

6. Wear protective gloves if handling a deployed airbag.

7. Always wash your hands or body well if exposed to a deployed airbag. The chemicals involved can cause skin irritation and possible rash development.

USED TIRE DISPOSAL

Used tires are an environmental concern because of several reasons, including the following:

1. In a landfill, they tend to "float" up through the other trash and rise to the surface.

2. The inside of tires traps and holds rainwater, which is a breeding ground for mosquitoes. Mosquito-borne diseases include encephalitis and dengue fever.

3. Used tires present a fire hazard and, when burned, create a large amount of black smoke that contaminates the air.

Used tires should be disposed of in one of the following ways:

1. Used tires can be reused until the end of their useful life.

2. Tires can be retreaded.

3. Tires can be recycled or shredded for use in asphalt.

4. Tires removed from the rims can be sent to a landfill (most landfill operators will shred the tires because it is illegal in many states to landfill whole tires).

5. Tires can be burned in cement kilns or other power plants where the smoke can be controlled.

6. A registered scrap tire handler should be used to transport tires for disposal or recycling.

AIR-CONDITIONING REFRIGERANT OIL DISPOSAL

Air-conditioning refrigerant oil contains dissolved refrigerant and is therefore considered to be hazardous waste. This oil must be kept separated from other waste oil or the entire amount of oil must be treated as hazardous. Used refrigerant oil must be sent to a licensed hazardous waste disposal company for recycling or disposal. ● **SEE FIGURE 3–10.**

WASTE CHART   All automotive service facilities create some waste and while most of it is handled properly, it is important that all hazardous and nonhazardous waste be accounted for and properly disposed. ● **SEE CHART 3–1** for a list of typical wastes generated at automotive shops, plus a checklist for keeping track of how these wastes are handled.

FIGURE 3–10 Air-conditioning refrigerant oil must be kept separated from other oils because it contains traces of refrigerant and must be treated as hazardous waste.

WASTE STREAM	TYPICAL CATEGORY IF NOT MIXED WITH OTHER HAZARDOUS WASTE	IF DISPOSED IN LANDFILL AND NOT MIXED WITH A HAZARDOUS WASTE	IF RECYCLED
Used oil	Used oil	Hazardous waste	Used oil
Used oil filters	Nonhazardous solid waste, if completely drained	Nonhazardous solid waste, if completely drained	Used oil, if not drained
Used transmission fluid	Used oil	Hazardous waste	Used oil
Used brake fluid	Used oil	Hazardous waste	Used oil
Used antifreeze	Depends on characterization	Depends on characterization	Depends on characterization
Used solvents	Hazardous waste	Hazardous waste	Hazardous waste
Used citric solvents	Nonhazardous solid waste	Nonhazardous solid waste	Hazardous waste
Lead–acid automotive batteries	Not a solid waste if returned to supplier	Hazardous waste	Hazardous waste
Shop rags used for oil	Used oil	Depends on used oil characterization	Used oil
Shop rags used for solvent or gasoline spills	Hazardous waste	Hazardous waste	Hazardous waste
Oil spill absorbent material	Used oil	Depends on used oil characterization	Used oil
Spill material for solvent and gasoline	Hazardous waste	Hazardous waste	Hazardous waste
Catalytic converter	Not a solid waste if returned to supplier	Nonhazardous solid waste	Nonhazardous solid waste
Spilled or unused fuels	Hazardous waste	Hazardous waste	Hazardous waste
Spilled or unusable paints and thinners	Hazardous waste	Hazardous waste	Hazardous waste
Used tires	Nonhazardous solid waste	Nonhazardous solid waste	Nonhazardous solid waste

CHART 3–1

Typical waste materials generated at auto repair shops and typical category (hazardous or nonhazardous) by disposal method.

Remove Components That Contain Mercury

Some vehicles have a placard near the driver's side door that lists the components that contain the heavy metal, mercury. **Mercury** can be absorbed through the skin and is a heavy metal that once absorbed by the body does not leave. ● **SEE FIGURE 3–11.**

These components should be removed from the vehicle before the rest of the body is sent to be recycled to help prevent releasing mercury into the environment.

What Every Technician Should Know

OSHA has adopted new hazardous chemical labeling requirements making it agree with global labeling standards established by the United Nations. As a result, workers will have better information available on the safe handling and use of hazardous chemicals, allowing them to avoid injuries and possible illnesses related to exposures to hazardous chemicals. ● **SEE FIGURE 3–12.**

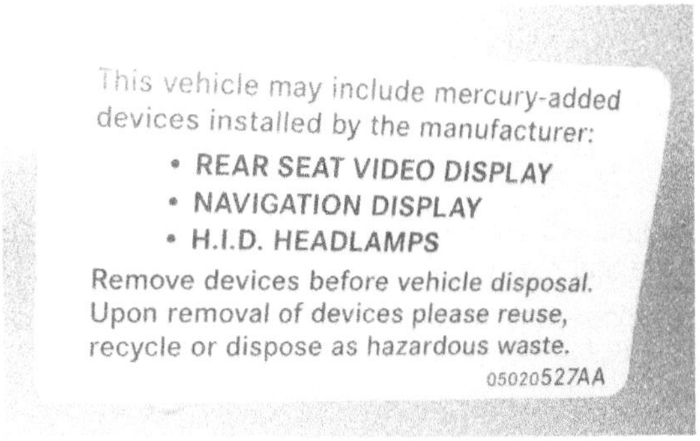

This vehicle may include mercury-added devices installed by the manufacturer:

* REAR SEAT VIDEO DISPLAY
* NAVIGATION DISPLAY
* H.I.D. HEADLAMPS

Remove devices before vehicle disposal. Upon removal of devices please reuse, recycle or dispose as hazardous waste.

05020527AA

FIGURE 3–11 Placard near driver's door, including what devices in the vehicle contain mercury.

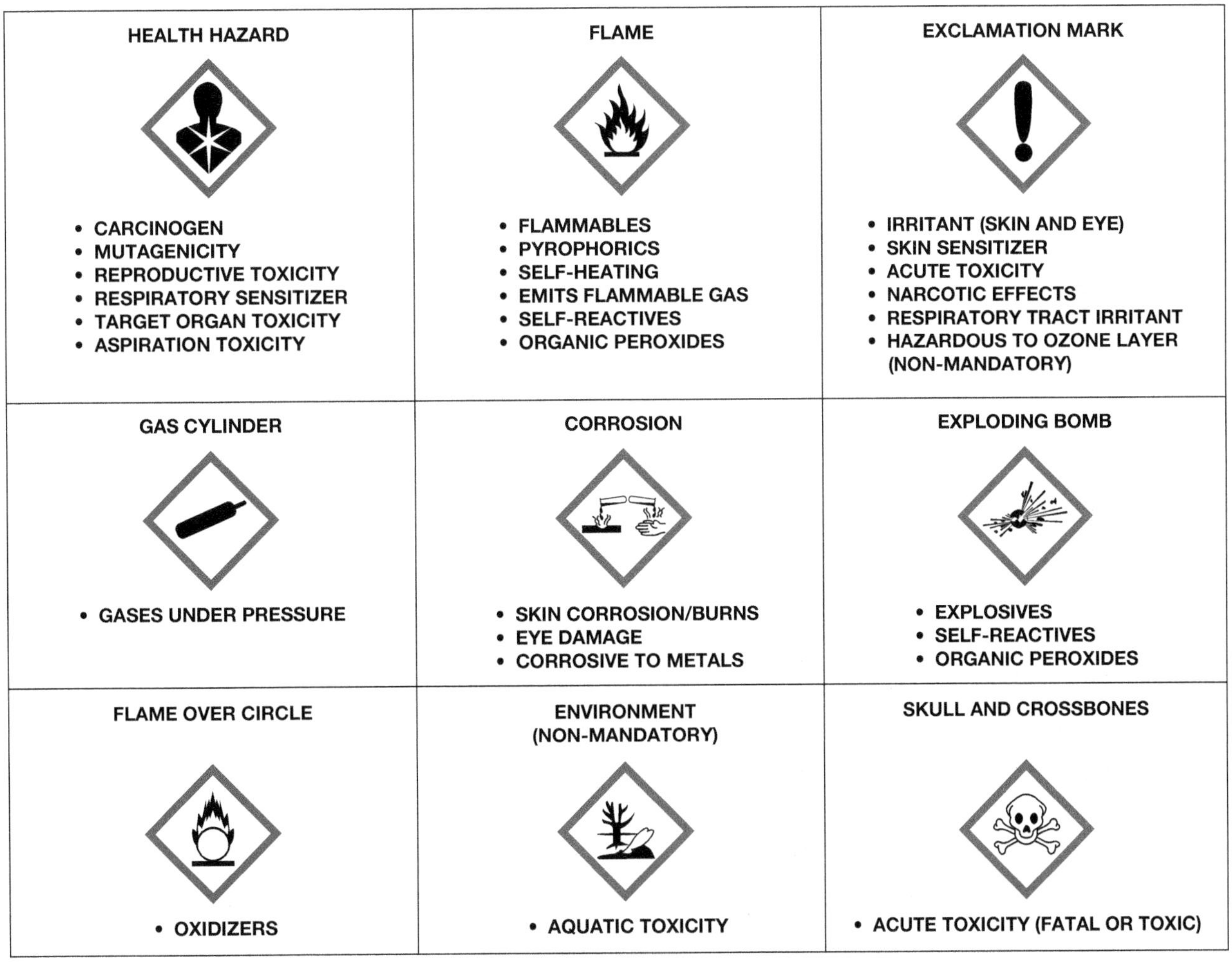

HEALTH HAZARD	FLAME	EXCLAMATION MARK
• CARCINOGEN • MUTAGENICITY • REPRODUCTIVE TOXICITY • RESPIRATORY SENSITIZER • TARGET ORGAN TOXICITY • ASPIRATION TOXICITY	• FLAMMABLES • PYROPHORICS • SELF-HEATING • EMITS FLAMMABLE GAS • SELF-REACTIVES • ORGANIC PEROXIDES	• IRRITANT (SKIN AND EYE) • SKIN SENSITIZER • ACUTE TOXICITY • NARCOTIC EFFECTS • RESPIRATORY TRACT IRRITANT • HAZARDOUS TO OZONE LAYER (NON-MANDATORY)
GAS CYLINDER	CORROSION	EXPLODING BOMB
• GASES UNDER PRESSURE	• SKIN CORROSION/BURNS • EYE DAMAGE • CORROSIVE TO METALS	• EXPLOSIVES • SELF-REACTIVES • ORGANIC PEROXIDES
FLAME OVER CIRCLE	ENVIRONMENT (NON-MANDATORY)	SKULL AND CROSSBONES
• OXIDIZERS	• AQUATIC TOXICITY	• ACUTE TOXICITY (FATAL OR TOXIC)

FIGURE 3–12 The OSHA global hazardous materials labels.

1. Hazardous materials include common automotive chemicals, liquids, and lubricants, especially those whose ingredients contain *chlor* or *fluor* in their name.
2. Right-to-know laws require that all workers have access to safety data sheets (SDS).
3. Asbestos fibers should be avoided and removed according to current laws and regulations.
4. Used engine oil contains metals worn from parts and should be handled and disposed of properly.
5. Solvents represent a serious health risk and should be avoided as much as possible.
6. Coolant should be disposed of properly or recycled.
7. Batteries are considered to be hazardous waste and should be discarded to a recycling facility.

REVIEW QUESTIONS

1. What are the five common automotive chemicals or products that may be considered hazardous?
2. Describe the labels used to identify flammables and explosive materials used by OSHA.
3. What is the proper disposal for used engine oil?
4. What is the correct disposal for used refrigerant oil?
5. What component(s) in a vehicle may contain the heavy metal mercury?

CHAPTER QUIZ

1. Hazardous materials include all of the following **except** _____.
   - a. engine oil
   - b. asbestos
   - c. water
   - d. brake cleaner

2. To determine if a product or substance being used is hazardous, consult _____.
   - a. a dictionary
   - b. an SDS
   - c. SAE standards
   - d. EPA guidelines

3. Exposure to asbestos dust can cause what condition?
   - a. Asbestosis
   - b. Mesothelioma
   - c. Lung cancer
   - d. All of the above

4. Wetted asbestos dust is considered to be _____.
   - a. solid waste
   - b. hazardous waste
   - c. toxic
   - d. poisonous

5. An oil filter should be hot-drained for how long before disposing of the filter?
   - a. 30 to 60 minutes
   - b. 4 hours
   - c. 8 hours
   - d. 12 hours

6. Used engine oil should be disposed of by all except the following method.
   - a. Disposed of in regular trash
   - b. Shipped offsite for recycling
   - c. Burned onsite in a waste oil-approved heater
   - d. Burned offsite in a waste oil-approved heater

7. All of the following are the proper ways to dispose of a drained oil filter **except** _____.
   - a. sent for recycling
   - b. picked up by a service contract company
   - c. disposed of in regular trash
   - d. considered to be hazardous waste and disposed of accordingly

8. Which act or organization regulates air-conditioning refrigerant?
   - a. Clean Air Act (CAA)
   - b. SDS
   - c. WHMIS
   - d. Code of Federal Regulations (CFR)

9. Gasoline should be stored in approved containers that include what color(s)?
   - a. A red container with yellow lettering
   - b. A red container
   - c. A yellow container
   - d. A yellow container with red lettering

10. What automotive devices may contain mercury?
   - a. Rear seat video displays
   - b. Navigation displays
   - c. HID headlights
   - d. All of the above

chapter
4

ELECTRICAL FUNDAMENTALS

LEARNING OBJECTIVES:

After studying this chapter, the reader should be able to:
Discuss the fundamentals of electricity and explain how electrons move through a conductor.
Explain the units of electrical measurement, and discuss the relationship among volts, amperes, and ohms.
Discuss the different sources of electricity.

Explain conductors and resistance, and describe the function of resistors.

This chapter will help you prepare for the ASE Electrical/ Electronic Systems (A6) certification test content area "A" (General Electrical/Electronic System Diagnosis).

KEY TERMS: Ammeter 57 • Ampere 57 • Bound electrons 55 • Conductors 55 • Conventional theory 56 • Coulomb 57 • Electrical potential 58 • Electricity 53 • Electrochemistry 60 • Electromotive force (EMF) 58 • Electron theory 57 • Free electrons 55 • Insulators 56 • Ion 54 • Neutral charge 54 • Ohmmeter 58 • Ohms 58 • Peltier effect 59 • Photoelectricity 59 • Piezoelectricity 60 • Positive temperature coefficient (PTC) 61 • Potentiometer 62 • Resistance 58 • Rheostat 62 • Semiconductor 56 • Static electricity 59 • Thermocouple 59 • Thermoelectricity 59 • Valence ring 55 • Voltmeter 58 • Watt 59

INTRODUCTION

The electrical system is one of the most important systems in a vehicle today. Every year more and more components and systems use electricity. Those technicians who really know and understand automotive electrical and electronic systems are in great demand.

Electricity may be difficult for some people to learn for the following reasons.

- It cannot be seen.
- Only the results of electricity can be seen.
- It has to be detected and measured.
- The test results have to be interpreted.

ELECTRICITY

BACKGROUND Our universe is composed of matter, which is *anything* that has mass and occupies space. All matter is made from slightly over 100 individual components called *elements*. The smallest particle that an element can be broken into and still retain the properties of that element is known as an atom. ● **SEE FIGURE 4–1**.

DEFINITION **Electricity** is the movement of electrons from one atom to another. The dense center of each atom is called the nucleus. The nucleus contains:

- *Protons*, which have a positive charge
- *Neutrons*, which are electrically neutral (have no charge)

Electrons, which have a negative charge, surround the nucleus in orbits. Each atom contains an equal number of electrons and protons. The physical aspect of all protons, electrons, and neutrons are the same for all atoms. It is the *number* of electrons and protons in the atom that determines the material and how electricity is conducted. Because the number of

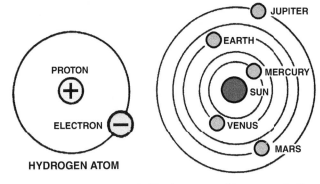

FIGURE 4–1 In an atom (left), electrons orbit protons in the nucleus just as planets orbit the sun in our solar system (right).

negative-charged electrons is balanced with the same number of positive-charged protons, an atom has a **neutral charge** (no charge).

NOTE: As an example of the relative sizes of the parts of an atom, consider that if an atom were magnified so that the nucleus were the size of the period at the end of this sentence, the whole atom would be bigger than a house.

POSITIVE AND NEGATIVE CHARGES The parts of the atom have different charges. The orbiting electrons are negatively charged, while the protons are positively charged. Positive charges are indicated by the "plus" sign (+) and negative charges by the "minus" sign (–), as shown in ● **FIGURE 4–2**.

These same + and – signs are used to identify parts of an electrical circuit. Neutrons have no charge at all. They are neutral. In a normal, or balanced, atom, the number of negative particles equals the number of positive particles. That is, there are as many electrons as there are protons. ● **SEE FIGURE 4–3**.

MAGNETS AND ELECTRICAL CHARGES An ordinary magnet has two ends, or poles. One end is called the south pole and the other is called the north pole. If two magnets are brought close to each other with like poles together (south to south or north to north), the magnets push each other apart, because like poles repel each other. If the opposite poles of the magnets are brought close to each other, south to north, the magnets snap together, because unlike poles attract each other.

The positive and negative charges within an atom are like the north and south poles of a magnet. Charges that are alike repel each other, similar to the poles of a magnet. ● **SEE FIGURE 4–4**.

That is why the negative electrons continue to orbit around the positive protons. They are attracted and held by the opposite charge of the protons. The electrons keep moving in orbit because they repel each other.

IONS When an atom loses any electrons, it becomes unbalanced. It has more protons than electrons, and therefore has a positive charge. If it gains more electrons than protons, the atom is negatively charged. When an atom is not balanced, it becomes a charged particle called an **ion**. Ions try to regain their balance of equal protons and electrons by exchanging electrons with neighboring atoms. The flow of electrons during the "equalization" process is defined as the flow of electricity. ● **SEE FIGURE 4–5**.

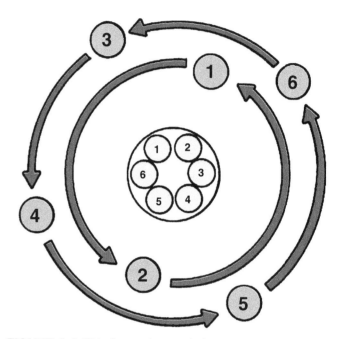

FIGURE 4–3 This figure shows a balanced atom. The number of electrons is the same as the number of protons in the nucleus.

FIGURE 4–4 Unlike charges attract and like charges repel.

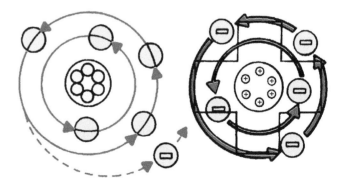

FIGURE 4–5 An unbalanced, positively charged atom (ion) attracts electrons from neighboring atoms.

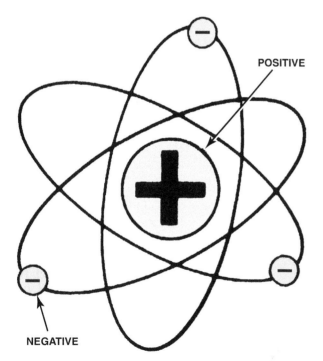

FIGURE 4–2 The nucleus of an atom has a positive (+) charge and the surrounding electrons have a negative (–) charge.

ELECTRON SHELLS
Electrons orbit around the nucleus in definite paths. These paths form shells, like concentric rings, around the nucleus. Only a specific number of electrons can orbit within each shell. If there are too many electrons for the first and closest shell to the nucleus, the others orbit in additional shells until all electrons have an orbit within a shell. There can be as many as seven shells around a single nucleus. ● **SEE FIGURE 4–6**.

FREE AND BOUND ELECTRONS
The outermost electron shell or ring, called the **valence ring**, is the most important part of understanding electricity. The number of electrons in this outer ring determines the valence of the atom and indicates its capacity to combine with other atoms.

If the valence ring of an atom has three or fewer electrons in it, the ring has room for more. The electrons there are held very loosely, and it is easy for a drifting electron to join the valence ring and push another electron away. ● **SEE FIGURE 4–7**. These loosely held electrons are called **free electrons.** When the valence ring has five or more electrons in it, it is fairly full. The electrons are held tightly, and it is hard for a drifting electron to push its way into the valence ring. These tightly held electrons are called **bound electrons**. ● **SEE FIGURE 4–8**.

The movement of these drifting electrons is called current. Current can be small, with only a few electrons moving, or it can be large, with a tremendous number of electrons moving. Electric current is the controlled, directed movement of electrons from atom to atom within a conductor.

CONDUCTORS
Conductors are materials with fewer than four electrons in their atom's outer orbit. ● **SEE FIGURE 4–9**.

Copper is an excellent conductor because it has only one electron in its outer orbit. This orbit is far enough away from the nucleus of the copper atom that the pull or force holding the outermost electron in orbit is relatively weak. ● **SEE FIGURE 4–10**.

Copper is the conductor most used in vehicles because the price of copper is reasonable compared to the relative cost of other conductors with similar properties. Examples of other commonly used conductors include:

- Silver
- Gold

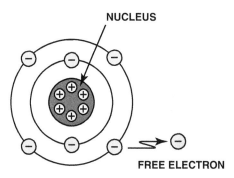

FIGURE 4–7 Electrons in the outer orbit, or shell, can often be drawn away from the atom and become free electrons.

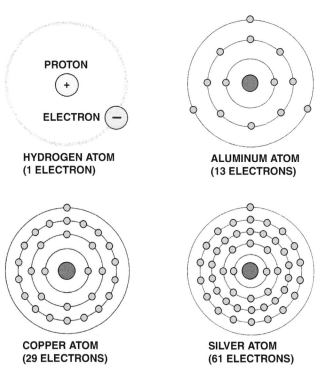

FIGURE 4–6 The hydrogen atom is the simplest atom, with only one proton, one neutron, and one electron. More complex elements contain higher numbers of protons, neutrons, and electrons.

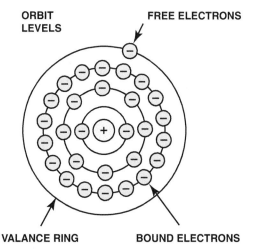

FIGURE 4–8 As the number of electrons increases, they occupy increasing energy levels that are farther from the center of the atom.

FIGURE 4–9 A conductor is any element that has one to three electrons in its outer orbit.

ELECTRICAL FUNDAMENTALS **55**

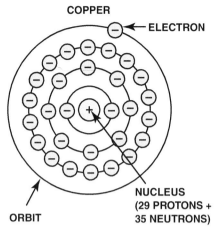

COPPER

ELECTRON

NUCLEUS
(29 PROTONS +
35 NEUTRONS)

ORBIT

FIGURE 4–10 Copper is an excellent conductor of electricity because it has just one electron in its outer orbit, making it easy to be knocked out of its orbit and flow to other nearby atoms. This causes electron flow, which is the definition of electricity.

INSULATORS

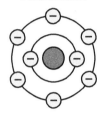

FIGURE 4–11 Insulators are elements with five to eight electrons in the outer orbit.

? FREQUENTLY ASKED QUESTION

Is Water a Conductor?

Pure water is an insulator; however, if anything is in the water, such as salt or dirt, then the water becomes conductive. Because it is difficult to keep it from becoming contaminated, water is usually thought of as being capable of conducting electricity, especially high-voltage household 110 or 220 volt outlets.

- Aluminum
- Steel
- Cast iron

INSULATORS Some materials hold their electrons very tightly; therefore, electrons do not move through them very well. These materials are called insulators. **Insulators** are materials with more than four electrons in their atom's outer orbit. Because they have more than four electrons in their outer orbit, it becomes easier for these materials to acquire (gain) electrons than to release electrons. ● **SEE FIGURE 4–11**.

SEMICONDUCTORS

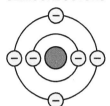

FIGURE 4–12 Semiconductor elements contain exactly four electrons in the outer orbit.

Examples of insulators include plastics, nylon, porcelain, fiberglass, wood, glass, rubber, ceramics (spark plugs), and varnish for covering (insulating) copper wires in alternators and starters.

SEMICONDUCTORS Materials with exactly four electrons in their outer orbit are neither conductors nor insulators, but are called **semiconductors.** Semiconductors can be either an insulator or a conductor in different design applications. ● **SEE FIGURE 4–12**.

Examples of semiconductors include:

- Silicon
- Germanium
- Carbon

Semiconductors are used mostly in transistors, computers, and other electronic devices.

HOW ELECTRONS MOVE THROUGH A CONDUCTOR

CURRENT FLOW The following events occur if a source of power, such as a battery, is connected to the ends of a conductor— a positive charge (lack of electrons) is placed on one end of the conductor and a negative charge (excess of electrons) is placed on the opposite end of the conductor. For current to flow, there *must* be an imbalance of excess electrons at one end of the circuit and a deficiency of electrons at the opposite end of the circuit.

- The negative charge repels the free electrons from the atoms of the conductor, whereas the positive charge on the opposite end of the conductor attracts electrons.
- As a result of this attraction of opposite charges and repulsion of like charges, electrons flow through the conductor. ● **SEE FIGURE 4–13**.

CONVENTIONAL THEORY VERSUS ELECTRON THEORY

- **Conventional theory.** It was once thought that electricity had only one charge and moved from positive to negative. This theory of the flow of electricity through a conductor is called the **conventional theory** of current flow. ● **SEE FIGURE 4–14**.

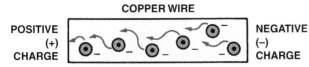

FIGURE 4-13 Current electricity is the movement of electrons through a conductor.

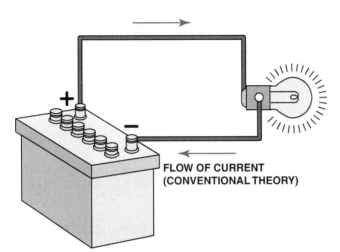

FIGURE 4-14 Conventional theory states that current flows through a circuit from positive (+) to negative (−). Automotive electricity uses the conventional theory in all electrical diagrams and schematics.

 FREQUENTLY ASKED QUESTION

What Is Static Electricity?

Static electricity means that isolated motionless electrical charges are present on an insulator. Static electricity is commonly created by friction. Static electricity occurs when an imbalance of electric charges is created on the surface of a material. This static charge can remain until it is discharged to a conductor. Static electricity can be created when using a hair comb or taking off a sweater. ● **SEE FIGURE 4-15.**

- **Electron theory.** The discovery of the electron and its negative charge led to the **electron theory,** which states that there is electron flow from negative to positive.
- Most automotive applications use the conventional theory. We use the conventional theory (positive to negative) unless stated otherwise.

UNITS OF ELECTRICITY

Electricity is measured using meters or other test equipment. The three fundamentals of electricity-related units include the ampere, volt, and ohm.

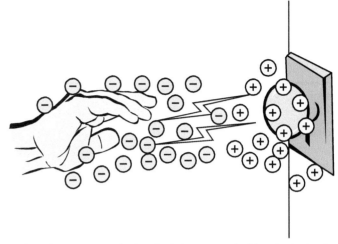

FIGURE 4-15 A static electrical charge can build up in the body if walking on an insulated floor such as on carpet. Then the static charge can discharge to a conductor such as a door knob resulting in a mild shock and often heard as a snapping sound too.

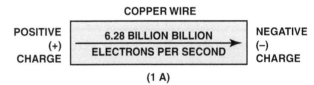

FIGURE 4-16 One ampere is the movement of 1 coulomb (6.28 billion billion electrons) past a point in 1 second.

AMPERES The **ampere** is the unit used throughout the world to measure current flow. When 6.28 billion billion electrons (the name for this large number of electrons is a **coulomb**) move past a certain point in 1 second, this represents 1 ampere of current. ● **SEE FIGURE 4-16.**

The ampere is the electrical unit for the amount of electron flow, just as "gallons per minute" is the unit that can be used to measure the quantity of water flow. It is named for the French electrician André Marie Ampére (1775–1836). The conventional abbreviations and measurement for amperes are as follows:

1. The ampere is the unit of measurement for the amount of current flow.
2. *A* and *amps* are acceptable abbreviations for *amperes*.
3. The capital letter *I*, for *intensity*, is used in mathematical calculations to represent amperes.
4. Amperes do the work in the circuit. It is the movement of the electrons through a lightbulb or motor that actually makes the electrical device work. Without amperage through a device, it will not work at all.
5. Amperes are measured by an **ammeter** (not ampmeter). ● **SEE FIGURE 4-17.**

VOLTS The **volt** is the unit of measurement for electrical pressure. It is named for an Italian physicist, Alessandro Volta

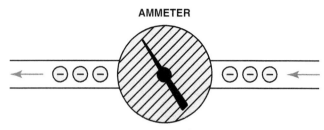

FIGURE 4–17 An ammeter is installed in the path of the electrons similar to a water meter used to measure the flow of water in gallons per minute. The ammeter displays current flow in amperes.

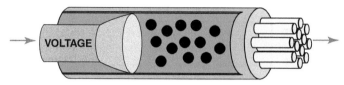

VOLTAGE IS PRESSURE

FIGURE 4–18 Voltage is the electrical pressure that causes the electrons to flow through a conductor.

FIGURE 4–19 This digital multimeter set to read DC volts is being used to test the voltage of a vehicle battery. Most multimeters can also measure resistance (ohms) and current flow (amperes).

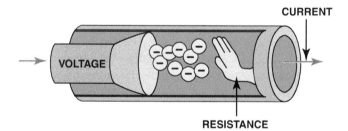

FIGURE 4–20 Resistance to the flow of electrons through a conductor is measured in ohms.

(1745–1827). The comparable unit using water pressure as an example would be pounds per square inch (psi). It is possible to have very high pressures (volts) and low water flow (amperes). It is also possible to have high water flow (amperes) and low pressures (volts). Voltage is also called **electrical potential**, because if there is voltage present in a conductor, there is a potential (possibility) for current flow. This electrical pressure is a result of the following:

- Excess electrons remain at one end of the wire or circuit.
- There is a lack of electrons at the other end of the wire or circuit.
- The natural effect is to equalize this imbalance, creating a pressure to allow the movement of electrons through a conductor.
- It is possible to have pressure (volts) without any flow (amperes). For example, a fully charged 12 volt battery placed on a workbench has 12 volts of pressure potential, but because there is no conductor (circuit) connected between the positive and negative terminals of the battery, there is no flow (amperes). Current only flows when there is pressure and a circuit for the electrons to flow in order to "equalize" to a balanced state.

Voltage does *not* flow through conductors, but voltage does cause current (in amperes) to flow through conductors. ● **SEE FIGURE 4–18.**

The conventional abbreviations and measurement for voltage are as follows:

1. The volt is the unit of measurement for the amount of electrical pressure.
2. **Electromotive force,** abbreviated **EMF,** is another way of indicating voltage.
3. *V* is the generally accepted abbreviation for *volts.*
4. The symbol used in calculations is *E,* for *electromotive force.*
5. Volts are measured by a **voltmeter.** ● **SEE FIGURE 4–19.**

OHMS **Resistance** to the flow of current through a conductor is measured in units called **ohms,** named after the German physicist George Simon Ohm (1787–1854). The resistance to the flow of free electrons through a conductor results from the countless collisions the electrons cause within the atoms of the conductor. ● **SEE FIGURE 4–20.**

The conventional abbreviations and measurement for resistance are as follows:

1. The ohm is the unit of measurement for electrical resistance.
2. The symbol for ohms is Ω (Greek capital letter omega), the last letter of the Greek alphabet.
3. The symbol used in calculations is *R,* for *resistance.*
4. Ohms are measured by an **ohmmeter.**
5. Resistance to electron flow depends on the material used as a conductor.

WATTS A **watt** is the electrical unit for *power*, the capacity to do work. It is named after a Scottish inventor, James Watt (1736–1819). The symbol for power is *P*. Electrical power is calculated as amperes times volts:

$$P \text{ (power)} = I \text{ (amperes)} \times E \text{ (volts)}$$

The formula can also be used to calculate the amperage if the wattage and the voltage are known. For example, a 100 watt lightbulb powered by 120 volt AC in the shop requires how many amperes?

A (amperes) = P (watts) $\div$ E (volts)

$A = 0.83$ amperes

● **SEE FIGURE 4–21**.

SOURCES OF ELECTRICITY

FRICTION When certain different materials are rubbed together, the friction causes electrons to be transferred from one to the other. Both materials become electrically charged. These charges are not in motion, but stay on the surface where they were deposited. Because the charges are stationary, or static, this type of voltage is called **static electricity.** Walking across a carpeted floor creates a buildup of a static charge in your body, which is an insulator, and then the charge is discharged when you touch a metal conductor.

FIGURE 4–21 A display at the Henry Ford Museum in Dearborn, Michigan, which includes a hand-cranked generator and a series of lightbulbs. This figure shows a young man attempting to light as many bulbs as possible. The crank gets harder to turn as more bulbs light because it requires more power to produce the necessary watts of electricity.

HEAT When pieces of two different metals are joined together at both ends and one junction is heated, current passes through the metals. The current is very small, only millionths of an ampere, but this is enough to use in a temperature-measuring device called a **thermocouple.** ● **SEE FIGURE 4–22**.

Some engine temperature sensors operate in this manner. This form of voltage is called **thermoelectricity**.

Thermoelectricity was discovered and has been known for over a century. In 1823, a German physicist, Thomas Johann Seebeck, discovered that a voltage was developed in a loop containing two dissimilar metals, provided the two junctions were maintained at different temperatures. A decade later, a French scientist, Jean Charles Athanase Peltier, found that electrons moving through a solid can carry heat from one side of the material to the other side. This effect is called the **Peltier effect**. A Peltier effect device is often used in portable coolers to keep food items cool if the current flows in one direction and keep items warm if the current flows in reverse.

LIGHT In 1839, Edmond Becquerel noticed that by shining a beam of sunlight over two different liquids, he could develop an electric current. When certain metals are exposed to light, some of the light energy is transferred to the free electrons of the metal. This excess energy breaks the electrons loose from the surface of the metal. They can then be collected and made to flow in a conductor. ● **SEE FIGURE 4–23**.

This **photoelectricity** is widely used in light-measuring devices.

PRESSURE The first experimental demonstration of a connection between the generation of a voltage due to pressure applied to a crystal was published in 1880 by Pierre and Jacques Curie. Their experiment consisted of voltage being produced when prepared crystals, such as quartz, topaz, and Rochelle salt, had a force applied. ● **SEE FIGURE 4–24**.

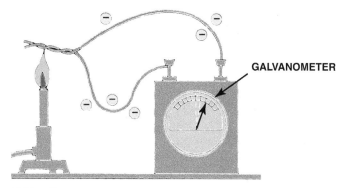

GALVANOMETER

FIGURE 4–22 Electron flow is produced by heating the connection of two different metals. A galvanometer is an analog (needle-type) meter designed to detect weak voltage signals.

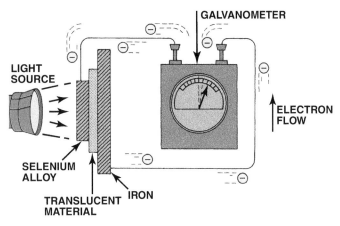

FIGURE 4–23 Electron flow is produced by light striking a light-sensitive material.

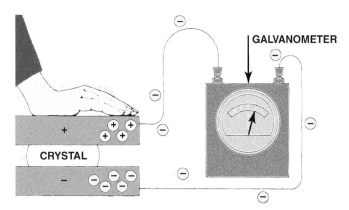

FIGURE 4–24 Electron flow is produced by pressure on certain crystals.

This current is used in crystal microphones, underwater hydrophones, and certain stethoscopes. The voltage created is called **piezoelectricity**. A gas-grill igniter uses the principle of piezoelectricity to produce a spark, and engine-knock sensors (KS) use piezoelectricity to create a voltage signal for use as an input for an engine computer input signal.

FREQUENTLY ASKED QUESTION

How Much Voltage and Current Is Discharged in a Lightning Strike?

Cloud-to-cloud and cloud-to-ground lightning bolts are common occurrences. Most lightning strikes carry from 5,000 amperes to over 200,000 amperes with voltages from 40,000 volts to over 120,000 volts. However, the lightning strike lasts for only a few microseconds so actual power in each strike is low. ● **SEE FIGURE 4–25**.

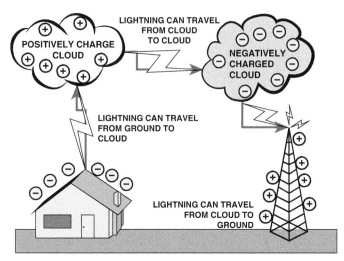

FIGURE 4–25 Lightning is created by the static charges that build up in clouds and can discharge to another cloud or to the earth.

CHEMICAL Two different materials (usually metals) placed in a conducting and reactive chemical solution create a difference in potential, or voltage, between them. This principle is called **electrochemistry** and is the basis of the automotive battery.

MAGNETISM Electricity can be produced if a conductor is moved through a magnetic field or a moving magnetic field is moved near a conductor. This is the principle on which many automotive devices work, including the following:

- Starter motor
- Alternator
- Ignition coils
- Solenoids and relays

CONDUCTORS AND RESISTANCE

All conductors have some resistance to current flow. The following are principles of conductors and their resistance.

- **If the conductor length is doubled, its resistance doubles.** This is the reason why battery cables are designed to be as short as possible.

- **If the conductor diameter is increased, its resistance is reduced.** This is the reason starter motor cables are larger in diameter than other wiring in the vehicle.

- **As the temperature increases, the resistance of the conductor also increases.** This is the reason for installing heat shields on some starter motors. The heat shield helps to protect the conductors (copper wiring inside the starter) from excessive engine heat, and so reduces the resistance of starter circuits. Because the resistance in a conductor increases with increase in temperature, the conductor is called a **positive temperature coefficient (PTC)** resistor.

■ **Materials used in the conductor have an impact on its resistance.** Silver has the lowest resistance among all materials used as conductors, but is expensive. Copper is the next lowest in resistance and is reasonably priced. ● **SEE CHART 4–1** for a comparison of materials.

● **SEE CHART 4–1** for a comparison of materials.

1	Silver
2	Copper
3	Gold
4	Aluminum
5	Tungsten
6	Zinc
7	Brass (copper and zinc)
8	Platinum
9	Iron
10	Nickel
11	Tin
12	Steel
13	Lead

CHART 4–1

Conductor ratings (starting with the best).

? FREQUENTLY ASKED QUESTION

Why Is Gold Used if Copper Has Lower Resistance?

Copper is used for most automotive electrical components and wiring because it has low resistance and is reasonably priced. Gold is used in airbag connections and sensors because it does not corrode. Gold can be buried for hundreds of years and when dug up, is just as shiny as ever.

RESISTORS

FIXED RESISTORS Resistance is the opposition to current flow. Resistors represent an electrical load, or resistance to current flow. Most electrical and electronic devices use resistors of specific values to limit and control the flow of current. Resistors can be made from carbon or other materials that restrict the flow of electricity and are available in various sizes and resistance values. Most resistors have a series of painted color bands around them. These color bands are coded to indicate the degree of resistance. ● **SEE FIGURES 4–26 AND 4–27.**

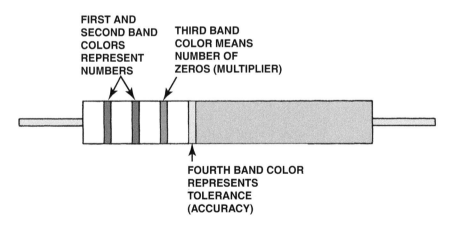

FIRST AND SECOND BAND COLORS REPRESENT NUMBERS

THIRD BAND COLOR MEANS NUMBER OF ZEROS (MULTIPLIER)

FOURTH BAND COLOR REPRESENTS TOLERANCE (ACCURACY)

BLACK = 0
BROWN = 1
RED = 2
ORANGE = 3
YELLOW = 4
GREEN = 5
BLUE = 6
VIOLET = 7
GRAY = 8
WHITE = 9

FOURTH BAND TOLERANCE CODE
NO FOURTH BAND = ±20%
SILVER = ±10%
* GOLD = ±5%
RED = ±2%
BROWN = ±1%

* GOLD IS THE MOST COMMONLY AVAILABLE RESISTOR TOLERANCE.

FIGURE 4–26 This figure shows a resistor color-code interpretation.

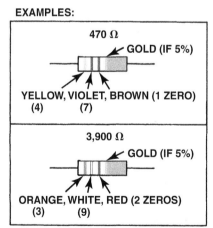

EXAMPLES:

470 Ω
GOLD (IF 5%)
YELLOW, VIOLET, BROWN (1 ZERO)
(4)   (7)

3,900 Ω
GOLD (IF 5%)
ORANGE, WHITE, RED (2 ZEROS)
(3)   (9)

(a)

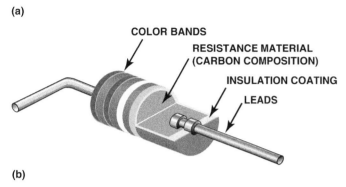

(b)

FIGURE 4–27 (a) A typical carbon resistor. (b) A cutaway view of a typical carbon resistor showing what is inside.

VARIABLE RESISTORS Two basic types of mechanically operated variable resistors are used in automotive applications.

■ A **potentiometer** is a three-terminal variable resistor where a wiper contact provides a variable voltage output. ● **SEE FIGURE 4–28**. Potentiometers are most commonly used as throttle position (TP) sensors on computer-equipped engines. A potentiometer is also used to control audio volume, bass, treble, balance, and fade.

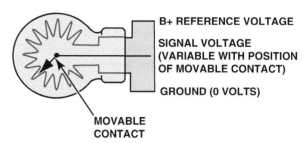

FIGURE 4–28 A three-wire variable resistor is called a potentiometer.

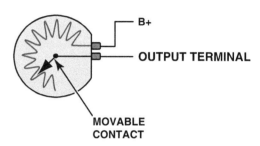

FIGURE 4–29 A two-wire variable resistor is called a rheostat.

■ Another type of mechanically operated variable resistor is the **rheostat.** A rheostat is a *two*-terminal unit in which all of the current flows through the movable arm. ● **SEE FIGURE 4–29**. A rheostat is commonly used for a dash light dimmer control.

SUMMARY

1. Electricity is the movement of electrons from one atom to another.
2. In order for current to flow in a circuit or wire, there must be an excess of electrons at one end and a deficiency of electrons at the other end.
3. Automotive electricity uses the conventional theory that electricity flows from positive to negative.
4. The ampere is the measure of the amount of current flow.
5. Voltage is the unit of electrical pressure.
6. Ohm is the unit of electrical resistance.
7. Sources of electricity include friction, heat, light, pressure, and chemical.

REVIEW QUESTIONS

1. What is electricity?
2. What are ampere, volt, and ohm?
3. What are three examples of conductors and three examples of insulators?
4. What are the five sources of electricity?
5. What is the relationship between the length of a wire and its resistance?

1. An electrical conductor is an element with _____ electrons in its outer orbit.
   - **a.** less than 2
   - **b.** less than 4
   - **c.** exactly 4
   - **d.** more than 4

2. Like charges _____.
   - **a.** attract
   - **b.** repel
   - **c.** neutralize each other
   - **d.** add

3. Carbon and silicon are examples of _____.
   - **a.** semiconductors
   - **b.** insulators
   - **c.** conductors
   - **d.** photoelectric materials

4. Which unit of electricity does the work in a circuit?
   - **a.** Volt
   - **b.** Ampere
   - **c.** Ohm
   - **d.** Coulomb

5. The _____ is a unit of electrical pressure.
   - **a.** coulomb
   - **b.** volt
   - **c.** ampere
   - **d.** ohm

6. Creating electricity by exerting a force on a crystal is called _____.
   - **a.** electrochemistry
   - **b.** piezoelectricity
   - **c.** thermoelectricity
   - **d.** photoelectricity

7. The fact that a voltage can be created by exerting force on a crystal is used in which type of sensor?
   - **a.** Throttle position (TP)
   - **b.** Manifold absolute pressure (MAP)
   - **c.** Barometric pressure (BARO)
   - **d.** Knock sensor (KS)

8. As temperature increases, _____.
   - **a.** the resistance of a conductor decreases
   - **b.** the resistance of a conductor increases
   - **c.** the resistance of a conductor remains the same
   - **d.** the voltage of the conductor decreases

9. Technician A says that a two-wire variable resistor is called a rheostat. Technician B says that a three-wire variable resistor is called a potentiometer. Which technician is correct?
   - **a.** Technician A only
   - **b.** Technician B only
   - **c.** Both Technicians A and B
   - **d.** Neither Technician A nor B

10. A potentiometer, a three-wire variable resistor, is used in which type of sensor?
    - **a.** Throttle position (TP)
    - **b.** Manifold absolute pressure (MAP)
    - **c.** Barometric pressure (BARO)
    - **d.** Knock sensor (KS)

chapter 5

ELECTRICAL CIRCUITS AND OHM'S LAW

LEARNING OBJECTIVES:

After studying this chapter, the reader should be able to:
Identify the parts of a complete circuit.
Describe the characteristics of different types of circuit faults.
Explain Ohm's law as it applies to automotive circuits.
Explain Watt's law as it applies to automotive circuits.

This chapter will help you prepare for the ASE Electrical/Electronic Systems (A6) certification test content area "A" (General Electrical/Electronic System Diagnosis).

KEY TERMS: Circuit 64 • Complete circuit 64 • Continuity 64 • Electrical load 64 • Grounded 66 • Load 64 • Ohm's law 67 • Open circuit 65 • Power source 64 • Return path (ground) 64 • Shorted 65 • Short-to-ground 66 • Short-to-voltage 65 • Watt 69 • Watt's law 69

CIRCUITS

DEFINITION A **circuit** is a complete path that electrons travel from a power source (such as a battery) through a **load,** such as a lightbulb, and back to the power source. It is called a *circuit* because the current must start and finish at the same place (power source).

For *any* electrical circuit to work at all, it must be continuous from the battery (power), through all the wires and components, and back to the battery (ground). A circuit that is continuous throughout is said to have **continuity.**

PARTS OF A COMPLETE CIRCUIT Every **complete circuit** contains the following parts. ● SEE FIGURE 5–1.

1. A **power source,** such as a vehicle's battery.

2. **Protection** from harmful overloads (excessive current flow). (Fuses, circuit breakers, and fusible links are examples of electrical circuit-protection devices.)

3. The **power path** for the current to flow through from the power source to the resistance. (This path from a power source to the load—a lightbulb in this example—is usually an insulated copper wire.)

4. The **electrical load** or resistance, which converts electrical energy into heat, light, or motion.

5. A **return path (ground)** for the electrical current from the load back to the power source so that there is a *complete* circuit. (This return, or ground, path is usually the metal body, frame, ground wires, and engine block of the vehicle. ● SEE FIGURE 5–2.)

6. Switches and controls that turn the circuit on and off. (● SEE FIGURE 5–3.)

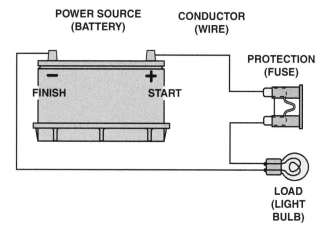

POWER SOURCE (BATTERY)   CONDUCTOR (WIRE)

PROTECTION (FUSE)

FINISH   START

LOAD (LIGHT BULB)

FIGURE 5–1 All complete circuits must have a power source, a power path, protection (fuse), an electrical load (lightbulb in this case), and a return path back to the power source.

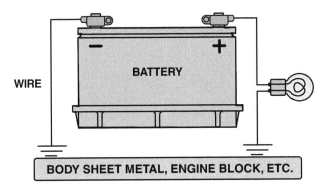

WIRE

BATTERY

− +

BODY SHEET METAL, ENGINE BLOCK, ETC.

FIGURE 5–2 The return path back to the battery can be any electrical conductor, such as a copper wire or the metal frame or body of the vehicle.

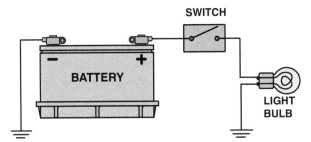

SWITCH

BATTERY

− +

LIGHT BULB

FIGURE 5–3 An electrical switch opens the circuit and no current flows. The switch could also be on the return (ground) path wire.

CIRCUIT FAULT TYPES

OPEN CIRCUITS An **open circuit** is any circuit that is *not* complete, or that lacks continuity, such as a broken wire.
● **SEE FIGURE 5–4.**

Open circuits have the following features.

1. *No current at all* flows through an open circuit.

2. An open circuit may be created by a break in the circuit or by a switch that opens (turns off) the circuit and prevents the flow of current.

3. In any circuit containing a power load and ground, an opening anywhere in the circuit causes the circuit not to work.

4. A light switch in a home and the headlight switch in a vehicle are examples of devices that open a circuit to control its operation.

5. A fuse blows (opens) when the current in the circuit exceeds the fuse rating. This stops the current flow to prevent any harm to the components or wiring as a result of the fault.

SHORT-TO-VOLTAGE *If a wire (conductor) or component is shorted to voltage*, it is commonly referred to as being **shorted.**

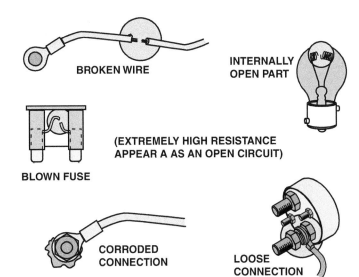

BROKEN WIRE

INTERNALLY OPEN PART

(EXTREMELY HIGH RESISTANCE APPEAR A AS AN OPEN CIRCUIT)

BLOWN FUSE

CORRODED CONNECTION

LOOSE CONNECTION

FIGURE 5–4 Examples of common causes of open circuits. Some of these causes are often difficult to find.

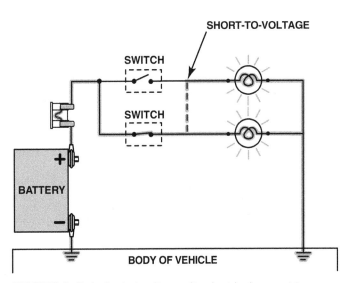

SHORT-TO-VOLTAGE

SWITCH

SWITCH

BATTERY

+

−

BODY OF VEHICLE

FIGURE 5–5 A short circuit permits electrical current to bypass some or all of the resistance in the circuit.

A **short-to-voltage** occurs when the power side of one circuit is electrically connected to the power side of another circuit.
● **SEE FIGURE 5–5.**

A short circuit has the following features.

1. It is a complete circuit in which the current usually bypasses *some* or *all* of the resistance in the circuit.

2. It involves the power side of the circuit.

3. It involves a copper-to-copper connection (two power-side wires touching together).

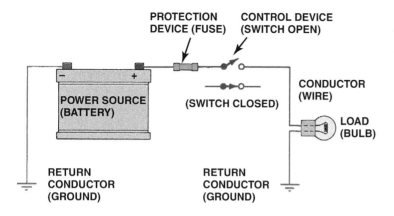

PROTECTION DEVICE (FUSE)   CONTROL DEVICE (SWITCH OPEN)

POWER SOURCE (BATTERY)

(SWITCH CLOSED)

CONDUCTOR (WIRE)

LOAD (BULB)

RETURN CONDUCTOR (GROUND)

RETURN CONDUCTOR (GROUND)

FIGURE 5–6 A fuse or circuit breaker opens the circuit to prevent possible overheating damage in the event of a short circuit.

4. It usually affects more than one circuit. In this case, if one circuit is electrically connected to another circuit, one of the circuits may operate when it is not supposed to because it is being supplied power from another circuit.

5. It *may* or *may not* blow a fuse. ● **SEE FIGURE 5–6.**

SHORT-TO-GROUND   A **short-to-ground** is a type of short circuit that occurs when the current bypasses part of the normal circuit and flows directly to ground. A short-to-ground has the following features.

1. Because the ground return circuit is metal (vehicle frame, engine, or body), it is often identified as having current flowing from copper to steel.

2. It occurs at any place where a power path wire accidentally touches a return path wire or conductor. ● **SEE FIGURE 5–7.**

3. A defective component or circuit that is shorted to ground is commonly called **grounded**.

4. A short-to-ground almost always results in a blown fuse, damaged connectors, or melted wires.

HIGH RESISTANCE   **High resistance** can be caused by any of the following:

- Corroded connections or sockets
- Loose terminals in a connector
- Loose ground connections

If there is high resistance anywhere in a circuit, it may cause the following problems.

1. Slow operation of a motor-driven unit, such as the windshield wipers or blower motor

2. Dim lights

3. "Clicking" of relays or solenoids

4. No operation of a circuit or electrical component

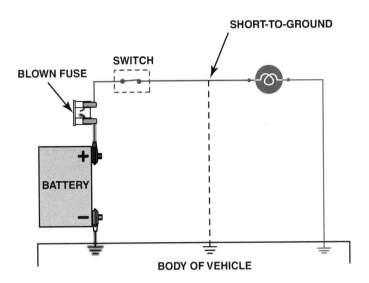

FIGURE 5–7 A short-to-ground affects the power side of the circuit. Current flows directly to the ground return, bypassing some or all of the electrical loads in the circuit. There is no current in the circuit past the short. A short-to-ground will also causes the fuse to blow.

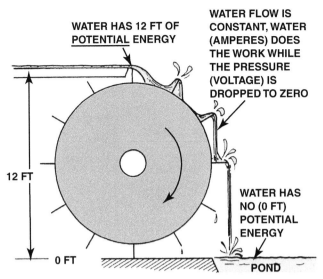

FIGURE 5–8 Electrical flow through a circuit is similar to water flowing over a waterwheel. The more water (amperes in electricity), the greater the amount of work (waterwheel). The amount of water remains constant, yet the pressure (voltage in electricity) drops as the current flows through the circuit.

 CASE STUDY

The Short-to-Voltage Story

A technician was working on a Chevrolet pickup truck with the following unusual electrical problems.
1. When the brake pedal was depressed, the dash light and the side marker lights would light.
2. The turn signals caused all lights to blink and the fuel gauge needle to bounce up and down.
3. When the brake lights were on, the front parking lights also came on.

NOTE: Using a single-filament bulb (such as a #1156) in the place of a dual-filament bulb (such as a #1157) could also cause many of these same problems.

Because most of the trouble occurred when the brake pedal was depressed, the technician decided to trace all the wires in the brake light circuit. The technician discovered the problem near the exhaust system. A small hole in the tailpipe (after the muffler) directed hot exhaust gases to the wiring harness containing all of the wires for circuits at the rear of the truck. The heat had melted the insulation and caused most of the wires to touch. Whenever one circuit was activated (such as when the brake pedal was applied), the current had a complete path to several other circuits. A fuse did not blow because there was enough resistance in the circuits being energized, so the current (in amperes) was too low to blow any fuses.

Summary:
- **Complaint**—Customer stated that the truck lights were doing strange things when the brake pedal was depressed.
- **Cause**—Melted wires caused by a small hole in the exhaust was found during a visual inspection.
- **Correction**—Performing a wire repair and fixing the exhaust leak corrected the customer concern.

OHM'S LAW

DEFINITION The German physicist George Simon Ohm established that electric pressure (electromotive force; EMF) in volts, electrical resistance in ohms, and the amount of current in amperes flowing through any circuit are all related. **Ohm's law** states:

It requires 1 volt to push 1 ampere through 1 ohm of resistance.

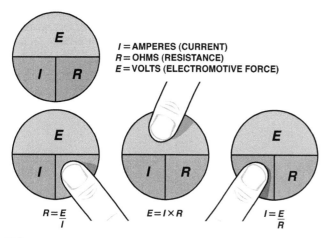

I = AMPERES (CURRENT)
R = OHMS (RESISTANCE)
E = VOLTS (ELECTROMOTIVE FORCE)

$R = \dfrac{E}{I}$ $E = I \times R$ $I = \dfrac{E}{R}$

FIGURE 5–9 To calculate one unit of electricity when the other two are known, simply use your finger and cover the unit you do not know. For example, if both voltage (*E*) and resistance (*R*) are known, cover the letter *I* (amperes). Notice that the letter *E* is above the letter *R*, so divide the resistor's value into the voltage to determine the current in the circuit.

This means that if the voltage is doubled, the number of amperes of current flowing through a circuit also doubles if the resistance of the circuit remains the same.

FORMULAS   Ohm's law can also be stated as a simple formula used to calculate one value of an electrical circuit if the other two are known. If, for example, the current (*I*) is unknown but the voltage (*E*) and resistance (*R*) are known, then Ohm's law can be used to find the answer. ● **SEE FIGURE 5–9**.

$$I = \frac{E}{R}$$

where

I = Current in amperes (A)

E = Electromotive force (EMF) in volts (V)

R = Resistance in ohms (Ω), represented by the Greek letter Omega (pronounced oh-MAY-guh).

1. Ohm's law can determine the resistance if the volts and amperes are known: $R = \dfrac{E}{I}$

2. Ohm's law can determine the *voltage* if the resistance (ohms) and amperes are known: $E = I \times R$

3. Ohm's law can determine the amperes if the resistance and voltage are known: $I = \dfrac{E}{R}$

NOTE: Before applying Ohm's law, be sure that each unit of electricity is converted into base units. For example, 10 KΩ should be converted to 10,000 Ω and 10 mA should be converted into 0.010 A.

● **SEE CHART 5–1**.

VOLTAGE	RESISTANCE	AMPERAGE
Up	Down	Up
Up	Same	Up
Up	Up	Same
Same	Down	Up
Same	Same	Same
Same	Up	Down
Down	Up	Down
Down	Same	Down

CHART 5–1

Ohm's law relationship with the three units of electricity.

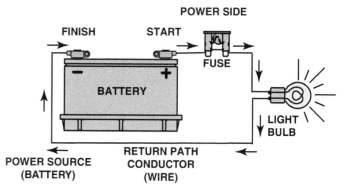

FIGURE 5–10 This closed circuit includes a power source, power-side wire, circuit protection (fuse), resistance (bulb), and return path wire. In this circuit, if the battery has 12 volts and the electrical load has 4 ohms, then the current through the circuit is 3 amperes.

OHM'S LAW APPLIED TO SIMPLE CIRCUITS   If a battery with 12 volts is connected to a resistor of 4 ohms, as shown in ● **FIGURE 5–10**, how many amperes flow through the circuit?

Using Ohm's law, we can calculate the number of amperes that flow through the wires and the resistor. Remember, if two factors are known (volts and ohms in this example), the remaining factor (amperes) can be calculated using Ohm's law.

$$I = \frac{E}{R} = \frac{12\,V}{4\,\Omega} = A$$

The values for the voltage (12) and the resistance (4) were substituted for the variables *E* and *R*, and *I* is thus 3 amperes

$$\left(\frac{12}{4} = 3 \right)$$

If we want to connect a resistor to a 12 volt battery, we now know that this simple circuit requires 3 amperes to operate. This may help us for two reasons.

1. We can now determine the wire diameter that we need based on the number of amperes flowing through the circuit.

2. The correct fuse rating can be selected to protect the circuit.

WATT'S LAW

BACKGROUND James Watt (1736–1819), a Scottish inventor, first determined the power of a typical horse while measuring the amount of coal being lifted out of a mine. The power of one horse was determined to be 33,000 foot-pounds per minute. Electricity can also be expressed in a unit of power called a watt and the relationship is known as **Watt's law,** which states:

A **watt** is a unit of electrical power represented by a current of 1 ampere through a circuit with a potential difference of 1 volt.

FORMULAS The symbol for a watt is the capital letter W. The formula for watts is:

$$W = I \times E$$

Another way to express this formula is to use the letter P to represent the unit of power. The formula then becomes:

$$P = I \times E$$

NOTE: An easy way to remember this equation is that it spells "pie."

Engine power is commonly rated in watts or kilowatts (1,000 watts equal 1 kilowatt), because 1 horsepower is equal to 746 watts. For example, a 200 horsepower engine can be rated as having the power equal to 149,200 watts or 149.2 kilowatts (kW).

To calculate watts, both the current in amperes and the voltage in the circuit must be known. If any two of these factors are known, then the other remaining factor can be determined by the following equations:

$P = I \times E$ **(watts equal amperes times voltage)**

$I = \dfrac{P}{E}$ **(amperes equal watts divided by voltage)**

$E = \dfrac{P}{I}$ **(voltage equals watts divided by amperes)**

For example, the amperage required to operate a 55 watt low beam headlight bulb can be calculated using Watt's law. The vehicle's 12 volt battery supplies the voltage to operate the lamp. Using the formula I = P/E, the calculation is 55/12 = 4.6 amperes.

A Watt's circle can be drawn and used like the Ohm's law circle diagram. ● **SEE FIGURE 5–11**.

MAGIC CIRCLE The formulas for calculating any combination of electrical units are shown in ● **FIGURE 5–12**.

It is almost impossible to remember all of these formulas, so this one circle showing all of the formulas is nice to have available if needed.

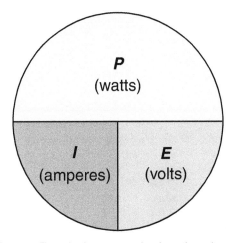

FIGURE 5–11 To calculate one unit when the other two are known, simply cover the unknown unit to see what unit needs to be divided or multiplied to arrive at the solution. The power of electric motors such as starter motors and propulsion (traction) motors used in electric and hybrid electric vehicles are rated in watts.

 TECH TIP

Wattage Increases by the Square of the Voltage

The brightness of a lightbulb, such as an automotive headlight or courtesy light, depends on the number of watts available. The watt is the unit by which electrical power is measured. If the battery voltage drops, even slightly, the light becomes noticeably dimmer. The formula for calculating power (P) in watts is $P = I \times E$. This can also be expressed as Watts = Amps × Volts.

According to Ohm's law, $I = \dfrac{E}{R}$. Therefore, $\dfrac{E}{R}$ can be substituted for I in the previous formula, resulting in $P = \dfrac{E}{R} \times E$ or $P = \dfrac{E^2}{R}$.

E^2 means E multiplied by itself. A small change in the voltage (E) has a big effect on the total brightness of the bulb. (Remember, household lightbulbs are sold according to their wattage.) Therefore, if the voltage to an automotive bulb is reduced, such as by a poor electrical connection, the brightness of the bulb is greatly affected. A poor electrical ground causes a voltage drop. The voltage at the bulb is reduced and the bulb's brightness is reduced.

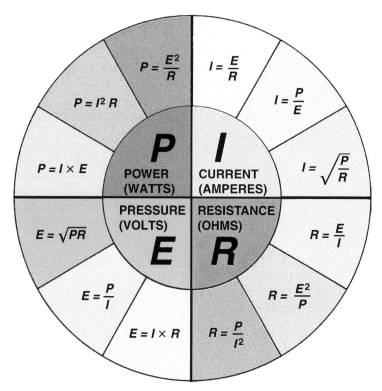

FIGURE 5–12 "Magic circle" of most formulas for problems involving Ohm's law. Each quarter of the "pie" has formulas used to solve for a particular unknown value: current (amperes), in the upper right segment; resistance (ohms), in the lower right; voltage (E), in the lower left; and power (watts), in the upper left.

SUMMARY

1. All complete electrical circuits have a power source (such as a battery), a circuit protection device (such as a fuse), a power-side wire or path, an electrical load, a ground return path, and a switch or a control device.

2. A short-to-voltage involves a copper-to-copper connection and usually affects more than one circuit.

3. A short-to-ground usually involves a power path conductor coming in contact with a return (ground) path conductor and usually causes the fuse to blow.

4. An open is a break in the circuit resulting in absolutely no current flow through the circuit.

5. Ohm's Law states "It requires 1 volt to push 1 ampere through 1 ohm of resistance".

6. Watt's Law states "A watt is a unit of electrical power represented by a current of 1 ampere through a circuit with a potential difference of 1 volt".

REVIEW QUESTIONS

1. What is included in a complete electrical circuit?

2. What is the difference between a short-to-voltage and a short-to-ground?

3. What is the difference between an electrical open and a short?

4. What is Ohm's law?

5. What happens to current flow (amperes) and wattage if the resistance of a circuit is increased because of a corroded connection?

1. If an insulated (power side) wire gets rubbed through a part of the insulation and the wire conductor touches the steel body of a vehicle, the type of failure would be called a(n) _____.
   a. short-to-voltage
   b. short-to-ground
   c. open
   d. chassis ground

2. If two insulated (power side) wires were to melt together at the point where the copper conductors touched each other, the type of failure would be called a(n) _____.
   a. short-to-voltage
   b. short-to-ground
   c. open
   d. floating ground

3. If 12 volts are being applied to a resistance of 3 ohms, _____ amperes will flow.
   a. 12
   b. 3
   c. 4
   d. 36

4. How many watts are consumed by a lightbulb if 1.2 amperes are measured when 12 volts are applied?
   a. 14.4 watts
   b. 144 watts
   c. 10 watts
   d. 0.10 watt

5. How many watts are consumed by a starter motor if it draws 150 amperes at 10 volts?
   a. 15 watts
   b. 150 watts
   c. 1,500 watts
   d. 15,000 watts

6. High resistance in an electrical circuit can cause _____.
   a. dim lights
   b. slow motor operation
   c. clicking of relays or solenoids
   d. All of the above

7. If the voltage increases in a circuit, what happens to the current (amperes) if the resistance remains the same?
   a. Increases
   b. Decreases
   c. Remains the same
   d. Cannot be determined

8. If 200 amperes flow from the positive terminal of a battery and operate the starter motor, how many amperes will flow back to the negative terminal of the battery?
   a. Cannot be determined
   b. Zero
   c. One half (about 100 amperes)
   d. 200 amperes

9. What is the symbol for voltage used in calculations?
   a. R
   b. E
   c. EMF
   d. I

10. Which circuit failure is most likely to cause the fuse to blow?
    a. Open
    b. Short-to-ground
    c. Short-to-voltage
    d. High resistance

LEARNING OBJECTIVES

After studying this chapter, the reader will be able to:

Explain series circuits laws and discuss series circuit examples.

Diagnose electrical/electronic integrity for series, parallel, and series–parallel circuits using Ohm's law.

Explain Kirchhoff's voltage law.

This chapter will help you prepare for the ASE Electrical/ Electronic Systems (A6) certification test content area "A" (General Electrical/Electronic System Diagnosis).

KEY TERMS Continuity 72 • Kirchhoff's voltage law 73 • Series circuit 72 • Series circuit laws 75 • Voltage drop 74

SERIES CIRCUITS

DEFINITION A **series circuit** is a complete circuit that has only one path for current to flow through all of the electrical loads. Electrical components such as fuses and switches are generally not considered to be included in the determination of a series circuit.

CONTINUITY The circuit must be continuous without any breaks. This is called **continuity.** Every circuit must have continuity in order for current to flow through the circuit. Because there is only one path for current to flow, the current is the same everywhere in a complete series circuit.

NOTE: Because an electrical load needs both a power and a ground to operate, a break (open) anywhere in a series circuit will cause the current in the circuit to stop.

OHM'S LAW AND SERIES CIRCUITS

SERIES CIRCUIT TOTAL RESISTANCE A series circuit is a circuit containing more than one resistance in which all current must flow through all resistances in the circuit. Ohm's law can be used to calculate the value of one unknown

(voltage, resistance, or amperes) if the other two values are known.

Because *all* current flows through all resistances, the total resistance is the sum (addition) of all resistances. ● **SEE FIGURE 6–1.**

The total resistance of the circuit shown here is 6 ohms ($1\ \Omega + 2\ \Omega + 3\ \Omega$). The formula for total resistance (R_T) for a series circuit is:

$$R_T = R_1 + R_2 + R_3 + \ldots$$

Using Ohm's law to find the current flow, we have:

$$I = \frac{E}{R} = \frac{12\ V}{6\ \Omega} = 2\ A$$

Therefore, with a total resistance of 6 ohms using a 12 volt battery in the series circuit shown, 2 amperes of current will flow through the entire circuit. If the amount of resistance in a series circuit is reduced, more current will flow.

For example, in ● **FIGURE 6–2**, one resistance (3 ohm bulb) has been eliminated compared to FIGURE 6–1, and now the total resistance is 3 ohms ($1\ \Omega + 2\ \Omega$).

Using Ohm's law to calculate current flow yields 4 amperes.

$$I = \frac{E}{R} = \frac{12\ V}{3\ \Omega} = 4\ A$$

Notice that the current flow was doubled (4 amperes instead of 2 amperes) when the resistance was cut in half (from 6 to 3 ohms). The current flow would also double if the applied voltage was doubled.

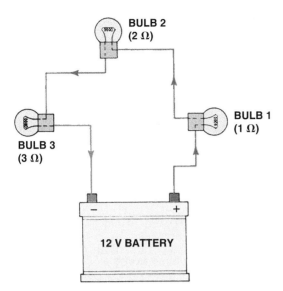

FIGURE 6–1 A series circuit with three bulbs. All current flows through all resistances (bulbs). The total resistance of the circuit is the sum of the individual resistances of each bulb, and the bulbs will light dimly because of the increased resistance and the reduction of current flow (amperes) through the circuit.

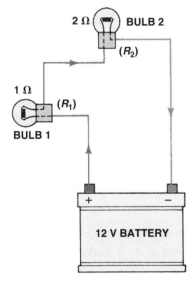

FIGURE 6–2 A series circuit with two bulbs.

KIRCHHOFF'S VOLTAGE LAW

DEFINITION A German physicist, Gustav Robert Kirchhoff (1824–1887), developed laws about electrical circuits. His second law, **Kirchhoff's voltage law,** concerns voltage drops. It states:

> The voltage around any closed circuit is equal to the sum (total) of the voltage drops across the resistances.

For example, the voltage that flows through a series circuit drops with each resistor in a manner similar to that in which

Farsighted Quality of Electricity

Electricity almost seems to act as if it knows what resistances are ahead on the long trip through a circuit. If the trip through the circuit has many high-resistance components, very few electrons (amperes) will choose to attempt to make the trip. If a circuit has little or no resistance (e.g., a short circuit), then as many electrons (amperes) as possible attempt to flow through the complete circuit. If another load, such as a lightbulb, were added in series, the current flow would decrease and the bulbs would be dimmer than before the other bulb was added. If the flow exceeds the capacity of the fuse or the circuit breaker, then the circuit is opened and all current flow stops.

the strength of an athlete drops each time a strenuous physical feat is performed. The greater the resistance is, the greater is the drop in voltage.

APPLYING KIRCHHOFF'S VOLTAGE LAW Kirchhoff states in his second law that the voltage will drop in proportion to the resistance and that the total of all voltage drops will equal the applied voltage. ● **SEE FIGURE 6–3**.

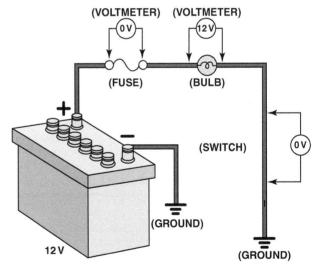

FIGURE 6–3 As current flows through a circuit, the voltage drops in proportion to the amount of resistance in the circuit. Most, if not all, of the resistance should occur across the load such as the bulb in this circuit. All of the other components and wiring should produce little, if any, voltage drop. If a wire or connection did cause a voltage drop, less voltage would be available to light the bulb and the bulb would be dimmer than normal.

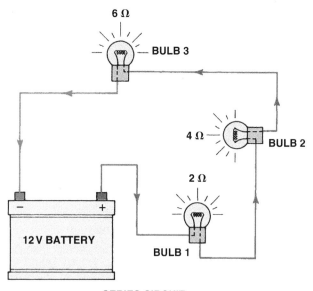

SERIES CIRCUIT

FIGURE 6–4 In a series circuit, the voltage is dropped or lowered by each resistance in the circuit. The higher the resistance is, the greater is the drop in voltage.

Using ● **FIGURE 6–4**, the total resistance of the circuit can be determined by adding the individual resistances 2 Ω + 4 Ω + 6 Ω = 12 Ω.

The current through the circuit is determined by using Ohm's law, $I = \dfrac{E}{R} = \dfrac{12\,V}{12\,\Omega} = 1\,A$

Therefore, in the circuit shown, the following values are known.

Resistance = 12 Ω

Voltage = 12 V

Current = 1 A

Everything is known *except* the voltage drop caused by each resistance. A **voltage drop** is the drop in voltage across a resistance when current flows through a complete circuit. In other words, a voltage drop is the amount of voltage (electrical pressure) required to push electrons through a resistance. The voltage drop can be determined by using Ohm's law and calculating for voltage (E) using the value of each resistance individually, as follows:

$$E = I \times R$$

where

E = Voltage

I = Current in the circuit (Remember, the current is constant in a series circuit; only the voltage varies.)

R = Resistance of only one of the resistances

The voltage drops are as follows:

Voltage drop for bulb 1: $E = I \times R = 1\,A \times 2\Omega = 2\,V$

Voltage drop for bulb 2: $E = I \times R = 1\,A \times 4\Omega = 4\,V$

Voltage drop for bulb 3: $E = I \times R = 1\,A \times 6\Omega = 6\,V$

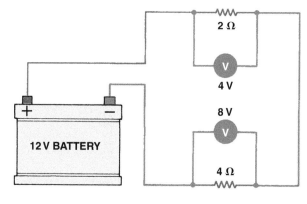

A. $I = E/R$ (TOTAL "R" = 6 Ω)
   12 V/6 Ω = 2 A

B. $E = I/R$ (VOLTAGE DROP)
   AT 2 Ω RESISTANCE =
   E = 2 × 2 = 4 V
   AT 4 Ω RESISTANCE =
   E = 2 × 4 = 8 V

C. 4 + 8 = 12 V
   SUM OF VOLTAGE DROP
   EQUALS APPLIED VOLTAGE

FIGURE 6–5 A voltmeter reads the differences of voltage between the test leads. The voltage read across a resistance is the voltage drop that occurs when current flows through a resistance. A voltage drop is also called an "IR" drop because it is calculated by multiplying the current (I) through the resistance (electrical load) by the value of the resistance (R).

NOTE: Notice that the voltage drop is proportional to the resistance. In other words, the higher the resistance is, the greater is the voltage drop. A 6 ohm resistance dropped the voltage three times as much as the voltage drop created by the 2 ohm resistance.

According to Kirchhoff, the sum (addition) of the voltage drops should equal the applied voltage (battery voltage).

Total of voltage drops = 2 V + 4 V
+ 6 V = 12 V = Battery voltage

This proves Kirchhoff's second (voltage) law. Another example is illustrated in ● **FIGURE 6–5**.

VOLTAGE DROPS

VOLTAGE DROPS USED IN CIRCUITS A voltage drop indicates resistance in the circuit. Often a voltage drop is not wanted in a circuit because it causes the electrical load to not operate correctly. Some automotive electrical systems use voltage drops in cases such as the following:

1. **Dash lights.** Most vehicles are equipped with a method of dimming the brightness of the dash lights by turning a variable resistor. This type of resistor can be adjusted and

therefore varies the voltage to the dash lightbulbs. A high voltage to the bulbs causes them to be bright, and a low voltage results in a dim light.

2. **Blower motor** (heater or air-conditioning fan). Speeds can be controlled by a fan switch sending current through high-, medium-, or low-resistance wire resistors. The highest resistance will drop the voltage the most, causing the motor to run at the lowest speed. The highest speed of the motor will occur when *no* resistance is in the circuit and full battery voltage is switched to the blower motor.

VOLTAGE DROPS AS A TESTING METHOD
Any resistance in a circuit causes the voltage to drop in proportion to the amount of the resistance. Because a high resistance will drop the voltage more than a lower resistance, a voltmeter, as well as an ohmmeter, can be used to measure resistance. In fact, measuring the voltage drop is the preferred method recommended by most vehicle manufacturers to locate or test a circuit for excessive resistance. The formula for voltage drop is $E = I \times R$, where E is the voltage drop and I is the current in the circuit. Notice that as the value of the resistance (R) increases, the voltage drop increases.

SERIES CIRCUIT LAWS

Electrical loads or resistances connected in series follow the following **series circuit laws**.

LAW 1 The total resistance in a series circuit is the sum total of the individual resistances. The resistance values of each electrical load are simply added together.

LAW 2 The current is the same throughout the circuit. ● **SEE FIGURE 6–6**.

If 2 amperes of current leave the battery, 2 amperes of current return to the battery.

LAW 3 Although the current (in amperes) is constant, the voltage drops across each resistance in the circuit can vary at each resistor. The voltage drop across each load is proportional to the value of the resistance compared to the total resistance. For example, if the resistance of each resistor in a two-resistor circuit is half of the total resistance, the voltage drop across that resistance will be half of the applied voltage. The sum total of all individual voltage drops equals the applied source voltage.

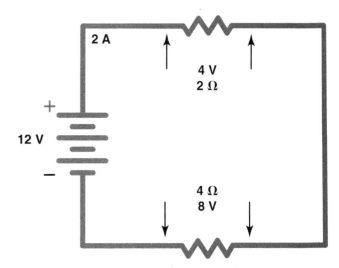

FIGURE 6–6 In this series circuit with a 2 ohm resistor and a 4 ohm resistor, current (2 amperes) is the same throughout, even though the voltage drops across each resistor are different.

? FREQUENTLY ASKED QUESTION

Why Check the Voltage Drop Instead of Measuring the Resistance?

Imagine a wire with all strands cut except for one. An ohmmeter can be used to check the resistance of this wire and the resistance would be low, indicating that the wire was okay, but this one small strand cannot properly carry the current (amperes) in the circuit. A voltage drop test is therefore a better test to determine the resistance in components for two reasons:

■ An ohmmeter can only test a wire or component that has been disconnected from the circuit and is not carrying current. The resistance can, and does, change when current flows.

■ A voltage drop test is a dynamic test because as the current flows through a component, the conductor increases in temperature, which in turn increases resistance. This means that a voltage drop test is testing the circuit during normal operation and is therefore the most accurate way of determining circuit conditions.

A voltage drop test is also easier to perform because the resistance does not have to be known, only that the loss of voltage in a circuit should be less than 3%, or less than about 0.36 volt for any 12 volt circuit.

Lightbulbs and Ohm's Law

If the resistance of a typical automotive lightbulb is measured at room temperature, the resistance will often be around 1 ohm. If 12 volts were to be applied to this bulb, a calculated current of 12 amperes would be expected ($I = \dfrac{E}{R} = 12 \div 1 = 12$ A). However, as current flows through the filament of the bulb, it heats up and becomes incandescent, thereby giving off light. When the bulb is first connected to a power source and current starts to flow, a high amount of current, called surge current, flows through the filament. Then, within a few thousandths of a second, the current flow is reduced to about 10% of the surge current due to the increasing resistance of the filament, resulting in an actual current flow of about 1.2 amperes or about 100 ohms of resistance when the bulb is working.

As a result, using Ohm's law to calculate current flow does not take into account the differences in temperature of the components during actual operation.

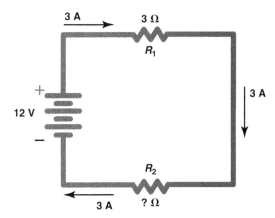

FIGURE 6–7 Example 1.

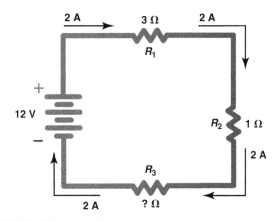

FIGURE 6–8 Example 2.

SERIES CIRCUIT EXAMPLES

Each of the four examples discussed below includes solving for the following:

- Total resistance in the circuit
- Current flow (amperes) through the circuit
- Voltage drop across each resistance

Example 1:
(● SEE FIGURE 6–7.)

The unknown in this problem is the value of R_2. Because the source voltage and the circuit current are known, the total circuit resistance can be calculated using Ohm's law.

$$R_{Total} = \frac{E}{I} = 12\,\text{V} \div 3\,\text{A} = 4\,\Omega$$

Because R_1 is 3 ohms and the total resistance is 4 ohms, the value of R_2 is 1 ohm.

Example 2:
(● SEE FIGURE 6–8.)

The unknown in this problem is the value of R_3. The total resistance, however, can be calculated using Ohm's law.

$$R_{Total} = \frac{E}{I} = 12\,\text{V} \div 2\,\text{A} = 6\,\Omega$$

The total resistance of R_1 (3 ohms) and R_2 (1 ohm) equals 4 ohms, so that the value of R_3 is the difference between the total resistance (6 ohms) and the value of the known resistance (4 ohms).

$$6 - 4 = 2\,\Omega = R_3$$

Example 3:
(● SEE FIGURE 6–9.)

The unknown value in this problem is the voltage of the battery. To solve for voltage, use Ohm's law ($E - I \times R$). The R in this problem refers to the total resistance (R_T). The total resistance of a series circuit is determined by adding the values of the individual resistors.

$$R_T = 1\,\Omega + 1\,\Omega + 1\,\Omega$$
$$R_T = 3\,\Omega$$

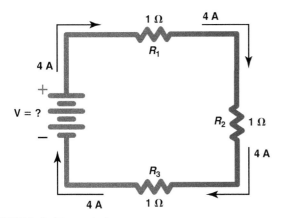

FIGURE 6–9 Example 3.

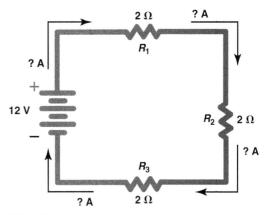

FIGURE 6–10 Example 4.

Placing the value for the total resistance (3 ohms) into the equation results in a battery voltage of 12 volts.

$$E = 4 A \times 3 \, \Omega$$
$$E = 12 V$$

Example 4:

(● **SEE FIGURE 6–10.**)

The unknown in this example is the current (amperes) in the circuit. To solve for current, use Ohm's law.

$$I = \frac{E}{R} = 12 V \div 6 \, \Omega = 2 A$$

Notice that the total resistance in the circuit (6 ohms) was used in this example, which is the total of the three individual resistors ($2 \, \Omega + 2 \, \Omega + 2 \, \Omega = 6 \, \Omega$). The current through the circuit is 2 amperes.

SUMMARY

1. In a simple series circuit, the current remains constant throughout, but the voltage drops as current flows through each of the resistances of the circuit.

2. The voltage drop across each resistance or load is directly proportional to the value of the resistance compared to the total resistance in the circuit.

3. The sum (total) of the voltage drops equals the applied voltage (Kirchhoff's voltage law).

4. An open or a break anywhere in a series circuit stops all current from flowing.

REVIEW QUESTIONS

1. What is Kirchhoff's voltage law?

2. What would happen to current (amperes) if the voltage were doubled in a circuit?

3. What would happen to current (amperes) if the resistance in the circuit were doubled?

4. What is the formula for voltage drop??

5. Why does the current through a circuit with a light bulb test lower than when calculated using an ohmmeter to measure the bulb resistance?

1. The amperage in a series circuit is _____.
   a. the same anywhere in the circuit
   b. variable in the circuit due to the different resistances
   c. high at the beginning of the circuit and decreases as the current flows through the resistance
   d. always less returning to the battery than leaving the battery

2. The sum of the voltage drops in a series circuit equals the _____.

   a. amperage
   b. resistance
   c. source voltage
   d. wattage

3. If the resistance and the voltage are known, what is the formula for finding the current (amperes)?
   a. $E = I \times R$
   b. $I = E \times R$
   c. $R = E \times I$
   d. $I = \dfrac{E}{R}$

4. A series circuit has three resistors of 4 ohms each. The voltage drop across each resistor is 4 volts. Technician A says that the source voltage is 12 volts. Technician B says that the total resistance is 18 ohms. Which technician is correct?
   a. Technician A only
   b. Technician B only
   c. Both Technicians A and B
   d. Neither Technician A nor B

5. If a 12 volt battery is connected to a series circuit with three resistors of 2, 4, and 6 ohms, how much current will flow through the circuit?
   a. 1 ampere
   b. 2 amperes
   c. 3 amperes
   d. 4 amperes

6. A series circuit has two 10 ohm bulbs. A third 10 ohm bulb is added in series. Technician A says that the three bulbs will be dimmer than when only two bulbs were in the circuit. Technician B says that the current in the circuit will increase. Which technician is correct?
   a. Technician A only
   b. Technician B only
   c. Both Technicians A and B
   d. Neither Technician A nor B

7. Technician A says that the sum of the voltage drops in a series circuit should equal the source voltage. Technician B says that the current (amperes) varies depending on the value of the resistance in a series circuit. Which technician is correct?
   a. Technician A only
   b. Technician B only
   c. Both Technicians A and B
   d. Neither Technician A nor B

8. Two lightbulbs are wired in series and one bulb burns out (opens). Technician A says that the other bulb will work. Technician B says that the current will increase in the circuit because one electrical load (resistance) is no longer operating. Which technician is correct?
   a. Technician A only
   b. Technician B only
   c. Both Technicians A and B
   d. Neither Technician A nor B

9. Four resistors are connected to a 12 volt battery in series. The values of the resistors are 10, 100, 330, and 470 ohms. Technician A says that the greatest voltage drop will occur across the 10 ohm resistor. Technician B says that the greatest voltage drop will occur across the 470 ohm resistor. Which technician is correct?
   a. Technician A only
   b. Technician B only
   c. Both Technicians A and B
   d. Neither Technician A nor B

10. Three lightbulbs are wired in series. A fourth bulb is connected to the circuit in series. Technician A says that the total voltage drop will increase. Technician B says that the current (amperes) will decrease. Which technician is correct?
    a. Technician A only
    b. Technician B only
    c. Both Technicians A and B
    d. Neither Technician A nor B

chapter 7
PARALLEL CIRCUITS

LEARNING OBJECTIVES

After studying this chapter, the reader will be able to:

State Kirchhoff's current law.

Explain parallel circuit laws.

This chapter will help you prepare for the ASE Electrical/ Electronic Systems (A6) certification test content area "A" (General Electrical/Electronic System Diagnosis).

KEY TERMS Branches 79 • Kirchhoff's current law 79 • Legs 79 • Parallel circuit 79 • Shunts 79 • Total circuit resistance (R_T) 81

PARALLEL CIRCUITS

DEFINITION A **parallel circuit** is a complete circuit that has more than one path for the current to flow. The separate paths that split and meet at junction points are called **branches, legs,** or **shunts.** The current flow through each branch or leg varies depending on the resistance in that branch. A break or open in one leg or section of a parallel circuit does not stop the current flow through the remaining legs of the parallel circuit. Most circuits in vehicles are parallel circuits and each branch is connected to the 12 volt power supply. ● **SEE FIGURE 7-1.**

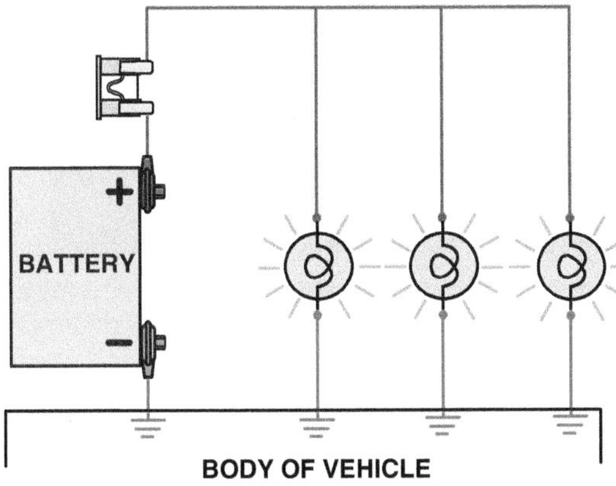

FIGURE 7–1 A typical parallel circuit used in vehicles includes many of the interior and exterior lights.

KIRCHHOFF'S CURRENT LAW

DEFINITION **Kirchhoff's current law** (his first law) states:

The current flowing into any junction of an electrical circuit is equal to the current flowing out of that junction.

Kirchhoff's law states that the amount of current flowing into junction A will equal the current flowing out of junction A.

Example:

Because the 6 ohm leg requires 2 amperes and the 3 ohm resistance leg requires 4 amperes, it is necessary that the wire from the battery to junction A be capable of handling

---

? **FREQUENTLY ASKED QUESTION**

Why Are Parallel Circuits Used Instead of Series Circuits?

Parallel circuits are used for most automotive circuits for the following reasons.

1. In a series circuit, any circuit fault such as an open would stop the flow of electricity to all of the electrical components in the circuit.

2. In a parallel circuit if one device fails, the other units will continue to work because each device has its own power supply wire.

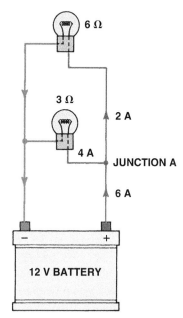

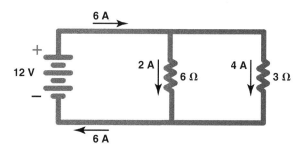

FIGURE 7–2 The amount of current flowing into junction A equals the total amount of current flowing out of the junction.

FIGURE 7–3 The current in a parallel circuit splits (divides) according to the resistance in each branch. Each branch has 12 volts applied to the resistors.

6 amperes. Also notice that the sum of the current flowing *out* of a junction (2 + 4 = 6 A) is equal to the current flowing *into* the junction (6 A), proving Kirchhoff's current law. ● **SEE FIGURE 7–2**.

PARALLEL CIRCUIT LAWS

LAW 1   The total resistance of a parallel circuit is always less than that of the smallest-resistance leg. This occurs because not all of the current flows through each leg or branch. With many branches, more current can flow from the battery just as more vehicles can travel on a road with five lanes compared to only one or two lanes.

LAW 2   The voltage is the same for each leg of a parallel circuit.

LAW 3   The sum of the individual currents in each leg will equal the total current. The amount of current flow through a parallel circuit may vary for each leg depending on the resistance of that leg. The current flowing through each leg results in the same voltage drop (from the power side to the ground side) as for every other leg of the circuit. ● **SEE FIGURE 7–3**.

NOTE: A parallel circuit drops the voltage from source voltage to zero (ground) across the resistance in each leg of the circuit.

🔧   TECH TIP

The Path of Least Resistance

There is an old saying that electricity will always take the path of least resistance. This is true, especially if there is a fault such as in the secondary (high-voltage) section of the ignition system. If there is a path to ground that is of lower resistance than the path to the spark plug, the high-voltage spark will take the path of least resistance. In a parallel circuit where there is more than one path for the current to flow, most of the current will flow through the branch with the lower resistance. This does not mean that all of the current will flow through the lowest resistance, because the other path provides a path to ground and the amount of current flow through the other branches is determined by the resistance and the applied voltage according to Ohm's law.

Therefore, the only place where electricity takes the path of least resistance is in a series circuit where there are no other paths for the current to flow.

DETERMINING TOTAL RESISTANCE IN A PARALLEL CIRCUIT

There are five methods commonly used to determine total resistance in a parallel circuit.

NOTE: Determining the total *resistance* of a parallel circuit is very important in automotive service. Electronic fuel injector and diesel engine glow-plug circuits are two of the most commonly tested circuits

where parallel circuit knowledge is required. Also, when installing extra lighting, the technician must determine the proper gauge wire and protection device.

METHOD 1 The total *current* (in amperes) can be calculated first by treating each leg of the parallel circuit as a simple circuit. ● **SEE FIGURE 7–4**.

Each leg has its own power (+) and ground (−) and, therefore, the current through each leg is independent of the current through any other leg.

Current through the 3 Ω resistance can be found using the equation $I = \dfrac{E}{R} = \dfrac{12 \text{ V}}{3 \text{ Ω}} = 4 \text{ A}$

Current through the 4 Ω resistance can be found using the equation $I = \dfrac{E}{R} = \dfrac{12 \text{ V}}{4 \text{ Ω}} = 3 \text{ A}$

Current through the 6 Ω resistance can be found using the equation $I = \dfrac{E}{R} = \dfrac{12 \text{ V}}{6 \text{ Ω}} = 2 \text{ A}$

The total current flowing from the battery is the sum total of the individual currents for each leg. Total current from the battery is, therefore, 9 amperes (4 A + 3 A + 2 A = 9 A).

If **total circuit resistance** (R_T) is needed, Ohm's law can be used to calculate it because voltage (E) and current (I) are now known.

$$R_T = \frac{E}{I} = \frac{12 \text{ V}}{9 \text{ A}} = \mathbf{1.33 \text{ Ω}}$$

Note that the total resistance (1.33 ohms) is smaller than that of the smallest-resistance leg of the parallel circuit. This characteristic of a parallel circuit holds true because not all of the total current flows through all resistances as in a series circuit.

Because the current has alternative paths to ground through the various legs of a parallel circuit, as additional resistances (legs) are added to a parallel circuit, the total current from the battery (power source) *increases.*

Additional current can flow when resistances are added in parallel, because each leg of a parallel circuit has its own power and ground and the current flowing through each leg is strictly dependent on the resistance of *that* leg.

METHOD 2 If only two resistors are connected in parallel, the total resistance (R_T) can be found using the formula $R_T = \left(\dfrac{R_1 \times R_2}{R_1 + R_2} \right)$. For example, using the circuit in ● **FIGURE 7–5** and substituting 3 ohms for R_1 and 4 ohms for R_2, $R_T = \dfrac{(3 \times 4)}{(3 + 4)} = \dfrac{12}{7} = 1.7 \text{ Ω}$.

Note that the total resistance (1.7 ohms) is smaller than that of the smallest-resistance leg of the circuit.

NOTE: Which resistor is R_1 and which is R_2 is not important. The position in the formula makes no difference in the multiplication and addition of the resistor values.

This formula can be used for more than two resistances in parallel, but only two resistances can be calculated at a time. After solving for R_T for two resistors, use the value of R_T as R_1 and the additional resistance in parallel as R_2. Then solve for another R_T. Continue the process for all resistance legs of the parallel circuit. However, note that it might be easier to solve for R_T when there are more than two resistances in parallel by using either Method 3 or Method 4.

METHOD 3 A formula that can be used to find the total resistance for any number of resistances in parallel is $\dfrac{1}{R_T} = \dfrac{1}{R_1} + \dfrac{1}{R_2} + \dfrac{1}{R_3} + \cdots$

To solve for R_T for the three resistance legs in ● **FIGURE 7–6**, substitute the values of the resistances for R_1, R_2, and R_3: $\dfrac{1}{R_T} = \dfrac{1}{3} + \dfrac{1}{4} + \dfrac{1}{6}$.

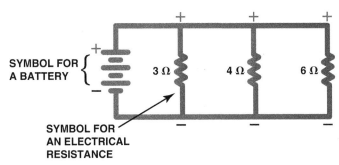

FIGURE 7–4 In a typical parallel circuit, each resistance has power and ground and each leg operates independently of the other legs of the circuit.

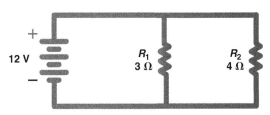

FIGURE 7–5 A schematic showing two resistors in parallel connected to a 12 volt battery.

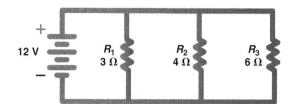

FIGURE 7-6 A parallel circuit with three resistors connected to a 12 volt battery.

The fractions cannot be added together unless they all have the same denominator. The lowest common denominator in this example is 12. Therefore, $\frac{1}{3}$ becomes $\frac{4}{12}$, $\frac{1}{4}$ becomes $\frac{3}{12}$, and $\frac{1}{6}$ becomes $\frac{2}{12}$.

$$\frac{1}{R_T} = \frac{4}{12} + \frac{3}{12} + \frac{2}{12} \text{ or } \frac{9}{12}.$$ Cross multiplying

$$R_T = \frac{12}{9} = 1.33 \ \Omega.$$

Note that the result (1.33 ohms) is the same regardless of the method used (see Method 1). The most difficult part of using this method (besides using fractions) is determining the lowest common denominator, especially for circuits containing a wide range of ohmic values for the various legs. For an easier method using a calculator, see Method 4.

METHOD 4 This method uses an electronic calculator, commonly available at very low cost. Instead of determining the lowest common denominator as in Method 3, one can use the electronic calculator to convert the fractions to decimal equivalents. The memory buttons on most calculators can be used to keep a running total of the fractional values. Using ● **FIGURE 7-7**, calculate the total resistance (R_T) by pushing the indicated buttons on the calculator. ● **ALSO SEE FIGURE 7-8**.

NOTE: This method can be used to find the total resistance of *any number* of resistances in parallel.

The memory recall (MRC) and equals (=) buttons invert the answer to give the correct value for total resistance (1.33 ohms). The inverse $\left(\frac{1}{X} \text{ or } X^{-1}\right)$ button can be used with the sum (SUM) button on scientific calculators without using the memory button.

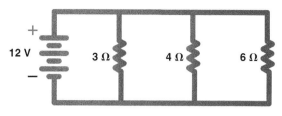

TO SOLVE THIS PARALLEL CIRCUIT PROBLEM FOR R_T (TOTAL RESISTANCE), PUSH THE EXACT BUTTONS ON AN ELECTRONIC CALCULATOR.

NOTE: BE CERTAIN TO PUSH THE ▤ BUTTON. FAILURE TO DO SO WILL RESULT IN INCORRECT ANSWERS WHEN USING MOST CALCULATORS.

(ANSWER = 1.3333)

FIGURE 7-7 Using an electronic calculator to determine the total resistance of a parallel circuit.

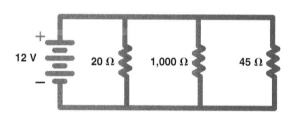

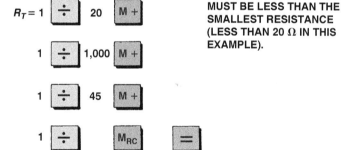

USE AN ELECTRONIC CALCULATOR TO SOLVE

NOTE: THE TOTAL RESISTANCE (R_T) MUST BE LESS THAN THE SMALLEST RESISTANCE (LESS THAN 20 Ω IN THIS EXAMPLE).

FIGURE 7-8 Another example of how to use an electronic calculator to determine the total resistance of a parallel circuit. The answer is 13.45 ohms. Notice that the effective resistance of this circuit is less than the resistance of the lowest branch (20 ohms).

METHOD 5 This method can be easily used when two or more resistances connected in parallel are of the same value. ● **SEE FIGURE 7-9**.

To calculate the total resistance (R_T) of equal-value resistors, divide the number of equal resistors into the value of the resistance: R_T = Value of equal resistance/Number of equal resistances $= \dfrac{12 \ \Omega}{4} = 3 \ \Omega$

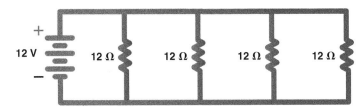

FIGURE 7–9 A parallel circuit containing four 12 ohm resistors. When a circuit has more than one resistor of equal value, the total resistance can be determined by simply dividing the value of the resistance (12 ohms in this example) by the number of equal-value resistors (4 in this example) to get 3 ohms.

NOTE: Because most automotive and light-truck electrical circuits involve multiple use of the same resistance, this method is the most useful. For example, if six additional 12 ohm lights were added to a vehicle, the additional lights would represent just 2 ohms of resistance $\left(\dfrac{12\ \Omega}{6}\ \text{lights} = 2\right)$. Therefore, 6 amperes of additional current would be drawn by the additional lights $\left(I = \dfrac{E}{R} = \dfrac{12\ V}{2\ \Omega} = 6\ A\right)$.

PARALLEL CIRCUIT CALCULATION EXAMPLES

Each of the four examples discussed below includes solving for the following:

- Total resistance
- Current flow (amperes) through each branch as well as total current flow
- Voltage drop across each resistance

Example 1:
(● SEE FIGURE 7–10.)

In this example, the voltage of the battery is unknown and the equation to be used is $E = I \times R$, where R represents the total resistance of the circuit. Using the equation for two resistors in parallel, the total resistance is 6 ohms.

$$R_T = \frac{R_1 \times R_2}{R_1 + R_2} = \frac{12 \times 12}{12 + 12} = \frac{144}{24} = 6\ \Omega$$

Placing the value of the total resistors into the equation results in a value for the battery voltage of 12 volts.

$$E = I \times R$$
$$E = 2\ A \times 6\Omega$$
$$E = 12\ V$$

Example 2:
(● SEE FIGURE 7–11.)

In this example, the value of R_3 is unknown. Because the voltage (12 volts) and the current (12 amperes) are known, it is easier to solve for the unknown resistance by treating each branch or leg as a separate circuit. Using Kirchhoff's law, the total current equals the total current flow through each branch. The current flow through R_1 is 3 amperes $\left(I = \dfrac{E}{R} = \dfrac{12\ V}{4\ \Omega} = 3\ A\right)$ and the current flow through R_2 is 6 amperes $\left(I = \dfrac{E}{R} = \dfrac{12\ V}{2\ \Omega} = 6\ A\right)$. Therefore, the total current through the two known branches equals 9 amperes (3 A + 6 A = 9 A). Because there are 12 amperes leaving and returning to the battery, the current flow through R_3 must be 3 amperes (12 A − 9 A = 3 A). The resistance must therefore be 4 ohms $\left(I = \dfrac{E}{R} = \dfrac{12\ V}{4\ \Omega} = 3\ A\right)$.

Example 3:
(● SEE FIGURE 7–12.)

In this example, the voltage of the battery is unknown. The equation to solve for voltage according to Ohm's law is:

$$E = I \times R$$

The R in this equation refers to the total resistance. Because there are four resistors of equal value, the total can be determined by the following equation.

$$R_{Total} = \frac{\textbf{Value of resistors}}{\textbf{Number of equal resistors}} = \frac{12\ \Omega}{4} = 3\ \Omega$$

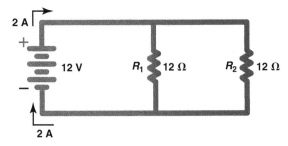

FIGURE 7–10 Example 1.

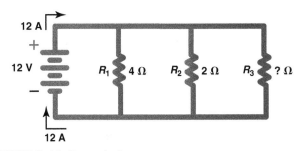

FIGURE 7–11 Example 2.

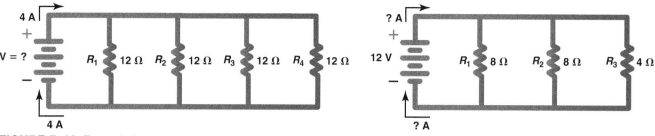

FIGURE 7-12 Example 3.

FIGURE 7-13 Example 4.

Inserting the value of the total resistance of the parallel circuit (3 ohms) into Ohm's law results in a battery voltage of 12 volts.

$$E = 4\,A \times 3\,\Omega$$
$$E = 12\,V$$

Example 4:

(● **SEE FIGURE 7-13.**)

The unknown value is the amount of current in the circuit. The Ohm's law equation for determining current is:

$$I = \frac{E}{R}$$

The R represents the total resistance. Because there are two equal resistances (8 ohms), these two can be replaced by one resistance of 4 ohms $\left(R_{Total} = \dfrac{Value}{Number} = \dfrac{8\,\Omega}{2} = 4\,\Omega \right)$.

The total resistance of this parallel circuit containing two 8 ohm resistors and one 4 ohm resistor is 2 ohms (two 8 ohm resistors in parallel equals 4 ohms. Then you have two 4 ohm resistors in parallel which equals 2 ohms). The current flow from the battery is then calculated to be 6 amperes.

$$I = \frac{E}{R} = \frac{12\,V}{2\,\Omega} = 6\,A$$

SUMMARY

1. Parallel circuits are used in most automotive applications.
2. The total resistance of a parallel circuit is always lower than the smallest resistance in the leg of the circuit.
3. The separate paths which split and meet at junction points are called branches, legs, or shunts.
4. Kirchhoff's current law states: The current flowing into any junction of an electrical circuit is equal to the current flowing out of that junction.
5. There are five basic methods that can be used to calculate the total resistance in a parallel circuit.

REVIEW QUESTIONS

1. Why is the total resistance of a parallel circuit less than the smallest resistance?
2. Why are parallel circuits (instead of series circuits) used in most automotive applications?
3. What does Kirchhoff's current law state?
4. What are three of the five ways to calculate the total resistance of a parallel circuit?
5. Why can't the resistances simply be added together when c`alculating total resistance in a parallel circuit?

1. Two bulbs are connected in parallel to a 12 volt battery. One bulb has a resistance of 6 ohms and the other bulb has a resistance of 2 ohms. Technician A says that only the 2 ohm bulb will light because all of the current will flow through the path with the least resistance and no current will flow through the 6 ohm bulb. Technician B says that the 6 ohm bulb will be dimmer than the 2 ohm bulb. Which technician is correct?
   a. Technician A only
   b. Technician B only
   c. Both Technicians A and B
   d. Neither Technician A nor B

2. Calculate the total resistance and current in a parallel circuit with three resistors of 4 Ω, 8 Ω, and 16 Ω, using any one of the five methods (calculator suggested). What are the values?
   a. 27 ohms (0.4 ampere)
   b. 14 ohms (0.8 ampere)
   c. 4 ohms (3 amperes)
   d. 2.3 ohms (5.3 amperes)

3. If an accessory such as an additional light is spliced into an existing circuit in parallel, what happens?
   a. The current increases in the circuit.
   b. The current decreases in the circuit.
   c. The voltage drops in the circuit.
   d. The resistance of the circuit increases.

4. A six-cylinder engine uses six fuel injectors connected electrically in two groups of three injectors in parallel. What would be the resistance if the three 12 ohm injectors were connected in parallel?
   a. 36 ohms
   b. 12 ohms
   c. 4 ohms
   d. 3 ohms

5. A vehicle has four taillight bulbs all connected in parallel. If one bulb burns out (opens), the total current flow in the circuit _____.
   a. increases and the other bulbs get brighter
   b. decreases because only three bulbs are operating
   c. remains the same because all the bulbs are wired in parallel
   d. drops to zero and the other three bulbs go out

6. Two identical bulbs are connected to a 12 volt battery in parallel. The voltage drop across the first bulb is 12 volts as measured with a voltmeter. What is the voltage drop across the other bulb?
   a. 0 volts
   b. 1 volt
   c. 6 volts
   d. 12 volts

7. Three resistors are connected to a 12 volt battery in parallel. The current flow through each resistor is 4 amperes. What is the value of the resistors?
   a. 1 ohm
   b. 2 ohms
   c. 3 ohms
   d. 4 ohms

8. Two bulbs are connected to a 12 volt battery in parallel. Another bulb is added in parallel. Technician A says that the third bulb will be dimmer than the other two bulbs due to reduced current flow through the filament of the bulb. Technician B says that the amount of current flowing from the battery will decrease due to the extra load. Which technician is correct?
   a. Technician A only
   b. Technician B only
   c. Both Technicians A and B
   d. Neither Technician A nor B

9. A vehicle has four parking lights all connected in parallel and one of the bulbs burns out. Technician A says that this could cause the parking light circuit fuse to blow (open). Technician B says that it would decrease the total current in the circuit. Which technician is correct?
   a. Technician A only
   b. Technician B only
   c. Both Technicians A and B
   d. Neither Technician A nor B

10. Three resistors are connected in parallel to a 12 volt battery. The total current flow from the battery is 12 amperes. The first resistor is 3 ohms and the second resistor is 6 ohms. What is the value of the third resistor?
    a. 1 Ω
    b. 2 Ω
    c. 3 Ω
    d. 4 Ω

chapter
8

SERIES–PARALLEL CIRCUITS

LEARNING OBJECTIVES

After studying this chapter, the reader will be able to:

Identify a series–parallel circuit.

Identify where faults in a series–parallel circuit can be detected.

This chapter will help you prepare for the ASE Electrical/Electronic Systems (A6) certification test content area "A" (General Electrical/Electronic System Diagnosis).

KEY TERMS Combination circuit 86 • Compound circuit 86 • Series–parallel circuits 86

SERIES–PARALLEL CIRCUITS

DEFINITION **Series–parallel circuits** are a combination of series and parallel segments in one complex circuit. A series–parallel circuit is also called a **compound** or **combination circuit.** Many automotive circuits include sections that are in parallel and in series.

TYPES OF SERIES–PARALLEL CIRCUITS A series–parallel circuit includes both parallel loads or resistances, plus additional loads or resistances that are electrically connected in series. There are two basic types of series–parallel circuits.

- A circuit where the load is in series with other loads in parallel. ● **SEE FIGURE 8–1.**

  An example of this type of series–parallel circuit is a dash light dimming circuit. The variable resistor is used to limit current flow to the dash light bulbs, which are wired in parallel.

- A circuit where a parallel circuit contains resistors or loads, which are in series with one or more branches.

A headlight and starter circuit is an example of this type of series–parallel circuit. A headlight switch is usually connected in series with a dimmer switch and in parallel with the dash light dimmer resistors. The headlights are also connected in parallel along with the taillights and side marker lights. ● **SEE FIGURE 8–2.**

SERIES–PARALLEL CIRCUIT FAULTS If a conventional parallel circuit, such as a taillight circuit, had an electrical fault that increased the resistance in one branch of the circuit, then the amount of current flow through that branch will be reduced.

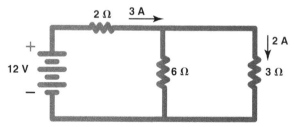

FIGURE 8–1 A series–parallel circuit.

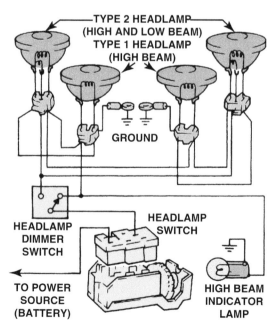

FIGURE 8–2 This complete headlight circuit with all bulbs and switches is a series–parallel circuit.

The added resistance, due to corrosion or other similar cause, would create a voltage drop. As a result of this drop in voltage, a lower voltage would be applied and the bulb in the taillight would be dimmer than normal because the brightness of the bulb depends on the voltage and current applied. If, however, the added resistance occurred in a part of the circuit that fed both taillights, then both taillights would be dimmer than normal. In this case, the added resistance created a series–parallel circuit that was originally just a simple parallel circuit.

SOLVING SERIES–PARALLEL CIRCUIT CALCULATION PROBLEMS

The key to solving series–parallel circuit problems is to combine or simplify as much as possible. For example, if there are two loads or resistances in series within a parallel branch or leg, then the circuit can be made simpler if the two are first added together before attempting to solve the parallel section. ● **SEE FIGURE 8–3.**

SERIES–PARALLEL CIRCUIT CALCULATION EXAMPLES

Each of the four examples discussed below solve for the following:

- Total resistance
- Current flow (amperes) through each branch, as well as total current flow
- Voltage drop across each resistance

Example 1
(● **SEE FIGURE 8–4.**)

The unknown resistor is in series with the other two resistances, which are connected in parallel. The Ohm's law equation to determine resistance is:

$$R = \frac{E}{I} = \frac{12 \text{ V}}{3} = 4 \ \Omega$$

The total resistance of the circuit is therefore 4 ohms and the value of the unknown can be determined by subtracting the value of the two resistors that are connected in parallel. The parallel branch resistance is 2 ohms.

$$R_T = \frac{4 \times 4}{4 + 4} = \frac{16}{8} = 2 \ \Omega$$

The value of the unknown resistance is therefore 2 ohms. Total $R = 4 \ \Omega - 2 \ \Omega = 2 \ \Omega$.

Example 2
(● **SEE FIGURE 8–5.**)

The unknown unit in this circuit is the voltage of the battery. The Ohm's law equation is:

$$E = I \times R$$

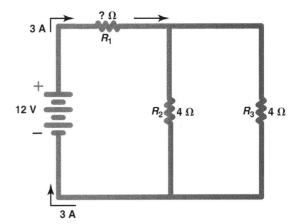

FIGURE 8–4 Example 1.

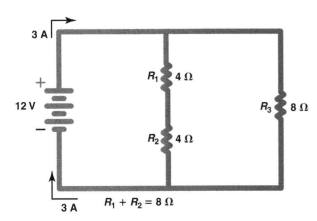

FIGURE 8–3 Solving a series–parallel circuit problem.

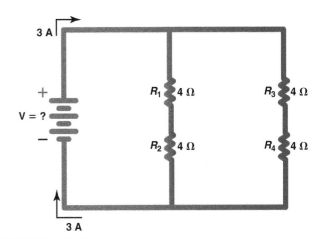

FIGURE 8–5 Example 2.

Before solving the problem, the total resistance must be determined. Because each branch contains two 4 ohm resistors in series, the value in each branch can be added to help simplify the circuit. By adding the resistors in each branch together, the parallel circuit now consists of two 8 ohm resistors.

$$R_T = \frac{R_1 \times R_2}{R_1 + R_2} = \frac{8 \times 8}{8 + 8} = \frac{64}{16} = 4\ \Omega$$

Inserting the value for the total resistance into the Ohm's law equation results in a value of 12 volts for the battery voltage.

$$E = I \times R$$
$$E = 3\ A \times 4\ \Omega$$
$$E = 12\ V$$

Example 3
(● SEE FIGURE 8–6.)

In this example, the total current through the circuit is unknown. The Ohm's law equation to solve this is:

$$I = \frac{E}{R}$$

The total resistance of the parallel circuit must be determined before the equation can be used to solve for current (amperes). To solve for total resistance, the circuit can first be simplified by adding R_3 and R_4 together, because these two resistors are in series in the same branch of the parallel circuit. To simplify even more, the resulting parallel section of the circuit, now containing two 8 ohm resistors in parallel, can be replaced with one 4 ohm resistor.

$$R_T = \frac{R_1 \times R_2}{R_1 + R_2} = \frac{8 \times 8}{8 + 8} = \frac{64}{16} = 4\ \Omega$$

With the parallel branches now reduced to just one 4 ohm resistor, this can be added to the 2 ohm (R_1) resistor because it is in series, creating a total circuit resistance of 6 ohms. Now the current flow can be determined from Ohm's law.

$$I = \frac{E}{R} = 12 \div 6 = 2\ A$$

Example 4
(● SEE FIGURE 8–7.)

In this example, the value of resistor R_1 is unknown. Using Ohm's law, the total resistance of the circuit is 3 ohms.

$$R = \frac{E}{I} = \frac{12\ V}{4\ A} = 3\ \Omega$$

However, knowing the total resistance is not enough to determine the value of R_1. To simplify the circuit, R_2 and R_5 can combine to create a parallel branch resistance value of 8 ohms because they are in series. To simplify even further, the two 8 ohm branches can be reduced to one branch of 4 ohms.

$$R_T = \frac{R_1 \times R_2}{R_1 + R_2} = \frac{8 \times 8}{8 + 8} = \frac{64}{16} = 4\ \Omega$$

Now the circuit has been simplified to one resistor in series (R_1) with two branches with 4 ohms in each branch. These two branches can be reduced to equal one 2 ohm resistor.

$$R_T = \frac{R_1 \times R_2}{R_1 + R_2} = \frac{4 \times 4}{4 + 4} = \frac{16}{8} = 2\ \Omega$$

Now the circuit includes just one 2 ohm resistor plus the unknown R_1. Because the total resistance is 3 ohms, the value of R_1 must be 1 ohm.

$$3\ \Omega - 2\ \Omega = 1\ \Omega$$

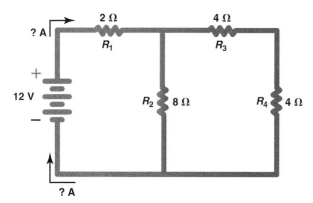

FIGURE 8–6 Example 3.

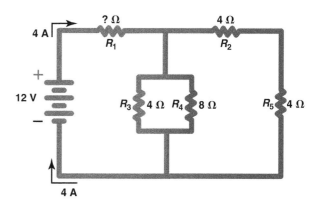

FIGURE 8–7 Example 4.

SUMMARY

1. A series–parallel circuit is called a compound circuit or a combination circuit.

2. A series–parallel circuit is a combination of a series and a parallel circuit.

3. A fault in a series portion of a series–parallel circuit would affect the entire circuit operation if the series part was in the power side or the ground side of the parallel portion of the circuit.

4. A fault in one leg of a series–parallel circuit will affect just the component(s) in that one leg.

REVIEW QUESTIONS

1. Explain why an increase in resistance in the series part of a series–parallel circuit will affect the current (amperes) through the parallel legs (branches).

2. What would be the effect of an open circuit in one leg of a parallel portion of a series–parallel circuit?

3. What would be the effect of an open circuit in a series portion of a series–parallel circuit?

4. What automotive circuits are in series-parallel?

5. Why are series-parallel circuits used in automotive applications?

CHAPTER QUIZ

1. Half of the dash is dark. Technician A says that a defective dash light dimmer can be the cause because it is in series with the bulbs that are in parallel. Technician B says that one or more bulbs could be defective. Which technician is correct?
   a. Technician A only
   b. Technician B only
   c. Both Technicians A and B
   d. Neither Technician A nor B

2. All brake lights are dimmer than normal. Technician A says that bad bulbs could be the cause. Technician B says that high resistance in the brake switch could be the cause. Which technician is correct?
   a. Technician A only
   b. Technician B only
   c. Both Technicians A and B
   d. Neither Technician A nor B

3. See ● **FIGURE 8–8** to solve for total resistance (R_T) and total current (I).
   a. 10 ohms and 1.2 amperes
   b. 4 ohms and 3 amperes
   c. 6 ohms and 2 amperes
   d. 2 ohms and 6 amperes

FIGURE 8–8 Chapter Quiz question 3.

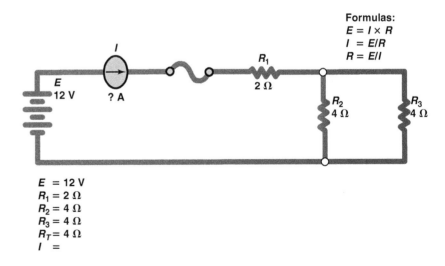

Formulas:
$E = I \times R$
$I = E/R$
$R = E/I$

$E = 12\ V$
$R_1 = 2\ \Omega$
$R_2 = 4\ \Omega$
$R_3 = 4\ \Omega$
$R_T = 4\ \Omega$
$I =$

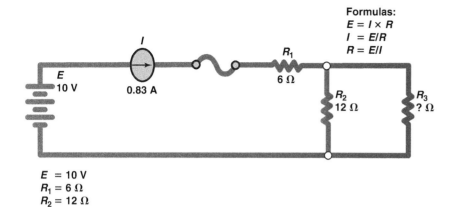

Formulas:
$E = I \times R$
$I = E/R$
$R = E/I$

FIGURE 8–9 Chapter Quiz question 4.

R_1
6 Ω

R_2
12 Ω

R_3
? Ω

E
10 V

I
0.83 A

E = 10 V
R_1 = 6 Ω
R_2 = 12 Ω
R_3 =
R_T =
I = 0.83 A

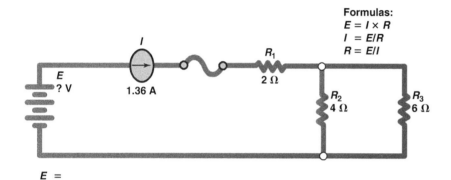

Formulas:
$E = I \times R$
$I = E/R$
$R = E/I$

FIGURE 8–10 Chapter Quiz question 5.

R_1
2 Ω

R_2
4 Ω

R_3
6 Ω

E
? V

I
1.36 A

E =
R_1 = 2 Ω
R_2 = 4 Ω
R_3 = 6 Ω
R_T =
I = 1.36 A

4. See ● **FIGURE 8–9** to solve for the value of R_3 and total resistance (R_T).
   a. 12 ohms and 12 ohms
   b. 1 ohm and 7 ohms
   c. 2 ohms and 8 ohms
   d. 6 ohms and 6 ohms

5. See ● **FIGURE 8–10** to solve for voltage (E) and total resistance (R_T).
   a. 16.3 volts and 12 ohms
   b. 3.3 volts and 2.4 ohms
   c. 1.36 volts and 1 ohm
   d. 6 volts and 4.4 ohms

6. See ● **FIGURE 8–11** to solve for R_1 and total resistance (R_T).
   a. 3 ohms and 15 ohms   c. 2 ohms and 5 ohms
   b. 1 ohm and 15 ohms   d. 5 ohms and 5 ohms

7. See ● **FIGURE 8–12** to solve for total resistance (R_T) and total current (I).
   a. 3.1 ohms and 7.7 amperes
   b. 5.1 ohms and 4.7 amperes
   c. 20 ohms and 1.2 amperes
   d. 6 ohms and 4 amperes

8. See ● **FIGURE 8–13** to solve for the value of E and total resistance (R_T).
   a. 13.2 volts and 40 ohms
   b. 11.2 volts and 34 ohms
   c. 8 volts and 24.2 ohms
   d. 8.6 volts and 26 ohms

FIGURE 8–11 Chapter Quiz question 6.

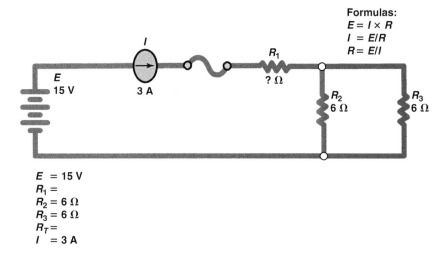

E = 15 V
R_1 =
R_2 = 6 Ω
R_3 = 6 Ω
R_T =
I = 3 A

FIGURE 8–12 Chapter Quiz question 7.

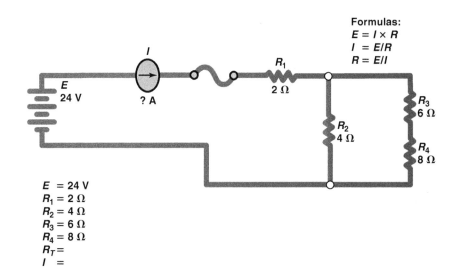

E = 24 V
R_1 = 2 Ω
R_2 = 4 Ω
R_3 = 6 Ω
R_4 = 8 Ω
R_T =
I =

FIGURE 8–13 Chapter Quiz question 8.

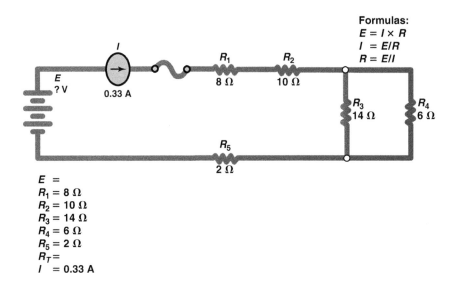

E =
R_1 = 8 Ω
R_2 = 10 Ω
R_3 = 14 Ω
R_4 = 6 Ω
R_5 = 2 Ω
R_T =
I = 0.33 A

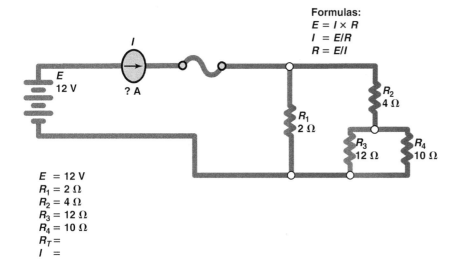

FIGURE 8–14 Chapter Quiz question 9.

Formulas:
$E = I \times R$
$I = E/R$
$R = E/I$

R_1 2 Ω

R_2 4 Ω

R_3 12 Ω

R_4 10 Ω

E 12 V
? A

$E = 12\ V$
$R_1 = 2\ \Omega$
$R_2 = 4\ \Omega$
$R_3 = 12\ \Omega$
$R_4 = 10\ \Omega$
$R_T =$
$I =$

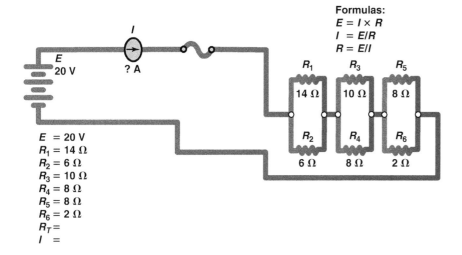

FIGURE 8–15 Chapter Quiz question 10.

Formulas:
$E = I \times R$
$I = E/R$
$R = E/I$

E 20 V
? A

R_1 14 Ω
R_3 10 Ω
R_5 8 Ω

R_2 6 Ω
R_4 8 Ω
R_6 2 Ω

$E = 20\ V$
$R_1 = 14\ \Omega$
$R_2 = 6\ \Omega$
$R_3 = 10\ \Omega$
$R_4 = 8\ \Omega$
$R_5 = 8\ \Omega$
$R_6 = 2\ \Omega$
$R_T =$
$I =$

9. See ● **FIGURE 8–14** to solve for total resistance (R_T) and total current (I).
   a. 1.5 ohms and 8 amperes
   b. 18 ohms and 0.66 ampere
   c. 6 ohms and 2 amperes
   d. 5.5 ohms and 2.2 amperes

10. See ● **FIGURE 8–15** to solve for total resistance (R_T) and total current (I).
   a. 48 ohms and 0.42 ampere
   b. 20 ohms and 1 ampere
   c. 30 ohms and 0.66 ampere
   d. 10.2 ohms and 1.96 amperes

chapter 9

CIRCUIT TESTERS AND DIGITAL METERS

LEARNING OBJECTIVES

After studying this chapter, the reader should be able to:

Discuss how to safely set up and use a fused jumper wire, a test light, and a logic probe.

Describe the uses of digital multimeters and inductive ammeters.

Discuss diode check and frequency.

Describe the prefixes used with electrical units and how to read digital meters.

Explain how to safely use a digital meter to read voltage, resistance, and current, and compare to factory specifications.

This chapter will help you prepare for the ASE Electrical/Electronic Systems (A6) certification test content area "A" (General Electrical/Electronic System Diagnosis).

KEY TERMS AC/DC clamp-on DMM 100 • DMM 95 • DVOM 95 • High-impedance test meter 95 • IEC 105 • Inductive ammeter 99 • Kilo (k) 101 • LED test light 94 • Logic probe 95 • Mega (M) 101 • Meter accuracy 104 • Meter resolution 103 • Milli (m) 101 • OL 97 • RMS 103 • Test light 94

FUSED JUMPER WIRE

DEFINITION A fused jumper wire is used to check a circuit by bypassing the switch or to provide a power or ground to a component. A fused jumper wire, also called a test lead, can be purchased or made by the service technician.
● **SEE FIGURE 9–1**.

It should include the following features.

■ **Fuse.** A typical fused jumper wire has a blade-type fuse that can be easily replaced. A 10 ampere fuse (red color) is often the value used.

■ **Alligator clip ends.** Alligator clips at the ends allow the fused jumper wire to be clipped to a ground or power source, while the other end is attached to the power side or ground side of the unit being tested.

■ **Good-quality insulated wire.** Most purchased jumper wire is about 14-gauge stranded copper wire with a flexible rubberized insulation to allow it to move easily, even in cold weather.

USES OF A FUSED JUMPER WIRE A fused jumper wire can be used to help diagnose a component or circuit by performing the following procedures.

■ **Supply power or ground.** If a component, such as a horn, does not work, a fused jumper wire can be used to supply a temporary power and/or ground. Start by unplugging the electrical connector from the device

FIGURE 9–1 A technician-made fused jumper lead, which is equipped with a red 10 ampere fuse. This fused jumper wire uses terminals for testing circuits at a connector instead of alligator clips.

and connect a fused jumper lead to the power terminal. Another fused jumper wire may be needed to provide the ground. If the unit works, the problem is in the power-side or ground-side circuit.

CAUTION: Never use a fused jumper wire to bypass any resistance or load in the circuit. The increased current flow could damage the wiring and could blow the fuse on the jumper lead.

TEST LIGHTS

NONPOWERED TEST LIGHT

A 12 volt test light is one of the simplest testers that can be used to detect electricity. A **test light** is simply a lightbulb with a probe and a ground wire attached. ● **SEE FIGURE 9–2**.

It is used to detect battery voltage potential at various test points. Battery voltage cannot be seen or felt and can be detected only with test equipment.

The ground clip is connected to a clean ground on either the negative terminal of the battery, or a clean metal part of the body, and the probe touched to terminals or components. If the test light comes on, this indicates that voltage is available. ● **SEE FIGURE 9–3**.

A purchased test light should be labeled a "12 volt test light." Do not purchase a test light designed for household current (110 or 220 volts), as it does not light with 12 to 14 volts.

USES OF A 12 VOLT TEST LIGHT

A 12 volt test light can be used to check the following:

- **Electrical power.** If the test light comes on, there is power available. It does not, however, indicate the voltage level, or if there is enough current available to operate an electrical load. This only indicates that there is enough voltage and current to light the test light (about 0.25 ampere).

- **Grounds.** A test light can be used to check for grounds by attaching the clip of the test light to the positive terminal of the battery or to any 12 volt electrical terminal. The tip of the test light can then be used to touch the ground wire. If there is a ground connection, the test light comes on.

HIGH-IMPEDANCE TEST LIGHT

A high-impedance test light has a high internal resistance and, therefore, draws very low current in order to light. High-impedance test lights are safe to use on computer circuits because they do not affect the circuit current in the same way as conventional 12 volt test lights when connected to a circuit. There are two types of high-impedance test lights.

- Some test lights use an electronic circuit to limit the current flow to avoid causing damage to electronic devices.

- An **LED test light** uses a light-emitting diode (LED), instead of a standard automotive bulb, for a visual indication of voltage. An LED test light requires only about 25 milliamperes (0.025 ampere) to light; therefore, it can be used on electronic circuits, as well as on standard circuits.

● **SEE FIGURE 9–4** for construction details for a homemade LED test light.

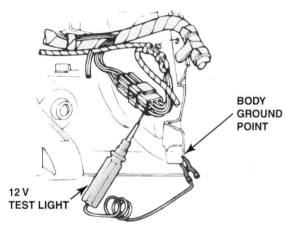

FIGURE 9–2 A 12 volt test light is attached to a good ground while probing for power.

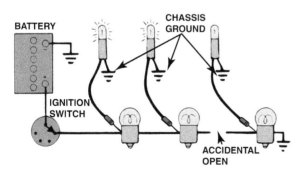

FIGURE 9–3 A test light can be used to locate an open in a circuit. Note that the test light is grounded at a different location than the circuit itself.

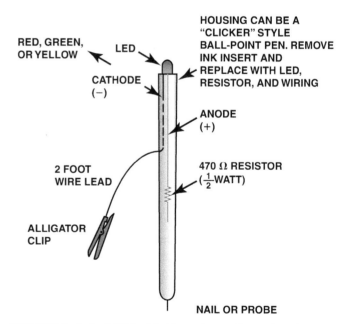

FIGURE 9–4 An LED test light can be easily made using low-cost components and an old ink pen. With the 470 ohm resistor in series with the LED, this tester only draws 0.025 ampere (25 milliamperes) from the circuit being tested. This low current draw helps assure the technician that the circuit or component being tested will not be damaged by excessive current flow.

LOGIC PROBE

PURPOSE AND FUNCTION

A **logic probe** is an electronic device that lights up a red (usually) LED if the probe is touched to battery voltage. If the probe is touched to ground, a green (usually) LED lights. ● **SEE FIGURE 9–5**.

A logic probe can "sense" the difference between high- and low-voltage levels, which explains the name *logic*.

- A typical logic probe can also light another light (often amber color) when a change in voltage occurs.
- Some logic probes flash the red light when a pulsing voltage signal is detected.
- Some flash the green light when a pulsing ground signal is detected.

This feature is helpful when checking for a variable voltage output from a computer or ignition sensor.

USING A LOGIC PROBE

A logic probe must first be connected to a power and ground source, such as the vehicle battery. This connection powers the probe and gives it a reference low (ground).

Most logic probes also make a distinctive sound for each high- and low-voltage level. This makes troubleshooting easier when probing connectors or component terminals. A sound (usually a beep) is heard when the probe tip is touched to a changing voltage source. The changing voltage also usually lights the pulse light on the logic probe.

Therefore, the probe can be used to check components, such as:

- Pickup coils
- Hall-effect sensors
- Magnetic sensors

DIGITAL MULTIMETERS

TERMINOLOGY

Digital multimeter (DMM) and **digital volt-ohm-meter (DVOM)** are terms commonly used for electronic **high-impedance test meters**. *High impedance* means that the electronic internal resistance of the meter is high enough to prevent excessive current draw from any circuit being tested. Most meters today have a minimum of 10 million ohms (10 megohms) of resistance. This high internal resistance between the meter leads is present only when measuring volts. The high resistance in the meter itself reduces the amount of current flowing through the meter when it is being used to measure voltage, leading to more accurate test results because the meter does not change the load on the circuit. High-impedance meters are required for measuring computer circuits.

CAUTION: Analog (needle-type) meters are almost always lower than 10 megohms and should not be used to measure any computer or electronic circuit. Connecting an analog meter to a computer circuit could damage the computer or other electronic modules.

A high-impedance meter can be used to measure any automotive circuit within the ranges of the meter. ● **SEE FIGURE 9–6**.

The common abbreviations for the units that many meters can measure are often confusing. ● **SEE CHART 9–1** for the most commonly used symbols and their meanings.

MEASURING VOLTAGE

A voltmeter measures the *pressure* or potential of electricity in units of volts. A voltmeter is connected to a circuit in parallel. Voltage can be measured by selecting either AC or DC volts.

- **DC volts (DCV).** This setting is the most common for automotive use. Use this setting to measure battery voltage and voltage to all lighting and accessory circuits.
- **AC volts (ACV).** This setting is used to check for unwanted AC voltage from alternators and some sensors.
- **Range.** The range is automatically set for most meters, but can be manually ranged, if needed.
  ● **SEE FIGURES 9–7 AND 9–8**.

MEASURING RESISTANCE

An ohmmeter measures the resistance in ohms of a component or circuit section when no current is flowing through the circuit. An ohmmeter contains a battery (or other power source) and is connected in series with

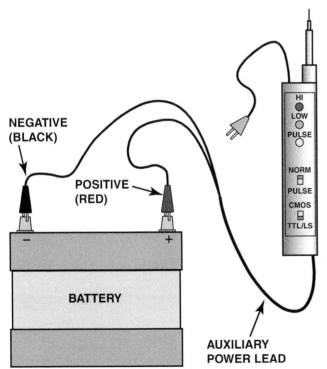

FIGURE 9–5 A logic probe connected to the vehicle battery. When the tip probe is connected to a circuit, it can check for power, ground, or a pulse.

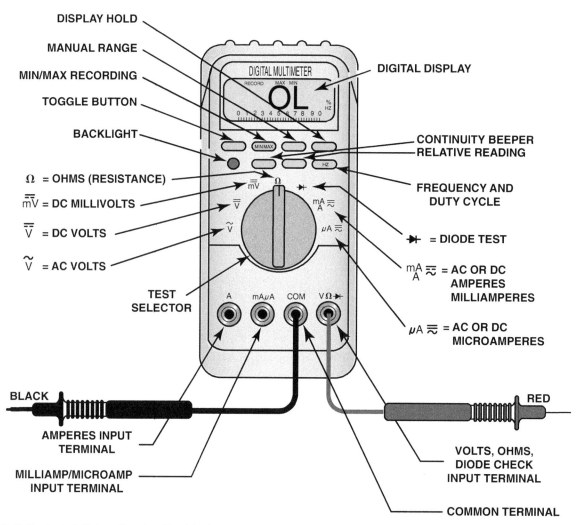

- DISPLAY HOLD
- MANUAL RANGE
- MIN/MAX RECORDING
- TOGGLE BUTTON
- BACKLIGHT
- DIGITAL DISPLAY
- CONTINUITY BEEPER RELATIVE READING
- FREQUENCY AND DUTY CYCLE

Ω = OHMS (RESISTANCE)
$\overline{mV}$ = DC MILLIVOLTS
$\overline{V}$ = DC VOLTS
$\widetilde{V}$ = AC VOLTS

TEST SELECTOR

➤┤ = DIODE TEST

$\frac{mA}{A}$ ≂ = AC OR DC AMPERES MILLIAMPERES

μA ≂ = AC OR DC MICROAMPERES

BLACK
RED

- AMPERES INPUT TERMINAL
- MILLIAMP/MICROAMP INPUT TERMINAL
- VOLTS, OHMS, DIODE CHECK INPUT TERMINAL
- COMMON TERMINAL

FIGURE 9–6 Typical digital multimeter. The black meter lead is always placed in the COM terminal. The red meter test lead should be in the volt-ohm terminal, except when measuring current in amperes.

SYMBOL	MEANING
AC	Alternating current or voltage
DC	Direct current or voltage
V	Volts
mV	Millivolts (1/1,000 volts)
A	Ampere (amps), current
mA	Milliampere (1/1,000 amps)
%	Percent (for duty-cycle readings only)
Ω	Ohms, resistance
kΩ	Kilohm (1,000 ohms), resistance
MΩ	Megohm (1,000,000 ohms), resistance
Hz	Hertz (cycles per second), frequency
kHz	Kilohertz (1,000 cycles/sec.), frequency
ms	Milliseconds (1/1,000 sec.) for pulse-width measurements

CHART 9–1

Common symbols and abbreviations used on digital meters.

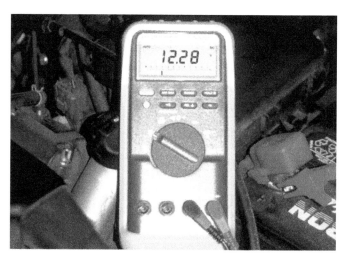

FIGURE 9–7 Typical digital multimeter (DMM) set to read DC volts.

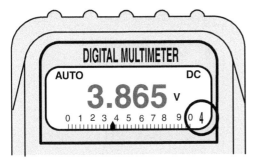

BECAUSE THE SIGNAL READING IS BELOW 4 V, THE METER AUTORANGES TO THE 4 V SCALE. IN THE 4 V SCALE, THIS METER PROVIDES THREE DECIMAL PLACES.

(a)

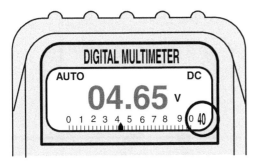

WHEN THE VOLTAGE EXCEEDS 4 V, THE METER AUTORANGES INTO THE 40 V SCALE. THE DECIMAL POINT MOVES ONE PLACE TO THE RIGHT, LEAVING ONLY TWO DECIMAL PLACES.

(b)

FIGURE 9–8 A typical autoranging digital multimeter automatically selects the proper scale to read the voltage being tested. The scale selected is usually displayed on the meter face. (a) Note that the display indicates "4," meaning that this range can read up to 4 volts. (b) The range is now set to the 40 volt scale, meaning that the meter can read up to 40 volts on the scale. Any reading above this level causes the meter to reset to a higher scale. If not set on autoranging, the meter display indicates OL if a reading exceeds the limit of the scale selected.

the component or wire being measured. When the leads are connected to a component, current flows through the test leads and the difference in voltage (voltage drop) between the leads is measured as resistance. Note the following facts about using an ohmmeter.

- Zero ohms on the scale means that there is no resistance between the test leads, thus indicating continuity or a continuous path for the current to flow in a closed circuit.
- Infinity means no connection, as in an open circuit.
- Ohmmeters have no required polarity, even though red and black test leads are used for resistance measurement.

CAUTION: The circuit must be electrically open with no current flowing when using an ohmmeter. If current is flowing when an ohmmeter is connected, the reading is incorrect and the meter can be destroyed.

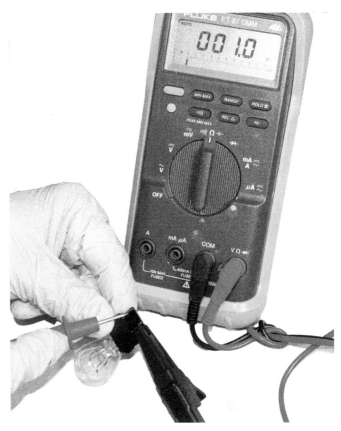

FIGURE 9–9 Using a digital multimeter set to read ohms (Ω) to test this lightbulb. The meter reads the resistance of the filament.

Different meters have different ways of indicating infinite resistance, or a reading higher than the scale allows. Examples of an over-limit display include:

- **OL**, meaning **over limit** or overload
- Flashing or solid number 1
- Flashing or solid number 3 on the left side of the display

Check the meter instructions for the exact display used to indicate an open circuit or over-range reading. ● **SEE FIGURES 9–9 AND 9–10.**

To summarize, open and zero readings are as follows:

0.00 Ω = Zero resistance (component or circuit has continuity)

OL = An open circuit or reading is higher than the scale selected (no current flows)

MEASURING AMPERES An ammeter measures the flow of *current* through a complete circuit in units of amperes. The ammeter has to be installed in the circuit (in series) so that it can measure all the current flow in that circuit, just as a water flow meter measures the amount of water flow (cubic feet per minute, for example). ● **SEE FIGURE 9–11.**

CAUTION: An ammeter must be installed in series with the circuit to measure the current flow in the circuit. If a meter set to read amperes is connected in parallel,

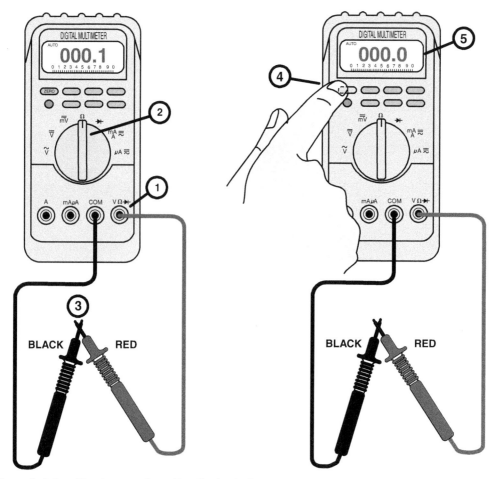

FIGURE 9–10 Many digital multimeters can have the display indicate zero to compensate for test lead resistance. (1) Connect leads in the V Ω and COM meter terminals. (2) Select the Ω scale. (3) Touch the two meter leads together. (4) Push the "zero" or "relative" button on the meter. (5) The meter display now indicates zero ohms of resistance.

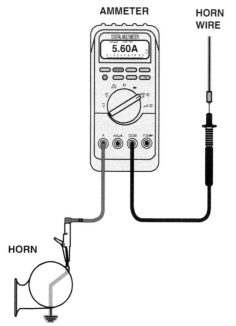

FIGURE 9–11 Measuring the current flow required by a horn requires that the ammeter be connected to the circuit in series and the horn button be depressed by an assistant.

? FREQUENTLY ASKED QUESTION

How Much Voltage Does an Ohmmeter Apply?

Most digital meters that are set to measure ohms (resistance) apply 0.3 to 1 volt to the component being measured. The voltage comes from the meter itself to measure the resistance. Two things are important to remember about an ohmmeter.

1. The component or circuit must be disconnected from any electrical circuit while the resistance is being measured.
2. Because the meter itself applies a voltage (even though it is relatively low), a meter set to measure ohms can damage electronic circuits. Computer or electronic chips can be easily damaged if subjected to only a few milliamperes of current, similar to the amount an ohmmeter applies when a resistance measurement is being performed.

Fuse Your Meter Leads!

Most digital meters include an ammeter capability. When reading amperes, the leads of the meter must be changed from volts or ohms (V or Ω) to amperes (A), milliamperes (mA), or microamperes (μA).

A common problem may occur the next time voltage is measured. Although the technician may switch the selector to read volts, often the leads are not switched back to the volt or ohm position. Because the ammeter lead position results in zero ohms of resistance to current flow through the meter, the meter or the fuse inside the meter is destroyed if the meter is connected to a battery. Many meter fuses are expensive and difficult to find.

To avoid this problem, simply solder an inline 10 ampere blade-fuse holder into one meter lead. ● **SEE FIGURE 9–12**.

Do not think that this technique is for beginners only. Experienced technicians often get in a hurry and forget to switch the lead. A blade fuse is faster, easier, and less expensive to replace than a meter fuse, or the meter itself. Also, if the soldering is done properly, the addition of an inline fuse holder and fuse does not increase the resistance of the meter leads.

WARNING Do not use a meter equipped with an external add-on fuse when testing a high-voltage circuit to prevent possible shock hazard.

such as across a battery, the meter or the leads may be destroyed, or the fuse blows, by the current available across the battery. Some digital multimeters (DMMs) beep if the unit selection does not match the test lead connection on the meter. However, in a noisy shop, this beep sound may be inaudible.

Digital meters require that the meter leads be moved to the ammeter terminals. Most digital meters have an ampere scale that can accommodate a maximum of 10 amperes. See the Tech Tip "Fuse Your Meter Leads!"

 FREQUENTLY ASKED QUESTION

What Does "CE" Mean on Many Meters?

The "CE" means that the meter meets the newest European Standards and the CE mark stands for Conformité Europeenne, which is French for "European Conformity."

INDUCTIVE AMMETERS

OPERATION **Inductive ammeters** do not make physical contact with the circuit. They measure the strength of the magnetic field surrounding the wire carrying the current, and use a Hall-effect sensor to measure current. The Hall-effect sensor detects the strength of the magnetic field that surrounds the wire carrying an electrical current. ● **SEE FIGURE 9–13**.

FIGURE 9–12 Note the blade-type fuse holder soldered in series with one of the meter leads. A 10 ampere fuse helps protect the internal meter fuse (if equipped), and the meter itself, from damage that may result from excessive current flow, if accidentally used incorrectly.

FIGURE 9–13 An inductive ammeter clamp is used with all starting and charging testers to measure the current flow through the battery cables.

This means that the meter probe surrounds the wire(s) carrying the current and measures the strength of the magnetic field that surrounds any conductor carrying a current.

AC/DC CLAMP-ON DIGITAL MULTIMETERS
An **AC/DC clamp-on digital multimeter (DMM)** is a useful meter for automotive diagnostic work. ● SEE FIGURE 9–14.

The major advantage of the clamp-on-type meter is that there is no need to break the circuit to measure current (amperes). Simply clamp the jaws of the meter around the power lead(s) or ground lead(s) of the component being measured and read the display. Most clamp-on meters can also measure alternating current, which is helpful in the diagnosis of an alternator problem. Volts, ohms, frequency, and temperature can also be measured with the typical clamp-on DMM, but use conventional meter leads. The inductive clamp is only used to measure amperes.

FIGURE 9–14 A typical mini clamp-on-type digital multimeter. This meter is capable of measuring alternating current (AC) and direct current (DC) without requiring that the circuit be disconnected to install the meter in series. The jaws are simply placed over the wire and current flow through the circuit is displayed.

DIODE CHECK Diode check is a meter function that can be used to check diodes, including light-emitting diodes (LEDs).

The meter is able to test diodes in the following way:

- The meter applies roughly a 3 volt DC signal to the text leads.
- The voltage is high enough to cause a diode to work and the meter displays:
  1. 0.4 to 0.7 volt when testing silicon diodes, such as those found in alternators
  2. 1.5 to 2.3 volts when testing LEDs, such as those found in some lighting applications

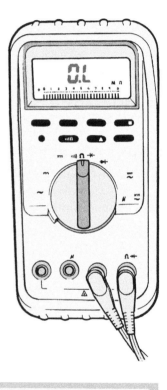

FIGURE 9–15 Typical digital multimeter showing OL (over limit) on the readout with the ohms (Ω) unit selected. This usually means that the unit being measured is open (infinite resistance) and has no continuity.

TECH TIP

Over-Limit Display Does Not Mean the Meter Is Reading "Nothing"

The meaning of the over-limit display on a digital meter often confuses beginning technicians. When asked what the meter is reading when an over limit (OL) is displayed on the meter face, the response is often, "Nothing." Many meters indicate over limit or over load, which simply means that the reading is over the maximum that can be displayed for the selected range. For example, the meter displays OL if 12 volts are being measured, but the meter has been set to read a maximum of 4 volts.

Autoranging meters adjust the range to match what is being measured. Here OL means a value higher than the meter can read (unlikely on the voltage scale for automobile usage), or infinity when measuring resistance (ohms). Therefore, OL means infinity when measuring resistance or an open circuit is being indicated. The meter reads 00.0 if the resistance is zero, so "nothing" in this case indicates continuity (zero resistance), whereas OL indicates infinite resistance. Therefore, when talking with another technician about a meter reading, make sure you know exactly what the reading on the face of the meter means. Also be sure that you are connecting the meter leads correctly. ● SEE FIGURE 9–15.

DUTY CYCLE Duty cycle is the amount of time, by percentage, that a signal is on compared to being off.

- 100% indicates that a device is being commanded on all of the time.
- 50% indicates that a device is being commanded on half of the time.
- 25% indicates that a device is being commanded on just 25% of the time.

Duty cycle is used to measure the on time for fuel injectors and other computer-controlled solenoid and devices.

FREQUENCY Frequency is a measure of how many times per second a signal changes. Frequency is measured in a unit called hertz, formerly termed "cycles per second."

Frequency measurements are used when checking the following:

- Mass airflow (MAF) sensors for proper operation
- Ignition primary pulse signals when diagnosing a no-start condition
- Checking a wheel speed sensor

ELECTRICAL UNIT PREFIXES

DEFINITIONS Electrical units are measured in numbers such as 12 volts, 150 amperes, and 470 ohms. Large units over 1,000 may be expressed in kilo units. **Kilo (k)** means 1,000. ● **SEE FIGURE 9–16.**

4,700 ohms = 4.7 kilohms (kΩ)

If the value is over 1 million (1,000,000), the prefix **mega (M)** is often used. For example:

1,100,000 volts = 1.1 megavolts (MV)

4,700,000 ohms = 4.7 megohms (MΩ)

Sometimes a circuit conducts so little current that a smaller unit of measure is required. Small units of measure expressed in 1/1,000 are prefixed by **milli (m)**. To summarize:

mega (M) = 1,000,000 (decimal point six places to the right = 1,000,000)

kilo (k) = 1,000 (decimal point three places to the right = 1,000)

milli (m) = 1/1,000 (decimal point three places to the left = 0.001)

NOTE: Lowercase _m_ equals a small unit (milli), whereas a capital _M_ represents a large unit (mega).

● **SEE CHART 9–2.**

PREFIXES The prefixes can be confusing because most digital meters can express values in more than one unit, especially if the meter is autoranging. For example, an ammeter reading may

THE SYMBOL ON THE RIGHT SIDE OF THE DISPLAY INDICATES WHAT RANGE THE METER HAS BEEN SET TO READ.

Ω **= OHMS**

IF THE ONLY SYMBOL ON THE DISPLAY IS THE OHMS SYMBOL, THE READING ON THE DISPLAY IS EXACTLY THE RESISTANCE IN OHMS.

kΩ **= KILOHMS = OHMS TIMES 1,000**

A "K" IN FRONT OF THE OHMS SYMBOL MEANS "KILOHMS"; THE READING ON THE DISPLAY IS IN KILOHMS. YOU HAVE TO MULTIPLY THE READING ON THE DISPLAY BY 1,000 TO GET THE RESISTANCE IN OHMS.

MΩ **= MEGOHMS = OHMS TIMES 1,000,000**

AN "M" IN FRONT OF THE OHMS SYMBOL MEANS "MEGOHMS"; THE READING ON THE DISPLAY IS IN MEGOHMS. YOU HAVE TO MULTIPLY THE READING ON THE DISPLAY BY 1,000,000 TO GET THE RESISTANCE IN OHMS.

FIGURE 9–16 Always look at the meter display when a measurement is being made, especially if using an autoranging meter.

TO/ FROM	MEGA	KILO	BASE	MILLI
Mega	0 places	3 places to the right	6 places to the right	9 places to the right
Kilo	3 places to the left	0 places	3 places to the right	6 places to the right
Base	6 places to the left	3 places to the left	0 places	3 places to the right
Milli	9 places to the left	6 places to the left	3 places to the left	0 places

CHART 9–2

A conversion chart showing the decimal point location for the various prefixes.

show 36.7 mA on autoranging. When the scale is changed to amperes ("A" in the window of the display), the number displayed is 0.037 A. Note that the resolution of the value is reduced.

NOTE: Always check the face of the meter display for the unit being measured. To best understand what is being displayed on the face of a digital meter, select a manual scale and move the selector until whole units appear, such as "A" for amperes instead of "mA" for milliamperes.

Think of Money

Digital meter displays can often be confusing. The display for a battery measured as 12 1/2 volts is 12.50 V, just as $12.50 is 12 dollars and 50 cents. A 1/2 volt reading on a digital meter is displayed as 0.50 V, just as $0.50 is half of a dollar.

It is more confusing when low values are displayed. For example, if a voltage reading is 0.063 volt, an autoranging meter displays 63 millivolts (63 mV), or 63/1,000 of a volt, or $63 of $1,000. (It takes 1,000 mV to equal 1 volt.) Think of millivolts as one-tenth of a cent, with 1 volt being $1.00. Therefore, 630 millivolts are equal to $0.63 of $1.00 (630 tenths of a cent, or 63 cents).

To avoid confusion, try to manually range the meter to read base units (whole volts). If the meter is ranged to base-unit volts, 63 millivolts is displayed as 0.063, or maybe just 0.06, depending on the display capabilities of the meter.

HOW TO READ DIGITAL METERS

STEPS TO FOLLOW Getting to know and use a digital meter takes time and practice. The first step is to read, understand, and follow all safety and operational instructions that come with the meter. Use of the meter usually involves the following steps.

STEP 1 **Select the proper unit of electricity for what is being measured.** This unit could be volts, ohms (resistance), or amperes (amount of current flow). If the meter is not autoranging, select the proper scale for the anticipated reading. For example, if a 12 volt battery is being measured, select a meter reading range that is higher than the voltage, but not too high. A 20 or 30 volt range accurately shows the voltage of a 12 volt battery. If a 1,000 volt scale is selected, a 12 volt reading may not be accurate.

STEP 2 **Place the meter leads into the proper input terminals.**

- The black lead is inserted into the common (COM) terminal. This meter lead usually stays in this location for all meter functions.
- The red lead is inserted into the volt, ohm, or diode check terminal, usually labeled "VΩ" when voltage, resistance, or diodes are being measured.
- When current flow in amperes is being measured, most digital meters require that the red test lead be inserted in the ammeter terminal, usually labeled "A" or "mA."

CAUTION: If the meter leads are inserted into ammeter terminals, even though the selector is set to volts, the meter may be damaged, or an internal fuse may blow, if the test leads touch both terminals of a battery.

STEP 3 Measure the component being tested. Carefully note the decimal point and the unit on the face of the meter.

- **Meter lead connections.** If the meter leads are connected to a battery backward (red to the battery negative, for example), the display still shows the correct reading, but a negative sign (–) is displayed in front of the number. The correct polarity is not important when measuring resistance (ohms), except where indicated, such as measuring a diode.
- **Autorange.** Many meters automatically default to the autorange position and the meter displays the value in the most readable scale. The meter can be manually ranged to select other levels, or to lock in a scale for a value that is constantly changing.

    If a 12 volt battery is measured with an autoranging meter, the correct reading of 12.0 is given. "AUTO" and "V" should show on the face of the meter. For example, if a meter is manually set to the 2 kilohm scale, the highest that the meter reads is 2,000 ohms. If the reading is over 2,000 ohms, the meter displays OL. ● **SEE CHART 9–3.**

STEP 4 Interpret the reading. This is especially difficult on autoranging meters, where the meter itself selects the proper scale. The following are two examples of different readings.

Example 1: A voltage drop is being measured. The specifications indicate a maximum voltage drop of 0.2 volt. The meter reads "AUTO" and "43.6 mV." This reading means that the voltage drop is 0.0436 volt, or 43.6 mV, which is far lower than the 0.2 volt (200 mV). Because the number showing on the meter face is much larger than the specifications, many beginner technicians believe that the voltage drop is excessive.

NOTE: Pay attention to the units displayed on the meter face and convert to whole units.

Example 2: A spark plug wire is being measured. The reading should be less than 10,000 ohms for each foot in length, if the wire is okay. The wire being tested is 3 foot long (maximum allowable resistance is 30,000 ohms). The meter reads "AUTO" and "14.85 kΩ." This reading is equivalent to 14,850 ohms.

NOTE: When converting from kilohms to ohms, make the decimal point a comma.

Because this reading is well below the specified maximum allowable, the spark plug wire is okay.

VOLTAGE BEING MEASURED

	0.01 V (10 mV)	0.150 V (150 mV)	1.5 V	10.0 V	12.0 V	120 V
Scale Selected	Voltmeter displays:					
200 mV	10.0	150.0	OL	OL	OL	OL
2 V	0.100	0.150	1.500	OL	OL	OL
20 V	0.1	1.50	1.50	10.00	12.00	OL
200 V	00.0	01.5	01.5	10.0	12.0	120.0
2 kV	00.00	00.00	000.1	00.10	00.12	0.120
Autorange	10.0 mV	15.0 mV	1.50	10.0	12.0	120.0

RESISTANCE BEING MEASURED

	10 OHMS	100 OHMS	470 OHMS	1 KILOHM	220 KILOHMS	1 MEGOHM
Scale Selected	Ohmmeter displays:					
400 ohms	10.0	100.0	OL	OL	OL	OL
4 kilohms	010	100	0.470 k	1000	OL	OL
40 kilohms	00.0	0.10 k	0.47 k	1.00 k	OL	OL
400 kilohms	000.0	00.1 k	00.5 k	0.10 k	220.0 k	OL
4 megohms	00.00	0.01 M	0.05 M	00.1 M	0.22 M	1.0 M
Autorange	10.0	100.0	470.0	1.00 k	220 k	1.00 M

CURRENT BEING MEASURED

	50 mA	150 mA	1.0 A	7.5 A	15.0 A	25.0 A
Scale Selected	Ammeter displays:					
40 mA	OL	OL	OL	OL	OL	OL
400 mA	50.0	150	OL	OL	OL	OL
4 A	0.05	0.00	1.00	OL	OL	OL
40 A	0.00	0.000	01.0	7.5	15.0	25.0
Autorange	50.0 mA	150.0 mA	1.00	7.5	15.0	25.0

CHART 9–3

Sample meter readings, using manually set and autoranging selection on the digital meter control.

RMS VERSUS AVERAGE Alternating-current voltage waveforms can be true sinusoidal or nonsinusoidal. A true sine wave pattern measurement is the same for both **root-mean-square (RMS)** and average-responding meters. RMS and averaging are two methods used to measure the true effective rating of a signal that is constantly changing. ● **SEE FIGURE 9–17**.

Only true RMS meters are accurate when measuring nonsinusoidal AC waveforms, which are seldom used in automotive applications.

RESOLUTION, DIGITS, AND COUNTS Meter resolution refers to how small or fine a measurement the meter can make. By knowing the resolution of a DMM, you can determine whether the meter could measure down to only 1 volt, or down to 1 millivolt (1/1,000 of a volt).

The terms *digits* and *counts* are used to describe a meter's resolution. DMMs are grouped by the number of counts or digits they display.

■ A 3 1/2-digit meter can display three full digits ranging from 0 to 9, and one "half" digit that displays only a 1 or is left blank. A 3 1/2-digit meter displays up to 1,999 counts of resolution.

■ A 4 1/2-digit meter can display up to 19,000 counts of resolution. It is more precise to describe a meter by counts of resolution than by 3 1/2 or 4 1/2 digits. Some 3 1/2-digit meters have enhanced resolution of up to 3,200 or 4,000 counts.

Meters with more counts offer better resolution for certain measurements. For example, a 1,999-count meter is not able to measure down to a tenth of a volt when measuring 200 volts or more. ● **SEE FIGURE 9–18**.

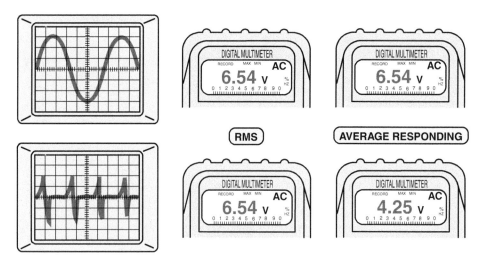

FIGURE 9–17 When reading AC voltage signals, a true RMS meter (such as a Fluke 87) provides a different reading than an average-responding meter (such as a Fluke 88). The only place this difference is important is when a reading is to be compared with a specification.

FIGURE 9–18 This meter display shows 052.2 AC volts. Notice that the zero beside the 5 indicates that the meter can read over 100 volts AC with a resolution of 0.1 volt.

However, a 3,200-count meter displays a tenth of a volt, up to 320 volts. Digits displayed to the far right of the display may at times flicker or constantly change. This is called *digit rattle* and represents a changing voltage being measured on the ground (COM terminal of the meter lead). High-quality meters are designed to reject this unwanted voltage.

ACCURACY **Meter accuracy** is the largest allowable error that occurs under specific operating conditions. In other

---

TECH TIP

Purchase a Digital Meter That Works for Automotive Use

Try to purchase a digital meter that is capable of reading the following:

- DC volts
- AC volts
- DC amperes (up to 10 A or more is helpful)
- Ohms (Ω) up to 40 MΩ (40 million ohms)
- Diode check

Additional features for advanced automotive diagnosis include:

- Frequency (hertz, abbreviated Hz)
- Temperature probe (°F and/or °C)
- Pulse width (millisecond, abbreviated ms)
- Duty cycle (%)

---

words, it is an indication of how close the DMM's displayed measurement is to the actual value of the signal being measured.

Accuracy for a DMM is usually expressed as a percent of reading. An accuracy of $\pm 1\%$ of reading means that for a displayed reading of 100.0 V, the actual value of the voltage could be anywhere between 99.0 V and 101.0 V. Thus, the lower the percent of accuracy is, the better.

- Unacceptable = 1.00%
- Okay = 0.50% (1/2%)
- Good = 0.25% (1/4%)
- Excellent = 0.10% (1/10%)

Meter Usage on Hybrid-Electric Vehicles

Many hybrid-electric vehicles use system voltage as high as 650 volts DC. Be sure to follow all vehicle manufacturer's testing procedures. If a voltage measurement is needed, be sure to use a meter and test leads that are designed to insulate against high voltages. The **International Electrotechnical Commission (IEC)** has several categories of voltage standards for meter and meter leads. These categories are ratings for overvoltage protection and are rated CAT I, CAT II, CAT III, and CAT IV. The higher the category rating, the greater the protection against voltage spikes caused by high-energy circuits. Under each category, there are various energy and voltage ratings.

CAT I Typically, a CAT I meter is used for low-energy voltage measurements, such as at wall outlets in the home. Meters with a CAT I rating are usually rated at 300 to 800 volts.

CAT II This higher rated meter is typically used for checking higher energy level voltages at the fuse panel in the home. Meters with a CAT II rating are usually rated at 300 to 600 volts.

CAT III This minimum-rated meter should be used for hybrid vehicles. The CAT III category is designed for high-energy levels and voltage measurements at the service pole at the transformer. Meters with this rating are usually rated at 600 to 1,000 volts.

CAT IV CAT IV meters are for clamp-on meters only. If a clamp-on meter also has meter leads for voltage measurements, that part of the meter is rated as CAT III.

NOTE: Always use the highest CAT rating meter, especially when working with hybrid vehicles. A CAT III, 600 volt meter is safer than a CAT II, 1,000 volt meter because of the energy level of the CAT ratings.

Therefore, for best personal protection, use only meters and meter leads that are CAT III or CAT IV rated when measuring voltage on a hybrid vehicle. ● **SEE FIGURES 9–19 AND 9–20.**

FIGURE 9–19 Be sure to use only a meter that is CAT III rated when taking electrical voltage measurements on a hybrid vehicle.

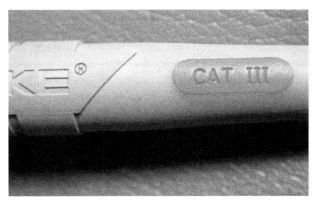

FIGURE 9–20 Always use meter leads that are CAT III rated on a meter that is also CAT III rated, to maintain the protection needed when working on hybrid vehicles.

For example, if a battery had 12.6 volts, a meter could read between the following, based on its accuracy.

± 0.1%	high =	12.61
	low =	12.59
± 0.25%	high =	12.63
	low =	12.57
± 0.50%	high =	12.66
	low =	12.54
± 1.00%	high =	12.73
	low =	12.47

Before you purchase a meter, check the accuracy. Accuracy is usually indicated on the specifications sheet for the meter.

DIGITAL METER USAGE

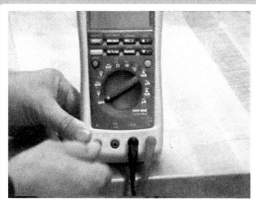

1 For most electrical measurements, the black meter lead is inserted in the terminal labeled "COM" and the red meter lead is inserted into the terminal labeled "V."

2 To use a digital meter, turn the power switch and select the unit of electricity to be measured. In this case, the rotary switch is turned to select DC volts V.

3 For most automotive electrical use, such as measuring battery voltage, select DC volts.

4 Connect the red meter lead to the positive (+) terminal of a battery and the black meter lead to the negative (−) terminal. The meter reads the voltage difference between the leads.

5 This jump-start battery unit measures 13.151 volts with the meter set on autoranging on the DC voltage scale.

6 Another meter (Fluke 87 III) displays four digits when measuring the voltage of the battery jump-start unit.

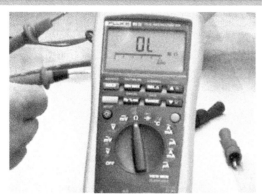

7 To measure resistance, turn the rotary dial to the ohm (Ω) symbol. With the meter leads separated, the meter display reads OL (over limit).

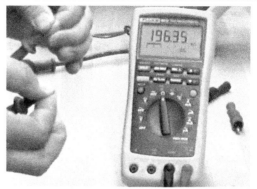

8 The meter can read your own body resistance if you grasp the meter lead terminals with your fingers. The reading on the display indicates 196.35 kΩ.

9 When measuring anything, be sure to read the symbol on the meter face. In this case, the meter reading is 291.10 kΩ.

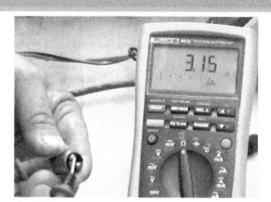

10 A meter set on ohms can be used to check the resistance of a light bulb filament. In this case, the meter reads 3.15 ohms. If the bulb were bad (filament open), the meter displays OL.

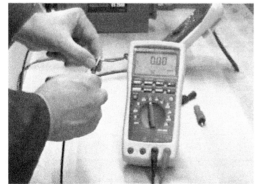

11 A digital meter set to read ohms should measure 0.00, as shown, when the meter leads are touched together.

12 The large letter V means volts and the wavy symbol over the V means that the meter measures alternating-current (AC) voltage, if this position is selected.

CONTINUED ▶

13 The next symbol is a V with a dotted and a straight line overhead. This symbol stands for direct-current (DC) volts. This position is most used for automotive service.

14 The symbol mV indicates millivolts or 1/1,000 of a volt (0.001). The solid and dashed line above the mV means DC mV.

15 The rotary switch is turned to Ω (ohms) unit of resistance measure. The symbol to the left of the Ω symbol is the beeper or continuity indicator.

16 Notice that AUTO is in the upper left and the MΩ is in the lower right. MΩ means megohms or that the meter is set to read in millions of ohms.

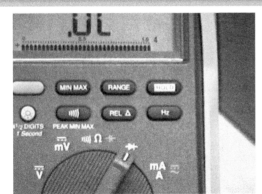

17 The symbol shown is that of a diode. In this position, the meter applies a voltage to a diode and the meter reads the voltage drop across the junction of a diode.

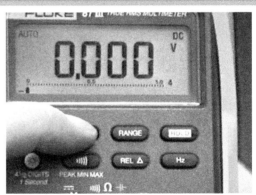

18 One of the most useful features of this meter is the MIN/MAX feature. By pushing the MIN/MAX button, the meter is able to display the highest (MAX) and the lowest (MIN) reading.

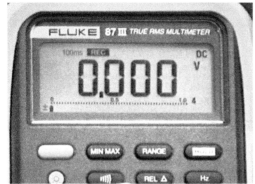

19 Pushing the MIN/MAX button puts the meter into record mode. Note the 100 ms and "rec" on the display. In this position, the meter is capturing any voltage change that lasts 100 ms (0.1 sec.) or longer.

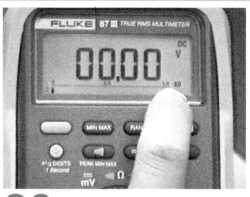

20 To increase the range of the meter, touch the range button. Now the meter is set to read voltage up to 40 volt DC.

21 Pushing the range button one more time changes the meter scale to the 400 volt range. Notice that the decimal point has moved to the right.

22 Pushing the range button again changes the meter to the 4,000 volt range. This range is not suitable to use in automotive applications.

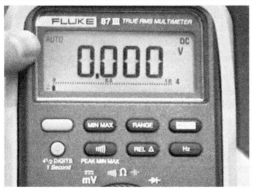

23 By pushing and holding the range button, the meter resets to autorange. Autorange is the preferred setting for most automotive measurements, except when using MIN/MAX record mode.

SUMMARY

1. Circuit testers include test lights and fused jumper leads.
2. Digital multimeter (DMM) and digital volt-ohm-meter (DVOM) are terms commonly used for electronic high-impedance test meters.
3. Use of a high-impedance digital meter is required on any computer-related circuit or component.
4. Ammeters measure current and must be connected in series in the circuit.
5. Voltmeters measure voltage and are connected in parallel.
6. Ohmmeters measure resistance of a component and must be connected in parallel, with the circuit or component disconnected from power.
7. Logic probes can indicate the presence of power, ground, or pulsed signals.

REVIEW QUESTIONS

1. Why should high-impedance meters be used when measuring voltage on computer-controlled circuits?
2. How is an ammeter connected to an electrical circuit?
3. Why must an ohmmeter be connected to a disconnected circuit or component?
4. How is a diode tested using a digital meter?
5. What is meant when a meter reads "OL" when measuring ohms?

CHAPTER QUIZ

1. How can a test light be used to test a ground connection?
   a. By touching both the tip and the ground clip to the positive terminal of a battery.
   b. By touching the ground lead to the tip of the test light.
   c. By connecting the tip of the test light to a good ground with the other end to the positive terminal of a battery.
   d. None of the above

2. A meter used to measure amperes is called a(n) _____.
   a. amp meter
   b. ampmeter
   c. ammeter
   d. coulomb meter

3. A voltmeter should be connected to the circuit being tested _____.
   a. in series
   b. in parallel
   c. only when no power is flowing
   d. both a and c

4. An ohmmeter should be connected to the circuit or component being tested _____.
   a. with current flowing in the circuit or through the component
   b. when connected to the battery of the vehicle to power the meter
   c. only when no power is flowing (electrically open circuit)
   d. both b and c

5. When testing a diode with the multimeter set on "Diode Check," a reading of 0.6 volt is obtained. This indicates that the diode being tested is a _____.
   a. tungsten bulb
   b. light-emitting diode
   c. silicon diode
   d. bad diode

6. If a digital meter face shows 0.93 when set to read kΩ, the reading means _____.
   a. 93 ohms
   b. 930 ohms
   c. 9,300 ohms
   d. 93,000 ohms

7. A reading of 432 shows on the face of the meter set to the millivolt scale. The reading means _____.
   a. 0.432 volt
   b. 4.32 volts
   c. 43.2 volts
   d. 4,320 volts

8. What could happen if the meter leads were connected to the positive and negative terminals of the battery while the meter and leads were set to read amperes?
   a. Could blow an internal fuse or damage the meter
   b. Would read volts instead of amperes
   c. Would display OL
   d. Would display 0.00

9. The highest amount of resistance that can be read by the meter set to the 2k scale is _____.
   a. 2,000 ohms
   b. 200 ohms
   c. 200k (200,000 ohms)
   d. 20,000,000 ohms

10. A high-impedance meter _____.
   a. measures a high amount of current flow
   b. measures a high amount of resistance
   c. can measure a high voltage
   d. has a high internal resistance

OSCILLOSCOPES AND GRAPHING MULTIMETERS

LEARNING OBJECTIVES

After studying this chapter, the reader should be able to:

Compare the different types of oscilloscopes.

Explain time base and volts per division settings.

Describe the use of DC or AC coupling when displaying waveforms on an oscilloscope.

Explain how to interpret pulse trains, channels, and triggers on a scope.

Explain how to use a scope and discuss graphing multimeters and scan tools.

This chapter will help you prepare for the ASE Electrical/ Electronic Systems (A6) certification test content area "A" (General Electrical/Electronic System Diagnosis).

KEY TERMS: AC coupling 113 • BNC connector 115 • Cathode ray tube (CRT) 111 • Channel 114 • DC coupling 113 • Digital storage oscilloscope (DSO) 111 • Division 112 • Duty cycle 114 • External trigger 114 • Frequency 114 • GMM 117 • Graticule 111 • Hertz 114 • Oscilloscope (scope) 111 • Pulse train 114 • Pulse width 114 • PWM 114 • Time base 112 • Trigger level 114 • Trigger slope 114

TYPES OF OSCILLOSCOPES

TERMINOLOGY An **oscilloscope** (usually called a **scope**) is a visual voltmeter with a timer that shows when a voltage changes. Following are two types of oscilloscopes.

- An *analog scope* uses a **cathode ray tube (CRT),** similar to some television screens, to display voltage patterns. The scope screen displays the electrical signal constantly.

- A *digital scope* commonly uses a liquid crystal display (LCD), but a CRT may also be used on some digital scopes. A digital scope takes samples of the signals that can be stopped or stored and is, therefore, called a **digital storage oscilloscope,** or **DSO.**

- A digital scope does not capture each change in voltage, but instead captures voltage levels over time and stores them as dots. Each dot is a voltage level. The scope displays the waveforms using the thousands of dots (each representing a voltage level) and electrically connects the dots to create a waveform.

- A DSO can be connected to a sensor output signal wire and can record over a long period of time the voltage signals. It can be replayed and a technician can see if any faults were detected. This feature makes a DSO the perfect tool to help diagnose intermittent problems.

- A digital storage scope, however, can sometimes miss faults called *glitches* that may occur between samples captured by the scope. This is why a DSO with a high

"sampling rate" is preferred. Sampling rate means that a scope is capable of capturing voltage changes that occur over a very short period of time. Some digital storage scopes have a capture rate of 25 million (25,000,000) samples per second. This means that the scope can capture a glitch (fault) that lasts just 40 nano (0.00000040) seconds.

- A scope has been called "a voltmeter with a clock."

- The voltmeter part means that a scope can capture and display changing voltage levels.

- The clock part means that the scope can display these changes in voltage levels within a specific time period and, with a DSO, it can be replayed so that any faults can be seen and studied.

OSCILLOSCOPE DISPLAY GRID A typical scope face usually has eight or ten grids vertically (up and down) and ten grids horizontally (left to right). The transparent scale (grid), used for reference measurements, is called a **graticule.** This arrangement is commonly 8 × 10 or 10 × 10 divisions. ● **SEE FIGURE 10–1.**

NOTE: These numbers originally referred to the metric dimensions of the graticule in centimeters. Therefore, an 8 × 10 display is 8 cm (80 mm or 3.14 inch) high and 10 cm (100 mm or 3.90 inch) wide.

- Voltage is displayed on a scope starting with zero volts at the bottom and higher voltage being displayed vertically.

- The scope illustrates time left to right. The pattern starts on the left and sweeps across the screen from left to right.

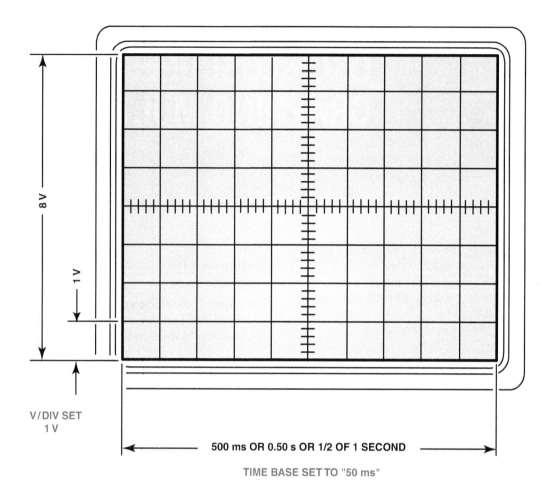

8 V

1 V

V/DIV SET
1 V

500 ms OR 0.50 s OR 1/2 OF 1 SECOND

TIME BASE SET TO "50 ms"

FIGURE 10–1 A scope display allows technicians to take measurements of voltage patterns. In this example, each vertical division is 1 volt and each horizontal division is set to represent 50 milliseconds.

SCOPE SETUP AND ADJUSTMENTS

SETTING THE TIME BASE Most scopes use 10 graticules from left to right on the display. Setting the **time base** means setting how much time is displayed in each block, called a **division**. For example, if the scope is set to read 2 seconds per division (referred to as *s/div*), the total time displayed is 20 seconds (2 × 10 divisions = 20 sec.). The time base should be set to an amount of time that allows two to four events to be displayed. Milliseconds (0.001 sec.) are commonly used in scopes when adjusting the time base. Sample time is milliseconds per division (indicated as *ms/div*) and total time. ● **SEE CHART 10–1.**

NOTE: Increasing the time base reduces the number of samples per second.

The horizontal scale is divided into 10 divisions (sometimes called *grats*). If each division represents 1 second of time, then the total time period displayed on the screen is 10 seconds. The time per division is selected so that several events of the

waveform are displayed. Time per division settings can vary greatly in automotive use, including:

- MAP/MAF sensors: 2 ms/div (20 ms total)
- Network (CAN) communications network: 2 ms/div (20 ms total)
- Throttle position (TP) sensor: 100 ms per division (1 sec. total)
- Fuel injector: 2 ms/div (20 ms total)

MILLISECONDS PER DIVISION (ms/DIV)	TOTAL TIME DISPLAYED
1 ms	10 ms (0.010 sec.)
10 ms	100 ms (0.100 sec.)
50 ms	500 ms (0.500 sec.)
100 ms	1 sec. (1.000 sec.)
500 ms	5 sec. (5.0 sec.)
1,000 ms	10 sec. (10.0 sec.)

CHART 10–1

The time base is milliseconds (ms) and total time of an event that can be displayed.

- Oxygen sensor: 1 sec. per division (10 sec. total)
- Primary ignition: 10 ms/div (100 ms total)
- Secondary ignition: 10 ms/div (100 ms total)
- Voltage measurements: 5 ms/div (50 ms total)

The total time displayed on the screen allows comparisons to see if the waveform is consistent or is changing. Multiple waveforms shown on the display at the same time also allow for measurements to be seen more easily. ● **SEE FIGURE 10–2** for an example of a throttle position sensor waveform created by measuring the voltage output as the throttle is depressed and then released.

VOLTS PER DIVISION The volts per division, abbreviated *V/div*, should be set so that the entire anticipated waveform can be viewed. Examples include:

Throttle position (TP) sensor: 1 V/div (8 V total)

Battery, starting and charging: 2 V/div (16 V total)

Oxygen sensor: 200 mV/div (1.6 V total)

Notice from the examples that the total voltage to be displayed exceeds the voltage range of the component being tested. This ensures that all the waveform is displayed. It also allows for some unexpected voltage readings. For example, an

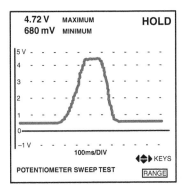

FIGURE 10–2 The digital storage oscilloscope (DSO) displays the entire waveform of a throttle position (TP) sensor from idle to wide-open throttle and returns to idle. The display also indicates the maximum (4.72 V) and minimum (680 mV or 0.68 V) readings. The display does not show anything until the throttle is opened, because the scope has been set up to start displaying a waveform only after a certain voltage level has been reached. This voltage is called the trigger or trigger point.

oxygen sensor should read between 0 V and 1 V (1,000 mV). By setting the V/div to 200 mV, up to 1.6 V (1,600 mV) is displayed.

AC VOLTAGE

DEFINITION Whereas direct current (DC) flows in one direction, alternating current (AC) voltage changes direction continuously. The voltage varies over time and the waveform is a sine wave. ● **SEE FIGURE 10–3**.

DC AND AC COUPLING

DC COUPLING **DC coupling** is the most used position on a scope because it allows the scope to display both AC and DC voltage signals present in the circuit. The AC part of the signal rides on top of the DC component. For example, if the engine is running and the charging voltage is 14.4 volt DC, this is displayed as a horizontal line on the screen. Any AC ripple voltage leaking past the alternator diodes is displayed as an AC signal on top of the horizontal DC voltage line. Therefore, both components of the signal can be observed at the same time.

AC COUPLING When the **AC coupling** position is selected, a capacitor is placed into the meter lead circuit, which effectively blocks all DC voltage signals, but allows the AC portion of the signal to pass and be displayed. AC coupling can be used to show output signal waveforms from sensors, such as:

- Distributor pickup coils
- Magnetic wheel speed sensors
- Magnetic crankshaft position sensors
- Magnetic camshaft position sensors
- The AC ripple from an alternator. ● **SEE FIGURE 10–4**.
- Magnetic vehicle speed sensors

NOTE: Check the instructions from the scope manufacturer for the recommended settings to use. Sometimes it is necessary to switch from DC coupling to AC coupling, or from AC coupling to DC coupling, to properly see some waveforms.

FIGURE 10–3 AC voltage varies over time from positive voltage to negative voltage. The effective value (0.707 of peak) is the level of DC required to deliver the same power.

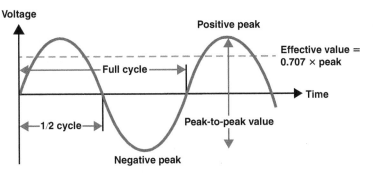

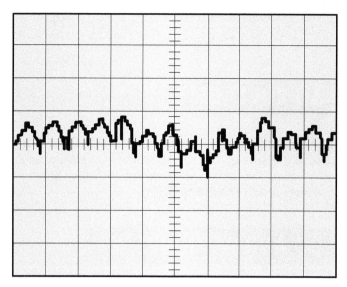

FIGURE 10–4 Ripple voltage is created from the AC voltage from an alternator. Some AC ripple voltage is normal, but if the AC portion exceeds 0.5 volt, then a bad diode is the most likely cause. Excessive AC ripple can cause many electrical and electronic devices to work incorrectly.

PULSE TRAINS

DEFINITION Scopes can show all voltage signals. Among the most commonly found in automotive applications is a DC voltage that varies up and down and does not go below zero, like an AC voltage. A DC voltage that turns on and off in a series of pulses is called a **pulse train**. Pulse trains differ from an AC signal in that they do not go below zero. An alternating voltage goes above and below zero voltage. Pulse train signals can vary in several ways. ● **SEE FIGURE 10–5.**

FREQUENCY **Frequency** is the number of cycles per second measured in **hertz**. The engine revolutions per minute (RPM) is an example of a signal that can occur at various frequencies. At low engine speed, the ignition pulses occur fewer times per second (lower frequency) than when the engine is operated at higher engine speeds (RPM).

DUTY CYCLE **Duty cycle** refers to the percentage of on-time of the signal during one complete cycle. As on-time increases, the amount of time the signal is off decreases and is usually measured in percentage. Duty cycle is also called **pulse-width modulation (PWM)** and can be measured in degrees. ● **SEE FIGURE 10–6.**

PULSE WIDTH The **pulse width** is a measure of the actual on-time measured in milliseconds. Fuel injectors are usually controlled by varying the pulse width. ● **SEE FIGURE 10–7.**

NUMBER OF CHANNELS

DEFINITION Scopes are available that allow the viewing of more than one sensor or event at the same time on the display. The number of events, which require leads for each, is called a **channel**. A channel is an input to a scope. Commonly available scopes include:

- **Single channel.** A single-channel scope is capable of displaying only one sensor signal waveform at a time.
- **Two channel.** A two-channel scope can display the waveform from two separate sensors or components at the same time. This feature is very helpful when testing the camshaft and crankshaft position sensors on an engine to see if they are properly timed. ● **SEE FIGURE 10–8.**
- **Four channel.** A four-channel scope allows the technician to view up to four different sensors or actuators on one display.

NOTE: **Often the capture speed of the signals is slowed when using more than one channel.**

TRIGGERS

EXTERNAL TRIGGER An **external trigger** is when the waveform starts when a signal is received from another external source, rather than from the signal pickup lead. A common example of an external trigger comes from the probe clamp around the cylinder #1 spark plug wire to trigger the start of an ignition pattern.

TRIGGER LEVEL **Trigger level** is the voltage that must be detected by the scope before the pattern is displayed. A scope starts displaying a voltage signal only when it is triggered or is told to start. The trigger level must be set to start the display. If the pattern starts at 1 volt, then the trace begins displaying on the left side of the screen *after* the trace has reached 1 volt.

TRIGGER SLOPE The **trigger slope** is the voltage direction that a waveform must have in order to start the display. Most often, the trigger to start a waveform display is taken from the signal itself. Besides trigger voltage level, most scopes can be adjusted to trigger only when the voltage rises past the trigger-level voltage. This is called a *positive slope*. When the voltage falling past the higher level activates the trigger, this is called a *negative slope*.

The scope display indicates both a positive and a negative slope symbol. For example, if a waveform, such as a magnetic sensor used for crankshaft position or wheel speed, starts moving upward, a positive slope should be selected. If a

1. FREQUENCY—FREQUENCY IS THE NUMBER OF CYCLES THAT TAKE PLACE PER SECOND. THE MORE CYCLES THAT TAKE PLACE IN 1 SECOND, THE HIGHER THE FREQUENCY READING. FREQUENCIES ARE MEASURED IN HERTZ, WHICH IS THE NUMBER OF CYCLES PER SECOND. AN 8 HERTZ SIGNAL CYCLES EIGHT TIMES PER SECOND.

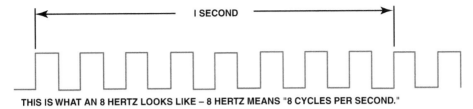

THIS IS WHAT AN 8 HERTZ LOOKS LIKE – 8 HERTZ MEANS "8 CYCLES PER SECOND."

2. DUTY CYCLE—DUTY CYCLE IS A MEASUREMENT COMPARING THE SIGNAL ON-TIME TO THE LENGTH OF ONE COMPLETE CYCLE. AS ON-TIME INCREASES, OFF-TIME DECREASES. DUTY CYCLE IS MEASURED IN PERCENTAGE OF ON-TIME. A 60% DUTY CYCLE IS A SIGNAL THAT IS ON 60% OF THE TIME AND OFF 40% OF THE TIME. ANOTHER WAY TO MEASURE DUTY CYCLE IS DWELL, WHICH IS MEASURED IN DEGREES INSTEAD OF PERCENT.

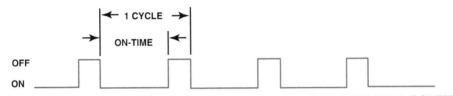

DUTY CYCLE IS THE RELATIONSHIP BETWEEN ONE COMPLETE CYCLE AND THE SIGNAL IS ON-TIME. A SIGNAL CAN VARY IN DUTY CYCLE WITHOUT AFFECTING THE FREQUENCY.

3. PULSE WIDTH—PULSE WIDTH IS THE ACTUAL ON-TIME OF A SIGNAL, MEASURED IN MILLISECONDS. WITH PULSE WIDTH MEASUREMENTS, OFF-TIME DOESN'T REALLY MATTER—THE ONLY REAL CONCERN IS HOW LONG THE SIGNAL IS ON. THIS IS A USEFUL TEST FOR MEASURING CONVENTIONAL INJECTOR ON-TIME, TO SEE THAT THE SIGNAL VARIES WITH LOAD CHANGE.

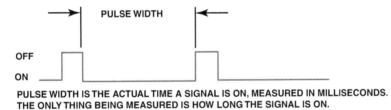

PULSE WIDTH IS THE ACTUAL TIME A SIGNAL IS ON, MEASURED IN MILLISECONDS. THE ONLY THING BEING MEASURED IS HOW LONG THE SIGNAL IS ON.

FIGURE 10–5 A pulse train is any electrical signal that turns on and off, or goes high and low in a series of pulses. Ignition module and fuel-injector pulses are examples of a pulse train signal.

negative slope is selected, the waveform does not start showing until the voltage reaches the trigger level in a downward direction. A negative slope should be used when a fuel-injector circuit is being analyzed. In this circuit, the computer provides the ground and the voltage level drops when the computer commands the injector on. Sometimes the technician needs to change from negative to positive, or positive to negative, trigger if a waveform is not being shown correctly. ● **SEE FIGURE 10–9**.

USING A SCOPE

USING SCOPE LEADS Most scopes, both analog and digital, normally use the same test leads. These leads usually attach to the scope through a **BNC connector**, which is

a miniature standard coaxial cable connector. BNC is an international standard that is used in the electronics industry. If using a BNC connector, be sure to connect one lead to a good clean, metal engine ground. The probe of the scope lead attaches to the circuit or component being tested. Many scopes use one ground lead and then each channel has its own signal pickup lead.

MEASURING BATTERY VOLTAGE WITH A SCOPE One of the easiest things to measure and observe on a scope is battery voltage. A lower voltage can be observed on the scope display as the engine is started, and a higher voltage should be displayed after the engine starts. ● **SEE FIGURE 10–10**.

An analog scope displays rapidly and cannot be set to show or freeze a display. Therefore, even though an analog scope shows all voltage signals, it is easy to miss a momentary glitch on an analog scope.

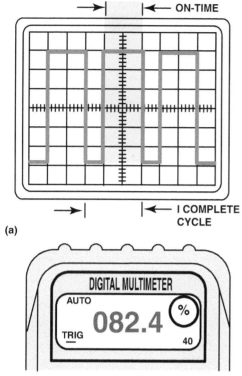

(a)

DIGITAL MULTIMETER

AUTO
082.4 %

TRIG
— 40

THE % SIGN IN THE UPPER RIGHT CORNER
OF THE DISPLAY INDICATES THAT THE METER
IS READING A DUTY CYCLE SIGNAL.

(b)

FIGURE 10–6 (a) A scope representation of a complete
cycle, showing both on-time and off-time. (b) A meter display,
indicating the on-time duty cycle in percentage (%). Note the
trigger and negative (–) symbol. This indicates that the meter
started recording the percentage of on-time when the voltage
dropped (start of on-time).

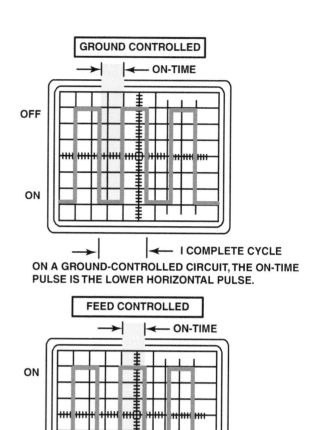

ON A GROUND-CONTROLLED CIRCUIT, THE ON-TIME
PULSE IS THE LOWER HORIZONTAL PULSE.

ON A FEED-CONTROLLED CIRCUIT, THE ON-TIME
PULSE IS THE UPPER HORIZONTAL PULSE.

FIGURE 10–7 Most automotive computer systems control the
device by opening and closing the ground to the component.

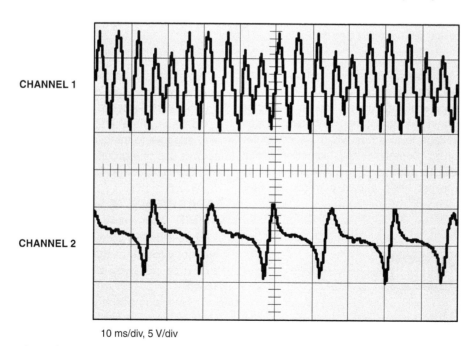

CHANNEL 1

CHANNEL 2

10 ms/div, 5 V/div

FIGURE 10–8 A two-channel scope being used to compare two signals on the same vehicle.

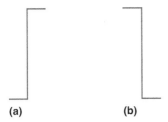

(a)   **(b)**

FIGURE 10–9 (a) A symbol for a positive trigger—a trigger occurs at a rising (positive) edge of the signal (waveform). (b) A symbol for a negative trigger—a trigger occurs at a falling (negative) edge of the signal (waveform).

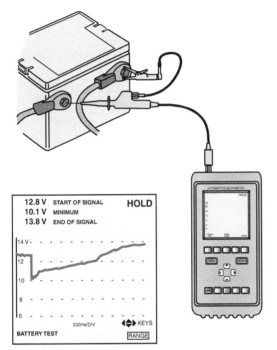

FIGURE 10–10 Constant battery voltage is represented by a flat horizontal line. In this example, the engine was started and the battery voltage dropped to about 10 V, as shown on the left side of the scope display. When the engine started, the alternator started to charge the battery and the voltage is shown as climbing.

CAUTION: Check the instructions for the scope being used before attempting to scope household AC circuits. Some scopes, such as the Snap-On MODIS, are not designed to measure high-voltage AC circuits.

FIGURE 10–11 A typical graphing multimeter that can be used as a digital meter, plus it can show the voltage levels on the display screen.

GRAPHING MULTIMETER

A **graphing multimeter**, abbreviated **GMM**, is a cross between a digital meter and a digital storage oscilloscope. A graphing multimeter displays the voltage levels at two places:

- On a display screen
- In a digital readout

It is usually not capable of capturing very short duration faults or glitches that are likely captured with a digital storage oscilloscope. ● **SEE FIGURE 10–11**.

GRAPHING SCAN TOOLS

Many scan tools are capable of displaying the voltage levels captured by the scan tool through the data link connector (DLC) on a screen. This feature is helpful where changes in voltage levels are difficult to detect by looking at numbers that are constantly changing. Read and follow the instructions for the scan tool being used.

1. Analog oscilloscopes use a cathode ray tube to display voltage patterns.

2. The waveforms shown on an analog oscilloscope cannot be stored for later viewing.

3. A digital storage oscilloscope (DSO) creates an image or waveform on the display by connecting thousands of dots captured by the scope leads.

4. An oscilloscope display grid is called a graticule. Each of the 8 x 10 or 10 x 10 dividing boxes is called a division.

5. Setting the time base means establishing the amount of time each division represents.

6. Setting the volts per division allows the technician to view either the entire waveform or just part of it.

7. DC coupling and AC coupling are two selections that can be made to observe different types of waveforms.

8. A graphing multimeter is not capable of capturing short duration faults but can display usable waveforms.

9. Oscilloscopes display voltage over time. A DSO can capture and store a waveform for viewing later.

REVIEW QUESTIONS

1. What are the differences between an analog and a digital oscilloscope?

2. What is the difference between DC coupling and AC coupling?

3. Why are DC signals that change called pulse trains?

4. What is the difference between an oscilloscope and a graphing multimeter?

5. What is the difference between a positive trigger and a negative trigger?

CHAPTER QUIZ

1. Technician A says an analog scope can store the waveform for viewing later. Technician B says that the trigger level has to be set on most scopes to be able to view a changing waveform. Which technician is correct?
   a. Technician A only
   b. Technician B only
   c. Both Technicians A and B
   d. Neither Technician A nor B

2. An oscilloscope display is called a _____.
   a. grid
   b. graticule
   c. division
   d. box

3. A signal showing the voltage of a battery displayed on a digital storage oscilloscope (DSO) is being discussed. Technician A says that the display shows one horizontal line above the zero line. Technician B says that the display shows a line sloping upward from zero to the battery voltage level. Which technician is correct?
   a. Technician A only
   b. Technician B only
   c. Both Technicians A and B
   d. Neither Technician A nor B

4. Setting the time base to 50 milliseconds per division allows the technician to view a waveform how long in duration?
   a. 50 ms
   b. 200 ms
   c. 400 ms
   d. 500 ms

5. A throttle position sensor waveform is going to be observed. At what setting should the volts per division be set to see the entire waveform from 0 to 5 volts?
   a. 0.5 V/div
   b. 1.0 V/div
   c. 2.0 V/div
   d. 5.0 V/div

6. Two technicians are discussing the DC coupling setting on a DSO. Technician A says that the position allows both the DC and AC signals of the waveform to be displayed. Technician B says that this setting allows just the DC part of the waveform to be displayed. Which technician is correct?
   a. Technician A only
   b. Technician B only
   c. Both Technicians A and B
   d. Neither Technician A nor B

7. Voltage signals (waveforms) that do not go below zero are called _____.
   a. AC signals
   b. pulse trains
   c. pulse width
   d. DC-coupled signals

8. Cycles per second are expressed in _____.
   a. hertz
   b. duty cycle
   c. pulse width
   d. slope

9. Oscilloscopes use what type of lead connector?
   a. Banana plugs
   b. Double banana plugs
   c. Single conductor plugs
   d. BNC

10. A digital meter that can show waveforms is called a _____.
    a. DVOM
    b. DMM
    c. GMM
    d. DSO

chapter 11

AUTOMOTIVE WIRING AND WIRE REPAIR

LEARNING OBJECTIVES:

After studying this chapter, the reader should be able to:

Explain automotive wiring and wire gauge systems.

Explain the purpose of ground wires, battery cables, and jumper cables.

Describe how fuses, fusible links, circuit breakers, and PTC circuit protector protect circuits and wiring.

List the steps for removing a terminal from a connector.

List the steps for performing each method of wire repair.

Explain the types of electrical conduit.

This chapter will help you prepare for the ASE Electrical/Electronic Systems (A6) certification test content area "A" (General Electrical/Electronic System Diagnosis).

KEY TERMS: Adhesive-lined heat shrink tubing 130 • American wire gauge (AWG) 119 • Auto link 123 • Battery cables 121 • Braided ground straps 121 • Circuit breakers 124 • Cold solder joint 129 • CPA 128 • Crimp-and-seal connectors 130 • Fuse link 123 • Fuses 122 • Fusible link 125 • Heat shrink tubing 129 • Jumper cables 122 • Lock tang 128 • Metric wire gauge 120 • Pacific fuse element 123 • Primary wire 120 • PTC circuit protection 125 • Rosin-core solder 129 • Terminal 128 • Twisted pair 121

AUTOMOTIVE WIRING

DEFINITION AND TERMINOLOGY Most automotive wire is made from strands of copper covered by plastic insulation. Copper is an excellent conductor of electricity that is reasonably priced and very flexible. However, solid copper wire can break when moved repeatedly. Therefore, most copper wiring is constructed of multiple small strands that allow for repeated bending and moving without breaking. Solid copper wire is generally used for components, such as starter armature and alternator stator windings that do not bend or move during normal operation. Copper is the best electrical conductor besides silver, which is a great deal more expensive. The conductivity of various metals is rated in ● **CHART 11–1**.

AMERICAN WIRE GAUGE Wiring is sized and purchased according to gauge size as assigned by the **American wire gauge (AWG)** system. AWG numbers can be confusing because as the gauge number *increases*, the size of the conductor wire *decreases*. Therefore, a 14-gauge wire is smaller than a 10-gauge wire. The *greater* the amount of current (in amperes) that is flowing through a wire, the *larger the diameter (smaller gauge number) that is required.* ● **SEE CHART 11–2**, which compares the AWG number to the actual wire diameter in inches. The diameter refers to the diameter of the metal conductor and does not include the insulation.

1. Silver
2. Copper
3. Gold
4. Aluminum
5. Tungsten
6. Zinc
7. Brass (copper and zinc)
8. Platinum
9. Iron
10. Nickel
11. Tin
12. Steel
13. Lead

CHART 11–1

The list of relative conductivity of metals, showing silver to be the best.

Following are general applications for the most commonly used wire gauge sizes. Always check the installation instructions or the manufacturer's specifications for wire gauge size before replacing any automotive wiring.

- 20 to 22 gauge: radio speaker wires
- 18 gauge: small bulbs and short leads

WIRE GAUGE DIAMETER TABLE	
AMERICAN WIRE GAUGE (AWG)	WIRE DIAMETER IN INCHES
20	0.03196118
18	0.040303
16	0.0508214
14	0.064084
12	0.08080810
10	0.10189
8	0.128496
6	0.16202
5	0.18194
4	0.20431
3	0.22942
2	0.25763
1	0.2893
0	0.32486
00	0.3648

CHART 11–2

American wire gauge (AWG) number and the actual conductor diameter in inches.

- 16 gauge: taillights, gas gauge, turn signals, windshield wipers
- 14 gauge: horn, radio power lead, headlights, accessory power socket, brake lights
- 12 gauge: headlight switch to fuse box, rear window defogger, power windows and locks
- 10 gauge: alternator to battery
- 4, 2, or 0 (1/0) gauge: battery cables

METRIC SIZE (MM^2)	AWG SIZE
0.5	20
0.8	18
1.0	16
2.0	14
3.0	12
5.0	10
8.0	8
13.0	6
19.0	4
32.0	2
52.0	0

CHART 11–3

Metric wire size in square millimeters (mm^2) conversion chart to American wire gauge (AWG).

METRIC WIRE GAUGE Most manufacturers indicate on the wiring diagrams the **metric wire gauge** sizes measured in square millimeters (mm^2) of cross-sectional area. The following chart gives conversions or comparisons between metric gauge and AWG sizes. Notice that the metric wire size increases with size (area), whereas the AWG size gets smaller with larger size wire. ● **SEE CHART 11–3**.

The AWG number should be decreased (wire size increased) with increased lengths of wire. ● **SEE CHART 11–4**.

For example, a trailer may require 14-gauge wire to light all the trailer lights, but if the wire required is over 25-feet long, 12-gauge wire should be used. Most automotive wire, except for spark plug wire, is often called **primary wire** (named for the voltage range used in the primary ignition circuit) because it is designed to operate at or near battery voltage.

FREQUENTLY ASKED QUESTION

Why Is There a Ground Strap on My Exhaust System?

The ground strap is only there to dissipate static electricity. Static electricity is created when the flow of the exhaust gases travels through the system. Using a ground strap connected to the exhaust system helps prevent the static charge from building up, which could cause a spark to jump to the body or frame of the vehicle.

The exhaust is insulated electrically from the rest of the vehicle by rubber hangers and gaskets at the exhaust manifold, causing the entire exhaust system to be electrically isolated from chassis ground.

If a vehicle is equipped with a ground strap, be sure that it is connected at both ends to help ensure long exhaust system life. If static electricity is allowed to discharge from the exhaust system to the body or frame of the vehicle, the resulting arcing points can cause rust or corrosion, shortening the life of the exhaust system.

If a new exhaust system is installed, be sure to reattach the ground strap. Most vehicles also use a ground strap connected to the fuel filler tube for the same reason.

12 V	RECOMMENDED WIRE GAUGE (AWG) (FOR LENGTH IN FEET)*						
AMPS	3'	5'	7'	10'	15'	20'	25'
5	18	18	18	18	18	18	18
7	18	18	18	18	18	18	16
10	18	18	18	18	16	16	16
12	18	18	18	18	16	16	14
15	18	18	18	18	14	14	12
18	18	18	16	16	14	14	12
20	18	18	16	16	14	12	10
22	18	18	16	16	12	12	10
24	18	18	16	16	12	12	10
30	18	16	16	14	10	10	10
40	18	16	14	12	10	10	8
50	16	14	12	12	10	10	8
100	12	12	10	10	6	6	4
150	10	10	8	8	4	4	2
200	10	8	8	6	4	4	2

* When mechanical strength is a factor, use the next larger wire gauge.

CHART 11–4

Recommended AWG wire size increases as the length increases because all wires have internal resistance. The longer the wire is, the greater the resistance. The larger the diameter is, the lower the resistance.

GROUND WIRES

PURPOSE AND FUNCTION All vehicles use ground wires between the engine and body and/or between the body and the negative terminal of the battery. The two types of ground wires are the following:

- Insulated copper wire
- Braided ground straps

Braided ground straps are uninsulated. It is not necessary to insulate a ground strap because it does not matter if it touches metal, as it already attaches to ground. Braided ground straps are more flexible than stranded wire. Because the engine moves slightly on its mounts, the braided ground strap must be able to flex without breaking. ● **SEE FIGURE 11–1.**

SKIN EFFECT The braided strap also dampens out some radio-frequency interference that otherwise might be transmitted through standard stranded wiring, due to the skin effect.

The *skin effect* is the term used to describe how high-frequency AC electricity flows through a conductor. Direct current flows through a conductor, but alternating current tends to travel through the outside (skin) of the conductor. Because of the skin effect, most audio (speaker) cable is

FIGURE 11–1 All lights and accessories ground to the body of the vehicle. Body ground wires, such as this one, are needed to conduct all of the current from these components back to the negative terminal of the battery. The body ground wire connects the body to the engine. Most battery negative cables attach to the engine.

? FREQUENTLY ASKED QUESTION

What Is a Twisted Pair?

A **twisted pair** is used to transmit low-voltage signals, using two wires that are twisted together. Electromagnetic interference can create a voltage in a wire and twisting the two signal wires cancels out the induced voltage. A twisted pair means that the two wires have at least nine turns per foot (turns per meter). A rule of thumb is a twisted pair should have one twist per inch of length.

constructed of many small-diameter copper wires, instead of fewer larger strands, because the smaller wire has a greater surface area and results in less resistance to the flow of AC voltage.

NOTE: Body ground wires are necessary to provide a circuit path for the lights and accessories that ground to the body and flow to the negative battery terminal.

BATTERY CABLES

Battery cables are the largest wires used in the automotive electrical system. The cables are usually 4-gauge, 2-gauge, or 1-gauge wires (19 mm^2 or larger). ● **SEE FIGURE 11–2.**

Wires larger than 1 gauge are called 0 gauge (pronounced "ought"). Larger cables are labeled 2/0 or 00 (2 ought) and 3/0

FIGURE 11–2 Battery cables are designed to carry heavy starter current and are, therefore, usually 4 gauge or larger wire. Note that this battery has a thermal blanket covering to help protect the battery from high underhood temperatures. The wiring is also covered with a plastic conduit called split-loom tubing.

or 000 (3 ought). Electrical systems that are 6 volts require battery cables two sizes larger than those used for 12 volt electrical systems, because the lower voltage used in antique vehicles resulted in twice the amount of current (amperes) to supply the same electrical power.

JUMPER CABLES

Jumper cables are 4- to 2/0-gauge electrical cables with large clamps attached, and are used to connect the discharged battery of one vehicle to the good battery of another vehicle. Good-quality jumper cables are necessary to prevent excessive voltage drops caused by cable resistance. Aluminum wire jumper cables should not be used, because, even though aluminum is a good electrical conductor (although not as good as copper), it is less flexible and can crack and break when bent or moved repeatedly. The size should be 6 gauge or larger.

1/0 AWG welding cable can be used to construct an excellent set of jumper cables using welding clamps on both ends. Welding cable is usually constructed of many very fine strands of wire, which allow for easier bending of the cable as the strands of fine wire slide against each other inside the cable.

NOTE: Always check the wire gauge of any battery cables or jumper cables and do not rely on the outside diameter of the wire. Many lower-cost jumper cables use smaller gauge wire, but may use thick insulation to make the cable look as if it is the correct size wire.

FUSES AND CIRCUIT PROTECTION DEVICES

CONSTRUCTION **Fuses** should be used in every circuit to protect the wiring from overheating and damage caused by excessive current flow as a result of a short circuit or other malfunction. The symbol for a fuse is a wavy line between two points: ⌇

A fuse is constructed of a fine tin conductor inside a glass, plastic, or ceramic housing. The tin is designed to melt and open the circuit if excessive current flows through the fuse. Each fuse is rated according to its maximum current-carrying capacity.

Many fuses are used to protect more than one circuit of the automobile. ● **SEE FIGURE 11–3**.

A typical example is the fuse for the accessory socket that also protects many other circuits, such as those for the courtesy lights, clock, and other circuits. A fault in one of these circuits can cause this fuse to melt, which prevents the operation of all other circuits that are protected by the fuse.

FUSE RATINGS Fuses are used to protect the wiring and components in the circuit from damage if an excessive amount of current flows. The fuse rating is normally about 20% higher than the normal current in the circuit. ● **SEE CHART 11–5** for a typical fuse rating based on the normal current in the circuit. In other words, the normal current flow should be about 80% of the fuse rating.

BLADE FUSES Colored blade-type fuses are also referred to as ATO fuses and have been used since 1977. The color of the plastic of blade fuses indicates the maximum current flow, measured in amperes.

● **SEE CHART 11–6** for the color and the amperage rating of blade fuses.

Each fuse has an opening in the top of its plastic portion to allow access to its metal contacts for testing purposes. ● **SEE FIGURE 11–4**.

MINI FUSES To save space, many vehicles use mini (small) blade fuses. Not only do they save space, but they also allow the vehicle design engineer to fuse individual circuits, instead of grouping many different components on one fuse. This improves customer satisfaction because if one component fails, it only affects that circuit, without stopping electrical power to several other circuits, as well. This makes troubleshooting much easier, too, because each circuit is separate. ● **SEE CHART 11–7** for the amperage rating and corresponding fuse color for mini fuses.

MAXI FUSES Maxi fuses are a large version of blade fuses and are used to replace fusible links in many vehicles. Maxi fuses are rated up to 80 amperes or more. ● **SEE CHART 11–8** for the amperage rating and corresponding color for maxi fuses.

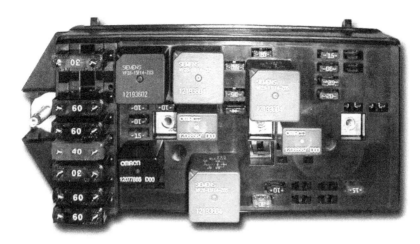

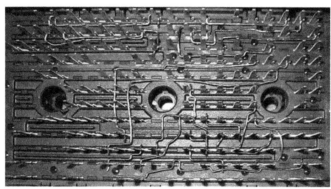

FIGURE 11–3 A typical Underhood Electrical Center (UHEC). Most are referred to as an "intelligent power distribution box" or a "smart junction box," because underneath (lower figure) are wires that join the circuits from the maxi fuses to other fuses and to or from relays. Because of these interconnected circuits, if there is a fault due to a collision or water intrusion, most experts suggest replacing the entire assembly rather than trying to repair the assembly. Always check service information for the exact procedures to follow when working with an underhood fuse panel.

NORMAL CURRENT IN THE CIRCUIT (AMPERES)	FUSE RATING (AMPERES)
7.5	10
16	20
24	30

CHART 11–5

The fuse rating should be 20% higher than the maximum current in the circuit to provide the best protection for the wiring and the component being protected.

● **SEE FIGURE 11–5** for a comparison of the various sizes of blade-type fuses.

PACIFIC FUSE ELEMENT First used in the late 1980s, **Pacific fuse elements** (also called a **fuse link** or **auto link**) are used to protect wiring from a direct short-to-ground. The housing contains a short link of wire sized for the rated current load. The transparent top allows inspection of the link inside. ● **SEE FIGURE 11–6**.

AMPERAGE RATING	COLOR
1	Dark green
2	Gray
2.5	Purple
3	Violet
4	Pink
5	Tan
6	Gold
7.5	Brown
9	Orange
10	Red
14	Black
15	Blue
20	Yellow
25	White
30	Green

CHART 11–6

The amperage rating and the color of the blade fuse are standardized.

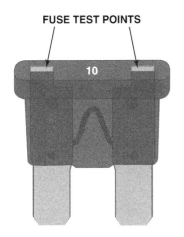

FIGURE 11–4 Blade-type fuses can be tested through openings in the plastic at the top of the fuse.

AMPERAGE RATING	COLOR
5	Tan
7.5	Brown
10	Red
15	Blue
20	Yellow
25	Natural
30	Green

CHART 11–7

Mini fuse amperage rating and colors.

AMPERAGE RATING	COLOR
20	Yellow
30	Green
40	Amber
50	Red
60	Blue
70	Brown
80	Natural

CHART 11–8

Maxi fuse amperage rating and colors.

TESTING FUSES

It is important to test the condition of a fuse if the circuit being protected by the fuse does not operate. Most blown fuses can be detected quickly because the center conductor is melted. Fuses can also fail and open the circuit because of a poor connection in the fuse itself or in the fuse holder. Therefore, just because a fuse "looks okay" does not mean that it *is* okay. All fuses should be tested with a test light. The test light should be connected to first one side of the fuse and then the other. A test light should light on both sides. If the test light only lights on one side, the fuse is blown or open. If

FIGURE 11–5 Three sizes of blade-type fuses: mini on the left, standard or ATO type in the center, and maxi on the right.

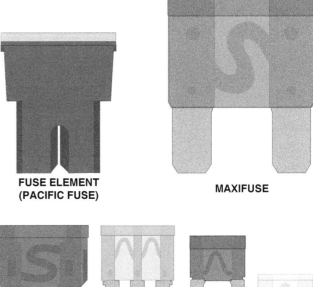

FUSE ELEMENT (PACIFIC FUSE) MAXIFUSE

ATO FUSE MICRO3 FUSE (THREE-LEGGED FUSE) MINIFUSE LOW PROFILE MINIFUSE

FIGURE 11–6 A comparison of the various types of protective devices used in most vehicles.

the test light does not light on either side of the fuse, then that circuit is not being supplied power. ● **SEE FIGURE 11–7**. An ohmmeter can be used to test fuses.

CAUTION: Only use name-brand fuses purchased from a known source. Some off-brand or no-brand fuses have been found to not blow until exposed to current levels far exceeding their rating. Fuses that do not blow at the designed rating could cause wiring to overheat and may even cause a fire.

CIRCUIT BREAKERS

Circuit breakers are used to prevent harmful overload (excessive current flow) in a circuit by opening the circuit and stopping the current flow to prevent overheating, and possible fire, caused by hot wires or electrical components. **Circuit breakers** are mechanical units made of two different metals (bimetallic) that deform when heated, and

FIGURE 11–7 To test a fuse, use a test light to check for power at the power side of the fuse. The ignition switch and lights may have to be on before some fuses receive power. If the fuse is good, the test light should light on both sides (power side and load side) of the fuse.

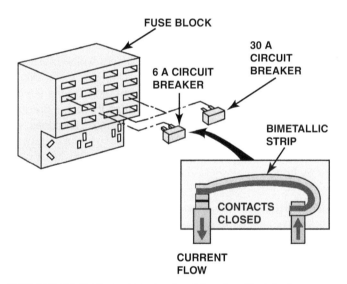

FUSE BLOCK

6 A CIRCUIT BREAKER

30 A CIRCUIT BREAKER

BIMETALLIC STRIP

CONTACTS CLOSED

CURRENT FLOW

FIGURE 11–8 Typical blade circuit breaker fits into the same space as a blade fuse. If excessive current flows through the bimetallic strip, the strip bends and opens the contacts and stops current flow. When the circuit breaker cools, the contacts close again, completing the electrical circuit.

open a set of contact points that work in the same manner as an "off" switch. ● SEE FIGURE 11–8.

Cycling-type circuit breakers, therefore, are reset when the current stops flowing, which causes the bimetallic strip to cool and the circuit to close again. A circuit breaker is used in circuits that could affect the safety of passengers if a conventional nonresetting fuse were used. The headlight circuit is an excellent example of the use of a circuit breaker, rather than a fuse. A short or grounded circuit anywhere in the headlight

CIRCUIT BREAKER

FIGURE 11–9 Electrical symbols used to represent circuit breakers.

circuit could cause excessive current flow and, therefore, the opening of the circuit. Obviously, a sudden loss of headlights at night could have disastrous results. A circuit breaker opens and closes the circuit rapidly, thereby protecting the circuit from overheating and also providing sufficient current flow to maintain at least partial headlight operation.

Circuit breakers are also used in other circuits where conventional fuses could not provide for the surges of high current commonly found in those circuits. ● SEE FIGURE 11–9 for the electrical symbols used to represent a circuit breaker.

Examples are the circuits for the following accessories.

1. Power seats
2. Power door locks
3. Power windows

PTC CIRCUIT PROTECTORS
Positive temperature coefficient (PTC) circuit protectors are solid state (without moving parts). Like all other circuit-protection devices, PTCs are installed in series in the circuit being protected. If excessive current flows, the temperature and resistance of the PTC increase.

This increased resistance reduces current flow (amperes) in the circuit and may cause the electrical component in the circuit not to function correctly. For example, when a PTC circuit protector is used in a power window circuit, the increased resistance causes the operation of the power window to be much slower than normal.

Unlike circuit breakers or fuses, PTC circuit-protection devices do not open the circuit, but rather provide a very high resistance between the protector and the component. ● SEE FIGURE 11–10.

In other words, voltage is available to the component. This fact has led to a lot of misunderstanding about how these circuit-protection devices actually work. It is even more confusing when the circuit is opened and the PTC circuit protector cools down. When the circuit is turned back on, the component may operate normally for a short time; however, the PTC circuit protector again get hot because of too much current flow. The resistance again increases to limit current flow.

The electronic control unit (computer) used in most vehicles today incorporates thermal-overload protection devices. ● SEE FIGURE 11–11.

Therefore, when a component fails to operate, do not blame the computer. The current-control device is controlling current flow to protect the computer. Components that do not operate correctly should be checked for proper resistance and current draw.

FUSIBLE LINKS
A fusible link is a type of fuse that consists of a short length (6 to 9 inches long) of standard

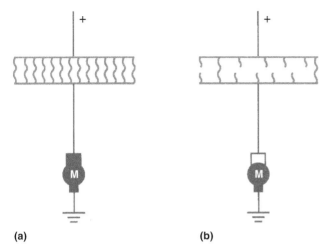

(a)   **(b)**

FIGURE 11–10 (a) The normal operation of a PTC circuit protector, such as in a power window motor circuit showing the many conducting paths. With normal current flow, the temperature of the PTC circuit protector remains normal. (b) When current exceeds the amperage rating of the PTC circuit protector, the polymer material that makes up the electronic circuit protector increases in resistance. As shown, a high-resistance electrical path still exists, even though the motor stops operating, as a result of the very low current flow through the very high resistance. The circuit protector does not reset or cool down until voltage is removed from the circuit.

FIGURE 11–11 PTC circuit protectors are used extensively in the power distribution center of this Chrysler vehicle.

copper-strand wire covered with a special nonflammable insulation. This wire is usually four wire numbers smaller than the wire of the circuits it protects. For example, a 12-gauge circuit is protected by a 16-gauge fusible link. The special thick insulation over the wire may make it look larger than other wires of the same gauge number. ● **SEE FIGURE 11–12.**

If excessive current flow (caused by a short-to-ground or a defective component) occurs, the fusible link melts in half and opens the circuit to prevent a fire hazard. Some fusible links are

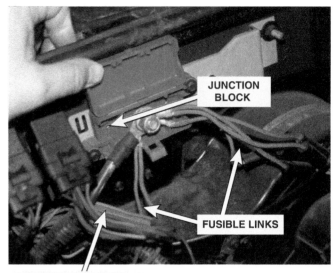

JUNCTION BLOCK

FUSIBLE LINKS

BATTERY CABLE (TO + TERMINAL OF BATTERY)

FIGURE 11–12 Fusible links are usually located close to the battery and are usually attached to a junction block. Notice they are only 6 to 9 inches long and feed more than one fuse from each fusible link.

identified with "fusible link" tags at the junction between the fusible link and the standard chassis wiring, which represent only the junction. Fusible links are the backup system for circuit protection. All current, except the current used by the starter motor, flows through fusible links and then through individual circuit fuses. It is possible that a fusible link melts and does not blow a fuse. Fusible links are installed as close to the battery as possible so that they can protect the wiring and circuits coming directly from the battery.

MEGA FUSES Many newer vehicles are equipped with mega fuses instead of fusible links to protect high-amperage circuits. Circuits often controlled by mega fuses include:

- Charging circuit
- HID headlights
- Heated front or rear glass
- Multiple circuits usually protected by mega fuses
- Mega fuse rating for vehicles, including 80, 100, 125, 150, 175, 225, 250, and 300 amperes
  ● **SEE FIGURE 11–13.**

CHECKING FUSIBLE LINKS AND MEGA FUSES Fusible links and mega fuses are usually located near where electrical power is sent to other fuses or circuits, such as:

- Starter solenoid battery terminals
- Power distribution centers
- Output terminals of alternators
- Positive terminals of the battery

(a)

(b)

FIGURE 11–13 (a) Several maxi fuses are used on this Chevrolet to protect all the circuits, including the 300 ampere fuse that is connected directly to the positive battery cable. (b) A close-up of the 300 ampere maxi fuse showing the marking that it is a 35 square millimeter (35 mm²) conductor being used to protect most of the electrical circuits at the battery.

  TECH TIP

Find the Root Cause

If a mega fuse or fusible link fails, find the root cause before replacing it. A mega fuse can fail due to vibration or physical damage as a result of a collision or corrosion. Check to see if the fuse itself is loose and can be moved by hand. If loose, simply replace the mega fuse. If a fusible link or mega fuse has failed due to excessive current, check for evidence of a collision or any other reason that could cause an excessive amount of current to flow. This inspection should include each electrical component being supplied current from the fusible link. After being sure that the root cause has been found and corrected, replace the fusible link or mega fuse.

 **TECH TIP**

Look for the "Green Crud"

Corroded connections are a major cause of intermittent electrical problems and open circuits. The usual sequence of conditions is as follows:

1. **Heat causes expansion.** This heat can be from external sources, such as connectors being too close to the exhaust system. Another possible source of heat is a poor connection at the terminal, causing a voltage drop and heat due to the electrical resistance.
2. **Condensation occurs when a connector cools.** The moisture from condensation causes rust and corrosion.
3. **Water gets into the connector.** If corroded connectors are noticed, the terminal should be cleaned and the condition of the electrical connection to the wire terminal end(s) confirmed. Many vehicle manufacturers recommend using a dielectric silicone or lithium-based grease inside connectors to prevent moisture from getting into and attacking the connector.

Fusible links can melt and not show any external evidence of damage. To check a fusible link, gently pull on each end to see if it stretches. If the insulation stretches, then the wire inside has melted and the fusible link must be replaced after determining what caused the link to fail.

Another way to check a fusible link is to use a test light or a voltmeter and check for available voltage at both ends of the fusible link. If voltage is available at only one end, then the link is electrically open and should be replaced.

REPLACING A FUSIBLE LINK   If a fusible link is found to be melted, perform the following steps.

STEP 1   Determine why the fusible link failed and repair the fault.

STEP 2   Check service information for the exact length, gauge, and type of fusible link required.

STEP 3   Replace the fusible link with the specified fusible link wire and according to the instructions found in the service information.

> **CAUTION: Always use the *exact* length of fusible link wire required because, if it is too short, it does not have enough resistance to generate the heat needed to melt the wire and protect the circuits or components. If the wire is too long, it could melt during normal operation of the circuits it is protecting. Fusible link wires are usually longer than 6 inches and shorter than 9 inches.**

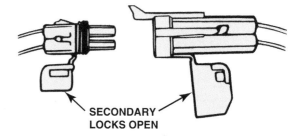

FIGURE 11–16 The secondary locks help retain the terminals in the connector.

TERMINALS AND CONNECTORS

A **terminal** is a metal fastener attached to the end of a wire, which makes the electrical connection. The term *connector* usually refers to the plastic portion that snaps or connects together, making the mechanical connection. Wire terminal ends usually snap into, and are held by, a connector. Male and female connectors can then be snapped together, completing an electrical connection. Connectors exposed to the environment are also equipped with a weather-tight seal. ● **SEE FIGURE 11–14**.

Terminals are retained in connectors by the use of a **lock tang.** Removing a terminal from a connector includes the following steps.

STEP 1 Release the **connector position assurance (CPA)**, if equipped, that keeps the latch of the connector from releasing accidentally.

STEP 2 Separate the male and female connector by opening the lock. ● **SEE FIGURE 11–15**.

STEP 3 Release the secondary lock, if equipped. ● **SEE FIGURE 11–16**.

STEP 4 Using a pick, look for the slot in the plastic connector where the lock tang is located, depress the lock tang, and gently remove the terminal from the connector. ● **SEE FIGURE 11–17**.

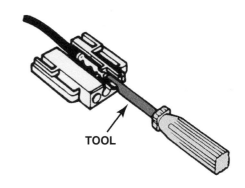

TOOL

RAISING RETAINING FINGERS TO REMOVE CONTACTS

LOCKING WEDGE CONNECTOR

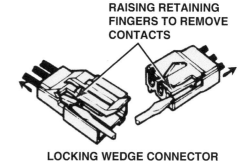

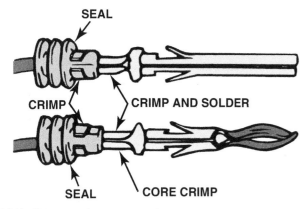

SEAL

CRIMP

CRIMP AND SOLDER

SEAL

CORE CRIMP

FIGURE 11–14 Some terminals have seals attached to help seal the electrical connections.

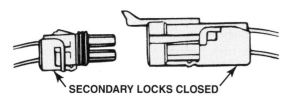

SECONDARY LOCKS CLOSED

FIGURE 11–15 Separate a connector by opening the lock and pulling the two apart.

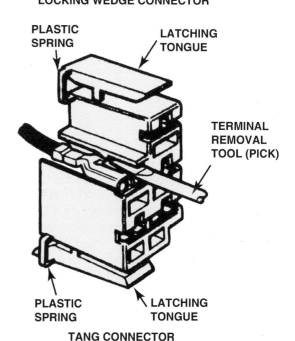

PLASTIC SPRING

LATCHING TONGUE

TERMINAL REMOVAL TOOL (PICK)

PLASTIC SPRING

LATCHING TONGUE

TANG CONNECTOR

FIGURE 11–17 Use a small removal tool, sometimes called a pick, to release terminals from the connector.

WIRE REPAIR

SOLDER Many manufacturers recommend that all wiring repairs be soldered. Solder is an alloy of tin and lead used to make a good electrical contact between two wires or connections in an electrical circuit. However, a flux must be used to help clean the area and to help make the solder flow. Therefore, solder is made with a resin (rosin) contained in the center, called **rosin-core solder.**

CAUTION: Never use acid-core solder to repair electrical wiring as the acid causes corrosion.

● **SEE FIGURE 11–18**.

An acid-core solder is also available, but should only be used for soldering sheet metal. Solder is available with various percentages of tin and lead in the alloy. Ratios are used to identify these various types of solder, with the first number denoting the percentage of tin in the alloy and the second number giving the percentage of lead. The most commonly used solder is 50/50, which means that 50% of the solder is tin and the other 50% is lead. The percentages of each alloy primarily determine the melting point of the solder.

- 60/40 solder (60% tin/40% lead) melts at 361°F (183°C).
- 50/50 solder (50% tin/50% lead) melts at 421°F (216°C).
- 40/60 solder (40% tin/60% lead) melts at 460°F (238°C).

NOTE: The melting points stated here can vary, depending on the purity of the metals used.

Because of the lower melting point, 60/40 solder is the most highly recommended solder to use, followed by 50/50.

SOLDERING GUNS When soldering wires, be sure to heat the wires (not the solder) using:

- An electric soldering gun or soldering pencil (60 to 150 watt rating)
- Butane-powered tool that uses a flame to heat the tip (about 60 watt rating) ● **SEE FIGURE 11–19**.

SOLDERING PROCEDURE Soldering a wiring splice includes the following steps.

STEP 1 While touching the soldering gun to the splice, apply solder to the junction of the gun and the wire.

STEP 2 The solder starts to flow. Do not move the soldering gun.

STEP 3 Just keep feeding more solder into the splice as it flows into and around the strands of the wire.

STEP 4 After the solder has flowed throughout the splice, remove the soldering gun and the solder from the splice and allow the solder to cool slowly.

The solder should have a shiny appearance. Dull-looking solder may be caused by not reaching a high enough temperature, which results in a **cold solder joint.** Reheating the splice and allowing it to cool often restores the shiny appearance.

CRIMPING TERMINALS Terminals can be crimped to create a good electrical connection if the proper type of crimping tool is used. Most vehicle manufacturers recommend that a W-shaped crimp be used to force the strands of the wire into a tight space. ● **SEE FIGURE 11–20**.

Most vehicle manufacturers also specify that all hand-crimped terminals or splices be soldered. ● **SEE FIGURE 11–21**.

HEAT SHRINK TUBING **Heat shrink tubing** is usually made from polyvinyl chloride (PVC) or polyolefin and shrinks to about half of its original diameter when heated; this is usually called a 2:1 shrink ratio. Heat shrink by itself does not provide protection against corrosion, because the ends of the

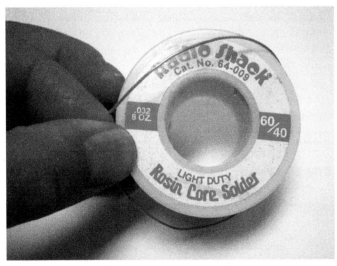

FIGURE 11–18 Always use rosin-core solder for electrical or electronic soldering. Also, use small-diameter solder for small soldering irons. Use large-diameter solder only for large-diameter (large-gauge) wire and higher-wattage soldering irons (guns).

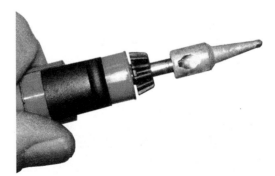

FIGURE 11–19 A butane-powered soldering tool. The cap has a built-in striker to light a converter in the tip of the tool. This handy soldering tool produces the equivalent of 60 watts of heat. It operates for about 1/2 hour on one charge from a commonly available butane refill dispenser.

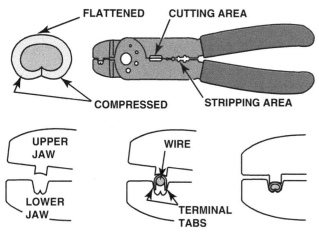

FIGURE 11–20 Notice that to create a good crimp the open part of the terminal is placed in the jaws of the crimping tool toward the anvil or the W-shape part.

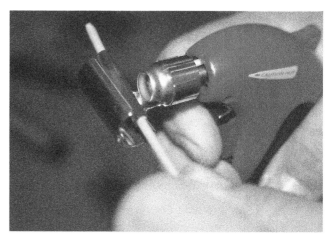

FIGURE 11–22 A butane torch especially designed for use on heat shrink applies heat without an open flame, which could cause damage.

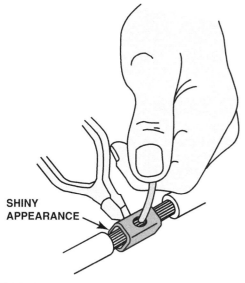

FIGURE 11–21 All hand-crimped splices or terminals should be soldered to be assured of a good electrical connection.

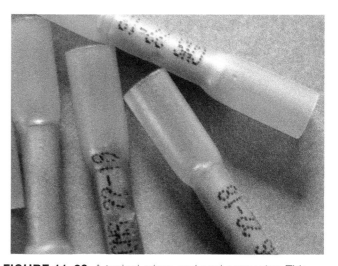

FIGURE 11–23 A typical crimp-and-seal connector. This type of connector is first lightly crimped to retain the ends of the wires and then it is heated. The tubing shrinks around the wire splice, and thermoplastic glue melts on the inside to provide an effective weather-resistant seal.

tubing are not sealed against moisture. Chrysler Corporation recommends that all wire repairs that may be exposed to the elements be repaired and sealed, using **adhesive-lined heat shrink tubing**. The tubing is usually made from flame-retardant flexible polyolefin with an internal layer of special thermoplastic adhesive. When heated, this tubing shrinks to one-third of its original diameter (3:1 shrink ratio) and the adhesive melts and seals the ends of the tubing. ● **SEE FIGURE 11–22.**

CRIMP-AND-SEAL CONNECTORS General Motors Corporation recommends the use of crimp-and-seal connectors as the method for wire repair. **Crimp-and-seal connectors** contain a sealant and shrink tubing in one piece and are *not* simply butt connectors. ● **SEE FIGURE 11–23.**

The usual procedure specified for making a wire repair using a crimp-and-seal connector is as follows:

STEP 1   Strip the insulation from the ends of the wire (about 5/16 inch or 8 mm).

STEP 2   Select the proper size of crimp-and-seal connector for the gauge of wire being repaired. Insert the wires into the splice sleeve and crimp.

NOTE: Use only the specified crimping tool to help prevent the pliers from creating a hole in the cover.

STEP 3   Apply heat to the connector until the sleeve shrinks down around the wire and a small amount of sealant is observed around the ends of the sleeve, as shown in ● **FIGURE 11–24.**

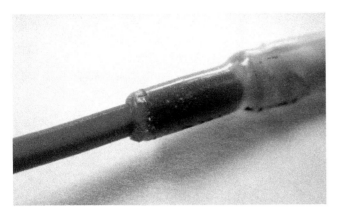

FIGURE 11–24 Heating the crimp-and-seal connector melts the glue and forms an effective seal against moisture.

 FREQUENTLY ASKED QUESTION

What Is in Lead-Free Solder?

Lead is an environmental and health concern and all vehicle manufacturers are switching to lead-free solder. Lead-free solder does not contain lead, but usually a very high percentage of tin. Several formulations of lead-free solder include the following:

- 95% tin; 5% antimony (melting temperature 450°F (245°C))
- 97% tin; 3% copper (melting temperature 441°F (227°C))
- 96% tin; 4% silver (melting temperature 443°F (228°C))

 FREQUENTLY ASKED QUESTION

What Method of Wire Repair Should I Use?

Good question. Vehicle manufacturers recommend all wire repairs performed under the hood, or where the repair could be exposed to the elements, be weatherproof. The most commonly recommended methods include the following:

- **Crimp-and-seal connector.** These connectors are special and are not like low-cost insulated-type crimp connectors. This type of connector is recommended by General Motors and others and is sealed using heat after the mechanical crimp has secured the wire ends together.

- **Solder and adhesive-lined heat shrink tubing.** This method is recommended by Chrysler and it uses the special heat shrink that has glue inside that melts when heated to form a sealed connection. Regular heat shrink tubing can be used inside a vehicle, but should not be used where it can be exposed to the elements.

- **Solder and electrical tape.** This is acceptable to use inside the vehicle where the splice is not exposed to the outside elements. It is best to use a crimp and seal, even on the inside of the vehicle, for best results.

ALUMINUM WIRE REPAIR Some vehicle manufacturers used plastic-coated solid aluminum wire for some body wiring. Because aluminum wire is brittle and can break as a result of vibration, it is used only where there is no possible movement of the wire, such as along the floor or sill area. This section of wire is stationary, and the wire changes back to copper at a junction terminal after the trunk or rear section of the vehicle, where movement of the wiring may be possible.

If any aluminum wire must be repaired or replaced, the following procedure should be used to be assured of a proper repair. The aluminum wire is usually found protected in a plastic conduit. This conduit is then slit, after which the wires can easily be removed for repair.

STEP 1 Carefully strip only about 1/4 inch (6 mm) of insulation from the aluminum wire, being careful not to nick or damage the aluminum wire case.

STEP 2 Use a crimp connector to join two wires together. Do *not* solder an aluminum wire repair. Solder does not readily adhere to aluminum because the heat causes an oxide coating on the surface of the aluminum.

STEP 3 The spliced, crimped connection must be coated with petroleum jelly to prevent corrosion.

STEP 4 The coated connection should be covered with shrinkable plastic tubing or wrapped with electrical tape to seal out moisture.

ELECTRICAL CONDUIT

Electrical conduit covers and protects wiring. The color used on electrical convoluted conduit tells the technician a lot if some information is known, such as the following:

- **Black conduit with a green or blue stripe.** This conduit is designed for high temperatures and is used under the hood and near hot engine parts. Do not replace high-temperature conduit with low-temperature conduit that does not have a stripe when performing wire repairs. ● **SEE FIGURE 11–25**.

- **Blue or yellow conduit.** This color conduit is used to cover wires that have voltages ranging from 12 to 42 volts. Circuits that use this high voltage usually are for the electric power steering. While 42 volts does not represent a shock hazard, an arc is maintained if a line circuit is disconnected. Use caution around these circuits. ● **SEE FIGURE 11–26** (a).

- **Orange conduit.** This color conduit is used to cover wiring that carries high-voltage current above 60 volts. These circuits are found in hybrid-electric vehicles

(HEVs). An electric shock from these wires can be fatal, so extreme caution has to be taken when working on or near the components that have orange conduit. Follow the vehicle manufacturer's instruction for de-powering the high-voltage circuits before work begins on any of the high-voltage components. ● **SEE FIGURE 11-27**.

FIGURE 11-27 Always follow the vehicle manufacturer's instructions, which include the use of linesman's (high-voltage) gloves, if working on circuits that are covered in orange conduit.

FIGURE 11-25 Conduit that has a paint stripe is constructed of plastic that can withstand high underhood temperatures.

(a)

(b)

FIGURE 11-26 (a) Blue conduit is used to cover circuits that carry up to 42 volts. (b) Yellow conduit can also be used to cover 42 volt wiring.

SUMMARY

1. The higher the AWG size number, the smaller the wire diameter.
2. Metric wire is sized in square millimeters (mm2) and the higher the number, the larger the wire.
3. All circuits should be protected by a fuse, fusible link, or circuit breaker. The current in the circuit should be about 80% of the fuse rating.
4. A terminal is the metal end of a wire, whereas a connector is the plastic housing for the terminal.
5. All wire repair should use either soldering or a crimp and seal connector.

1. What is the difference between the American wire gauge (AWG) system and the metric system?
2. What is the difference between a wire and a cable?
3. What is the difference between a terminal and a connector?

4. How do fuses, PTC circuit protectors, circuit breakers, and fusible links protect a circuit?
5. How should a wire repair be done if the repair is under the hood where it is exposed to the outside?

CHAPTER QUIZ

1. The higher the AWG number, _____.
   a. the smaller the wire diameter
   b. the larger the wire diameter
   c. the thicker the insulation
   d. the more strands in the conductor core

2. Metric wire size is measured in units of _____.
   a. meters
   b. cubic centimeters
   c. square millimeters
   d. cubic millimeters

3. Which statement is true about fuse ratings?
   a. The fuse rating should be less than the maximum current for the circuit.
   b. The fuse rating should be higher than the normal current for the circuit.
   c. Of the fuse rating, 80% should equal the current in the circuit.
   d. Both b and c

4. Which statements are true about wire, terminals, and connectors?
   a. Wire is called a lead, and the metal end is a connector.
   b. A connector is usually a plastic piece where terminals lock in.
   c. A lead and a terminal are the same thing.
   d. Both a and c

5. The type of solder that should be used for electrical work is _____.
   a. rosin core
   b. acid core
   c. 60/40 with no flux
   d. 50/50 with acid paste flux

6. A technician is performing a wire repair on a circuit under the hood of the vehicle. Technician A says to use solder and adhesive-lined heat shrink tubing or a crimp-and-seal connector. Technician B says to solder and use electrical tape. Which technician is correct?
   a. Technician A only
   b. Technician B only
   c. Both Technicians A and B
   d. Neither Technician A nor B

7. Two technicians are discussing fuse testing. Technician A says that a test light should light on both test points of the fuse if it is okay. Technician B says the fuse is defective if a test light only lights on one side of the fuse. Which technician is correct?
   a. Technician A only
   b. Technician B only
   c. Both Technicians A and B
   d. Neither Technician A nor B

8. Many ground straps are uninsulated and braided because _____.
   a. they are more flexible to allow movement of the engine without breaking the wire
   b. they are less expensive than conventional wire
   c. they help dampen radio-frequency interference (RFI)
   d. Both a and c

9. What causes a fuse to blow?
   a. A decrease in circuit resistance
   b. An increase in the current flow through the circuit
   c. A sudden decrease in current flow through the circuit
   d. Both a and b

10. A vehicle has some wiring covered with orange conduit. This indicates a _____ circuit.
    a. 42 volt
    b. 12 to 16 volt
    c. variable voltage
    d. high-voltage

WIRING SCHEMATICS AND CIRCUIT TESTING

LEARNING OBJECTIVES:

After studying this chapter, the reader should be able to:

Interpret wiring schematics and explain the procedure to identify relay terminals.

Locate shorts, grounds, opens, and resistance problems in electrical circuits, and determine necessary action.

Explain the different methods to locate a short circuit, and the procedure to troubleshoot an electrical problem.

This chapter will help you prepare for the ASE Electrical/Electronic Systems (A6) certification test content area "A" (General Electrical/Electronic System Diagnosis).

KEY TERMS: Coil 140 • DPDT 139 • DPST 139 • Gauss gauge 147 • Momentary switch 139 • N.C. 139 • N.O. 139 • Poles 139 • Relay 140 • Short circuit 145 • SPDT 139 • SPST 139 • Terminal 135 • Throws 139 • Tone generator tester 148 • Wiring schematic 134

WIRING SCHEMATICS AND SYMBOLS

TERMINOLOGY The service manuals of automotive manufacturers include wiring schematics of every electrical circuit in a vehicle. A **wiring schematic**, sometimes called a *diagram*, shows electrical components and wiring using symbols and lines to represent components and wires. A typical wiring schematic may include all of the circuits combined on several large foldout sheets, or they may be broken down to show individual circuits. All circuit schematics or diagrams include the following:

- Power-side wiring of the circuit
- All splices
- Connectors
- Wire size
- Wire color
- Trace color (if any)
- Circuit number
- Electrical components
- Ground return paths
- Fuses and switches

CIRCUIT INFORMATION Many wiring schematics include numbers and letters near components and wires that may confuse readers of the schematic. Most letters used near or on a wire identify the color or colors of the wire.

- The first color or color abbreviation is the color of the wire insulation.
- The second color (if mentioned) is the color of the stripe or tracer on the base color. ● **SEE FIGURE 12–1**.

Wires with different color tracers are indicated by a slash (/) between them. For example, GRN/WHT means a green wire with a white stripe or tracer. ● **SEE CHART 12–1**.

WIRE SIZE Wire size is shown on all schematics. ● **FIGURE 12–2** illustrates a rear side-marker bulb circuit diagram where "0.8" indicates the metric wire gauge size in square millimeters (mm^2) and "PPL" indicates a solid purple wire.

The wire diagram also shows that the color of the wire changes at number C210. This stands for "connector #210" and is used for reference purposes. The symbol for the connection can vary depending on the manufacturer. The color change from purple (PPL) to purple with a white tracer (PPL/WHT) is not important

FIGURE 12–1 The center wire is a solid color wire, meaning that the wire has no other identifying tracer or stripe color. The two end wires could be labeled "BLU/WHT," indicating a blue wire with a white tracer or stripe.

ABBREVIATION	COLOR
BRN	Brown
BLK	Black
GRN	Green
WHT	White
PPL	Purple
PNK	Pink
TAN	Tan
BLU	Blue
YEL	Yellow
ORN	Orange
DK BLU	Dark blue
LT BLU	Light blue
DK GRN	Dark green
LT GRN	Light green
RED	Red
GRY	Gray
VIO	Violet

CHART 12–1

Typical abbreviations used on schematics to show wire color. Some vehicle manufacturers use two letters to represent a wire color. Check service information for the color abbreviations used.

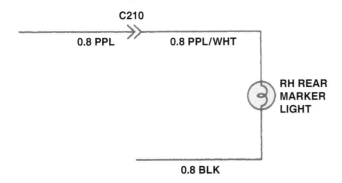

FIGURE 12–2 Typical section of a wiring diagram. Notice that the wire color changes at connection C210. The "0.8" represents the metric wire size in square millimeters.

except for knowing where the wire changes color in the circuit. The wire gauge has remained the same on both sides of the connection (0.8 mm^2 or 18 gauge). The ground circuit is the "0.8 BLK" wire. ● **FIGURE 12–3** shows many of the electrical and electronic symbols that are used in wiring and circuit diagrams.

SCHEMATIC SYMBOLS

In a schematic drawing, photos or line drawings of actual components are replaced with a symbol that represents the actual component. The following discussion centers on these symbols and their meanings.

 **TECH TIP**

Read the Arrows

Wiring diagrams indicate connections by symbols that look like arrows. ● **SEE FIGURE 12–4**.

Do *not* read these "arrows" as pointers showing the direction of current flow. Also observe that the power side (positive side) of the circuit is usually the female end of the connector. If a connector becomes disconnected, it is difficult for the circuit to become shorted to ground or to another circuit because the wire is recessed inside the connector.

BATTERY The plates of a battery are represented by long and short lines. ● **SEE FIGURE 12–5**.

The longer line represents the positive plate of a battery and the shorter line represents the negative plate. Therefore, each pair of short and long lines represents one cell of a battery. Because each cell of a typical automotive lead–acid battery has 2.1 volts, a battery symbol showing a 12 volt battery should have six pairs of lines. However, most battery symbols simply use two or three pairs of long and short lines and list the voltage of the battery next to the symbol. As a result, the battery symbols are shorter and yet clear, because the voltage is stated. The positive terminal of the battery is often indicated with a plus sign (+), representing the positive post of the battery, and is placed next to the long line of the end cell. The negative terminal of the battery is represented by a negative sign (−) and is placed next to the shorter cell line. The negative battery terminal is connected to ground. ● **SEE FIGURE 12–6**.

WIRING Electrical wiring is shown as straight lines and with a few numbers and/or letters to indicate the following:

- **Wire size.** This can be either AWG, such as 18 gauge, or in square millimeters, such as 0.8 mm^2.

- **Circuit numbers.** Each wire in part of a circuit is labeled with the circuit number to help the service technician trace the wiring and to provide an explanation of how the circuit should work.

- **Wire color.** Most schematics also indicate an abbreviation for the color of the wire and place it next to the wire. Many wires have two colors: a solid color and a stripe color. In this case, the solid color is listed, followed by a slash (/) and the color of the stripe. For example, Red/ Wht indicates a red wire with a white tracer. ● **SEE FIGURE 12–7**.

- **Terminals.** The metal part attached at the end of a wire is called a **terminal**. A symbol for a terminal is shown in ● **FIGURE 12–8**.

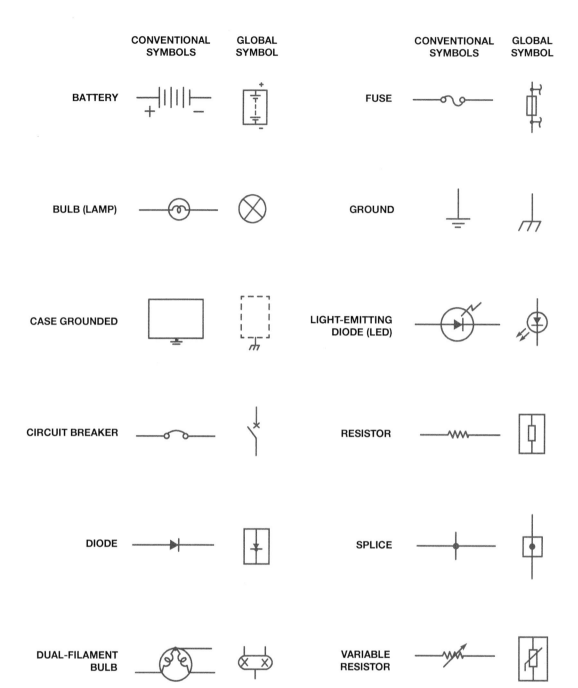

	CONVENTIONAL SYMBOLS	GLOBAL SYMBOL		CONVENTIONAL SYMBOLS	GLOBAL SYMBOL
BATTERY			FUSE		
BULB (LAMP)			GROUND		
CASE GROUNDED			LIGHT-EMITTING DIODE (LED)		
CIRCUIT BREAKER			RESISTOR		
DIODE			SPLICE		
DUAL-FILAMENT BULB			VARIABLE RESISTOR		

FIGURE 12–3 Typical electrical and electronic symbols used in automotive wiring and circuit diagrams. Both the conventional and the global symbols are shown side by side to make reading schematics easier. The global symbols are used by many vehicle manufacturers.

FIGURE 12–4 In this typical connector, note that the positive terminal is usually a female connector.

FIGURE 12–5 The symbol for a battery. The positive plate of a battery is represented by the longer line and the negative plate by the shorter line. The voltage of the battery is usually stated next to the symbol.

FIGURE 12–6 The ground symbol on the left represents an earth ground. The ground symbol on the right represents a chassis ground.

■ **Splices.** When two wires are electrically connected, the junction is shown with a black dot. The identification of the splice is an "S" followed by three numbers, such as S103. ● **SEE FIGURE 12–9**. When two wires cross in a schematic that are not electrically connected, one of

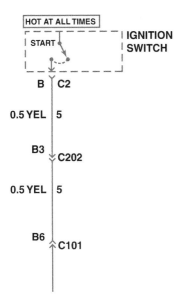

FIGURE 12–7 Starting at the top, the wire from the ignition switch is attached to terminal B of connector C2, the wire is 0.5 mm^2 (20-gauge AWG), and is yellow. The circuit number is 5. The wire enters connector C202 at terminal B3.

FIGURE 12–8 The electrical terminals are usually labeled with a letter or number.

the wires is shown as going over the other wire and does not connect. ● **SEE FIGURE 12–10.**

■ **Connectors.** An electrical connector is a plastic part that contains one or more terminals. Although the terminals provide the electrical connection in a circuit, it is the plastic connector that keeps the terminals together mechanically.

■ **Location.** Connections are usually labeled "C" followed by three numbers. The three numbers indicate the general location of the connector. Normally, the connector vehicle, such as:

100–199	Under the hood
200–299	Under the dash
300–399	Passenger compartment
400–499	Rear package or trunk area
500–599	Left-front door
600–699	Right-front door
700–799	Left-rear door
800–899	Right-rear door

FIGURE 12–9 Two wires that cross at the dot indicate that the two are electrically connected.

FIGURE 12–10 Wires that cross, but do not electrically contact each other, are shown with one wire bridging over the other.

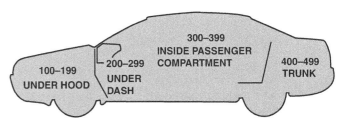

FIGURE 12–11 Connectors (C), grounds (G), and splices (S) are followed by a number, generally indicating the location in the vehicle. For example, G209 is a ground connection located under the dash.

Even-numbered connectors are on the right (passenger side) of the vehicle and odd-numbered connectors are on the left (driver's side) of the vehicle. For example, C102 is a connector located under the hood (between 100 and 199) on the right side of the vehicle (even number 102). ● **SEE FIGURE 12–11.**

■ **Grounds and splices.** These are also labeled using the same general format as connectors. Therefore, a ground located in the passenger compartment could be labeled G305 (*G* means "ground" and "305" means that it is located in the passenger compartment). ● **SEE FIGURE 12–12.**

ELECTRICAL COMPONENTS Most electrical components have their own unique symbol that shows the basic function or parts.

■ **Bulbs.** Lightbulbs often use a filament, which heats and gives off light when electrical current flows. The symbol used for a lightbulb is a circle with a filament inside. A dual-filament bulb, such as is used for taillights and brake light/turn signals, is shown with two filaments. ● **SEE FIGURE 12–13.**

ELECTRIC MOTORS An electric motor symbol shows a circle with the letter *M* in the center and two electrical connections, one at the top and the other at the bottom. ● **SEE FIGURE 12–14** for an example of a cooling fan motor.

RESISTORS Although resistors are usually part of another component, the symbol appears on many schematics and

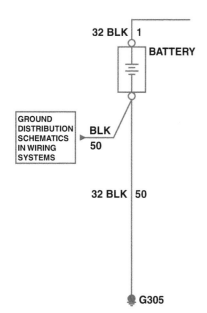

FIGURE 12–12 The ground for the battery is labeled G305, indicating the ground connector is located in the passenger compartment of the vehicle. The ground wire is black (BLK), the circuit number is 50, and the wire is 32 mm² (2-gauge AWG).

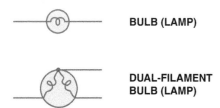

FIGURE 12–13 The symbol for lightbulbs shows the filament inside a circle, which represents the glass ampoule of the bulb.

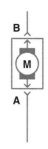

FIGURE 12–14 An electric motor symbol shows a circle with the letter *M* in the center and two black sections that represent the brushes of the motor. This symbol is used even though the motor is a brushless design.

wiring diagrams. A resistor symbol is a jagged line representing resistance to current flow. If the resistor is variable, such as a thermistor, an arrow is shown running through the symbol of a fixed resistor. A potentiometer is a three-wire variable resistor, shown with an arrow pointing toward the resistance part of a fixed resistor. ● SEE FIGURE 12–15.

A two-wire rheostat is usually shown as part of another unit, such as a fuel-level sensing unit. ● SEE FIGURE 12–16.

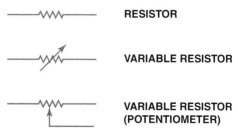

FIGURE 12–15 Resistor symbols vary, depending on the type of resistor.

FIGURE 12–16 A rheostat uses only two wires—one is connected to a voltage source and the other is attached to the movable arm.

FIGURE 12–17 Symbols used to represent capacitors. If one of the lines is curved, this indicates that the capacitor being used has a polarity, while the one without a curved line can be installed in the circuit without concern about polarity.

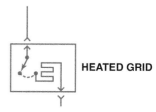

FIGURE 12–18 The grid-like symbol represents an electrically heated element.

CAPACITORS Capacitors are usually part of an electronic component, but not a replaceable component, unless the vehicle is an older model. Many older vehicles used capacitors to reduce radio interference and were installed inside alternators or were attached to wiring connectors. ● SEE FIGURE 12–17.

ELECTRIC HEATED UNIT Electric grid-type rear window defoggers and heated outside mirrors are shown with a square box–type symbol. ● SEE FIGURE 12–18.

BOXED COMPONENTS If a component is shown in a box using a solid line, the box is the entire component. If a box uses dashed lines, it represents part of a component. A commonly used dashed-line box is a fuse panel. Often, just one or two fuses are shown in a dashed-line box. This means that a fuse panel has more fuses than shown. ● SEE FIGURES 12–19 AND 12–20.

FIGURE 12–19 A dashed outline represents a portion (part) of a component.

FIGURE 12–20 A solid box represents an entire component.

FIGURE 12–21 This symbol represents a component that is case grounded.

SEPARATE REPLACEABLE PART Often components are shown on a schematic that cannot be replaced, but are part of a complete assembly. When looking at a schematic of General Motors vehicles, the following is shown.

- If a part name is underlined, it is a replaceable part.
- If a part is not underlined, it is not available as a replaceable part, but is included with other components shown and sold as an assembly.
- If the case itself is grounded, the ground symbol is attached to the component as shown in ● **FIGURE 12–21**.

SWITCHES Electrical switches are drawn on a wiring diagram in their normal position. This can be one of two possible positions.

- **Normally open.** The switch is not connected to its internal contacts and no current flows. This type of switch is labeled **N.O.**
- **Normally closed.** The switch is electrically connected to its internal contacts and current flows through the switch. This type of switch is labeled **N.C.**

Other switches can use more than two contacts.

The **poles** refer to the number of circuits completed by the switch and the **throws** refer to the number of output circuits. A **single-pole, single-throw (SPST)** switch has only two positions, on or off. A **single-pole, double-throw (SPDT)** switch has three terminals, one wire in and two wires out. A headlight dimmer switch is an example of a typical SPDT switch. In one position, the current flows to the low-filament headlight; in the other, the current flows to the high-filament headlight.

NOTE: A SPDT switch is not an on or off type of switch, but instead directs power from the source to either the high-beam lamps or the low-beam lamps.

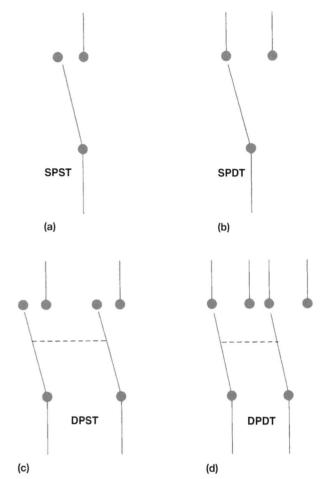

FIGURE 12–22 (a) A symbol for a single-pole, single-throw (SPST) switch. This type of switch is normally open (N.O.) because nothing is connected to the terminal that the switch is contacting in its normal position. (b) A single-pole, double-throw (SPDT) switch has three terminals. (c) A double-pole, single-throw (DPST) switch has two positions (off and on) and can control two separate circuits. (d) A double-pole, double-throw (DPDT) switch has six terminals—three for each pole. Note: Both (c) and (d) also show a dotted line between the two arms indicating that they are mechanically connected, called a "ganged switch."

There are also **double-pole, single-throw (DPST)** switches and **double-pole, double-throw (DPDT)** switches. ● **SEE FIGURE 12–22**.

NOTE: All switches are shown on schematics in their normal position. This means that the headlight switch is shown normally off, as are most other switches and controls.

MOMENTARY SWITCH A **momentary switch** is a switch primarily used to send a voltage signal to a module or controller to request that a device be turned on or off. The switch makes momentary contact and returns to the open position. A horn switch is a commonly used momentary switch. The symbol that represents a momentary switch uses two dots for the contact with a switch above them. A momentary switch can be either normally open or normally closed. ● **SEE FIGURE 12–23**.

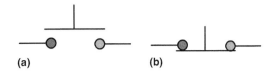

(a)   (b)

FIGURE 12–23 (a) A symbol for a normally open (N.O.) momentary switch. (b) A symbol for a normally closed (N.C.) momentary switch.

 TECH TIP

Color-Coding Is Key to Understanding

Whenever diagnosing an electrical problem, it is common practice to print out the schematic of the circuit and take it to the vehicle. A meter is then used to check for voltage at various parts of the circuit to help determine if there is a fault. The diagnosis can be made easier if the parts of the circuit are first color-coded using markers or color pencils.

The colors represent voltage conditions in various parts of a circuit. Once the circuit has been color-coded, it can be tested using the factory wire colors as a guide. ● **SEE FIGURE 12–24.**

A momentary switch, for example, can be used to lock or unlock a door or to turn the air conditioning on or off. If the device is currently operating, the signal from the momentary switch turns it off, and if it is off, the switch signals the module to turn it on. The major advantage of momentary switches is that they can be lightweight and small, because the switch does not carry any heavy electrical current, just a small voltage signal. Most momentary switches use a membrane constructed of foil and plastic.

RELAY TERMINAL IDENTIFICATION

DEFINITION A **relay** is a magnetic switch that uses a movable armature to control a high-amperage circuit by using a low-amperage electrical switch.

ISO RELAY TERMINAL IDENTIFICATION Most automotive relays adhere to common terminal identification. The primary source for this common identification comes from the standards established by the International Standards Organization (ISO). Knowing this terminal information helps in the correct diagnosis and troubleshooting of any circuit containing a relay. ● **SEE FIGURES 12–25 AND 12–26.**

Relays are found in many circuits because they are capable of being controlled by computers, yet are able to handle enough current to power motors and accessories. Relays include the following components and terminals.

RELAY OPERATION

1. **Coil** (terminals 85 and 86)
   - A coil provides the magnetic pull to a movable armature (arm).
   - The resistance of most relay coils ranges from 50 to 150 ohms, but is usually between 60 and 100 ohms.
   - The ISO identification of the coil terminals are 86 and 85. The terminal number 86 represents the power to the relay coil and the terminal labeled 85 represents the ground side of the relay coil.
   - The relay coil can be controlled by supplying either power or ground to the relay coil winding.
   - The coil winding represents the *control circuit,* which uses low current to control the higher current through the other terminals of the relay. ● **SEE FIGURE 12–27.**

  TECH TIP

Divide the Circuit in Half

When diagnosing any circuit that has a relay, start testing at the relay and divide the circuit in half.

- **High-current portion:** Remove the relay and check that there are 12 volts at the terminal 30 socket. If there is, the power side is okay. Use an ohmmeter and check between terminal 87 socket and ground. If the load circuit has continuity, there should be some resistance. If OL, the circuit is electrically open.
- **Control circuit (low current):** With the relay removed from the socket, check that there are 12 volts to terminal 86 with the ignition on and the control switch on. If not, check service information to see if power should be applied to terminal 86, and continue troubleshooting the switch power and related circuit.
- **Check the relay itself:** Use an ohmmeter and measure for continuity and resistance.
  - Between terminals 85 and 86 (coil), there should be 60 to 100 ohms. If not, replace the relay.
  - Between terminals 30 and 87 (high-amperage switch controls), there should be continuity (low ohms) when there is power applied to terminal 85 and a ground applied to terminal 86 that operates the relay. If OL is displayed on the meter set to read ohms, the circuit is open, which requires that the relay be replaced.
  - Between terminals 30 and 87a (if equipped), with the relay turned off, there should be low resistance (less than 5 ohms).

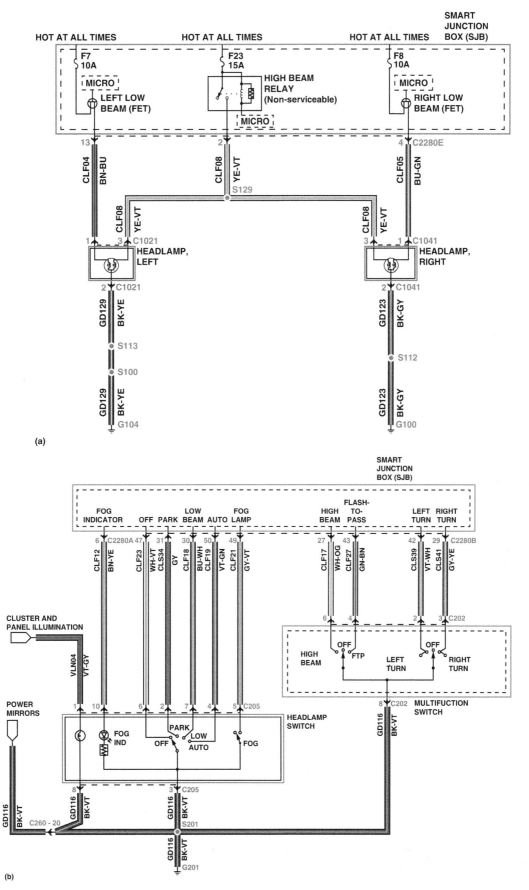

FIGURE 12–24 (a) A typical headlight circuit showing the colors of the wires. (b) A more complex circuit using colored pencils to indicate where there is voltage in the circuit will help diagnose the system if there is a fault.

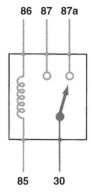

86 87 87a

85 30

86—POWER SIDE OF THE COIL
85—GROUND SIDE OF THE COIL

(MOST RELAY COILS
HAVE BETWEEN
60–100 Ω
OF RESISTANCE)

30—COMMON POWER FOR RELAY CONTACTS
87—NORMALLY OPEN OUTPUT (N.O.)
87a—NORMALLY CLOSED OUTPUT (N.C.)

FIGURE 12–25 A relay uses a movable arm to complete a circuit whenever there is a power at terminal 86 and a ground at terminal 85. A typical relay only requires about 1/10 ampere through the relay coil. The movable arm then closes the contacts (#30 to #87) and can relay 30 amperes or more.

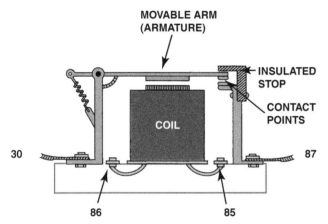

MOVABLE ARM
(ARMATURE)

INSULATED
STOP

CONTACT
POINTS

COIL

30   87

86   85

FIGURE 12–26 A cross-sectional view of a typical four-terminal relay. Current flowing through the coil (terminals 86 and 85) causes the movable arm (called the armature) to be drawn toward the coil magnet. The contact points complete the electrical circuit connected to terminals 30 and 87.

2. Other terminals used to control the load current
   ■ The higher amperage current flow through a relay flows through terminals 30 and 87, and often 87a.
   ■ Terminal 30 is usually where power is applied to a relay. Check service information for the exact operation of the relay being tested.
   ■ When the relay is at rest without power and ground to the coil, the armature inside the relay electrically connects terminals 30 and 87a if the relay has five terminals. When there is power at terminal 85 and a ground at terminal 86 of the relay, a magnetic field is created in the coil winding, which draws the armature of the relay toward the coil. The armature, when energized electrically, connects terminals 30 and 87.

RELAY   RELAY SOCKET

FIGURE 12–27 A typical relay showing the schematic of the wiring in the relay.

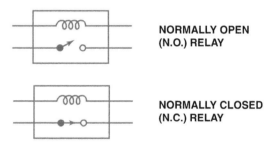

NORMALLY OPEN
(N.O.) RELAY

NORMALLY CLOSED
(N.C.) RELAY

FIGURE 12–28 All schematics are shown in their normal, nonenergized position.

The maximum current through the relay is determined by the resistance of the circuit, and relays are designed to safely handle the designed current flow. ● **SEE FIGURES 12–28 AND 12–29**.

RELAY VOLTAGE SPIKE CONTROL Relays contain a coil and, when power is removed, the magnetic field surrounding the coil collapses, creating a voltage to be induced in the coil winding. This induced voltage can be as high as 100 volts or more and can cause problems with other electronic devices in the vehicle. For example, the short high-voltage surge can be heard as a "pop" in the radio. To reduce the induced voltage, some relays contain a diode connected across the coil. ● **SEE FIGURE 12–30**.

When the current flows through the coil, the diode is not part of the circuit because it is installed to block current. However, when the voltage is removed from the coil, the resulting voltage induced in the coil windings has a reversed polarity to the applied voltage. Therefore, the voltage in the coil is applied to the coil in a forward direction through the diode,

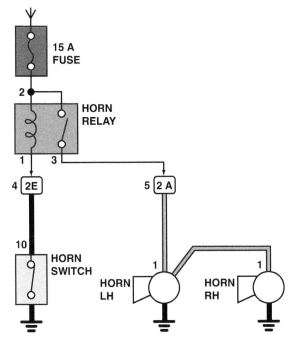

FIGURE 12–29 A horn circuit. Note that the relay contacts supply the heavy current to operate the horn when the horn switch simply completes a low-current circuit to ground, causing the relay contacts to close.

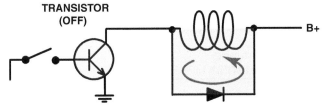

FIGURE 12–30 When the relay or solenoid coil current is turned off, the stored energy in the coil flows through the clamping diode and effectively reduces voltage spike.

FREQUENTLY ASKED QUESTION

What Is the Difference Between a Relay and a Solenoid?

Often, these terms are used differently among vehicle manufacturers, which can lead to some confusion.

Relay: A relay is an electromagnetic switch that uses a movable arm. Because a relay uses a movable arm, it is generally limited to current flow not exceeding 30 amperes.

Solenoid: A solenoid is an electromagnetic switch that uses a movable core. Because of this type of design, a solenoid is capable of handling 200 amperes or more. It is used in the starter motor circuit and other high-amperage applications, such as in the glow plug circuit of diesel engines.

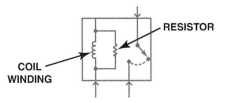

FIGURE 12–31 A resistor used in parallel with the coil windings is a common spike reduction method used in many relays.

which conducts the current back into the winding. As a result, the induced voltage spike is eliminated.

Most relays use a resistor connected in parallel with the coil winding. The use of a resistor, typically about 400 to 600 ohms, reduces the voltage spike by providing a path for the voltage created in the coil to flow back through the coil windings when the coil circuit is opened. See ● FIGURE 12–31.

LOCATING AN OPEN CIRCUIT

TERMINOLOGY An open circuit is a break in the electrical circuit that prevents current from flowing and operating an electrical device. Examples of open circuits include the following:

- Blown (open) lightbulbs
- Cut or broken wires
- Disconnected or partially disconnected electrical connectors
- Electrically open switches
- Loose or broken ground connections or wires
- Blown fuse

PROCEDURE TO LOCATE AN OPEN CIRCUIT The typical procedure for locating an open circuit involves the following steps.

STEP 1 **Perform a thorough visual inspection.** Check the following:
- Look for evidence of a previous repair. Often, an electrical connector or ground connection can be accidentally left disconnected.
- Look for evidence of recent body damage or body repairs. Movement due to a collision can cause metal to move, which can cut wires or damage connectors or components.

STEP 2 **Print out the schematic.** Trace the circuit and check for voltage at certain places. This helps pinpoint the location of the open circuit.

STEP 3 **Check everything that does and does not work.** Often, an open circuit affects more than one component. Check the part of the circuit that is common to the other components that do not work.

STEP 4 **Check for voltage.** Voltage is present up to the location of the open circuit fault. For example, if there is battery voltage at the positive terminal and the negative (ground) terminal of a two-wire lightbulb socket with the bulb plugged in, the ground circuit is open.

COMMON POWER OR GROUND

When diagnosing an electrical problem that affects more than one component or system, check the electrical schematic for a common power source or a common ground. ● **SEE FIGURE 12–32** for an example of lights being powered by one fuse (power source).

- Underhood light
- Inside lighted mirrors
- Dome light
- Left-side courtesy light
- Right-side courtesy light

If a customer complains about one or more of the items listed, check the fuse and the common part of the circuit that feeds all of the affected lights. Check for a common ground if several components that seem unrelated are not functioning correctly.

TECH TIP

Do It Right—Install a Relay

Often the owners of vehicles, especially owners of pickup trucks and sport utility vehicles (SUVs), want to add additional electrical accessories or lighting. It is tempting in these cases to simply splice into an existing circuit. However, when another circuit or component is added, the current that flows through the newly added component is also added to the current for the original component. This additional current can easily overload the fuse and wiring. Do not simply install a larger amperage fuse; the wire gauge size was not engineered for the additional current and could overheat.

The solution is to install a relay, which uses a small coil to create a magnetic field that causes a movable arm to switch on a higher current circuit. The typical relay coil has 50 to 150 ohms (usually 60 to 100 ohms) of resistance and requires just 0.24 to 0.08 ampere when connected to a 12 volt source. This small additional current is not enough to overload the existing circuit. ● **SEE FIGURE 12–33** for an example of how additional lighting can be added.

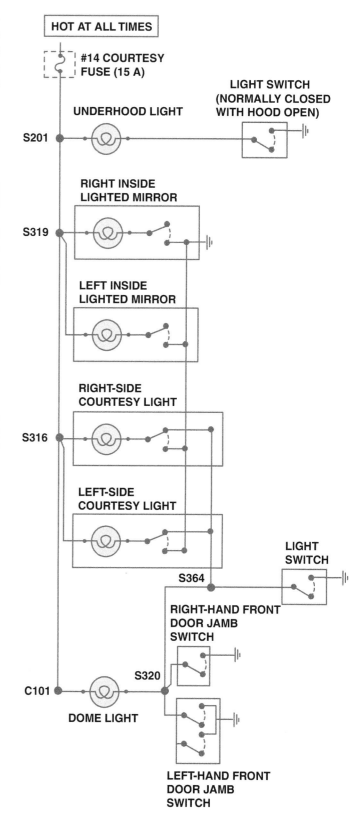

FIGURE 12–32 A typical wiring diagram showing multiple switches and bulbs powered by one fuse.

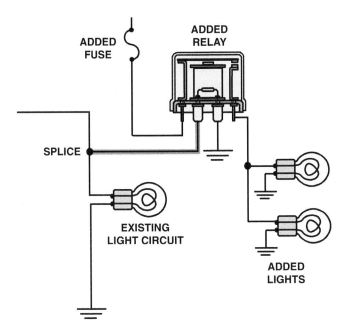

FIGURE 12–33 To add additional lighting, simply tap into an existing light wire and connect a relay. Whenever the existing light is turned on, the coil of the relay is energized. The arm of the relay then connects power from another circuit (fuse) to the auxiliary lights without overloading the existing light circuit.

CIRCUIT TROUBLESHOOTING PROCEDURE

Follow these steps when troubleshooting wiring problems.

STEP 1   Verify the malfunction. If, for example, the backup lights do not operate, make certain that the ignition is on (key on, engine off), with the gear selector in reverse, and check for operation of the backup lights.

STEP 2   Check everything else that does or does not operate correctly. For example, if the taillights are also not working, the problem could be a loose or broken ground connection in the trunk area that is shared by both the backup lights and the taillights.

STEP 3   Check the fuse for the backup lights. ● **SEE FIGURE 12–34**.

STEP 4   Check for voltage at the backup light socket. This can be done using a test light or a voltmeter.

If voltage is available at the socket, the problem is either a defective bulb or a poor ground at the socket or a ground wire connection to the body or frame. If no voltage is available at the socket, consult a wiring diagram for the type of vehicle being tested. The wiring diagram should show all of the wiring and components included in the circuit. For example, the backup light current must flow through the fuse and ignition switch to the gear selector switch before traveling to

CASE STUDY

The Electric Mirror Fault Story

A customer noticed that the electric mirrors stopped working. The service technician checked all electrical components in the vehicle and discovered that the interior lights were also not working.

The interior lights were not mentioned by the customer as being a problem most likely because the driver only used the vehicle in daylight hours.

The service technician found the interior light and power accessory fuse blown. Replacing the fuse restored the proper operation of the electric outside mirror and the interior lights. However, what caused the fuse to blow? A visual inspection of the dome light, next to the electric sunroof, showed an area where a wire was bare. Evidence showed the bare wire had touched the metal roof, which could cause the fuse to blow. The technician covered the bare wire with a section of vacuum hose and then taped the hose with electrical tape to complete the repair.

Summary:

- **Complaint**—The electric power mirrors stopped working.
- **Cause**—A blown fuse due to a fault in the wiring at the dome light.
- **Correction**—Repaired the wiring at the dome light, which restored the proper operation of the electric mirrors that shared the same fuse as the dome light.

the rear backup light socket. As stated in the second step, the fuse used for the backup lights may also be used for other vehicle circuits.

The wiring diagram can be used to determine all other components that share the same fuse. If the fuse is blown (open circuit), the cause can be a short in any of the circuits sharing the same fuse. Because the backup light circuit current must be switched on and off by the gear selector switch, an open in the switch can also prevent the backup lights from functioning.

LOCATING A SHORT CIRCUIT

TERMINOLOGY   A short circuit usually blows a fuse, and a replacement fuse often also blows in the attempt to locate the source of the short circuit. A **short circuit** is an electrical connection to another wire or to ground before the current flows through some or all of the resistance in the circuit. A short-to-ground always blows a fuse, and usually involves a wire on the power side of the circuit coming in contact with metal.

FIGURE 12–34 Always check the simple things first. Check the fuse for the circuit you are testing. Maybe a fault in another circuit controlled by the same fuse could have caused the fuse to blow. Use a test light to check that both sides of the fuse have voltage.

 FREQUENTLY ASKED QUESTION

Where to Start?

The common question is where does a technician start the troubleshooting when using a wiring diagram (schematic)?

HINT 1 If the circuit contains a relay, start your diagnosis at the relay. The entire circuit can be tested at the terminals of the relay.

HINT 2 The easiest first step is to locate the unit on the schematic that is not working or not working correctly.
  a. Trace where the unit gets its ground connection.
  b. Trace where the unit gets its power connection.

Often a ground is used by more than one component. Therefore, ensure that everything else is working correctly. If not, the fault may lie at the common ground (or power) connection.

HINT 3 Divide the circuit in half by locating a connector or a part of the circuit that can be accessed easily. Then check for power and ground at this midpoint. This step could save you time.

HINT 4 Use a fused jumper wire to substitute a ground or a power source to replace a suspected switch or section of wire.

Therefore, a thorough visual inspection should be performed around areas involving heat or movement, especially if there is evidence of a previous collision or previous repair that may not have been properly completed.

A short-to-voltage may or may not cause the fuse to blow and usually affects another circuit. Look for areas of heat or movement where two power wires could come in contact with each other. Several methods can be used to locate the short.

FUSE REPLACEMENT METHOD Disconnect one component at a time and then replace the fuse. If the new fuse blows, continue the process until you determine the location of the short. This method uses many fuses and is *not* a preferred method for finding a short circuit.

CIRCUIT BREAKER METHOD Another method is to connect an automotive circuit breaker to the contacts of the fuse holder with alligator clips. Circuit breakers are available that plug directly into the fuse panel, replacing a blade-type fuse. The circuit breaker alternately opens and closes the circuit, protecting the wiring from possible overheating damage, while still providing current flow through the circuit.

NOTE: A heavy-duty (HD) flasher can also be used in place of a circuit breaker to open and close the circuit. Wires and terminals must be made to connect the flasher unit where the fuse normally plugs in.

All components included in the defective circuit should be disconnected one at a time until the circuit breaker stops clicking. The unit that was disconnected and stopped the circuit breaker clicking is the unit causing the short circuit. If the circuit breaker continues to click with all circuit components unplugged, the problem is in the wiring *from* the fuse panel *to* any one of the units in the circuit. Visual inspection of all the wiring or further disconnecting is necessary to locate the problem.

TEST LIGHT METHOD To use the test light method, simply remove the blown fuse and connect a test light to the terminals of the fuse holder (polarity does not matter). If there is a short circuit, current flows from the power side of the fuse holder through the test light and on to ground through the short circuit, and the test light lights. Unplug the connectors or components protected by the fuse until the test light goes out. The circuit that was disconnected, which caused the test light to go out, is the circuit that is shorted.

BUZZER METHOD The buzzer method is similar to the test light method, but uses a buzzer to replace a fuse and act as an electrical load. The buzzer sounds if the circuit is shorted and stops when the part of the circuit that is grounded is unplugged.

OHMMETER METHOD The fifth method uses an ohmmeter connected to the fuse holder and ground. This is the recommended method of finding a short circuit, as an ohmmeter indicates low ohms when connected to a short circuit. However, an ohmmeter should never be connected to an operating circuit. The correct procedure for locating a short using an ohmmeter is as follows:

1. Connect one lead of an ohmmeter (set to a low scale) to a good clean metal ground and the other lead to the circuit (load) side of the fuse holder.

   CAUTION: Connecting the lead to the power side of the fuse holder causes current to flow through and damages the ohmmeter.

2. The ohmmeter reads zero, or almost zero, ohms if the circuit or a component in the circuit is shorted.

3. Disconnect one component in the circuit at a time and watch the ohmmeter. If the ohmmeter reading shoots to a high value or infinity, the component just unplugged was the source of the short circuit.

4. If all of the components have been disconnected and the ohmmeter still reads low ohms, disconnect electrical connectors until the ohmmeter reads high ohms. The location of the short-to-ground is between the ohmmeter and the disconnected connector.

NOTE: Some meters, such as the Fluke 87, can be set to beep (alert) when the circuit closes or when the circuit opens — a very useful feature.

GAUSS GAUGE METHOD If a short circuit blows a fuse, a special pulsing circuit breaker (similar to a flasher unit) can be installed in the circuit in place of the fuse. Current flows through the circuit until the circuit breaker opens the circuit. As soon as the circuit breaker opens the circuit, it closes again. This on-and-off current flow creates a pulsing magnetic field around the wire carrying the current. A **Gauss gauge** is a handheld meter that responds to weak magnetic fields. It is used to observe this pulsing magnetic field, which is indicated on the gauge as needle movement. This pulsing magnetic field registers on the Gauss gauge, even through the metal body of the vehicle. A needle-type compass can also be used to observe the pulsing magnetic field. ● **SEE FIGURES 12–35 AND 12–36.**

CIRCUIT TRACER An electronic tone generator tester can be used to locate a short-to-ground or an open circuit. Similar to test equipment used to test telephone and cable

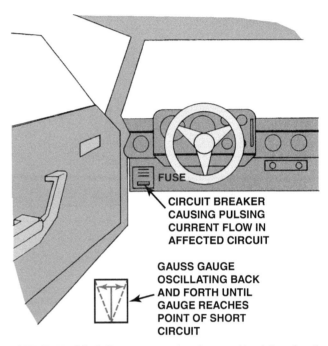

FIGURE 12–36 A Gauss gauge can be used to determine the location of a short circuit even behind a metal panel.

(a)

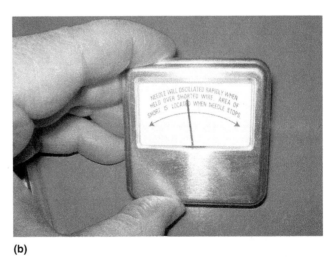

(b)

FIGURE 12–35 (a) After removing the blown fuse, a pulsing circuit breaker is connected to the terminals of the fuse. (b) The circuit breaker causes current to flow, then stop, then flow again, through the circuit up to the point of the short-to-ground. By observing the Gauss gauge, the location of the short is indicated near where the needle stops moving due to the magnetic field created by the flow of current through the wire.

television lines, a **tone generator tester** generates a tone that can be heard through a receiver (probe). ● **SEE FIGURE 12–37**.

The tone is generated as long as there is a continuous electrical path along the circuit. The signal stops if there is a short-to-ground or an open in the circuit. ● **SEE FIGURE 12–38**.

The windings in the solenoids and relays increase the strength of the signal in these locations.

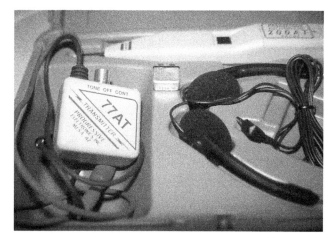

FIGURE 12–37 A tone generator–type tester used to locate open circuits and circuits that are shorted-to-ground. Included with this tester is a transmitter (tone generator), receiver probe, and headphones for use in noisy shops.

ELECTRICAL TROUBLE-SHOOTING GUIDE

When troubleshooting any electrical component, remember the following hints to identify the problem faster and more easily.

1. For a device to work, it must have two things: power and ground. Often more than one circuit shares a single ground connector.

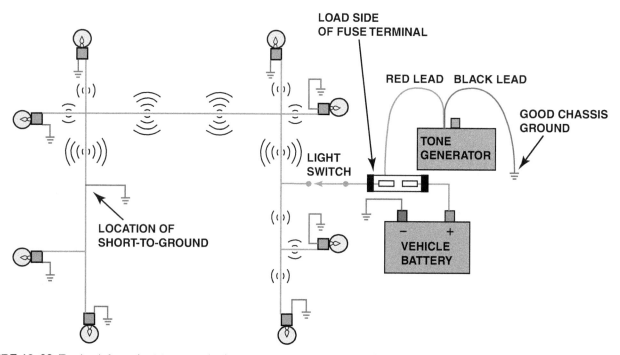

FIGURE 12–38 To check for a short-to-ground using a tone generator, connect the black transmitter lead to a good chassis ground and the red lead to the load side of the fuse terminal. Turn the transmitter on and check for tone signal with the receiver. Using a wiring diagram, follow the strongest signal to the location of the short-to-ground. There is no signal beyond the fault, either a short-to-ground, as shown, or an open circuit.

2. If there is no power to a device, an open power side (blown fuse, etc.) is indicated. Often more than one circuit is being protected by each fuse.

3. If there is power on both sides of a device, an open ground is indicated.

4. If a fuse blows immediately, a grounded power-side wire is indicated.

5. Most electrical faults result from heat or movement.

6. Most noncomputer–controlled devices operate by opening and closing the power side of the circuit (power-side switch).

7. Most computer-controlled devices operate by opening and closing the ground side of the circuit (ground-side switch).

STEP-BY-STEP TROUBLESHOOTING PROCEDURE

Knowing what should be done and when it should be done is a major concern for many technicians trying to repair an electrical problem. The following field-tested procedure provides a step-by-step guide for troubleshooting an electrical fault.

STEP 1 Determine the customer concern (complaint) and get as much information as possible from the customer or service advisor.

    a. When did the problem start?

    b. Under what conditions does the problem occur?

    c. Have there been any recent previous repairs to the vehicle that could have created the problem?

 TECH TIP

Wiggle Test

Intermittent electrical problems are common, yet difficult to locate. To help locate these hard-to-find problems, try operating the circuit and start wiggling the wires and connections that control the circuit. If in doubt where the wiring goes, try moving all the wiring starting at the battery. Pay particular attention to wiring running near the battery or the windshield washer container. Corrosion can cause wiring to fail, and battery acid fumes and alcohol-based windshield washer fluid can start or contribute to the problem. If you notice any change in the operation of the device being tested while wiggling the wiring, look closer in the area you were wiggling until you locate and correct the actual problem.

 CASE STUDY

Shocking Experience

A customer complained that after driving for a while, he got a static shock whenever he grabbed the door handle when exiting the vehicle. The customer thought that there must be an electrical fault and that the shock was coming from the vehicle itself. In a way, the shock was caused by the vehicle, but it was not a fault. The service technician sprayed the cloth seats with an antistatic spray and the problem did not reoccur. Obviously, a static charge was being created by the movement of the driver's clothing on the seats and then discharged when the driver touched the metal door handle. ● **SEE FIGURE 12–39**.

Summary:

▪ **Complaint**–Vehicle owner complained that he got shocked when the door handle was touched.

▪ **Cause**–Static electricity was found to be the cause, not a fault with the vehicle.

▪ **Correction**–The seats and carpet were sprayed with an antistatic spray and this corrected the concern.

STEP 2 Verify the customer's concern by actually observing the fault.

STEP 3 Perform a thorough visual inspection and be sure to check everything that does and does not work.

STEP 4 Check for technical service bulletins (TSBs).

FIGURE 12–39 Antistatic spray can be used by customers to prevent being shocked when they touch a metal object like the door handle.

STEP 5 Locate the wiring schematic for the circuit being diagnosed.

STEP 6 Check the factory service information and follow the troubleshooting procedure.

    a. Determine how the circuit works.

    b. Determine which part of the circuit is good, based on what works and what does not work.

    c. Isolate the problem area.

NOTE: Split the circuit in half to help isolate the problem and start at the relay (if the circuit has a relay).

STEP 7 Determine the root cause and repair the vehicle.

STEP 8 Verify the repair and complete the work order by listing the three Cs (complaint, cause, and correction).

SUMMARY

1. Most wiring diagrams include the wire color, circuit number, and wire gauge.

2. The number used to identify connectors, grounds, and splices usually indicates where they are located in the vehicle.

3. All switches and relays on a schematic are shown in their normal position either normally closed (N.C.) or normally open (N.O.).

4. A typical relay uses a small current through a coil (terminals 85 and 86) to operate the higher current part (terminals 30 and 87).

5. A short-to-voltage affects the power side of the circuit and usually involves more than one circuit.

6. A short-to-ground usually causes the fuse to blow and usually affects only one circuit.

7. Most electrical faults are a result of heat or movement.

REVIEW QUESTIONS

1. What do the circuit numbers shown on schematics usually mean?

2. What do the terminal numbers on an ISO relay mean?

3. What is used to control voltage spikes inside a relay?

4. How can a tone generator be used to locate a short circuit?

5. What is the difference between a relay and a solenoid?

CHAPTER QUIZ

1. On a wiring diagram, S110 with a "0.8 BRN/BLK" means _____.

    a. circuit #.8, spliced under the hood

    b. a connector with 0.8 mm^2 wire

    c. a splice of a brown with black stripe, wire size being 0.8 mm^2 (18-gauge AWG)

    d. both a and b

2. Where is connector C250?

    a. Under the hood

    b. Under the dash

    c. In the passenger compartment

    d. In the trunk

3. All switches illustrated in schematics are _____.

    a. shown in their normal position

    b. always shown in their on position

    c. always shown in their off position

    d. shown in their on position except for lighting switches

4. When testing a relay using an ohmmeter, which two terminals should be touched to measure the coil resistance?

    a. 87 and 30   **c.** 87a and 87

    b. 86 and 85   **d.** 86 and 87

5. Technician A says that a good relay should measure between 60 and 100 ohms across the coil terminals. Technician B says that OL should be displayed on an ohmmeter when touching terminals 30 and 87. Which technician is correct?

    a. Technician A only

    b. Technician B only

    c. Both Technicians A and B

    d. Neither Technician A nor B

6. Which relay terminal is the normally closed (N.C.) terminal?

    a. 30   **c.** 87

    b. 85   **d.** 87a

7. Technician A says that there is often more than one circuit being protected by each fuse. Technician B says that more than one circuit often shares a single ground connector. Which technician is correct?

    a. Technician A only

    b. Technician B only

    c. Both Technicians A and B

    d. Neither Technician A nor B

8. Two technicians are discussing finding a short-to-ground using a test light. Technician A says that the test light, connected in place of the fuse, lights when the circuit that has the short is disconnected. Technician B says that the test light should be connected to the positive (+) and negative (−) terminals of the battery during this test. Which technician is correct?
   a. Technician A only
   b. Technician B only
   c. Both Technicians A and B
   d. Neither Technician A nor B

9. A short circuit can be located using a _____.
   a. test light
   b. gauss gauge
   c. tone generator
   d. Any of the above

10. For an electrical device to operate, it must have _____.
   a. power and a ground
   b. a switch and a fuse
   c. a ground and fusible link
   d. a relay to transfer the current to the device

chapter 13

CAPACITANCE AND CAPACITORS

LEARNING OBJECTIVES:

After studying this chapter, the reader should be able to:

Explain capacitance and the construction and operation of capacitors, and factors of capacitance.

Explain the uses of capacitors and discuss capacitors in series and parallel circuits.

This chapter will help you prepare for the ASE Electrical/Electronic Systems (A6) certification test content area "A" (General Electrical/Electronic System Diagnosis).

KEY TERMS: Capacitance 152 • Condenser 152 • Dielectric 152 • Farads 155 • Leyden jar 152

CAPACITANCE

DEFINITION **Capacitance** is the ability of an object or surface to store an electrical charge. Around 1745, Ewald Christian von Kliest and Pieter van Musschenbroek independently discovered capacitance in an electric circuit. While engaged in separate studies of electrostatics, they discovered that an electric charge could be stored for a period of time. They used a device, now called a **Leyden jar,** for their experimentation, which consisted of a glass jar filled with water, with a nail piercing the stopper and dipping into the water. ● **SEE FIGURE 13–1**.

The two scientists connected the nail to an electrostatic charge. After disconnecting the nail from the source of the charge, they felt a shock by touching the nail, demonstrating that the device had stored the charge.

In 1747, John Bevis lined both the inside and outside of the jar with foil. This created a capacitor with two conductors (the inside and outside metal foil layers) equally separated by the insulating glass. The Leyden jar was also used by Benjamin Franklin to store the charge from lightning, as well as in other experiments. The natural phenomenon of lightning includes capacitance, because huge electrical fields develop between cloud layers or between clouds and the earth prior to a lightning strike.

NOTE: Capacitors are also called **condensers. This term developed because electric charges collect, or condense, on the plates of a capacitor, much like water vapor collects and condenses on a cold bottle or glass.**

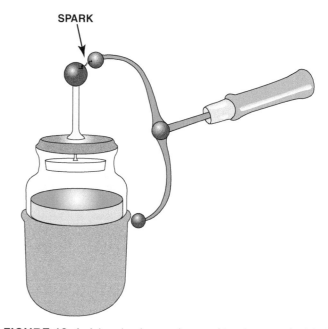

SPARK

FIGURE 13–1 A Leyden jar can be used to store an electrical charge.

CAPACITOR CONSTRUCTION AND OPERATION

CONSTRUCTION A capacitor (also called a condenser) consists of two conductive plates with an insulating material between them. The insulating material is commonly called a **dielectric.** This substance is a poor conductor of electricity and can include air, mica, ceramic, glass, paper, plastic, or any similar nonconductive material. The dielectric constant is the relative strength of a material against the flow of electrical current. The higher the number is, the better are the insulating properties. ● **SEE CHART 13–1.**

OPERATION When a capacitor is placed in a closed circuit, the voltage source (battery) forces electrons around the circuit. Because electrons cannot flow through the dielectric of the capacitor, excess electrons collect on what becomes the negatively charged plate. At the same time, the other plate loses electrons and, therefore, becomes positively charged. ● **SEE FIGURE 13–2.**

Current continues until the voltage charge across the capacitor plates becomes the same as the source voltage. At that time, the negative plate of the capacitor and the negative terminal of the battery are at the same negative potential. ● **SEE FIGURE 13–3.**

The positive plate of the capacitor and the positive terminal of the battery are also at equal positive potentials. There is a voltage charge across the battery terminals and an equal voltage charge across the capacitor plates. The circuit is in balance, and there is no current. An electrostatic field now exists between the capacitor plates because of their opposite charges. It is this field that stores energy. In other words,

a charged capacitor is similar to a charged battery. ● **SEE FIGURE 13–4.**

If the circuit is opened, the capacitor holds its charge until it is connected into an external circuit through which it can discharge. When the charged capacitor is connected to an external circuit, it discharges. After discharging, both plates of the capacitor are neutral because all the energy from a circuit stored in a capacitor is returned when it is discharged. ● **SEE FIGURE 13–5.**

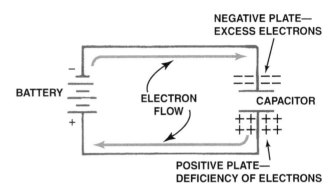

FIGURE 13–3 As the capacitor is charging, the battery forces electrons through the circuit.

MATERIAL	DIELECTRIC CONSTANT
Vacuum	1
Air	1.00059
Polystyrene	2.5
Paper	3.5
Mica	5.4
Flint glass	9.9
Methyl alcohol	35
Glycerin	56.2
Pure water	81

CHART 13–1

The higher the dielectric constant is, the better are the insulating properties between the plates of the capacitor.

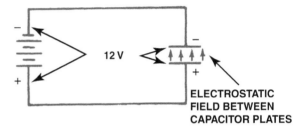

FIGURE 13–4 When the capacitor is charged, there is equal voltage across the capacitor and the battery. An electrostatic field exists between the capacitor plates. No current flows in the circuit.

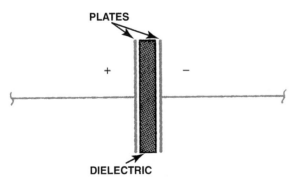

FIGURE 13–2 This simple capacitor is made of two plates separated by an insulating material, called a dielectric.

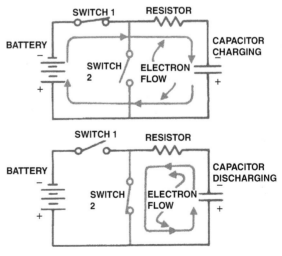

FIGURE 13–5 The capacitor is charged through one circuit (top) and discharged through another (bottom).

Theoretically, a capacitor holds its charge indefinitely. Actually, the charge slowly leaks off the capacitor through the dielectric. The better the dielectric, the longer the capacitor holds its charge. To avoid an electrical shock, any capacitor should be treated as if it were charged until it is proven to be discharged. To safely discharge a capacitor, use a test light with the clip attached to a good ground, and touch the pigtail or terminal with the point of the test light. ● **SEE FIGURE 13–6** for the symbol for capacitors as used in electrical schematics.

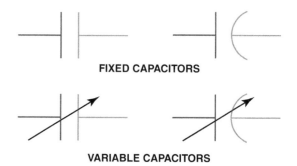

FIXED CAPACITORS

VARIABLE CAPACITORS

FIGURE 13–6 Capacitor symbols as shown in electrical diagrams. The negative plate is often shown curved.

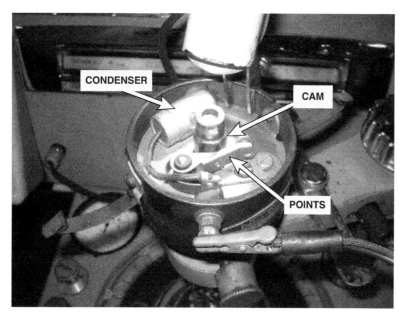

FIGURE 13–7 A point-type distributor shown with the condenser from an old vehicle being tested on a distributor machine.

? **FREQUENTLY ASKED QUESTION**

What Are "Points and Condenser"?

Points and condenser are used in point-type ignition systems.

Points. A set of points use one stationary contact and
a movable contact that is opened by a cam lobe inside the ignition distributor. When the points are closed, current flows through the primary windings of the ignition coil and creates a strong magnetic field. As the engine rotates, the distributor can open the contact points, which opens the circuit to the coil. The stored magnetic field in the coil collapses and generates a high-voltage arc from the secondary winding of the coil. It is this spark that is sent to the spark plugs that ignites the air-fuel mixture inside the engine.

Condenser. The condenser (capacitor) is attached to the points and the case of the condenser is grounded. When the points start to open, the charge built up in the primary winding of the coil likely starts to arc across the opening points. To prevent the points from arcing and to increase how rapidly the current is turned off, the condenser stores the current temporarily.

Points and condenser were used in vehicles and small gasoline engines until the mid-1970s. ● **SEE FIGURE 13–7**.

FACTORS OF CAPACITANCE

Capacitance is governed by three factors.

- The surface area of the plates
- The distance between the plates
- The dielectric material

The larger the surface area of the plates is, the greater the capacitance, because more electrons collect on a larger plate area than on a small one. The closer the plates are to each other, the greater the capacitance, because a stronger electrostatic field exists between charged bodies that are close together. The insulating qualities of the dielectric material also affect capacitance. The capacitance of a capacitor is higher if the dielectric is a very good insulator.

MEASUREMENT OF CAPACITANCE Capacitance is measured in **farads,** which is named after Michael Faraday (1791–1867), an English physicist. The symbol for farads is the letter F. If a charge of 1 coulomb is placed on the plates of a capacitor and the potential difference between them is 1 volt, the capacitance is defined to be 1 farad, or 1 F. One coulomb is equal to the charge of 6.25×10^{18} electrons. One farad is an extremely large quantity of capacitance. Microfarads (0.000001 farad), or µF, are more commonly used.

The capacitance of a capacitor is proportional to the quantity of charge that can be stored in it for each volt difference in potential.

USES FOR CAPACITORS

SPIKE SUPPRESSION A capacitor can be used in parallel to a coil to reduce the resulting voltage spike that occurs when the circuit is opened. The energy stored to the magnetic field of the coil is rapidly released at this time. The capacitor acts to absorb the high voltage produced and stop it from interfering with other electronic devices, such as automotive radio and video equipment.

NOISE FILTERING Interference in a sound system or radio is usually due to alternating current (AC) voltage created somewhere in the vehicle, such as in the alternator. A capacitor does the following:

- Blocks the flow of direct current (DC)
- Allows AC to pass

By connecting a capacitor (condenser) to the power lead of the radio or sound system amplifier, the AC voltage passes through the capacitor to the ground, where the other end of the capacitor is connected. Therefore, the capacitor provides a path for the AC without affecting the DC power circuit. ● **SEE FIGURE 13–8.**

Because a capacitor stores a voltage charge, it opposes or slows any voltage change in a circuit. Therefore, capacitors are often used as voltage "shock absorbers." You sometimes find a capacitor attached to one terminal of an ignition coil. In this application, the capacitor absorbs and dampens changes in ignition voltage that interfere with radio reception.

SUPPLEMENTAL POWER SOURCE A capacitor can be used to supply electrical power for short bursts in an audio system to help drive the speakers. Woofers and subwoofers require a lot of electrical current that often cannot be delivered by the amplifier itself. ● **SEE FIGURE 13–9.**

TIMER CIRCUITS Capacitors are used in electronic circuits as part of a timer, to control window defoggers, interior lighting, pulse wipers, and automatic headlights. The capacitors store energy and are allowed to discharge through a resistance load. The greater the capacity of the capacitor and the higher the resistance load, the longer the time it takes for the capacitor to discharge.

COMPUTER MEMORY In most cases, the main memory of a computer is a high-speed random-access memory (RAM). One type of main memory called dynamic random-access

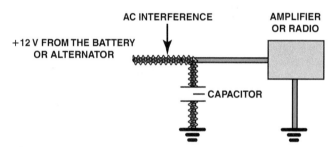

FIGURE 13–8 A capacitor blocks direct current (DC), but passes alternating current (AC). A capacitor makes a very good noise suppressor because most of the interference is AC, and the capacitor conducts this AC to ground before it can reach the radio or amplifier.

FIGURE 13–9 A 1 farad capacitor used to boost the power to large speakers.

memory (DRAM) is the most commonly used type of RAM. A single memory chip is made up of several million memory cells. In a DRAM chip, each memory cell consists of a capacitor. When a capacitor is electrically charged, it is said to store the binary digit 1, and when discharged, it represents 0.

CONDENSER MICROPHONES A microphone converts sound waves into an electric signal. All microphones have a diaphragm that vibrates as sound waves strike. The vibrating diaphragm in turn causes an electrical component to create an output flow of current at a frequency proportional to the sound waves. A condenser microphone uses a capacitor for this purpose.

In a condenser microphone, the diaphragm is the negatively charged plate of a charged capacitor. When a sound wave compresses the diaphragm, the diaphragm is moved closer to the positive plate. Decreasing the distance between the plates increases the electrostatic attraction between them, which results in a flow of current to the negative plate. As the diaphragm moves out in response to sound waves, it also moves further from the positive plate. Increasing the distance between the plates decreases the electrostatic attraction between them. This results in a flow of current back to the positive plate. These alternating flows of current provide weak electronic signals that travel to an amplifier and then to a loudspeaker.

CAPACITORS IN CIRCUITS

CAPACITORS IN PARALLEL CIRCUITS Capacitance can be increased in a circuit by connecting capacitors in parallel. For example, if a greater boost is needed for a sound system, then additional capacitors should be connected in parallel because their value adds together. ● SEE FIGURE 13–10.

We know that capacitance of a capacitor can be increased by increasing the size of its plates. Connecting two or more capacitors in parallel in effect increases plate size. Increasing plate area makes it possible to store more charge, and therefore, creates greater capacitance. To determine total capacitance of several parallel capacitors, simply add up their individual values. The following is the formula for

calculating total capacitance in a circuit containing capacitors in parallel.

$$C_T = C_1 + C_2 + C_3 \ldots$$

For example, 220 µF + 220 µF = 400 µF when connected in parallel.

CAPACITORS IN SERIES CIRCUITS Capacitance in a circuit can be decreased by placing capacitors in series, as shown in ● **FIGURE 13–11**.

We know that capacitance of a capacitor can be decreased by placing the plates further apart. Connecting two or more capacitors in series in effect increases the distance between the plates and thickness of the dielectric, decreasing the amount of capacitance.

Following is the formula for calculating total capacitance in a circuit containing two capacitors in series.

$$C_T = \frac{C_1 \times C_2}{C_1 + C_2}$$

For example, $\dfrac{220\ \mu F \times 220\ \mu F}{220\ \mu F + 220\ \mu F} = \dfrac{48,400}{440} = 110\ \mu F$

NOTE: Capacitors are often used to reduce radio interference or to improve the performance of a high-power sound system. Additional capacitance can, therefore, be added by attaching another capacitor in parallel.

SUPPRESSION CAPACITORS Capacitors are installed across many circuits and switching points to absorb voltage fluctuations. Among other applications, they are used across the following:

- The primary circuit of some electronic ignition modules
- The output terminal of most alternators
- The armature circuit of some electric motors

Radio choke coils reduce current fluctuations resulting from self-induction. They are often combined with capacitors to act as electromagnetic interference (EMI) filter circuits for windshield wiper and electric fuel pump motors. Filters also may be incorporated in wiring connectors.

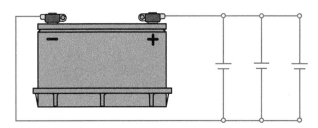

FIGURE 13–10 Capacitors in parallel effectively increase the capacitance.

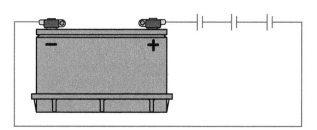

FIGURE 13–11 Capacitors in series decrease the capacitance.

SUMMARY

1. Capacitors (condensers) are used in numerous automotive applications.
2. Capacitors can block direct current and pass alternating current.
3. Capacitors are used to control radio-frequency interference and are installed in various electronic circuits to control unwanted noise.
4. Capacitors connected in series reduce the capacitance, whereas if connected in parallel increase the capacitance.

REVIEW QUESTIONS

1. How does a capacitor store an electrical charge?
2. How should two capacitors be electrically connected if greater capacitance is needed?
3. Where can a capacitor be used as a power source?
4. How can a capacitor be used as a noise filter?
5. Why is a large capacitor used in some high-powered sound systems?

CHAPTER QUIZ

1. A capacitor _____.
   a. stores electrons
   b. passes AC
   c. blocks DC
   d. All of the above

2. Capacitors are often used as "suppression capacitors." What does a capacitor suppress?
   a. Excessive current
   b. Voltage fluctuations
   c. Resistance
   d. Noise

3. Capacitors are commonly used as a _____.
   a. voltage supply
   b. timer
   c. noise filter
   d. All of the above

4. A charged capacitor acts like a _____.
   a. switch
   b. battery
   c. resistor
   d. coil

5. The unit of measurement for capacitor rating is the _____.
   a. ohm
   b. volt
   c. farad
   d. ampere

6. Two technicians are discussing the operation of a capacitor. Technician A says that a capacitor can create electricity. Technician B says that a capacitor can store electricity. Which technician is correct?
   a. Technician A only
   b. Technician B only
   c. Both Technicians A and B
   d. Neither Technician A nor B

7. Capacitors block the flow of _____ current but allow _____ current to pass.
   a. strong; weak
   b. AC; DC
   c. DC; AC
   d. weak; strong

8. To increase the capacity, what could be done?
   a. Connect another capacitor in series
   b. Connect another capacitor in parallel
   c. Add a resistor between two capacitors
   d. Both a and b

9. A capacitor can be used in what components?
   a. Microphone
   b. Radio
   c. Speaker
   d. All of the above

10. A capacitor used for spike protection is normally placed in _____ to the load or circuit.
    a. series
    b. parallel
    c. either series or parallel
    d. parallel with a resistor in series

chapter 14

MAGNETISM AND ELECTROMAGNETISM

LEARNING OBJECTIVES

After studying this chapter, the reader should be able to:

Define magnetism and explain the concepts of magnetic induction, permeability, and reluctance.

Explain how an electromagnet works.

Explain how electromagnetism is used in relays and solenoids.

Explain how magnetism and voltage are related.

Describe how an ignition coil works.

Describe ways to reduce electromagnetic interference.

This chapter will help you prepare for the ASE Electrical/ Electronic Systems (A6) certification test content area "A" (General Electrical/Electronic System Diagnosis).

KEY TERMS Ampere-turns 162 • Counter electromotive force (CEMF) 165 • Electromagnetic interference (EMI) 168 • Flux density 159 • Flux lines 159 • Ignition control module (ICM) 167 • Left-hand rule 161 • Lenz's law 165 • Magnetic flux 159 • Magnetic induction 159 • Magnetism 158 • Mutual induction 165 • Permeability 159 • Pole 159 • Relay 162 • Reluctance 160 • Residual magnetism 159 • Turns ratio 167

FUNDAMENTALS OF MAGNETISM

DEFINITION **Magnetism** is a form of energy that is caused by the motion of electrons in some materials. It is recognized by the attraction it exerts on other materials. Like electricity, magnetism cannot be seen. It can be explained in theory, however, because it is possible to see the results of magnetism and recognize the actions that it causes. Magnetite is the most naturally occurring magnet. Naturally magnetized pieces of magnetite, called *lodestone*, attract and hold small pieces of iron. ● **SEE FIGURE 14–1**.

Many other materials can be artificially magnetized to some degree, depending on their atomic structure. Soft iron is

---

TECH TIP

A Cracked Magnet Becomes Two Magnets

Magnets are commonly used in vehicle crankshaft, camshaft, and wheel speed sensors. If a magnet is struck and cracks or breaks, the result is two smaller-strength magnets. Because the strength of the magnetic field is reduced, the sensor output voltage is also reduced. A typical problem occurs when a magnetic crankshaft sensor becomes cracked, resulting in a no-start condition. Sometimes the cracked sensor works well enough to start an engine that is cranking at normal speeds, but does not work when the engine is cold. ● **SEE FIGURE 14–2**.

FIGURE 14–1 A freely suspended natural magnet (lodestone) points toward the magnetic north pole.

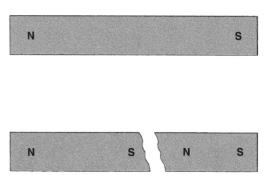

FIGURE 14–2 If a magnet breaks or is cracked, it becomes two weaker magnets.

very easy to magnetize, whereas some materials, such as aluminum, glass, wood, and plastic, cannot be magnetized at all.

LINES OF FORCE   The lines that create a field of force around a magnet are believed to be caused by the way groups of atoms are aligned in the magnetic material. In a bar magnet, the lines are concentrated at both ends of the bar and form closed, parallel loops in three dimensions around the magnet. Force does not flow along these lines the way electrical current flows, but the lines *do* have direction. They come out of the north end, or **pole**, of the magnet and enter at the other end. ● **SEE FIGURE 14–3**.

The opposite ends of a magnet are called its north and south poles. In reality, they should be called the "north-seeking" and "south-seeking" poles, because they seek the earth's North Pole and South Pole, respectively.

The more lines of force that are present, the stronger the magnet becomes. The magnetic lines of force, also called **magnetic flux** or **flux lines**, form a magnetic field. The terms *magnetic field*, *lines of force*, *flux*, and *flux lines* are used interchangeably.

Flux density refers to the number of flux lines per unit area. A magnetic field can be measured using a Gauss gauge, named for German scientist Johann Carl Friedrick Gauss (1777–1855).

Magnetic lines of force can be seen by spreading fine iron filings or dust on a piece of paper laid on top of a magnet. A magnetic field can also be observed by using a compass. A compass is simply a thin magnet or magnetized iron needle balanced on a pivot. The needle rotates to point toward the opposite pole of a magnet. The needle can be very sensitive to small magnetic fields. Because it is a small magnet, a compass usually has one north end (marked N) and one south end (marked S). ● **SEE FIGURE 14–4**.

MAGNETIC INDUCTION   If a piece of iron or steel is placed in a magnetic field, it also becomes magnetized. This process of creating a magnet by using a magnetic field is called **magnetic induction.**

If the metal is then removed from the magnetic field, and it retains some magnetism, this is called **residual magnetism.**

ATTRACTING OR REPELLING   The poles of a magnet are called north (N) and south (S) because when a magnet is suspended freely, the poles tend to point toward the earth's North Pole and South Pole. Magnetic flux lines exit from the north pole and bend around to enter the south pole. An equal number of lines exit and enter, so magnetic force is equal at both poles of a magnet. Flux lines are concentrated at the poles and, therefore, magnetic force (flux density) is stronger at the ends.

Magnetic poles behave like positively and negatively charged particles. When unlike poles are placed close together, the lines exit from one magnet and enter the other. The two magnets are pulled together by flux lines. If like poles are placed close together, the curving flux lines meet head-on, forcing the magnets apart. Therefore, like poles of a magnet repel and unlike poles attract. ● **SEE FIGURE 14–5**.

PERMEABILITY   Magnetic flux lines cannot be insulated. There is no known material through which magnetic force does not pass, if the force is strong enough. However, some materials allow the force to pass through more easily than others. This degree of passage is called **permeability.** Iron allows magnetic flux lines to pass through much more easily than air, so iron is highly permeable.

An example of this characteristic is the use of a reluctor wheel in magnetic-type camshaft position (CMP) and crankshaft position (CKP) sensors. The teeth on a reluctor cause the magnetic field to increase as each tooth gets closer to the sensor, and decrease as

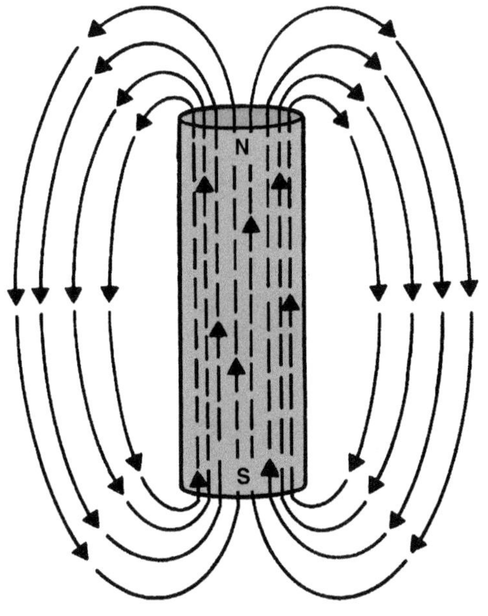

FIGURE 14–3 Magnetic lines of force leave the north pole and return to the south pole of a bar magnet.

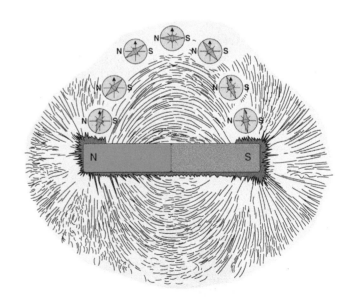

FIGURE 14–4 Iron filings and a compass can be used to observe the magnetic lines of force.

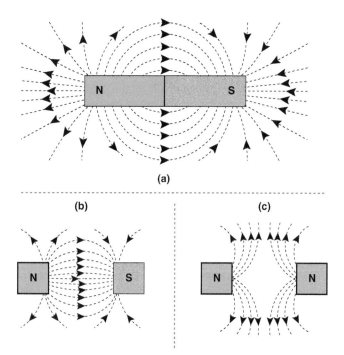

FIGURE 14–5 (a) Magnetic lines of force spread out from around an isolated magnet. (b) Opposite poles attract. (c) Similar poles repel.

TECH TIP

Magnetize a Steel Needle

A piece of steel can be magnetized by rubbing a magnet in one direction along the steel. This causes the atoms to line up in the steel, so it acts like a magnet. The steel often does not remain magnetized, whereas the true magnet is permanently magnetized.

When soft iron or steel is used, such as a paper clip, it loses its magnetism quickly. The atoms in a magnetized needle can be disturbed by heating it or by dropping the needle on a hard object, which causes the needle to lose its magnetism. Soft iron is used inside ignition coils because it does not keep its magnetism.

the tooth moves away, thus creating an AC voltage signal. ● **SEE FIGURE 14–6**.

RELUCTANCE Although there is no absolute insulation for magnetism, certain materials resist the passage of magnetic force. This can be compared to resistance without an electrical circuit. Air does not allow easy passage, so air has a high **reluctance.** Magnetic flux lines tend to concentrate in permeable materials and avoid materials with high reluctance. As with electricity, magnetic force follows the path of least resistance.

ELECTROMAGNETISM

DEFINITION Scientists did not discover that current-carrying conductors also are surrounded by a magnetic field until 1820. These fields may be made many times stronger than those surrounding conventional magnets. Also, the magnetic

FIGURE 14–6 A crankshaft position sensor and reluctor (notched wheel).

CRANKSHAFT POSITION (CKP) SENSOR

RELUCTOR

field strength around a conductor may be controlled by changing the current.

- As current increases, more flux lines are created and the magnetic field expands.
- As current decreases, the magnetic field contracts. The magnetic field collapses when the current is shut off.
- The interaction and relationship between magnetism and electricity is known as electromagnetism.

CREATING AN ELECTROMAGNET An easy way to create an electromagnet is to wrap a nail with 20 turns of insulated wire and connect the ends to the terminals of a 1.5 volt dry cell battery. When energized, the nail becomes a magnet and is able to pick up tacks or other small steel objects.

STRAIGHT CONDUCTOR The magnetic field surrounding a straight, current-carrying conductor consists of several concentric cylinders of flux that are the length of the wire. The amount of current flow (amperes) determines how many flux lines (cylinders) there are and how far out they extend from the surface of the wire. ● **SEE FIGURE 14–7.**

LEFT-HAND AND RIGHT-HAND RULES Magnetic flux cylinders have direction, just as the flux lines surrounding a bar magnet have direction. The **left-hand rule** is a simple way to determine this direction. When you grasp a conductor with your left hand so that your thumb points in the direction of electron flow (– to +) through the conductor, your fingers curl around the wire in the direction of the magnetic flux lines. ● **SEE FIGURE 14–8.**

Most automotive circuits use the conventional theory of current (+ to –) and, therefore, the right-hand rule is used to determine the direction of the magnetic flux lines. ● **SEE FIGURE 14–9.**

FIELD INTERACTION The cylinders of flux surrounding current-carrying conductors interact with other magnetic fields. In the following illustrations, the cross symbol (+) indicates current moving inward, or away from you. It represents the tail of an arrow. The dot symbol (●) represents an arrowhead and indicates current moving outward. If two conductors carry current in opposite directions, their magnetic fields also carry current in opposite directions (according to the left-hand rule). If they are placed side by side, then the opposing flux lines between the conductors create a strong magnetic field. Current-carrying conductors tend to move out of a strong field into a weak field, so the conductors move away from each other. ● **SEE FIGURE 14–10.**

If the two conductors carry current in the same direction, their fields are in the same direction. The flux lines between the two conductors cancel each other out, leaving a very weak field between them. The conductors are drawn into this weak field, and they tend to move toward each other.

MOTOR PRINCIPLE Electric motors, such as vehicle starter motors, use this magnetic field interaction to convert electrical energy into mechanical energy. If two conductors carrying current in opposite directions are placed between strong north and south poles, the magnetic field of the conductor interacts with the magnetic fields of the poles. The counterclockwise field of the top conductor adds to the fields of the poles and creates a strong field beneath the conductor. The conductor then tries to move up to get out of this strong field. The clockwise field of the lower conductor adds to the field of the poles and creates

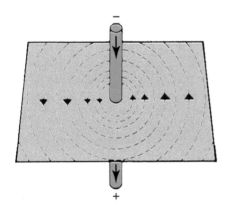

FIGURE 14–7 A magnetic field surrounds a straight, current-carrying conductor.

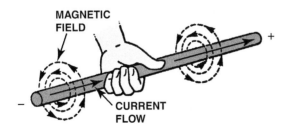

FIGURE 14–8 The left-hand rule for magnetic field direction is used with the electron flow theory.

FIGURE 14–9 The right-hand rule for magnetic field direction is used with the conventional theory of electron flow.

FIGURE 14–10 Conductors with opposing magnetic fields move apart into weaker fields.

Electricity and Magnetism

Electricity and magnetism are closely related because any electrical current flowing through a conductor creates a magnetic field. Any conductor moving through a magnetic field creates an electrical current. This relationship can be summarized as follows:

- Electricity creates magnetism.
- Magnetism creates electricity.

From a service technician's point of view, this relationship is important because wires carrying current should always be routed as the factory intended to avoid causing interference with another circuit or electronic component. This is especially important when installing or servicing spark plug wires, which carry high voltages and can cause high electromagnetic interference.

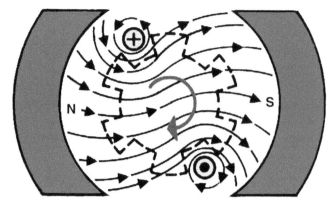

FIGURE 14–11 Electric motors use the interaction of magnetic fields to produce mechanical energy.

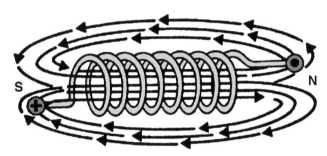

FIGURE 14–12 The magnetic lines of flux surrounding a coil look like those surrounding a bar magnet.

a strong field above the conductor. The conductor then tries to move down to get out of this strong field. These forces cause the center of the motor, where the conductors are mounted, to turn clockwise. ● **SEE FIGURE 14–11**.

COIL CONDUCTOR If several loops of wire are made into a coil, then the magnetic flux density is strengthened. Flux lines around a coil are the same as the flux lines around a bar magnet. ● **SEE FIGURE 14–12**.

They exit from the north pole and enter at the south pole. Use the left-hand rule to determine the north pole of a coil, as shown in ● **FIGURE 14–13**.

Grasp the coil with your left hand so that your fingers point in the direction of electron flow; your thumb points toward the north pole of the coil.

ELECTROMAGNETIC STRENGTH The magnetic field surrounding a current-carrying conductor can be strengthened (increased) in three ways.

- Place a soft iron core in the center of the coil.
- Increase the number of turns of wire in the coil.
- Increase the current flow through the coil windings.

Because soft iron is highly permeable, magnetic flux lines pass through it easily. If a piece of soft iron is placed inside a coiled conductor, the flux lines concentrate in the iron core, rather than pass through the air, which is less permeable. The concentration of force greatly increases the strength of the magnetic field inside the coil. Increasing the number of turns in a coil and/or increasing the current flow through the coil results in greater field strength and is proportional to the number of turns. The magnetic field strength is often expressed in the units called **ampere-turns.** Coils with an iron core are called electromagnets. ● **SEE FIGURE 14–14**.

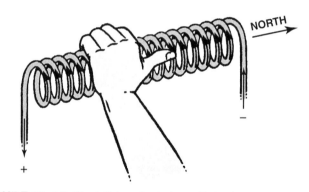

FIGURE 14–13 The left-hand rule for coils is shown.

USES OF ELECTROMAGNETISM

RELAYS As mentioned in the previous chapter, a **relay** is a control device that allows a small amount of current to control a large amount of current in another circuit. A simple relay contains an electromagnetic coil in series with a battery and a switch. Near the electromagnet is a movable flat arm, called an *armature*, of some material that is attracted by a magnetic field. ● **SEE FIGURE 14–15**.

The armature pivots at one end and is held a small distance away from the electromagnet by a spring (or by the spring steel of the movable arm itself). A contact point, made of a good conductor, is attached to the free end of the armature. Another

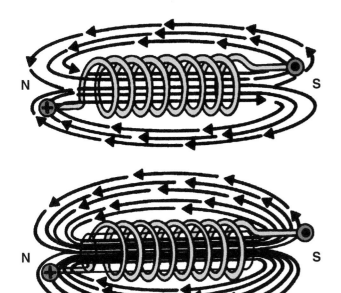

FIGURE 14–14 An iron core concentrates the magnetic lines of force surrounding a coil.

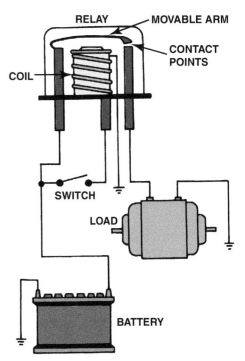

FIGURE 14–15 An electromagnetic switch that has a movable arm is referred to as a relay.

 FREQUENTLY ASKED QUESTION

Solenoid or Relay?

Often, either term is used to describe the same part in service information. ● **SEE CHART 14–1** for a summary of the differences.

contact point is fixed a small distance away. The two contact points are wired in series with an electrical load and the battery.

When the switch is closed, the following occurs.

1. Current travels from the battery through a coil, creating an electromagnet.

2. The magnetic field created by the current attracts the armature, pulling it down until the contact points close.

3. Closing the contacts allows current in the heavy current circuit from the battery to the load.

When the switch is open, the following occurs.

1. The electromagnet loses its magnetism when the current is shut off.

2. Spring pressure lifts the arm backup.

3. The heavy current circuit is broken by the opening of the contact points.

Relays may also be designed with normally closed contacts that open when current passes through the electromagnetic coil.

SOLENOID A solenoid is an example of an electromagnetic switch. A solenoid uses a movable core rather than a movable arm and is generally used in higher-amperage applications. A solenoid can be a separate unit or attached to a starter, such as a starter solenoid. ● **SEE FIGURE 14–16.**

	CONSTRUCTION	AMPERAGE RATING (AMPERE)	USES	CALLED IN SERVICE INFORMATION
Relay	Uses a movable arm Coil: 60–100 ohms requiring 0.12–0.20 ampere to energize	1–30	Lower current switching, lower cost, more commonly used	Electromagnetic switch or relay
Solenoid	Uses a movable core Coil(s): 0.2–0.6 ohm requiring 20–60 amperes to energize	30–400	Higher cost, used in starter motor circuits and other high-amperage applications	Solenoid, relay, or electromagnetic switch

CHART 14–1

Comparison between a relay and a solenoid.

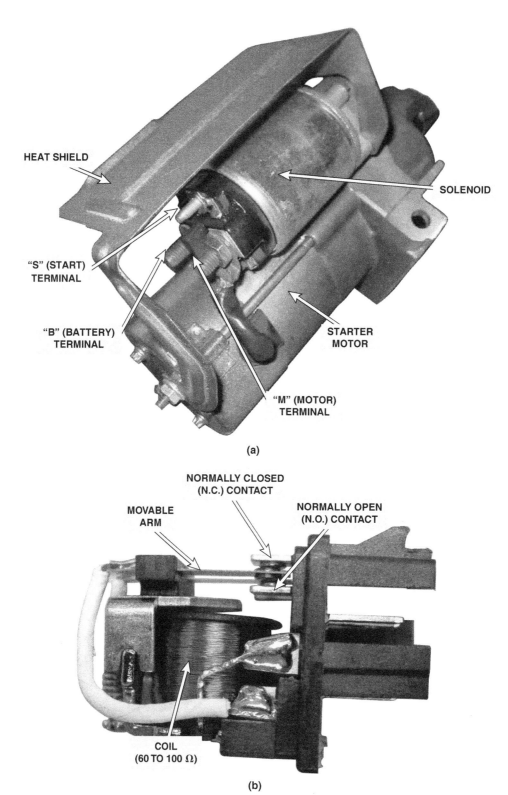

HEAT SHIELD

SOLENOID

"S" (START)
TERMINAL

"B" (BATTERY)
TERMINAL

STARTER
MOTOR

"M" (MOTOR)
TERMINAL

(a)

NORMALLY CLOSED
(N.C.) CONTACT

MOVABLE
ARM

NORMALLY OPEN
(N.O.) CONTACT

COIL
(60 TO 100 Ω)

(b)

FIGURE 14–16 (a) A starter with attached solenoid. All the current needed by the starter flows through the two large terminals of the solenoid and through the solenoid contacts inside. (b) A relay is designed to carry lower current, compared to a solenoid, and uses a movable arm.

ELECTROMAGNETIC INDUCTION

PRINCIPLES INVOLVED Electricity can be produced by using the relative movement of an electrical conductor and a magnetic field. The following three items are necessary to produce electricity (voltage) from magnetism.

1. Electrical conductor (usually a coil of wire)
2. Magnetic field
3. Movement of either the conductor or the magnetic field
   Therefore:
   - Electricity creates magnetism.
   - Magnetism can create electricity.

Magnetic flux lines create an electromotive force, or voltage, in a conductor if either the flux lines or the conductor is moving. This movement is called *relative motion*. This process is called induction, and the resulting electromotive force is called *induced voltage*. This creation of a voltage (electricity) in a conductor by a moving magnetic field is called electromagnetic induction. ● **SEE FIGURE 14–17**.

VOLTAGE INTENSITY Voltage is induced when a conductor cuts across magnetic flux lines. The amount of the voltage depends on the rate at which the flux lines are broken. The more flux lines that are broken per unit of time, the greater the induced voltage. If a single conductor breaks 1 million flux lines per second, 1 volt is induced.

There are four ways to increase induced voltage.

- Increase the strength of the magnetic field, so there are more flux lines.
- Increase the number of conductors that are breaking the flux lines.
- Increase the speed of the relative motion between the conductor and the flux lines so that more lines are broken per time unit.
- Increase the angle between the flux lines and the conductor to a maximum of 90 degrees. There is no voltage induced if the conductors move parallel to, and do not break, any flux lines.

Maximum voltage is induced if the conductors break flux lines at 90 degrees. Induced voltage varies proportionately at angles between 0 and 90 degrees. ● **SEE FIGURE 14–18**.

Voltage can be induced electromagnetically and can be measured. Induced voltage creates current. The direction of induced voltage (and the direction in which current moves) is called *polarity* and depends upon the direction of the flux lines, as well as the direction of relative motion.

LENZ'S LAW An induced current moves so that its magnetic field opposes the motion that induced the current. This principle is called **Lenz's law.** The relative motion of a conductor and a magnetic field is opposed by the magnetic field of the current it has induced.

SELF-INDUCTION When current begins to flow in a coil, the flux lines expand as the magnetic field forms and strengthens. As current increases, the flux lines continue to expand, cutting across the wires of the coil and actually inducing another voltage within the same coil. Following Lenz's law, this self-induced voltage tends to *oppose* the current that produces it. If the current continues to increase, the second voltage opposes the increase. When the current stabilizes, the counter voltage is no longer induced because there are no more expanding flux lines (no relative motion). When current to the coil is shut off, the collapsing magnetic flux lines self-induce a voltage in the coil that tries to maintain the original current. The self-induced voltage *opposes* and *slows* the *decrease* in the original current. The self-induced voltage that opposes changes in current flow is an inductor called **counter electromotive force (CEMF).**

MUTUAL INDUCTION When two coils are close together, energy may be transferred from one to the other by magnetic coupling, called mutual induction. **Mutual induction** means

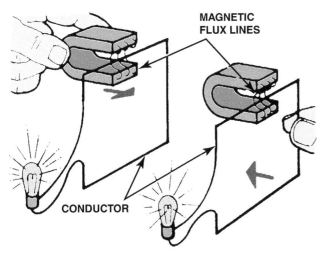

FIGURE 14–17 Voltage can be induced by the relative motion between a conductor and magnetic lines of force.

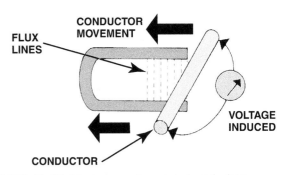

FIGURE 14–18 Maximum voltage is induced when conductors cut across the magnetic lines of force (flux lines) at a 90 degree angle.

that the expansion or collapse of the magnetic field around one coil induces a voltage in the second coil.

IGNITION COILS

IGNITION COIL WINDINGS Ignition coils use two windings and are wound on the same iron core.

- One coil winding is connected to a battery through a switch and is called the *primary winding*.
- The other coil winding is connected to an external circuit and is called the *secondary winding*.

When the switch is open, there is no current in the primary winding. There is no magnetic field and, therefore, no voltage in the secondary winding. When the switch is closed, current is introduced and a magnetic field builds up around both windings. The primary winding thus changes electrical energy from the battery into magnetic energy of the expanding field. As the field expands, it cuts across the secondary winding and induces a voltage in it. A meter connected to the secondary circuit shows current. ● SEE FIGURE 14–19.

When the magnetic field has expanded to its full strength, it remains steady as long as the same amount of current exists. The flux lines have stopped their cutting action. There is no relative motion and no voltage in the secondary winding, as shown on the meter.

When the switch is opened, primary current stops and the field collapses. As it does, flux lines cut across the secondary winding, but in the opposite direction. This induces a secondary voltage with current in the opposite direction, as shown on the meter.

Mutual induction is used in ignition coils. In an ignition coil, low-voltage primary current induces a very high secondary voltage because of the different number of turns in the primary and secondary windings. Because the voltage is increased, an ignition coil is also called a *step-up transformer*.

- **Electrically connected windings.** Many ignition coils contain two separate, but electrically connected, windings of copper wire. This type of coil is called a "married" type and is used in older distributor-type ignition systems and in many coil-on-plug (COP) designs.
- **Electrically insulated windings.** Other coils are true transformers in which the primary and secondary windings are not electrically connected. This type of coil is often called a "divorced" type and is used in all waste-spark-type ignition systems.
  - ● SEE FIGURE 14–20.

IGNITION COIL CONSTRUCTION The center of an ignition coil contains a core of laminated soft iron (thin strips of soft iron). This core increases the magnetic strength of the coil. Surrounding the laminated core are approximately 20,000 turns of fine wire (approximately 42 gauge). These windings are called the secondary coil windings. Surrounding the

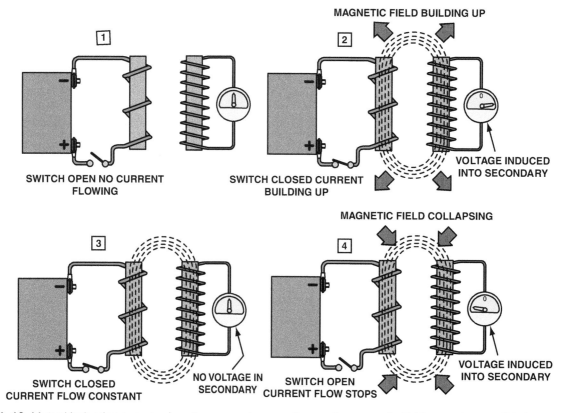

FIGURE 14–19 Mutual induction occurs when the expansion or collapse of a magnetic field around one coil induces a voltage in a second coil.

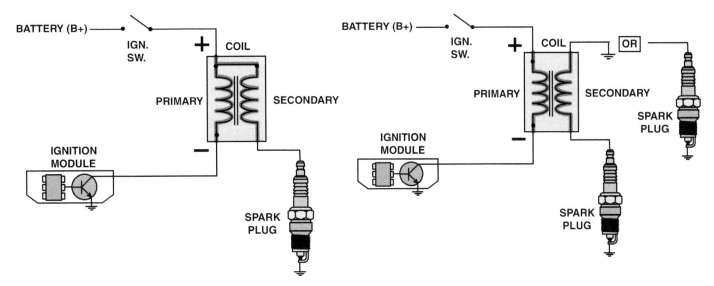

FIGURE 14–20 Some ignition coils are electrically connected, called "married" (left figure), whereas others use separated primary and secondary windings, called "divorced" (lower figure).

secondary windings are approximately 150 turns of heavy wire (approximately 21 gauge). These windings are called the primary coil windings. The secondary winding has about 100 times the number of turns of the primary winding, referred to as the **turns ratio** (approximately 100:1). In many coils, these windings are surrounded with a thin metal shield and insulating paper and placed into a metal container. The metal container and shield help retain the magnetic field produced in the coil windings. The primary and secondary windings produce heat because of the electrical resistance in the turns of wire. Many coils contain oil to help cool the ignition coil. Other coil designs include the following:

- **Air-cooled, epoxy-sealed E coil.** The *E coil* is so named because the laminated, soft iron core is E shaped, with the coil wire turns wrapped around the center "finger" of the E and the primary winding wrapped inside the secondary winding. ● **SEE FIGURE 14–21.**

- **Spool design.** Used mostly for coil-on-plug design, the coil windings are wrapped around a nylon or plastic spool or bobbin. ● **SEE FIGURE 14–22.**

IGNITION COIL OPERATION The negative terminal is attached to an **ignition control module (ICM, or igniter)**, which opens and closes the primary ignition circuit by opening or closing the ground return path of the circuit. When the ignition switch is on, voltage should be available at *both* the positive terminal and the negative terminal of the coil if the primary windings of the coil have continuity.

A spark is created by the following sequence of events.

- A magnetic field is created in the primary winding of the coil when there are 12 volts applied to the primary coil winding and the ignition control module grounds the other end on the coil.

FIGURE 14–21 A GM waste-spark ignition coil showing the section of laminations that is shaped like the letter *E*. These mild steel laminations improve the efficiency of the coil.

- When the ignition control module (or powertrain control module) opens the ground circuit, the stored magnetic field collapses and creates a high voltage (up to 40,000 volts or more) in the secondary winding.

- The high-voltage pulse then flows to the spark plug and creates a spark at the ground electrode inside the engine that ignites the air–fuel mixture inside the cylinder.

FIGURE 14–22 The coil-on-plug (COP) design typically uses a bobbin-type coil.

ELECTROMAGNETIC INTERFERENCE

DEFINITION Until the advent of onboard computers, **electromagnetic interference (EMI)** was not a source of real concern to automotive engineers. The problem was mainly one of *radio-frequency interference* (RFI), caused primarily by the use of secondary ignition cables. Using spark plug wires that contained a high-resistance, nonmetallic core made of carbon, linen, or fiberglass strands impregnated with graphite mostly solved RFI from the secondary ignition system. RFI is a part of electromagnetic interference, which deals with interference that affects radio reception. All electronic devices used in vehicles are affected by EMI/RFI.

HOW EMI IS CREATED Whenever there is current in a conductor, an electromagnetic field is created. When current stops and starts, as in a spark plug cable or a switch that opens and closes, the field strength changes. Each time this happens, it creates an electromagnetic signal wave. If it happens rapidly enough, the resulting high-frequency signal waves, or EMI, interfere with radio and television transmission or with other electronic systems, such as those under the hood. This is an undesirable side effect of the phenomenon of electromagnetism.

Static electric charges caused by friction of the tires with the road, or the friction of engine drive belts contacting their pulleys, also produce EMI. Drive axles, driveshafts, and clutch or brake-lining surfaces are other sources of static electric charges.

There are four ways of transmitting EMI, all of which can be found in a vehicle.

- Conductive coupling is actual physical contact through circuit conductors.
- Capacitive coupling is the transfer of energy from one circuit to another through an electrostatic field between two conductors.
- Inductive coupling is the transfer of energy from one circuit to another as the magnetic fields between two conductors form and collapse.
- Electromagnetic radiation is the transfer of energy by the use of radio waves from one circuit or component to another.

EMI SUPPRESSION DEVICES There are four general ways in which EMI is reduced.

- **Resistance suppression.** Adding resistance to a circuit to suppress RFI works only for high-voltage systems. This has been done by the use of resistance spark plug cables, resistor spark plugs, and the silicone grease used on the distributor cap and rotor of some electronic ignitions.

- **Suppression capacitors and coils.** Capacitors are installed across many circuits and switching points to absorb voltage fluctuations. Among other applications, they are used across the following:
  - The primary circuit of some electronic ignition modules
  - The output terminal of most alternators
  - The armature circuit of some electric motors

Coils reduce current fluctuations resulting from self-induction. They are often combined with capacitors to act as EMI filter circuits for windshield wiper and electric fuel pump motors. Filters also may be incorporated in wiring connectors.

- **Shielding.** The circuits of onboard computers are protected to some degree from external electromagnetic waves by their metal housings.

- **Ground wires or straps.** Ground wires or braided straps between the engine and chassis of an automobile help suppress EMI conduction and radiation by providing a low-resistance circuit ground path. Such suppression ground straps are often installed between rubber-mounted components and body parts. On some models, ground straps are installed between body parts, such as between the hood and a fender panel, where no electrical circuit exists. The strap has no other job than to suppress EMI. Without it, the sheet-metal body and hood could function as a large capacitor. The space between the fender and hood could form an electrostatic field and couple with the computer circuits in the wiring harness routed near the fender panel. ● **SEE FIGURE 14–23.**

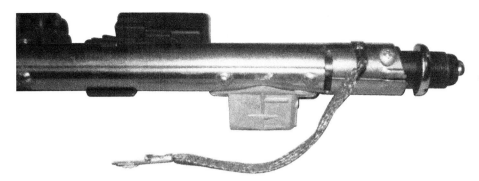

FIGURE 14–23 To help prevent underhood electromagnetic devices from interfering with the antenna input, it is important that all ground wires, including the one from this power antenna, be properly grounded.

SUMMARY

1. Most automotive electrical components use magnetism, the strength of which depends on both the amount of current (amperes) and the number of turns of wire of each electromagnet.
2. The strength of electromagnets is increased by using a soft iron core.
3. Voltage can be induced from one circuit to another.
4. Electricity creates magnetism and magnetism creates electricity.
5. Radio-frequency interference (RFI) is a part of electromagnetic interference (EMI).

REVIEW QUESTIONS

1. What is the relationship between electricity and magnetism?
2. What is the difference between mutual induction and self-induction?
3. What is the result if a magnet cracks?
4. How can EMI be reduced or controlled?
5. What is the difference between a "married" ignition coil and a "divorced" ignition coil?

CHAPTER QUIZ

1. Technician A says that magnetic lines of force can be seen by placing iron filings on a piece of paper and then holding them over a magnet. Technician B says that the effects of magnetic lines of force can be seen using a compass. Which technician is correct?
   a. Technician A only
   b. Technician B only
   c. Both Technicians A and B
   d. Neither Technician A nor B
2. Unlike magnetic poles _____, and like magnetic poles _____.
   a. repel; attract
   b. attract; repel
   c. repel; repel
   d. attract; attract
3. The conventional theory for current flow is being used to determine the direction of magnetic lines of force. Technician A says that the left-hand rule should be used. Technician B says that the right-hand rule should be used. Which technician is correct?
   a. Technician A only
   b. Technician B only
   c. Both Technicians A and B
   d. Neither Technician A nor B
4. Technician A says that a relay is an electromagnetic switch. Technician B says that a solenoid uses a movable core. Which technician is correct?
   a. Technician A only
   b. Technician B only
   c. Both Technicians A and B
   d. Neither Technician A nor B
5. Two technicians are discussing electromagnetic induction. Technician A says that the induced voltage can be increased if the speed is increased between the conductor and the magnetic lines of force. Technician B says that the induced voltage can be increased by increasing the strength of the magnetic field. Which technician is correct?
   a. Technician A only
   b. Technician B only
   c. Both Technicians A and B
   d. Neither Technician A nor B

6. An ignition coil operates using the principle(s) of _____.
   a. electromagnetic induction
   b. self-induction
   c. mutual induction
   d. all of the above

7. Electromagnetic interference can be reduced by using a _____.
   a. resistance
   b. capacitor
   c. coil
   d. any of the above

8. An ignition coil is an example of a _____.
   a. solenoid
   b. step-down transformer
   c. step-up transformer
   d. relay

9. Magnetic field strength is measured in _____.
   a. ampere-turns
   b. flux
   c. density
   d. coil strength

10. Two technicians are discussing ignition coils. Technician A says that some ignition coils have the primary and secondary windings electrically connected. Technician B says that some coils have totally separate primary and secondary windings that are not electrically connected. Which technician is correct?
    a. Technician A only
    b. Technician B only
    c. Both Technicians A and B
    d. Neither Technician A nor B

chapter 15

ELECTRONIC FUNDAMENTALS

LEARNING OBJECTIVES:

After studying this chapter, the reader should be able to:

Identify semiconductor components.

Describe how diodes and transistors work, and how to test them. Identify the causes of failure of electronic components. Explain how converters and inverters are used, and precautions for working with semiconductor circuits.

List ways to avoid electrostatic discharge.

This chapter will help you prepare for the ASE Electrical/ Electronic Systems (A6) certification test content area "A" (General Electrical/Electronic System Diagnosis).

KEY TERMS: Anode 173 • Base 179 • Bipolar transistor 179 • Burn in 174 • Cathode 173 • CHMSL 178 • Clamping diode 174 • Collector 179 • Darlington pair 180 • Despiking diode 174 • Diode 173 • Doping 171 • Dual inline pins (DIP) 181 • Emitter 179 • ESD 186 • FET 180 • Forward bias 173 • Germanium 171 • Heat sink 181 • Hole theory 172 • Impurities 171 • Integrated circuit (IC) 181 • Inverter 186 • Junction 173 • Light-emitting diode (LED) 176 • MOSFET 181 • NPN transistor 179 • NTC 178 • N-type material 171 • Op-amps 182 • Photodiodes 177 • Photons 177 • Photoresistor 177 • Phototransistor 181 • Peak inverse voltage (PIV) 176 • Peak reverse voltage (PRV) 176 • PNP transistor 179 • P-type material 172 • PWM 184 • Rectifier bridge 178 • Reverse bias 173 • SCR 178 • Semiconductors 171 • Silicon 171 • Spike protection resistor 175 • Suppression diode 174 • Thermistor 178 • Threshold voltage 180 • Transistor 179 • Zener diode 174

SEMICONDUCTORS

DEFINITION Semiconductors are neither conductors nor insulators. The flow of electrical current is caused by the movement of electrons in materials known as conductors, having *fewer* than four electrons in their atom's outer orbit. Insulators contain *more* than four electrons in their outer orbit and cannot conduct electricity because their atomic structure is stable (no free electrons).

Semiconductors are materials that contain exactly four electrons in the outer orbit of their atom structure and are, therefore, neither good conductors nor good insulators.

EXAMPLES OF SEMICONDUCTORS Two examples of semiconductor materials are **germanium** and **silicon**, which have exactly four electrons in their valance ring and no free electrons to provide current flow. However, both of these semiconductor materials can be made to conduct current if another material is added to provide the necessary conditions for electron movement.

CONSTRUCTION When another material is added to a semiconductor material in very small amounts, it is called

doping. The doping elements are called **impurities**; therefore, after their addition, the germanium and silicon are no longer considered *pure* elements. The material added to pure silicon or germanium to make it electrically conductive represents only one atom of impurity for every *100 million* atoms of the pure semiconductor material. The resulting atoms are still electrically *neutral*, because the number of electrons still equals the number of protons of the combined materials. These combined materials are classified into two groups depending on the number of electrons in the bonding between the two materials.

■ N-type materials

■ P-type materials

N-TYPE MATERIAL **N-type material** is silicon or germanium that is doped with an element such as *phosphorus*, *arsenic*, or *antimony*, each having five electrons in its outer orbit. These five electrons are combined with the four electrons of the silicon or germanium to total nine electrons. There is room for only eight electrons in the bonding between the semiconductor material and the doping material. This leaves extra electrons, and even though the material is still electrically neutral, these extra electrons tend to repel other electrons outside the material. ● **SEE FIGURE 15–1.**

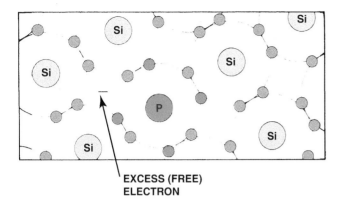

FIGURE 15–1 N-type material. Silicon (Si) doped with a material (such as phosphorus) with five electrons in the outer orbit results in an extra free electron.

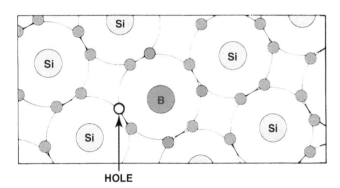

FIGURE 15–2 P-type material. Silicon (Si) doped with a material, such as boron (B), with three electrons in the outer orbit results in a hole capable of attracting an electron.

P-TYPE MATERIAL **P-type material** is produced by doping silicon or germanium with the element *boron* or the element *indium*. These impurities have only three electrons in their outer shell and, when combined with the semiconductor material, result in a material with seven electrons, one electron *less* than is required for atom bonding. This lack of one electron makes the material able to attract electrons, even though the material still has a neutral charge. This material tends to attract electrons to fill the holes for the missing eighth electron in the bonding of the materials. ● **SEE FIGURE 15–2**.

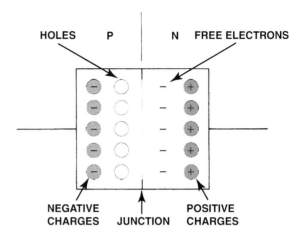

FIGURE 15–3 Unlike charges attract and the current carriers (electrons and holes) move toward the junction.

SUMMARY OF SEMICONDUCTORS

The following is a summary of semiconductor fundamentals.

1. The two types of semiconductor materials are P type and N type. N-type material contains extra electrons; P-type material contains holes due to missing electrons. The number of excess electrons in an N-type material must remain constant, and the number of holes in the P-type material must also remain constant. Because electrons are interchangeable, movement of electrons in or out of the material is possible to maintain a balanced material.

2. In P-type semiconductors, electrical conduction occurs mainly as a result of holes (absence of electrons). In N-type semiconductors, electrical conduction occurs mainly as a result of electrons (excess of electrons).

3. Hole movement results from the jumping of electrons into new positions.

4. Under the effect of a voltage applied to the semiconductor, electrons travel toward the positive terminal and holes move toward the negative terminal. The direction of hole current agrees with the conventional direction of current flow.

 FREQUENTLY ASKED QUESTION

What Is the Hole Theory?

Current flow is expressed as the movement of electrons from one atom to another. In semiconductor and electronic terms, the movement of electrons fills the holes of the P-type material. Therefore, as the holes are filled with electrons, the unfilled holes move opposite to the flow of the electrons. This concept of hole movement is called the **hole theory** of current flow. The holes move in the direction opposite to that of electron flow. For example, think of an egg carton, where if an egg is moved in one direction, the holes created move in the opposite direction. ● **SEE FIGURE 15–3**.

DIODES

CONSTRUCTION A **diode** is an electrical one-way check valve made by combining a P-type material and an N-type material. The word *diode* means "having two electrodes." Electrodes are electrical connections: The positive electrode is called the **anode**; the negative electrode is called the **cathode**. The point where the two types of materials join is called the **junction**. ● **SEE FIGURE 15–4**.

OPERATION The N-type material has one extra electron, which can flow into the P-type material. The P type requires electrons to fill its holes. If a battery's positive terminal (+) is connected to the diode's P-type material and negative (−) to the N-type material, the electrons that left the N-type material and flowed into the P-type material to fill the holes are quickly replaced by the electron flow from the battery. Current flows through a forward-bias diode for the following reasons.

■ Electrons move toward the holes (P-type material).

■ Holes move toward the electrons (N-type material).

As a result, current flows through the diode with low resistance. This condition is called **forward bias**.

If the battery connections are reversed and the positive side of the battery is connected to the N-type material, the electrons are pulled toward the battery, and away from the junction of the N-type and P-type materials. (Remember, unlike charges attract, whereas like charges repel.) Because electrical conduction requires the flow of electrons across the junction of the N-type and P-type materials, and because the battery connections are actually reversed, the diode offers very high resistance to current flow. This condition is called **reverse bias**. ● **SEE FIGURE 15–5**.

Therefore, diodes allow current flow only when current of the correct polarity is connected to the circuit.

■ Diodes are used in alternators to control current flow in one direction, which changes the AC voltage generated into DC voltage.

■ Diodes are also used in computer controls, relays, air-conditioning circuits, and many other circuits to prevent possible damage due to reverse current flows that may be generated within the circuit. ● **SEE FIGURE 15–6**.

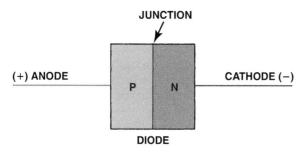

FIGURE 15–4 A diode is a component with P-type and N-type materials together. The negative electrode is called the cathode and the positive electrode is called the anode.

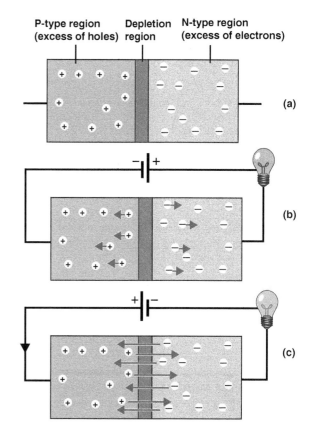

FIGURE 15–5 (a) A diode consist of P-type and N-type materials separated by a depletion region. (b) When connected to a voltage source in the reverse bias situation, the charge carriers are forced apart and no current flows across the depletion region. (c) When the diode is connected in the forward bias direction, the charge carriers are allowed to cross the depletion region and current can flow from the anode (+) to the cathode (−).

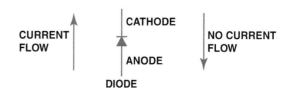

FIGURE 15–6 Diode symbol and electrode names. The stripe on one end of a diode represents the cathode end of the diode.

"Burn In" to Be Sure

A common term heard in the electronic and computer industry is **burn in**, which means to operate an electronic device, such as a computer, for a period from several hours to several days.

Most electronic devices fail in infancy, or during the first few hours of operation. This early failure occurs if there is a manufacturing defect, especially at the P-N junction of any semiconductor device. The junction usually fails after only a few operating cycles.

What does this information mean to the average person? When purchasing a personal or business computer, have the computer burned in before delivery. This step helps ensure that all of the circuits have survived infancy and that the chances of chip failure are greatly reduced. Purchasing sound or television equipment that has been on display may be a good value, because during its operation as a display model, the burn-in process has been completed. The automotive service technician should be aware that if a replacement electronic device fails shortly after installation, the problem may be a case of early electronic failure.

NOTE: Whenever there is a failure of a replacement part, the technician should always check for excessive voltage or heat to and around the problem component.

FIGURE 15–7 A zener diode blocks current flow until a certain voltage is reached, then it permits current to flow.

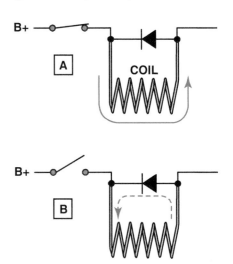

FIGURE 15–8 (a) Notice that when the coil is being energized, the diode is reverse biased and the current is blocked from passing through the diode. The current flows through the coil in the normal direction. (b) When the switch is opened, the magnetic field surrounding the coil collapses, producing a high-voltage surge in the reverse polarity of the applied voltage. This voltage surge forward biases the diode, and the surge is dissipated harmlessly back through the windings of the coil.

ZENER DIODES

CONSTRUCTION A **zener diode** is a specially constructed diode designed to operate with a reverse-bias current. Zener diodes were named in 1934 for their inventor, Clarence Melvin Zener, an American professor of physics.

OPERATION A zener diode acts as any diode in that it blocks reverse-bias current, but only up to a certain voltage. Above this certain voltage (called the *breakdown voltage* or the zener region), a zener diode conducts current in the opposite direction without damage to the diode. A zener diode is heavily doped, and the reverse-bias voltage does not harm the material. The voltage drop across a zener diode remains practically the same before and after the breakdown voltage, and this factor makes a zener diode perfect for voltage regulation. Zener diodes can be constructed for various breakdown voltages and can be used in a variety of automotive and electronic applications, especially for electronic voltage regulators used in the charging system. ● **SEE FIGURE 15–7**.

HIGH-VOLTAGE SPIKE PROTECTION

CLAMPING DIODES Diodes can be used as a high-voltage clamping device when the power (+) is connected to the cathode (−) of the diode. If a coil is pulsed on and off, a high-voltage spike is produced whenever the coil is turned off. To control and direct this possibly damaging high-voltage spike, a diode can be installed across the leads to the coil to redirect the high-voltage spike back through the coil windings to prevent possible damage to the rest of the vehicle's electrical or electronic circuits. A diode connected across the terminals of a coil to control voltage spikes is called a **clamping diode**. Clamping diodes can also be called **despiking** or **suppression diodes**. ● **SEE FIGURE 15–8**.

CLAMPING DIODE APPLICATION The diode is used to help prevent the high-voltage spike generated inside the A/C clutch coil from damaging delicate electronic circuits anywhere in the vehicle's electrical system. ● **SEE FIGURE 15–9**.

FIGURE 15–9 A diode connected to both terminals of the air-conditioning compressor clutch used to reduce the high-voltage spike that results when a coil (compressor clutch coil) is de-energized.

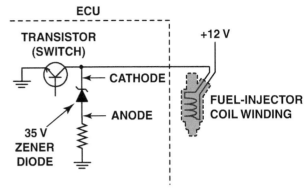

FIGURE 15–11 A zener diode is commonly used inside automotive computers to protect delicate electronic circuits from high-voltage spikes. A 35 volt zener diode conducts any voltage spike higher than 35 volts resulting from the discharge of the fuel-injector coil safely to ground through a current-limiting resistor in series with the zener diode.

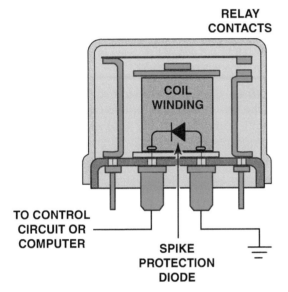

FIGURE 15–10 Spike protection diodes are commonly used in computer-controlled circuits to prevent damaging high-voltage surges that occur any time current flowing through a coil is stopped.

Because most automotive circuits eventually are electrically connected to each other in parallel, a high-voltage surge anywhere in the vehicle could damage electronic components in other circuits.

The circuits most likely to be affected by the high-voltage surge, if the diode fails, are the circuits controlling the operation of the A/C compressor clutch and any component that uses a coil, such as those of the blower motor and climate control units.

Many relays are equipped with a diode to prevent a voltage spike when the contact points open and the magnetic field in the coil winding collapses. ● **SEE FIGURE 15–10**.

DESPIKING ZENER DIODES Zener diodes can also be used to control high-voltage spikes and keep them from damaging delicate electronic circuits. Zener diodes are

most commonly used in electronic fuel-injection circuits that control the firing of the injectors. If clamping diodes were used in parallel with the injection coil, the resulting clamping action tends to delay the closing of the fuel-injector nozzle. A zener diode is commonly used to clamp only the higher voltage portion of the resulting voltage spike without affecting the operation of the injector. ● **SEE FIGURE 15–11**.

DESPIKING RESISTORS All coils must use some protection against high-voltage spikes that occur when the voltage is removed from any coil. Instead of a diode installed in parallel with the coil windings, a resistor can be used, called a **spike protection resistor**. ● **SEE FIGURE 15–12**.

Resistors are preferred instead of diodes for voltage spike protection for two reasons:

Reason 1	Coils usually fail when shorted, rather than open, as this shorted condition results in greater current flow in the circuit. A diode installed in the reverse-bias direction cannot control this extra current, whereas a resistor in parallel can help reduce potentially damaging current flow if the coil becomes shorted.
Reason 2	The protective diode can also fail, and diodes usually fail by shorting before they blow open. If a diode becomes shorted, excessive current can flow through the coil circuit, perhaps causing damage. A resistor usually fails open and, therefore, even in failures could not in itself cause a problem.

Resistors on coils are often used in relays and in climate-control circuit solenoids to control vacuum to the various air-management system doors, as well as other electronically controlled appliances.

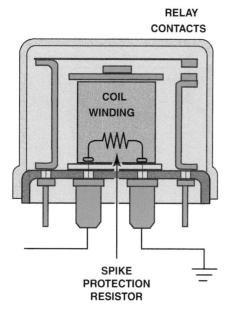

RELAY
CONTACTS

COIL
WINDING

SPIKE
PROTECTION
RESISTOR

FIGURE 15–12 A despiking resistor is used in many automotive applications to help prevent harmful high-voltage surges from being created when the magnetic field surrounding a coil collapses when the coil circuit is opened.

DIODE RATINGS

SPECIFICATIONS Most diodes are rated according to the following:

- Maximum current flow in the forward-bias direction. Diodes are sized and rated according to the amount of current they are designed to handle in the forward-bias direction. This rating is normally from 1 to 5 amperes for most automotive applications.

- This rating of resistance to reverse-bias voltage is called the **peak inverse voltage (PIV)** rating, or the **peak reverse voltage (PRV)** rating. It is important that the service technician specifies and uses only a replacement diode that has the same or a higher rating than specified by the vehicle manufacturer for both amperage and PIV rating. Typical 1 ampere diodes use an industry numbering code that indicates the PIV rating. For example:

  1N 4001-50 V PIV

  1N 4002-100 V PIV

  1N 4003-200 V PIV (most commonly used)

  1N 4004-400 V PIV

  1N 4005-600 V PIV

- "1N" means that the diode has one P-N junction. A higher-rating diode can be used with no problems (except for slightly higher cost, even though the highest rated diode generally costs less than $1). Never substitute a *lower*-rated diode than is specified.

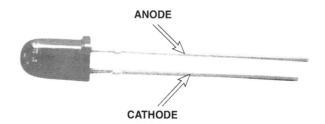

ANODE

CATHODE

FIGURE 15–13 A typical light-emitting diode (LED). This particular LED is designed with a built-in resistor so that 12 volt DC may be applied directly to the leads without an external resistor. Normally a 300 to 500 ohm, 0.5 watt resistor is required to be attached in series with the LED, to control current flow to about 0.020 ampere (20 milliamperes), or damage to the P-N junction may occur.

DIODE VOLTAGE DROP The voltage drop across a diode is about the same voltage as that required to forward bias the diode. If the diode is made from germanium, the forward voltage is 0.3 to 0.5 volt. If the diode is made from silicon, the forward voltage is 0.5 to 0.7 volt.

NOTE: When diodes are tested using a digital multimeter, the meter displays the voltage drop across the P-N junction (about 0.5 to 0.7 volt) when the meter is set to the *diode-check* position.

LIGHT-EMITTING DIODES

OPERATION All diodes radiate some energy during normal operation. Most diodes radiate heat because of the junction barrier voltage drop (typically 0.6 volt for silicon diodes). **Light-emitting diodes (LED)** radiate light when current flows through the diode in the forward-bias direction. ● **SEE FIGURE 15–13.**

The forward-bias voltage required for an LED ranges between 1.5 and 2.2 volts.

An LED only lights if the voltage at the anode (positive electrode) is at least 1.5 to 2.2 volts higher than the voltage at the cathode (negative electrode).

NEED FOR CURRENT LIMITING If an LED is connected across a 12 volt automotive battery, the LED lights brightly, but only for a second or two. Excessive current (amperes) that flows across the P-N junction of any electronic device can destroy the junction. A resistor *must* be connected in series with every diode (including LEDs) to control current flow across the P-N junction. This protection should include the following:

1. The value of the resistor should be from 300 to 500 ohms for each P-N junction. Commonly available resistors in this range include 470, 390, and 330 ohm resistors.

2. The resistors can be connected to either the anode or the cathode end. (Polarity of the resistor does not matter.)

How Does an LED Emit Light?

An LED contains a chip that houses P-type and N-type materials. The junction between these regions acts as a barrier to the flow of electrons between the two materials. When a voltage of 1.5 to 2.2 volts is applied to the correct polarity, current flows across the junction. As the electrons enter the P-type material, it combines with the holes in the material and releases energy in the form of light (called **photons**). The intensity and color the light produces depends on materials used in the manufacture of the semiconductor.

LEDs are very efficient compared to conventional incandescent bulbs, which depend on heat to create light. LEDs generate very little heat, with most of the energy consumed converted directly into light. LEDs are reliable and are being used for taillights, brake lights, daytime running lights, and headlights in some vehicles.

Current flows through the LED in series with the resistor, and the resistor controls the current flow through the LED, regardless of its position in the circuit.

3. Resistors protecting diodes can be actual resistors or other current-limiting loads, such as lamps or coils. With the current-limiting devices to control the current, the average LED requires about 20 to 30 milliamperes (mA), or 0.020 to 0.030 ampere.

PHOTODIODES

PURPOSE AND FUNCTION All semiconductor P-N junctions emit energy, mostly in the form of heat or light, such as with an LED. In fact, if an LED is exposed to bright light, a voltage potential is established between the anode and the cathode. **Photodiodes** are specially constructed to respond to various wavelengths of light with a "window" built into the housing. ● SEE FIGURE 15–14.

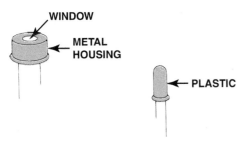

FIGURE 15–14 Typical photodiodes. They are usually built into a plastic housing so that the photodiode itself may not be visible.

Photodiodes are frequently used in steering wheel controls for transmitting tuning, volume, and other information from the steering wheel to the data link and the unit being controlled. If several photodiodes are placed on the steering column end and LEDs or phototransistors are placed on the steering wheel side, data can be transmitted between the two moving points without the interference that could be caused by physical contact-types of units.

CONSTRUCTION A photodiode is sensitive to light. When light energy strikes the diode, electrons are released and the diode conducts in the forward-bias direction. (The light energy is used to overcome the barrier voltage.)

The resistance across the photodiode decreases as the intensity of the light increases. This characteristic makes the photodiode a useful electronic device for controlling some automotive lighting systems, such as automatic headlights. The symbol for a photodiode is shown in ● FIGURE 15–15.

PHOTORESISTORS

A **photoresistor** is a semiconductor material (usually cadmium sulfide) that changes resistance with the presence or absence of light.

Dark = High resistance

Light = Low resistance

Because resistance is reduced when the photoresistor is exposed to light, the photoresistor can be used to control headlight dimmer relays and automotive headlights. ● SEE FIGURE 15–16.

FIGURE 15–15 Symbol for a photodiode. The arrows represent light striking the P-N junction of the photodiode.

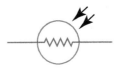

FIGURE 15–16 Either symbol may be used to represent a photoresistor.

SILICON-CONTROLLED RECTIFIERS

CONSTRUCTION A **silicon-controlled rectifier (SCR)** is commonly used in the electronic circuits of various automotive applications. An SCR is a semiconductor device that looks like two diodes connected end to end. ● **SEE FIGURE 15–17.**

If the anode is connected to a higher voltage source rather than the cathode in a circuit, no current flows, as occurs with a diode. If, however, a positive voltage source is connected to the gate of the SCR, current can flow from anode to cathode with a typical voltage drop of 1.2 volts (double the voltage drop of a typical diode, at 0.6 volt).

Voltage applied to the gate is used to turn the SCR on. However, if the voltage source at the gate is shut off, the current still continues to flow through the SCR until the source current is stopped.

USES OF AN SCR SCRs can be used to construct a circuit for a **center high-mounted stoplight (CHMSL)**. If this third stoplight is wired into either the left- or the right-side brake light circuit, the CHMSL also flashes whenever the turn signals are used for the side that was connected to the CHMSL. When two SCRs are used, both brake lights must be activated to supply current to the CHMSL. The current to the CHMSL is shut off when both SCRs lose their power source (when the brake pedal is released, which stops the current flow to the brake lights). ● **SEE FIGURE 15–18.**

THERMISTORS

CONSTRUCTION A **thermistor** is a semiconductor material, such as silicon, that has been doped to provide a given resistance. When the thermistor is heated, the electrons within the crystal gain energy and electrons are released. This means that a thermistor actually produces a small voltage when heated. If voltage is applied to a thermistor, its resistance decreases because the thermistor itself is acting as a current carrier rather than as a resistor at higher temperatures.

USES OF THERMISTORS A thermistor is commonly used as a temperature-sensing device for coolant temperature and intake manifold air temperature. Because

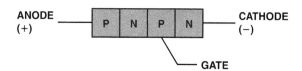

FIGURE 15–17 Symbol and terminal identification of an SCR.

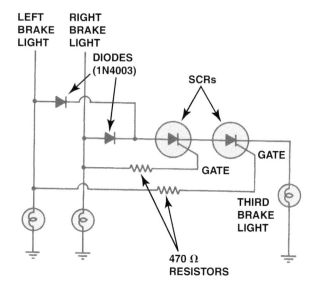

FIGURE 15–18 Wiring diagram for a center high-mounted stoplight (CHMSL) using SCRs.

	COPPER WIRE	NTC THERMISTOR
Cold	Lower resistance	Higher resistance
Hot	Higher resistance	Lower resistance

CHART 15–1

The resistance changes opposite to that of a copper wire with changes in temperature.

FIGURE 15–19 Symbols used to represent a thermistor.

thermistors operate in a manner opposite to that of a typical conductor, they are called **negative temperature coefficient (NTC)** thermistors; their resistance decreases as the temperature increases. ● **SEE CHART 15–1.**

Thermistor symbols are shown in ● **FIGURE 15–19.**

RECTIFIER BRIDGES

DEFINITION The word *rectify* means "to set straight"; therefore, a rectifier is an electronic device (such as a diode) used to convert a changing voltage into a straight or constant voltage. A **rectifier bridge** is a group of diodes that is used to change an AC circuit into a DC circuit. A rectifier bridge is used in alternators to rectify the AC voltage produced in the stator

FIGURE 15–20 This rectifier bridge contains six diodes; the three on each side are mounted in an aluminum-finned unit to help keep the diode cool during alternator operation.

(stationary windings) of the alternator into DC voltage. These rectifier bridges contain six diodes: one pair of diodes (one positive and one negative) for each of the three stator windings. ● **SEE FIGURE 15–20.**

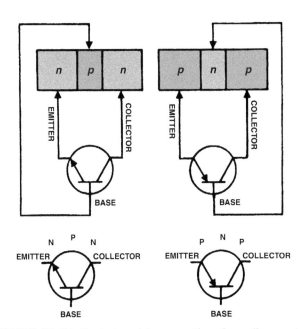

FIGURE 15–21 Basic transistor operation. A small current flowing through the base and emitter of the transistor turns on the transistor and permits a higher amperage current to flow from the collector and the emitter.

TRANSISTORS

PURPOSE AND FUNCTION
A **transistor** is a semiconductor device that can perform the following electrical functions.

1. Act as an electrical switch in a circuit
2. Act as an amplifier of current in a circuit
3. Regulate the current in a circuit

The word *transistor*, derived from the words *transfer* and *resistor*, is used to describe the transfer of current across a resistor. A transistor is made of three alternating sections or layers of P-type and N-type materials. This type of transistor is usually called a **bipolar transistor**.

CONSTRUCTION
A transistor that has P-type material on each end with N-type material in the center is called a **PNP transistor**. Another type, with the exact opposite arrangement, is called an **NPN transistor**.

The material at one end of a transistor is called the **emitter** and the material at the other end is called the **collector**. The **base** is in the center and the voltage applied to the base is used to control current through a transistor.

TRANSISTOR SYMBOLS
All transistor symbols contain an arrow indicating the emitter part of the transistor. The arrow points in the direction of current flow (conventional theory).

When an arrowhead appears in any semiconductor symbol, it stands for a P-N junction and it points from the P-type material toward the N-type material. The arrow on a transistor

is always attached to the *emitter* side of the transistor. ● **SEE FIGURE 15–21.**

HOW A TRANSISTOR WORKS
A transistor is similar to two back-to-back diodes that can conduct current in only one direction. As in a diode, N-type material can conduct electricity by means of its supply of free electrons, and P-type material conducts by means of its supply of positive holes.

 FREQUENTLY ASKED QUESTION

Is a Transistor Similar to a Relay?
Yes, in many cases a transistor is similar to a relay.
Both use a low current to control a higher current circuit. ● **SEE CHART 15–2.**
A relay can only be on or off. A transistor can provide a variable output if the base is supplied a variable current input.

	RELAY	TRANSISTOR
Low-current circuit	Coil (terminals 85 and 86)	Base and emitter
High-current circuit	Contacts terminals 30 and 87	Collector and emitter

CHART 15–2

Comparison between the control (low-current) and high-current circuits of a transistor compared to a mechanical relay.

A transistor allows current flow if the electrical conditions allow it to switch on, in a manner similar to the working of an electromagnetic relay. The electrical conditions are determined, or switched, by means of the base, or *B*. The base carries current only when the proper voltage and polarity are applied. The main circuit current flow travels through the other two parts of the transistor: the emitter *E* and the collector *C*. ● **SEE FIGURE 15–22.**

If the base current is turned off or on, the current flow from collector to emitter is turned off or on. The current controlling the base is called the control current. The control current must be high enough to switch the transistor on or off. (This control voltage, called the **threshold voltage**, must be above approximately 0.3 volt for germanium and 0.6 volt for silicon transistors.) This control current can also "throttle" or regulate the main circuit, in a manner similar to the operation of a water faucet.

HOW A TRANSISTOR AMPLIFIES A transistor can amplify a signal if the signal is strong enough to trigger the base of a transistor on and off. The resulting on–off current flow

through the transistor can be connected to a higher-powered electrical circuit. This results in a higher-powered circuit being controlled by a lower-powered circuit. This low-powered circuit's cycling is exactly duplicated in the higher-powered circuit and, therefore, any transistor can be used to amplify a signal. However, because some transistors are better than others for amplification, specialized types of transistors are used for each specialized circuit function.

FIELD-EFFECT TRANSISTORS

Field-effect transistors (FETs) have been used in most automotive applications since the mid-1980s. They use less electrical current and rely mostly on the strength of a small voltage signal to control the output. The parts of a typical FET include the *source, gate,* and *drain.* ● **SEE FIGURE 15–23.**

 FREQUENTLY ASKED QUESTION

What Does the Arrow Mean on a Transistor Symbol?

The arrow on a transistor symbol is always on the emitter and points toward the N-type material. The arrow on a diode also points toward the N-type material. To know which type of transistor is being shown, note which direction the arrow points.

- PNP: pointing in
- NPN: not pointing in

 FREQUENTLY ASKED QUESTION

What Is a Darlington Pair?

A **Darlington pair** consists of two transistors wired together. This arrangement permits a very small current flow to control a large current flow. The Darlington pair is named for Sidney Darlington, an American physicist for Bell Laboratories from 1929 to 1971. Darlington amplifier circuits are commonly used in electronic ignition systems, computer engine control circuits, and many other electronic applications. ● **SEE FIGURE 15–24.**

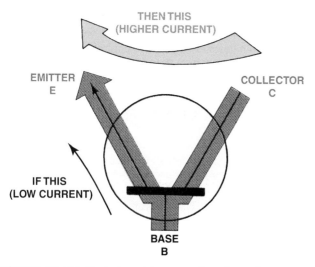

FIGURE 15–22 Basic transistor operation. A small current flowing through the base and emitter of the transistor turns on the transistor and permits a higher amperage current to flow from the collector and the emitter.

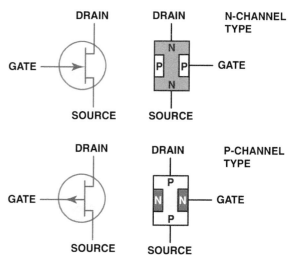

FIGURE 15–23 The three terminals of a field-effect transistor (FET) are called the source, gate, and drain.

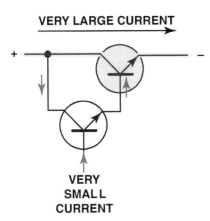

VERY LARGE CURRENT

VERY SMALL CURRENT

FIGURE 15–24 A Darlington pair consists of two transistors wired together, allowing for a very small current to control a larger current flow circuit.

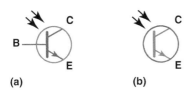

(a)   (b)

FIGURE 15–25 Symbols for a phototransistor. (a) This symbol uses the line for the base; (b) this symbol does not.

Many FETs are constructed of metal oxide semiconductor (MOS) materials, called **MOSFETs**. MOSFETs are highly sensitive to static electricity and can be easily damaged if exposed to excessive current or high-voltage surges (spikes). Most automotive electronic circuits use MOSFETs, which explains why it is vital for the service technician to use caution to avoid doing anything that could result in a high-voltage spike, and perhaps destroy an expensive computer module. Some vehicle manufacturers recommend that technicians wear an antistatic wristband when working with modules that contain MOSFETs. Always follow the vehicle manufacturer's instructions found in service information to avoid damaging electronic modules or circuits.

PHOTOTRANSISTORS

Similar in operation to a photodiode, a **phototransistor** uses light energy to turn on the base of a transistor. A phototransistor is an NPN transistor that has a large exposed base area to permit light to act as the control for the transistor. Therefore, a phototransistor may or may not have a base lead. If not, then it has only a collector and emitter lead. When the phototransistor is connected to a powered circuit, the light intensity is amplified by the gain of the transistor. Phototransistors, along with photo diodes, are frequently used in steering wheel controls. ● **SEE FIGURE 15–25.**

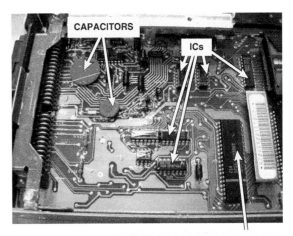

CAPACITORS

ICs

CENTRAL PROCESSING UNIT (CPU)

FIGURE 15–26 A typical automotive computer with the case removed to show all of the various electronic devices and integrated circuits (ICs). The CPU is an example of a DIP chip and the large red and orange devices are ceramic capacitors.

INTEGRATED CIRCUITS

PURPOSE AND FUNCTION Solid-state components are used in many electronic semiconductors and/or circuits. They are called "solid-state" because they have no moving parts, just higher or lower voltage levels within the circuit. Discrete (individual) diodes, transistors, and other semiconductor devices were often used to construct early electronic ignition and electronic voltage regulators. Newer-style electronic devices use the same components, but they are now combined (integrated) into one group of circuits, and are thus called an **integrated circuit (IC)**.

CONSTRUCTION Integrated circuits are usually encased in a plastic housing called a CHIP with two rows of inline pins. This arrangement is called the **dual inline pins (DIP)** chips. ● **SEE FIGURE 15–26.**

Therefore, most computer circuits are housed as an integrated circuit in a DIP chip.

HEAT SINK Heat sink is a term used to describe any area around an electronic component that, because of its shape or design, can conduct damaging heat away from electronic parts. Examples of heat sinks include the following:

1. Ribbed electronic ignition control units
2. Cooling slits and cooling fan attached to an alternator
3. Special heat-conducting grease under the electronic ignition module in General Motors HEI distributor ignition systems and other electronic systems

Heat sinks are necessary to prevent damage to diodes, transistors, and other electronic components due to heat buildup. Excessive heat can damage the junction between the N-type and P-type materials used in diodes and transistors.

What Causes a Transistor or Diode to Blow?

Every automotive diode and transistor is designed to operate within certain voltage and amperage ranges for individual applications. For example, transistors used for switching are designed and constructed differently from transistors used for amplifying signals.

Because each electronic component is designed to operate satisfactorily for its particular application, any severe change in operating current (amperes), voltage, or heat can destroy the *junction*. This failure can cause either an open circuit (no current flows) or a short (current flows through the component all the time when the component should be blocking the current flow).

TRANSISTOR GATES

PURPOSE AND FUNCTION Knowledge of the basic operation of electronic gates is important in understanding how computers work. A gate is an electronic circuit whose output depends on the location and voltage of two inputs.

CONSTRUCTION Whether a transistor is on or off depends on the voltage at the base of the transistor. For the transistor to turn on, a voltage difference between the base of the transmitter and the emitter should be at least a 0.6 volt. Most electronic and computer circuits use 5 volts as a power source. If two transistors are wired together, several different outputs can be received, depending on how the two transistors are wired. ● **SEE FIGURE 15-27**.

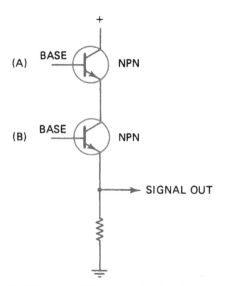

FIGURE 15--27 Typical AND gate circuit using two transistors. The emitter is always the line with the arrow. Notice that both transistors must be turned on before there is voltage present at the point labeled "signal out."

OPERATION If the voltage at *A* is higher than that of the emitter, the top transistor is turned on; however, the bottom transistor is off unless the voltage at *B* is also higher. If both transistors are turned on, the output signal voltage is high. If only one of the two transistors is on, the output is zero (off or no voltage). Because it requires both *A* and *B* to be on to result in a voltage output, this circuit is called an *AND gate*. In other words, both transistors have to be on before the gate opens and allows a voltage output. Other types of gates can be constructed using various connections to the two transistors. For example:

AND gate. Requires both transistors to be on to get an output.

OR gate. Requires either transistor to be on to get an output.

NAND (NOT-AND) gate. Output is on unless both transistors are on.

NOR (NOT-OR) gate. Output is on only when both transistors are off.

Gates represent logic circuits that can be constructed so that the output depends on the voltage (on or off; high or low) of the inputs to the bases of transistors. Their inputs can come from sensors or other circuits that monitor sensors, and their outputs can be used to operate an output device, if amplified and controlled by other circuits. For example, the blower motor is commanded on when the following events occur, to cause the control module to turn it on.

1. The ignition must be on (input).
2. The air-conditioning is commanded on.
3. The engine coolant temperature is within a predetermined limit.

If all of these conditions are met, the control module commands the blower motor on. If any of the input signals are incorrect, the control module cannot perform the correct command.

OPERATIONAL AMPLIFIERS

Operational amplifiers (op-amps) are used in circuits to control and amplify digital signals. Op-amps are frequently used for motor control for airflow door operation as part of the climate control system. Op-amps can provide the proper voltage polarity and current (amperes) to control the direction of permanent magnetic (PM) motors. The symbol for an op-amp is shown in ● **FIGURE 15-28**.

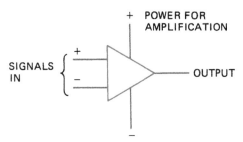

FIGURE 15-28 Symbol for an operational amplifier (op-amp).

FREQUENTLY ASKED QUESTION

What Are Logic Highs and Lows?

All computer circuits and most electronic circuits (such as gates) use various combinations of high and low voltages. High voltages are typically those above 5 volts, and low is generally considered zero (ground). However, high voltages do not *have* to begin at 5 volts. *High, or the number 1, to a computer is the presence of voltage above a certain level.* For example, a circuit could be constructed where any voltage higher than 3.8 volts is considered high. *Low, or the number 0, to a computer is the absence of voltage or a voltage lower than a certain value.* For example, a voltage of 0.62 volt may be considered low. Various associated names and terms can be summarized.

- Logic low = Low voltage = Number 0 = Reference low
- Logic high = Higher voltage = Number 1 = Reference high

TECH TIP

Blinking LED Theft Deterrent

A blinking (flashing) LED consumes only about 5 milliamperes (5/1,000 of 1 ampere, or 0.005 ampere). Most alarm systems use a blinking red LED to indicate that the system is armed. A fake alarm indicator is easy to make and install.

A 470 ohm, 0.5 watt resistor limits current flow to prevent battery drain. The positive terminal (anode) of the diode is connected to a fuse that is hot at all times, such as the cigarette lighter. The negative terminal (cathode) of the LED is connected to any ignition-controlled fuse.

● **SEE FIGURE 15–29**.

When the ignition is turned off, the power flows through the LED to ground and the LED flashes. To prevent distraction during driving, the LED goes out when the ignition is on. Therefore, this fake theft deterrent is "auto setting," and no other action is required to activate it when you leave your vehicle except to turn off the ignition and remove the key, as usual.

ELECTRONIC COMPONENT FAILURE CAUSES

Electronic components, such as electronic ignition modules, electronic voltage regulators, onboard computers, and any other electronic circuit are generally quite reliable; however, failure can occur. Frequent causes of premature failure include the following:

- **Poor connections.** It has been estimated that most engine computers returned as defective have simply had poor connections at the wiring harness terminal ends. These faults are often intermittent and hard to find.

  NOTE: When cleaning electronic contacts, use a pencil eraser. This cleans the contacts without harming the thin, protective coating used on most electronic terminals.

- **Heat.** The operation and resistance of electronic components and circuits are affected by heat. Electronic components should be kept as cool as possible and never hotter than 260°F (127°C).

- **Voltage spikes.** A high-voltage spike can literally burn a hole through semiconductor material. The source of these high-voltage spikes is often the discharge of a coil without proper (or with defective) despiking protection. A poor electrical connection at the battery or other major electrical connection can cause high-voltage spikes to occur, because the *entire wiring harness creates its own magnetic field,* similar

BLINKING LED THEFT DETERRENT*

RED LED STARTS TO FLASH WHENEVER IGNITION IS TURNED OFF

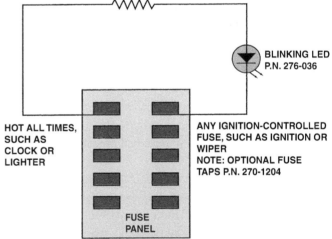

FIGURE 15–29 Schematic for a blinking LED theft deterrent.

to that formed around a coil. If the connection is loose and momentary loss of contact occurs, a high-voltage surge can occur through the entire electrical system. To help prevent this type of damage, ensure that all electrical connections, including grounds, are properly clean and tight.

CAUTION: One of the major causes of electronic failure occurs during jump starting a vehicle. Always check that the ignition switch is off on both vehicles when making the connection. Always double-check that the correct battery polarity (+ to + and − to −) is being performed.

■ **Excessive current.** All electronic circuits are designed to operate within a designated range of current (amperes). If a solenoid or relay is controlled by a computer circuit, the resistance of that solenoid or relay becomes part of that control circuit. If a coil winding inside the solenoid or relay becomes shorted, the resulting lower resistance increases the current through the circuit. Even though individual components are used with current-limiting resistors in series, the coil winding resistance is also used as a current-control component in the circuit. If a computer fails, always measure the resistance across all computer-controlled relays and solenoids. The resistance should be within specifications (generally *over* 20 ohms) for each component that is computer controlled.

NOTE: Some computer-controlled solenoids are pulsed on and off rapidly. This type of solenoid is used in many electronically shifted transmissions. Their resistance is usually about half of the resistance of a simple on–off solenoid— usually between 10 and 15 ohms. Because the computer controls the on-time of the solenoid, the solenoid and its circuit control are called **pulse-width modulated (PWM)**.

HOW TO TEST DIODES AND TRANSISTORS

TESTERS Diodes and transistors can be tested with an ohmmeter. The diode or transistor being tested must be disconnected from the circuit for the results to be meaningful.

■ Use the *diode-check* position on a digital multimeter.

■ In the diode-check position on a digital multimeter, the meter applies a higher voltage than when the ohms test function is selected.

■ This slightly higher voltage (about 2 to 3 volts) is enough to forward bias a diode or the P-N junction of transistors.

DIODES Using the diode test position, the meter applies a voltage. The display shows the voltage drop across the diode P-N junction. A good diode should give an over limit (OL) reading with the test leads attached to each lead of the diode in one way, and a voltage reading of 0.400 to 0.600 volt when the leads are reversed. This reading is the voltage drop or the barrier voltage across the P-N junction of the diode.

1. A low-voltage reading with the meter leads attached both ways across a diode means that the diode is *shorted* and must be replaced.

2. An OL reading with the meter leads attached both ways across a diode means that the diode is *open* and must be replaced.

● **SEE FIGURE 15–30.**

TRANSISTORS Using a digital meter set to the diode-check position, a good transistor should show a voltage drop of 0.400 to 0.600 volt between the following:

■ The emitter (*E*) and the base (*B*) and between the base (*B*) and the collector (*C*) with a meter connected one way, and OL when the meter test leads are reversed.

■ An OL reading (no continuity) in both directions when a transistor is tested between the emitter (*E*) and the collector (*C*). (A transistor tester can also be used if available.)

● **SEE FIGURE 15—31.**

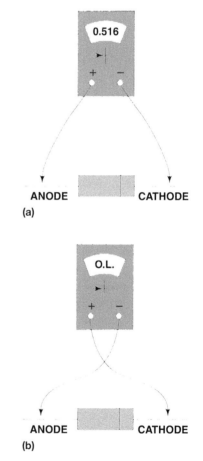

FIGURE 15–30 To check a diode, select "diode check" on a digital multimeter. The display indicates the voltage drop (difference) between the meter leads. The meter itself applies a low-voltage signal (usually about 3 volts) and displays the difference on the display. (a) When the diode is forward biased, the meter should display a voltage between 0.500 and 0.700 volt (500 to 700 millivolts). (b) When the meter leads are reversed, the meter should read OL (over limit) because the diode is reverse biased and blocking current flow.

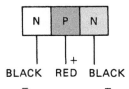

BLACK   RED   BLACK

FIGURE 15–31 If the red (positive) lead of the ohmmeter (or a multimeter set to diode check) is touched to the center and the black (negative lead) touched to either end of the electrode, the meter should forward bias the P-N junction and indicate on the meter as low resistance. If the meter reads high resistance, reverse the meter leads, putting the black on the center lead and the red on either end lead. If the meter indicates low resistance, the transistor is a good PNP type. Check all P-N junctions in the same way.

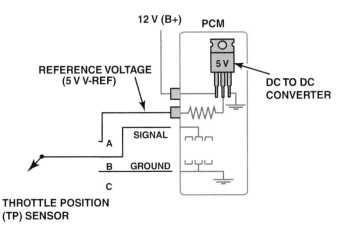

THROTTLE POSITION
(TP) SENSOR

FIGURE 15––32 A DC to DC converter is built into most powertrain control modules (PCMs) and is used to supply the 5 volt reference, called V-ref, to many sensors used to control the internal combustion engine.

CONVERTERS AND INVERTERS

CONVERTERS DC to DC converters (usually written as DC–DC converter) are electronic devices used to transform DC voltage from one level to another higher or lower level. They are used to distribute various levels of DC voltage throughout a vehicle from a single power bus (or voltage source).

EXAMPLES OF USE One example of a DC–DC converter circuit is the circuit the PCM uses to convert 14 to 5 volts. The 5 volts are called the reference voltage, abbreviated V-ref, and used to power many sensors in a computer-controlled engine management system. The schematic of a typical 5 volt V-ref interfacing with the TP sensor circuit is shown in ● **FIGURE 15–32**.

The PCM operates on 14 volts, using the principle of DC conversion, to provide a constant 5 volts of sensor reference

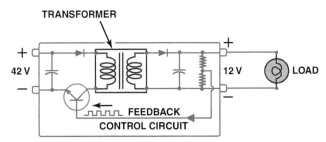

FIGURE 15–33 This DC–DC converter is designed to convert 42 volts to 14 volts, to provide 12 volt power to accessories on a hybrid-electric vehicle operating with a 42 volt electrical system.

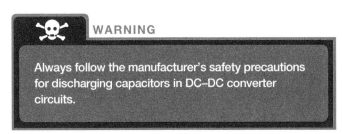

WARNING

Always follow the manufacturer's safety precautions for discharging capacitors in DC–DC converter circuits.

voltage to the TP sensor and others. The TP sensor demands little current, so the V-ref circuit is a low-power DC voltage converter in the range of 1 watt. The PCM uses a DC–DC converter, which is a small semiconductor device called a voltage regulator, and is designed to convert battery voltage to a constant 5 volts, regardless of changes in the charging voltage.

Hybrid-electric vehicles use DC–DC converters to provide higher or lower DC voltage levels and current requirements.

A high-power DC–DC converter schematic is shown in ● **FIGURE 15–33** and represents how a nonelectronic DC–DC converter works.

The central component of a converter is a transformer that physically isolates the input (42 volts) from the output (14 volts). The power transistor pulses the high-voltage coil of the transformer, and the resulting changing magnetic field induces a voltage in the coil windings of the lower voltage side of the transformer. The diodes and capacitors help control and limit the voltage and frequency of the circuit.

DC–DC CONVERTER CIRCUIT TESTING Usually a DC control voltage is used, which is supplied by a digital logic circuit to shift the voltage level to control the converter. A voltage test can indicate if the correct voltages are present when the converter is on and off.

Voltage measurements are usually specified to diagnose a DC–DC converter system. A digital multimeter (DMM) that is CAT III rated should be used.

HIGH-VOLTAGE CIRCUIT PRECAUTIONS Whenever working on or near potential high-voltage circuits, adhere to the following:

1. Always follow the manufacturer's safety precautions when working with high-voltage circuits. These circuits are usually indicated by orange wiring.

WARNING

Do not touch the terminals of a battery that are being used to power an inverter. There is always a risk that those battery terminals could deliver a much greater shock than from batteries alone, if a motor or inverter should develop a fault.

2. Never tap into wires in a DC–DC converter circuit to access power for another circuit.

3. Never tap into wires in a DC–DC converter circuit to access a ground for another circuit.

4. Never block airflow to a DC–DC converter heat sink.

5. Never use a heat sink for a ground connection for a meter, scope, or accessory connection.

6. Never connect or disconnect a DC–DC converter while the converter is powered up.

7. Never connect a DC–DC converter to a larger voltage source than specified.

INVERTERS An **inverter** is an electronic circuit that changes DC into AC. In most DC-AC inverters, the switching transistors, which are usually MOSFETs, are turned on alternately for short pulses. As a result, the transformer produces a modified sine wave output, rather than a true sine wave. ● **SEE FIGURE 15—34.**

The waveform produced by an inverter is not the perfect sine wave of household AC, but is rather more like a pulsing DC that reacts similar to sine wave AC in transformers and in induction motors. ● **SEE FIGURE 15—35.**

Inverters power AC motors. An inverter converts DC power to AC power at the required frequency and amplitude. The inverter consists of three half-bridge units, and the output voltage is mostly created by a pulse-width modulation (PWM) technique. The three-phase voltage waves are shifted 120 degrees to each other to power each of the three phases.

ELECTROSTATIC DISCHARGE

DEFINITION **Electrostatic discharge (ESD)** is created when static charges build up on the human body when movement occurs. The friction of the clothing and the movement of shoes against carpet or vinyl floors cause a high voltage to build. Then when we touch a conductive material, such as a doorknob, the static charge is rapidly discharged. These charges, although just slightly painful to us, can cause severe damage to delicate electronic components. The following are typical static voltages.

■ If you can feel it, it is at least 3,000 volts.

■ If you can hear it, it is at least 5,000 volts.

■ If you can see it, it is at least 10,000 volts.

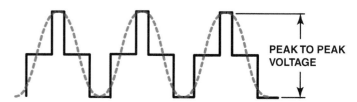

FIGURE 15—35 The switching (pulsing) MOSFETs create a waveform called a modified sine wave (solid lines), compared to a true sine wave (dotted lines).

FIGURE 15–34 A typical circuit for an inverter designed to change direct current from a battery to alternating current for use by the electric motors used in a hybrid-electric vehicle.

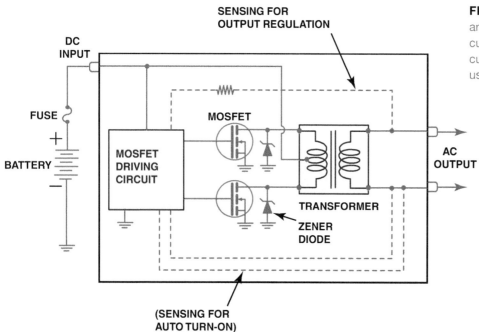

Although these voltages seem high, the current, in amperes, is extremely low. However, sensitive electronic components, such as vehicle computers, radios, and instrument panel clusters, can be ruined if exposed to as little as 30 volts. This is a problem because components can be harmed at voltages lower than we can feel.

AVOIDING ESD To help prevent damage to components, follow these easy steps.

1. Keep the replacement electronic component in the protective wrapping until just before installation.

2. Before handling any electronic component, ground yourself by touching a metal surface to drain away any static charge.

3. Do not touch the terminals of electronic components.

4. If working in an area where you could come in contact with terminals, wear a static electrically grounding wrist strap available at most electronic parts stores, such as Radio Shack.

If these precautions are observed, ESD damage can be eliminated or reduced. Remember, just because the component works even after being touched does not mean that damage has not occurred. Often, a section of the electronic component may be damaged, yet does not fail until several days or weeks later.

SUMMARY

1. Semiconductors are constructed by doping semiconductor materials such as silicon.

2. N-type and P-type materials can be combined to form diodes, transistors, SCRs, and computer chips.

3. Diodes can be used to direct and control current flow in circuits and to provide despiking protection.

4. Transistors are electronic relays that can also amplify signals.

5. All semiconductors can be damaged if subjected to excessive voltage, current, or heat.

6. Never touch the terminals of a computer or electronic device; static electricity can damage electronic components.

REVIEW QUESTIONS

1. What is the difference between P-type material and N-type material?

2. How can a diode be used to suppress high-voltage surges in automotive components or circuits containing a coil?

3. How does a transistor work?

4. To what precautions should all service technicians adhere, to avoid damage to electronic and computer circuits?

5. What is the difference between forward bias and reverse bias when discussing a diode?

CHAPTER QUIZ

1. A semiconductor is a material _____.
   a. with fewer than four electrons in the outer orbit of its atoms
   b. with more than four electrons in the outer orbit of its atoms
   c. with exactly four electrons in the outer orbit of its atoms
   d. determined by other factors besides the number of electrons

2. The arrow in a symbol for a semiconductor device _____.
   a. points toward the negative
   b. points away from the negative
   c. is attached to the emitter on a transistor
   d. both a and c

3. A diode installed across a coil with the cathode toward the battery positive is called a(n) _____.
   a. clamping diode
   b. forward-bias diode
   c. SCR
   d. transistor

4. A transistor is controlled by the polarity and current at the _____.
   a. collector
   b. emitter
   c. base
   d. Both a and b

5. A transistor can _____.
   a. switch on and off
   b. amplify
   c. throttle
   d. all of the above

6. A zener diode is normally used for voltage regulation. A zener diode, however, can also be used for high-voltage spike protection, if connected _____.
   a. positive to anode, negative to cathode
   b. positive to cathode, ground to anode
   c. negative to anode, cathode to a resistor, then to a lower voltage terminal
   d. both a and c

7. The forward-bias voltage required for an LED is _____.
   a. 0.3 to 0.5 volt
   b. 0.5 to 0.7 volt
   c. 1.5 to 2.2 volts
   d. 4.5 to 5.1 volts

8. Faults or failures in electronic components could be caused by all of the following EXCEPT _____.
   a. loose connector terminals
   b. a loose alternator belt
   c. jumper cables reversed when jump-starting
   d. a voltage spike

9. What is the purpose and function of an inverter?
   a. To change the polarity of DC voltages
   b. To change low DC voltage to high DC voltage
   c. To change DC voltage to AC voltage
   d. To change AC voltage to DC voltage

10. To avoid damage from an electrostatic discharge, the technician should _____ before handling sensitive electronic components.
    a. wear dark clothing
    b. be sure to wear insulated shoes
    c. touch the housing of the component before removing it from the protective cover
    d. touch a metal surface on the vehicle

COMPUTER FUNDAMENTALS

After studying this chapter, the reader should be able to:
List the various parts of onboard computers.
Explain the purpose and function of onboard computers.
List to an automotive computer's input sensors and the output devices (actuators) it controls.

This chapter will help you prepare for the ASE Electrical/Electronic Systems (A6) certification test content area "A" (General Electrical/Electronic System Diagnosis).

KEY TERMS: Actuator 190 • Analog-to-digital (AD) converter 190 • Baud rate 192 • Binary system 192 • Clock generator 191 • Controller 189 • CPU 191 • Digital computer 191 • Duty cycle 194 • E²PROM 190 • ECA 189 • ECM 189 • ECU 189 • EEPROM 190 • Engine mapping 191 • Input 189 • Input conditioning 190 • KAM 190 • Nonvolatile RAM 190 • Output drivers 194 • Powertrain control module (PCM) 189 • PROM 190 • PWM 194 • RAM 190 • ROM 190 • SAE 189

COMPUTER FUNDAMENTALS

PURPOSE AND FUNCTION Modern automotive control systems consist of a network of electronic sensors, actuators, and computer modules designed to regulate the powertrain and vehicle support systems. The onboard automotive computer has many names. It may be called an **electronic control unit (ECU), electronic control module (ECM), electronic control assembly (ECA)**, or a **controller**, depending on the manufacturer and the computer application. The **Society of Automotive Engineers (SAE)** bulletin J1930 standardizes the name as a **powertrain control module (PCM)**. The PCM coordinates engine and transmission operation, processes data, maintains communications, and makes the control decisions needed to keep the vehicle operating. Not only is it capable of operating the engine and transmission, but it is also able to perform the following:

- Undergo self-tests (40% of the computing power is devoted to diagnosis)
- Set and store diagnostic trouble codes (DTCs)
- Communicate with the technician using a scan tool

VOLTAGE SIGNALS Automotive computers use voltage to send and receive information. Voltage is electrical pressure and does not flow through circuits, but voltage can be used as a signal. A computer converts input information or data into voltage signal combinations that represent number combinations. A computer processes the input voltage signals it receives by computing what they represent, and then delivering the data in computed or processed form.

COMPUTER FUNCTIONS

BASIC FUNCTIONS The operation of every computer can be divided into four basic functions. ● **SEE FIGURE 16–1.**

- **Input.** Receives voltage signals from sensors
- **Processing.** Performs mathematical calculations
- **Storage.** Includes short-term and long-term memory
- **Output.** Controls an output device by either turning it on or off

INPUT FUNCTIONS First, the computer receives a voltage signal (input) from an input device. **Input** is a signal from

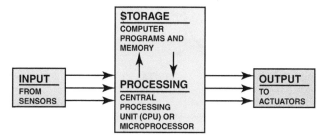

FIGURE 16–1 All computer systems perform four basic functions: input, processing, storage, and output.

a device that can be as simple as a button or a switch on an instrument panel, or a sensor on an automotive engine. ● **SEE FIGURE 16–2** for a typical type of automotive sensor.

Vehicles use various mechanical, electrical, and magnetic sensors to measure factors, such as vehicle speed, throttle position, engine RPM, air pressure, oxygen content of exhaust gas, airflow, engine coolant temperature, and status of electrical circuits (on-off). Each sensor transmits its information in the form of voltage signals. The computer receives these voltage signals, but before it can use them, the signals must undergo a process called **input conditioning**. This process includes amplifying voltage signals that are too small for the computer circuitry to handle. Input conditioners generally are located inside the computer, but a few sensors have their own input conditioning circuitry.

A digital computer changes the analog input signals (voltage) to digital bits (*binary digits*) of information through an **analog-to-digital (AD) converter** circuit. The binary digital number is used by the computer in its calculations or logic networks. ● **SEE FIGURE 16–3.**

PROCESSING The term *processing* is used to describe how input voltage signals received by a computer are handled through a series of electronic logic circuits maintained in its programmed instructions. These logic circuits change the input voltage signals, or data, into output voltage signals or commands.

STORAGE Storage is the place where the program instructions for a computer are stored in electronic memory. Some programs may require that certain input data be stored for later reference or future processing. In others, output commands may be delayed or stored before they are transmitted to devices elsewhere in the system.

Computers have two types of memory.

1. Permanent memory is called **read-only memory (ROM)** because the computer can only read the contents; it cannot change the data stored in it. This data is retained even when power to the computer is shut off. Part of the ROM is built into the computer, and the rest is located in an integrated circuit (IC) chip called a **programmable read-only memory (PROM)** or calibration assembly. Many chips are erasable, meaning that the program can be changed. These chips are called erasable programmable read-only memory, or EPROM. Since the early 1990s, most programmable memory has been electronically erasable, meaning that the program in the chip can be reprogrammed by using a scan tool and the proper software. This computer reprogramming is usually called *reflashing*. These chips are electrically erasable programmable read-only memory, abbreviated **EEPROM** or **E²PROM**.

   All vehicles equipped with onboard diagnosis second generation, called OBD-II, are equipped with EEPROMs.

2. Temporary memory is called **random-access memory (RAM)**, because the computer can write or store new data into it as directed by the computer program, as well as read the data already in it. Automotive computers use two types of RAM memory.

   ■ Volatile RAM memory is lost whenever the ignition is turned off. However, a type of volatile RAM called **keep-alive memory (KAM)** can be wired directly to battery power. This prevents its data from being erased when the ignition is turned off. One example of RAM and KAM is the loss of station settings in a programmable radio when the battery is disconnected. Because all the settings are stored in RAM, they have to be reset when the battery is reconnected. System trouble codes are commonly stored in RAM and can be erased by disconnecting the battery.

   ■ **Nonvolatile RAM** memory can retain its information even when the battery is disconnected. One use for this type of RAM is the storage of odometer information in an electronic speedometer. The memory chip retains the mileage accumulated by the vehicle. When speedometer replacement is necessary, the odometer chip is removed and installed in the new speedometer unit. KAM is used primarily in conjunction with adaptive strategies.

OUTPUT FUNCTIONS After the computer has processed the input signals, it sends voltage signals or commands to other devices in the system, such as system actuators. An **actuator** is

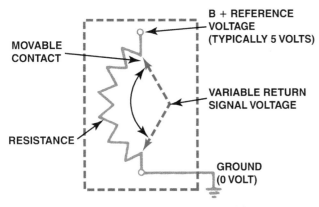

FIGURE 16–2 A potentiometer uses a movable contact to vary resistance and send an analog voltage right to the PCM.

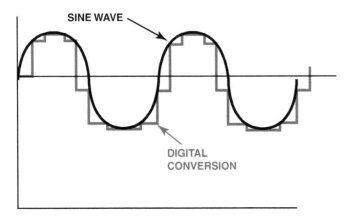

FIGURE 16–3 An AD converter changes analog (variable) voltage signals into digital signals that the PCM can process.

an electrical or mechanical output device that converts electrical energy into a mechanical action, such as:

- Adjusting engine idle speed
- Operating fuel injectors
- Ignition timing control
- Altering suspension height

COMPUTER COMMUNICATION A typical vehicle can have many computers, also called modules or controllers. Computers also can communicate with, and control, each other through their output and input functions. This means that the output signal from one computer system can be the input signal for another computer system through a data network.

DIGITAL COMPUTERS

PARTS OF A COMPUTER The software consists of the programs and logic functions stored in the computer's circuitry. The hardware is the mechanical and electronic parts of a computer.

- **Central processing unit.** The microprocessor is the **central processing unit (CPU)** of a computer. Because it performs the essential mathematical operations and logic decisions that make up its processing function, the CPU can be considered the brain of a computer. Some computers use more than one microprocessor, called a coprocessor. The digital computer can process thousands of digital signals per second because its circuits are able to switch voltage signals on and off in billionths of a second. It is called a **digital computer** because it processes zeros and ones (digits) and needs to have any variable input signals, called analog inputs, converted to digital form before it can function. ● **SEE FIGURE 16–4.**

- **Computer memory.** Other integrated circuit (IC) devices store the computer operating program, system sensor input data, and system actuator output data—information that is necessary for CPU operation.

- **Computer programs.** By operating a vehicle on a dynamometer and manually adjusting the variable factors, such as speed, load, and spark timing, it is possible to determine the optimum output settings for the best driveability, economy, and emission control. This is called engine mapping. ● **SEE FIGURE 16–5.**

Engine mapping creates a three-dimensional performance graph that applies to a given vehicle and powertrain combination. Each combination is mapped in this manner to produce a PROM or EEPROM calibration. This allows an automaker to use one basic computer for all models.

Many older-vehicle computers used a single PROM that plugged into the computer.

NOTE: If the computer needs to be replaced, the PROM or calibration module must be removed from the defective unit and installed in the replacement computer. Since the mid-1990s, PCMs do not have removable calibration PROMs, and must be programmed or flashed using a scan tool before being put into service.

CLOCK RATES AND TIMING The microprocessor receives sensor input voltage signals, processes them by using information from other memory units, and then sends voltage signals to the appropriate actuators. The microprocessor communicates by transmitting long strings of 0s and 1s in a language called binary code, but the microprocessor must have some way of knowing when one signal ends and another begins. That is the job of a crystal oscillator called a **clock generator**. ● **SEE FIGURE 16–6.**

The computer's crystal oscillator generates a steady stream of one-bit-long voltage pulses. Both the microprocessor and the memories monitor the clock pulses while they are com-

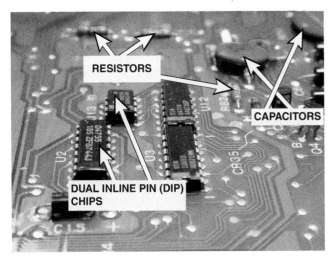

FIGURE 16–4 Many electronic components are used to construct a typical vehicle computer, including chips, resistors, and capacitors.

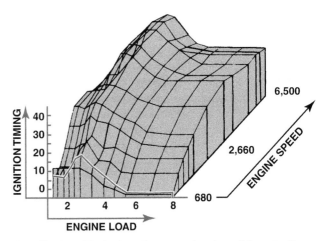

FIGURE 16–5 Typical engine map developed from testing and used by the vehicle computer to provide the optimum ignition timing for all engine speeds and load combinations.

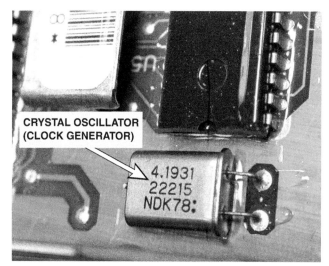

CRYSTAL OSCILLATOR
(CLOCK GENERATOR)

4.1931
22215
NDK78:

FIGURE 16–6 The clock generator produces a series of pulses that are used by the microprocessor and other components to stay in step with each other at a steady rate.

PCM

FIGURE 16–7 A powertrain control module (PCM) under the hood where it can be exposed to air for cooling.

municating. Because they know how long each voltage pulse should be, they can distinguish between a 01 and a 0011. To complete the process, the input and output circuits also watch the clock pulses.

COMPUTER SPEEDS Not all computers operate at the same speed; some are faster than others. The speed at which a computer operates is specified by the cycle time, or clock speed, required to perform certain measurements. Cycle time or clock speed is measured in megahertz (4.7 MHz, 8 MHz, 15 MHz, 18 MHz, and 32 MHz, which is the clock speed of most vehicle computers today).

BAUD RATE The computer transmits bits of a serial datastream at precise intervals. The computer's speed is called the **baud rate**, or bits per second. The term *baud* was named after J. M. Emile Baudot (1845–1903), a French telegraph operator who developed a five-bit-per-character code of telegraph. Just as mph helps in estimating the length of time required to travel a certain distance, the baud rate is useful in estimating how long a given computer needs to transmit a specified amount of data to another computer.

Automotive computers have evolved from a baud rate of 160 used in the early 1980s to a baud rate as high as 500,000 for some networks. The speed of data transmission is an important factor both in system operation and in system troubleshooting.

CONTROL MODULE LOCATIONS The computer hardware is all mounted on one or more circuit boards and installed in a metal case to help shield it from electromagnetic interference (EMI). The wiring harnesses that link the computer to sensors and actuators connect to multipin connectors or edge connectors on the circuit boards.

Onboard computers range from single-function units that control a single operation to multifunction units that manage all of the separate (but linked) electronic systems in the vehicle. They vary in size from a small module to a notebook-size box. Most other computers are installed in the passenger compartment, either under the instrument panel, or in a side kick panel, where they can be shielded from physical damage caused by temperature extremes, dirt, and vibration, or interference by the high currents and voltages of various underhood systems. ● **SEE FIGURE 16–7.**

? **FREQUENTLY ASKED QUESTION**

What Is a Binary System?

In a digital computer, the signals are simple high–low, yes–no, on–off signals. The digital signal voltage is limited to two voltage levels: high voltage and low voltage. Since there is no stepped range of voltage or current in between, a digital binary signal is a "square wave." The signal is called "digital" because the on and off signals are processed by the computer as the digits or numbers 0 and 1. The number system containing only these two digits is called the **binary system**. Any number or letter from any number system or language alphabet can be translated into a combination of binary 0s and 1s for the digital computer. A digital computer changes the analog input signals (voltage) to digital bits (binary digits) of information through an analog-to-digital (AD) converter circuit. The binary digital number is used by the computer in its calculations or logic networks. Output signals usually are digital signals that turn system actuators on and off.

COMPUTER INPUT SENSORS

The vehicle computer uses signals (voltage levels) from the following sensors.

- **Engine speed (revolutions per minute, or RPM) sensor.** This signal comes from the primary ignition signal in the ignition control module (ICM) or directly from the crankshaft position (CKP) sensor.

- **Switches or buttons for accessory operation.** Many accessories use control buttons that signal the body computer to turn on or off an accessory, such as the windshield wiper or heated seats.

- **Manifold absolute pressure (MAP) sensor.** This sensor detects engine load by using a signal from a sensor that measures the vacuum in the intake manifold.

- **Mass airflow (MAF) sensor.** This sensor measures the mass (weight and density) of the air flowing through the sensor and entering the engine.

- **Engine coolant temperature (ECT) sensor.** This sensor measures the temperature of the engine coolant. This is a sensor used for engine controls and for automatic air-conditioning control operation.

- **Oxygen sensor (O2S).** This sensor measures the oxygen in the exhaust stream. There are as many as four oxygen sensors in some vehicles.

- **Throttle position (TP) sensor.** This sensor measures the throttle opening and is used by the computer for engine control and the shift points of the automotive transmission/transaxle.

- **Vehicle speed (VS) sensor.** This sensor measures the vehicle speed using a sensor located at the output of the transmission/transaxle or by monitoring sensors at the wheel speed sensors. This sensor is used by the speedometer, cruise control, and airbag systems.

COMPUTER OUTPUTS

OUTPUT CONTROLS After the computer has processed the input signals, it sends voltage signals or commands to other devices in the system, as follows:

- **Operate actuators.** An actuator is an electrical or mechanical device that converts electrical energy into heat, light, or motion to control engine idle speed, suspension height, ignition timing, and other output devices.

- **Network communication.** Computers also can communicate with another computer system through a network.

A vehicle computer can do only two things.

1. Turn a device on.
2. Turn a device off. ● **SEE FIGURE 16–8.**

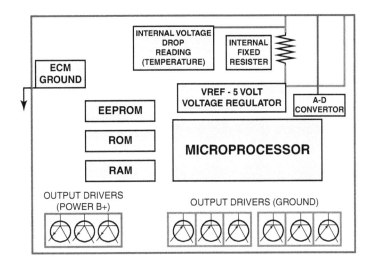

FIGURE 16–8 The microprocessor is the brain inside the computer which then can command the operation of output devices through either power or ground control drivers.

Typical output devices include the following:

- **Fuel injectors.** The computer can vary the amount of time in milliseconds the injectors are held open, thereby controlling the amount of fuel supplied to the engine.

- **Blower motor control.** Many blower motors are controlled by the body computer by pulsing the current on and off to maintain the desired speed.

- **Transmission shifting.** The computer provides a ground to the shift solenoids and torque converter clutch (TCC) solenoid. The operation of the automatic transmission/transaxle is optimized based on vehicle sensor information.

- **Idle speed control.** The computer can control the idle air control (IAC) or electronic throttle control (ETC) to maintain engine idle speed and to provide an increased idle speed, as needed.

- **Evaporative emission control solenoids.** The computer can control the flow of gasoline fumes from the charcoal canister to the engine and seal off the system to perform a fuel system leak detection test as part of the OBD-II system requirements.

Most outputs work electrically in one of three ways:

1. Digital
2. Pulse-width modulated
3. Switched

Digital control is mostly used for computer communications and involves voltage signals that are transmitted and received in packets.

Pulse-width control allows a device, such as a blower motor, to be operated at variable speed by changing the amount of time electrical power is supplied to the device.

A switched output is an output that is either on or off. In many circuits, the PCM uses a relay to switch a device on or off, because the relay is a low-current device that can switch to a higher current device. Most computer circuits cannot handle high amounts of current. By using a relay circuit, the PCM provides the output control to the relay, which in turn provides the output control to the device.

The relay coil, which the PCM controls, typically draws less than 0.5 ampere. The device that the relay controls may draw 30 amperes or more. The PCM switches are actually transistors, and are often called **output drivers**. ● **SEE FIGURE 16–9.**

OUTPUT DRIVERS There are two basic types of output drivers.

1. **Low-side drivers.** The low-side drivers (LSDs) are transistors inside the computer that complete the ground path of relay coil. Ignition (key-on) voltage and battery voltage are supplied to the relay. The ground side of the relay coil is connected to the transistor inside the computer. In the example of a fuel pump relay, when the transistor turns "on," it completes the ground for the relay coil, and the relay then completes the power circuit between the battery power and the fuel pump. A relatively low current flows through the relay coil and transistor that is inside the computer. This causes the relay to switch and provides the fuel pump with battery voltage. The majority of switched outputs have typically been low-side drivers. ● **SEE FIGURE 16–10.**

Low-side drivers can often perform a diagnostic circuit check by monitoring the voltage from the relay to check that the control circuit for the relay is complete. A low-side driver, however, cannot detect a short-to-ground.

2. **High-side drivers.** The high-side drivers (HSDs) control the power side of the circuit. In these applications, when the transistor is switched on, voltage is applied to the device. A ground has been provided to the device, so when the high-side driver switches, the device is energized. In some applications, high-side drivers are used instead of low-side drivers to provide better circuit protection. General Motors vehicles have used a high-side driver to control the fuel pump relay instead of a low-side driver. In the event of an accident, should the circuit to the fuel pump relay become grounded, a high-side driver causes a short circuit, which causes the fuel pump relay to de-energize. High-side drivers inside modules can detect electrical faults, such as a lack of continuity when the circuit is not energized. ● **SEE FIGURE 16–11.**

PULSE-WIDTH MODULATION Pulse-width modulation (PWM) is a method of controlling an output using a digital signal. Instead of just turning devices on or off, the computer can control the amount of on-time. For example, a solenoid could be a PWM device. If, for example, a vacuum solenoid is controlled by a switched driver, switching either on or off would mean that either full vacuum would flow through the solenoid or no vacuum would flow through the solenoid. However, to control the amount of vacuum that flows through the solenoid, pulse-width modulation could be used. A PWM signal is a digital signal, usually 0 and 12 volts, which is cycling at a fixed frequency. Varying the length of time that the signal is on provides a signal that can vary the on- and off-time of an output. The ratio of on-time relative to the period of the cycle is referred to as **duty cycle**. ● **SEE FIGURE 16–12.**

Depending on the frequency of the signal, which is usually fixed, this signal turns the device on and off a fixed number of times per second. When, for example, the voltage is high

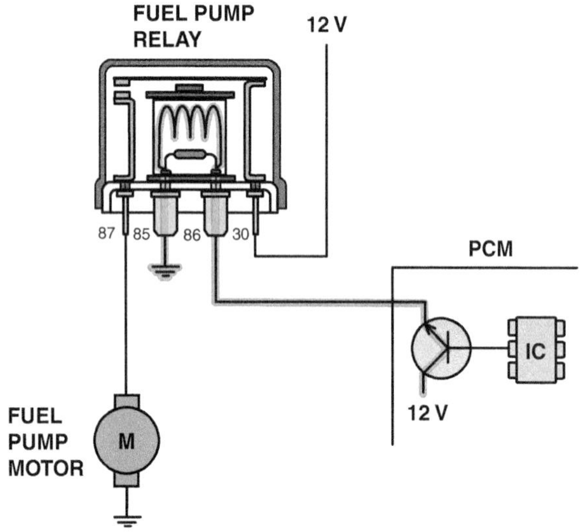

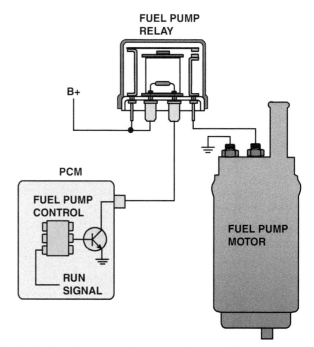

FIGURE 16–9 A typical output driver. In this case, the PCM applies voltage to the fuel pump relay coil to energize the fuel pump.

FIGURE 16–10 A typical low-side driver (LSD), which uses a control module to control the ground side of the relay coil.

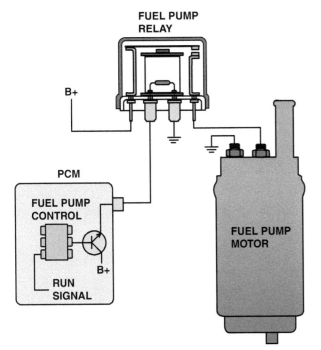

FIGURE 16–11 A typical module-controlled high-side driver (HSD) where the module itself supplies the electrical power to the device. The logic circuit inside the module can detect circuit faults, including continuity of the circuit, and if there is a short-to-ground in the circuit being controlled.

(12 volts) 90% of the time and low (0 volt) the other 10% of the time, the signal has a 90% duty cycle. In other words, if this signal were applied to the vacuum solenoid, the solenoid is on 90% of the time. This allows more vacuum to flow through the solenoid. The computer has the ability to vary this on- and off-time or pulse-width modulation at any rate between 0% and 100%. A good example of pulse-width modulation is the cooling fan speed control. The speed of the cooling fan is controlled

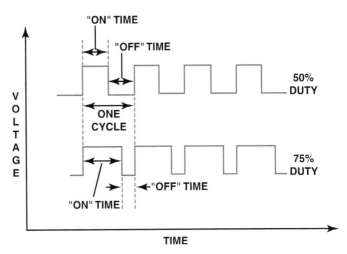

FIGURE 16–12 Both the top and bottom pattern have the same frequency. However, the amount of on-time varies. Duty cycle is the percentage of the time during a cycle that the signal is turned on.

by varying the amount of on-time that the battery voltage is applied to the cooling fan motor.

- 100% duty cycle: fan runs at full speed
- 75% duty cycle: fan runs at 3/4 speed
- 50% duty cycle: fan runs at 1/2 speed
- 25% duty cycle: fan runs at 1/4 speed

The use of PWM, therefore, results in precise control of an output device to achieve the amount of cooling needed and conserve electrical energy compared to simply timing the cooling fan on high when needed. PWM may be used to control vacuum through a solenoid, the amount of purge of the evaporative purge solenoid, the speed of a fuel pump motor, control of a linear motor, or even the intensity of a light bulb.

SUMMARY

1. The Society of Automotive Engineers (SAE) standard J1930 specifies that the term *powertrain control module* (PCM) be used for the computer that controls the engine and transmission in a vehicle.

2. The four basic computer functions are input, processing, storage, and output.

3. Types of memory include read-only memory (ROM) which can be programmable (PROM), erasable (EPROM), or electrically erasable (EEPROM); random-access memory (RAM); and keep-alive memory (KAM).

4. Computer input sensors include engine speed (RPM), MAP, MAF, ECT, O2S, TP, and VS.

5. A computer can only turn a device on or turn a device off, but it can do either operation rapidly.

1. What part of the vehicle computer is considered to be the brain?

2. What is the difference between volatile and nonvolatile RAM?

3. What are the four input sensors?

4. What are the four output devices?

5. How does using pulse-width modulation control devices?

CHAPTER QUIZ

1. What unit of electricity is used as a signal for a computer?
   a. Volt
   b. Ohm
   c. Ampere
   d. Watt

2. The four basic computer functions include _____.
   a. writing, processing, printing, and remembering
   b. input, processing, storage, and output
   c. data gathering, processing, output, and evaluation
   d. sensing, calculating, actuating, and processing

3. All OBD-II vehicles use what type of read-only memory?
   a. ROM
   b. PROM
   c. EPROM
   d. EEPROM

4. The "brain" of the computer is the_____.
   a. PROM
   b. RAM
   c. CPU
   d. AD converter

5. Computer speed is measured in _____.
   a. baud rate
   b. clock speed (Hz)
   c. voltage
   d. bytes

6. Which item is a computer input sensor?
   a. RPM
   b. Throttle position
   c. Engine coolant temperature
   d. All of the above

7. Which item is a computer output device?
   a. Fuel injector
   b. Transmission shift solenoid
   c. Evaporative emission control solenoid
   d. All of the above

8. The SAE term for the vehicle computer is _____.
   a. PCM
   b. ECM
   c. ECA
   d. controller

9. What two things can a vehicle computer actually perform (output)?
   a. Store and process information
   b. Turn something on or turn something off
   c. Calculate and vary temperature
   d. Control fuel and timing only

10. Analog signals from sensors are changed to digital signals for processing by the computer through which type of circuit?
    a. Digital
    b. Analog
    c. Analog-to-digital converter
    d. PROM

chapter 17

CAN AND NETWORK COMMUNICATIONS

LEARNING OBJECTIVES:

After studying this chapter, the reader should be able to:

Discuss how networks connect to the data link connector and to other modules.

Describe the types of networks and serial communications used on vehicles.

Describe the features of a controller area network.

Compare the network communications of common U.S., Asian, and European vehicle brands.

Explain how to diagnose module communication faults.

List the shared features of all OBD-II vehicles.

This chapter will help you prepare for the ASE Electrical/Electronic Systems (A6) certification test content area "A" (General Electrical/Electronic System Diagnosis).

KEY TERMS: Breakout box (BOB) 208 • BUS 199 • CAN 200 • Class 2 200 • E & C 200 • GMLAN 201 • Keyword 200 • Multiplexing 198 • Network 198 • Node 197 • Programmable controller interface (PCI) 205 • Serial communications interface (SCI) 205 • Serial data 198 • Splice pack 199 • Standard corporate protocol (SCP) 203 • State of health (SOH) 209 • SWCAN 201 • Terminating resistors 209 • Twisted pair 197 • UART 200 • UART-based protocol (UBP) 203

MODULE COMMUNICATIONS AND NETWORKS

NEED FOR NETWORK Since the 1990s, vehicles have used modules to control the operation of most electrical components. A typical vehicle has 10 or more modules, and they communicate with each other over data lines or hard wiring, depending on the application.

ADVANTAGES Most modules are connected together in a network because of the following advantages.

- A decreased number of wires are needed, thereby saving weight and cost, as well as helping with installation at the factory and decreased complexity, making servicing easier.

- Common sensor data can be shared with those modules that may need the information, such as vehicle speed, outside air temperature, and engine coolant temperature.

- ● SEE FIGURE 17–1.

NETWORK FUNDAMENTALS

MODULES AND NODES Each module, also called a **node**, must communicate to other modules. For example, if the driver depresses the window-down switch, the power window switch sends a window-down message to the body control module. The body control module then sends the request to the driver's side window module. This module is responsible for actually performing the task by supplying power and ground to the window lift motor in the current polarity to cause the window to go down. The module also contains a circuit that monitors the current flow through the motor and stops and/or reverses the window motor if an obstruction causes the window motor to draw more than the normal amount of current.

TYPES OF COMMUNICATION The types of communications include the following:

- **Differential.** In the differential form of BUS communication, a difference in voltage is applied to two wires, which are twisted to help reduce electromagnetic interference (EMI). These transfer wires are called a **twisted pair**.

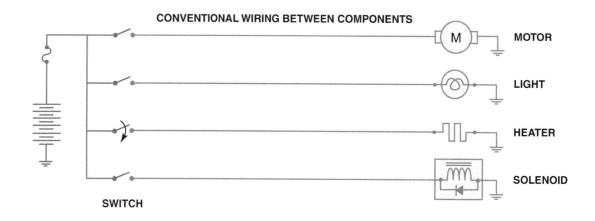

CONVENTIONAL WIRING BETWEEN COMPONENTS

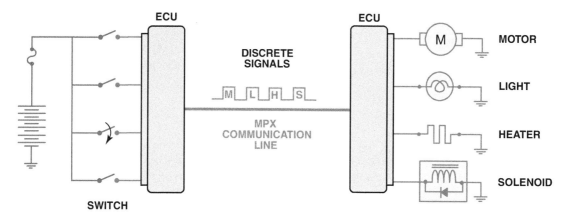

FIGURE 17–1 Module communications makes controlling multiple electrical devices and accessories easier by utilizing simple low-current switches to signal another module, which does the actual switching of the current to the device.

- **Parallel.** In the parallel type of BUS communication, the send and receive signals are on different wires.
- **Serial data.** The **serial data** is data transmitted by a series of rapidly changing voltage signals pulsed from low to high or from high to low.
- **Multiplexing.** The process of **multiplexing** involves the sending of multiple signals of information at the same time over a signal wire and separating the signals at the receiving end.

This system of intercommunication of computers or processors is referred to as a **network**. ● **SEE FIGURE 17–2**.

By connecting the computers together on a communications network, they can easily share information back and forth. This multiplexing has the following advantages.

- Elimination of redundant sensors and dedicated wiring for these multiple sensors
- Reduction of the number of wires, connectors, and circuits
- Addition of more features and option content to new vehicles
- Weight reduction due to fewer components, wires, and connectors, thereby increasing fuel economy
- Changeable features with software upgrades versus component replacement

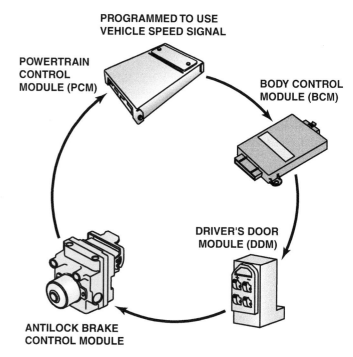

FIGURE 17–2 A network allows all modules to communicate with other modules.

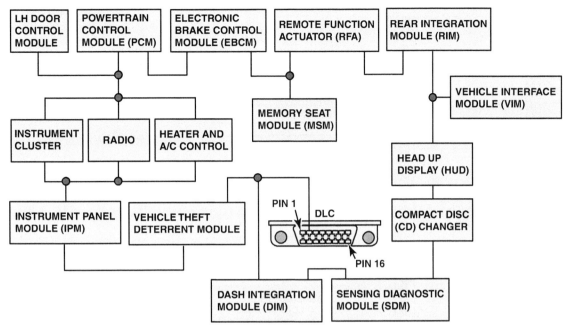

FIGURE 17–3 A ring link network reduces the number of wires it takes to interconnect all of the modules.

MODULE COMMUNICATIONS CONFIGURATION

The three most common types of networks used on vehicles include the following:

1. **Ring link networks.** In a ring-type network, all modules are connected to each other by a serial data line (in a line) until all are connected in a ring. ● **SEE FIGURE 17–3**.

2. **Star link networks.** In a star link network, a serial data line attaches to each module and then each is connected to a central point. This central point is called a **splice pack**, abbreviated SP, such as in "SP 306." The splice pack uses a bar to splice all of the serial lines together. Some GM vehicles use two or more splice packs to tie the modules together. When more than one splice pack is used, a serial data line connects one splice pack to the others. In most applications, the BUS bar used in each splice pack can be removed. When the BUS bar is removed, a special tool (J 42236) can be installed in place of the removed BUS bar.

 FREQUENTLY ASKED QUESTION

What Is a BUS?

A **BUS** is a term used to describe a communications network. Therefore, there are *connections to the BUS* and *BUS communications,* both of which refer to digital messages being transmitted among electronic modules or computers.

 FREQUENTLY ASKED QUESTION

What Is a Protocol?

A protocol is a set of rules or a standard used between computers or electronic control modules. Protocols include the type of electrical connectors, voltage levels, and frequency of the transmitted messages. Protocols, therefore, include both the hardware and software needed to communicate between modules.

Using this tool, the serial data line for each module can be isolated and tested for a possible problem. Using the special tool at the splice pack makes diagnosing this type of network easier than many others. ● **SEE FIGURE 17–4**.

3. **Ring/star hybrid.** In a ring/star network, the modules are connected using both types of network configurations. Check service information (SI) for details on how this network is connected on the vehicle being diagnosed and always follow the recommended diagnostic steps.

NETWORK COMMUNICATIONS CLASSIFICATIONS

The Society of Automotive Engineers (SAE) standards include the following three categories of in-vehicle network communications.

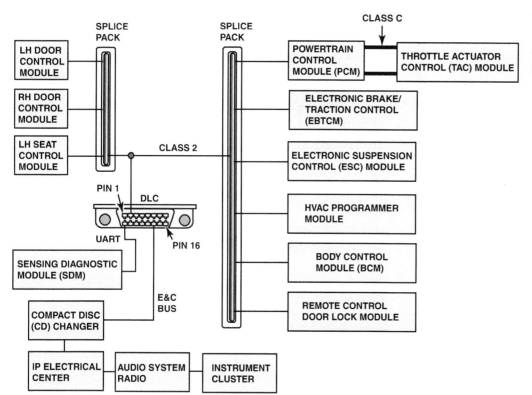

SPLICE PACK

LH DOOR CONTROL MODULE

RH DOOR CONTROL MODULE

LH SEAT CONTROL MODULE

CLASS 2

PIN 1

DLC

UART

PIN 16

SENSING DIAGNOSTIC MODULE (SDM)

E&C BUS

COMPACT DISC (CD) CHANGER

IP ELECTRICAL CENTER

AUDIO SYSTEM RADIO

INSTRUMENT CLUSTER

SPLICE PACK

CLASS C

POWERTRAIN CONTROL MODULE (PCM)

THROTTLE ACTUATOR CONTROL (TAC) MODULE

ELECTRONIC BRAKE/ TRACTION CONTROL (EBTCM)

ELECTRONIC SUSPENSION CONTROL (ESC) MODULE

HVAC PROGRAMMER MODULE

BODY CONTROL MODULE (BCM)

REMOTE CONTROL DOOR LOCK MODULE

FIGURE 17–4 In a star link network, all of the modules are connected using splice packs.

CLASS A Low-speed networks, meaning less than 10,000 bits per second (bps, or 10 Kbs), are generally used for trip computers, entertainment, and other convenience features.

CLASS B Medium-speed networks, meaning 10,000 to 125,000 bps (10 to 125 Kbs), are generally used for information transfer among modules, such as instrument clusters, temperature sensor data, and other general uses.

CLASS C High-speed networks, meaning 125,000 to 1,000,000 bps, are generally used for real-time powertrain and vehicle dynamic control. High-speed BUS communication systems now use a **controller area network (CAN)**. ● **SEE FIGURE 17–5**.

GENERAL MOTORS COMMUNICATIONS PROTOCOLS

UART General Motors and others use UART communications for some electronic modules or systems. **UART** is a serial data communications protocol that stands for **universal asynchronous receive and transmit**. UART uses a master control module connected to one or more remote modules. The master control module is used to control message traffic on the data line by poling all of the other UART modules. The remote modules send a response message back to the master module.

UART uses a fixed pulse-width switching between 0 and 5 volts. The UART data BUS operates at a baud rate of 8,192 bps. ● **SEE FIGURE 17–6**.

ENTERTAINMENT AND COMFORT COMMUNICATION
The GM **entertainment and comfort (E & C)** serial data is similar to UART, but uses a 0 to 12 volts toggle. Like UART, the E & C serial data uses a master control module connected to other remote modules, which could include the following:

- Compact disc (CD) player
- Instrument panel (IP) electrical center
- Audio system (radio)
- Heating, ventilation, and air-conditioning (HVAC) programmer and control head
- Steering wheel controls

 ● **SEE FIGURE 17–7**.

CLASS 2 COMMUNICATIONS Class 2 is a serial communications system that operates by toggling between 0 and 7 volts at a transfer rate of 10.4 Kbs. Class 2 is used for most high-speed communications between the powertrain control module and other control modules, plus to the scan tool. Class 2 is the primary high-speed serial communications system used by GMCAN (CAN) and is connected to terminal 2 of the DLC. ● **SEE FIGURE 17–8**.

KEYWORD COMMUNICATION Keyword 81, 82, and 2000 serial data are also used for some module-to-module communication on GM vehicles. Keyword data BUS signals are toggled from 0 to 12 volts when communicating. The voltage

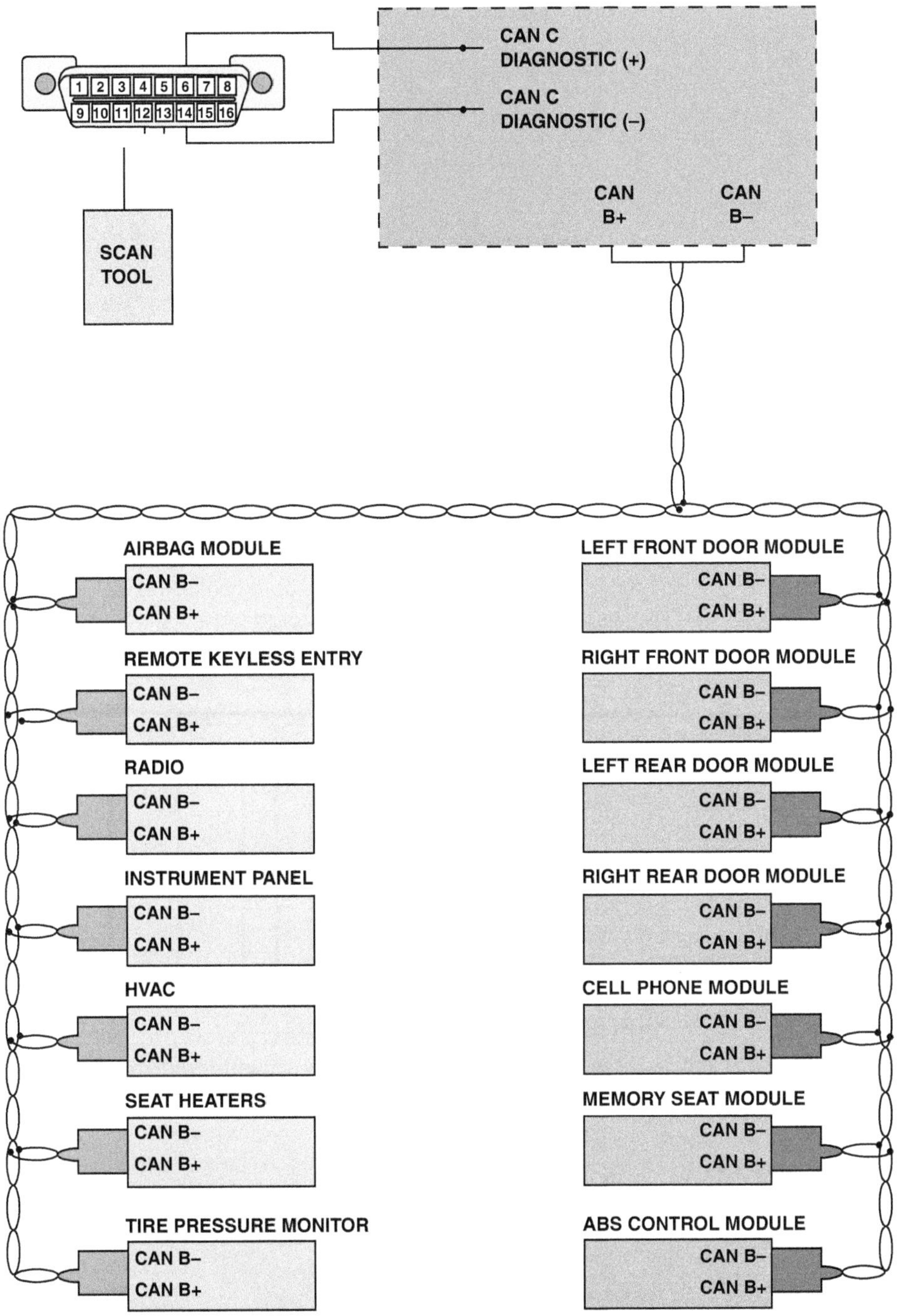

FIGURE 17-5 A typical BUS system showing module CAN communications and twisted pairs of wire.

or the datastream is 0 volt when not communicating. Keyword serial communication is used by the seat heater module and others, but is not connected to the data link connector (DLC). ● **SEE FIGURE 17–9.**

GMLAN General Motors, like all vehicle manufacturers, must use high-speed serial data to communicate with scan tools on all vehicles effective with the 2008 model year. As mentioned, the standard is called controller area network (CAN), which General Motors calls **GMLAN,** which stands for **GM local area network.** General Motors uses two versions of GMLAN.

- **Low-speed GMLAN.** The low-speed version is used for driver-controlled functions, such as power windows

and door locks. The baud rate for low-speed GMLAN is 33,300 bps. The GMLAN low-speed serial data is not connected directly to the data link connector and uses one wire. The voltage toggles between 0 and 5 volts after an initial 12 volt spike, which indicates to the modules to turn on or wake up and listen for data on the line. Low-speed GMLAN is also known as **single-wire CAN,** or **SWCAN,** and is located at pin 1 of the DLC.

- **High-speed GMLAN.** The baud rate is almost real time at 500 Kbs. This serial data method uses a two-twisted-wire circuit, which is connected to the data link connector on pins 6 and 14. ● **SEE FIGURE 17–10.**

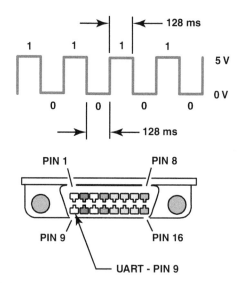

FIGURE 17–6 UART serial data master control module is connected to the data link connector (DLC) at pin 9.

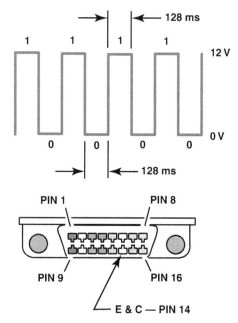

FIGURE 17–7 The E & C serial data is connected to the data link connector at pin 14.

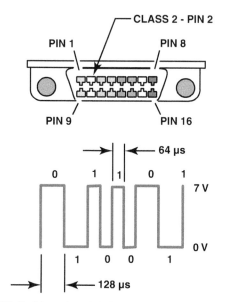

FIGURE 17–8 Class 2 serial data communication is accessible at the data link connector at pin 2.

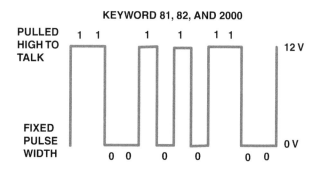

FIGURE 17–9 Keyword 82 operates at a rate of 8,192 bps, similar to UART, and keyword 2000 operates at a baud rate of 10,400 bps (the same as a Class 2 communicator).

? FREQUENTLY ASKED QUESTION

Why Is a Twisted Pair Used?

A twisted pair is where two wires are twisted to prevent electromagnetic radiation from affecting the signals passing through the wires. By twisting the two wires about once every inch (9 to 16 times per foot), the interference is canceled by the adjacent wire. ● **SEE FIGURE 17–11.**

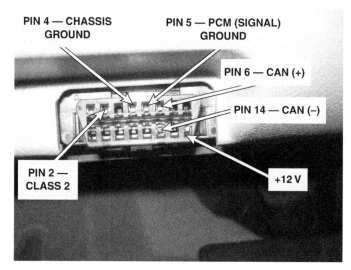

FIGURE 17–10 GMLAN uses pins at terminals 6 and 14. Pin 1 is used for low-speed GMLAN on 2006 and newer GM vehicles.

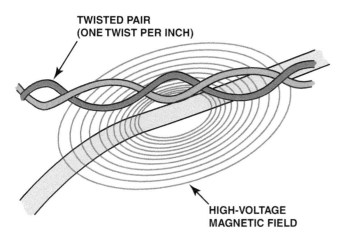

FIGURE 17–11 A twisted pair is used by several different network communications protocols to reduce interference that can be induced in the wiring from nearby electromagnetic sources.

FIGURE 17–12 A CANDi module flashes the green LED rapidly if communication is detected.

A CANDi (CAN diagnostic interface) module is required to be used with the Tech 2 to be able to connect a GM vehicle equipped with GMLAN. ● **SEE FIGURE 17–12**.

FORD NETWORK COMMUNICATIONS PROTOCOLS

STANDARD CORPORATE PROTOCOL Only a few Fords had scan tool data accessible through the OBD-I data link connector. To identify an OBD-I (1988–1995) on a Ford vehicle that is equipped with **standard corporate protocol (SCP)**, and be able to communicate through a scan tool, look for terminals in cavities 1 and 3 of the DLC. ● **SEE FIGURE 17–13**.

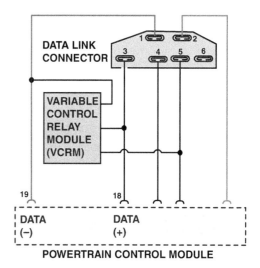

FIGURE 17–13 A Ford OBD-I diagnostic link connector showing that SCP communication uses terminals in cavities 1 (upper left) and 3 (lower left).

 FREQUENTLY ASKED QUESTION

What Are U Codes?

The U diagnostic trouble codes were at first "undefined" but are now network-related codes. Use the network codes to help pinpoint the circuit or module that is not working correctly.

SCP uses the J-1850 protocol and is active with the key on. The SCP signal is from 4 volts negative to 4.3 volts positive, and a scan tool does not have to be connected for the signal to be detected on the terminals. OBD-II (EECV) Ford vehicles use terminals 2 (positive) and 10 (negative) of the 16-pin data link connector for network communication, using the SCP module communications.

UART-BASED PROTOCOL Newer Fords use the CAN for scan tool diagnosis, but still retain SCP and **UART-based protocol (UBP)** for some modules. ● **SEE FIGURES 17–14 AND 17–15**.

CHRYSLER COMMUNICATIONS PROTOCOLS

CCD Since the late 1980s, the Chrysler Collision Detection (CCD) multiplex network is used for scan tool and module communications. It is a differential-type communication and uses a twisted pair of wires. The modules connected to the network apply a bias voltage on each wire. CCD signals are divided into

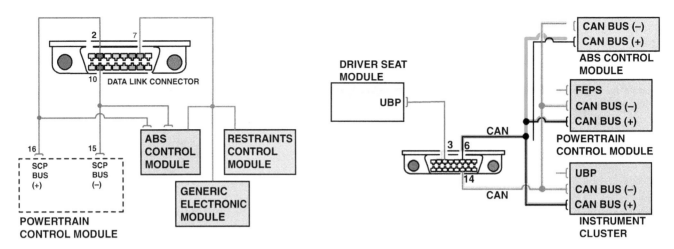

FIGURE 17–14 A scan tool can be used to check communications with the SCP BUS through terminals 2 and 10 and to the other modules connected to terminal 7 of the data link connector.

FIGURE 17–15 Many Fords use UBP module communications along with CAN.

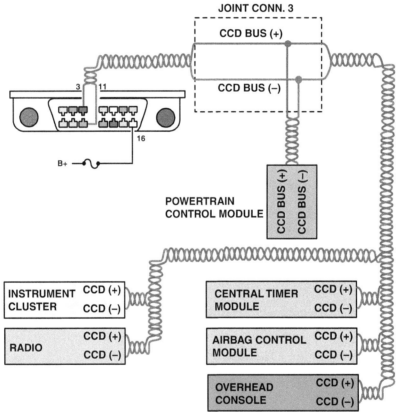

FIGURE 17–16 CCD signals are labeled plus (+) and minus (–) and use a twisted pair of wires. Notice that terminals 3 and 11 of the data link connector are used to access the CCD BUS from a scan tool. Pin 16 is used to supply 12 volts to the scan tool.

plus and minus (CCD+ and CCD–) and the voltage difference does not exceed 0.02 volt. The baud rate is 7,812.5 bps.

NOTE: The "collision" in the Chrysler Collision detection BUS communications refers to the program that avoids conflicts of information exchange within the BUS, and does not refer to airbags or other accident-related circuits of the vehicle.

The circuit is active without a scan tool command. ● **SEE FIGURE 17–16**.

The modules on the CCD BUS apply a bias voltage on each wire by using termination resistors. ● **SEE FIGURE 17–17**.

The difference in voltage between CCD+ and CCD– is less than 20 millivolts. For example, using a digital meter with the black meter lead attached to ground and the red meter lead attached at the data link connector, a normal reading could include:

- Terminal 3 = 2.45 volts
- Terminal 11 = 2.47 volts

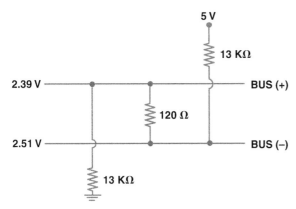

FIGURE 17-17 The differential voltage for the CCD BUS is created by using resistors in a module.

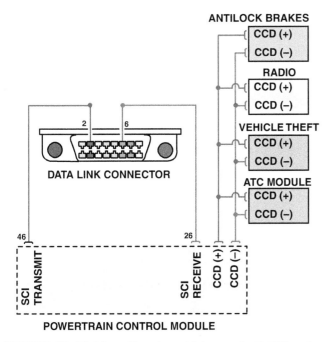

FIGURE 17-18 Many Chrysler vehicles use both SCI and CCD for module communication.

This is an acceptable reading because the readings are 20 millivolts (0.020 volt) of each other. If both had been exactly 2.5 volts, then this could indicate that the two data lines are shorted together. The module providing the bias voltage is usually the body control module on passenger cars and the front control module on Jeeps and trucks.

PROGRAMMABLE CONTROLLER INTERFACE

The Chrysler **programmable controller interface (PCI)** is a one-wire communication protocol that connects at the OBD-II DLC at terminal 2. The PCI BUS is connected to all modules on the BUS in a star configuration and operates at a baud rate of 10,200 bps. The voltage signal toggles between 7.5 and 0 volt. If this voltage is checked at terminal 2 of the OBD-II DLC, a voltage of about 1 volt indicates the average voltage, and means that the BUS is functioning and is not shorted-to-ground. PCI and CCD are often used in the same vehicle. ● **SEE FIGURE 17-18**.

SERIAL COMMUNICATIONS INTERFACE

Chrysler used **serial communications interface (SCI)** for most scan tool and flash reprogramming functions until it was replaced with CAN. SCI is connected at the OBD-II data link connector (DLC) at terminals 6 (SCI receive) and 2 (SCI transmit). A scan tool must be connected to test the circuit.

CONTROLLER AREA NETWORK

BACKGROUND
Robert Bosch Corporation developed the CAN protocol, which was called CAN 1.2, in 1993. The CAN protocol was approved by the Environmental Protection Agency (EPA) for 2003 and newer vehicle diagnostics, and became a legal requirement for all vehicles by 2008. The CAN diagnostic systems use pins 6 and 14 in the standard 16-pin OBD-II (J-1962) connector. Before CAN, the scan tool protocol had been manufacturer-specific.

CAN FEATURES
The CAN protocol offers the following features.

- Faster than other BUS communication protocols
- Cost-effective because it is an easier system than others to use
- Less affected by electromagnetic interference (Data is transferred on two wires that are twisted together, called twisted pair, to help reduce EMI interference.)
- Message-based rather than address-based, which makes it easier to expand
- No wake-up needed because it is a two-wire system
- Supports up to 15 modules plus a scan tool
- Uses a 120 ohm resistor at the ends of each pair to reduce electrical noise
- Applies 2.5 volts on both wires:
  H (high) goes to 3.5 volts when active
  L (low) goes to 1.5 volts when active
  ● **SEE FIGURE 17-19**.

CAN CLASS A, B, AND C
There are three classes of CAN and they operate at different speeds. The CAN A, B, and C networks can all be linked using a gateway within the same vehicle. The gateway is usually one of the many modules in the vehicle.

- **CAN A.** This class operates on only one wire at slow speeds and is, therefore, less expensive to build. CAN A operates a data transfer rate of 33.33 Kbs in normal mode and up to 83.33 Kbs during reprogramming mode. CAN A uses the vehicle ground as the signal return circuit.
- **CAN B.** This class operates on a two-wire network and does not use the vehicle ground as the signal return circuit.

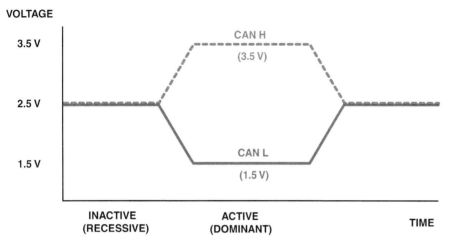

FIGURE 17–19 CAN uses a differential type of module communication where the voltage on one wire is the equal, but opposite, voltage on the other wire. When no communication is occurring, both wires have 2.5 volts applied. When communication is occurring, CAN H goes up 1 to 3.5 volts and CAN L goes down 1 to 1.5 volts.

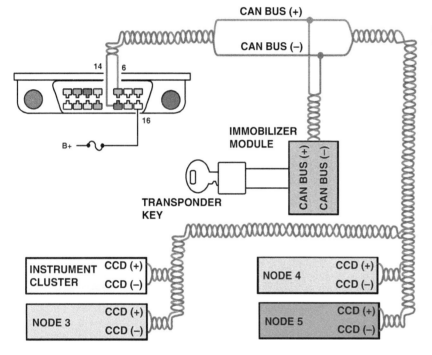

FIGURE 17–20 A typical (generic) system showing how the CAN BUS is connected to various electrical accessories and systems in the vehicle.

CAN B uses a data transfer rate of 95.2 Kbs. Instead, CAN B (and CAN C) uses two network wires for differential signaling. This means that the two data signal voltages are opposite to each other and used for error detection by constantly being compared. In this case, when the signal voltage at one of the CAN data wires goes high (CAN H), the other one goes low (CAN L), hence the name *differential signaling*. Differential signaling is also used for redundancy, in case one of the signal wires shorts out.

■ **CAN C.** This class is the highest speed CAN protocol, with speeds up to 500 Kbs. Beginning with 2008 models, all vehicles sold in the United States must use CAN BUS for scan tool communications. Most vehicle manufacturers started using CAN in older models; it is easy to determine if a vehicle is equipped with CAN. The CAN BUS communicates to the scan tool through terminals 6 and 14 of the DLC, indicating that the vehicle is equipped with CAN. ● **SEE FIGURE 17–20.**

The total voltage remains constant at all times and the electromagnetic field effects of the two data BUS lines cancel each other out. The data BUS line is protected against received radiation and is virtually neutral in sending radiation.

HONDA/TOYOTA COMMUNICATIONS

The primary BUS communication on pre-CAN-equipped vehicles is ISO 9141-2 using terminals 7 and 15 at the OBD-II DLC. ● **SEE FIGURE 17–21.**

A factory scan tool or an aftermarket scan tool equipped with enhanced original equipment (OE) software is needed to access many of the BUS messages. ● **SEE FIGURE 17–22.**

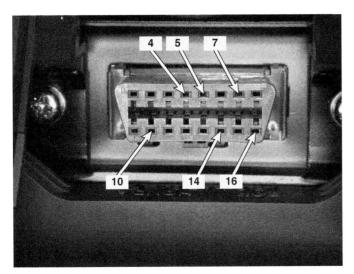

FIGURE 17–21 A DLC from a pre-CAN Acura. It shows terminals in cavities 4, 5 (grounds), 7, 10, 14, and 16 (B+).

FIGURE 17–23 A typical 38-cavity diagnostic connector as found on many BMW and Mercedes vehicles under the hood. The use of a breakout box (BOB) connected to this connector can help gain access to module BUS information.

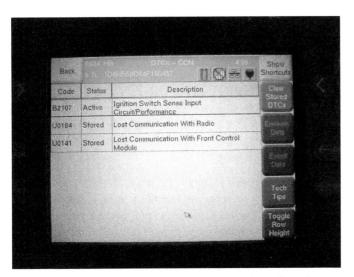

FIGURE 17–22 A Honda scan display showing a B and two U codes, all indicating a BUS-related problem(s).

EUROPEAN BUS COMMUNICATIONS

UNIQUE DIAGNOSTIC CONNECTOR Many different types of module communications protocols are used on European vehicles, such as Mercedes and BMW.

Most of these communication BUS messages cannot be accessed through the data link connector. To check the operation of the individual modules, a scan tool equipped with factory-type software is needed to communicate with the module through the gateway module. ● **SEE FIGURE 17–23** for an alternative access method to the modules.

MEDIA-ORIENTED SYSTEM TRANSPORT BUS The media-oriented system transport (MOST) BUS uses fiber optics for module-to-module communications in a ring or star configuration. This BUS system is currently being used for entertainment equipment data communications for videos, CDs, and other media systems in the vehicle.

MOTOROLA INTERCONNECT BUS Motorola interconnect (MI) is a single-wire serial communications protocol, using one master control module and many slave modules. Typical

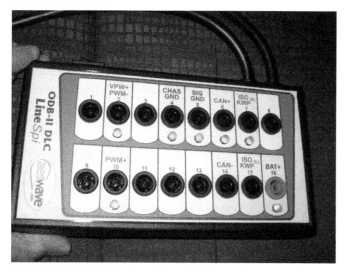

FIGURE 17–24 A breakout box (BOB) used to access the BUS terminals while using a scan tool to activate the modules. This breakout box is equipped with LEDs that light when data circuits are active.

application of the MI BUS protocol is with power and memory mirrors, seats, windows, and headlight levelers.

DISTRIBUTED SYSTEM INTERFACE BUS
Distributed system interface (DSI) BUS protocol was developed by Motorola and uses a two-wire serial BUS. This BUS protocol is currently being used for safety-related sensors and components.

BOSCH-SIEMANS-TEMIC BUS
The Bosch-Siemans-Temic (BST) BUS is another system that is used for safety-related components and sensors in a vehicle, such as airbags. The BST BUS is a two-wire system and operates up to 250,000 bps.

BYTEFLIGHT BUS
The byteflight BUS is used in safety critical systems, such as airbags, and uses the time division multiple access (TDMA) protocol, which operates at 10 million bps using a plastic optical fiber (POF).

FLEXRAY BUS
FlexRay BUS is a version of byteflight and is a high-speed serial communication system for in-vehicle networks. FlexRay is commonly used for steer-by-wire and brake-by-wire systems.

DOMESTIC DIGITAL BUS
The domestic digital BUS, commonly designated D2B, is an optical BUS system connecting audio, video, computer, and telephone components in a single-ring structure with a speed of up to 5,600,000 bps.

LOCAL INTERCONNECT NETWORK BUS
Local interconnect network (LIN) is a BUS protocol used between intelligent sensors and actuators and has a BUS speed of 19,200 bps.

NETWORK COMMUNICATIONS DIAGNOSIS

STEPS TO FINDING A FAULT When a network communications fault is suspected, perform the following steps.

STEP 1 **Check everything that does and does not work.** Often accessories that do not seem to be connected can help identify which module or BUS circuit is at fault.

STEP 2 **Perform module status test.** Use a factory-level scan tool or an aftermarket scan tool equipped with enhanced software that allows OE-like functions. Check if the components or systems can be operated through the scan tool. ● **SEE FIGURE 17–25.**

■ **Ping modules.** Start the Class 2 diagnosis by using a scan tool and select *diagnostic circuit check*. If no diagnostic trouble codes (DTCs) are shown, there could be a communication problem. Select *message monitor,* which displays the status of all of the modules on the Class 2 BUS circuit. The modules that are awake are shown as active and the scan tool can be used to ping individual modules or command all modules. The ping command should change the status from "active" to "inactive." ● **SEE FIGURE 17–26.**

NOTE: If an excessive parasitic draw is being diagnosed, use a scan tool to ping the modules in one way to determine if one of the modules is not going to sleep and cause excessive battery drain.

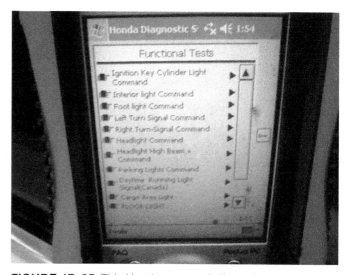

FIGURE 17–25 This Honda scan tool allows the technician to turn on individual lights and operate individual power windows and other accessories that are connected to the BUS system.

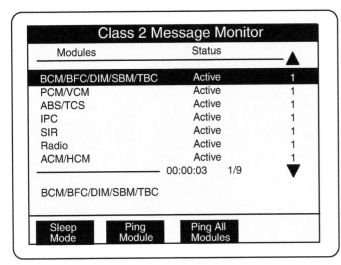

FIGURE 17–26 Modules used in a General Motors vehicle can be "pinged" using a Tech 2 scan tool.

- **Check state of health.** All modules on the Class 2 BUS circuit have at least one other module responsible for reporting **state of health (SOH)**. If a module fails to send a state of health message within five seconds, the companion module sets a diagnostic trouble code for the module that did not respond. The defective module is not capable of sending this message.

STEP 3 **Check the resistance of the terminating resistors.** Most high-speed BUS systems use resistors at each end, called **terminating resistors**. These resistors are used to help reduce interference into other systems in the vehicle. Usually two 120 ohm resistors are installed at each end and are, therefore, connected electrically in parallel. Two 120 ohm resistors connected in parallel measure 60 ohms if tested using an ohmmeter. ● **SEE FIGURE 17–27.**

STEP 4 **Check data BUS for voltages.** Use a digital multimeter set to DC volts to monitor communications and

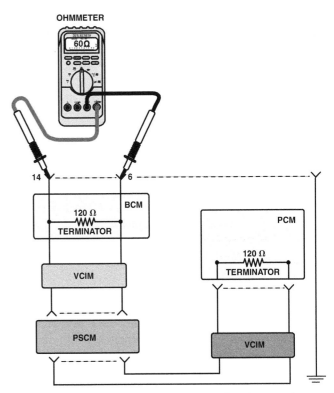

FIGURE 17–27 Checking the terminating resistors using an ohmmeter at the DLC.

 CASE STUDY

The Radio Caused No-Start Story

A 2012 GMC pickup truck did not start. A technician checked with a subscription-based helpline service and discovered that a fault with the Class 2 data circuit could prevent the engine from starting. The advisor suggested that a module should be disconnected one at a time to see if one of them was taking the data line to ground. The first one the technician disconnected was the radio. The engine started and ran. Apparently the Class 2 serial data line was shorted-to-ground inside the radio, which took the entire BUS down. When BUS communication is lost, the PCM is not able to energize the fuel pump, ignition, or fuel injectors, so the engine does not start. The radio was replaced to solve the no-start condition.

Summary:
- **Complaint**—The engine did not start.
- **Cause**—A hotline service helped the technician narrow the cause to a fault in the radio that took the Class 2 data line to ground.
- **Correction**—The radio was replaced, which restored proper operation of the Class 2 data bus.

check the BUS for proper operation. Some BUS conditions and possible causes include the following:

- **Signal is zero volt all of the time.** Check for short-to-ground by unplugging modules one at a time to check if one module is causing the problem.
- **Signal is high or 12 volts all of the time.** The BUS circuit could be shorted to 12 volts. Check with the customer to see if any service or body repair work was done recently. Try unplugging each module one at a time to pin down which module is causing the communications problem.
- **A variable voltage usually indicates that messages are being sent and received.** CAN and Class 2 can be identified by looking at the data link connector for a terminal in cavity number 2. Class 2 is active all of the time the ignition is "on," and, therefore, voltage variation between zero and seven volts can be measured using a DMM set to read DC volts. ● **SEE FIGURE 17–28.**

STEP 5 **Use a digital storage oscilloscope to monitor the waveforms of the BUS circuit.** Using a scope on the data line terminals can show if communication is being transmitted. Typical faults and their causes include the following:

- **Normal operation.** Normal operation shows variable voltage signals on the data lines. It is impossible to know what information is being transmitted, but, if there is activity with short sections of inactivity, this indicates normal data line transmission activity. ● **SEE FIGURE 17–29.**

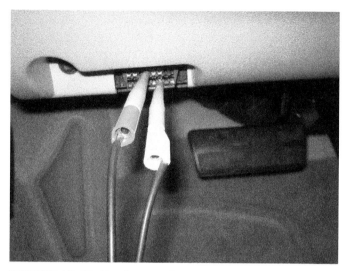

FIGURE 17–28 Use front-probe terminals to access the data link connector. Always follow the specified back-probe and front-probe procedures as found in service information.

(a)

CAN BUS LOOKS GOOD

FIGURE 17–29 (a) Data is sent in packets, so it is normal to see activity and then a flat line between messages. (b) A CAN BUS should show voltages that are opposite when there is normal communications. CAN H circuit should go from 2.5 volts at rest to 3.5 volts when active. The CAN L circuit goes from 2.5 volts at rest to 1.5 volts when active.

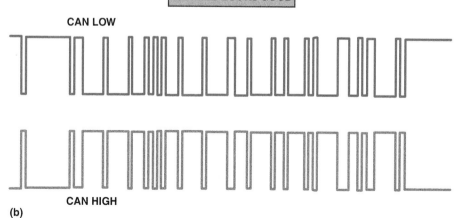

CAN LOW

CAN HIGH

(b)

- **High voltage.** If there is a constant high-voltage signal without any change, this indicates that the data line is shorted-to-voltage.
- **Zero or low voltage.** If the data line voltage is zero or almost zero and not showing any higher voltage signals, the data line is short-to-ground.

STEP 6 **Follow factory service information instructions to isolate the cause of the fault.** This step often involves disconnecting one module at a time to see if it is the cause of a short-to-ground or an open in the BUS circuit.

OBD-II DATA LINK CONNECTOR

All OBD-II vehicles use a 16-pin connector that includes the following:

Pin 4 = chassis ground

Pin 5 = signal ground

Pin 16 = battery power (4 A max)

● **SEE FIGURE 17–30.**

GENERAL MOTORS VEHICLES

- SAE J-1850 (VPW, Class 2, 10.4 Kbs) standard, which uses pins 2, 4, 5, and 16, but not 10
- GM Domestic OBD-II

Pins 1 and 9: CCM (comprehensive component monitor) slow baud rate, 8,192 UART (prior to 2006)

PIN	DESCRIPTION	PIN	DESCRIPTION
1	Vendor Option	9	Vendor Option
2	J1850 Bus+	10	J1850 Bus–
3	Vendor Option	11	Vendor Option
4	Chassis Ground	12	Vendor Option
5	Signal Ground	13	Vendor Option
6	CAN (J-2234) High	14	CAN (J-2234) Low
7	ISO 9141-2 K-Line	15	ISO 9141-2 L-Line
8	Vendor Option	16	Battery Power

FIGURE 17–30 A 16-pin OBD-II DLC with terminals identified. Scan tools use the power pin (16) and ground pin (4) for power so that a separate cigarette lighter plug is not necessary on OBD-II vehicles.

FREQUENTLY ASKED QUESTION

Which Module Is the Gateway Module?

The gateway module is responsible for communicating with other modules and acts as the main communications module for scan tool data. Most General Motors vehicles use the body control module (BCM) or the instrument panel control (IPC) module as the gateway. To verify which module is the gateway, check the schematic and look for one that has voltage applied during all of the following conditions.

- Key on, engine off
- Engine cranking
- Engine running

Pin 1 (2006+): low-speed GMLAN

Pins 2 and 10: OEM enhanced, fast rate, 40,500 baud rate

Pins 7 and 15: generic OBD-II, ISO 9141, 10,400 baud rate

Pins 6 and 14: GMLAN

ASIAN, CHRYSLER, AND EUROPEAN VEHICLES

- ISO 9141-2 standard, which uses pins 4, 5, 7, 15, and 16
- Chrysler Domestic Group OBD-II

Pins 2 and 10: CCM

Pins 3 and 14: OEM enhanced, 60,500 baud rate

Pins 7 and 15: generic OBD-II, ISO 9141, 10,400 baud rate

FORD VEHICLES

- SAE J-1850 (PWM, 41.6 Kbs) standard, which uses pins 2, 4, 5, 10, and 16
- Ford Domestic OBD-II

Pins 2 and 10: CCM

Pins 6 and 14: OEM enhanced, Class C, 40,500 baud rate

Pins 7 and 15: generic OBD-II, ISO 9141, 10,400 baud rate

TECH TIP

Check Computer Data Line Circuit Schematic

Many General Motors vehicles use more than one type of BUS communications protocol. Check service information (SI) and look at the schematic for computer data line circuits, which should show all of the data BUSes and their connectors to the diagnostic link connector (DLC). ● **SEE FIGURE 17–31.**

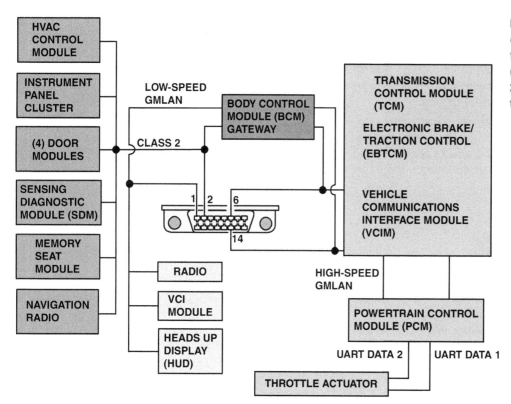

FIGURE 17–31 This schematic of a Chevrolet Equinox shows that the vehicle uses a GMLAN BUS (DLC pins 6 and 14), plus a Class 2 (pin 2) and UART. Pin 1 connects to the low-speed GMLAN network.

SUMMARY

1. The use of a network for module communications reduces the number of wires and connections needed.

2. Module communication configurations include ring link, star link, and ring/star hybrid systems.

3. The SAE communication classifications for vehicle communications systems include Class A (low speed), Class B (medium speed), and Class C (high speed).

4. Various module communications used on General Motors vehicles include UART, E & C, Class 2, keyword communications, and GMLAN (CAN).

5. Types of module communications used on Ford vehicles include SCP, UBP, and CAN.

6. Chrysler brand vehicles use SCI, CCD, PCI, and CAN communications protocols.

7. Many European vehicles use an underhood electrical connector that can be used to access electrical components and modules using a breakout box (BOB) or special tester.

8. Diagnosis of network communications includes checking the terminating resistor value and checking for changing voltage signals at the DLC.

REVIEW QUESTIONS

1. Why is a communication network used?

2. Why are the two wires twisted if used for network communications?

3. Why is a gateway module used?

4. What are U codes?

5. What is the purpose of the terminating resistors?

1. Technician A says that module communications networks are used to reduce the number of wires in a vehicle. Technician B says that a communications network is used to share data from sensors, which can be used by many different modules. Which technician is correct?
   a. Technician A only
   b. Technician B only
   c. Both Technicians A and B
   d. Neither Technician A nor B

2. A module is also known as a _____.
   a. bus
   b. node
   c. terminator
   d. resistor pack

3. A high-speed CAN BUS communicates with a scan tool through which terminal(s)?
   a. 6 and 14
   b. 2
   c. 7 and 15
   d. 4 and 16

4. In a star link network, a serial data line connects all of the modules to _____.
   a. a central point
   b. each other
   c. the vehicle fuse box
   d. chassis ground

5. Network diagnosis is being discussed. Technician A says that a test light can be used at the DLC to determine if the CAN bus has activity. Technician B says that a break-out box can be used to determine if there is activity on the CAN bus. Which technician is correct?
   a. Technician A only
   b. Technician B only
   c. Both technicians are correct
   d. Neither technician is correct

6. Which terminal of the data link connector does General Motors use for Class 2 communication?
   a. 1
   b. 2
   c. 3
   d. 4

7. GMLAN is the General Motors term for which type of module communication?
   a. UART
   b. Class 2
   c. High-speed CAN
   d. Keyword 2000

8. How do CAN H and CAN L operate?
   a. CAN H is at 2.5 volts when not transmitting.
   b. CAN L is at 2.5 volts when not transmitting.
   c. CAN H goes to 3.5 volts when transmitting.
   d. All of the above

9. Which terminal of the OBD-II data link connector is the signal ground for all vehicles?
   a. 1
   b. 3
   c. 4
   d. 5

10. Terminal 16 of the OBD-II data link connector is used for what?
    a. Chassis ground
    b. 12 volt positive
    c. Module (signal ground)
    d. Manufacturer's discretion**(b)**

chapter 18

BATTERIES

LEARNING OBJECTIVES:

After studying this chapter, the reader should be able to:

Describe the construction of a battery.

Describe how a battery works.

Discuss how charge indicators work.

Discuss valve regulated batteries and the causes of battery failure.

List battery ratings and battery sizes.

This chapter will help you prepare for the ASE Electrical/Electronic Systems (A6) certification test content area "B" (Battery Diagnosis and Service).

KEY TERMS: AGM 219 • Ampere hour 221 • Battery Council International (BCI) 221 • CA 220 • CCA 220 • Cells 216 • Deep cycling 221 • Electrolyte 216 • Enhanced Flooded Batteries (EFB) 218 • Flooded lead acid (FLA) 218 • Gassing 215 • Gel battery 219 • Grid 215 • Low-water-loss battery 215 • Maintenance-free battery 215 • MCA 220 • Partitions 216 • Porous lead 215 • Recombinant battery 219 • Reserve capacity 220 • Sediment chamber 214 • SLA 219 • SLI 214 • Specific gravity 217 • Sponge lead 215 • SVR 219 • VRLA 219

INTRODUCTION

PURPOSE AND FUNCTION Every electrical component in a vehicle is supplied current from the battery. The battery is one of the most important parts of a vehicle because it is the heart or foundation of the electrical system. The primary purpose of an automotive battery is to provide a source of electrical power for starting, and for electrical demands that exceed alternator output.

WHY BATTERIES ARE IMPORTANT The battery also acts as a voltage stabilizer for the entire electrical system. The battery is a voltage stabilizer because it acts as a reservoir from where large amounts of current (amperes) can be used quickly during starting, and replaced back gradually by the alternator during charging.

- The battery *must* be in good (serviceable) condition before the charging and cranking systems can be tested. For example, if a battery is discharged, the cranking circuit (starter motor) could test as being defective because the battery voltage might drop below specifications.

- The charging circuit could also test as being defective because of a weak or discharged battery. It is important to test the vehicle battery before further testing of the cranking or charging system.

BATTERY CONSTRUCTION

CASE Most automotive battery cases (container or covers) are constructed of polypropylene, a thin (approximately 0.08 inch or 0.02 millimeter thick), strong, and lightweight plastic. In contrast, containers for industrial batteries and some truck batteries are constructed of a hard, thick rubber material.

Inside the case are six cells (for a 12 volt battery). Each cell has positive and negative plates. Built into the bottom of many batteries are ribs that support the lead-alloy plates and provide a space for sediment to settle, called the **sediment chamber**. This space prevents spent active material from causing a short circuit between the plates at the bottom of the battery. **SEE FIGURE 18–1**.

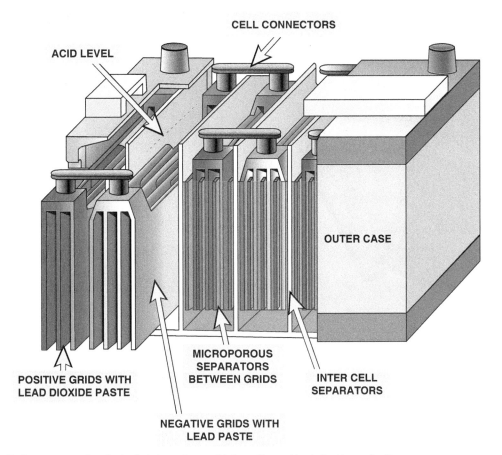

FIGURE 18–1 Batteries are constructed of plates grouped into cells and installed in a plastic case.

CELL CONNECTORS

ACID LEVEL

OUTER CASE

POSITIVE GRIDS WITH
LEAD DIOXIDE PASTE

MICROPOROUS
SEPARATORS
BETWEEN GRIDS

INTER CELL
SEPARATORS

NEGATIVE GRIDS WITH
LEAD PASTE

A **maintenance-free battery** uses little water during normal service because of the alloy material used to construct the battery plate grids. Maintenance-free batteries are also called **low-water-loss batteries**.

GRIDS Each positive and negative plate in a battery is constructed on a framework, or **grid**, made primarily of lead. Lead is a soft material and must be strengthened for use in an automotive battery grid. Adding antimony or calcium to the pure lead adds strength to the lead grids. ● **SEE FIGURE 18–2**.

Battery grids hold the active material and provide the electrical pathways for the current created in the plate.

Maintenance-free batteries use calcium instead of antimony, because 0.2% calcium has the same strength as 6% antimony. A typical lead–calcium grid uses only 0.09% to 0.12% calcium. Using low amounts of calcium instead of higher amounts of antimony reduces **gassing**. Gassing is the release of hydrogen and oxygen from the battery that occurs during charging and results in water usage.

Low-maintenance batteries use a low percentage of antimony (about 2% to 3%), or use antimony only in the positive grids and calcium in the negative grids. *The percentages that make up the alloy of the plate grids constitute the major difference between standard and maintenance-free batteries.* The chemical reactions that occur inside each battery are identical, regardless of the type of material used to construct the grid plates.

FIGURE 18–2 A grid from a battery used in both positive and negative plates.

POSITIVE PLATES The positive plates have *lead dioxide (peroxide)* placed onto the grid framework. This process is called *pasting*. This active material can react with the sulfuric acid of the battery and is dark brown in color.

NEGATIVE PLATES The negative plates are pasted to the grid with a pure **porous lead**, called **sponge lead**, and are gray in color.

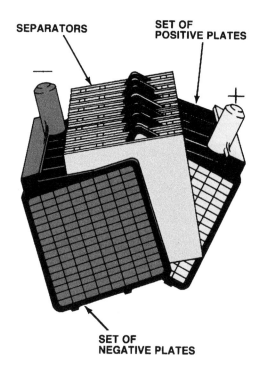

FIGURE 18–3 Two groups of plates are combined to form a battery element.

SEPARATORS

The positive and the negative plates must be installed alternately next to each other without touching. Nonconducting *separators* are used, which allow room for the reaction of the acid with both plate materials, yet insulate the plates to prevent shorts. These separators are porous (with many small holes) and have ribs facing the positive plate. Separators can be made from resin-coated paper, porous rubber, fiberglass, or expanded plastic. Many batteries use envelope-type separators that encase the entire plate. This helps prevent any material that may shed from the plates from causing a short circuit between plates at the bottom of the battery.

CELLS

Cells are constructed of positive and negative plates with insulating separators between each plate. Most batteries use one more negative plate than positive plate in each cell. However, many newer batteries use the same number of positive and negative plates. A cell is also called an element. Each cell is actually a 2.1 volt battery, regardless of the number of positive or negative plates used. The greater the number of plates used in each cell, the greater the amount of *current* that can be produced. Typical batteries contain four positive plates and five negative plates per cell. A 12 volt battery contains six cells connected in series, which produce 12.6 volts ($6 \times 2.1 = 12.6$) and contain 54 plates (9 plates per cell × 6 cells). If the same 12 volt battery had five positive plates and six negative plates, for a total of 11 plates per cell (5 + 6), or 66 plates (11 plates × 6 cells), it has the same voltage, but the amount of current that the battery could produce is increased. ● **SEE FIGURE 18–3**.

The amperage capacity of a battery is determined by the amount of active plate material in the battery and the area of the plate material exposed to the electrolyte in the battery.

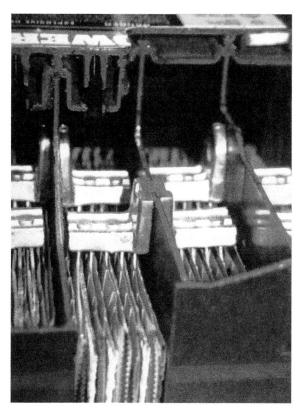

FIGURE 18–4 A cutaway battery showing the connection of the cells to each other through the partition.

PARTITIONS

Each cell is separated from the other cells by **partitions**, which are made of the same material as that used for the outside case of the battery. Electrical connections between cells are provided by lead connectors that loop over the top of the partition and connect the plates of the cells together. Many batteries connect the cells directly through the partition connectors, which provide the shortest path for the current and the lowest resistance. ● **SEE FIGURE 18–4**.

ELECTROLYTE

Electrolyte is the term used to describe the acid solution in a battery. The electrolyte used in automotive batteries is a solution (liquid combination) of 36% sulfuric acid and 64% water. This electrolyte is used for both lead–antimony and lead–calcium (maintenance-free) batteries. The chemical symbol for this sulfuric acid solution is H_2SO_4.

> H_2 = Symbol for hydrogen (the subscript 2 means that there are two atoms of hydrogen)
>
> S = Symbol for sulfur
>
> O_4 = Symbol for oxygen (the subscript 4 indicates that there are four atoms of oxygen)

Electrolyte is sold premixed in a proper proportion and is factory installed or added to the battery when the battery is sold. Additional electrolyte must *never* be added to any battery after the original electrolyte fill. It is normal for some water (H_2O) to escape during charging as a result of the chemical reactions. The escape of gases from a battery during charging or discharging is called gassing. Only pure distilled water should be added to a battery. If distilled water is not available, clean drinking water can be used.

HOW A BATTERY WORKS

PRINCIPLE INVOLVED The principle on which a battery works is based on a scientific principle discovered years ago, which states that:

- When two dissimilar metals are placed in an acid, electrons flow between the metals if a circuit is connected between them.
- This can be demonstrated by pushing a steel nail and a piece of solid copper wire into a lemon. Connect a voltmeter to the ends of the copper wire and the nail, and voltage is displayed.

A fully charged lead–acid battery has a positive plate of lead dioxide (peroxide) and a negative plate of lead surrounded by a sulfuric acid solution (electrolyte). The difference in potential (voltage) between lead peroxide and lead in acid is approximately 2.1 volts.

DURING DISCHARGING The positive plate lead dioxide (PbO_2) combines with the SO_4, forming $PbSO_4$ from the electrolyte and releases its O_2 into the electrolyte, forming H_2O. The negative plate also combines with the SO_4 from the electrolyte and becomes lead sulfate ($PbSO_4$). ● **SEE FIGURE 18–5.**

FULLY DISCHARGED STATE When the battery is fully discharged, both the positive and the negative plates are $PbSO_4$ (lead sulfate) and the electrolyte has become water (H_2O). As the battery is being discharged, the plates and the electrolyte approach the completely discharged state. There is also the

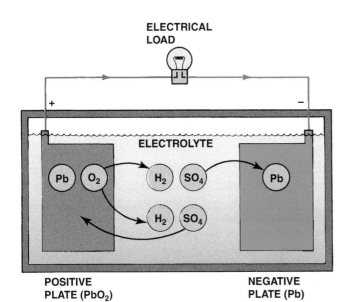

FIGURE 18–5 Chemical reaction for a lead–acid battery that is fully charged being discharged by the attached electrical load.

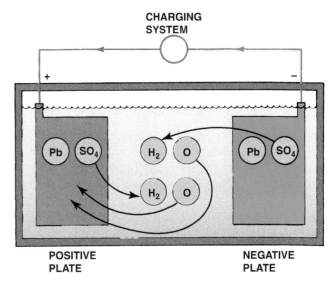

FIGURE 18–6 Chemical reaction for a lead–acid battery that is fully discharged being charged by the attached generator.

? FREQUENTLY ASKED QUESTION

Is There an Easy Way to Remember How a Battery Works?

Yes. Think of the sulfuric acid solution in the electrolyte being deposited, then removed from the plates.

- **During discharge.** The acid (SO_4) is leaving the electrolyte and getting onto both plates.
- **During charging.** The acid (SO_4) is being forced from both plates and enters the electrolyte.

danger of freezing when a battery is discharged, because the electrolyte is mostly water.

CAUTION: Never charge or jump-start a frozen battery because the hydrogen gas can get trapped in the ice and ignite if a spark is caused during the charging process. The result can be an explosion.

DURING CHARGING During charging, the sulfate from the acid leaves both the positive and the negative plates and returns to the electrolyte, where it becomes a normal-strength sulfuric acid solution. The positive plate returns to lead dioxide (PbO_2), the negative plate is again pure lead (Pb), and the electrolyte becomes H_2SO_4. ● **SEE FIGURE 18–6.**

SPECIFIC GRAVITY

DEFINITION The amount of sulfate in the electrolyte is determined by the electrolyte's **specific gravity**, which is the ratio of the weight of a given volume of a liquid to the weight

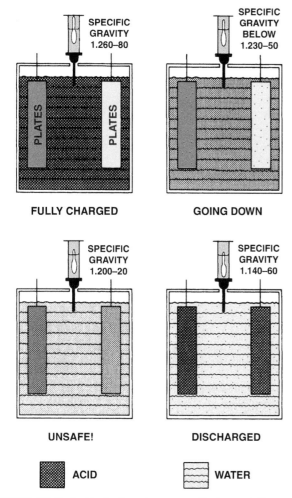

FIGURE 18–7 As the battery becomes discharged, the specific gravity of the battery acid decreases. Because the electrolyte is close to water when discharged, a dead battery can freeze in cold weather.

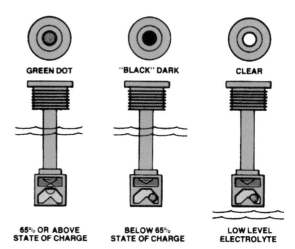

FIGURE 18–8 Typical battery charge indicator. If the specific gravity is low (battery discharged), the ball drops away from the reflective prism. When the battery is charged enough, the ball floats and reflects the color of the ball (usually green) back up through the sight glass and the sight glass is dark.

SPECIFIC GRAVITY	STATE OF CHARGE	BATTERY VOLTAGE (V)
1.265	Fully charged	12.6 or higher
1.225	75% charged	12.4
1.190	50% charged	12.2
1.155	25% charged	12.0
Lower than 1.120	Discharged	11.9 or lower

CHART 18–1

A comparison showing the relationship among specific gravity, battery voltage, and state of charge.

of an equal volume of water. In other words, the denser the liquid is, the higher its specific gravity. Pure water is the basis for this measurement and is given a specific gravity of 1.000 at 80°F (27°C). Pure sulfuric acid has a specific gravity of 1.835; the *correct* concentration of water and sulfuric acid (called electrolyte—64% water, 36% acid) is 1.260 to 1.280 at 80°F. The higher the battery's specific gravity, the more fully it is charged. ● **SEE FIGURE 18–7**.

CHARGE INDICATORS Some batteries are equipped with a built-in state-of-charge indicator, commonly called *green eyes*. This indicator is simply a small, ball-type hydrometer that is installed in one cell. This hydrometer uses a plastic ball that floats if the electrolyte density is sufficient (which it is when the battery is about 65% charged). When the ball floats, it appears in the hydrometer's sight glass, changing its color. ● **SEE FIGURE 18–8**.

Because the hydrometer is testing only one cell (out of six on a 12 volt battery), and because the hydrometer ball can easily stick in one position, do not trust that this is accurate information about a state of charge (SOC) of the battery.

Values of specific gravity, state of charge, and battery voltage at 80°F (27°C) are given in ● **CHART 18–1**.

BATTERY CONSTRUCTION TYPES

FLOODED BATTERIES Conventional batteries use a liquid electrolyte and are called **flooded lead acid (FLA)** batteries. In this design, vents are used to allow the gases (hydrogen and oxygen) to escape. It is this loss of the hydrogen and oxygen that results in a battery using water during normal use.

ENHANCED FLOODED BATTERIES **Enhanced Flooded Battery (EFB)** is a flooded battery (NOT an absorbed glass mat battery) that is optimized to work with stop/start vehicle systems. Using wet cells, the design allows for improved charge acceptance and greater durability when being operated in a vehicle that uses a stop/start system. In stop/start vehicle, the engine stops running when at idle speed, then restarts when the driver releases the brake pedal. This operation requires a robust battery and starter motor to function correctly over an estimated life of over 500,000 stops and starts.

ABSORBED GLASS MAT The acid used in an **absorbed glass mat (AGM)** battery is totally absorbed into the separator, making the battery leak proof and spill proof. The battery is assembled by compressing the cell about 20%, then inserting it into the container. The compressed cell helps reduce damage caused by vibration and helps keep the acid tightly against the plates. The sealed maintenance-free design uses a pressure release valve in each cell. Unlike conventional batteries that use a liquid electrolyte, called flooded cell batteries, most of the hydrogen and oxygen given off during charging remains inside the battery. The separator or mat is only 90% to 95% saturated with electrolyte, thereby allowing a portion of the mat to be filled with gas. The gas spaces provide channels to allow the hydrogen and oxygen gases to recombine rapidly and safely. Because the acid is totally absorbed into the glass mat separator, an AGM battery can be mounted in any direction. AGM batteries also have a longer service life, often lasting 7 to 10 years. Absorbed glass mat batteries are used as standard equipment in some vehicles, such as the Chevrolet Corvette, and in most Toyota/Lexus hybrid-electric vehicles. ● **SEE FIGURES 18–9 AND 18–10.**

GELLED ELECTROLYTE BATTERY In a gelled electrolyte battery, silica is added to the electrolyte, which turns the electrolyte into a substance similar to gelatin. This type of battery is also called a **gel battery**. Gel batteries are usually not used in automotive applications but instead are used in electric wheelchairs and scooters.

VALVE-REGULATED LEAD–ACID BATTERIES Both AGM and gel batteries are called **valve-regulated lead–acid (VRLA)**, also called **sealed valve-regulated (SVR)** or **sealed**

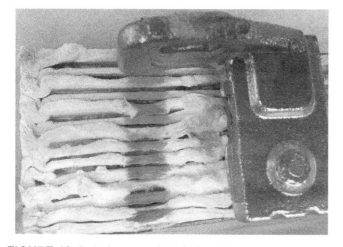

FIGURE 18–9 A close up of a AGM cell showing the mat totally encasing the plates.

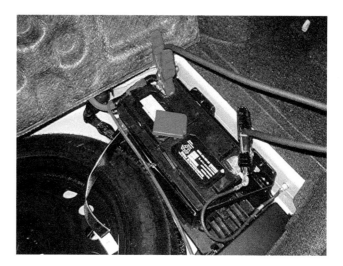

FIGURE 18–10 A AGM battery under the floor next to the spare tire on a Lexus NX300h hybrid-electric vehicle.

lead–acid (SLA), batteries. These batteries use a low-pressure venting system that releases excess gas and automatically reseals if a buildup of gas is created due to overcharging.

Both types of valve-regulated lead–acid batteries are also called **recombinant battery** design. A recombinant-type battery means that the oxygen gas generated at the positive plate travels through the dense electrolyte to the negative plate. When the oxygen reaches the negative plate, it reacts with the lead, which consumes the oxygen gas and prevents the formation of hydrogen gas. It is because of this oxygen recombination that VRLA batteries do not use water.

CAUSES AND TYPES OF BATTERY FAILURE

NORMAL LIFE Most automotive batteries have a useful service life of three to seven years; however, proper care can help increase the life of a battery, but abuse can shorten it. The major cause of premature battery failure is overcharging.

BATTERY SULFATION During charging of a battery, the lead sulfate is converted back to lead. When a battery is left in a discharged condition, the lead sulfate re-crystallizes into hard lead sulfate. This process is called sulfation or a *sulfated battery*.

CHARGING VOLTAGE The automotive charging circuit, consisting of an alternator and connecting wires, must operate correctly to prevent damage to the battery.

- Charging voltages higher than 15.5 volts can damage a battery by warping the plates as a result of the heat of overcharging.
- AGM batteries can be damaged if charged at a voltage higher than 14.5 volts.

FIGURE 18–11 A typical battery hold-down bracket. All batteries should use a bracket to prevent battery damage due to vibration and shock.

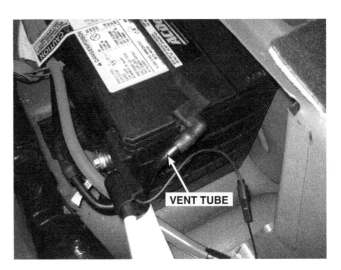

FIGURE 18–12 A battery installed under the rear seat of a Cadillac showing the vent tubes.

Overcharging also causes the active plate material to disintegrate and fall out of the supporting grid framework. Vibration or bumping can also cause internal damage similar to that caused by overcharging. It is important, therefore, to ensure that all automotive batteries are securely clamped with the battery hold-down bracket in the vehicle. The shorting of cell plates can occur without notice. If one of the six cells of a 12 volt battery is shorted, the resulting voltage of the battery is only 10 volts (12 − 2 = 10). With only 10 volts available, the starter *usually* is not able to start the engine.

BATTERY HOLD-DOWNS All batteries must be attached securely to the vehicle to prevent battery damage. Normal vehicle vibrations can cause the active materials inside the battery to shed. Battery hold-down clamps or brackets help reduce vibration, which can greatly reduce the capacity and life of any battery. ● **SEE FIGURE 18–11.**

BATTERY VENT TUBES If a battery is installed inside a vehicle, vent tubes are used to route battery fumes to the outside so they don't get into the passenger compartment. ● **SEE FIGURE 18–12.**

BATTERY RATINGS

Batteries are rated according to the amount of current they can produce under specific conditions.

COLD-CRANKING AMPERES Every automotive battery must be able to supply electrical power to crank the engine in cold weather and still provide battery voltage high enough to operate the ignition system for starting. The cold-cranking ampere rating

of a battery is the number of amperes that can be supplied by a battery at 0°F (−18°C) for 30 seconds while the battery still maintains a voltage of 1.2 volts per cell or higher. This means that the battery voltage is 7.2 volts for a 12 volt battery and 3.6 volts for a 6 volt battery. The cold-cranking performance rating is called **cold-cranking amperes (CCA)**. Try to purchase a battery with the highest CCA for the money. See the vehicle manufacturer's specifications for recommended battery capacity.

CRANKING AMPERES The designation **CA** refers to the number of amperes that can be supplied by a battery at 32°F (0°C). This rating results in a higher number than the more stringent CCA rating. ● **SEE FIGURE 18–13.**

MARINE CRANKING AMPERES Marine cranking amperes (MCA) is similar to cranking amperes and is tested at 32°F (0°C).

RESERVE CAPACITY The **reserve capacity** rating for batteries is *the number of minutes* that the battery can produce 25 amperes and still have a battery voltage of

FIGURE 18–13 This battery has a cranking amperes (CA) rating of 1,000. This means that this battery is capable of cranking an engine for 30 seconds at a temperature of 32°F (0°C) at a minimum of 1.2 volts per cell (7.2 volts for a 12 volt battery).

1.75 volts per cell (10.5 volts for a 12 volt battery). This rating is actually a measurement of the time a vehicle can be driven in the event of a charging system failure.

AMPERE HOUR Ampere hour is an older battery rating system that measures how many amperes of current the battery can produce over a period of time. For example, a battery that has a 50 amp-hour (A-H) rating can deliver 50 amperes for 1 hour or 1 ampere for 50 hours or any combination that equals 50 amp-hours.

BATTERY SIZES

BCI GROUP SIZES Battery sizes are standardized by the **Battery Council International (BCI)**. When selecting a replacement battery, check the specified group number in service information, battery application charts at parts stores, or the owner's manual.

TYPICAL GROUP SIZE APPLICATIONS

- **24/24F (top terminals).** Fits many Honda, Acura, Infiniti, Lexus, Nissan, and Toyota vehicles.
- **34/78 (dual terminals, both side and top posts).** Fits many General Motors pickups and SUVs, as well as midsize and larger GM sedans and large Chrysler/Dodge vehicles.
- **35 (top terminals).** Fits many Japanese-brand vehicles.
- **65 (top terminals).** Fits most large Ford/Mercury passenger cars, trucks, and SUVs.
- **75 (side terminals).** Fits some General Motors small- and midsize cars, and some Chrysler/Dodge vehicles.
- **78 (side terminals).** Fits many General Motors pickups and SUVs, as well as midsize and larger GM sedans.

Exact dimensions can be found on the Internet by searching for BCI battery sizes.

? FREQUENTLY ASKED QUESTION

What Is Deep Cycling?

Deep cycling is almost fully discharging a battery and then completely recharging it. Golf cart batteries are an example of lead–acid batteries that must be designed to be deep cycled. A golf cart must be able to cover two 18-hole rounds of golf and then be fully recharged overnight. Charging is hard on batteries because the internal heat generated can cause plate warpage, so these specially designed batteries use thicker plate grids that resist warpage. Normal automotive batteries are not designed for repeated deep cycling.

SUMMARY

1. Maintenance-free batteries use lead–calcium grids instead of lead–antimony grids to reduce gassing.
2. When a battery is being discharged, the acid (SO4) is leaving the electrolyte and being deposited on the plates.

   When the battery is being charged, the acid (SO4) is forced off the plates and goes back into the electrolyte.

3. All batteries give off hydrogen and oxygen when being charged.
4. Batteries are rated according to CCA and reserve capacity.

1. Why can discharged batteries freeze?
2. What are the battery-rating methods?
3. Why can a battery explode if it is exposed to an open flame or spark?
4. What is meant by a sulfated battery?
5. What does the BCI group number mean?

1. When a battery becomes completely discharged, both positive and negative plates become _____ and the electrolyte becomes _____.
   a. H_2SO_4; Pb
   b. $PbSO_4$; H_2O
   c. PbO_2; H_2SO_4
   d. $PbSO_4$; H_2SO_4

2. A fully charged 12 volt battery should indicate _____.
   a. 12.6 volts or higher
   b. a specific gravity of 1.265 or higher
   c. 12 volts
   d. both a and b

3. Some vehicles use an AGM-type battery. This means the electrolyte is _____ inside the battery.
   a. a dry powder
   b. liquid
   c. absorbed into the separator
   d. a gel-like form

4. What makes a battery "low maintenance" or "maintenance free"?
   a. The material that is used to construct the grids.
   b. The plates are constructed of different metals.
   c. The electrolyte is hydrochloric acid solution.
   d. The battery plates are smaller, making more room for additional electrolytes.

5. The positive battery plate is _____.
   a. lead dioxide
   b. brown in color
   c. sometimes called lead peroxide
   d. all of the above

6. Which battery rating is tested at 0°F (−18°C)?
   a. Cold-cranking amperes (CCA)
   b. Cranking amperes (CA)
   c. Reserve capacity
   d. Battery voltage test

7. Which battery rating is expressed in minutes?
   a. Cold-cranking amperes (CCA)
   b. Cranking amperes (CA)
   c. Reserve capacity
   d. Battery voltage test

8. What battery rating is tested at 32°F (0°C)?
   a. Cold-cranking amperes (CCA)
   b. Cranking amperes (CA)
   c. Reserve capacity
   d. Battery voltage test

9. What gases are released from a battery when it is being charged?
   a. Oxygen
   b. Hydrogen
   c. Nitrogen and oxygen
   d. Hydrogen and oxygen

10. A charge indicator (eye) operates by showing green or red when the battery is charged and dark if the battery is discharged. This charge indicator detects _____.
    a. battery voltage
    b. specific gravity
    c. electrolyte water pH
    d. internal resistance of the cells

chapter 19

BATTERY TESTING AND SERVICE

LEARNING OBJECTIVES:

After studying this chapter, the reader should be able to:

List the precautions for working with batteries.

List the symptoms of a weak or defective battery.

Describe how to inspect and clean terminals and hold-downs.

Discuss how to test batteries for open circuit voltage and specific gravity.

Describe how to perform a battery load test and a conductance test.

Explain how to safely charge or jump start a battery.

Discuss how to perform a battery drain test.

Describe how to prevent loss of memory functions and reinitialize memory functions.

This chapter will help you prepare for the ASE Electrical/Electronic Systems (A6) certification test content area "B" (Battery Diagnosis and Service).

KEY TERMS: Battery electrical drain test 231 • Dynamic voltage 224 • Hydrometer 226 • IOD 231 • Load test 226 • Open circuit voltage 224 • Parasitic load test 231 • Three-minute charge test 226

BATTERY SERVICE SAFETY CONSIDERATIONS

HAZARDS Batteries contain acid and release explosive gases (hydrogen and oxygen) during normal charging and discharging cycles.

SAFETY PROCEDURES To help prevent physical injury or damage to the vehicle, always adhere to the following safety procedures.

1. When working on any electrical component on a vehicle, disconnect the negative battery cable from the battery. When the negative cable is disconnected, all electrical circuits in the vehicle are open, which prevents accidental electrical contact between an electrical component and ground. Any electrical spark has the potential to cause explosion and personal injury.

2. Wear eye protection (goggles preferred) when working around any battery.

3. Wear protective clothing to avoid skin contact with battery acid.

4. Always adhere to all safety precautions as stated in the service procedures for the equipment used for battery service and testing.

5. Never smoke or use an open flame around any battery.

6. Never attempt to jump start or charge a frozen battery.

SYMPTOMS OF A WEAK OR DEFECTIVE BATTERY

The following warning signs indicate that a battery is near the end of its useful life.

■ **Uses water in one or more cells.** This indicates that the plates are sulfated and that, during the charging process, the water in the electrolyte is being turned into separate hydrogen and oxygen gases. ● SEE FIGURE 19–1.

■ **Excessive corrosion on battery cables or connections.** Corrosion is more likely to occur if the battery is sulfated, creating hot spots on the plates. When the battery is being charged, the acid fumes are forced out of the vent holes and onto the battery cables, connections, and even on the battery tray underneath the battery. ● SEE FIGURE 19–2.

■ **Slower than normal engine cranking.** When the capacity of the battery is reduced due to damage or age, it is less likely to be able to supply the necessary current for starting the engine, especially during cold weather.

FIGURE 19–1 A visual inspection on this battery shows the electrolyte level is below the plates in all cells. Not many batteries can be checked for the electrolyte level and, if low, the battery is likely at the end of its normal service life.

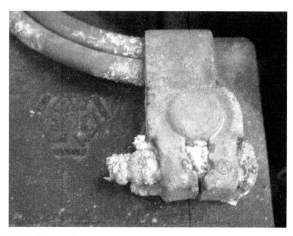

FIGURE 19–2 Corrosion on a battery cable could be an indication that the battery itself is either being overcharged or is sulfated, creating a lot of gassing of the electrolyte.

🔧 **TECH TIP**

Dynamic versus Open Circuit Voltage

Open circuit voltage is the voltage (usually of a battery) that exists without a load being applied. **Dynamic voltage** is the voltage of the power source (battery) with the circuit in operation. A vehicle battery, for example, may indicate that it has 12.6 volts or more, but that voltage drops when the battery is put under a load, such as cranking the engine. If the battery voltage drops too much, the starter motor rotates more slowly and the engine may not start.

If the dynamic voltage is lower than specified, the battery may be weak or defective or the circuit may be defective.

BATTERY MAINTENANCE

NEED FOR MAINTENANCE Most new-style batteries are of a maintenance-free design that uses lead–calcium, instead of lead–antimony, plate grid construction. Because lead–calcium batteries do not release as much gas as the older-style, lead–antimony, batteries, there is less consumption of water during normal service. Also, with less gassing, less corrosion is observed on the battery terminals, wiring, and support trays. If the electrolyte level can be checked, and if it is low, add only distilled water. Distilled water is recommended by all battery manufacturers, but if distilled water is not available, clean ordinary drinking water, low in mineral content, can be used.

Battery maintenance includes making certain that the battery case is clean, and checking that the battery cables and hold-down fasteners are clean and tight.

BATTERY TERMINAL CLEANING Many battery-related faults are caused by poor electrical connections at the battery. Battery cable connections should be checked and cleaned to prevent voltage drop at the connections. One common reason for an engine to not start is loose or corroded battery cable connections. Perform an inspection and check for the following conditions.

- Loose or corroded connections at the battery terminals (should not be able to be moved by hand)
- Loose or corroded connections at the ground connector on the engine block
- Wiring that has been modified to add auxiliary power for a sound system or other electrical accessory

If the connections are loose or corroded, use 1 tablespoon of baking soda in 1 quart (liter) of water and brush this mixture onto the battery and housing to neutralize the acid. Mechanically clean the connections and wash the area with water. ● **SEE FIGURE 19–3**.

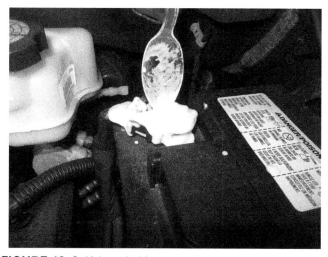

FIGURE 19–3 Using a baking soda and water paste to remove the corrosion on a battery terminal.

BATTERY HOLD-DOWN The battery should also be secured with a hold-down bracket to prevent vibration from damaging the plates inside the battery. The hold-down bracket should be snug enough to prevent battery movement, yet not so tight as to cause the case to crack. Factory-original hold-down brackets are often available through local automobile dealers, and universal hold-down units are available through local automotive parts stores.

BATTERY VOLTAGE TEST

STATE OF CHARGE Testing the battery voltage with a voltmeter is a simple method for determining the state of charge of any battery. ● **SEE FIGURE 19–4.** The voltage of a battery does not necessarily indicate whether the battery can perform satisfactorily, but it does indicate to the technician more about the battery's condition than a simple visual inspection. A battery that "looks good" may not be good. This test is commonly called an *open circuit battery voltage test* because it is conducted with an open circuit, no current flowing, and no load applied to the battery.

1. If the battery has just been charged or the vehicle has recently been driven, it is necessary to remove the surface charge from the battery before testing. A surface charge is a charge of higher-than-normal voltage that is just on the surface of the battery plates. The surface charge is quickly removed when the battery is loaded and, therefore, does not accurately represent the true state of charge of the battery.

2. To remove the surface charge, turn the headlights on high beam (brights) for one minute, then turn the headlights off and wait two minutes.

3. With the engine and all electrical accessories off, and the doors shut (to turn off the interior lights), connect a voltmeter to the battery posts. Connect the red positive lead to the positive post and the black negative lead to the negative post.

   NOTE: If the meter reads negative (−), the battery has been reverse charged (has reversed polarity) and should be replaced, or the meter has been connected incorrectly.

4. Read the voltmeter and compare the results with the state of charge (SOC). The voltages shown are for a battery at or near room temperature (70°F to 80°F, or 21°C to 27°C). ● **SEE CHART 19–1.**

BATTERY VOLTAGE (V)	STATE OF CHARGE
12.6 or higher	100% charged
12.4	75% charged
12.2	50% charged
12.0	25% charged
11.9 or lower	Discharged

CHART 19–1

The estimated state of charge of a 12 volt battery after the surface charge has been removed.

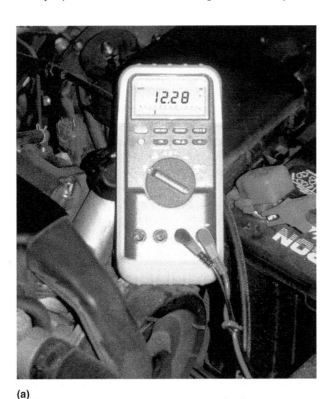

(a)

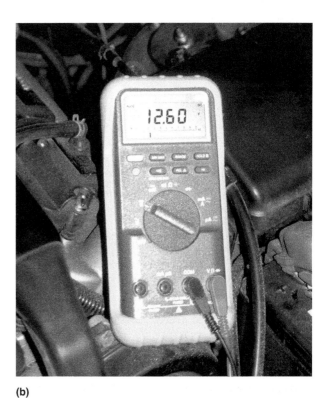

(b)

FIGURE 19–4 (a) A voltage reading of 12.28 volts indicates that the battery is not fully charged and should be charged before testing. (b) A battery that measures 12.6 volts or higher after the surface charge has been removed is 100% charged.

HYDROMETER TESTING

If the battery has removable filler caps, the specific gravity of the electrolyte can also be checked. A **hydrometer** is a tester that measures the specific gravity. ● **SEE FIGURE 19–5**.

This test can also be performed on most maintenance-free batteries because their filler caps are removable, except for those produced by Delco (Delphi) Battery. The specific gravity test indicates the state of battery charge and can indicate a defective battery if the specific gravity of one or more cells varies by more than 0.050 from the value of the highest-reading cell. ● **SEE CHART 19–2**.

SPECIFIC GRAVITY	BATTERY VOLTAGE (V)	STATE OF CHARGE
1.265	12.6 or higher	100% charged
1.225	12.4	75% charged
1.190	12.2	50% charged
1.155	12.0	25% charged
Lower than 1.120	11.9 or lower	Discharged

CHART 19–2

Measuring the specific gravity can detect a defective battery. A battery should be at least 75% charged before being load tested.

? FREQUENTLY ASKED QUESTION

What Is the Three-Minute Charge Test?

A **three-minute charge test** is used to check if a battery is sulfated and is performed as follows:

- Connect a battery charger and a voltmeter to the battery terminals.
- Charge the battery at a rate of 40 amperes for three minutes.
- At the end of three minutes, read the voltmeter.

Results: If the voltage is above 15.5 volts, replace the battery. If the voltage is below 15.5 volts, the battery is not sulfated and should be charged and retested.

This is not a valid test for many maintenance-free batteries. Due to the high internal resistance, a discharged battery may not start to accept a charge for several hours. Always use another alternative battery test before discarding a battery based on the results of the three-minute charge test.

FIGURE 19–6 This battery has a CCA rating of 600 amperes and a reserve capacity (RC) of 110 minutes.

BATTERY LOAD TESTING

TERMINOLOGY One test to determine the condition of any battery is the **load test.** Most automotive starting and charging testers use a carbon pile to create an electrical load on the battery. The amount of the load is determined by the original CCA rating of the battery, which should be at least 75% charged before performing a load test. The capacity is measured in cold-cranking amperes, which is the number of amperes that a battery can supply at 0°F (−18°C) for 30 seconds.

TEST PROCEDURE To perform a battery load test, take the following steps.

STEP 1 **Determine the CCA rating of the battery.** The proper electrical load used to test a battery is half of the CCA rating, or three times the ampere-hour rating, with a minimum 150 ampere load. ● **SEE FIGURE 19–6**.

STEP 2 **Connect the load tester to the battery.** Follow the instructions for the tester being used.

STEP 3 **Apply the load for a full 15 seconds.** Observe the voltmeter during the load testing and check the voltage at the end of the 15 second period, while

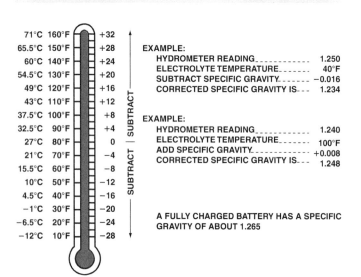

71°C	160°F	+32
65.5°C	150°F	+28
60°C	140°F	+24
54.5°C	130°F	+20
49°C	120°F	+16
43°C	110°F	+12
37.5°C	100°F	+8
32.5°C	90°F	+4
27°C	80°F	0
21°C	70°F	−4
15.5°C	60°F	−8
10°C	50°F	−12
4.5°C	40°F	−16
−1°C	30°F	−20
−6.5°C	20°F	−24
−12°C	10°F	−28

SUBTRACT | SUBTRACT

```
EXAMPLE:
HYDROMETER READING _____ 1.250
ELECTROLYTE TEMPERATURE _____ 40°F
SUBTRACT SPECIFIC GRAVITY _____ −0.016
CORRECTED SPECIFIC GRAVITY IS ___ 1.234

EXAMPLE:
HYDROMETER READING _____ 1.240
ELECTROLYTE TEMPERATURE _____ 100°F
ADD SPECIFIC GRAVITY _____ +0.008
CORRECTED SPECIFIC GRAVITY IS ___ 1.248


A FULLY CHARGED BATTERY HAS A SPECIFIC
GRAVITY OF ABOUT 1.265
```

FIGURE 19–5 When testing a battery using a hydrometer, the reading must be corrected if the temperature is above or below 80°F (27°C).

the battery is still under load. A good battery should indicate above 9.6 volts.

STEP 4   Repeat the test. Many battery manufacturers recommend performing the load test twice, using the first load period to remove the surface charge on the battery and the second test to provide a truer indication of the condition of the battery. Wait 30 seconds between tests to allow time for the battery to recover. ● **SEE FIGURE 19-7**.

Results: If the battery fails the load test, recharge the battery and retest. If the load test is failed again, replacement of the battery is required.

FIGURE 19-7 A Snap-on battery tester that is capable of performing a battery load test, as well as starter and alternator amperage tests.

 FREQUENTLY ASKED QUESTION

How Should You Test a Vehicle Equipped with Two Batteries?

Many vehicles equipped with a diesel engine use two batteries. These batteries are usually electrically connected in parallel to provide additional current (amperes) at the same voltage. ● **SEE FIGURE 19-8**.

Some heavy-duty trucks and buses connect two batteries in series to provide about the same current as one battery, but with twice the voltage, as shown in ● **FIGURE 19-9**.

To successfully test the batteries, they should be disconnected and tested separately. If just one battery is found to be defective, most experts recommend that both be replaced to help prevent future problems. Because the two batteries are electrically connected, a fault in one battery can cause the good battery to discharge into the defective battery, thereby affecting both, even if just one battery is defective.

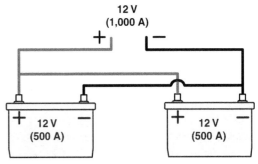

FIGURE 19-8 Most light-duty vehicles equipped with two batteries are connected in parallel as shown. Two 500 ampere, 12 volt batteries are capable of supplying 1,000 amperes at 12 volts, which is needed to start many diesel engines.

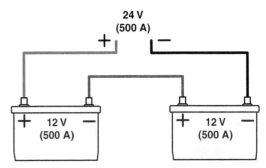

FIGURE 19-9 Many heavy-duty trucks and buses use two 12 volt batteries connected in series to provide 24 volts.

ELECTRONIC CONDUCTANCE TESTING

TERMINOLOGY   General Motors Corporation, Chrysler Corporation, and Ford specify that an electronic conductance tester be used to test batteries in vehicles still under factory warranty. Conductance is a measure of how well a battery can create current. This tester sends a small signal through the battery and then measures a part of the AC response. As a battery ages, the plates can become sulfated and shed active materials from the grids, thus reducing the battery capacity. Conductance testers can be used to test flooded or absorbed glass mat-type (AGM) batteries. The unit can determine the following information about a battery.

- CCA
- State of charge
- Voltage of the battery
- Defects such as shorts and opens

However, a conductance tester is not designed to accurately determine the state of charge or CCA rating of a new battery. Unlike a battery load test, a conductance tester can be used on a battery that is discharged. This type of tester should only be used to test batteries that have been in service. ● **SEE FIGURE 19-10**.

FIGURE 19–10 A conductance tester is very easy to use and has proved to accurately determine battery condition, if the connections are properly made. Follow the instructions on the display exactly for best results.

TEST PROCEDURE

STEP 1 Connect the unit to the positive and negative terminals of the battery. If testing a side-post battery, always use the lead adapters, and *never* use steel bolts, as these can cause an incorrect reading.

NOTE: **Test results can be incorrectly reported on the display if proper, clean connections to the battery are not made. Also, be sure that all accessories and the ignition switch are in the off position.**

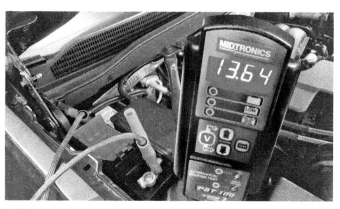

FIGURE 19–11 A Midtronics tester that can not only test the battery but can also detect faults with the starter and alternator.

STEP 2 Enter the CCA rating (if known) and push the arrow keys.

STEP 3 The tester determines and displays one of the following:
- **Good battery.** The battery can return to service.
- **Charge and retest.** Fully recharge the battery and return it to service.
- **Replace the battery.** The battery is not serviceable and should be replaced.
- **Bad cell–replace.** The battery is not serviceable and should be replaced.

Some conductance testers can check the charging and cranking circuits, too. ● **SEE FIGURE 19–11.**

BATTERY CHARGING

CHARGING PROCEDURE If the state of charge of a battery is low, it must be recharged. It is best to slow charge any battery to prevent possible overheating damage to the battery. Perform the following steps.

STEP 1 **Determine the charge rate.** The charge rate is based on the current state of charge and charging rate. ● **SEE CHART 19–3** for the recommended charging rate.

STEP 2 **Connect a battery charger to the battery.** Be sure the charger is not plugged in when connecting a charger to a battery. Always follow the battery charger's instructions for proper use.

STEP 3 **Set the charging rate.** The initial charge rate should be about 35 amperes for 30 minutes to help start the charging process. Fast charging a battery increases the temperature of the battery and can cause warping of the plates inside the battery. Fast charging also increases the amount of gassing (release of hydrogen and oxygen), which can create a health and fire

OPEN CIRCUIT VOLTAGE	BATTERY SPECIFIC GRAVITY*	STATE OF CHARGE	CHARGING TIME TO FULL CHARGE AT 80°F**					
			at 60 amps	at 50 amps	at 40 amps	at 30 amps	at 20 amps	at 10 amps
12.6	1.265	100%	FULL CHARGE					
12.4	1.225	75%	15 min.	20 min.	27 min.	35 min.	48 min.	90 min.
12.2	1.190	50%	35 min.	45 min.	55 min.	75 min.	95 min.	180 min.
12.0	1.155	25%	50 min.	65 min.	85 min.	115 min.	145 min.	260 min.
11.8	1.120	0%	65 min.	85 min.	110 min.	150 min.	195 min.	370 min.

CHART 19–3

Battery charging guideline showing the charging times that vary according to state of charge, temperature, and charging rate. It may take eight hours or more to charge a fully discharged battery.

*Correct for temperature.

**If colder, it'll take longer.

 TECH TIP

Charge Batteries at 1% of Their CCA Rating

Many batteries are damaged due to overcharging. To help prevent damages, such as warped plates and excessive release of sulfur smell gases, charge batteries at a rate equal to 1% of the battery's CCA rating. For example, a battery with a 700 CCA rating should be charged at 7 amperes $(700 \times 0.01 = 7$ amperes). No harm occurs to the battery at this charge rate, even though it may take longer to achieve a full charge. This means that a battery may require eight or more hours to become fully charged, depending on the battery capacity and state of charge (SOC).

 TECH TIP

Always Use Adapters on Side-Post Batteries

Side-post batteries require that an adapter be used when charging the battery, if it is removed from the vehicle. Do not use steel bolts. If a bolt is threaded into the terminal, only the parts of the threads that contact the battery terminal are conducting all of the charging current. An adapter or a bolt with a nut attached is needed to achieve full contact with the battery terminals. ● **SEE FIGURE 19–13.**

hazard. The battery temperature should not exceed 125°F (52°C) (hot to the touch).
- Fast charge: 15 amperes maximum
- Slow charge: 5 amperes maximum

● **SEE FIGURE 19–12.**

CHARGING AGM BATTERIES
Charging an AGM battery requires a different charger than is used to recharge a flooded-type battery. The differences include the following:

- The AGM can be charged with high current, up to 75% of the ampere-hour rating due to lower internal resistance.

- The charging voltage has to be kept at or below 14.4 volts to prevent damage.

Because most conventional battery chargers use a charging voltage of 16 volts or higher, a charger specifically designed to charge AGM batteries must be used.

Absorbed glass mat batteries are often used as auxiliary batteries in hybrid electric vehicles when the battery is located inside the vehicle.

FIGURE 19–12 A typical industrial battery charger. Be sure that the ignition switch is in the off position before connecting any battery charger. Connect the cables of the charger to the battery before plugging the charger into the outlet. This helps prevent a voltage spike and spark that could occur if the charger happened to be accidentally left on. Always follow the battery charger manufacturer's instructions.

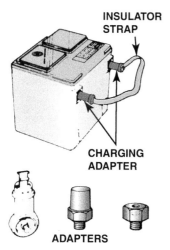

FIGURE 19–13 Adapters should be used on side-terminal batteries whenever charging.

BATTERY CHARGE TIME

The time needed to charge a completely discharged battery can be estimated by using the reserve capacity rating of the battery in minutes divided by the charging rate.

Hours needed to charge the battery =
Reserve capacity ÷ Charge current

For example, if a 10 ampere charge rate is applied to a discharged battery that has a 90 minute reserve capacity, the time needed to charge the battery is nine hours.

90 minutes ÷ 10 amperes = 9 hours

FLOAT-TYPE BATTERY CHARGERS

PURPOSE AND FUNCTION A float-type charger, sometimes referred to by the brand name "Battery Tender," will only turn on and charge a battery when it has self-discharged below a certain level. This is not the same as a trickle charger which will continuously apply a small current to the battery regardless of the charge level. A float-type battery charger is often referred to as a "smart battery charger." While a float-type charger can be used to charge a battery during normal service operations, it is usually used when a vehicle is being stored for an extended period of time. ● **SEE FIGURE 19–14.**

OPERATION The operational modes or stages of a typical float-type battery charger include the following:

1. **Constant current or bulk charging** (battery 0–80% state-of-charge): In this mode of operation, the charger supplying a constant current to the battery. In this mode, the battery voltage is allowed to rise as it is being recharged.
2. **Absorption stage** (battery 80–95% state-of-charge): This mode switches mode switches to where the charger voltage is held constant and the battery current is allowed to reduce. This stage is reached when the battery voltage reaches about 2.4 volts per cell (14.6 volts for a 12 volt battery). It is this region where the last 20% of battery capacity is returned.

FIGURE 19–14 A typical float-type battery charger connected to a vehicle placed in storage for the winter. This type of charger can be left connected to the battery all winter long without it causing any harm to the battery.

3. **Float mode** (battery from 95–100% state-of-charge): In this mode, the voltage applied to the battery is maintained at about 2.25 volts per cell (13.5 volts for a 12 volt battery). During this mode of operation, the charger will maintain the full charge without boiling the electrolyte or overcharging the battery.

JUMP STARTING

To jump start another vehicle with a dead battery, connect good-quality copper jumper cables or a jump box to the good battery and the dead battery, as shown in ● **FIGURE 19–15**.

FIGURE 19–15 A typical battery jump box used to jump start vehicles. These hand-portable units have almost made jumper cables obsolete.

When using jumper cables or a battery jump box, the last connection made should always be on the engine block or an engine bracket on the dead vehicle as far from the battery as possible.

It is normal for a spark to occur when the jumper cables finally complete the jumping circuit, and this spark could cause an explosion of the gases around the battery. Many newer vehicles have special ground and/or positive power connections built away from the battery just for the purpose of jump starting. Check the owner's manual or service information for the exact location.

BATTERY ELECTRICAL DRAIN TEST

TERMINOLOGY The **battery electrical drain test** determines if any component or circuit in a vehicle is causing a drain on the battery when everything is off. This test is also called the **ignition off draw (IOD)** or **parasitic load test.**

Many electronic components draw a continuous, slight amount of current from the battery when the ignition is off.

This test should be performed when one of the following conditions exists.

1. When a battery is being charged or replaced (a battery drain could have been the cause for charging or replacing the battery)

2. When the battery is suspected of being drained

PROCEDURE FOR BATTERY ELECTRICAL DRAIN TEST

■ **Inductive DC ammeter.** The fastest and easiest method to measure battery electrical drain is to connect an inductive DC ammeter that is capable of measuring low current (10 milliamperes). ● **SEE FIGURE 19–17** for an example of a clamp-on digital multimeter (DMM) being used to measure battery drain.

 TECH TIP

Look at the Battery Date Code

All major battery manufacturers' stamp codes on the battery case give the date of manufacture and other information about the battery. Most battery manufacturers use a number to indicate the year of manufacture and a letter to indicate the month of manufacture, except the letter I, because it can be confused with the number 1. For example:

A = January   G = July
B = February   H = August
C = March   J = September
D = April   K = October
E = May   L = November
F = June   M = December

The shipping date from the manufacturing plant is usually indicated by a sticker on the body of the battery. Almost every battery manufacturer uses just one letter and one number to indicate the month and year. ● **SEE FIGURE 19–16.**

FIGURE 19–16 The sticker on this battery indicates that it was shipped from the factory July, 2019.

FIGURE 19–17 This mini clamp-on digital multimeter is being used to measure the amount of battery electrical drain that is present. In this case, a reading of 20 milliamperes (displayed on the meter as 00.02 ampere) is within the normal range of 20 to 30 milliamperes. Be sure to clamp around all of the positive battery cables or all of the negative battery cables, whichever is easiest to get the clamp around.

■ **DMM set to read milliamperes.** Following is the procedure for performing the battery electrical drain test using a DMM set to read DC amperes.

STEP 1 Make certain that all lights, accessories, and ignition are off.

STEP 2 Check all vehicle doors to be certain that the interior courtesy (dome) lights are off.

STEP 3 Disconnect the *negative* (−) battery cable and install a parasitic load tool, as shown in ● **FIGURE 19–18**.

STEP 4 Start the engine and drive the vehicle about 10 minutes, being sure to turn on all the lights and accessories, including the radio.

STEP 5 Turn the engine and all accessories off, including the underhood light.

STEP 6 Connect an ammeter across the parasitic load tool switch and wait 20 minutes for all computers and circuits to shut down.

STEP 7 Open the switch on the load tool and read the battery electrical drain on the meter display.

SPECIFICATIONS Results:

■ Normal = 20 to 30 milliamperes (0.02 to 0.03 ampere)

■ Maximum allowable = 50 milliamperes (0.05 ampere)

BATTERY DRAIN AND RESERVE CAPACITY It is normal for a battery to self-discharge, even if there is not an electrical load, such as computer memory, to drain the battery. According to General Motors, this self-discharge is about 13 milliamperes (0.013 ampere).

Some vehicle manufacturers specify a maximum allowable parasitic draw or battery drain be based on the reserve capacity of the battery. The calculation used is the reserve capacity of the battery divided by 4; this equals the maximum allowable battery drain. For example, a battery rated at 120 minutes reserve capacity should have a maximum battery drain of 30 milliamperes.

120 minutes reserve capacity ÷ 4 = 30 mA

🚗 **CASE STUDY**

The Chevrolet Battery Story

A 2011 Chevrolet Impala was being diagnosed for a dead battery. Testing for a battery drain (parasitic draw) showed 2.25 amperes, which was clearly over the acceptable value of 0.050 or less. At the suggestion of the shop foreman, the technician used a Tech 2 scan tool to check if all of the computers and modules went to sleep after the ignition was turned off. The scan tool display indicated that the instrument panel (IP) showed that it remained awake after all of the others had gone into sleep mode. The IP cluster was unplugged and the vehicle was tested for an electrical drain again. This time, it was only 32 milliamperes (0.032 ampere), well within the normal range. Replacing the IP cluster solved the excessive battery drain.

Summary:

• **Complaint**—The battery was dead.

• **Cause**—Excessive battery drain (parasitic draw) was found. Using a scan tool to test the modules, it was discovered that the instrument panel cluster (IPC) remained awake and never powered down when the ignition was turned off.

• **Correction**—The IPC was replaced, which corrected the excessive battery drain problem.

FIGURE 19–18 After connecting the shut-off tool, start the engine and operate all accessories. Stop the engine and turn off everything. Connect the ammeter across the shut-off switch in parallel. Wait 20 minutes. This time allows all electronic circuits to "time out" or shut down. Open the switch—all; current now flows through the ammeter. A reading greater than specified (usually greater than 50 milliamperes, or 0.05 ampere) indicates a problem that should be corrected.

FINDING THE SOURCE OF THE DRAIN If there is a drain, check and temporarily disconnect the following components.

1. Underhood light
2. Glove compartment light
3. Trunk light

If after disconnecting these three components the battery drain draws more than 50 milliamperes (0.05 ampere), disconnect one fuse at a time from the fuse box until the excessive drain drops to normal.

NOTE: Do not reinsert fuses after they have been removed as this action can cause modules to "wake up," leading to an inconclusive test.

If the excessive battery drain stops after one fuse is disconnected, the source of the drain is located in that particular circuit, as labeled on the fuse box. Continue to disconnect the *power-side* wire connectors from each component included in that particular cir-cuit until the test light goes off. The source of the battery drain can then be traced to an individual component or part of one circuit.

WHAT TO DO IF A BATTERY DRAIN STILL EXISTS
If all the fuses have been disconnected and the drain still exists, the source of the drain has to be between the battery and the fuse box. The most common sources of drain under the hood include the following:

1. **The alternator.** Disconnect the alternator wires and retest. If the ammeter now reads a normal drain, the problem is a defective diode(s) in the alternator.
2. **PCM or control module** staying on and not going to sleep. The procedure usually involves disconnecting one module at a time, then checking to see if the battery drain has been

reduced or eliminated. Check service information for the exact procedures to follow to determine if the modules are staying awake.

MAINTAINING ELECTRONIC MEMORY FUNCTIONS

BATTERY DISCONNECT ISSUES Whenever a battery is disconnected or replaced, many electrical/electronic modules may lose their memory including:

Radio presets and clock functions plus antitheft (if equipped) ● **SEE FIGURE 19–19.**

1. Security system
2. PCM engine idle learn
3. Auto power windows/sunroof

? **FREQUENTLY ASKED QUESTION**

How Is a New Battery Registered?

Some vehicles require that a new battery be *registered* so that the Powertrain Control Module (PCM) "knows" that the battery has been replaced. Overtime, every battery loses capacity and as a result, the charging voltage usually needs to be increased to keep the battery performing correctly. If a new battery is installed without being registered, the PCM may overcharge the new battery leading to a possible premature battery failure. The steps needed to be performed to resister a battery include the following:

Step 1 When installing a new battery, ensure that the replacement battery is the same type (AGM or flooded) as the original plus the same size and capacity as the original.

Step 2 Use a factory or factory level aftermarket scan tool to the DLC and turn the ignition on (KOEO).

Step 3 Check the instructions for the scan tool to where to precede to register the battery and follow the on-screen directions.

The scan tool will perform the following:

- Sets the battery capacity to 80% (charging to a higher state-of-charge than 80% shortens the life of any battery)
- The current battery statistics such as the charge level and calculated battery temperature are deleted.

If a different size or type of battery is being installed, then the PCM needs to be coded to match the specifications of the new and different battery.

FIGURE 19–19 The battery was replaced in this Ford Focus and the radio displayed "enter code" when the replacement battery was installed. Thankfully, the owner had the code required to unlock the radio.

FIGURE 19–21 A memory saver tool that uses a 12 volt battery to connect to the power (terminal 16) and ground (terminals 4 and 5) of the DLC.

REINITIALIZATION If a memory saver was not used and the battery was disconnected, then the memory functions need to be reinitialized, which can include the following:

1. **Auto power windows** To reset proper operation, use the window control for each window and hold the down button for a few seconds after the window reaches the bottom. Repeat for the up button, if the vehicle is equipped with auto up function.

2. **Radio antitheft** To unlock an antitheft radio that has lost power, a code number is needed to get the radio to function again. Check service information for the exact procedure to follow if the owner does not have the radio code number, which is usually with the owner's manual.

3. **Intelligent battery systems** Some vehicles, usually European brands, use an intelligent battery system that monitors the battery operation including state of charge, voltage, and temperature. As the battery ages, the system can compensate by changing the charging voltage. When a new battery is installed, the vehicle must have the new battery *registered* so that the system does not overcharge the new battery. The replacement battery must be the same type (flooded or AGM) as the original to avoid potential issues.

FIGURE 19–20 A special tool that includes a lighter plug that can be plugged into a jump-start battery unit and the other end connected to the data link connector (DLC) of the vehicle to maintain the memory functions.

To prevent having to reinitialize these modules, a "memory saver" can be used keep power applied to the electrical system when the battery is disconnected.

MAINTAINING MEMORY METHODS There are two ways to connect power to prevent the loss of memory function.

Connect a battery (9 volt dry cell or 12 volt auxiliary battery) to the power (cigarette lighter) plug. ● **SEE FIGURE 19–20.**

Connect a 12 volt auxiliary battery to terminals 4 and 16 of the data link connector (DLC). Use a commercially available memory saver for this procedure to help prevent possible damage that could occur if 12 volt power is accidently applied to data lines at the DLC.

Make the connections to the vehicle, using either method, before disconnecting the vehicle battery. The applied voltage, which is connected the electrical system through the power plug or DLC, will keep all memory functions, so they do not need to be reset. ● **SEE FIGURES 19–21 AND 19–22.**

 **TECH TIP**

Dead Batteries Can Freeze

If a battery becomes discharged, the electrolyte can freeze. This can occur because, when a battery is discharged, the "acid" ($PbSO_4$) leaves the electrolyte and is deposited on both the negative and positive plates, leaving just water. Never attempt to charge or place into service a battery that is frozen. Often the case is split, requiring the battery to be replaced. If a battery is found to be frozen, place the battery into a warm room with good ventilation and allow to thaw.

If the case is not cracked, then it may be able to be restored to useful service, if charged at a low rate for several hours. Connect the load tester to.

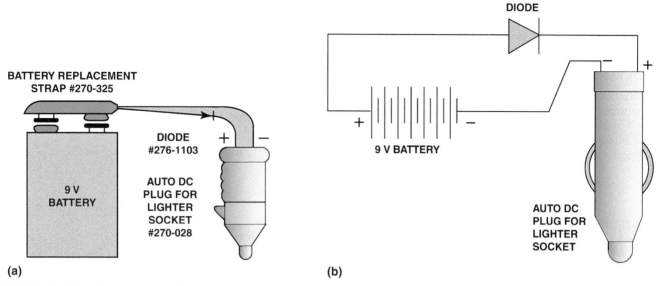

(a)   **(b)**

FIGURE 19–22 (a) Memory saver. The part numbers represent components from RadioShack. (b) A schematic drawing of the same memory saver. Some experts recommend using a 12 volt lantern battery, instead of a small 9 volt battery, to help ensure there is enough voltage in the event that a door is opened while the vehicle battery is disconnected. Interior lights could quickly drain a small 9 volt battery.

? FREQUENTLY ASKED QUESTION

Where Is the Battery?

Many vehicle manufacturers today place the battery under the backseat, under the front fender, or in the trunk. ● **SEE FIGURE 19–23**.

Often, the battery is not visible, even if it is located under the hood. When testing or jump starting a vehicle, look for a battery access point.

FIGURE 19–23 Many newer vehicles have batteries that are sometimes difficult to find. Some are located under plastic panels under the hood, under the front fender, or even under the rear seat, as shown here.

A scan tool is needed to register the new battery to the vehicle. Always follow the vehicle manufacturer's recommended procedures when replacing a battery.

BATTERY SYMPTOM GUIDE

The following list assists technicians in troubleshooting batteries.

Problem	Possible Causes and/or Solutions
1. Headlights are dimmer than normal	1. Discharged battery or poor connections on the battery, engine, or body
2. Solenoid clicks	2. Discharged battery or poor connections on the battery, or an engine fault, such as coolant on top of the pistons, causing a hydrostatic lock
3. Engine is slow in cranking	3. Discharged battery, high-resistance battery cables, or defective starter or solenoid
4. Battery does not accept a charge	4. Possible loose battery cable connections. (If the battery is a maintenance-free type, attempt to fast charge the battery for several hours. If the battery still does not accept a charge, replace the battery.)
5. Battery is using water	5. Check charging system for too high a voltage. (If the voltage is normal, the battery is showing signs of gradual failure. Load test and replace the battery, if necessary.)

SUMMARY

1. All batteries should be securely attached to the vehicle with hold-down brackets to prevent vibration damage.

2. Batteries can be tested with a voltmeter to determine the state of charge. A battery load test loads the battery to half of its CCA rating. A good battery should be able to maintain higher than 9.6 volts for the entire 15 second test period.

3. Batteries can be tested with a conductance tester even if discharged.

4. A battery drain test should be performed if the battery runs down.

5. Be sure that the battery charger is unplugged from power outlet when making connections to a battery.

REVIEW QUESTIONS

1. What are the results of a voltmeter test of a battery and its state of charge?

2. What are the steps for performing a battery load test?

3. How is a battery drain test performed?

4. Why should a battery not be fast charged?

5. Why do some vehicles need to have a new battery registered?

CHAPTER QUIZ

1. Technician A says that distilled or clean drinking water should be added to a battery when the electrolyte level is low. Technician B says that fresh electrolyte (solution of acid and water) should be added. Which technician is correct?
   a. Technician A only
   b. Technician B only
   c. Both Technicians A and B
   d. Neither Technician A nor B

2. A battery should be checked for _____.
   a. being securely held down
   b. should have clean and tight battery terminals
   c. the battery case being clean
   d. All of the above

3. What precautions are needed when charging an AGM-type battery?
   a. Keep the charger away from the battery as far as possible.
   b. Charging amperage should be set to less than 10 amperes.
   c. Charging voltage should be at or below 14.4 volts.
   d. Keep the charging time to less than one hour.

4. A battery has just been changed on a popular European vehicle. What service should the technician perform before returning the vehicle to the owner?
   a. Charge the battery overnight
   b. Register the new battery to the vehicle
   c. Allow the vehicle to sit overnight with the headlights on, then recharge the battery
   d. No additional steps are required, other than just installing the battery

5. A defective battery causes which of the following symptoms?
   a. Slow cranking
   b. Excessive voltage (over 16 volts)
   c. Smooth, clean connectors, indicating overheating of the cables
   d. None of these

6. When measuring the specific gravity of the electrolyte, the maximum allowable difference between the highest and lowest hydrometer reading is _____.
   a. 0.010
   b. 0.020
   c. 0.050
   d. 0.50

7. A battery high-rate discharge (load capacity) test is being performed on a 12 volt battery. Technician A says that a good battery should have a voltage reading of higher than 9.6 volts, while under load, at the end of the 15 second test. Technician B says that a battery conductance tester is often used to load the battery to two times the CCA rating of the battery. Which technician is correct?
   a. Technician A only
   b. Technician B only
   c. Both Technicians A and B
   d. Neither Technician A nor B

8. When charging a lead–acid (flooded-type) battery, _____.
   a. the initial charging rate should be about 35 amperes for 30 minutes
   b. the battery may not accept a charge for several hours, yet may still be a good (serviceable) battery
   c. the battery temperature should not exceed 125°F (52°C) (hot to the touch)
   d. All of the above

9. Normal battery drain (parasitic drain) in a vehicle with many computer and electronic circuits is _____.
   a. 20 to 30 milliamperes
   b. 2 to 3 amperes
   c. 150 to 300 milliamperes
   d. None of the above

10. When jump starting, _____.
   a. the last connection should be the positive post of the dead battery
   b. the last connection should be the engine block of the dead vehicle
   c. the alternator must be disconnected on both vehicles
   d. Both a and c

chapter 20

CRANKING SYSTEM

LEARNING OBJECTIVES:

After studying this chapter, the reader should be able to:

Describe the parts and operation of a cranking circuit and explain computer-controlled starting.

Discuss how a starter motor converts electrical power into mechanical power.

List the different types of starter motors.

Describe gear reduction starters.

Describe the function of starter drives and solenoids.

Discuss stop-start system operation.

This chapter will help prepare for the ASE Electrical/Electronic Systems (A6) certification test content area "C" (Starting System Diagnosis and Repair).

KEY TERMS: Advanced Engagement (AE) Starter 248 • Armature 243 • Brush-end housing 242 • Brushes 243 • CEMF 241 • Commutator-end housing 242 • Commutator segments 243 • Compression spring 246 • Drive-end housing 242 • Engine stop/start (ESS) 248 • Field coils 243 • Field housing 242 • Field poles 243 • Ground brushes 244 • Hold-in winding 247 • Insulated brushes 244 • Mesh spring 246 • Neutral safety switch 239 • Overrunning clutch 246 • Permanently Engaged (PE) Starter 249 • Pole shoes 243 • Pull-in winding 247 • RVS 240 • Starter drive 245 • Starter solenoid 247 • Tandem Solenoid (TS) Starter 248 • Through bolts 242

CRANKING CIRCUIT

PARTS INVOLVED For any engine to start, it must first be rotated using an external power source. It is the purpose and function of the cranking circuit to create the necessary power and transfer it from the battery to the starter motor, which rotates the engine.

The cranking circuit includes those mechanical and electrical components that are required to crank the engine for starting. The control circuit includes those wires and components that carry a relatively small current such as the ignition switch, safety switch, and solenoid. The power circuit carries the heavy current needed to crank the engine and includes the battery itself, plus the battery cables, solenoid, and starter motor. Modern cranking circuits include the following:

1. **Starter motor.** The starter is normally a 0.5 to 2.6 horsepower (0.4 to 2 kilowatts) electric motor that can develop nearly 8 horsepower (6 kilowatts) for a very short time when first cranking a cold engine. ● SEE FIGURE 20–1.

2. **Battery.** The battery must be of the correct capacity and be at least 75% charged to provide the necessary current and voltage for correct starter operation.

3. **Starter solenoid or relay.** The high current required by the starter must be able to be turned on and off. A large switch would be required if the current were controlled by the driver directly. Instead, a small current switch (ignition

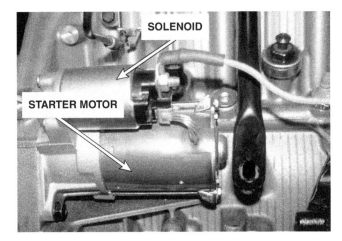

FIGURE 20–1 A typical solenoid-operated starter.

switch) operates a solenoid or relay that controls the high current to the starter.

4. **Starter drive.** The starter drive uses a small pinion gear that contacts the engine flywheel gear teeth and transmits starter motor power to rotate the engine.

5. **Ignition switch.** The ignition switch and safety control switches control the starter motor operation. ● SEE FIGURE 20–2.

CONTROL CIRCUIT PARTS AND OPERATION The engine is cranked by an electric motor that is controlled by a key-operated ignition switch. The ignition switch does not operate the

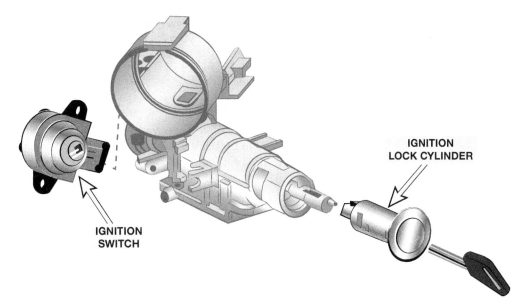

FIGURE 20–2 The lock cylinder is often a separate part from the electrical ignition switch and operates it directly or uses a link between two components.

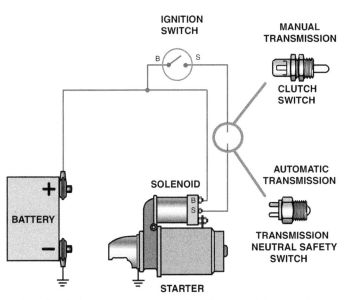

FIGURE 20–3 To prevent the engine from cranking, an electrical switch is usually installed to open the circuit between the ignition switch and the starter solenoid. The control circuit includes the small wiring and components needed to control the solenoid. The starter solenoid controls the electrical current flow through the large battery cables of the power circuit that operates the starter motor.

starter unless the automatic transmission is in neutral or park, or the clutch pedal is depressed on manual transmission/transaxle vehicles. This is to prevent any accident that might result from the vehicle moving forward or rearward when the engine is started. The types of controls that are used to be sure that the vehicle does not move when being cranked include the following:

■ Many automobile manufacturers use an electric switch called a **neutral safety switch**, which opens the circuit

between the ignition switch and the starter to prevent starter motor operation, unless the gear selector is in neutral or park. The safety switch can be attached either to the steering column inside the vehicle near the floor or on the side of the transmission.

■ Many manufacturers use a mechanical blocking device in the steering column to prevent the driver from turning the key switch to the start position unless the gear selector is in neutral or park.

■ Many manual transmission vehicles also use a safety switch to permit cranking only if the clutch is depressed. This switch is commonly called the *clutch safety switch*. ● **SEE FIGURE 20–3**.

COMPUTER-CONTROLLED STARTING

OPERATION Push button start systems and many key operated systems use the computer to crank the engine. The ignition switch start position on the push-to-start button is used as an input signal to the powertrain control module (PCM). Before the PCM cranks the engine, the following conditions must be met.

■ The brake pedal is depressed.

■ The gear selector is in park or neutral.

■ The correct key fob (code) is present in the vehicle.

A typical push-button-to-start system includes the following sequence.

■ When the start button is depressed, or the key is turned to the start position, the PCM cranks the engine until it senses that the engine has started.

FIGURE 20–4 Instead of using an ignition key to start the engine, some vehicles are using a start button, which is also used to stop the engine, as shown on this Jaguar.

- The PCM can detect that the engine has started by looking at the engine speed signal.
- Normal cranking speed can vary between 100 and 250 RPM. If the engine speed exceeds 400 RPM, the PCM determines that the engine has started and opens the circuit to the "S" (start) terminal of the starter solenoid that stops the starter motor.

Computer-controlled starting is almost always part of the system if a push-button start is used. ● **SEE FIGURE 20–4.**

REMOTE STARTING Remote starting, sometimes called **remote vehicle start (RVS)**, is a system that allows the driver to start the engine of the vehicle from inside the house or a building at a distance of about 200 feet (65 m). The doors remain locked to reduce the possibility of theft. This feature allows the heating or air-conditioning system to start before the driver arrives. ● **SEE FIGURE 20–5.**

NOTE: **Most remote start systems turn off the engine after 10 minutes of run time unless reset by using the remote.**

FIGURE 20–5 The top button on this key fob is the remote start button.

STARTER MOTOR OPERATION

PRINCIPLES A starter motor uses electromagnetic principles to convert electrical energy from the battery (up to 300 amperes) to mechanical power (up to 8 horsepower [6 kilowatts]) to crank the engine. Current for the starter motor or power circuit is controlled by a solenoid or relay, which is itself controlled by the driver-operated ignition switch.

The current travels through the brushes and into the armature windings, where other magnetic fields are created around each copper wire loop in the armature. The two strong magnetic fields created inside the starter housing create the force that rotates the armature.

Inside the starter housing is a strong magnetic field created by the field coil magnets. The armature, a conductor, is installed inside this strong magnetic field, with little clearance between the armature and the field coils.

The two magnetic fields act together, and their lines of force "bunch up" or are strong on one side of the armature loop wire and become weak on the other side of the conductor. This causes the conductor (armature) to move from the area of strong magnetic field strength toward the area of weak magnetic field strength. ● **SEE FIGURES 20–6 AND 20–7.**

The difference in magnetic field strength causes the armature to rotate. This rotation force (torque) is increased as

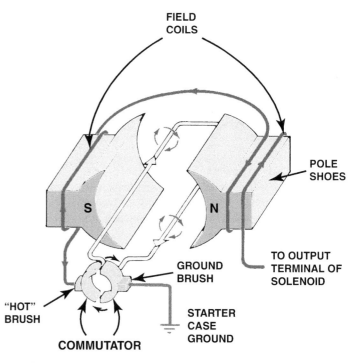

FIGURE 20–6 This series-wound electric motor shows the basic operation with only two brushes: one hot brush and one ground brush. The current flows through both field coils, then through the hot brush and the loop winding of the armature, before reaching ground through the ground brush.

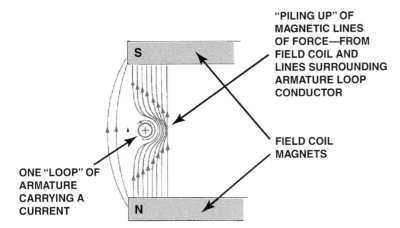

FIGURE 20–7 The interaction of the magnetic fields of the armature loops and field coils creates a stronger magnetic field on the right side of the conductor, causing the armature loop to move toward the left.

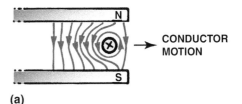

(a)

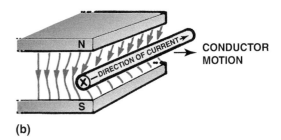

(b)

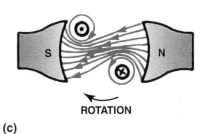

(c)

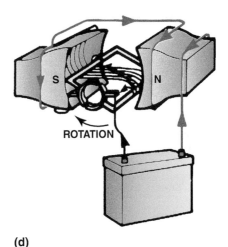

(d)

the current flowing through the starter motor increases. The torque of a starter is determined by the strength of the magnetic fields inside the starter. Magnetic field strength is measured in ampere-turns. If the current or the number of turns of wire is increased, the magnetic field strength is increased.

The magnetic field of the starter motor is provided by two or more pole shoes and field windings. The pole shoes are made of iron and are attached to the frame with large screws. ● **SEE FIGURE 20–8**.

● **FIGURE 20–9** shows the paths of magnetic flux lines within a four-pole motor.

The field windings are usually made of a heavy copper ribbon to increase their current-carrying capacity and electromagnetic field strength. ● **SEE FIGURE 20–10**.

Automotive starter motors usually have four pole shoes and two to four field windings to provide a strong magnetic field within the motor. Pole shoes that do not have field windings are magnetized by flux lines from the wound poles.

SERIES MOTORS A series motor develops its maximum torque at the initial start (0 RPM) and develops less torque as the speed increases.

- A series motor is commonly used for an automotive starter motor because of its high starting power characteristics.

- A series starter motor develops less torque at high RPM, because a current is produced in the starter itself that acts against the current from the battery. Because this current works against battery voltage, it is called **counter-electromotive force**, or **CEMF**. This CEMF is produced by electromagnetic induction in the armature conductors, which are cutting across the magnetic lines of force formed by the field coils. This induced voltage operates against the applied voltage supplied by the battery, which reduces the strength of the magnetic field in the starter.

- Because the power (torque) of the starter depends on the strength of the magnetic fields, the torque of the starter decreases as the starter speed increases. A

FIGURE 20–8 The armature loops rotate due to the difference in the strength of the magnetic field. The loops move from a strong magnetic field strength toward a weaker magnetic field strength.

series-wound starter also draws less current at higher speeds and keeps increasing in speed under light loads. This could lead to the destruction of the starter motor unless controlled or prevented. ● **SEE FIGURE 20–11**.

SHUNT MOTORS Shunt-type electric motors have the field coils in parallel (or shunt) across the armature.

A shunt-type motor has the following features.

- A shunt motor does not decrease in torque at higher motor RPM, because the CEMF produced in the armature does not decrease the field coil strength.

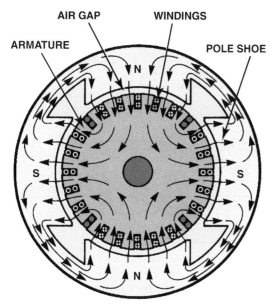

FIGURE 20–9 Magnetic lines of force in a four-pole motor.

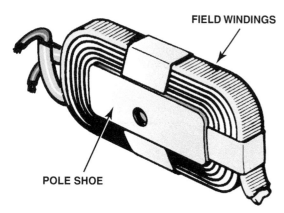

FIGURE 20–10 A pole shoe and field winding.

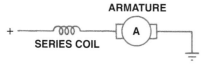

FIGURE 20–11 This wiring diagram illustrates the construction of a series-wound electric motor. Notice that all current flows through the field coils, then through the armature (in series) before reaching ground.

■ A shunt motor, however, does not produce as high a starting torque as that produced by a series-wound motor and is not used for starters. Some small electric motors, such as those used for windshield wipers, use a shunt motor, but most use permanent magnets rather than electromagnets.
● SEE FIGURE 20–12.

PERMANENT MAGNET MOTORS A permanent magnet (PM) starter uses permanent magnets that maintain constant field strength, the same as a shunt-type motor, so they have similar operating characteristics. To compensate for the lack

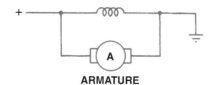

FIGURE 20–12 This wiring diagram illustrates the construction of a shunt-type electric motor and shows the field coils in parallel (or shunt) across the armature.

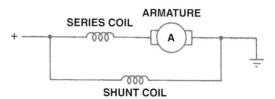

FIGURE 20–13 A compound motor is a combination of series and shunt types, using part of the field coils connected electrically in series with the armature and part in parallel (shunt).

of torque, all PM starters use gear reduction to multiply starter motor torque. The permanent magnets used are an alloy of neodymium, iron, and boron and are almost 10 times more powerful than previously used permanent magnets.

COMPOUND MOTORS A compound-wound, or compound, motor has the operating characteristics of a series motor *and* a shunt-type motor, because some of the field coils are connected to the armature in series and some (usually only one) are connected directly to the battery in parallel (shunt) with the armature.

Compound-wound starter motors are commonly used in Ford, Chrysler, and some GM starters. The shunt-wound field coil is called a shunt coil and is used to limit the maximum speed of the starter. Because the shunt coil is energized as soon as the battery current is sent to the starter, it is used to engage the starter drive on older Ford positive engagement-type starters. ● SEE FIGURE 20–13.

HOW THE STARTER MOTOR WORKS

PARTS INVOLVED A starter consists of the main structural support called the **field housing**, one end of which is called a **commutator-end** (or **brush-end**) **housing** and the other end a **drive-end housing**. The drive-end housing contains the drive pinion gear, which meshes with the engine flywheel gear teeth to start the engine. The commutator-end plate supports the end containing the starter brushes. **Through bolts** hold the three components together. ● SEE FIGURE 20–14.

■ **Field coils.** The steel housing of the starter motor contains permanent magnets or four electromagnets that are connected directly to the positive post of the battery to provide a strong magnetic field inside the starter. The

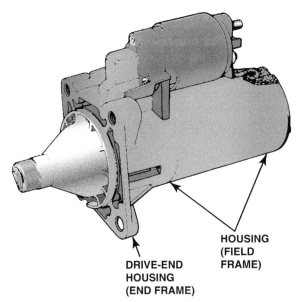

FIGURE 20-14 A typical starter motor showing the drive-end housing.

HOUSING
(FIELD
FRAME)

DRIVE-END
HOUSING
(END FRAME)

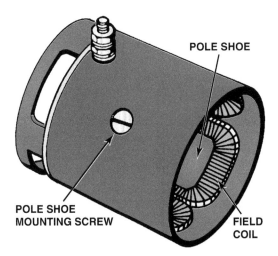

POLE SHOE

POLE SHOE
MOUNTING SCREW

FIELD
COIL

FIGURE 20-15 Pole shoes and field windings installed in the housing.

four electromagnets use heavy copper or aluminum wire wrapped around a soft-iron core, which is contoured to fit against the rounded internal surface of the starter frame. The soft-iron cores are called **pole shoes**. Two of the four pole shoes are wrapped with copper wire in one direction to create a north pole magnet, and the other two pole shoes are wrapped in the opposite direction to create a south pole magnet. These magnets, when energized, create strong magnetic fields inside the starter housing and, therefore, are called **field coils**. The soft-iron cores (pole shoes) are often called **field poles**. ● **SEE FIGURE 20-15**.

■ **Armature.** Inside the field coils is an **armature** that is supported with either bushings or ball bearings at both ends, which permit it to rotate. The armature is constructed of thin, circular discs of steel laminated together and wound lengthwise with heavy-gauge insulated copper wire. The laminated iron core supports the copper loops of wire and helps concentrate the magnetic field produced by the coils. ● **SEE FIGURE 20-16**.

Insulation between the laminations helps increase the magnetic efficiency in the core. For reduced resistance, the armature conductors are made of a thick copper wire. The two ends of each conductor are attached to two adjacent commutator bars.

The commutator is made of copper bars insulated from each other by mica or some other insulating material. ● **SEE FIGURE 20-17**.

The armature core, windings, and commutator are assembled on a long armature shaft. This shaft also carries the pinion gear that meshes with the engine flywheel ring gear.

STARTER BRUSHES To supply the proper current to the armature, a four-pole motor must have four brushes riding on the commutator. Most automotive starters have two grounded and two insulated brushes, which are held against the commutator by spring force.

The ends of the copper armature windings are soldered to **commutator segments**. The electrical current that passes through the field coils is then passed to the commutator of the armature by brushes that can move over the segments of the rotating armature. These **brushes** are made of a combination of copper and carbon.

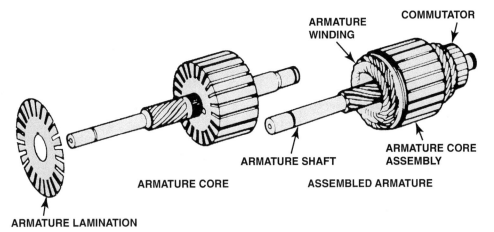

ARMATURE
WINDING

COMMUTATOR

ARMATURE SHAFT

ARMATURE CORE
ASSEMBLY

ARMATURE CORE

ASSEMBLED ARMATURE

ARMATURE LAMINATION

FIGURE 20-16 A typical starter motor armature. The armature core is made from thin sheet metal sections assembled on the armature shaft, which is used to increase the magnetic field strength.

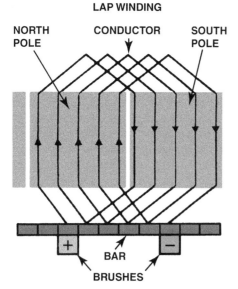

LAP WINDING

NORTH POLE　　CONDUCTOR　　SOUTH POLE

+ BAR − BRUSHES

FIGURE 20–17 An armature showing how its copper wire loops are connected to the commutator.

- The copper used here is a good conductor material.
- The carbon added to the starter brushes helps provide the graphite-type lubrication needed to reduce wear of the brushes and the commutator segments.

The starter uses four brushes—two brushes to transfer the current from the field coils to the armature and two brushes to provide the ground return path for the current that flows through the armature.

The two sets of brushes include the following:

1. Two **insulated brushes**, which are in holders and are insulated from the housing.
2. Two **ground brushes**, which use bare, stranded copper wire connections to the brushes. The ground brush holders are not insulated and attach directly to the field housing or brush-end housing. ● **SEE FIGURE 20–18.**

🔧 TECH TIP

Don't Hit That Starter!

In the past, it was common to see service technicians hitting a starter in their effort to diagnose a no-crank condition. Often the shock of the blow to the starter aligned or moved the brushes, armature, and bushings. Many times, the starter functioned after being hit, even if only for a short time.

However, most starters today use permanent magnet fields, and the magnets can be easily broken if hit. A magnet that is broken becomes two weaker magnets. Some early permanent magnet starters used magnets that were glued or bonded to the field housing. If struck with a heavy tool, the magnets could be broken with parts of the magnet falling onto the armature and into the bearing pockets, making the starter impossible to repair or rebuild. ● **SEE FIGURE 20–19.**

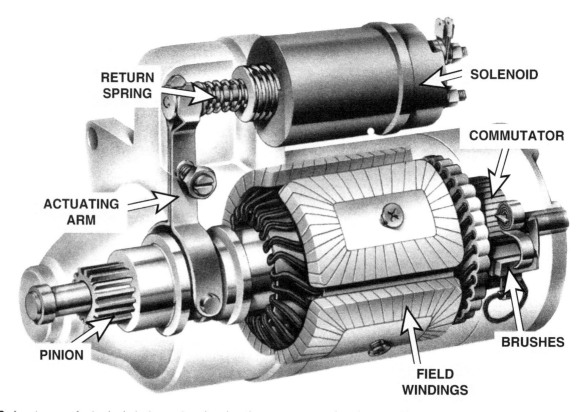

RETURN SPRING　　SOLENOID

COMMUTATOR

ACTUATING ARM

PINION　　FIELD WINDINGS　　BRUSHES

FIGURE 20–18 A cutaway of a typical starter motor showing the commutator, brushes, and brush spring.

FIGURE 20–19 This starter permanent magnet field housing was ruined when someone used a hammer on the field housing in an attempt to "fix" a starter that did not work. A total replacement is the only solution in this case.

PERMANENT MAGNET FIELDS Permanent magnets are used in place of the electromagnetic field coils and pole shoes in many starters today. This eliminates the motor field circuit, which in turn eliminates the potential for field coil faults and other electrical problems. The motor has only an armature circuit.

GEAR-REDUCTION STARTERS

PURPOSE AND FUNCTION Gear-reduction starters are used by many automotive manufacturers. The purpose of the gear reduction (typically 2:1 to 4:1) is to increase starter motor speed and provide the torque multiplication necessary to crank an engine.

As a series-wound motor increases in rotational speed, the starter produces less power, and less current is drawn from the battery because the armature generates greater CEMF as the starter speed increases. However, a starter motor's maximum torque occurs at 0 RPM and torque decreases with increasing RPM. A smaller starter using a gear-reduction design can produce the necessary cranking power with reduced starter amperage requirements. Lower current requirements mean that smaller battery cables can be used. Many permanent magnet starters use a planetary gear set (a type of gear reduction) to provide the necessary torque for starting. ● **SEE FIGURE 20–20.**

STARTER DRIVES

PURPOSE AND FUNCTION A **starter drive** includes small pinion gears that mesh with and rotate the larger gear on the engine flywheel or flex plate for starting. The pinion gear must engage with the engine gear slightly *before* the starter motor rotates to prevent serious damage to either the starter gear or the engine, but must be disengaged after the engine starts. The ends of the starter pinion gear are tapered to help the teeth mesh more easily without damaging the flywheel ring gear teeth. ● **SEE FIGURE 20–21.**

STARTER DRIVE GEAR RATIO The ratio of the number of teeth on the engine ring gear to the number on the starter pinion is between 15:1 and 20:1. A typical small starter pinion gear has 9 teeth that turn an engine ring gear with 166 teeth. This provides an 18:1 gear reduction; thus, the starter motor is rotating approximately 18 times faster than the engine. Normal cranking speed for the engine is 200 RPM (varies from 70 to 250

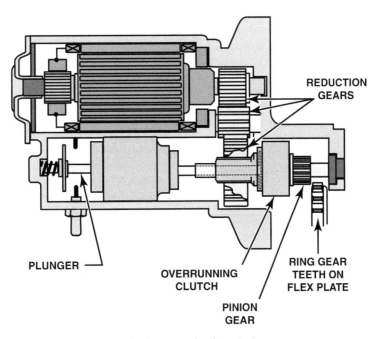

REDUCTION GEARS

PLUNGER

OVERRUNNING CLUTCH

PINION GEAR

RING GEAR TEETH ON FLEX PLATE

FIGURE 20–20 A typical gear-reduction starter.

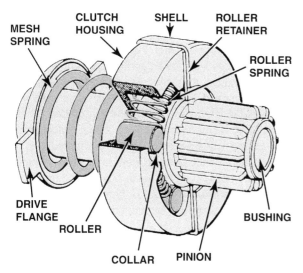

FIGURE 20–21 A cutaway of a typical starter drive showing all of the internal parts.

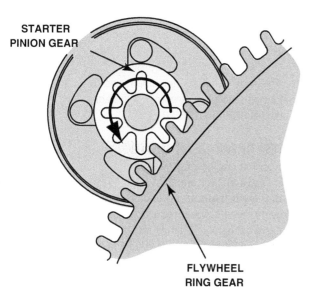

FIGURE 20–22 The ring gear to pinion gear ratio is usually 15:1 to 20:1.

RPM). This means that the starter motor speed is 18 times faster, or 3,600 starter RPM ($200 \times 18 = 3,600$). If the engine starts and is accelerated to 2,000 RPM (normal cold engine speed), the starter is destroyed by the high speed (36,000 RPM), if the starter was not disengaged from the engine. ● SEE FIGURE 20–22.

STARTER DRIVE OPERATION
All starter drive mechanisms use a type of one-way clutch that allows the starter to rotate the engine, but then turns freely if the engine speed is greater than the starter motor speed. This clutch, called an **overrunning clutch**, protects the starter motor from damage if the ignition switch is held in the start position after the engine starts. The overrunning clutch, which is built in as a part of the starter drive unit, uses steel balls or rollers installed in tapered notches. ● SEE FIGURE 20–23.

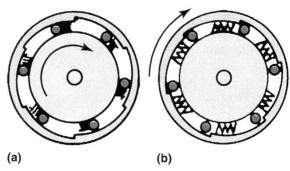

(a)   (b)

FIGURE 20–23 Operation of the overrunning clutch. (a) Starter motor is driving the starter pinion and cranking the engine. The rollers are wedged against spring force into their slots. (b) The engine has started and is rotating faster than the starter armature. Spring force pushes the rollers so they can rotate freely.

This taper forces the balls or rollers tightly into the notch when rotating in the direction necessary to start the engine. When the engine rotates faster than the starter pinion, the balls or rollers are forced out of the narrow tapered notch, allowing the pinion gear to turn freely (overrun).

The spring between the drive tang or pulley and the overrunning clutch and pinion is called a **mesh spring**. It helps cushion and control the engagement of the starter drive pinion with the engine flywheel gear. This spring is also called a **compression spring**, because the starter solenoid or starter yoke compresses the spring and the spring tension causes the starter pinion to engage the engine flywheel.

FAILURE MODE A starter drive is generally a dependable unit and does not require replacement unless defective or worn. The major wear occurs in the overrunning clutch section of the starter drive unit. The steel balls or rollers wear and often do not wedge tightly into the tapered notches as is necessary for engine cranking.

 FREQUENTLY ASKED QUESTION

What Is a Bendix?
Older-model starters often used a Bendix drive mechanism, which used inertia to engage the starter pinion with the engine flywheel gear. Inertia is the tendency of a stationary object to remain stationary, because of its weight, unless forced to move. On these older-model starters, the small starter pinion gear was attached to a shaft with threads, and the weight of this gear caused it to be spun along the threaded shaft and mesh with the flywheel whenever the starter motor spun. If the engine speed was greater than the starter speed, the pinion gear was forced back along the threaded shaft and out of mesh with the flywheel gear. The Bendix drive mechanism has generally not been used since the early 1960s, but some technicians use this term when describing a starter drive.

A worn starter drive can cause the starter motor to operate and then stop cranking the engine further, creating a "whining" noise. The whine indicates that the starter motor is operating and that the starter drive is not rotating the engine flywheel. The entire starter drive is replaced as a unit. The overrunning clutch section of the starter drive cannot be serviced or repaired separately because the drive is a sealed unit. Starter drives are most likely to fail intermittently at first and then more frequently, until replacement becomes necessary to start the engine. Intermittent starter drive failure (starter whine) is often most noticeable during cold weather.

STARTER SOLENOIDS

SOLENOID OPERATION A **starter solenoid** is an electromagnetic switch containing two separate, but connected, electromagnetic windings. This switch is used to engage the starter drive and control the current from the battery to the starter motor.

SOLENOID WINDINGS The two internal windings contain approximately the same number of turns but are made from different-gauge wire. Both windings together produce a strong magnetic field that pulls a metal plunger into the solenoid. The plunger is attached to the starter drive through a shift fork lever. When the ignition switch is turned to the start position, the motion of the plunger into the solenoid causes the starter drive to move into mesh with the flywheel ring gear.

1. The heavier-gauge winding (called the **pull-in winding**) is needed to draw the plunger into the solenoid and is grounded through the starter motor.

2. The lighter-gauge winding (called the **hold-in winding**), which is grounded through the starter frame, produces enough magnetic force to keep the plunger in position. The main purpose of using two separate windings is to permit as much current as possible to operate the starter and yet provide the strong magnetic field required to move the starter drive into engagement. ● **SEE FIGURE 20–24.**

 FREQUENTLY ASKED QUESTION

How Are Starters Made So Small?

Starters and most components in a vehicle are being made as small and as light in weight as possible to help increase vehicle performance and fuel economy. A starter can be constructed smaller due to the use of gear reduction and permanent magnets to achieve the same cranking torque as a straight drive starter, but using much smaller components. ● **SEE FIGURE 20–25** for an example of an automotive starter armature that is palm size.

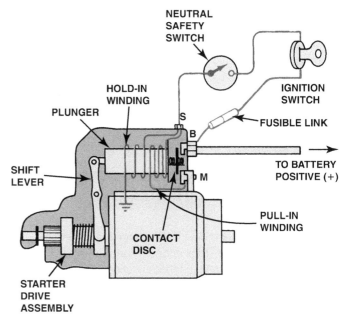

FIGURE 20–24 Wiring diagram of a typical starter solenoid. Notice that both the pull-in winding and the hold-in winding are energized when the ignition switch is first turned to the "start" position. As soon as the solenoid contact disc makes electrical contact with both the B and M terminals, the battery current is conducted to the starter motor and electrically neutralizes the pull-in winding.

FIGURE 20–25 A palm-size starter armature.

OPERATION

1. The solenoid operates as soon as the ignition or computer-controlled relay energizes the "S" (start) terminals. At that instant, the plunger is drawn into the solenoid enough to engage the starter drive.

2. The plunger makes contact with a metal disc that connects the battery terminal post of the solenoid to the motor

terminal. This permits full battery current to flow through the solenoid to operate the starter motor.

3. The contact disc also electrically disconnects the pull-in winding. The solenoid *has* to work to supply current to the starter. Therefore, if the starter motor operates at all, the solenoid is working, even though it may have high external resistance that could cause slow starter motor operation.

STOP-START SYSTEMS

PURPOSE AND FUNCTION **Stop-start** systems are designed to increase fuel economy and reduce exhaust emissions. Fuel economy and the reduction of CO_2 emissions are estimated to be 5% to 10%, depending on the vehicle and how it is being operated. With stop-start mechanism, the engine is stopped to reduce the fuel consumption when the vehicle is stopped at traffic signals or in stop and go traffic conditions. Various vehicle manufacturers refer to stop-start systems using different terms including:

- Auto Stop (● **SEE FIGURE 20–26.**)
- Stop-Start
- Idle-Stop (Honda)
- Smart Stop (Toyota)
- Intelligent Stop and Go (Kia)
- Auto Start/Stop (BMW)
- Engine Stop-Start (ESS)-Chrysler

FIGURE 20–26 A Buick Auto Stop system lets the driver know when the engine is stopped.

CONDITIONS FOR STOP-START TO OCCUR Before the PCM engages the stop-start function, the following parameters must be achieved:

Engine speed is within idling range.

- Accelerator pedal is not depressed.
- Vehicle speed is low or zero, depending on the type of starter used.
- Battery state-of-charge (SOC) is above threshold.
- Hood is closed.

STOP-START SYSTEM COMPONENTS It is estimated that a stop-start system starts the engine about 500,000 times in the life of the vehicle compared to about 5,000 times for a conventional starting system. A typical stop-start system includes the following components:

1. An absorbed glass-mat (AGM) or enhanced lead–acid (ELA) battery.

2. Battery sensor—Used by the PCM to determine the current entering and leaving the battery in order to estimate the battery SOC.

3. Hood switch—Used by the PCM to disengage stop-start if the hood is open.

4. HVAC control unit—Used to start the engine if cooling or heat is required in the passenger compartment.

STARTER MOTOR DESIGNS Because the engine needs to be restarted many times a day, if driving in heavy congested traffic, the starter used must be robust and capable of starting the engine over 500,000 times during the life of the system. There are three designs of starters used in stop-start system including:

1. **Advanced Engagement (AE) Starter.** An advanced engagement starter works like a typical starter. When energized, the pinion shifts forward by the starter solenoid and engages with the engine's ring gear/flywheel, and immediately spins. This starter design requires that the engine speed is zero before re-engagement and engine restart can occur. To survive, the increased usage requires long-life electrical brushes, plus an enhanced pinion spring mechanism that reduces ring gear/flywheel wear.

2. **Tandem Solenoid (TS) Starter.** Using a starter that has two solenoids allows the starter to engage the flywheel of the engine when it is still moving, such as when the vehicle is coasting to a stop. A tandem solenoid starter design is also able to start the engine within 0.5 and 1.5 seconds, compared to about 3 seconds for a conventional starter. A conventional starter uses the solenoid to engage the starter pinion, then, when it is being held by the hold-in winding, the solenoid energizes the starter motor cranking the engine. The use of a dual solenoid allows the two functions of the starter solenoid to work independently:

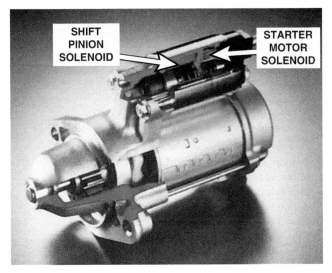

FIGURE 20-27 Using two solenoids allows independent control of the pinion gear and motor energization.

FIGURE 20-28 The stop-start system on this Ford F-150 pickup truck can be turned off using a switch on the dash.

One solenoid is used to engage the starter drive into the engine ring gear.

The other solenoid is used to engage the operation of the starter motor. ● SEE FIGURE 20-27.

This allows the engine to be re-engaged (and restarted) by the starter motor when the engine RPM is falling from idle (about 600 RPM) to zero RPM. A tandem solenoid starter is almost identical in size and shape, so it can be used on almost any engine.

3. **Permanently Engaged (PE) Starter.** A permanently engaged starter delivers the quickest and quietest restart times of all starter motor-based systems. In this system, the starter and flywheel gears are permanently connected, so there are no concerns with gear engagement

 FREQUENTLY ASKED QUESTION

Can a Stop-Start System Be Turned Off?

Sometimes. Some vehicles equipped with a stop-start system can be turned off using a button on the dash or center stack. ● SEE FIGURE 20-28.

and disengagement. The PE starter eliminates the starter pinion gear shifting mechanism with its slight delay in activating by mounting the starter to the engine permanently engaged with the flywheel. When a restart is needed, the motor is simply energized, which immediately re-cranks the engine. There is no waiting or delay since the starter gear is already mated to the flywheel. The flywheel does require a special clutching mechanism to disconnect it from engine RPM after engine start.

SUMMARY

1. All starter motors use the principle of magnetic interaction between the field coils attached to the housing and the magnetic field of the armature.

2. The control circuit includes the ignition switch, neutral safety (clutch) switch, and solenoid.

3. The power circuit includes the battery, battery cables, solenoid, and starter motor.

4. The parts of a typical starter include the main field housing, commutator-end (or brush-end) housing, drive-end housing, brushes, armature, and starter drive.

REVIEW QUESTIONS

1. What is the difference between the control circuit and the power (motor) circuit sections of a typical cranking circuit?

2. What are the parts of a typical starter?

3. Why does a gear-reduction unit reduce the amount of current required by the starter motor?

4. What are the symptoms of a defective starter drive?

5. Why are there two windings in the starter solenoid?

CHAPTER QUIZ

1. Starter motors operate on the principle that _____.
   a. the field coils rotate in the opposite direction from the armature
   b. opposite magnetic poles repel
   c. like magnetic poles repel
   d. the armature rotates from a strong magnetic field toward a weaker magnetic field

2. Series-wound electric motors _____.
   a. produce electrical power
   b. produce maximum power at 0 RPM
   c. produce maximum power at high RPM
   d. use a shunt coil

3. Technician A says that a defective solenoid can cause a starter whine. Technician B says that a defective starter drive can cause a starter whining noise. Which technician is correct?
   a. Technician A only
   b. Technician B only
   c. Both Technicians A and B
   d. Neither Technician A nor B

4. The neutral safety switch is located _____.
   a. between the starter solenoid and the starter motor
   b. inside the ignition switch itself
   c. between the ignition switch and the starter solenoid
   d. in the battery cable between the battery and the starter solenoid

5. The brushes are used to transfer electrical power between _____.
   a. field coils and the armature
   b. the commutator segments
   c. the solenoid and the field coils
   d. the armature and the solenoid

6. The faster a starter motor rotates, _____.
   a. the more current it draws from the battery
   b. the less CEMF is generated
   c. the less current it draws from the battery
   d. the greater the amount of torque produced

7. Normal cranking speed of the engine is about _____.
   a. 2,000 RPM   c. 1,000 RPM
   b. 1,500 RPM   d. 200 RPM

8. A starter motor rotates about _____ times faster than the engine.
   a. 18   c. 5
   b. 10   d. 2

9. Permanent magnets are commonly used for what part of the starter?
   a. Armature   c. Field coils
   b. Solenoid   d. Commutator

10. A stop-start system includes what components?
    a. A special starter
    b. An AGM or ELA battery
    c. A switch to turn the system off in some vehicles
    d. All of the above

chapter 21

CRANKING SYSTEM DIAGNOSIS AND SERVICE

LEARNING OBJECTIVES:

After studying this chapter, the reader should be able to:

Explain the procedure to troubleshoot a starting system problem.

Discuss how to perform a voltage drop test on the cranking circuit.

Perform control circuit testing and starter amperage test, and determine necessary action.

Describe the procedure to remove a starter motor.

Explain starter motor service and bench testing.

Describe the procedure to install a starter motor.

Describe how to ensure proper clearance between the starter pinion and the engine flywheel.

This chapter will help prepare for the ASE Electrical/Electronic Systems (A6) certification test content area "C" (Battery and Starting Systems Diagnosis and Repair).

KEY TERMS: Bench testing 257 • Growler 256 • Shims 257 • Voltage drop 252

STARTING SYSTEM TROUBLESHOOTING PROCEDURE

OVERVIEW The proper operation of the starting system depends on a good battery, good cables and connections, and a good starter motor. Because a starting problem can be caused by a defective component anywhere in the starting circuit, it is important to check for the proper operation of each part of the circuit to diagnose and repair the problem quickly.

STEPS INVOLVED Following are the steps involved in the diagnosis of a fault in the cranking circuit.

STEP 1 Verify the customer concern. Sometimes the customer is not aware of how the cranking system is supposed to work, especially if it is computer controlled.

STEP 2 Visually inspect the battery and battery connections. The starter is the highest amperage draw device used in a vehicle and any faults, such as corrosion on battery terminals, can cause cranking system problems.

STEP 3 Test battery condition. Perform a battery load or conductance test on the battery to be sure that the battery is capable of supplying the necessary current for the starter.

STEP 4 Check the control circuit. An open or high resistance anywhere in the control circuit can cause the starter motor to not engage. Items to check include:

THEFT DETERRENT INDICATOR LAMP

FIGURE 21–1 A theft deterrent indicator lamp of the dash. A flashing lamp usually indicates a fault in the system, and the engine may not start.

- "S" terminal of the starter solenoid
- Neutral safety or clutch switch
- Starter enable relay (if equipped)
- Antitheft system fault (If the engine does not crank or start and the theft indicator light is on or flashing, there is likely a fault in the theft deterrent system. Check service information for the exact procedures to follow before attempting to service the cranking circuit. ● **SEE FIGURE 21–1.**)

Voltage Drop Is Resistance

Many technicians have asked, "Why measure voltage drop when the resistance can be easily measured using an ohmmeter?" Think of a battery cable with all the strands of the cable broken, except for one strand. If an ohmmeter were used to measure the resistance of the cable, the reading would be very low, probably less than 1 ohm. However, the cable is not capable of conducting the amount of current necessary to crank the engine. In less severe cases, several strands can be broken, thereby affecting the operation of the starter motor. Although the resistance of the battery cable does not indicate an increase, the restriction to current flow causes heat and a drop of voltage available at the starter. Because resistance is not effective until current flows, measuring the voltage drop (differences in voltage between two points) is the most accurate method of determining the true resistance in a circuit.

How much is too much? According to Bosch Corporation, all electrical circuits should have a maximum of 3% loss of the circuit voltage to resistance. Therefore, in a 12 volt circuit, the maximum loss of voltage in cables and connections should be 0.36 volt (12 × 0.03 = 0.36 volt). The remaining 97% of the circuit voltage (11.64 volts) is available to operate the electrical device (load). Just remember:

- Low-voltage drop = Low resistance
- High-voltage drop = High resistance

STEP 5 **Check voltage drop of the starter circuit.** Any high resistance in either the power side or ground side of the starter circuit causes the starter to rotate slowly or not at all.

VOLTAGE DROP TESTING

PURPOSE **Voltage drop** is the drop in voltage that occurs when current is flowing through a resistance. That is, a voltage drop is the difference between voltage at the source and voltage at the electrical device to which it is flowing. The higher the voltage drop is, the greater is the resistance in the circuit. Even though voltage drop testing can be performed on any electrical circuit, the most common areas of testing include the cranking circuit and the charging circuit wiring and connections. Voltage drop testing should be performed on both the power side and ground side of the circuit.

A high-voltage drop (high resistance) in the cranking circuit wiring can cause slow engine cranking with less than normal starter amperage drain as a result of the excessive circuit resistance. If the voltage drop is high enough, such as that caused by dirty battery terminals, the starter may not operate. A typical symptom of high resistance in the cranking circuit is a "clicking" of the starter solenoid.

TEST PROCEDURE Voltage drop testing of the wire involves connecting a voltmeter set to read DC volts to the suspected high-resistance cable ends and cranking the engine. ● **SEE FIGURES 21–2 THROUGH 21–4.**

NOTE: **Before a difference in voltage (voltage drop) can be measured between the ends of a battery cable, current must be flowing through the cable. Resistance is not effective unless current is flowing. If the engine**

is not being cranked, current is not flowing through the battery cables and the voltage drop cannot be measured.

STEP 1 Disable the ignition or fuel injection as follows:
- Disconnect the primary (low-voltage) electrical connection(s) from the ignition module or ignition coils.
- Remove the fuel-injection fuse or relay, or the electrical connection leading to all of the fuel injectors.

CAUTION: **Never disconnect the high-voltage ignition wires unless they are connected to ground. The high voltage that could occur when cranking can cause the ignition coil to fail (arc internally).**

STEP 2 Connect one lead of the voltmeter to the starter motor battery terminal and the other end to the positive battery terminal.

STEP 3 Crank the engine and observe the reading while cranking. (Disregard the first higher reading.) The reading should be less than 0.20 volt (200 millivolts).

STEP 4 If accessible, test the voltage drop across the "B" and "M" terminals of the starter solenoid with the engine cranking. The voltage drop should be less than 0.20 volt (200 millivolts).

TECH TIP

A Warm Cable Equals High Resistance

If a cable or connection is warm to the touch, there is electrical resistance in the cable or connection. The resistance changes electrical energy into heat energy. Therefore, if a voltmeter is not available, touch the battery cables and connections while cranking the engine. If any cable or connection is hot to the touch, it should be cleaned or replaced.

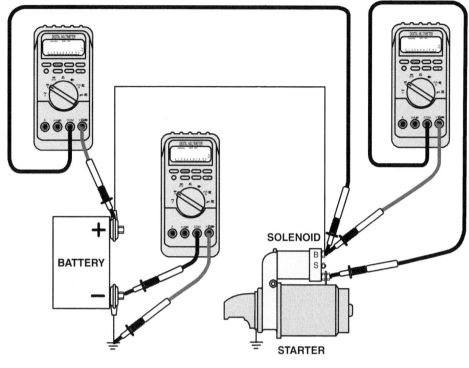

FIGURE 21–2 Voltmeter hookups for voltage drop testing of a solenoid-type cranking circuit.

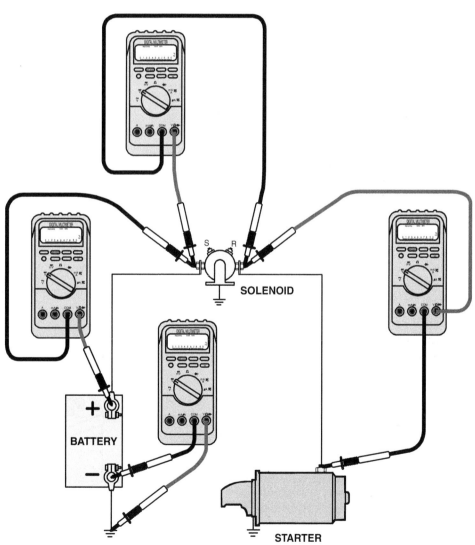

FIGURE 21–3 Voltmeter hookups for voltage drop testing of a Ford cranking circuit.

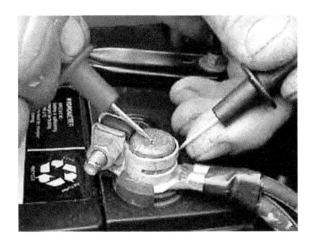

FIGURE 21–4 To test the voltage drop of the battery cable connection, place one voltmeter lead on the battery terminal and the other voltmeter lead on the cable end and crank the engine. The voltmeter reads the difference in voltage between the two leads, which should not exceed 0.20 volt (200 millivolts).

STEP 5 Repeat the voltage drop on the ground side of the cranking circuit by connecting one voltmeter lead to the negative battery terminal and the other at the starter housing. Crank the engine and observe the voltmeter display. The voltage drop should be less than 0.2 volt (200 millivolts).

CONTROL CIRCUIT TESTING

PARTS INVOLVED The control circuit for the starting circuit includes the battery, ignition switch, neutral or clutch safety switch, theft deterrent system, and starter solenoid. When the ignition switch is rotated to the start position, current flows through the ignition switch and neutral safety switch to activate the solenoid. High current then flows directly from the battery through the solenoid and to the starter motor. Therefore, an open or break anywhere in the control circuit prevents the operation of the starter motor.

If a starter is inoperative, first check for voltage at the "S" (start) terminal of the starter solenoid. Check for faults with the following:

- Neutral safety or clutch switch
- Blown crank fuse
- Open at the ignition switch in the crank position
- Starter relay or module, if equipped

Some models with antitheft controls use a relay to open this control circuit to prevent starter operation.

STARTER AMPERAGE TEST

REASON FOR A STARTER AMPERAGE TEST
A starter should be tested to see if the reason for slow or no cranking is due to a fault with the starter motor or another problem. A

voltage drop test is used to find out if the battery cables and connections are okay. A starter amperage draw test determines if the starter motor is the cause of a no or slow cranking concern.

TEST PREPARATION Before performing a starter amperage test, be certain that the battery is sufficiently charged (75% or more) and capable of supplying adequate starting current. Connect a starter amperage tester following the tester's instructions. ● **SEE FIGURE 21–5**.

A starter amperage test should be performed when the starter fails to operate normally (is slow in cranking) or as part of a routine electrical system inspection.

SPECIFICATIONS Some service manuals specify normal starter amperage for starter motors being tested on the vehicle; however, most service manuals only give the specifications for bench testing a starter without a load applied. These specifications are helpful in making certain that a repaired starter meets exact specifications, but they do not apply to starter testing on the vehicle. If exact

 TECH TIP

Watch the Dome Light

When diagnosing any starter-related problem, open the door of the vehicle and observe the brightness of the dome or interior light(s).

The brightness of any electrical lamp is proportional to the voltage of the battery.

Normal operation of the starter results in a slight dimming of the dome light.

If the light remains bright, the problem is usually an open in the control circuit.

If the light goes out or almost goes out, there could be a problem with the following:

- A shorted or grounded armature of field coils inside the starter
- Loose or corroded battery connections or cables
- Weak or discharged battery

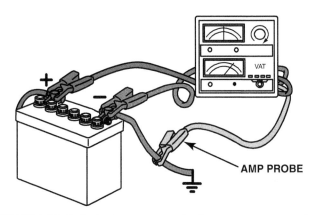

FIGURE 21–5 A starter amperage tester uses an amp probe around the positive or negative battery cables.

specifications are not available, the following can be used as general *maximum* amperage draw specifications for testing a starter on the vehicle. (Ignore the initial current surge when the starter is first engaged and just record the cranking amperage)

- **4-cylinder engines** = 150 to 185 amperes (normally less than 100 amperes) at room temperature

- **6-cylinder engines** = 160 to 200 amperes (normally less than 125 amperes) at room temperature

- **8-cylinder engines** = 185 to 250 amperes (normally less than 150 amperes) at room temperature

Excessive current draw may indicate one or more of the following:

1. Binding of starter armature as a result of worn bushings
2. Oil too thick (viscosity too high) for weather conditions
3. Shorted or grounded starter windings or cables
4. Tight or seized engine
5. Shorted starter motor (usually caused by fault with the field coils or armature)
    - High mechanical resistance = High starter amperage draw
    - High electrical resistance = Low starter amperage draw

Lower amperage draw and slow or no cranking may indicate one or more of the following:

- Dirty or corroded battery connections
- High internal resistance in the battery cable(s)
- High internal starter motor resistance
- Poor ground connection between the starter motor and the engine block

 CASE STUDY

The Case of the No-Crank Camaro

The owner of a Camaro SS equipped with a 6.2 liter V-8 and a six-speed manual transmission had the car towed to a shop for a no crank, no start condition. The technician used a scan tool and was able to retrieve a stored diagnostic trouble code (DTC) P0807. This code indicated a fault with the clutch pedal position (CPP) sensor. The clutch pedal position sensor was removed and it was found to be internally shorted. A new sensor was installed and the technician performed a relearn procedure as specified in service information. The car was then able to crank and start and verified that no codes were present.

Summary:

- **Complaint**—The customer stated that the engine would not crank or start.
- **Cause**—A shorted clutch pedal position (CPP) sensor.
- **Correction**—The clutch pedal position sensor was replaced and a relearn procedure was performed.

STARTER REMOVAL

PROCEDURE After testing has confirmed that a starter motor may need to be replaced, most vehicle manufacturers recommend the following general steps and procedures.

STEP 1 Disconnect the negative battery cable.

STEP 2 Hoist the vehicle safely.

> NOTE: This step may not be necessary. Check service information for the specified procedure for the vehicle being serviced. Some starters are located under the intake manifold. ● SEE FIGURE 21–6.

STEP 3 Remove the starter retaining bolts and lower the starter to gain access to the wire(s) connection(s) on the starter.

STEP 4 Disconnect and label the wire(s) from the starter and remove the starter.

STEP 5 Inspect the flywheel (flexplate) for ring gear damage. Also check that the mounting holes are clean and the mounting flange is clean and smooth. Service as needed.

STARTER MOTOR SERVICE

PURPOSE Most starter motors are replaced as an assembly or not easily disassembled or serviced. However, some starters, especially on classic muscle or collector vehicles, can be serviced.

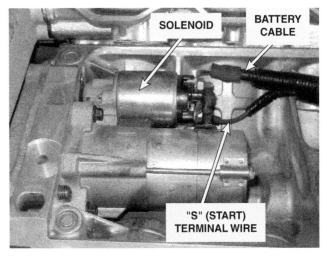

FIGURE 21–6 The starter is located under the intake manifold on this Cadillac Northstar engine.

DISASSEMBLY PROCEDURE Disassembly of a starter
motor usually includes the following steps.

STEP 1 Remove the starter solenoid assembly.

STEP 2 Mark the location of the through bolts on the field
housing to help align them during reassembly.

STEP 3 Remove the drive-end housing and then the armature
assembly.

   ● **SEE FIGURE 21–7**.

INSPECTION AND TESTING The various parts should be
inspected and tested to see if the components can be used to
restore the starter to serviceable condition.

 ▪ **Solenoid.** Check the resistance of the solenoid winding. The solenoid can be tested using an ohmmeter to
   check for the proper resistance in the hold-in and pull-in
   windings. ● **SEE FIGURE 21–8**.

   Most technicians replace the solenoid whenever the starter
is replaced and is usually included with a replacement starter.

 ▪ **Starter armature.** After the starter drive has been removed
   from the armature, it can be checked for runout using a
   dial indicator and V-blocks, as shown in ● **FIGURE 21–9**.

 ▪ **Growler.** Because the loops of copper wire are interconnected in the armature of a starter, an armature can
   be accurately tested only by use of a **growler**. A growler
   is a 110 volt AC test unit that generates an alternating
   (60 hertz) magnetic field around an armature. A starter

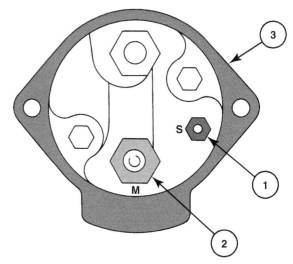

FIGURE 21–8 GM solenoid ohmmeter check. The reading
between 1 and 3 (S terminal and ground) should be 0.4 to 0.6
ohm (hold-in winding). The reading between 1 and 2 (S terminal
and M terminal) should be 0.2 to 0.4 ohm (pull-in winding).

armature is placed into the V-shaped top portion of a
laminated soft-iron core surrounded by a coil of copper
wire. Plug the growler into a 110 volt outlet and then follow the instructions for testing the armature.

 ▪ **Starter motor field coils.** With the armature removed
   from the starter motor, the field coils should be tested
   for opens and grounds using a powered test light or an

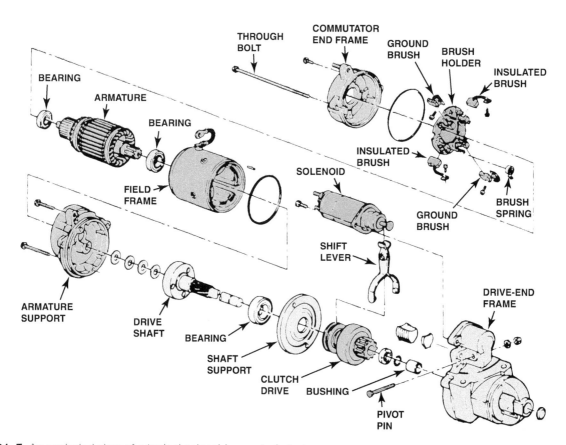

FIGURE 21–7 An exploded view of a typical solenoid-operated starter.

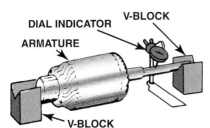

FIGURE 21–9 Measuring an armature shaft for runout using a dial indicator and V-blocks.

ohmmeter. To test for a grounded field coil, touch one lead of the tester to a field brush (insulated or hot) and the other end to the starter field housing. The ohmmeter should indicate infinity (no continuity), and the test light should *not* light. If there is continuity, replace the field coil housing assembly. The ground brushes should show continuity to the starter housing.

NOTE: Many starters use removable field coils. These coils must be rewound using the proper equipment and insulating materials. Usually, the cost involved in replacing defective field coils exceeds the cost of a replacement starter.

- **Starter brush inspection.** Starter brushes should be replaced if the brush length is less than half of its original length (less than 0.5 inch [13 millimeters]). On some models of starter motors, the field brushes are serviced with the field coil assembly and the ground brushes with the brush holder. Many starters use brushes that are held in with screws and are easily replaced, whereas other starters may require soldering to remove and replace the brushes. ● **SEE FIGURE 21–10.**

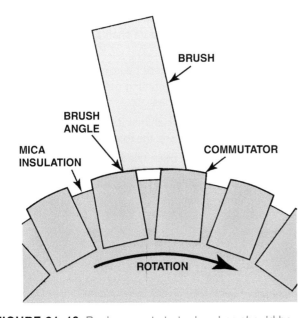

FIGURE 21–10 Replacement starter brushes should be installed so the beveled edge matches the rotation of the commutator.

Every starter should be tested before installation in a vehicle. **Bench testing** is the usual method and involves clamping the starter in a vise to prevent rotation during operation and connecting heavy-gauge jumper wires (minimum 4 gauge) to both a good battery and the starter. The starter motor should rotate as fast as specifications indicate and not draw more than the free-spinning amperage permitted. A typical amperage specification for a starter being tested on a bench (not installed in a vehicle) usually ranges from 60 to 100 amperes.

STARTER INSTALLATION

After verifying that the starter assembly is functioning correctly, verify that the negative battery cable has been disconnected. Then safely hoist the vehicle, if necessary. Following are the usual steps to install a starter. Be sure to check service information for the exact procedures to follow for the vehicle being serviced.

STEP 1 Check service information for the exact wiring connections to the starter and/or the solenoid.

STEP 2 Verify that all electrical connections on the starter-motor and/or the solenoid are correct for the vehicle and that they are in good condition.

> **NOTE: Be sure that the locking nuts for the studs are tight. Often, the retaining nut that holds the wire to the stud is properly tightened, but if the stud itself is loose, cranking problems can occur.**

STEP 3 Attach the power and control wires.

STEP 4 Install the starter, and torque all the fasteners to factory specifications and tighten evenly.

STEP 5 Perform a starter amperage draw test and check for proper engine cranking.

CAUTION: Be sure to install all factory heat shields to help ensure problem-free starter operation under all weather and driving conditions.

STARTER DRIVE-TO-FLYWHEEL CLEARANCE

NEED FOR SHIMS For the proper operation of the starter and absence of abnormal starter noise, there must be a slight clearance between the starter pinion and the engine flywheel ring gear. Many starters use **shims**, which are thin metal strips,

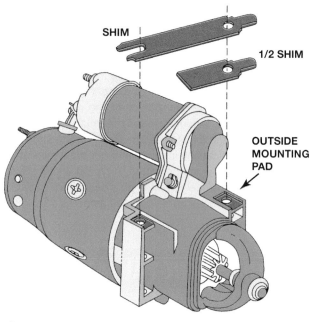

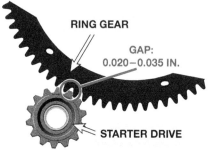

FIGURE 21–11 A shim (or half shim) may be needed to provide the proper clearance between the flywheel teeth of the engine and the pinion teeth of the starter.

between the flywheel and the engine block mounting pad to provide the proper clearance. ● **SEE FIGURE 21–11**.

Some manufacturers use shims under the starter drive-end housings during production. Other manufacturers *grind* the mounting pads at the factory for proper starter pinion gear clearance. If a GM starter is replaced, the starter pinion should be checked and corrected, as necessary, to prevent starter damage and excessive noise.

 **TECH TIP**

Reuse Drive-End Housing to Be Sure

Most GM starter motors use a pad mount and attach to the engine with bolts through the drive-end (nose) housing. Many times when a starter is replaced on a GM vehicle, the starter makes noise because of improper starter pinion-to-engine flywheel ring gear clearance. Instead of spending a lot of time shimming the new starter, simply remove the drive-end housing from the original starter and install it on the replacement starter. Service the bushing in the drive-end housing, if needed. Because the original starter did not produce excessive gear engagement noise, the replacement starter is also okay. Reuse any shims that were used with the original starter. This is preferable to removing and reinstalling the replacement starter several times until the proper clearance is determined.

SYMPTOMS OF CLEARANCE PROBLEMS

- If the clearance is too great, the starter produces a high-pitched whine *during* cranking.
- If the clearance is too small, the starter may bind, crank slowly, or produce a high-pitched whine *after* the engine starts, just as the ignition key is released.

PROCEDURE FOR PROPER CLEARANCE   To be sure that the starter is shimmed correctly, use the following procedure.

STEP 1   Place the starter in position and finger-tighten the mounting bolts.

STEP 2   Use a 1/8 inch diameter drill bit (or gauge tool) and insert between the armature shaft and a tooth of the engine flywheel.

STEP 3   If the gauge tool cannot be inserted, use a full-length shim across both mounting holes to move the starter away from the flywheel.

STEP 4   Remove a shim (or shims) if the gauge tool is loose between the shaft and the tooth of the engine flywheel.

STEP 5   If no shims have been used and the fit of the gauge tool is too loose, add a half shim to the outside pad only. This moves the starter closer to the teeth of the engine flywheel.

STARTING SYSTEM SYMPTOM GUIDE

The following list assists technicians in troubleshooting starting systems.

Problem	Possible Causes
1. Starter motor whines	1. Possible defective starter drive; worn starter drive engagement yoke; defective flywheel; improper starter drive to flywheel clearance
2. Starter rotates slowly	2. Possible high resistance in the battery cables or connections; possible defective or discharged battery; possible worn starter bushings, causing the starter armature to drag on the field coils; possible worn starter brushes or weak brush springs; possible defective (open or shorted) field coil
3. Starter fails to rotate	3. Possible defective ignition switch or neutral safety switch, or open in the starter motor control circuit; theft deterrent system fault; possible defective starter solenoid
4. Starter produces grinding noise	4. Possible defective starter drive unit; possible defective flywheel; possible incorrect distance between the starter pinion and the flywheel; possible cracked or broken starter drive-end housing; worn or damaged flywheel or ring gear teeth
5. Starter clicks when engaged	5. Low battery voltage; loose or corroded battery connections

1 This dirty and greasy starter can be restored to useful service.

2 The connecting wire between the solenoid and the starter is removed.

3 An old starter field housing is being used to support the drive-end housing of the starter as it is being disassembled. This rebuilder is using an electric impact wrench to remove the solenoid fasteners.

4 A Torx driver is used to remove the solenoid attaching screws.

5 After the retaining screws have been removed, the solenoid can be separated from the starter motor. This rebuilder always replaces the solenoid.

6 The through bolts are being removed.

7 The brush end plate is removed.

8 The armature assembly is removed from the field frame.

9 Notice that the length of a direct-drive starter armature (top) is the same length as the overall length of a gear-reduction armature, except smaller in diameter.

10 A light tap with a hammer dislodges the armature thrust ball (in the palm of the hand) from the center of the gear-reduction assembly.

11 This figure shows the planetary ring gear and pinion gears.

12 A close-up of one of the planetary gears, which shows the small needle bearings on the inside.

CONTINUED ▶

13 The clip is removed from the shaft so the planetary gear assembly can be separated and inspected.

14 The shaft assembly is being separated from the stationary gear assembly.

15 The commutator on the armature is discolored and the brushes may not have been making good contact with the segments.

16 All of the starter components are placed in a tumbler with water-based cleaner. The armature is installed in a lathe and the commutator is resurfaced using emery cloth.

17 The finished commutator looks like new.

18 Starter reassembly begins by installing a new starter drive on the shaft assembly. The stop ring and stop ring retainer are then installed.

19 The gear-reduction assembly is positioned along with the shift fork (drive lever) into the cleaned drive-end housing.

20 After gear retainer has been installed over the gear-reduction assembly, the armature is installed.

21 New brushes are being installed into the brush holder assembly.

22 The brush end plate and the through bolts are installed, being sure that the ground connection for the brushes is clean and tight.

23 This starter was restored to useful service by replacing the solenoid, the brushes, and the starter drive assembly, plus a thorough cleaning and attention to detail in the reassembly.

1. Proper operation and testing of the starter motor depends on the battery being at least 75% charged and the battery cables being of the correct size (gauge) and having no more than a 0.2 volt drop.

2. Voltage drop testing includes cranking the engine, measuring the drop in voltage from the battery to the starter, and measuring the drop in voltage from the negative terminal of the battery to the engine block.

3. The cranking circuit should be tested for proper amperage draw.

4. An open in the control circuit can prevent starter motor operation.

REVIEW QUESTIONS

1. What are the steps involved in the diagnosis of a fault in the cranking circuit?

2. What are the steps taken to perform a voltage drop test of the cranking circuit?

3. What are the steps necessary to replace a starter?

4. What are typical starter amperage draw for four-, six-, and eight-cylinder engines?

5. What could be the cause of excessive starter current draw?

CHAPTER QUIZ

1. Which one of these would NOT be a diagnostic step when diagnosing a "no crank" customer concern?
   a. Check the condition of the engine oil
   b. Check operation of the theft deterrent systems
   c. Check the battery with a load test
   d. Test for proper operation of the starter enable relay

2. Two technicians are discussing what could be the cause of slow cranking and excessive current draw. Technician A says that an engine mechanical fault could be the cause. Technician B says that the starter motor could be binding or defective. Which technician is correct?
   a. Technician A only
   b. Technician B only
   c. Both Technicians A and B
   d. Neither Technician A nor B

3. A V-6 is being checked for starter amperage draw. The initial surge current was about 210 amperes and about 160 amperes during cranking. Technician A says the starter is defective and should be replaced because the current flow exceeds 200 amperes. Technician B says this is normal current draw for a starter motor on a V-6 engine. Which technician is correct?
   a. Technician A only
   b. Technician B only
   c. Both Technicians A and B
   d. Neither Technician A nor B

4. What is the first step for removing a starter?
   a. Hoist the vehicle
   b. Disconnect the battery positive cable
   c. Disconnect the battery negative cable
   d. Remove the battery cable from the starter

5. Technician A says that a discharged battery (lower than normal battery voltage) can cause solenoid clicking. Technician B says that a discharged battery or dirty (corroded) battery cables can cause solenoid clicking. Which technician is correct?
   a. Technician A only
   b. Technician B only
   c. Both Technicians A and B
   d. Neither Technician A nor B

6. Slow cranking by the starter can be caused by all of these EXCEPT _____.
   a. a low or discharged battery
   b. corroded or dirty battery cables
   c. engine mechanical problems
   d. an open neutral safety switch

7. Bench testing of a starter should be done _____.
   a. after reassembling an old starter
   b. before installing a new starter
   c. after removing the old starter
   d. Both a and b

8. If the clearance between the starter pinion and the engine flywheel is too great, _____.
   a. the starter produces a high-pitched whine during cranking
   b. the starter produces a high-pitched whine after the engine starts
   c. the starter drive does not rotate at all
   d. the solenoid does not engage the starter drive unit

9. A technician connects one lead of a digital voltmeter to the positive (+) terminal of the battery and the other meter lead to the battery terminal (B) of the starter solenoid and then cranks the engine. During cranking, the voltmeter displays a reading of 878 millivolts. Technician A says that this reading indicates that the positive battery cable has too high resistance. Technician B says that this reading indicates that the starter is defective. Which technician is correct?
   a. Technician A only
   b. Technician B only
   c. Both Technicians A and B
   d. Neither Technician A nor B

10. After installing the starter, the technician should perform which of the following?
    a. Attach the negative battery cable
    b. Check the starter for proper operation
    c. Perform a starter voltage drop test before starting the engine
    d. Both a and b

chapter 22

CHARGING SYSTEM

LEARNING OBJECTIVES:

After studying this chapter, the reader should be able to:

Explain why an alternator generates an AC and changes it to DC.

Describe an alternator's construction, including overrunning pulleys.

Describe the components and operation of an alternator.

Discuss how an alternator works.

List the factors determining an alternator's output voltage and current.

Explain how the voltage and heat produced by an alternator are regulated.

Discuss computer-controlled alternators.

This chapter will help prepare for the ASE Electrical/ Electronic Systems (A6) certification test content area "C" (Starting System Diagnosis and Repair).

KEY TERMS: Alternator 266 • Claw poles 269 • Delta winding 272 • Diodes 270 • Drive-end (DE) housing 266 • Duty cycle 276 • EPM 275 • OAD 268 • OAP 267 • Rotor 269 • Slip-ring-end (SRE) housing 266 • Stator 269 • Thermistor 274

PRINCIPLE OF ALTERNATOR OPERATION

PURPOSE AND FUNCTION It is the purpose and function of the charging system to keep the battery fully charged. The Society of Automotive Engineers (SAE) term for the unit that generates electricity is *generator*. The term **alternator** is most commonly used in the trade and is used here as well.

PRINCIPLES All electrical alternators use the principle of electromagnetic induction to generate electrical power from mechanical power. Electromagnetic induction involves the generation of electric current in a conductor when the conductor is moved through a magnetic field. The amount of current generated can be increased by the following factors.

1. Increasing the *speed* of the conductors through the magnetic field
2. Increasing the *number* of conductors passing through the magnetic field
3. Increasing the *strength* of the magnetic field

CHANGING AC TO DC An alternator generates an alternating current (AC) because the current changes polarity during the alternator's rotation. However, a battery cannot "store" AC; therefore, this AC is changed to direct current (DC) by diodes inside the alternator. Diodes are one-way electrical check valves that permit current to flow in only one direction.

ALTERNATOR CONSTRUCTION

HOUSING An alternator is constructed using a two-piece cast aluminum housing. Aluminum is used because of its lightweight, nonmagnetic properties, and heat transfer properties needed to help keep the alternator cool. A front ball bearing is pressed into the front housing, called the **drive-end (DE) housing**, to provide the support and friction reduction necessary for the belt-driven rotor assembly. The rear housing, or the **slip-ring-end (SRE) housing**, usually contains either a roller bearing or ball bearing support for the rotor and mounting for the brushes, diodes, and internal voltage regulator (if so equipped). ● **SEE FIGURES 22–1 AND 22–2.**

ALTERNATOR OVERRUNNING PULLEYS

PURPOSE AND FUNCTION Many alternators are equipped with an **overrunning alternator pulley (OAP)**, also called an *overrunning clutch pulley* or an *alternator clutch pulley*. The purpose of this pulley is to help eliminate noise and vibration in the accessory drive belt system, especially when the engine is at idle speed. At idle, engine impulses are

FIGURE 22–1 A typical alternator on a Chevrolet V-8 engine that is driven by the accessory drive belt at the front of the engine.

 TECH TIP

Alternator Horsepower and Engine Operation

Many technicians are asked how much power certain accessories require. A 100 ampere alternator requires about 2 horsepower from the engine. One horsepower is equal to 746 watts. Watts are calculated by multiplying amperes times volts.

$$\text{Power in watts} = 100\,\text{A} \times 14.5\,\text{V} = 1,450\,\text{W}$$
$$1\,\text{hp} = 746\,\text{W}$$

Therefore, 1,450 watts is about 2 horsepower.

Allowing about 20% for mechanical and electrical losses adds another 0.4 horsepower. Therefore, when someone asks how much power it takes to produce 100 amperes from an alternator, the answer is 2.4 horsepower.

Many alternators delay the electrical load to prevent the engine from stumbling when a heavy electrical load is applied. The voltage regulator or vehicle computer is capable of gradually increasing the output of the alternator over a period of several minutes. Even though 2 horsepower does not sound like much, a sudden demand for 2 horsepower from an idling engine can cause the engine to run rough or stall. The difference in part numbers of various alternators is often an indication of the time interval over which the load is applied. Therefore, using the wrong replacement alternator could cause the engine to stall!

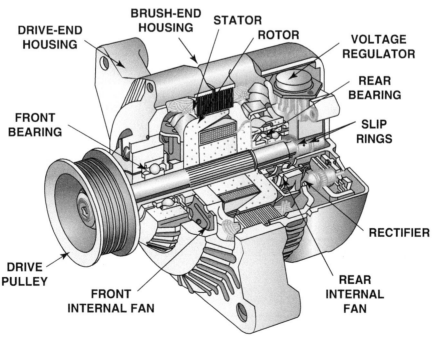

FIGURE 22–2 The end frame toward the drive belt is called the drive-end housing and the rear section is called the slip-ring-end housing.

transmitted to the alternator through the accessory drive belt. The mass of the rotor of the alternator tends to want to keep spinning, but the engine crankshaft speeds up and slows down slightly due to the power impulses. Using a one-way clutch in the alternator pulley allows the belt to apply power to the alternator in only one direction, thereby reducing fluctuations in the belt. ● **SEE FIGURES 22–3 AND 22–4.**

A conventional drive pulley attaches to the alternator (rotor) shaft with a nut and lock washer. In the overrunning clutch pulley, the inner race of the clutch acts as the nut as it screws on to the shaft. Special tools are required to remove and install this type of pulley.

Another type of alternator pulley uses a dampener spring inside, plus a one-way clutch. These units have the following names. ● **SEE FIGURES 22–5.**

- Isolating Decoupler Pulley (IDP)
- Active Alternator Pulley (AAP)
- Alternator Decoupler Pulley (ADP)
- Alternator Overrunning Decoupler Pulley
- **Overrunning Alternator Dampener (OAD)** (most common term)

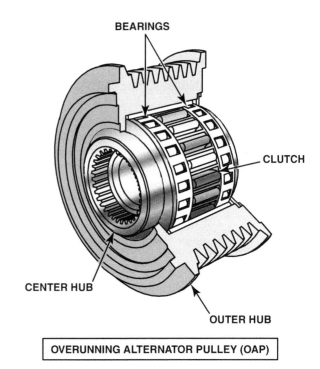

OVERUNNING ALTERNATOR PULLEY (OAP)

FIGURE 22–4 An exploded view of an overrunning alternator pulley showing all of the internal parts.

? FREQUENTLY ASKED QUESTION

Can I Install an OAP or an OAD to My Alternator?

Usually, no. An alternator needs to be equipped with the proper shaft to allow the installation of an OAP or OAD. This also means that a conventional pulley often cannot be used to replace a defective overrunning alternator pulley or dampener. Check service information for the exact procedure to follow.

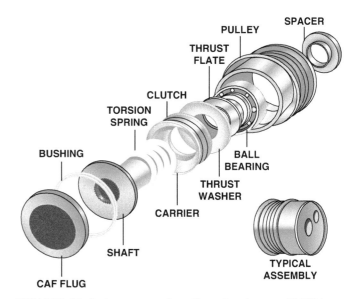

FIGURE 22–5 An overrunning alternator damper (OAD) is not a simple one-way clutch or a solid pulley, but instead is engineered to dampen noises and vibrations in the front accessory drive belt system.

OAP or OAD pulleys are primarily used on vehicles equipped with diesel engines or on luxury vehicles where noise and vibration need to be kept at a minimum. Both are designed to:

- Reduce accessory drive belt noise
- Improve the life of the accessory drive belt
- Improve fuel economy by allowing the engine to be operated at a low idle speed

FIGURE 22–3 An OAP on a Chevrolet Corvette alternator.

ALTERNATOR COMPONENTS AND OPERATION

ROTOR CONSTRUCTION The **rotor** is the rotating part of the alternator and is driven by the accessory drive belt. The rotor creates the magnetic field of the alternator and produces a current by electromagnetic induction in the stationary stator windings. The rotor is constructed of many turns of copper wire coated with a varnish insulation wound over an iron core. The iron core is attached to the rotor shaft.

At both ends of the rotor windings are heavy-gauge metal plates bent over the windings with triangular fingers called **claw poles**. These pole fingers do not touch, but alternate or interlace, as shown in ● **FIGURE 22–6**.

HOW ROTORS CREATE MAGNETIC FIELDS The two ends of the rotor winding are connected to the rotor's slip rings. Current for the rotor flows from the battery into one brush that rides on one of the slip rings, then flows through the rotor winding, then exits the rotor through the other slip ring and brush. One alternator brush is considered to be the "positive" brush and one is considered to be the "negative" or "ground" brush. The voltage regulator is connected to either the positive or the negative brush and controls the field current through the rotor that controls the output of the alternator.

If current flows through the rotor windings, the metal pole pieces at each end of the rotor become electromagnets. Whether a north or a south pole magnet is created depends on the *direction* in which the wire coil is wound. Because the pole pieces are attached to each end of the rotor, one pole piece is a north pole magnet. The other pole piece is on the opposite end of the rotor and, therefore, is viewed as being wound in the opposite direction, creating a south pole. Therefore, the rotor fingers are alternating north and south magnetic poles. The magnetic fields are created between the alternating pole piece fingers. These individual magnetic fields produce a current by electromagnetic induction in the stationary stator windings. ● **SEE FIGURE 22–7**.

ROTOR CURRENT The current necessary for the field (rotor) windings is conducted through slip rings with carbon brushes. The maximum rated alternator output in amperes depends on the number and gauge of the rotor windings. Substituting rotors from one alternator to another can greatly affect maximum output. Many commercially rebuilt alternators are tested and then display a sticker to indicate their tested output. The original rating stamped on the housing is then ground off.

The current for the field is controlled by the voltage regulator and is conducted to the slip rings through carbon brushes. The brushes conduct only the field current, which is usually between 2 and 5 amperes.

STATOR CONSTRUCTION The **stator** consists of the stationary coil windings inside the alternator. The stator is supported between the two halves of the alternator housing,

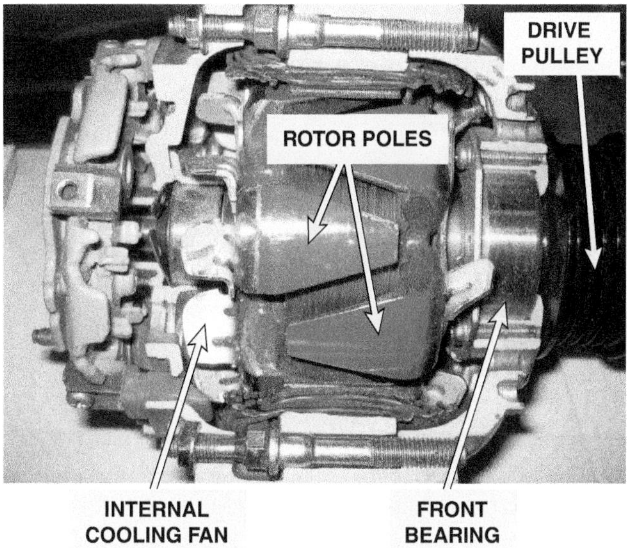

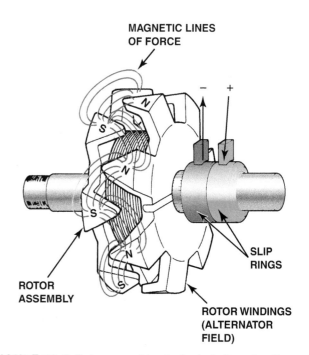

FIGURE 22–7 Rotor assembly of a typical alternator. Current through the slip rings causes the "fingers" of the rotor to become alternating north and south magnetic poles. As the rotor revolves, these magnetic lines of force induce a current in the stator windings.

FIGURE 22–6 A cutaway of an alternator, showing the rotor and cooling fan that is used to force air through the unit to remove the heat created when it is charging the battery and supplying electrical power for the vehicle.

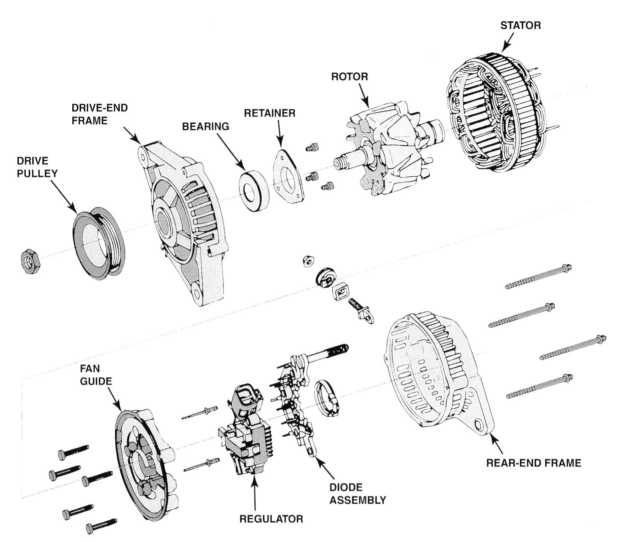

FIGURE 22–8 An exploded view of a typical alternator showing all of its internal parts including the stator windings.

with three copper wire windings that are wound on a laminated metal core.

As the rotor revolves, its moving magnetic field induces a current in the stator windings. ● **SEE FIGURE 22–8**.

DIODES **Diodes** are constructed of a semiconductor material (usually silicon) and operate as a one-way electrical check valve that permits the current to flow in only one direction. Alternators often use six diodes (one positive and one negative set for each of the three stator windings) to convert alternating current to direct current.

Diodes used in alternators are included in a single part called a rectifier, or *rectifier bridge*. A rectifier includes not only the diodes (usually six), but also the cooling fins and connections for the stator windings and the voltage regulator. ● **SEE FIGURE 22–9**.

DIODE TRIO Some alternators are equipped with a diode trio that supplies current to the brushes from the stator

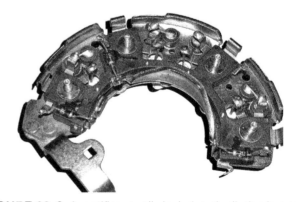

FIGURE 22–9 A rectifier usually includes six diodes in one assembly and is used to rectify AC voltage from the stator windings into DC voltage suitable for use by the battery and electrical devices in the vehicle.

windings. A diode trio uses three diodes in one housing, with one diode for each of the three stator windings and then one output terminal.

HOW AN ALTERNATOR WORKS

FIELD CURRENT IS PRODUCED A rotor inside an alternator is turned by a belt and drive pulley that are turned by the engine. Field current flowing through the slip rings to the rotor creates an alternating north and south pole on the rotor, with a magnetic field between each finger of the rotor. The magnetic field of the rotor generates a current in the stator windings by electromagnetic induction. ● **SEE FIGURE 22–10**.

CURRENT IS INDUCED IN THE STATOR The induced current in the stator windings is an alternating current because of the alternating magnetic field of the rotor. The induced

current starts to increase as the magnetic field starts to induce current in each winding of the stator. The current then peaks when the magnetic field is the strongest and starts to decrease as the magnetic field moves away from the stator winding. Therefore, the current generated is described as being of a sine wave or alternating current pattern. ● **SEE FIGURE 22–11**.

As the rotor continues to rotate, this sine wave current is induced in each of the three windings of the stator.

Because each of the three windings generates a sine wave current, as shown in ● **FIGURE 22–12**, the resulting currents combine to form a three-phase voltage output.

The current induced in the stator windings connects to diodes (one-way electrical check valves) that permit the alternator output current to flow in only one direction, thereby changing AC voltage to DC voltage. All alternators contain six diodes, one pair (a positive and a negative diode) for each of the three stator windings. Some alternators contain eight diodes with another pair connected to the center connection of a wye-type stator.

WYE-CONNECTED STATORS The Y (pronounced "wye" and generally so written) type or star pattern is the most commonly used alternator stator winding connection. ● **SEE FIGURE 22–13**.

The output current with a wye-type stator connection is constant over a broad alternator speed range.

Current is induced in each winding by electromagnetic induction from the rotating magnetic fields of the rotor. In a wye-type stator connection, the currents must combine because two windings are always connected in series. ● **SEE FIGURE 22–14**.

The current produced in each winding is added to the other windings' current and then flows through the diodes to the alternator output terminal. One-half of the current

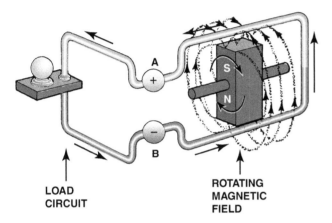

FIGURE 22–10 Magnetic lines of force cutting across a conductor induce a voltage and current in the conductor.

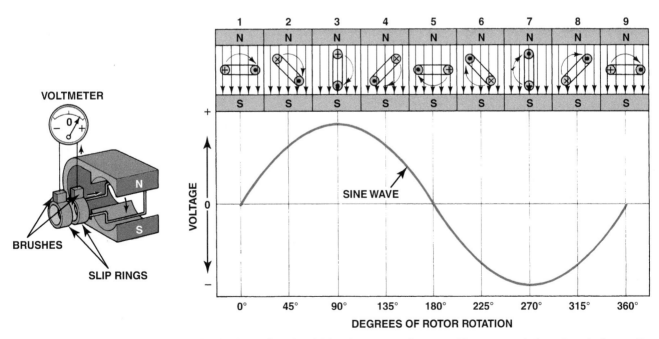

FIGURE 22–11 A sine wave (shaped like the letter *S* on its side) voltage curve is created by one revolution of a winding as it rotates in a magnetic field.

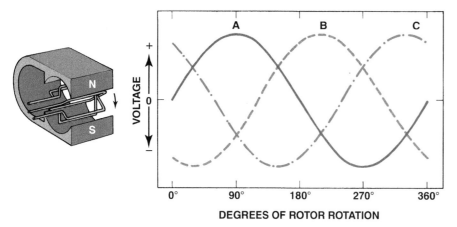

FIGURE 22–12 When three windings (A, B, and C) are present in a stator, the resulting current generation is represented by the three sine waves. The voltages are 120 degrees out of phase. The connection of the individual phases produces a three-phase alternating voltage.

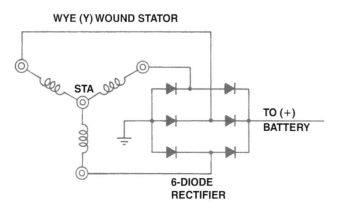

FIGURE 22–13 Wye-connected stator winding.

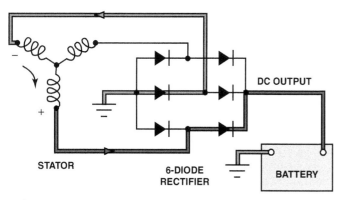

FIGURE 22–14 As the magnetic field, created in the rotor, cuts across the windings of the stator, a current is induced. Notice that the current path includes passing through one positive (+) diode on the way to the battery and one negative (−) diode as a complete circuit is completed through the rectifier and stator. It is the flow of current through the diodes that converts the AC voltage produced in the stator windings to DC voltage available at the output terminal of the alternator.

produced is available at the neutral junction (usually labeled "STA" for stator).

DELTA-CONNECTED STATORS The **delta winding** is connected in a triangular shape. Delta is a Greek letter shaped like a triangle. ● **SEE FIGURE 22–15**.

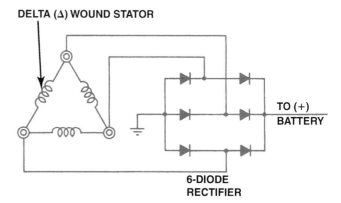

FIGURE 22–15 Delta-connected stator winding.

Current induced in each winding flows to the diodes in a parallel circuit. More current can flow through two parallel circuits than can flow through a series circuit (as in a wye-type stator connection).

Delta-connected stators are used on alternators where high output at high-alternator revolutions per minute (RPM) is required. The delta-connected alternator can produce 73% more current than the same alternator with wye-type stator connections. For example, if an alternator with a wye-connected stator can produce 55 amperes, the *same* alternator with delta-connected stator windings can produce 73% more current, or 95 amperes (55 × 1.73 = 95). The delta-connected alternator, however, produces lower current at low speed and must be operated at high speed to produce its maximum output.

ALTERNATOR OUTPUT FACTORS

The output voltage and current of an alternator depend on the following factors.

1. **Speed of rotation.** Alternator output is increased with alternator rotational speed up to the alternator's maximum possible ampere output. Alternators normally rotate

at a speed two to three times faster than engine speed, depending on the relative pulley sizes used for the belt drive. For example, if an engine is operating at 5,000 RPM, the alternator is rotating at about 15,000 RPM.

2. **Number of conductors.** A high-output alternator contains more turns of wire in the stator windings. Stator winding connections (whether wye or delta) also affect the maximum alternator output. ● **SEE FIGURE 22–16** for an example of a stator that has six, rather than three windings, which greatly increase the amperage output of the alternator.

3. **Strength of the magnetic field.** If the magnetic field is strong, a high output is possible because the current generated by electromagnetic induction is dependent on the number of magnetic lines of force that are cut.

   a. The strength of the magnetic field can be increased by increasing the number of turns of conductor wire wound on the rotor. A higher output alternator rotor has more turns of wire than an alternator rotor with a low-rated output.

   b. The strength of the magnetic field also depends on the current through the field coil (rotor). Because magnetic field strength is measured in ampere-turns, the greater the amperage or the number of turns, or both, the greater the alternator output.

ALTERNATOR VOLTAGE REGULATION

PRINCIPLES An automotive alternator must be able to produce electrical pressure (voltage) higher than battery voltage to charge the battery. Excessively high voltage can damage the battery, electrical components, and the lights of a vehicle. Basic principles include the following:

- If no (zero) amperes of current exists throughout the field coil of the alternator (rotor), alternator output is zero, because without field current, a magnetic field does not exist.

- The field current required by most automotive alternators is less than 3 amperes. It is the *control* of the *field* current that controls the output of the alternator.

- Current for the rotor flows from the battery positive post, through the rotor positive brush, into the rotor field winding, and exits the rotor winding through the rotor ground brush. Most voltage regulators control field current by controlling the amount of field current through the ground brush.

- The voltage regulator simply opens the field circuit if the voltage reaches a predetermined level, then closes the field circuit again, as necessary, to maintain the correct charging voltage. ● **SEE FIGURE 22–17**.

- The electronic circuit of the voltage regulator cycles between 10 and 7,000 times per *second*, as needed, to accurately control the field current through the rotor and, therefore, control the alternator output.

REGULATOR OPERATION

- The control of the field current is accomplished by opening and closing the *ground* side of the field circuit through the rotor on most alternators.

- The zener diode is a major electronic component that makes voltage regulation possible. A zener diode blocks current flow until a specific voltage is reached, then it permits current to flow. Alternator voltage from the stator and diodes is first sent through a thermistor, which changes resistance with temperature, and then to a zener diode. When the upper-limit voltage is reached, the zener diode conducts current to a transistor, which then opens the field (rotor) circuit. The electronics are usually housed in a separate part inside the alternator. ● **SEE FIGURES 22–18 AND 22–19**.

BATTERY CONDITION AND CHARGING VOLTAGE

If the automotive battery is discharged, its voltage is lower than the voltage of a fully charged battery. The alternator supplies charging current, but it may not reach the maximum charging voltage. For example, if a vehicle is jump started and run at

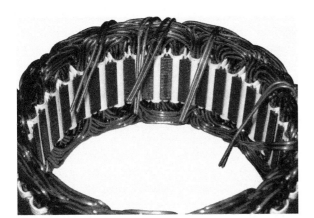

FIGURE 22–16 A stator assembly with six, rather than the normal three, windings.

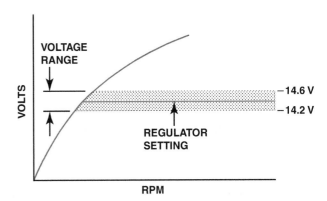

FIGURE 22–17 Typical voltage regulator range.

FIGURE 22–18 A typical electronic voltage regulator with the cover removed showing the circuits inside.

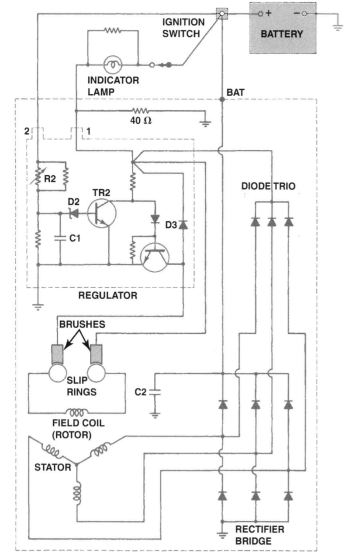

FIGURE 22–19 Typical General Motors SI-style alternator with an integral voltage regulator. Voltage present at terminal 2 is used to reverse bias the zener diode (D2) that controls TR2. The positive brush is fed by the ignition current (terminal 1) plus current from the diode trio.

a fast idle (2,000 RPM), the charging voltage may be only 12 volts. In this case, the following may occur.

- As the battery becomes charged and the battery voltage increases, the charging voltage also increases, until the voltage regulator limit is reached.

- Then, the voltage regulator starts to control the charging voltage. A good, but discharged, battery should be able to convert into chemical energy all the current the alternator can produce. As long as alternator voltage is higher than battery voltage, current flows from the alternator (high voltage) to the battery (lower voltage).

- Therefore, if a voltmeter is connected to a discharged battery with the engine running, it may indicate charging voltage that is lower than normally acceptable.

In other words, the condition and voltage of the battery *do* determine the charging rate of the alternator. It is often stated that the battery is the true "voltage regulator" and that the voltage regulator simply acts as the upper-limit voltage control. This is the reason why all charging system testing *must* be performed with a reliable and known to be good battery, at least 75% charged, to be assured of accurate test results. If a discharged battery is used during charging system testing, tests could mistakenly indicate a defective alternator and/or voltage regulator.

TEMPERATURE COMPENSATION All voltage regulators (mechanical or electronic) provide a method for increasing the charging voltage slightly at low temperatures and for lowering the charging voltage at high temperatures. A battery requires a higher charging voltage at low temperatures because of the resistance to chemical reaction changes. However, the battery is overcharged if the charging voltage is not reduced during warm weather. Electronic voltage regulators use a temperature-sensitive resistor in the regulator circuit. This resistor, called a **thermistor**, provides lower resistance as the temperature increases. A thermistor is used in the electronic circuits of the voltage regulator to control charging voltage over a wide range of underhood temperatures.

NOTE: Voltmeter test results may vary according to temperature. Charging voltage tested at 32°F (0°C) is higher than for the same vehicle tested at 80°F (27°C) because of the temperature-compensation factors built into voltage regulators.

ALTERNATOR COOLING

Alternators create heat during normal operation and this heat must be removed to protect the components inside, especially the diodes and voltage regulator. The types of cooling include the following:

- External fan
- Internal fan(s)

FIGURE 22–20 A coolant-cooled alternator showing the hose connections where coolant from the engine flows through the rear frame of the alternator.

- Both an external fan and an internal fan
- Coolant cooled (● **SEE FIGURE 22–20**.)

COMPUTER-CONTROLLED CHARGING SYSTEMS

ADVANTAGES Computer control of the charging system has the following advantages.

1. The computer controls the field of the alternator, which can pulse it on or off, as needed, for maximum efficiency, thereby saving fuel.

NOTE: Some vehicle manufacturers, such as Honda/ Acura, use an electronic load control (ELC), which turns on the alternator when decelerating, where the additional load on the engine is simply used to help slow the vehicle. This allows the battery to be charged without placing a load on the engine, helping to increase fuel economy.

2. Engine idle can also be improved by turning on the alternator slowly, rather than all at once, if an electrical load is switched on, such as the air-conditioning system.

3. Most computers can also reduce the load on the electrical system if the demand exceeds the capacity of the charging system, by reducing fan speed, shutting off rear window defoggers, or increasing engine speed to cause the alternator to increase the amperage output.

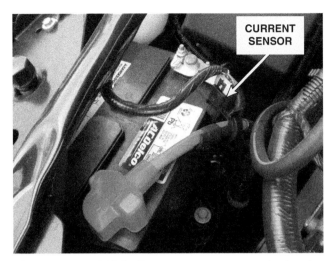

FIGURE 22–21 A Hall-effect current sensor attached to the positive battery cable is used as part of the EPM system.

NOTE: A commanded higher-than-normal idle speed may be the result of the computer compensating for an abnormal electrical load. This higher idle speed could indicate a defective battery or other electrical system faults.

4. The computer can monitor the charging system and set diagnostic trouble codes (DTCs) if a fault is detected. Many systems allow the service technician to control the charging of the alternator using a scan tool.

5. Because the charging system is computer controlled, it can be checked using a scan tool. Some vehicle systems allow the scan tool to activate the alternator field and then monitor the output to help detect fault locations. Always follow the vehicle manufacturer's diagnostic procedure.

TYPES OF SYSTEMS Computers can interface with the charging system in three ways.

1. The computer can *activate* the charging system by turning on and off the field current to the rotor. In other words, the computer, usually the powertrain control module (PCM), controls the field current to the rotor.

2. The computer can *monitor* the operation of the alternator and increase engine speed, if needed, during conditions when a heavy load is demanded by the alternator.

3. The computer can *control* the alternator by controlling alternator output to match the needs of the electrical system. This system detects the electrical needs of the vehicle and commands the alternator to charge only when needed to improve fuel economy.

GM ELECTRICAL POWER MANAGEMENT SYSTEM A typical system used on some General Motors vehicles is called **electrical power management (EPM)**. It uses a Hall-effect sensor attached to the negative or positive battery cable to measure the current leaving and entering the battery. ● **SEE FIGURE 22–21**.

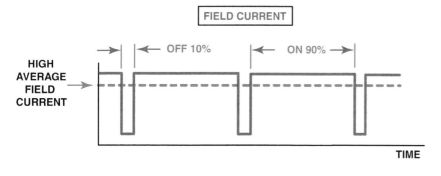

FIGURE 22–22 The amount of time current flowing through the field (rotor) determines the alternator output.

COMMAND DUTY CYCLE	ALTERNATOR OUTPUT VOLTAGE
10%	11.0 V
20%	11.6 V
30%	12.1 V
40%	12.7 V
50%	13.3 V
60%	13.8 V
70%	14.4 V
80%	14.9 V
90%	15.5 V

CHART 22–1

The output voltage is controlled by varying the duty cycle as controlled by the PCM.

The engine control module (ECM) controls the alternator by changing the on-time of the current through the rotor.
● **SEE FIGURE 22–22**.

The on-time, called **duty cycle**, varies from 5% to 95%.
● **SEE CHART 22–1**.

This system has six modes of operation.

1. **Charge mode.** The charge mode is activated when any of the following occurs.
   ▪ Electric cooling fans are on high speed.
   ▪ Rear window defogger is on.
   ▪ Battery state of charge (SOC) is less than 80%.
   ▪ Outside (ambient) temperature is less than 32°F (0°C).

2. **Fuel economy mode.** This mode reduces the load on the engine from the alternator for maximum fuel economy. This mode is activated when the following conditions are met.
   ▪ Ambient temperature is above 32°F (0°C).
   ▪ The SOC of the battery is 80% or higher.
   ▪ The cooling fans and rear defogger are off.
   The target voltage is 13 volts and returns to the charge mode, if needed.

3. **Voltage reduction mode.** This mode is commanded to reduce the stress on the battery during low-load conditions. This mode is activated when the following conditions are met.
   ▪ Ambient temperature is above 32°F (0°C).
   ▪ Battery discharge rate is less than 7 amperes.
   ▪ Rear defogger is off.
   ▪ Cooling fans are on low or off.
   ▪ Target voltage is limited to 12.7 volts.

4. **Start-up mode.** This mode is selected after engine start and commands a charging voltage of 14.5 volts for 30 seconds. After 30 seconds, the mode is changed, depending on conditions.

5. **Battery sulfation mode.** This mode is commanded if the output voltage is less than 13.2 volts for 45 minutes, which can indicate that sulfated plates could be the cause. The target voltage is 13.9 to 15.5 volts for three minutes. After three minutes, the system returns to another mode, based on conditions.

6. **Headlight mode.** This mode is selected when the headlights are on and the target voltage is 14.5 volts.

SUMMARY

1. Alternator output is increased if the speed of the alternator is increased.
2. The parts of a typical alternator include the drive-end (DE) housing, slip-ring-end (SRE) housing, rotor assembly, stator, rectifier bridge, brushes, and voltage regulator.
3. The magnetic field is created in the rotor.
4. The alternator output current is created in the stator windings.
5. The voltage regulator controls the current flow through the rotor winding.

REVIEW QUESTIONS

1. How can a small electronic voltage regulator control the output of a typical 100 ampere alternator?
2. What are the component parts of a typical alternator?
3. How is the computer used to control an alternator?
4. How is AC voltage inside the alternator changed to DC voltage at the output terminal?
5. What is the purpose of an OAP or OAD?

CHAPTER QUIZ

1. Technician A says that the diodes regulate the alternator output voltage. Technician B says that the field current can be computer controlled. Which technician is correct?
   a. Technician A only
   b. Technician B only
   c. Both Technicians A and B
   d. Neither Technician A nor B

2. A magnetic field created in the_____is used to induce a voltage in the _____.
   a. stator; rear housing
   b. diodes; stator
   c. rotor; stator
   d. drive-end frame; OAD

3. How is the AC voltage produced in the alternator changed to DC voltage?
   a. Mechanical switches
   b. Alternating brushes
   c. Slip ring rotation
   d. Diodes inside the alternator

4. Technician A says that two diodes are required for each stator winding lead. Technician B says that diodes change alternating current into direct current. Which technician is correct?
   a. Technician A only
   b. Technician B only
   c. Both Technicians A and B
   d. Neither Technician A nor B

5. The alternator output current is produced in the _____.
   a. stator
   b. rotor
   c. brushes
   d. diodes (rectifier bridge)

6. The output of an alternator can be increased by increasing the _____ of the alternator.
   a. speed of rotation
   b. number of conductors in the starter
   c. current in the rotor
   d. any of these would increase the output

7. How much current flows through the alternator brushes?
   a. All of the alternator output flows through the brushes
   b. 25 to 35 amperes, depending on the vehicle
   c. 10 to 15 amperes
   d. Less than 3 amperes

8. Technician A says that an alternator overrunning pulley is used to reduce vibration and noise. Technician B says that an overrunning alternator pulley or dampener uses a one-way clutch. Which technician is correct?
   a. Technician A only
   b. Technician B only
   c. Both Technicians A and B
   d. Neither Technician A nor B

9. What is/are used to help control the heat created in the alternator?
   a. External fan
   b. Internal fan
   c. Coolant cooled
   d. Any of the above

10. How does the computer interface with the alternator?
    a. The computer can actuate the charging system
    b. The computer can monitor the operation of the alternator
    c. The computer can control the operation of the alternator
    d. Any of the above

chapter 23
CHARGING SYSTEM DIAGNOSIS AND SERVICE

LEARNING OBJECTIVES:

After studying this chapter, the reader should be able to:

Discuss the various methods to test the charging system.

Describe how to inspect and adjust the drive belts.

Discuss the alternator output test and minimum required output.

Explain how to remove, disassemble, reassemble, and install an alternator and test its component parts.

Describe remanufactured alternators.

This chapter will help prepare for the ASE Electrical/ Electronic Systems (A6) certification test content area "D" (Charging System Diagnosis and Repair).

KEY TERMS: AC ripple voltage 283 • Charging voltage test 279 • Cores 291

CHARGING SYSTEM TESTING AND SERVICE

BATTERY STATE OF CHARGE The charging system can be tested as part of a routine vehicle inspection or to determine the reason for a no-charge or reduced charging circuit performance. The battery *must* be at least 75% charged before testing the alternator and the charging system. A weak or defective battery causes inaccurate test results. If in doubt, replace the battery with a known good shop battery for testing.

CHARGING VOLTAGE TEST The **charging voltage test** is the easiest way to check the charging system voltage at the battery. Use a digital multimeter to check the voltage, as follows:

STEP 1 Select DC volts.

STEP 2 Connect the red meter lead to the positive (+) terminal of the battery and the black meter lead to the negative (−) terminal of the battery.

> **NOTE: The polarity of the meter leads is not too important when using a digital multimeter. If the meter leads are connected backward on the battery, the resulting readout simply has a negative (−) sign in front of the voltage reading.**

STEP 3 Start the engine and increase the engine speed to about 2,000 RPM (fast idle) and record the charging voltage.
● **SEE FIGURE 23–1**.

FIGURE 23–1 The digital multimeter should be set to read DC volts, with the red lead connected to the positive (+) battery terminal and the black meter lead connected to the negative (−) battery terminal.

Specifications for charging voltage = 13.5 to 15 volts

- If the voltage is too high, check that the alternator is properly grounded.
- If the voltage is lower than specifications, then there is a fault with the wiring or the alternator.
- If the wiring, fuses, and the connections are okay, then additional testing is required to help pinpoint the root cause. Replacement of the alternator and/or battery is

often required if the charging voltage is not within factory specifications.

■ If the alternator is computer-controlled, a defective current sensor or PCM could be the reason for a no-charge condition.

SCAN TESTING THE CHARGING CIRCUIT

Most vehicles that use a computer-controlled charging system can be diagnosed using a scan tool. Not only can the charging voltage be monitored, but also, in many vehicles, the field circuit can be controlled and the output voltage monitored to check that the system is operating correctly. ● **SEE FIGURE 23–2**.

NOTE: Some charging systems, such as those on many Honda/Acura vehicles, use an electronic load detection circuit that energizes the field circuit only when an electrical load is detected. For example, if the engine is running and there are no accessories on, the voltage read at the battery may be 12.6 volts, which could indicate that the charging system is not operating. In this situation, turning on the headlights or an accessory should cause the computer to activate the field circuit, and the alternator should produce normal charging voltage.

FIGURE 23–2 A scan tool can be used to diagnose charging system problems.

 CASE STUDY

The Case of the Overcharging Chevrolet Truck

The owner of a Chevrolet Silverado 2500 HD, equipped with a 6.6L diesel V8, stated that the ABS, Battery, and many other dash warning lights would come on when accelerating hard. The technician retrieved a C0800 diagnostic trouble code. (The module detects that the system voltage is greater than 16 volts.) The technician measured the voltage at the battery terminal with the engine operating above the idle speed and recorded a reading of a 17.7 volts. Because the voltage output of the alternator is controlled by the voltage regulator and it is built in the alternator, the technician replaced the alternator. The technician checked the charging voltage and it was now within factory specification. The diagnostic trouble code was cleared and the vehicle returned to the customer.

Summary:

■ **Complaint**—Customer asked to check the engine light and stated that several other warning lights would come on when accelerating rapidly.

■ **Cause**—The voltage regulator inside the alternator was not working as designed.

■ **Correction**—The alternator was replaced which corrected the customer concern.

 FREQUENTLY ASKED QUESTION

What Is a Full-Fielding Test?

Full fielding is a procedure used on older noncomputerized vehicles for bypassing the voltage regulator that could be used to determine if the alternator is capable of producing its designed output. This test is no longer performed for the following reasons.

• The voltage regulator is built into the alternator, requiring that the entire assembly be replaced even if just the regulator is defective.

• When the regulator is bypassed, the alternator can produce a high voltage (over 100 volts in some cases), which could damage all of the electronic circuits in the vehicle.

Always follow the vehicle manufacturer's recommended testing procedures.

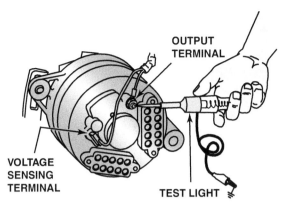

OUTPUT TERMINAL

VOLTAGE SENSING TERMINAL

TEST LIGHT

FIGURE 23–3 Before replacing an alternator, the wise technician checks that battery voltage is present at the output and battery voltage sense terminals. if no voltage is detected, then there is a fault in the wiring.

TECH TIP

Use a Test Light to Check for a Defective Fusible Link

Most alternators use a fusible link or mega fuse between the output terminal and the positive (+) terminal of the battery. If this fusible link or fuse is defective (blown), then the charging system does not operate at all. Many alternators have been replaced repeatedly because of a blown fusible link that was not discovered until later. A quick and easy test to check if the fusible link is okay is to touch a test light to the output terminal. With the other end of the test light attached to a good ground, the fusible link or mega fuse is okay if the light comes on. This test confirms that the circuit between the alternator and the battery has continuity. ● **SEE FIGURE 23–3.**

DRIVE BELT INSPECTION AND ADJUSTMENT

BELT VISUAL INSPECTION It is generally recommended that all belts be inspected regularly and replaced as needed. Replace any serpentine belt that has more than three cracks in any one rib that appears in a 3 inch span. Check service information for the specified procedure and recommended replacement interval. ● **SEE FIGURE 23–4.**

BELT TENSION MEASUREMENT If the vehicle does not use a belt tensioner, then a belt tension gauge is needed to achieve the specified belt tension. Install the belt and operate

(a)

(b)

FIGURE 23–4 (a) This accessory drive belt is worn and requires replacement. Newer belts are made from ethylene propylene diene monomer (EPDM). This rubber does not crack like older belts and may not show wear, even though the ribs do wear and can cause slippage. (b) A belt wear gauge being used to check a belt. It should fit tightly but if it is able to be moved side to side, then the belt is worn and should be replaced.

the engine with all of the accessories turned on to "run-in" the belt for at least five minutes. Adjust the tension of the accessory drive belt to factory specifications or use the following table for an example of the proper tension based on the size of the belt. ● **SEE FIGURE 23–5.**

There are four ways that vehicle manufacturers specify that the belt tension is within factory specifications.

1. **Belt tension gauge.** A belt tension gauge is needed to determine if it is at the specified belt tension. Install the belt and operate the engine with all of the accessories turned on to "run-in" the belt for at least five minutes. Adjust the tension of the accessory drive belt to factory specifications, or see ● **CHART 23–1** for an example of the proper tension based on the size of the belt.

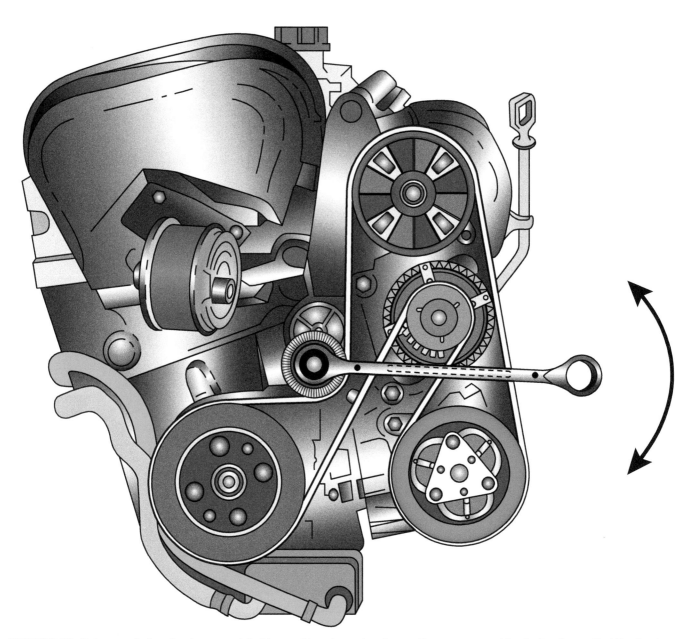

FIGURE 23–5 A wrench, breaker bar, or ratchet is used to release tension on the accessory drive belt, often called the front engine accessory drive (FEAD). Many experts recommend replacing the tensioner at the same time as the accessory drive belt.

2. **Marks on a tensioner.** Many tensioners have marks that indicate the normal operating tension range for the accessory drive belt. Check service information for the preferred location of the tensioner mark. ● **SEE FIGURE 23–6**.

3. **Torque wrench reading.** Some vehicle manufacturers specify that a beam-type torque wrench be used to determine the torque needed to rotate the tensioner. If the torque reading is below specifications, the tensioner must be replaced.

4. **Deflection.** Depress the belt between the two pulleys that are the farthest apart; the flex or deflection should be 1/2 inch (13 mm).

OVERRUNNING CLUTCH If low or no alternator output is found, remove the alternator drive belt and check the

overrunning alternator pulley (OAP) or overrunning alternator dampener (OAD) for proper operation. Both types of overrunning clutches use a one-way clutch. Therefore, the pulley should freewheel in one direction and rotate the alternator rotor when rotated in the opposite direction. ● **SEE FIGURE 23–7**

A special tool, such as Lisle No. 57650 or Gates No. 91024, is needed to repair the alternator. ● **SEE FIGURE 23–8**

AC RIPPLE VOLTAGE CHECK

PRINCIPLES A good alternator should produce very little AC voltage or current output. It is the purpose of the diodes

SERPENTINE BELTS	
NUMBER OF RIBS USED	TENSION RANGE (LB)
3	45–60
4	60–80
5	75–100
6	90–125
7	105–145
V-BELTS	
V-BELT TOP WIDTH (IN.)	TENSION RANGE (LB)
1/4	45–65
5/16	60–85
25/64	85–115
31/64	105–145

CHART 23–1

Typical belt tension for various widths of belts. Tension is the force needed to depress the belt as displayed on a belt tension gauge.

OVERRUNNING ALTERNATOR PULLEY (OAP)

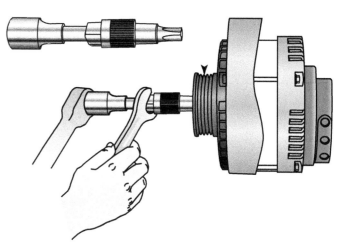

FIGURE 23–8 A special tool is needed to remove and install overrunning alternator pulleys or dampeners.

FIGURE 23–6 Check service information for the exact marks where the tensioner should be located for proper belt tension.

FIGURE 23–7 This overrunning alternator dampener (OAD) is longer than an overrunning alternator pulley (OAP) because it contains a dampener spring, as well as a one-way clutch. Be sure to check that it locks in one direction.

in the alternator to rectify or convert most AC voltage into DC voltage. While it is normal to measure some AC voltage from an alternator, excessive AC voltage, called AC ripple, is undesirable and indicates a fault with the rectifier diodes or stator windings inside the alternator.

TESTING AC RIPPLE VOLTAGE The procedure to check for **AC ripple voltage** includes the following steps.

STEP 1 Set the digital meter to read AC volts.

STEP 2 Start the engine and operate it at 2,000 RPM (fast idle).

STEP 3 Connect the voltmeter leads to the positive and negative battery terminals.

STEP 4 Turn on the headlights to provide an electrical load on the alternator.

NOTE: A more accurate reading can be obtained by touching the meter lead to the output or "battery" terminal of the alternator. ● SEE FIGURE 23–9.

TECH TIP

The Lighter Plug Trick

Battery voltage measurements can be read through the lighter socket. Simply construct a test tool using a lighter plug at one end of a length of two-conductor wire and the other end connected to a double banana plug. The double banana plug fits most meters in the common (COM) terminal and the volt terminal of the meter. This is handy to use while road testing the vehicle under real-life conditions. Both DC voltage and AC ripple voltage can be measured. ● **SEE FIGURE 23–10.**

MEASURING THE AC RIPPLE FROM THE ALTERNATOR TELLS A LOT ABOUT ITS CONDITION. IF THE AC RIPPLE IS ABOVE 500 MILLIVOLTS, OR 0.5 VOLT, LOOK FOR A PROBLEM IN THE DIODES OR STATOR. IF THE RIPPLE IS BELOW 500 MILLIVOLTS, CHECK THE ALTERNATOR OUTPUT TO DETERMINE ITS CONDITION.

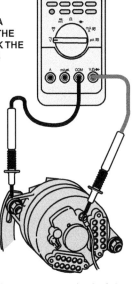

FIGURE 23–9 Testing AC ripple at the output terminal of the alternator is more accurate than testing at the battery due to the resistance of the wiring between the alternator and the battery. The reading shown on the meter, set to AC volts, is only 78 millivolts (0.078 volt), far below what the reading is if a diode is defective.

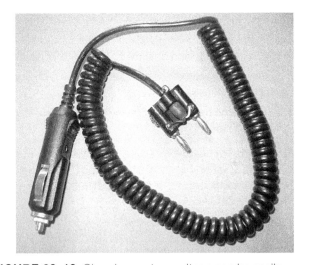

FIGURE 23–10 Charging system voltage can be easily checked at the lighter plug by connecting a lighter plug to the voltmeter through a double banana plug.

The results should be interpreted as follows: If the rectifier diodes are good, the voltmeter should read *less* than 400 millivolts (0.4 volt) AC. If the reading is over 500 millivolts (0.5 volt) AC, the rectifier diodes are defective.

NOTE: Many conductance testers, such as Midtronic and Snap-On, automatically test for AC ripple.

TESTING AC RIPPLE CURRENT

All alternators should create direct current (DC) if the diodes and stator windings are functioning correctly. A mini clamp-on meter capable of measuring AC amperes can be used to check the alternator. A good alternator should produce less than 10% of its rated amperage output in AC ripple amperes. For example, an alternator rated at 100 amperes should not produce more than 10 amperes AC ripple (100 × 10% = 10). It is normal for a good alternator to produce 3 or 4 amperes of AC ripple current to the battery. Only if the AC ripple current exceeds 10% of the rating of the alternator should the alternator be repaired or replaced.

TEST PROCEDURE To measure the AC current to the battery, perform the following steps.

STEP 1 Start the engine and turn on the lights to create an electrical load on the alternator.

STEP 2 Using a mini clamp-on digital multimeter, place the clamp around either all of the positive (+) battery cables or all of the negative (–) battery cables.

An AC/DC current clamp adapter can also be used with a conventional digital multimeter set on the DC millivolts scale.

STEP 3 To check for AC current ripple, switch the meter to read AC amperes and record the reading. Read the meter display.

STEP 4 The results should be within 10% of the specified alternator rating. A reading of greater than 10 amperes AC indicates defective alternator diodes. ● **SEE FIGURE 23–11.**

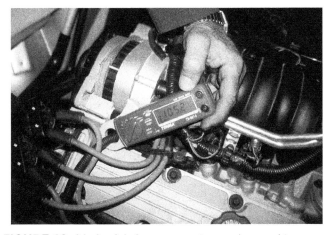

FIGURE 23–11 A mini clamp-on meter can be used to measure alternator output, as shown here (105.2 amperes). Then the meter can be used to check AC ripple by selecting AC amps on the rotary dial. AC ripple should be less than 10% of the DC output.

CHARGING SYSTEM VOLTAGE DROP TESTING

ALTERNATOR WIRING For the proper operation of any charging system, there must be good electrical connections between the battery positive terminal and the alternator output terminal. The alternator must also be properly grounded to the engine block.

Many manufacturers of vehicles run the lead from the output terminal of the alternator to other connectors or junction blocks that are electrically connected to the positive terminal of the battery. If there is high resistance (a high voltage drop) in these connections or in the wiring itself, the battery is not properly charged.

VOLTAGE DROP TEST PROCEDURE When there is a suspected charging system problem (with or without a charge indicator light on), simply follow these steps to measure the voltage drop of the insulated (power-side) charging circuit.

STEP 1 Start the engine and run it at a fast idle (about 2,000 engine RPM).

STEP 2 Turn on the headlights to ensure an electrical load on the charging system.

STEP 3 Using any voltmeter set to read DC volts, connect the positive test lead (red) to the output terminal of the alternator. Attach the negative test lead (black) to the positive post of the battery.

The results should be interpreted as follows:

1. If there is less than a 0.4 volt (400 millivolts) reading, then all wiring and connections are satisfactory.

2. If the voltmeter reads higher than 0.4 volt, there is excessive resistance (voltage drop) between the alternator output terminal and the positive terminal of the battery.

3. If the voltmeter reads battery voltage (or close to battery voltage), there is an open circuit between the battery and the alternator output terminal.

To determine whether the alternator is correctly grounded, maintain the engine speed at 2,000 RPM with the headlights on. Connect the positive voltmeter lead to the case of the alternator and the negative voltmeter lead to the negative terminal of the battery. The voltmeter should read less than 0.2 volt (200 millivolts) if the alternator is properly grounded. If the reading is over 0.2 volt, connect one end of an auxiliary ground wire to the case of the alternator and the other end to a good engine ground. ● **SEE FIGURE 23–12**.

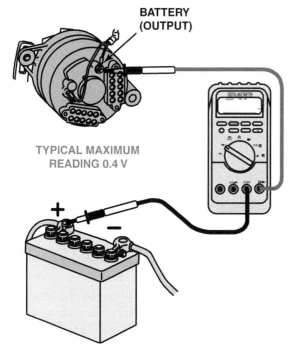

BATTERY (OUTPUT)

TYPICAL MAXIMUM READING 0.4 V

VOLTAGE DROP—INSULATED CHARGING CIRCUIT

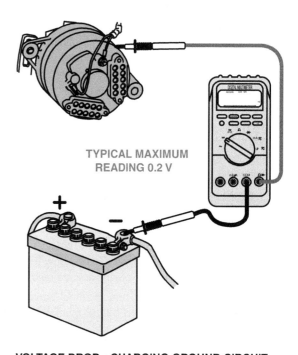

ENGINE AT 2,000 RPM. CHARGING SYSTEM LOADED TO 20 A

TYPICAL MAXIMUM READING 0.2 V

VOLTAGE DROP—CHARGING GROUND CIRCUIT

FIGURE 23–12 Voltmeter hookup to test the voltage drop of the charging circuit.

Use a Fused Jumper Wire as a Diagnostic Tool

When diagnosing an alternator charging problem, try using a fused jumper wire to connect the positive and negative terminals of the alternator directly to the positive and negative terminals of the battery. If a definite improvement is noticed, the problem is in the wiring of the vehicle. High resistance, due to corroded connections or loose grounds, can cause low alternator output, repeated regulator failures, slow cranking, and discharged batteries. A voltage drop test of the charging system can also be used to locate excessive resistance (high voltage drop) in the charging circuit, but using a fused jumper wire is often faster and easier.

FIGURE 23–13 A typical tester used to test batteries as well as the cranking and charging system. Always follow the operating instructions.

ALTERNATOR OUTPUT TEST

PRELIMINARY CHECKS An alternator output test measures the current (amperes) of the alternator. A charging circuit may be able to produce correct charging circuit voltage, but not be able to produce adequate amperage output. If in doubt about charging system output, first check the condition of the alternator drive belt. With the engine off, attempt to rotate the fan of the alternator by hand. Replace or tighten the drive belt if the alternator fan can be rotated this way.

CARBON PILE TEST PROCEDURE A carbon pile tester uses plates of carbon to create an electrical load. A carbon pile test is used to load test a battery and/or an alternator. ● **SEE FIGURE 23–13**.

The testing procedure for alternator output is as follows:

STEP 1 Connect the starting and charging test leads according to the manufacturer's instructions, which usually include installing the amp clamp around the output wire near the alternator.

STEP 2 Turn off all electrical accessories to be sure that the tester is measuring the true output of the alternator.

STEP 3 Start the engine and operate it at 2,000 RPM (fast idle). Turn the load increase control slowly to obtain the highest reading on the ammeter scale. Do not allow the voltage to drop below 12.6 volts. Note the ampere reading.

STEP 4 Add 5 to 7 amperes to the reading because this amount of current is used by the ignition system to operate the engine.

STEP 5 Compare the output reading to factory specifications. The rated output may be stamped on the alternator or can be found in service information.

CAUTION: *NEVER* **disconnect a battery cable with the engine running. All vehicle manufacturers warn not to do this, because this was an old test, before alternators, to see if a generator could supply current to operate the ignition system without a battery. When a battery cable is removed, the alternator (or PCM) loses the battery voltage sense signal. Without a battery voltage sense circuit, the alternator does one of two things, depending on the make and model of vehicle.**

- **The alternator output can exceed 100 volts. This high voltage may damage not only the alternator, but also electrical components in the vehicle, including the PCM and all electronic devices.**
- **The alternator stops charging as a fail-safe measure to protect the alternator and all of the electronics in the vehicle from being damaged due to excessively high voltage.**

MINIMUM REQUIRED ALTERNATOR OUTPUT

PURPOSE All charging systems must be able to supply the electrical demands of the electrical system. If lights and accessories are used constantly and the alternator cannot supply the necessary ampere output, the battery is drained. To determine the minimum electrical load requirements, connect an inductive ammeter probe around either battery cable or the alternator output cable. ● **SEE FIGURE 23–14.**

NOTE: If using an inductive pickup ammeter, be certain that the pickup is over *all* the wires leaving the battery terminal.

Bigger Is Not Always Better

Many technicians are asked to install a higher output alternator to allow the use of emergency equipment or other high-amperage equipment, such as a high-wattage sound system.

Although many higher output units can be physically installed, it is important not to forget to upgrade the wiring and the fusible link(s) in the alternator circuit. Failure to upgrade the wiring could lead to overheating. The usual failure locations are at junctions or electrical connectors.

Failure to include the small body ground wire from the negative battery terminal to the body or the small positive wire (if testing from the positive side) *greatly decreases* **the current flow readings.**

PROCEDURE After connecting an ammeter correctly in the battery circuit, continue as follows:

1. Start the engine and operate to about 2,000 RPM (fast idle).
2. Turn the heat selector to air-conditioning (if the vehicle is so equipped).
3. Turn the blower motor to high speed.
4. Turn the headlights on bright.
5. Turn on the rear defogger.
6. Turn on the windshield wipers.
7. Turn on any other accessories that may be used continuously (do not operate the horn, power door locks, or other units that are not used for more than a few seconds).

FIGURE 23–14 The best place to install a charging system tester amp probe is around the alternator output terminal wire, as shown in the figure.

8. Observe the ammeter. The current indicated is the electrical load that the alternator is able to exceed to keep the battery fully charged.

TEST RESULTS The minimum acceptable alternator output is 5 amperes greater than the accessory load. A negative (discharge) reading indicates that the alternator is not capable of supplying the current (amperes) that may be needed.

ALTERNATOR REMOVAL

After diagnosis of the charging system has determined that there is a fault with the alternator, it must be removed safely from the vehicle. Always check service information for the exact procedure to follow on the vehicle being serviced. A typical removal procedure includes the following steps.

STEP 1 Before disconnecting the negative battery cable, use a test light or a voltmeter and check for battery voltage at the output terminal of the alternator. A complete circuit must exist between the alternator and the battery. If there is no voltage at the alternator output terminal, check for a blown fusible link or other electrical circuit fault.

STEP 2 Disconnect the negative (−) terminal from the battery. (Use a memory saver to maintain radio, memory seats, and other functions.)

STEP 3 Remove the accessory drive belt that drives the alternator.

STEP 4 Remove electrical wiring, fasteners, spacers, and brackets, as necessary, and remove the alternator from the vehicle. ● **SEE FIGURE 23–15**.

FIGURE 23–15 Replacing an alternator is not always as easy as it is from a Buick with a 3800 V-6, where the alternator is easy to access. Many alternators are difficult to access and require the removal of other components.

The Sniff Test

When checking for the root cause of an alternator failure, one test that a technician could do is to sniff (smell) the alternator. If the alternator smells like a dead rat (rancid smell), the stator windings have been overheated by trying to charge a discharged or defective battery. If the battery voltage is continuously low, the voltage regulator continues supplying full-field current to the alternator. The voltage regulator is designed to cycle on and off to maintain a narrow charging system voltage range.

If the battery voltage is continually below the cutoff point of the voltage regulator, the alternator is continually producing current in the stator windings. This constant charging can often overheat the stator and burn the insulating varnish covering the stator windings. If the alternator fails the sniff test, the technician should replace the stator and other alternator components that are found to be defective *and* replace or recharge and test the battery.

What Is a "Clock Position"?

Most alternators of a particular manufacturer can be used on a variety of vehicles, which may require wiring connections placed in various locations. For example, a Chevrolet and a Buick alternator may be identical except for the position of the rear section containing the electrical connections. The four through bolts that hold the two halves together are equally spaced; therefore, the rear alternator housing *can* be installed in any one of four positions to match the wiring needs of various models. Always check the clock position of the original and be sure that it matches the replacement unit. ● **SEE FIGURE 23–16.**

ALTERNATOR DISASSEMBLY

DISASSEMBLY PROCEDURE

STEP 1 Mark the case with a scratch or with chalk to ensure proper reassembly of the alternator case.

STEP 2 After the through bolts have been removed, carefully separate the two halves. The stator windings must stay

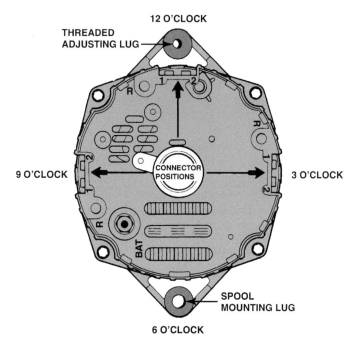

FIGURE 23–16 Explanation of clock positions. Because the four through bolts are equally spaced, it is possible for an alternator to be installed in one of four different clock positions. The connector position is determined by viewing the alternator from the diode end with the threaded adjusting lug in the up or 12 o'clock position. Select the 3 o'clock, 6 o'clock, 9 o'clock, or 12 o'clock position to match the unit being replaced.

with the rear case. When this happens, the brushes and springs fall out.

STEP 3 Remove the rectifier assembly and voltage regulator.

ROTOR TESTING The slip rings on the rotor should be smooth and round (within 0.002 inch of being perfectly round).

- ■ If grooved, the slip rings can be machined to provide a suitable surface for the brushes. Do not machine beyond the minimum slip-ring dimension as specified by the manufacturer.

- ■ If the slip rings are discolored or dirty, they can be cleaned with 400-grit or fine emery (polishing) cloth. The rotor must be turned while being cleaned to prevent flat spots on the slip rings.

- ■ Measure the resistance between the slip rings using an ohmmeter. Typical resistance values and results include the following:

  1. The resistance measured between either slip ring and the steel rotor shaft should be infinity (OL). If there is continuity, then the rotor is shorted-to-ground.

  2. Rotor resistance range is normally between 2.4 and 6 ohms.

  3. If the resistance is below specification, the rotor is shorted.

TESTING AN ALTERNATOR ROTOR USING AN OHMMETER

**CHECKING FOR GROUNDS
(SHOULD READ INFINITY IF
ROTOR IS NOT GROUNDED)**

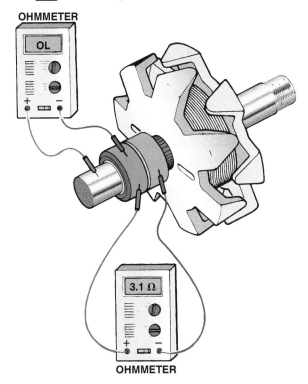

FIGURE 23–17 Testing an alternator rotor using an ohmmeter.

4. If the resistance is above specification, the rotor connections are corroded or open.

If the rotor is found to be bad, it must be replaced or repaired at a specialized shop. ● **SEE FIGURE 23–17**.

NOTE: The cost of a replacement rotor may exceed the cost of an entire rebuilt alternator. Be certain, however, that the rebuilt alternator is rated at the same output as the original or higher.

STATOR TESTING The stator must be disconnected from the diodes (rectifiers) before testing. Because all three windings of the stator are electrically connected (either wye or delta), an ohmmeter can be used to check a stator.

- There should be low resistance at all three stator leads (continuity).

- There should *not* be continuity (in other words, there should be a meter reading of infinity ohms) when the stator is tested between any stator lead and the metal stator core.

- If there is continuity, the stator is shorted-to-ground and must be repaired or replaced. ● **SEE FIGURE 23–18**.

NOTE: Because the resistance is very low for a normal stator, it is generally *not* possible to test for a *shorted* (copper-to-copper) stator. A shorted stator does,

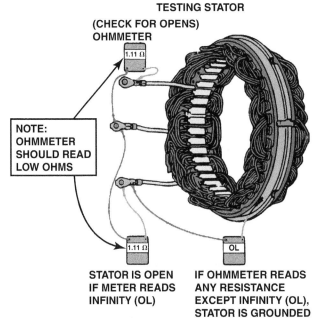

FIGURE 23–18 If the ohmmeter reads infinity between any two of the three stator windings, the stator is open and, therefore, defective. The ohmmeter should read infinity between any stator lead and the steel laminations. If the reading is less than infinity, the stator is grounded. Stator windings cannot be tested if shorted because the normal resistance is very low.

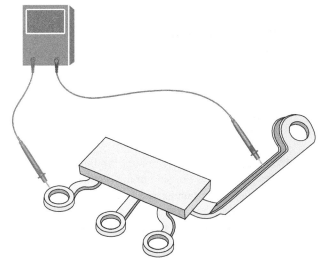

FIGURE 23–19 A diode trio can be tested using an analog (needle-type) ohmmeter or a digital meter set to "diode check."

however, greatly reduce alternator output. An ohmmeter cannot detect an open stator if the stator is delta wound. The ohmmeter still indicates low resistance because all three windings are electrically connected.

TESTING THE DIODE TRIO Many alternators are equipped with a diode trio. A diode is an electrical one-way check valve that permits current to flow in only one direction. Because *trio* means "three," a diode trio is three diodes connected together. ● **SEE FIGURE 23–19**.

The diode trio is connected to all three stator windings. The current generated in the stator flows through the diode trio to the internal voltage regulator. The diode trio is designed to supply current for the field (rotor) and turns off the charge indicator light when the alternator voltage equals or exceeds the battery voltage. If one of the three diodes in the diode trio is defective (usually open), the alternator may produce close-to-normal output; however, the charge indicator light is "on" dimly.

A diode trio should be tested with a digital multimeter. The meter should be set to the diode-check position. The multimeter should indicate 0.5 to 0.7 volt (500 to 700 millivolts) one way and OL (overlimit) after reversing the test leads and touching all three connectors of the diode trio.

TESTING THE RECTIFIER

TERMINOLOGY The rectifier assembly usually is equipped with six diodes, including three positive diodes and three negative diodes (one positive and one negative for each winding of the stator).

METER SETUP The rectifier(s) (diodes) should be tested using a multimeter that is set to "diode check" position on the digital multimeter (DMM).

Because a diode (rectifier) should allow current to flow in only one direction, each diode should be tested to determine if the diode allows current flow in one direction and blocks current flow in the opposite direction. To test some alternator diodes, it may be necessary to unsolder the stator connections. ● SEE FIGURE 23–20.

Accurate testing is not possible unless the diodes are separated electrically from other alternator components.

TESTING PROCEDURE Connect the leads to the leads of the diode (pigtail and housing of the rectifier bridge). Read the meter. Reverse the test leads. A good diode should have high resistance (OL) one way (reverse bias) and low voltage drop of 0.5 to 0.7 volt (500 to 700 millivolts) the other way (forward bias).

FIGURE 22–20 A typical rectifier bridge that contains all six diodes in one replaceable assembly.

RESULTS Open or shorted diodes must be replaced. Most alternators group or combine all positive and all negative diodes in one replaceable rectifier component.

REASSEMBLING THE ALTERNATOR

BRUSH HOLDER REPLACEMENT Alternator carbon brushes often last for many years and require no scheduled maintenance. The life of the alternator brushes is extended because they conduct only the field (rotor) current, which is normally only 2 to 5 amperes. The alternator brushes should be inspected when the alternator is disassembled and should be replaced when worn to less than 1/2 inch long. Brushes are commonly purchased and assembled together in a brush holder. After the brushes are installed (usually retained by two or three screws) and the rotor is installed in the alternator housing, a brush retainer pin can be pulled out through an access hole in the rear of the alternator, allowing the brushes to be pressed against the slip rings by the brush springs. ● SEE FIGURE 23–21.

BEARING SERVICE AND REPLACEMENT The bearings of an alternator must be able to support the rotor and reduce friction. An alternator must be able to rotate at up to 15,000 RPM and withstand the forces created by the drive belt. The front bearing is usually a ball bearing type and the rear can be either a smaller roller or ball bearing.

The old or defective bearing can sometimes be pushed out of the front housing and the replacement pushed in by applying pressure with a socket or pipe against the outer edge of the bearing (outer race). Replacement bearings are usually

BRUSH RETAINER PIN HOLE

FIGURE 23–21 A brush holder assembly with new brushes installed. The holes in the brushes are used to hold the brushes up in the holder when it is installed in the alternator. After the rotor has been installed, the retaining pin is removed, which allows the brushes to contact the slip rings of the rotor.

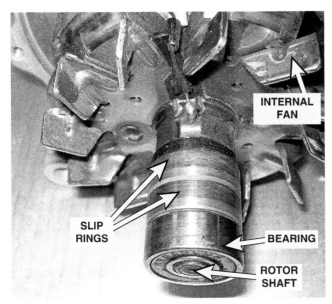

SLIP RINGS
INTERNAL FAN
BEARING
ROTOR SHAFT

FIGURE 23–22 An example of a rotor assembly that, if tested to be within specification, is suitable to be reinstalled after the slip rings have been cleaned.

 FREQUENTLY ASKED QUESTION

What is Considered to be Normal Rotor Slip Ring Wear?

Many alternators can be restored to useful service by replacing the only wear item that they have, which are the brushes. The brushes ride on the surface of the slip rings of the rotor and these need to be round with a surface that is free from grooves that would reduce the contact surface area where the brushes ride. Slight wear or discoloration is usually normal and can be cleaned using fine sandpaper. The slip rings also need to be perfectly round. ● **SEE FIGURE 23–22**.

prelubricated and seated. Many alternator front bearings must be removed from the rotor using a special puller.

ALTERNATOR ASSEMBLY After testing or servicing, the alternator rectifier(s), regulator, stator, and brush holder must be reassembled using the following steps.

STEP 1 If the brushes are internally mounted, insert a wire through the holes in the brush holder to hold the brushes against the springs.

STEP 2 Install the rotor and front-end frame in proper alignment with the mark made on the outside of the alternator housing. Install the through bolts. Before removing the wire pin holding the brushes, spin the alternator pulley. If the alternator is noisy or not rotating freely, the alternator can easily be disassembled again to check for the

cause. After making certain the alternator is free to rotate, remove the brush holder pin and spin the alternator again by hand. The noise level may be slightly higher with the brushes released onto the slip rings.

STEP 3 Alternators should be tested on a bench tester, if available, before they are reinstalled on a vehicle. When installing the alternator on the vehicle, be certain that all mounting bolts and nuts are tight. The battery terminal should be covered with a plastic or rubber protective cap to help prevent accidental shorting to ground, which could seriously damage the alternator.

REMANUFACTURED ALTERNATORS

Remanufactured or rebuilt alternators are totally disassembled and rebuilt. Even though there are many smaller rebuilders who may not replace all worn parts, the major national remanufacturers *totally* remanufacture the alternator. Old alternators (called **cores**) are totally disassembled and cleaned. Both bearings are replaced and all components are tested. Rotors are rewound to original specifications, if required. The rotor windings are not counted but are rewound on the rotor "spool," using the correct-gauge copper wire, to the *weight* specified by the original manufacturer. New slip rings are replaced as required, soldered to the rotor spool windings, and machined. The rotors are also balanced and measured to ensure that the outside diameter of the rotor meets specifications. An undersized rotor produces less alternator output because the field must be close to the stator windings for maximum output. Bridge rectifiers are replaced, if required. Every alternator is then assembled and tested for proper output, boxed, and shipped to a warehouse. Individual parts stores (called jobbers) purchase parts from various regional or local warehouses.

ALTERNATOR INSTALLATION

Before installing a replacement alternator, check service information for the exact procedure to follow for the vehicle being serviced. A typical installation procedure includes the following steps.

STEP 1 Verify that the replacement alternator is the correct unit for the vehicle.

STEP 2 Install the alternator wiring on the alternator and install the alternator.

The Two-Minute Alternator Repair

A Chevrolet pickup truck was brought to a shop for routine service. The customer stated that the battery required a jump start after a weekend of sitting. The technician tested the battery and the charging system voltage using a small handheld digital multimeter. The battery voltage was 12.4 volts (about 75% charged), but the charging voltage was also 12.4 volts at 2,000 RPM. Because normal charging voltage should be 13.5 to 15 volts, it was obvious that the charging system was not operating correctly.

The technician checked the dash and found that the "charge" light was *not* on. Before removing the alternator for service, the technician checked the wiring connection on the alternator. When the connector was removed, it was discovered to be rusty. After the contacts were cleaned, the charging system was restored to normal operation. The technician had learned that the simple things should always be checked first before tearing into a big or expensive repair.

Summary:

- **Complaint**—Customer stated that the truck battery had to be jump-started after sitting for a weekend.

- **Cause**—Tests confirmed that the alternator was not charging and a rusty connection at the alternator was found during a visual inspection.

- **Correction**—Cleaning the electrical terminals at the alternator restored proper operation of the charging system.

STEP 3 Check the condition of the drive belt and replace, if necessary. Install the drive belt over the drive pulley.

STEP 4 Properly tension the drive belt.

STEP 5 Tighten all fasteners to factory specifications.

STEP 6 Double-check that all fasteners are correctly tightened and remove all tools from the engine compartment area.

STEP 7 Reconnect the negative battery cable.

STEP 8 Start the engine and verify proper charging circuit operation.

1 Before the alternator is disassembled, it is spin tested and connected to a scope to check for possible defective components.

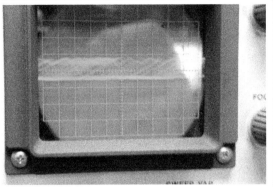

2 The scope pattern shows that the voltage output is far from being a normal pattern. This pattern indicates serious faults in the rectifier diodes.

3 The first step is to remove the drive pulley. This rebuilder is using an electric impact wrench to accomplish the task.

4 Carefully inspect the drive galley for damage of embedded rubber from the drive belt. The slightest fault can cause a vibration, noise, or possible damage to the alternator.

5 Remove the external fan (if equipped) and then the spacers, as shown.

6 Next pop off the plastic cover (shield) covering the stator/rectifier connection.

CONTINUED ▶

7 After the cover has been removed, the stator connections to the rectifier can be seen.

8 Using a diagonal cutter, cut the weld to separate the stator from the rectifier.

9 Before separating the halves of the case, this technician uses a punch to mark both halves.

10 After the case has been marked, the through bolts are removed.

11 The drive-end (DE) housing and the stator are being separated from the rear (slip-ring-end) housing.

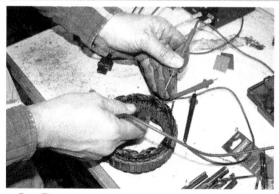

12 The stator is checked by visual inspection for discoloration or other physical damage, and then checked with an ohmmeter to see if the windings are shorted-to-ground.

13 The front bearing is removed from the drive-end housing using a press.

14 A view of the slip-ring-end (SRE) housing showing the black plastic shield, which helps direct air flow across the rectifier.

15 A punch is used to dislodge the plastic shield retaining clips.

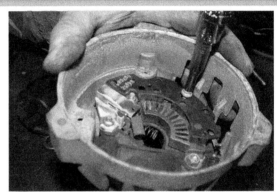

16 After the shield has been removed, the rectifier, regulator, and brush holder assembly can be removed by removing the retaining screws.

17 The heat transfer grease is visible when the rectifier assembly is lifted out of the rear housing.

18 The parts are placed into a tumbler where ceramic stones and a water-based solvent are used to clean the parts.

CONTINUED ▶

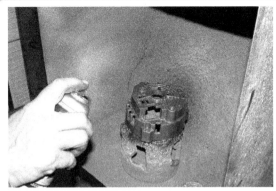

19 This rebuilder is painting the housing using a high-quality industrial grade spray paint to make the rebuilt alternator look like new.

20 The slip rings on the rotor are being machined on a lathe.

21 The rotor is being tested using an ohmmeter. The specifications for the resistance between the slip rings on the CS-130 are 2.2 to 3.5 ohms.

22 The rotor is also tested between the slip ring and the rotor shaft. This reading should be infinity.

23 A new rectifier. This replacement unit is significantly different than the original but is designed to replace the original unit and meets the original factory specifications.

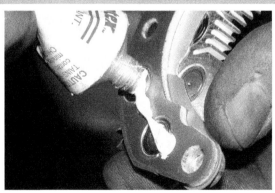

24 Silicone heat transfer compound is applied to the heat sink of the new rectifier.

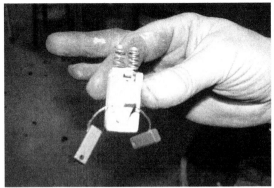

25 Replacement brushes and springs are assembled into the brush holder.

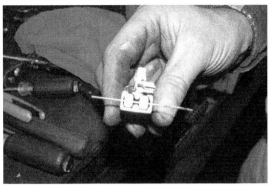

26 The brushes are pushed into the brush holder and retained by a straight wire, which extends through the rear housing of the alternator. This wire is then pulled out when the unit is assembled.

27 Here is what the CS alternator looks like after installing the new brush holder assembly, rectifier bridge, and voltage regulator.

28 The junction between the rectifier bridge and the voltage regulator is soldered.

29 The plastic deflector shield is snapped back into location using a blunt chisel and a hammer. This shield directs the airflow from the fan over the rectifier bridge and voltage regulator.

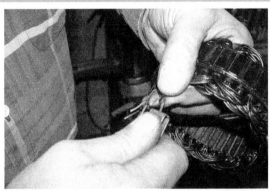

30 Before the stator windings can be soldered to the rectifier bridge, the varnish insulation is removed from the ends of the leads.

CONTINUED ▶

31 After the stator has been inserted into the rear housing, the stator leads are soldered to the copper lugs of the rectifier bridge.

32 New bearings are installed. A spacer is placed between the bearing and the slip rings to help prevent the possibility that the bearing could move on the shaft and short against the slip ring.

33 The slip-ring-end housing is aligned with the marks made during disassembly and is pressed into the drive-end housing.

34 The retaining bolts, which are threaded into the drive-end housing from the back of the alternator, are installed.

35 The external fan and drive pulley are installed and the retaining nut is tightened on the rotor shaft.

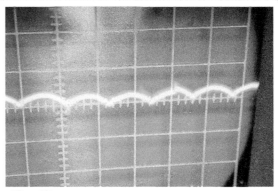

36 The scope pattern shows that the diodes and stator are functioning correctly and voltage check indicates that the voltage regulator is also functioning correctly.

1. Charging system testing requires that the battery be at least 75% charged to be assured of accurate test results. Normal charging voltage (at 2,000 engine RPM) is 13.5 to 15 volts.

2. To check for excessive resistance in the wiring between the alternator and the battery, a voltage drop test should be performed.

3. Alternators do not produce their maximum rated output unless required by circuit demands. Therefore, to test for maximum alternator output, the battery must be loaded to force the alternator to produce its maximum output.

4. Each alternator should be marked across its case before disassembly to ensure proper clock position during reassembly. After disassembly, all alternator internal components should be tested using an ohmmeter. The following components should be tested.
   a. Stator
   b. Rotor
   c. Diodes
   d. Diode trio (if the alternator is so equipped)
   e. Bearings
   f. Brushes (should be more than 1/2 inch long)

REVIEW QUESTIONS

1. How does a technician test the voltage drop of the charging circuit?

2. How does a technician measure the amperage output of an alternator?

3. What tests can be performed to determine whether a diode or stator is defective before removing the alternator from the vehicle?

4. Why could a defective overrunning alternator pulley (OAP) or dampener (OAD) cause a lack of proper charging?

5. What is procedure for replacing an alternator?

CHAPTER QUIZ

1. To check the charging voltage, connect a digital multimeter (DMM) to the positive (+) and the negative (−) terminals of the battery and select _____.
   a. DC volts
   b. AC volts
   c. DC amps
   d. AC amps

2. To check for ripple voltage from the alternator, connect a digital multimeter (DMM) and select _____.
   a. DC volts
   b. AC volts
   c. DC amps
   d. AC amps

3. Which of the following would NOT be used to check drive belt wear?
   a. Groove color change
   b. A tension gauge
   c. A belt wear gauge
   d. Belt deflection between two pulleys

4. When performing an alternator output test, which tool should the technician choose?
   a. An electronic torque wrench
   b. An ohmmeter
   c. A load tester
   d. A vacuum gauge

5. An acceptable charging circuit voltage on a 12 volt system is _____.
   a. 13.5 to 15 volts
   b. 12.6 to 15.6 volts
   c. 12 to 14 volts
   d. 14.9 to 16.1 volts

6. The diodes are usually replaced_____
   a. individually only if open
   b. individually only if shorted
   c. as a replaceable rectifier component
   d. as part of the stator assembly

7. Technician A says that a voltage drop test of the charging circuit should only be performed when current is flowing through the circuit. Technician B says to connect the leads of a voltmeter to the positive and negative terminals of the battery to measure the voltage drop of the charging system. Which technician is correct?
   a. Technician A only
   b. Technician B only
   c. Both Technicians A and B
   d. Neither Technician A nor B

8. When testing an alternator minimum required output, what is the acceptable reading?
   a. 2 to 5 amperes
   b. Five amperes grater than the accessory load
   c. Over 100 amperes higher than the accessory load
   d. Less than 3 amperes

9. An alternator diode is being tested using a digital multimeter set to the diode-check position. A good diode reads _____ if the leads are connected one way across the diode and _____ if the leads are reversed.
   a. 300;300
   b. 0.475;0.475
   c. OL;OL
   d. 0.551;OL

10. How are new slip rings attached to the rotor core during alternator rebuilding?
    a. Machine clamped
    b. Soldered on
    c. Crimped on
    d. Epoxy glue

chapter 24

LIGHTING AND SIGNALING CIRCUITS

LEARNING OBJECTIVES:

After studying this chapter, the reader should be able to:

Explain lighting systems in an automobile and list the advantages of using LED lights.

Read and interpret a bulb chart.

Discuss the operation of brake lights and turn signals.

Describe daytime running lights, fog lights, driving lights, types of headlights, adaptive headlights, and how to aim headlights.

Describe automatic dimming mirrors, courtesy lights, and illuminated entry.

Explain the procedures to inspect and troubleshoot lighting and signaling systems.

This chapter will help you prepare for the ASE Electrical/Electronic Systems (A6) certification test content area "E" (Lighting Systems Diagnosis and Repair).

KEY TERMS: Adaptive Front Lighting Systems (AFS) 312 • Automatic headlights 313 • Composite headlight 308 • Courtesy lights 316 • Daytime running lights (DRLs) 308 • Hazard warning 308 • High-intensity discharge (HID) 309 • Kelvin (K) 311 • Light-emitting diode (LED) 302 • Trade number 304 • Troxler effect 316

LIGHTING SYSTEMS

CIRCUITS INVOLVED A vehicle has many different lighting and signaling systems, each with its own specific components and operating characteristics. The major light-related circuits and systems covered in this chapter include the following:

- Exterior lighting
- Headlights
- Bulb trade numbers
- Brake lights
- Turn signals and flasher units
- Courtesy lights
- Light-dimming rearview mirrors

NON-COMPUTER-CONTROLLED LIGHTING Older vehicles used the headlight switch to operate all the lights, including:

1. Headlights
2. Taillights
3. Side-marker lights
4. Front parking lights
5. Dash lights
6. Interior (dome) light(s)

The headlight switch assembly on older vehicles carried a heavy current and was mechanical. Most contained a built-in circuit breaker for the headlights that caused them to flicker on and off if a short circuit occurred in the headlight circuit. ● **SEE FIGURE 24–1.**

BODY CONTROL MODULE-CONTROLLED LIGHTING

The **Body Control Module (BCM)** is often referred to as a *central organizational module.* Using a BCM results in the following benefits:

1. It simplifies the manufacturing and troubleshooting aspects of electronic modules.
2. It coordinates the operating functions of many related items, as well as security features.

All recent vehicles use a controller, usually the body control module (BCM), to control the lights. The switches to turn on the lights are simply a request from the switch to the BCM to turn on the lights. The communication between the switches and the BCM is over serial data lines. Many vehicles use front and rear lighting modules, so the BCM sends a message over the data lines to the front or rear lighting module to turn on the commanded lights. The controller can control either the power side or the ground side of the circuit and performs the following:

- Monitors the current flow through the circuit and turns on a bulb failure warning light if it detects an open bulb or a fault in the circuit.

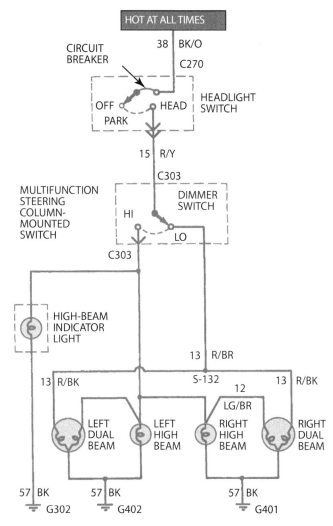

FIGURE 24–1 A typical headlight circuit diagram on an older vehicle that does not use a controller, such as the body control module (BCM) to control the operation of the lights. Note that the headlight switch is represented by a dotted outline indicating that other circuits (such as dash lights) also operate from the switch.

- After the ignition has been turned off, the modules turn off the lights after a time delay to prevent the battery from being drained.
- In the event of a communication failure, most module-controlled exterior lighting systems default to on position for safety.

Many electronic components are controlled by the BCM, including the following lighting circuits:

- Brake lights
- Courtesy lamps
- Dome lamps
- Exterior and interior lamps
- Fog lamps
- Hazard warning lamps

- Low- and high-beam head lamps
- Parking lamps
- Turn-signal lamps
  - ● **SEE FIGURE 24–2.**

LED LIGHTING

PARTS AND OPERATION A **light-emitting diode (LED)** is a two-lead semiconductor light source. An LED is a P–N junction diode that emits light when a suitable voltage is applied to the leads. The electrons are able to recombine with electron holes within the device, releasing energy in the form of photons. ● **SEE FIGURE 24–3.**

LED FEATURES LED lights are frequently used in newer vehicles for the following reasons.

1. **Faster illumination.** Using LEDs in brake lights light up 200 ms faster than an incandescent bulb, which requires some time to heat the filament before it is hot enough to create light. This faster illumination, when used in brake lights, can mean the difference in stopping distances at 60 MPH (100 km/h) by about 18 feet (6 m) due to the reduced reaction time for the driver of the vehicle behind.

2. **Longer service life.** LEDs are solid-state devices that do not use a filament to create light. As a result, they are less susceptible to vibration and often last the life of the vehicle.

3. **Lower current draw.** LEDs draw less current compared to incandescent bulbs and the result is less electrical drain from the charging system to operate all the lights in the vehicle. This helps improve fuel economy and lowers exhaust emissions by reducing the electrical load created by the alternator on the engine.

NOTE: Aftermarket replacement LED bulbs that are used to replace conventional bulbs may require the use of a different type of flasher unit due to the reduced current draw of the LED bulbs. ● SEE FIGURE 24–4.

TESTING BULBS Bulbs can be tested using two basic tests.

1. Perform a visual inspection of any bulb. Many faults, such as a shorted filament, a corroded connector, or moisture, can cause weird problems that are often thought to be wiring issues.

2. Bulbs can be tested using an ohmmeter and checking the resistance of the filament(s). Most bulbs read low resistance, between 0.5 and 20 ohms (incandescent bulbs), at room temperature, depending on the bulb. Test results include the following:

    - Normal resistance. The bulb is good. Check both filaments if it is a two-filament bulb.
      - ● **SEE FIGURE 24–5.**

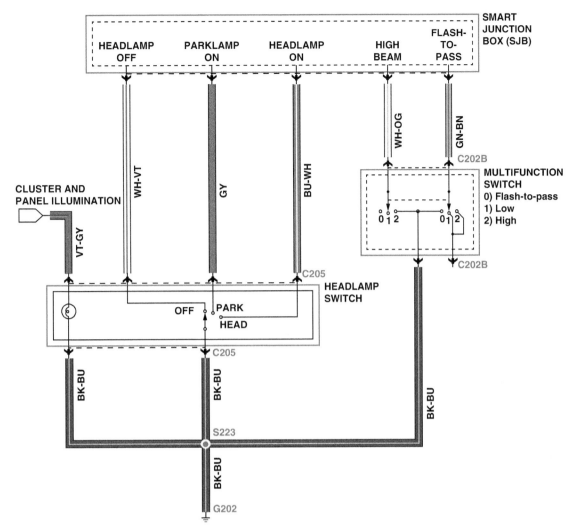

FIGURE 24–2 A schematic showing the inputs from the multi-function switch and the headlight switch to the smart junction box (SJB). The SJB then uses the body control module (BCM) to operate the lights.

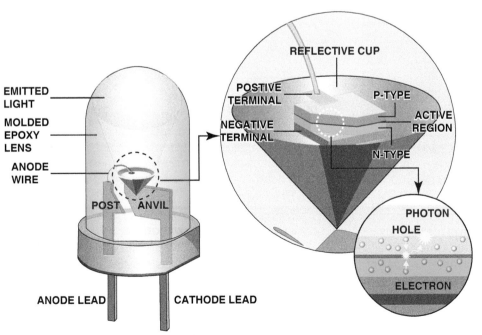

FIGURE 24–3 An LED emits light when a photon is released at the P–N junction.

- Zero ohms. It is unlikely, but possible for the bulb filament to be shorted.
- OL (electrically open). The reading indicates that the bulb filament is broken.

NOTE: If testing LED lights, check service information for the specified testing procedure.

FIGURE 24–4 A replacement LED taillight bulb is constructed of many small, individual light-emitting diodes.

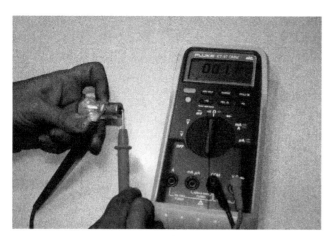

FIGURE 24–5 This single-filament bulb is being tested with a digital multimeter set to read resistance in ohms. The reading of 1.1 ohms is the resistance of the bulb when cold. As soon as current flows through the filament, the resistance increases about 10 times. It is the initial surge of current flowing through the filament, when the bulb is cool, that causes many bulbs to fail in cold weather as a result of the reduced resistance. As the temperature increases, the resistance increases.

BULB NUMBERS

TRADE NUMBER The number used on automotive bulbs is called the bulb **trade number**, as recorded with the American National Standards Institute (ANSI). The number is the same regardless of the manufacturer. ● **SEE FIGURE 24–6.**

The amount of light produced by a bulb is determined by the resistance of the filament wire, which also affects the amount of current (in amperes) required by the bulb. The correct trade number of a bulb should always be used for replacement to prevent circuit or component damage. Check service information or the owner's manual for the exact replacement bulb to use. ● **SEE CHART 24–1.**

BULB NUMBER SUFFIXES Many bulbs have suffixes that indicate some feature of the bulb, while keeping the same size and light output specifications. Typical bulb suffixes include the following:

- A—amber (painted glass)
- B—blue
- G—green
- HD—heavy duty
- IF—inside frosted
- LL—long life
- NA—natural amber (amber glass)
- Q—Quartz halogen
- R—red

● **SEE FIGURE 24–7.**

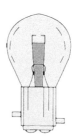
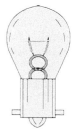

DOUBLE-CONTACT 1157/2057 BULBS

SINGLE-CONTACT 1156 BULBS

WEDGE 194 BULB

FIGURE 24–6 Dual-filament (double-contact) bulbs contain both a low-intensity filament for taillights or parking lights, and a high-intensity filament for brake lights and turn signals. Bulbs come in a variety of shapes and sizes. The numbers shown are the trade numbers.

BULB NUMBER	FILAMENTS	AMPERAGE	WATTAGE
1156	1	2.1	26.9
1157	2	0.6/2/1	8.3/26.9
2057	2	0.5/2.1	6.9/26.9
3057	2	0.5/2.1	6.7/26.9
4157	2	0.6/2/1	8.3/26.9
7440	1	1.8	21.0
7443	2	0.4/1.8	5.0/21.0
67	1	0.6	8.0
161	1	0.2	2.7
168	1	0.4	4.9
192	1	0.3	4.3
194	1	0.3	3.8
585	1	0.04	1.1
921	1	1.4	18
9003	2	4.6/5.0	55.0/60.0
9006	1	4.3	55.0

CHART 24–1

Some automotive bulb trade numbers with their amperage and wattage rating. Check service information for the exact bulb to use.

FIGURE 24–7 Bulbs that have the same trade number have the same operating voltage and wattage. NA means that the bulb uses a natural amber glass ampoule with clear turn-signal lenses.

BRAKE LIGHTS

TERMINOLOGY Brake lights, also called *stop lights*, use the high-intensity filament of a double-filament bulb or LEDs. The brake lights are lit when the driver depresses the brake pedal. On older vehicles, the brake switch receives current from a fuse that is hot all the time. The brake light switch is a normally open (N.O.) switch, but is closed when the driver depresses the brake pedal. Newer brake switches have more than one set of contacts. In many cases, one set is normally open and the other set is normally closed.

- **One-Filament Stop/Turn Bulbs**—In some vehicles, the stop and turn signals are both provided by one filament.
- **Two-Filament Stop/Turn Bulbs**—In systems using separate filaments for the stop and turn lamps, the brake and turn-signal switches are not connected.

All vehicles sold in the United States have a third brake light commonly referred to as the *center high-mounted stop light (CHMSL)*. ● SEE FIGURE 24–8.

BCM-CONTROLLED BRAKE LIGHTS When the brake pedal is depressed, the signal is sent to the brake light controller, usually the BCM, which then signals the rear light module to actuate the brake lights. The input from the brake pedal switch or sensor is used by other systems in the vehicle as an input signal for the following systems:

1. **Shift interlock**—On vehicles equipped with an automatic transmission, the gear selector cannot be moved out of the park position unless the brake pedal is depressed.
2. **Push-button start**—Vehicles equipped with a push-button start do not start unless the brake pedal is depressed.
3. **Cruise control**—If the brake pedal is depressed, the cruise control function is disabled.
4. **Antilock braking system (ABS)**—When the brake pedal is depressed, the ABS system is ready to intervene, if needed, to control wheel slippage.

On some vehicles, the key must be in the on position for all the brake lights to illuminate. This is particularly important to know when performing diagnostics. Check service information for the specified procedure to follow on the vehicle being tested. ● SEE FIGURE 24–9.

TURN SIGNALS

MECHANICAL SYSTEM OPERATION In older systems, the turn-signal circuit is supplied power from the ignition switch and operated by a lever and a switch. When the turn-signal switch is moved in either direction, the corresponding turn-signal lamps receive current through the flasher unit. The flasher unit causes the current to start and stop as the turn-signal lamp flashes on and off with the interrupted current.

A turn-signal flasher unit is a metal or plastic can, containing a switch that opens and closes the turn-signal circuit. It is often installed in a metal clip attached to the dash panel to allow the "clicking" noise of the flasher to be heard by the driver.

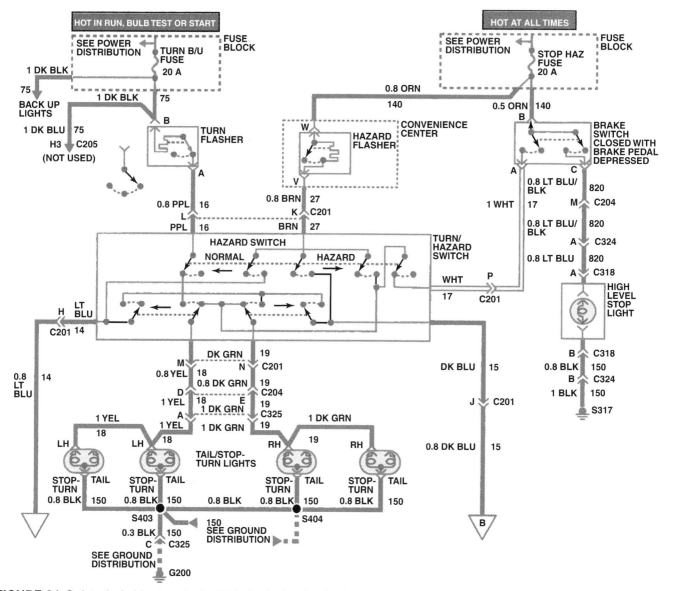

FIGURE 24–8 A typical older-type brake light circuit showing the brake switch and all of the related circuit components.

Most flashers have a lamp current-sensing circuit, which cause the flash rate to double when a bulb is burned out. ● **SEE FIGURE 24–10.**

BCM-CONTROLLED TURN SIGNALS Starting in the early 2000s, many vehicles use the turn signal as an input to the body control module (BCM). ● **SEE FIGURE 24–11.**

The BCM sends a signal through the data lines to the lighting module(s) to flash the lights. With these systems, the BCM also sends a signal to the radio, which sends a clicking sound to the driver's side speaker, even if the radio is off.

BULB OUTAGE WARNING The lighting module, usually the BCM, monitors the current flow though all of the lights. These circuits measure the current and, if there is a change that is not expected, it can turn on a warning light to warn the driver. If this current is below some threshold value, the bulb is

assumed to be burned out. The bulb failure system works using a resistance value for each circuit. When diagnosing a bulb outage concern, perform the following steps:

STEP 1 Visually check the exterior lights for proper operation. Check all of the following:

- Backup light(s)
- Brake lights, including the center high-mounted stop light
- Driving lights, if equipped
- Fog lights, if equipped
- High-beam headlights
- License plate light(s)
- Low-beam headlights
- Park lights
- Puddle lights
- Side marker lights, front and rear, and left and right sides

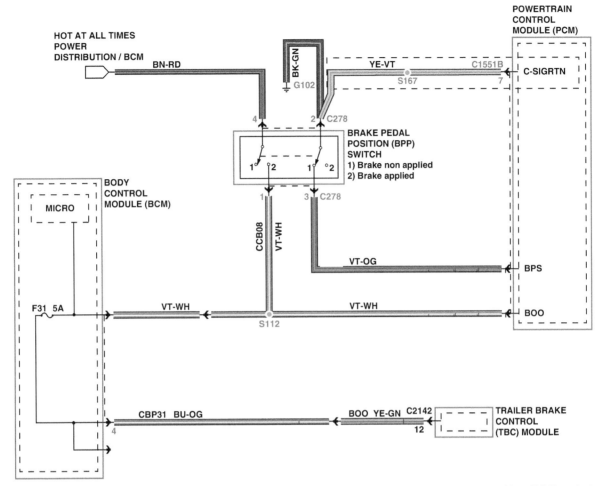

FIGURE 24–9 A schematic of the BCM-controlled brake light circuit that includes the brake pedal position (BPP) switch, which creates signals to the powertrain control module (PCM) with inputs labeled BPS (brake pedal position) and BOO (brake on-off).

FIGURE 24–10 Three styles of flasher units.

- Taillights
- Turn signals front and rear

STEP 2 If one or more are not lighting, check or replace the bulb. Verify that the affected bulb is not an LED where a non-LED bulb is specified. ● **SEE FIGURE 24–12.**

STEP 3 If the warning lamp is still on, check the sockets for corrosion, proper voltage, and ground at the socket.

FIGURE 24–11 A steering column with the steering wheel removed, showing the turn signal canceling cam used to return the lever to the neutral position after a turn. The switches are an input to the body control module for left and right turn-signal operation.

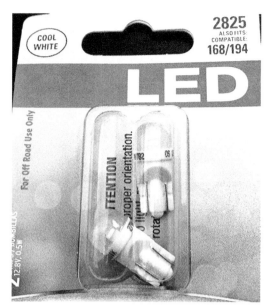

FIGURE 24–12 Replacement side marker LED lamps that could be used to replace standard bulbs. However, the current draw is lower and using these bulbs could cause the lamp outage warning lamp to be turned on.

HAZARD WARNING LIGHTS The **hazard warning**, also called *four-way flashers*, is a device installed in a vehicle lighting system with the primary function of causing both the left and right turn-signal lamps to flash when the hazard warning switch is activated. Secondary functions may include visible dash indicators for the hazard system and an audible signal to indicate when the flasher is operating. In older systems, a separate hazard warning flasher is used. Current vehicles use the BCM to operate all four turn-signal lights when the hazard (four-way) flasher switch is turned on by the driver.

DAYTIME RUNNING LIGHTS

PURPOSE AND FUNCTION **Daytime running lights (DRLs)** are lights at the front of the vehicle that are on all the time the engine is running, unless they are turned off, or when the headlights are on. DRLs involve operation of the following:

- Front parking lights
- Separate DRL lamps
- Headlights (usually at reduced current and voltage) when the vehicle is running

Studies have shown that DRLs have reduced accidents where used. DRLs primarily use a control module that turns on either the low- or high-beam headlights wired in series or separate daytime running lights. The lights on some vehicles come on when the engine starts. Other vehicles turn on the lamps when the engine is running but delay their operation until a signal from the vehicle speed sensor indicates that the vehicle is moving. To avoid having the lights on during servicing, some

systems turn off the headlights when the parking brake is applied, and the ignition switch is cycled off and then back on. Others only light the headlights when the vehicle is in a drive gear. ● **SEE FIGURE 24–13.**

The DRLs operate when the following conditions are met:

- The ignition is in the RUN or CRANK position
- The shift lever is out of the PARK position for vehicles equipped with automatic transmissions, or the parking brake is released for vehicles with manual transmissions
- The low- and high-beam headlamps are OFF

HEADLIGHTS

HEADLIGHT SWITCHES Older vehicles use the headlight switch to operate the exterior and interior lights. On these systems, the headlight switch is connected directly to the battery through a fusible link, and has continuous power or is "hot" all the time. ● **SEE FIGURE 24–14.**

COMPOSITE HEADLIGHTS Sealed beam headlights were used for many years and then, in the 1990s, were replaced with composite headlights. **Composite headlights** are constructed using a replaceable bulb and a fixed lens cover that is part of the vehicle. Composite headlights are the result of changes in the aerodynamic styling of vehicles where sealed beam lamps could no longer be used. ● **SEE FIGURE 24–15.**

The replaceable bulbs are usually bright halogen bulbs. Halogen bulbs get very hot during operation, between 500°F and 1,300°F (260°C and 704°C). It is important to never touch the glass of any halogen bulb with bare fingers because the natural oils of the skin on the glass bulb can cause the bulb to break when it heats during normal operation. ● **SEE FIGURE 24–16.**

BULB FAULTS Halogen bulbs can fail for various reasons. Some causes for halogen bulb failure and their indications include the following:

- **Gray color.** Low voltage to the bulb (check for corroded socket or connector)
- **White (cloudy) color.** Indication of an air leak
- **Broken filament.** Usually caused by excessive vibration
- **Blistered glass.** Indication that someone has touched the glass

CLOUDY HEADLIGHT RESTORATION The bulb covering of composite headlights is made from acrylic plastic. This material tends to fade, turn yellow, and discolor over a period of time due primarily to constant exposure to the sun's ultraviolet (UV) rays. The problem tends to be most serious in warmer, sunny climates. This clouding of the surface is more than a cosmetic issue because it can reduce the available light, reducing night vision. There are many brands and types of headlight restoration products available. Most products involve sanding

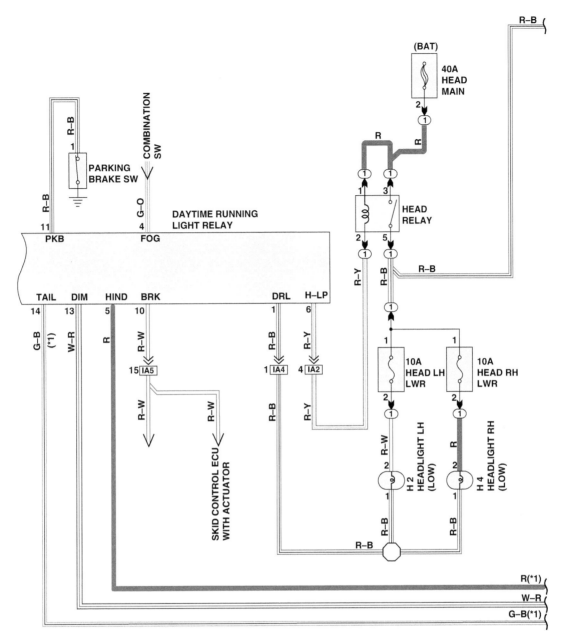

FIGURE 24–13 A schematic showing a DRL circuit that uses the headlights. Also notice that each headlight has its own fuse to protect the circuit. Check service information for how the DRLs operate on the vehicle being serviced.

the surface of the lens using fine sandpaper and applying a UV protectant to help prevent further damage to the plastic lens. Always follow the instructions for the product or procedure used to restore the headlights. ● **SEE FIGURE 24–17.**

HIGH-INTENSITY DISCHARGE HEADLIGHTS

PARTS AND OPERATION **High-intensity discharge (HID)** headlights produce light that is crisper, clearer, and brighter than light produced by a halogen headlight. HID lamps do not

use a filament like conventional electrical bulbs, but contain two electrodes about 0.2 inch (5 mm) apart. A high-voltage pulse is sent to the bulb, which arcs across the tips of electrodes, producing light. It creates light from an electrical discharge between two electrodes in a gas-filled arc tube. A HID lamp produces twice the light with less electrical current (amperage) than conventional halogen bulbs. The HID lighting system consists of the discharge arc source, igniter, ballast, and headlight assembly. ● **SEE FIGURE 24–18.**

The two electrodes are contained in a tiny quartz capsule filled with xenon gas, mercury, and metal halide salts. HID headlights are also called *xenon* headlights. The lights and support electronics are expensive, but they should last the life of the vehicle, unless physically damaged. HID head-

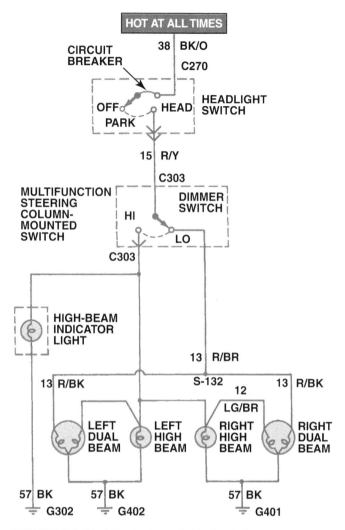

FIGURE 24–16 Handle a halogen bulb by the base to prevent the skin's oil from getting on the glass.

FIGURE 24–14 A Typical headlight circuit diagram on an older vehicle that does not use a controller, such as the BCM, to control the operation of the lights. Note that the headlight switch is represented by a dotted outline, indicating that other circuits (such as dash lights) also operate from the switch.

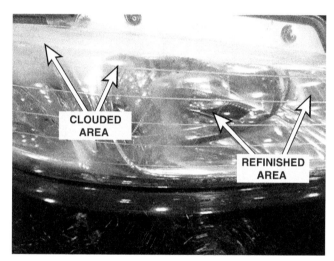

FIGURE 24–17 The right side of this headlight assembly has been restored, but still needs to be polished. The left side is cloudy and not yet restored.

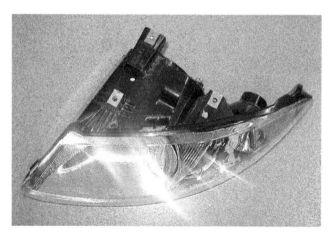

FIGURE 24–15 A typical composite headlamp assembly. The lens, housing, and bulb sockets are usually included as a complete assembly.

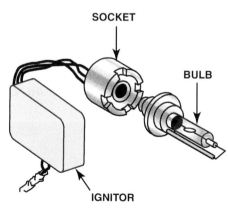

FIGURE 24–18 The igniter contains the ballast and transformer needed to provide high-voltage pulses to the arc-tube bulb.

FREQUENTLY ASKED QUESTION

What Is the Difference between the Temperature of the Light and the Brightness of the Light?

The temperature of the light indicates the color of the light. The brightness of the light is measured in lumens. A standard 100 watt incandescent light bulb emits about 1,700 lumens. A typical halogen head-light bulb produces about 2,000 lumens, and a typical HID bulb produces about 2,800 lumens.

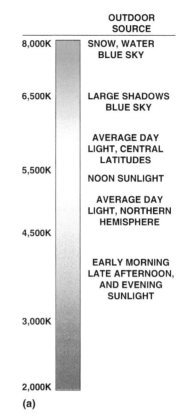

(a)

lights produce a white light giving the lamp a blue-white color. The color of light is expressed in temperature using the Kelvin scale. **Kelvin (K)** temperature is the Celsius temperature plus 273 degrees. Typical color temperatures include the following:

- Daylight—5,400°K
- HID—4,100°K
- Halogen—3,200°K
- Incandescent (tungsten)—2,800°K
- ● **SEE FIGURE 24–19.**

STAGES OF HID HEADLIGHT OPERATION The HID ballast is powered by voltage from the headlight switch or the BCM. The HID headlights operate in three stages or states.

1. **Start-up or stroke state**—When the headlight switch is turned to the on position, the ballast may draw up to 20 amperes at 12 volts. The ballast sends multiple high-voltage pulses to the arc tube to start the arc inside the bulb. The voltage provided by the ballast during the start-up state ranges from –600 to +600 volts, which is increased by a transformer to about 25,000 volts. The increased voltage is used to create an arc between the electrodes in the bulb.

2. **Run-up state**—After the arc is established, the ballast provides a higher-than-steady-state voltage to the arc tube to keep the bulb illuminated. On a cold bulb, this state could last as long as 40 seconds. On a hot bulb, the run-up state may last only 15 seconds. The current requirements during the run-up state are about 360 volts from the ballast and a power level of about 75 watts.

3. **Steady state**—The steady-state phase begins when the power requirement of the bulb drops to 35 watts. The ballast provides a minimum of 55 volts to the bulb during steady-state operation.

BI-XENON HEADLIGHTS Some vehicles are equipped with bi-xenon headlights, which use a shutter to block some of the light during low-beam operation, and then mechanically move

(b)

FIGURE 24–19 (a) The color of light is measured in degrees Kevin (K). The higher the temperature of the light, the bluer the appearance. (Line drawing to be drafted.) (b) HID (xenon) headlights emit a whiter light than halogen headlights and usually look blue compared to halogen bulbs.

to expose more of the light from the bulb for high-beam operation. Because xenon lights are relatively slow to start working, vehicles equipped with bi-xenon headlights use two halogen lights for the "flash-to-pass" feature.

HID HEADLIGHT FAILURE SYMPTOMS The following symptoms indicate bulb failure.

- A light flickers
- Lights go out (caused when the ballast assembly detects repeated bulb restrikes)
- Color changes to a dim pink glow

Bulb failures are often intermittent and difficult to repeat. However, bulb failure is likely if the symptoms get worse over time. Always follow the vehicle manufacturer's recommended testing and service procedures.

DIAGNOSIS AND SERVICE HID headlights change slightly in color with age. This color shift is usually not noticeable unless one headlight arc-tube assembly has been replaced due to a collision repair, and then the difference in color may be noticeable. The difference in color gradually changes as the arc tube ages and should not be too noticeable by most customers. If the arc-tube assembly is near the end of its life, it may not light immediately if it is turned off and then back on immediately. This test is called a "hot restrike" and, if it fails, a replacement arc-tube assembly may be needed, or there is another fault, such as a poor electrical connection, that should be checked.

LED HEADLIGHTS

Many newer vehicles use LED headlights either as standard equipment or optional equipment. ● **SEE FIGURE 24–20.**

The advantages of LED headlights compared to other types are as follows:

■ Long service life
■ Reduced electrical power required

The disadvantages of LED headlights are as follows:

■ Higher cost
■ Many small LEDs are required to create the necessary light output

ADAPTIVE FRONT LIGHTING SYSTEM

PURPOSE AND FUNCTION An **adaptive (or advanced) front lighting system**, or **AFS**, is a system that mechanically moves the headlights to follow the direction of the front wheels. The purpose is to provide improved lighting during cornering. The AFS headlights are usually capable of rotating 15 degrees to the left and 5 degrees to the right (some systems rotate 14 degrees and 9 degrees, respectively). Vehicles that use AFS include Lexus, Mercedes, and certain domestic models, usually as an extra cost option. ● **SEE FIGURE 24–21.**

NOTE: These angles are reversed on vehicles sold in countries that drive on the left side of the road, such as Great Britain, Japan, Australia, and New Zealand.

PARTS AND OPERATION The vehicle has to be moving above a predetermined speed, usually above 20 MPH (30 km/h), and the lights stop moving when the speed drops below about 3 MPH (5 km/h). AFS is often used in addition to self-leveling motors so that the headlights remain properly aimed, regardless of how the vehicle is loaded. Without self-leveling, headlights shine higher than normal if the rear of the vehicle is heavily loaded. ● **SEE FIGURE 24–22.**

When a vehicle is equipped with an AFS, the lights are moved by the headlight controller outward and then inward,

FIGURE 24–20 LED headlights usually require multiple units to provide the needed light, as seen on this Lexus LS600h.

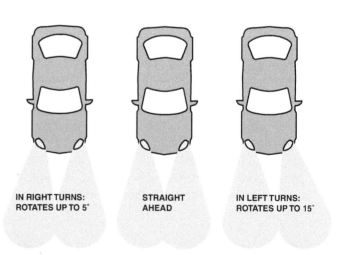

IN RIGHT TURNS: ROTATES UP TO 5° STRAIGHT AHEAD IN LEFT TURNS: ROTATES UP TO 15°

FIGURE 24–21 Adaptive front lighting systems rotate the low-beam headlight in the direction of travel.

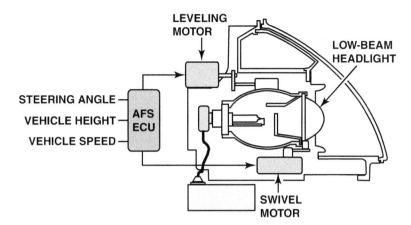

FIGURE 24–22 A typical adaptive front lighting system uses two motors: one for the up-and-down movement and the other for rotating the low-beam headlight to the left and right.

FIGURE 24–23 Typical dash-mounted switch that allows the driver to turn off the front lighting system.

FIGURE 24–24 A dash symbol used to inform the driver that the automatic headlights are on.

as well as up and down, as a test of the system. This action is quite noticeable to the driver and is a normal operation of the system.

DIAGNOSIS AND SERVICE The first step when diagnosing an AFS fault is to perform the following visual inspection.

- Start by checking that the AFS is switched on. Most AFS headlights are equipped with a switch that allows the driver to turn the system on and off. ● SEE FIGURE 24–23.
- Check that the system performs a self-test during start-up.
- Verify that both low-beam and high-beam lights function correctly. The system may be disabled if a fault with one of the headlights is detected.
- Use a scan tool to test for any AFS-related diagnostic trouble codes. Some systems allow the AFS to be checked and operated using a scan tool.

Always follow the recommended testing and service procedures as specified by the vehicle manufacturer in service information.

AUTOMATIC HEADLIGHTS

PURPOSE AND FUNCTION Automatic headlights automatically turn on the headlights when the light sensor detects low ambient light level. These sensors are usually located on the dash of the vehicle. If the light level is low, the headlights turn on automatically when the engine starts. The ambient light sensor is used to monitor outside lighting conditions. The ambient light sensor provides a voltage signal that varies between 0.2 and 4.9 volts, depending on outside lighting conditions. The BCM provides a 5 volt reference signal to the ambient light sensor. The BCM monitors the ambient light sensor signal circuit to determine if outside lighting conditions are correct for either daytime running lights, or automatic lamp control (ALC) when the headlamp switch is in the AUTO position.

CONTROLS Most vehicles allow the driver to select the headlights in the "AUTO" position or turn them on and off manually. If the headlights are on, a dash symbol is often displayed on the dash to inform the driver. ● SEE FIGURE 24–24.

HEADLIGHT HIGH/LOW BEAM SWITCH

DIMMER SWITCH Headlights use a high-intensity bulb or lamp and a low-intensity bulb or lamp. The switch used to switch between the two circuits is often called the *dimmer switch* or the high/low switch. An indicator light illuminates on the dash when the high beams are selected. The dimmer switch is usually hand-operated by a lever on the steering column. Some steering column switches are attached to the outside of the steering column and are spring-loaded. To replace these types of dimmer switches, the steering column needs to be lowered slightly to gain access to the switch itself.

AUTO DIMMING HEADLIGHTS

PURPOSE AND FUNCTION An **automatic headlight dimmer** (also called *automatic beam control* or *automatic high beams*) is a system that causes the headlights to switch from high-intensity beams to low-intensity beams when the system detects the headlights from an approaching vehicle.

TYPES OF SYSTEMS Types of automatic headlight dimming include the following:

- **Photo resistor-based system**—A system that uses a photo resistor is usually mounted at the top of the windshield inside the vehicle. This system automatically adjusts the headlight beams from "high-beam" to "low-beam" when approaching oncoming vehicles during nighttime driving. The system also switches back to high-beam after the vehicles have passed. Drivers can also use standard headlight dimmers to override the automatic headlight dimmer on vehicles so equipped.
- **Camera-based systems**—Some vehicles use the camera and lasers already fitted for collision avoidance. These systems can detect an oncoming vehicle from 400 yards (366 m) away, and detect the tail lights of a car in front from more than 120 yards (110 m).

CONDITIONS NEEDED TO FUNCTION For the automatic operation to turn on the high beams, the following conditions are usually required:

- Vehicle speed above 20 MPH
- Dark conditions with few streetlights
- There are no approaching vehicles with the headlights on
- There are no taillights from the vehicle in front

NOTE: High beams may not automatically turn off when an approaching vehicle is hidden from view due to a hill or a curve. This inability is not a fault with the system, but instead is due to the limiting factors of the system.

HEADLIGHT AIMING

According to U.S. federal law, all headlights, regardless of shape, must be able to be aimed using headlight-aiming equipment. The headlights are equipped with adjusting screws that can be used to aim the headlights. Some are also equipped with a bubble level to help make sure that the lights are level. Older vehicles equipped with sealed beam headlights used a headlight-aiming system that is attached to the headlight itself. Check service information for the exact procedure and specifications to follow when aiming headlights. ● **SEE FIGURE 24–25.**

FOG AND DRIVING LIGHTS

FOG LIGHTS The light from regular headlights can reflect off the fog, snow, or dust particles in the air, causing glare. When driving in fog, the use of fog lights reduces the glare. Fog lights have a unique beam that is flat and wide, and is positioned low on the vehicle, usually near the front bumper. Fog lights are also useful where there is dust and snow on the road, either drifting in through the air or being churned up from the surface of the road. Fog lights are usually white, though they can also be yellow or blue. Fog lights in the rear are always red. ● **SEE FIGURE 24–26.**

NOTE: Fog lights should only be used when poor visibility is present and then turned off.

DRIVING LIGHTS Driving lights have a narrow, straight beam, and are used while off-roading or traversing dark, deserted country roads. Driving lights are designed to send powerful beams far ahead, illuminating the next stretch of road. Driving lights are usually installed by the vehicle owner and are usually not available from the factory unless a special off-road equipment package is ordered. If installed, they should be wired to work only when the high beams are in use. Check local and state regulations in regards to the mounting and use of driving lights.

AUTOMATIC DIMMING MIRRORS

PARTS AND OPERATION Automatic dimming mirrors use electrochromic technology to dim the mirror in proportion to the amount of headlight glare from other vehicles at the rear. The

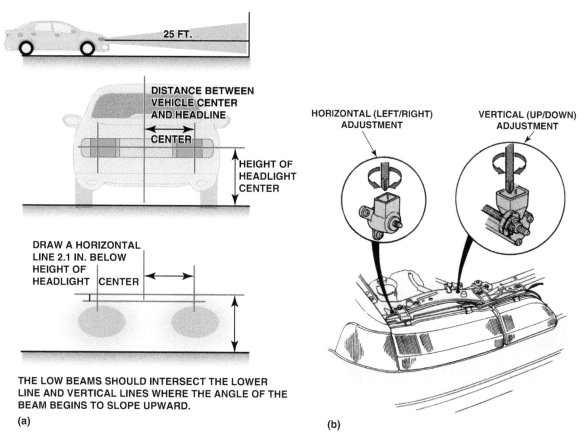

FIGURE 24–25 (a) A typical headlight-aiming diagram as found in service information. (b) Adjustments to move the headlight-aiming point left or right or up and down are usually made using a screwdriver to move the headlight housing.

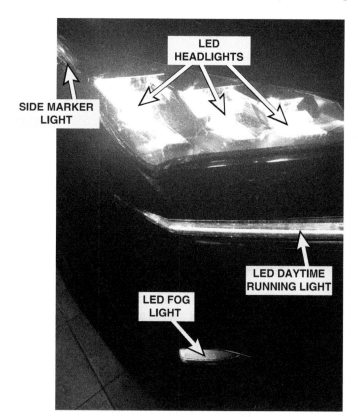

FIGURE 24–26 Fog lights are often included on many vehicles, such as these on a Lexus SUV.

 FREQUENTLY ASKED QUESTION

What Are Rear Fog Lights?

Some vehicles, usually European vehicles, are equipped with rear (red) fog lights. These are used so that drivers behind can see the vehicle in front. These could be on whenever the fog lights are turned on, or they could be on a separate switch. These rear fog lights are sometimes confused with brake lights being on because they are often as bright as brake lights. Check the owner's manual or service information if a fault is reported about the rear fog lights.

electrochromic technology developed by Gentex Corporation uses a gel that changes with light between two pieces of glass. One piece of glass acts as a reflector and the other has a transparent (clear) electrically conductive coating. The inside rearview mirror also has a forward-facing light sensor that is used to detect darkness. It signals the rearward-facing sensor to begin to check for excessive glare from headlights behind the vehicle. The rearward-facing sensor sends a voltage to the electrochromic gel in the mirror that is in proportion to the amount of glare detected. The mirror dims in proportion to the glare, and becomes like a standard rearview mirror when the glare is no longer detected. If automatic dimming mirrors are used on the exterior, the sensors

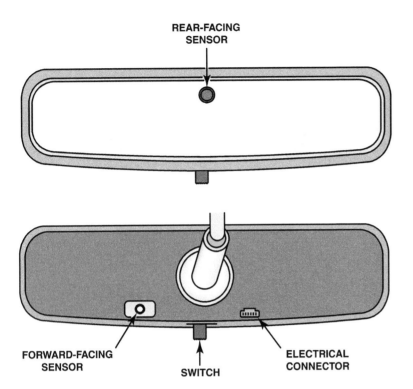

REAR-FACING SENSOR

FORWARD-FACING SENSOR

SWITCH

ELECTRICAL CONNECTOR

FIGURE 24–27 An automatic dimming mirror compares the amount of light toward the front of the vehicle to the rear of the vehicle and allows a voltage to cause the gel to darken the mirror.

What Is the Troxler Effect?

The **Troxler effect**, also called *Troxler fading*, is a visual effect where an image remains on the retina of the eye for a short time after the image has been removed. The effect was discovered in 1804 by Ignaz Paul Vital Troxler (1780–1866), a Swiss physician. Because of the Troxler effect, headlight glare can remain on the retina of the eye and create a blind spot. At night, this fading away of the bright light from the vehicle in the rear reflected by the rearview mirror can cause a hazard.

in the interior mirror and electronics are used to control both the interior and exterior mirrors. ● **SEE FIGURE 24–27.**

DIAGNOSIS AND SERVICE If a customer concern states that the mirrors do not dim when exposed to bright headlights from the vehicle behind, the cause could be sensors or the mirror itself. Be sure that the mirror is getting electrical power. Most automotive dimming mirrors have a green light to indicate the presence of electrical power. If no voltage is found at the mirror, follow standard troubleshooting procedures to find the cause. If the mirror is getting voltage, start the diagnosis by placing a strip of tape over the forward-facing light sensor. Turn the ignition key on, engine off (KOEO), and observe the operation of the mirror when a flashlight or trouble light is directed onto the mirror. If the mirror reacts and dims, the forward-facing sensor is defective. Most often, the entire mirror assembly must be replaced, if any sensor or mirror faults are found.

One typical fault with automatic dimming mirrors is that a crack can occur in the mirror assembly, allowing the gel to escape from between the two layers of glass. This gel can drip onto the dash or center console and harm these surfaces. The mirror should be replaced at the first sign of any gel leakage.

COURTESY LIGHTS

Courtesy lights are a generic term primarily used for interior lights, including overhead (dome) and under-the-dash (courtesy) lights. These interior lights are controlled by switches located in the door handle of the vehicle or by a switch on the dash. Many newer vehicles operate the interior lights through the BCM or through an electronic module. Because the exact wiring and operation of these units differ, check the service information for the exact model of the vehicle being serviced.

ILLUMINATED ENTRY

Some vehicles are equipped with illuminated entry, meaning the interior lights are turned on for a given amount of time when the outside door handle or remote keyless entry (RKE) fob is operated while the doors are locked.

Most vehicles equipped with illuminated entry also light the exterior door lights, called "puddle lights," that shine downward so people entering a vehicle in the dark can see the ground near the vehicle. The input from the door handle or key fob remote is used to "wake up" the power supply for the BCM and usually turns on the interior lights.

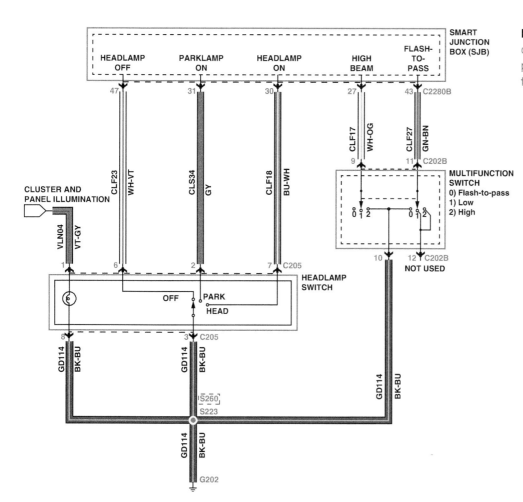

FIGURE 24–28 A Ford headlight circuit showing the control of the power side of the circuit comes from the smart junction box (SJB).

HEADLIGHT SYSTEM DIAGNOSIS

VISUAL INSPECTION All of the lights, including the operation of the headlights, should be a part of any vehicle inspection process. During a visual inspection, check the headlights for the following:

- Are they functioning as designed? (Check service information or a similar vehicle to make sure that the system is not working as designed.)
- Check the brightness to see if they are dim.
- Check if the headlights are too bright.

DIAGNOSTIC PROCEDURE If the headlights are not working at all, perform the following steps:

STEP 1 Use a factory or factory-level scan tool to turn the headlights on using the bi-directional command from the scan tool. If the headlights work, the headlights and the headlight circuit are working normally. The problem is likely the control input to the controller that operates the headlights.

STEP 2 Check the schematic for the headlight circuit and check for voltage at various parts to help pinpoint the location

of the open circuit. Always follow the vehicle manufacturer's specified procedures. ● **SEE FIGURE 24–28.**

- If the headlights are brighter than normal, the battery voltage may be higher than normal. Check the charging system voltage to make sure that it is less than 15.5 volts (on most vehicles). Check service information for the exact specifications.
- If the headlight(s) is/are dimmer than normal, check the electrical circuits to the headlights for excessive circuit resistance, such as any of the following:
  1. Loose electrical connector
  2. Corroded socket
  3. Poor electrical ground connection

LIGHTING SYSTEM DIAGNOSIS

Diagnosing any faults in the lighting and signaling systems usually includes the following steps.

STEP 1 Verify the customer concern.

STEP 2 Perform a visual inspection, checking for collision damage or other possible causes that would affect the operation of the lighting circuit.

The Weirder the Problem, the More Likely It Is a Poor Ground Connection

Bad grounds are often the cause for feedback or lamps operating at full or partial brilliance. At first, the problem looks weird, because often the switch for the lights that are on dimly is not even turned on. When an electrical device is operating, and it lacks a proper ground connection, the current tries to find ground and often causes other circuits to work. Check all grounds before replacing parts.

STEP 3 Connect a factory or enhanced scan tool with bidirectional control of the control modules to check for proper operation of the affected lighting circuit.

STEP 4 Follow the diagnostic procedure, as found in service information, to determine the root cause of the problem.

LIGHTING SYSTEM SYMPTOM GUIDE

The following list assists technicians in determining lighting systems faults by symptom.

PROBLEM/CONCERN	POSSIBLE CAUSE
One headlight dim	1. Poor ground connection on body
	2. Corroded connector
One headlight out (low or high beam)	1. Burned out headlight filament (Check the headlight with an ohmmeter. There should be a low ohm reading between the power-side connection and the ground terminal of the bulb.)
	2. Open circuit (no 12 volts to the bulb)
Both high- and low-beam headlights out	1. Burned out bulbs
	2. Open circuit (Check for voltage at the wiring connector to the headlights for a possible open circuit to the headlights or open [defective] dimmer switch.)
All headlights inoperative	1. Burned out filaments in all headlights (Check for excessive charging-system voltage.)
	2. Defective dimmer switch
	3. Defective headlight switch
Slow turn-signal operation	1. Defective flasher unit (if equipped)
	2. High resistance in sockets or ground wire connections
	3. Incorrect bulb numbers
Turn signals operating on one side only	1. Burned out bulb on the affected side
	2. Poor ground connection or defective socket on the affected side
	3. Incorrect bulb number on the affected side
	4. Defective turn-signal switch
Interior light(s) inoperative	1. Burned out bulb(s)
	2. Open in the power-side circuit (blown fuse)
	3. Open in door switch(es)
Brake lights inoperative	1. Defective brake switch
	2. Defective turn-signal switch (mechanical system)
	3. Burned out brake light bulbs
	4. Open circuit or poor ground connection
	5. Blown fuse
Hazard warning lights inoperative	1. Defective hazard flasher unit (if equipped)
	2. Open in hazard circuit
	3. Blown fuse
	4. Defective hazard switch

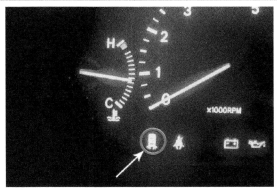

1 The driver noticed that the taillight fault indicator (icon) on the dash was on any time the lights were on.

2 A visual inspection at the rear of the vehicle indicated that the right rear taillight bulb did not light. Removing a few screws from the plastic cover revealed the taillight assembly.

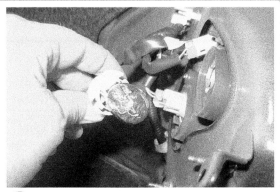

3 The bulb socket is removed from the taillight assembly by gently twisting the base of the bulb counterclockwise.

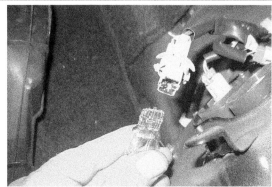

4 The bulb is removed from the socket by gently grasping the bulb and pulling the bulb straight out of the socket. Many bulbs required that you rotate the bulb 90° (1/4 turn) to release the retaining bulbs.

5 The new 7443 replacement bulb is being checked with an ohmmeter to be sure that it is okay before it is installed in the vehicle.

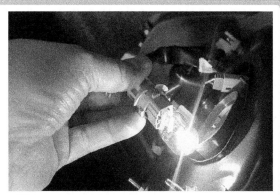

6 The replacement bulb is inserted into the taillight socket and the lights are turned on to verify proper operation before putting the components back together.

1. Automotive bulbs are identified by trade numbers.
2. A bulb trade number means that the specifications for that number are the same regardless of the bulb manufacturer.
3. Daytime running lights (DRLs) are used on many vehicles.
4. High-intensity discharge (HID) headlights are brighter and have a blue tint.
5. Turn-signal flashers come in many different types and construction.

REVIEW QUESTIONS

1. Why should the exact same trade number of bulb be used as a replacement?
2. Why is it important to avoid touching a halogen bulb with your fingers?
3. What are the advantages of LED lights?
4. Why are lights controlled by the BCM in many vehicles?
5. What are the conditions needed for an auto dimming headlight system to work?

CHAPTER QUIZ

1. Technician A says that the bulb trade number is the same for all bulbs of the same size. Technician B says that a dual-filament bulb has different wattage ratings for each filament. Which technician is correct?
   a. Technician A only
   b. Technician B only
   c. Both Technicians A and B
   d. Neither Technician A nor B

2. Light-emitting diodes (LEDs) are used for lighting because they _____.
   a. light quicker (faster illumination)
   b. have longer service life
   c. have lower current draw
   d. Any of the above

3. The correct trade number of bulb always is used for replacement because it _____.
   a. prevents circuit or component damage
   b. keeps the circuit resistance the same
   c. keeps the circuit current (amperes) the same
   d. All of the above

4. Which of the following will cause the brake lights to turn on when the brake pedal is depressed?
   a. A brake light switch
   b. The pedal sensor
   c. A pressure sensor on the brake pedal itself
   d. Either a or b depending on the vehicle

5. Vehicles equipped with the illuminated entry feature typically use _____ to command the interior lights ON.
   a. the BCM
   b. RKE fob
   c. outside door handle
   d. Any of the above

6. Which of the lighting systems could result in an electrical shock hazard if proper precautions are not followed?
   a. LED lights
   b. HID lights
   c. Rear fog lights
   d. Driving lights

7. What type of light bulb should not be touched using bare hands?
   a. 1157 or 2057 bulbs
   b. Halogen bulbs
   c. LED bulbs
   d. HID bulbs

8. The "color" of light produced by a light bulb is measured in what unit?
   a. Kelvin degrees
   b. Amperes
   c. Watts
   d. Volts

9. An automatically dimming mirror is used to _____.
   a. automatically dim the headlights
   b. help prevent the Troxler effect
   c. operate the fog lights when needed
   d. operate the daytime running lights (DRLs)

10. Technician A says that a scan tool is usually needed to aim headlights. Technician B says that the keyless entry key fob is used to wake up the BCM which usually is responsible to turn on the interior lights. Which technician is correct?
    a. Technician A only
    b. Technician B only
    c. Both Technicians A and B
    d. Neither Technician A nor B

chapter 25

DRIVER INFORMATION AND NAVIGATION SYSTEMS

LEARNING OBJECTIVES:

After studying this chapter, the reader should be able to:

Identify the meaning of dash warning symbols.

Describe steering wheel controls, voice activation, and maintenance indicators.

Discuss the operation of head-up display, night vision, and digital electronic displays.

Describe how speedometers and odometers work.

Discuss the diagnosis of oil pressure lamp, temperature lamp, brake warning lamp, and other analog dash instruments.

Describe how a navigation system works.

Explain the operation and diagnosis of Telematics systems, backup camera, and backup sensor.

Help prepare for the ASE Electrical/Electronic Systems (A6) certification test content area "F" (Gauges, Warning Devices, and Driver Information System Diagnosis and Repair).

KEY TERMS: Analog display 323 • Backup camera 321 • Blind spot monitor 321 • Bulb test 321 • Digital display 323 • EEPROM 321 • Electromagnetic parking sensors (EPS) 321 • Global positioning system (GPS) 331 • Head-up display (HUD) 324 • Instrument panel (IP) 321 • Instrument panel cluster (IPC) 323 • Lane departure warning system (LDWS) 321 • Liquid crystal display (LCD) 327 • Light emitting diode (LED) 326 • Night vision 325 • Nonvolatile random access memory (NVRAM) 328 • OnStar 321 • Parking assist systems 321 • Steering wheel controls 322 • Stepper motor 324 • Telematics 333 • Thin-film-transistor (TFT) 327 • Virtual display 327 • Voice activation 322 • Vacuum tube fluorescent (VTF) 326 • WOW display 327

DASH WARNING SYMBOLS

PURPOSE AND FUNCTION All vehicles are equipped with warning lights on the **instrument panel (IP)** and they are often confusing to drivers. Symbols are used instead of words because they are universal in a global vehicle market. The dash warning lights are often called *telltale* lights as they are used to notify the driver of a situation or fault.

NOTE: Not all vehicles use all the symbols. Check the owner's manual or service information for the symbols used on the vehicle being checked.

BULB TEST A **bulb test** is performed when the ignition is first turned on. All of the warning lights come on as part of a self-test, and to help the driver or technician spot any warning light that may be burned out or not operating. Technicians or drivers who are familiar with what lights should light may be able to determine if one or more warning lights are not on when the ignition is first turned on. Most factory scan tools can be used

to command all of the warning lights on to help determine if one is not working.

GREEN OR WHITE SYMBOLS Green or white symbols are used to notify the driver that certain functions are working, such as the headlights are on, or the turn signals have been activated. None of the green or white symbols need any further action by the driver. The blue symbol is used to indicate the high-beam headlights are on. ● **SEE FIGURE 25–1.**

AMBER SYMBOLS Amber-colored symbols mean that a fault or an issue has occurred that may require attention soon. These can include a warning of low air pressure in a tire, or that the powertrain control module (PCM) has detected a fault in the engine that could affect the exhaust emissions.

While these issues should be addressed, there is no urgency and it is not necessary to stop the vehicle. ● **SEE FIGURE 25–2.**

RED WARNING SYMBOLS Red symbols mean that a serious fault has been detected and that immediate attention is required.

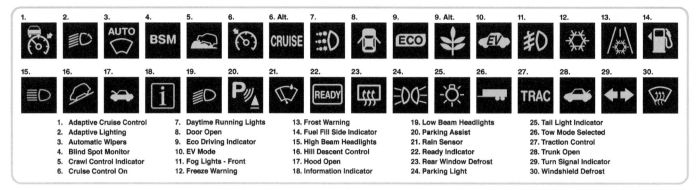

FIGURE 25–1 Green and blue symbols are used to inform the driver what is in operation.

1. Adaptive Cruise Control
2. Adaptive Lighting
3. Automatic Wipers
4. Blind Spot Monitor
5. Crawl Control Indicator
6. Cruise Control On
7. Daytime Running Lights
8. Door Open
9. Eco Driving Indicator
10. EV Mode
11. Fog Lights - Front
12. Freeze Warning
13. Frost Warning
14. Fuel Fill Side Indicator
15. High Beam Headlights
16. Hill Descent Control
17. Hood Open
18. Information Indicator
19. Low Beam Headlights
20. Parking Assist
21. Rain Sensor
22. Ready Indicator
23. Rear Window Defrost
24. Parking Light
25. Tail Light Indicator
26. Tow Mode Selected
27. Traction Control
28. Trunk Open
29. Turn Signal Indicator
30. Windshield Defrost

FIGURE 25–2 Amber warning symbols inform the driver of a potential concern.

1. Adaptive Cruise Control
2. Alert Notice
3. All Wheel Lock
4. All Wheel Steer
5. Anti-Lock Brake System Warning
6. Auto Braking Indicator
7. Auxiliary Brake Active
8. Blind Spot Indicator
9. Brake Fluid Low
10. Brake Warning Light Fault
11. Brake Pad Wear Warning
12. Brake Pad Warning - Front
13. Brake Pad Warning - Rear
14. Collision Warning Off
15. Convertible Top Warning
16. Crosswind Assist
17. Diesel Engine Preheat
18. Diesel Particulate Filter Warning
19. Dirty Air Filter
20. Electric Shift Malfunction
21. Exterior Light Fault
22. Four-Wheel-Drive Fault
23. Gas Cap Loose
24. Glow Plug
25. Headlight Range Control
26. Key Fob Battery Low
27. Key Not In Vehicle
28. Lane Departure Warning
29. Low Coolant Level Detected
30. Low Fuel
31. Malfunction Indicator Lamp (MIL)
32. Needs To Be Towed
33. Parking Brake
34. Passenger Airbag Deactivated
35. Press Brake Pedal
36. Press Clutch Pedal
37. Rear Differential Lock
38. Reduced Power
39. Service Required
40. Speed Reduced
41. Stability Control Activated
42. TPMS Warning Lamp
43. Tail Light Out
44. Theft Deterrent
45. Time for Maintenance Indicator
46. Traction Control Fault
47. Trailer Towing Mode
48. Transmission Warning
49. Washer Fluid Low
50. Water in Diesel Fuel
51. Water in Fuel Filter

An example of a serious fault that requires the driver's attention is the red brake warning light, or the oil pressure warning light. Both of these indicate that a fault has been detected and the vehicle should not be driven further until the cause has been found and corrected. ● **SEE FIGURE 25–3.**

STEERING WHEEL CONTROLS

PURPOSE **Steering wheel controls** are steering wheels that include buttons to allow the driver to control certain audio, vehicle information, and HVAC functions. The purpose of having steering wheel controls is to allow the driver to keep their hands on the wheel and their eyes on the road at all times. Steering wheels that have controls are often called *multi-function steering wheels*. ● **SEE FIGURE 25–4.**

FUNCTIONS Some of the functions on the steering wheel include the following:

- Radio controls, such as volume up and down and mode selection
- Cruise control
- Telephone answering and calling
- Voice Commands

Check service information for the specified tests and procedures to follow if the steering wheel controls do not operate as designed.

VOICE ACTIVATION

PURPOSE Most recent vehicles include *voice commands*, commonly called **voice activation**, that can be used to perform

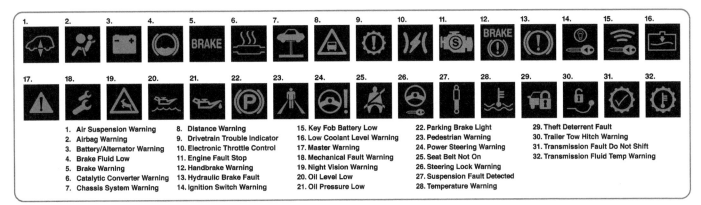

1. Air Suspension Warning
2. Airbag Warning
3. Battery/Alternator Warning
4. Brake Fluid Low
5. Brake Warning
6. Catalytic Converter Warning
7. Chassis System Warning
8. Distance Warning
9. Drivetrain Trouble Indicator
10. Electronic Throttle Control
11. Engine Fault Stop
12. Handbrake Warning
13. Hydraulic Brake Fault
14. Ignition Switch Warning
15. Key Fob Battery Low
16. Low Coolant Level Warning
17. Master Warning
18. Mechanical Fault Warning
19. Night Vision Warning
20. Oil Level Low
21. Oil Pressure Low
22. Parking Brake Light
23. Pedestrian Warning
24. Power Steering Warning
25. Seat Belt Not On
26. Steering Lock Warning
27. Suspension Fault Detected
28. Temperature Warning
29. Theft Deterrent Fault
30. Trailer Tow Hitch Warning
31. Transmission Fault Do Not Shift
32. Transmission Fluid Temp Warning

FIGURE 25–3 Red dash symbols are used to warn the driver of a fault requiring immediate action.

FIGURE 25–4 Steering wheel controls allow the driver to select a function while keeping their hands on the wheel and their eyes on the road.

FIGURE 25–5 Maintenance reminders are often messages displayed on the instrument panel informing the driver of needed service, such as the need to change the engine oil.

various functions or settings in the vehicle. Most systems include a list of phrases to use to achieve the best results.

FUNCTIONS The typical functions that can be performed using voice commands include the following:

- Phone calls with outgoing or incoming calls usually tied by Bluetooth to a cell phone in the vehicle
- Text messages can be read, and a response sent, using Bluetooth
- Climate-control settings, including desired temperature, in many vehicles
- Select source of audio, such as radio, USB, or satellite
- Navigation system, including destination and points of interest

Check service information for the specified tests and procedures to follow if the voice commands or the controls do not operate as designed.

MAINTENANCE INDICATORS

PURPOSE AND FUNCTION The purpose of the maintenance reminders is to inform the driver that routine maintenance is needed. The message can include what type of maintenance is needed, such as a minor or a major service, but most messages simply state that service is required soon or service is required now. ● **SEE FIGURE 25–5.**

RESET MAINTENANCE INDICATORS To reset the maintenance reminder light or message, check the owner's manual, service information. Or visit www.jameshalderman. com and click on "classroom content," and then select "service information" for the procedure to follow for all vehicles.

ANALOG AND DIGITAL DISPLAYS

TERMINOLOGY Vehicle information is displayed on the **instrument panel cluster (IPC)**.

- An **analog display** uses a needle to show the values, such as engine RPM
- A **digital display** uses numbers to indicate values, such as vehicle speed

Analog electromagnetic dash instruments use small electromagnetic coils that are connected to a sending unit for such things as fuel level, water temperature, and oil pressure. The sensors are the same, regardless of the type of display used. The resistance of the sensor varies with what is being measured.

STEPPER MOTOR ANALOG GAUGES
Most analog dash displays use a stepper motor to move the needle. A **stepper motor** is a type of electric motor that is designed to rotate in small steps based on the signal from a computer. This type of gauge is very accurate. A digital output is used to control stepper motors. Stepper motors are direct current motors that move in fixed steps or increments from de-energized (no voltage) to fully energized (full voltage). A stepper motor often has as many as 120 steps of motion.

A typical stepper motor uses a permanent magnet and two electromagnets. Each of the two electromagnetic windings is controlled by the computer. The computer pulses the windings and changes the polarity of the windings to cause the armature of the stepper motor to rotate a degree at a time. Each degree pulse is recorded by the computer as a "count" or "step," which explains the name given to this type of motor. ● **SEE FIGURE 25–6.**

NOTE: **Many electronic-gauge clusters are checked when the ignition is first turned on; the dash display needles** are commanded to 1/4, 1/2, 3/4, and full positions before returning to their normal readings. This self-test allows the service technician to check the operation of each individual gauge, even though replacing the entire instrument panel cluster is usually necessary to repair an inoperative gauge.

NETWORK COMMUNICATION
Many instrument panels are operated by electronic control units that communicate with the powertrain control module (PCM) for engine data, such as revolutions per minute (RPM) and engine coolant temperature (ECT). The PCM uses the voltage changes from variable-resistance sensors, such as that of the fuel gauge, to determine fuel level. The data is transmitted to the instrument cluster, as well as to the PCM through serial data lines. Because all sensor inputs are interconnected, the technician should always follow the factory recommended diagnostic procedures. ● **SEE FIGURE 25–7.**

HEAD-UP DISPLAY

PURPOSE
The **head-up display (HUD)**, also called a *heads-up display*, is a supplemental display that projects the vehicle speed and sometimes other data, such as turn-signal information, onto the windshield. The projected image looks as if it is some distance ahead, making it easy for the driver to see without having to refocus on a closer dash display. ● **SEE FIGURES 25–8 AND 25–9.**

OPERATION
On many vehicles, the brightness of the head-up display can be controlled to make it easier for the driver to see the information. The HUD unit is installed in the instrument panel (IP) and uses a mirror to project vehicle information onto the inside surface of the windshield. ● **SEE FIGURE 25–10.**

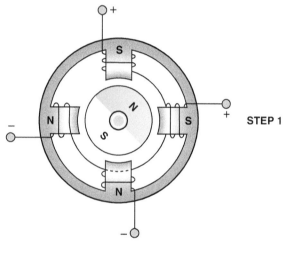

STEP 1

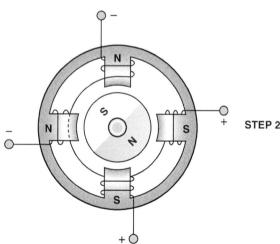

STEP 2

FIGURE 25–6 Most stepper motors use four wires that are pulsed by the computer to rotate the armature in steps.

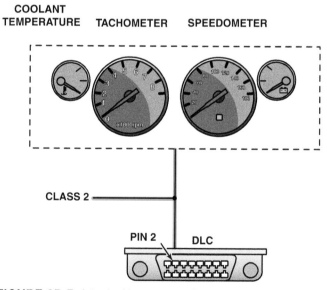

FIGURE 25–7 A typical instrument display uses data from the sensors over serial data lines to the individual gauges.

FIGURE 25–8 A typical head-up display showing zero miles per hour, which is actually projected on the windshield from the head-up display in the dash.

FIGURE 25–9 The dash-mounted control for the head-up display on this Cadillac allows the driver to move the image up and down on the windshield for best viewing.

Follow the vehicle manufacturer's recommended diagnostic and testing procedures if any faults are found with the head-up display.

NIGHT VISION

PURPOSE AND FUNCTION **Night vision** systems use a camera that is capable of observing objects in the dark to assist the driver while driving at night. The primary night-

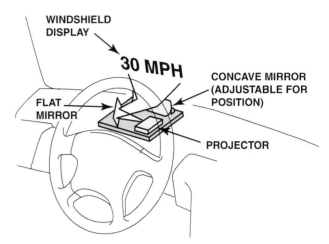

FIGURE 25–10 A typical head-up display (HUD) unit.

FIGURE 25–11 A night vision camera behind the grille of a Cadillac.

viewing illumination devices are the headlights. The night vision option uses a HUD to improve the vision of the driver beyond the scope of the headlights. Using a HUD allows the driver to keep eyes on the road and hands on the wheel for maximum safety. Besides the HUD, the night vision camera uses a special thermal imaging or infrared technology. The camera is mounted behind the grille in the front of the vehicle. ● **SEE FIGURES 25–11 AND 25–12.**

OPERATION The camera creates pictures based on the heat energy emitted by objects, rather than from light reflected on an object, as in a normal optical camera. The image looks like a black and white photo negative when hot objects (higher thermal energy) appear light or white, and cool objects appear dark or black. Other parts of the night vision system include the following:

- On/off and dimming switch. This allows the driver to adjust the brightness of the display and to turn it on or off, as needed.

- Up/down switch. The night vision HUD system has an electric tilt-adjust motor that allows the driver to adjust the image up or down on the windshield within a certain image.

FIGURE 25–12 A view of a person walking in front of a Cadillac equipped with night vision.

CAUTION: Becoming accustomed to night vision can be difficult and may take several nights to get used to looking at the HUD.

DIAGNOSIS AND SERVICE The first step when diagnosing a fault with the night vision system is to verify the concern. Check the owner's manual or service information for proper operation. For example, the Cadillac night vision system requires the following actions to function.

1. The ignition has to be in the on (run) position.
2. The Twilight Sentinel photo cell must indicate that it is dark.
3. The headlights must be on.
4. The switch for the night vision system must be on and the brightness adjusted so the image is properly displayed.

Even though the night vision system camera is protected from road debris by a grille, small stones or other debris can get past the grille and damage the lens of the camera. The operation of the night vision can also be affected by an accumulation of heavy ice or snow. If the camera is damaged, it must be replaced as an assembly because no separate parts are available. Always follow the vehicle manufacturer's recommended testing and servicing procedures.

ELECTRONIC DISPLAYS

LIGHT-EMITTING DIODE (LED) All diodes emit some form of energy during operation. The **light-emitting diode (LED)** is a semiconductor that is constructed to release energy in the form of light. Many colors of LEDs can be constructed, but the most popular are red, green, and yellow. Red is difficult to see in direct sunlight; therefore, if an LED is used, most

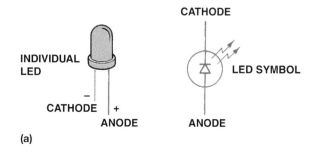

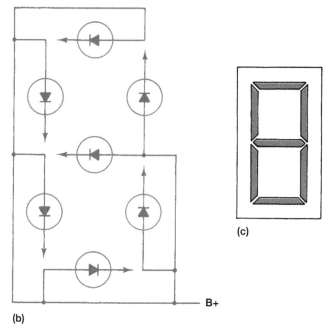

FIGURE 25–13 (a) Symbol and line drawing of a typical light-emitting diode (LED). (b) Grouped in seven segments, this array is called a seven-segment LED display with a common anode (positive connection). The dash computer toggles the cathode (negative) side of each individual segment to display numbers and letters. (c) When all segments are turned on, the number 8 is displayed.

vehicle manufacturers use yellow. LEDs can be arranged in a group of seven, which then can be used to display both numbers and letters. ● **SEE FIGURE 25–13.**

An LED display requires more electrical power than other types of electronic displays. A typical LED display requires 30 milliamperes for each *segment;* therefore, each number or letter displayed could require 210 milliamperes (0.210 ampere).

VACUUM TUBE FLUORESCENT DISPLAYS The **vacuum tube fluorescent (VTF)** display is a popular automotive and household appliance display because it is very bright and can easily be viewed in strong sunlight.

- The VTF display generates its bright light in a manner similar to that of a TV screen, where a chemical-coated light-emitting element called phosphor is hit with high-speed electrons.

- VTF displays are very bright and must be dimmed by use of dense filters or by controlling the voltage applied to the display. A typical VTF dash is dimmed to 75% brightness whenever the parking lights or headlights are turned on. Some displays use a photocell to monitor and adjust the intensity of the display during daylight viewing. Most VTF displays are green for best viewing under most lighting conditions.

LIQUID CRYSTAL DISPLAYS A **liquid crystal display (LCD)** can be arranged into a variety of forms, letters, numbers, and bar graph displays.

- LCD construction consists of a special fluid sandwiched between two sheets of polarized glass. The special fluid between the glass plates permit light to pass if a small voltage is applied to the fluid through a conductive film laminated to the glass plates.
- The light from a very bright halogen bulb behind the LCD shines through those segments of the LCD that have been polarized to let the light through, which then show numbers or letters.
- **Thin-film-transistor (TFT)** liquid-crystal display (LCD) is a type of a liquid-crystal display that uses thin-film-transistor (TFT) technology. This type of display has enhanced image qualities and contrast compared to simple light-driven LCDs.
- LCD displays can be used to present data in the form of numbers, text messages, or graphical gauges. The high-resolution screen can be programmed to show several functions, such as navigation, radio and media, as well as Google Earth 3-D graphics, and traffic data. This is in addition to the usual functions of showing speed, engine revolutions, outside temperature, and fuel level.

CAUTION: When cleaning an LCD, be careful not to push on the glass plate covering the special fluid. If excessive pressure is exerted on the glass, the display may be permanently distorted. If the glass breaks, the fluid escapes and could damage other components in the vehicle, due to its strong alkaline nature. Use only a soft, damp cloth to clean these displays.

- The major disadvantage of an LCD digital dash is that the numbers or letters are slow to react or change at low temperatures. ● **SEE FIGURE 25–14.**

WOW DISPLAY When a vehicle equipped with a digital dash is started, all segments of the electronic display are turned on at full brilliance for 1 or 2 seconds. This is commonly called the **WOW display** and is used to show off the brilliance of the display. If numbers are part of the display, the number 8 is shown, because this number uses all segments of a number display. Technicians can also use the WOW display to determine if all segments of the electronic display are functioning correctly.

FIGURE 25–14 A typical LCD navigation system display.

VIRTUAL DISPLAY

PURPOSE AND FUNCTION A **virtual display** is a dash that allows the driver to select what data is being displayed. Many vehicles are equipped with an LCD dash display that can be changed to display various functions based on the driver's preference. This allows the dash display to be totally customized to what the driver wishes to see displayed. For example, a typical display can show any four of the following:

- Coolant temperature
- Voltmeter
- Oil pressure
- Vehicle speed (speedometer)
- Engine speed (tachometer)
- Automatic transmission fluid temperature
- Tire pressures for all four tires

OPERATION The dash display is all that is really different because all the data comes to the IPC on the data bus. The only difference is that the display can be changed to meet the needs of the driver. For example, if a driver is towing a trailer, displaying the automatic transmission fluid temperature is very helpful so that overheating of the transmission is avoided. ● **SEE FIGURE 25–15.**

TOUCH SCREENS

PURPOSE A **touch screen** is a dash display, usually LCD, that allows the driver or passenger to use a finger to perform functions that are displayed on the screen.

OPERATION A capacitive touchscreen panel consists of an insulator, such as glass, coated with a transparent conductor,

FIGURE 25–15 A virtual dash on this Volvo is able to display a speedometer (left) in both analog (needle-type) and digital (number) as well as a tachometer on the right. In the center of the display, this virtual dash is displaying the navigation screen. What is displayed can be changed by the driver to match what is important to them.

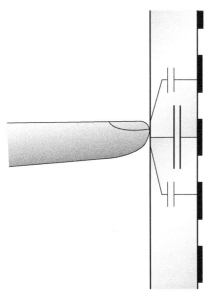

FIGURE 25–16 Schematic of a capacitive touchscreen.

such as indium tin oxide (ITO). Because the human body is also an electrical conductor, touching the surface of the screen results in a distortion of the screen's electrostatic field. The location is then sent to the controller for processing. Placing a finger near the electric fields adds conductive surface area to the capacitive system. This is measurable as a change in capacitance. The capacitance can be changed and measured at every individual point on the grid (intersection). ● **SEE FIGURE 25–16.**

TOUCH SCREEN FEEDBACK Many touch screens include feedback to the user by either using a beep or a small vibration when the screen is touched. This is called *haptic* response system and helps improve the user experience by giving immediate feedback.

SPEEDOMETERS/ODOMETERS

OPERATION Dash displays use an electric vehicle speed sensor on the output of the transmission or from the input from the wheel speed sensors (WSS). Some vehicles use the ABS wheel speed sensors to get vehicle speed, rather than a dedicated vehicle speed sensor. Many speed sensors contain a permanent magnet and generate a voltage in proportion to the vehicle speed. These speed sensors are commonly called permanent magnet (PM) generators. ● **SEE FIGURE 25–17.**

The output of a PM generator speed sensor is an AC voltage that varies in frequency and amplitude with increasing vehicle speed. The PM generator speed signal is sent to the instrument cluster electronic circuits. These specialized electronic circuits include a buffer amplifier circuit that converts the variable sine wave voltage from the speed sensor to an on/off signal that can be used by other electronic circuits to indicate a vehicle's speed. The vehicle speed is then displayed by either an electronic needle-type speedometer or by numbers on a digital display.

ODOMETERS An odometer is a dash display that indicates the total miles traveled by the vehicle. Electronic dash displays can use either an electrically driven mechanical odometer or a digital display odometer to indicate miles traveled. On mechanical-type odometers, a small electric motor, called a stepper motor, is used to turn the number wheels of a mechanical-style odometer. A pulsed voltage is fed to this stepper motor, which moves in relation to the miles traveled. ● **SEE FIGURE 25–18.**

Digital odometers use LED, LCD, or VTF displays to indicate miles traveled in the instrument cluster. Because total miles must be retained when the ignition is turned off or the battery is disconnected, a special electronic chip must be used that retains the miles traveled. These special chips are called **nonvolatile random access memory (NVRAM)**. *Nonvolatile* means that the information stored in the electronic chip is not

FIGURE 25–17 A vehicle speed sensor located in the extension housing of the transmission. Some vehicles use the wheel speed sensors for vehicle speed information.

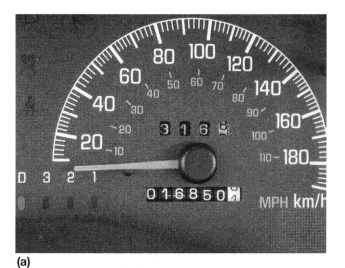

(a)

(b)

FIGURE 25–18 (a) Some odometers are mechanical and are operated by a stepper motor. (b) Many vehicles are equipped with an electronic odometer.

 **TECH TIP**

Keep the Same Overall Tire Diameter

Whenever larger (or smaller) wheels or tires are installed, the speedometer and odometer calibration are thrown off. This can be summarized as follows:

- **Larger diameter tires.** The speed showing on the speedometer is slower than the actual speed.

  The odometer reading shows fewer miles than actual.

- **Smaller diameter tires.** The speed showing on the speedometer is faster than the actual speed. The odometer reading shows more miles than actual.

To avoid speedometer and odometer issues, select a wheel/tire combination that has the same outside diameter (OD) of the original wheel/tire combination. Many newer vehicles can use the scan tool to change the tire size (from a select group of sizes) to minimize the effects of tires size change on odometer and speedometer readings.

To determine the exact effects of a replacement size wheel or tire, perform an Internet search for a tire size comparison chart.

 CASE STUDY

The Speedometer Works as if It Is a Tachometer

The owner of a Ford F-150 pickup truck complained that all of a sudden the speedometer needle went up and down with engine speed, rather than vehicle speed. In fact, the speedometer needle went up and down with engine speed, even though the gear selector was in "park" and the vehicle was not moving. After hours of troubleshooting, the service technician went back and started checking the basics and discovered that the alternator had a bad diode. The technician measured over 1 volt AC and over 10 ampere AC ripple current using a clamp-on AC/DC ammeter. Replacing the alternator restored the proper operation of the speedometer.

Summary:

- **Complaint**—Customer stated that the speedometer moves in relation to engine speed and not vehicle speed.
- **Cause**—Tests confirmed that the alternator was producing excessive AC voltage due to a bad diode.
- **Correction**—Replacing the alternator restored proper operation of the speedometer.

lost when electrical power is removed. Some vehicles use a chip called electronically erasable programmable read-only memory (EEPROM). Most digital odometers can read up to 999,999.9 miles or kilometers (km), and then the display indicates error. If the chip is damaged or exposed to static electricity, it may fail to operate and "error" may appear.

SPEEDOMETER/ODOMETER SERVICE If the speedometer and odometer fail to operate, check the following:

- Use a scan tool and monitor the vehicle speed as displayed on the scan tool. If the speed is zero, then check the output from the vehicle speed sensor. With the vehicle safely raised off the ground and supported so the drive wheels rotate, check the vehicle speed using a scan tool.

- If a scan tool is not available, disconnect the wires from the speed sensor near the output shaft of the transmission. Connect a multimeter set on AC volts to the terminals of the speed sensor, and rotate the drive wheels with the transmission in neutral. A good speed sensor should indicate approximately 2 volt AC if the drive wheels are rotated by hand.

- If the speed sensor is working, check the wiring from the speed sensor to the dash cluster. If the wiring is good, the instrument panel (IP) should be sent to a specialized repair facility.

- If the speedometer operates correctly, but the mechanical odometer does not work, the odometer stepper motor, the number wheel assembly, or the circuit controlling the stepper motor is defective. If the digital odometer does not operate, but the speedometer operates correctly, the dash cluster must be removed and sent to a specialized repair facility.

DASH GAUGES

FUEL LEVEL Fuel level gauges use a fuel tank sending unit that consists of a float attached to a variable resistor. When the fuel level changes, the resistance of the fuel level sending unit also changes. As the resistance of the tank unit changes, the dash-mounted gauge also changes to show the level of the fuel in the tank.

OIL PRESSURE The oil pressure lamp operates through use of an oil pressure sending unit, which is a switch screwed into the engine block, and grounds the electrical circuit. It lights the dash warning lamp in the event of low oil pressure, that is, 3 to 7 PSI (20 to 50 kilopascals [kPa]). Normal oil pressure is generally between 10 and 60 PSI (70 and 400 kPa). Some vehicles are equipped with variable-voltage oil pressure sensors rather than a simple pressure switch. ● **SEE FIGURE 25–19.**

To test the operation of the oil pressure warning circuit, unplug the wire from the oil pressure sending unit, usually located near the oil filter, with the ignition switch on. With the

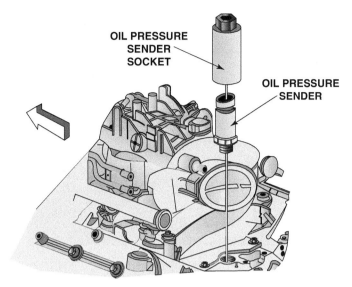

FIGURE 25–19 A sending unit socket being used to remove an oil pressure sender unit.

 CASE STUDY

Electronic Devices Cannot Swim

The owner of a Dodge minivan complained that after the vehicle was cleaned inside and outside, the temperature gauge, fuel gauge, and speedometer stopped working. The vehicle speed sensor was checked and found to be supplying a square wave signal that changed with vehicle speed. A scan tool indicated a speed, yet the speedometer displayed zero all the time. Finally, the service technician checked the body control module (BCM) to the right of the accelerator pedal and noticed that it had been wet, from the interior cleaning. Drying the BCM did not fix the problem, but a replacement BCM fixed all the problems. The owner discovered that electronic devices do not like water and that computers cannot swim.

Summary:

- **Complaint**—Customer complained that many gauges stopped working after the vehicle was cleaned.
- **Cause**—The body control module (BCM) was found to be wet and had to be replaced to fix the problems.
- **Correction**—Replacing the BCM was needed to fix the problems.

wire disconnected from the sending unit, the warning lamp should be off. If the wire is touched to a ground, the warning lamp should be on. If there is *any* doubt of the operation of the oil pressure warning lamp, always check the actual engine oil pressure, using a mechanical gauge that can be screwed

FIGURE 25–20 The arrow next to the fuel pump symbol shows which side of the vehicle the fuel cap is located.

FIGURE 25–21 A temperature gauge showing normal operating temperature between 180°F and 215°F, depending on the specific vehicle and engine.

into the opening that is left after unscrewing the oil pressure sending unit. For removing the sending unit, special sockets are available at most auto parts stores, or a 1 inch or 1 1/16 inch 6-point socket may be used for most sending units.

COOLANT TEMPERATURE The "hot" lamp, or engine coolant overheat warning lamp, warns the driver whenever the engine coolant temperature is between 248°F and 258°F (120°C and 126°C). Most vehicles use the engine coolant temperature (ECT) sensor for engine temperature gauge operation. To test this sensor, use a scan tool to verify proper engine temperature and follow the vehicle manufacturer's recommended testing procedures. ● **SEE FIGURE 25–21.**

DASH INSTRUMENT DIAGNOSIS If one or more electronic dash gauges do not work correctly, first perform a bulb check. If on a digital dash, check the WOW display that lights all segments to full brilliance whenever the ignition switch is first switched on. If all segments of the display do not operate, the entire electronic cluster must be replaced in most cases. If all segments operate during the WOW display, but do not function correctly afterward, the problem is most often a defective sensor or defective wiring to the sensor. All dash instruments, except the voltmeter, use a variable-resistance unit as a sensor for the system being monitored. The electronic dash instruments can be tested using the following procedure.

1. Use a factory or factory-level scan tool to check for any "B" (body) or "C" (chassis) diagnostic trouble codes (DTCs) that may be set and stored. If a DTC is stored, follow the service information instructions to find the root cause.

2. Use the bidirectional control features on the scan tool to actuate the dash display to see if they function. If not, the replacement of the entire IPC may be required.

3. If just one gauge works when commended, but does not work in the vehicle, unplug the wire(s) from the sensor for the function being tested. For example, if the oil pressure gauge is not functioning correctly, unplug the wire connector at the oil pressure sending unit.

4. With the sensor wire unplugged, turn the ignition switch on and wait until the WOW display stops. The display for the affected unit should show either fully lighted segments, or no lighted segments, depending on the make of the vehicle and the type of sensor.

Always follow the specified testing and diagnostic procedures found in service information for the vehicle being tested.

NAVIGATION AND GPS

PURPOSE AND FUNCTION The **global positioning system (GPS)** uses 24 satellites in orbit around the earth to provide signals for navigation devices. GPS is funded and controlled by the U.S. Department of Defense (DOD). While the system can be used by anyone with a GPS receiver, it was designed for and is operated by the U.S. military. ● **SEE FIGURE 25–22.**

NAVIGATION SYSTEM PARTS AND OPERATION Navigation systems use the GPS satellites for basic location information. The navigation controller uses other sensors, including a digitized map to display the location of the vehicle.

- **GPS satellite signals.** Signals from at least three satellites are needed to locate the vehicle.

- **Yaw sensor.** This sensor is often used inside the navigation unit to detect movement of the vehicle during cornering. This sensor is also called a *"g" sensor* because it measures force; 1 g is the force of gravity.

- **Vehicle speed sensor.** A yaw sensor is a device, usually a chip that measures the movement of a vehicle around its vertical axis. This sensor input is used by the navigation controller to determine the speed and distance the vehicle

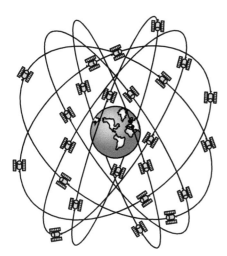

FIGURE 25–22 Global positioning systems use 24 satellites in high earth orbit whose signals are picked up by navigation systems. The navigation system computer then calculates the location based on the position of the satellite overhead.

FIGURE 25–23 A typical GPS display screen showing the location of the vehicle.

travels. This information is compiled and compared to the digital map and GPS satellite inputs to locate the vehicle.

■ **Audio output/input.** Voice-activated factory units use a built-in microphone at the center top of the windshield and the audio speakers speech output.

Navigation systems include the following components.

1. Screen display ● **SEE FIGURE 25–23.**
2. GPS antenna
3. Navigation control unit, usually with map information on a DVD or memory card.

The memory card includes street names and the following information:

1. Points of interest (POI), including automated teller machines (ATMs), restaurants, schools, colleges, museums, shopping mall, and airports, as well as vehicle dealer locations.

 FREQUENTLY ASKED QUESTION

What Is Navigation-Enhanced Climate Control?

Some vehicles use data from the navigation system to help control the automatic climate control system. Data about the location of the vehicle includes:

• Time and date. This information allows the automatic climate control system to determine where the sun is located.
• Direction of travel. The navigation system can also help the climate control system determine the direction of travel.

As a result of the input from the navigation system, the automatic climate control system can control cabin temperature, in addition to various other sensors in the vehicle. For example, if the vehicle is traveling south in the late afternoon in July, the climate control system could assume that the passenger side of the vehicle is warmed more by the sun than the driver's side, and could increase the airflow to the passenger side to help compensate for the additional solar heating.

2. Business addresses and telephone numbers, including hotels and restaurants. (If the telephone number is listed in the business telephone book, it can usually be displayed on the navigation screen. If the telephone number of the business is known, the location can be displayed.)

Note: Private residences or cellular telephone numbers are not included in the database of telephone numbers stored on the navigation system memory card.

3. Turn-by-turn directions to addresses that are selected by:

■ Points of interest (POI)

■ Typed in using a keyboard shown on the display

The navigation unit then often allows the user to select the fastest way to the destination, as well as the shortest way, or assists in how to avoid toll roads. ● **SEE FIGURE 25–24.**

DIAGNOSIS AND SERVICE For the correct functioning of the navigation system, three inputs are needed.

■ Location

■ Direction

■ Speed

The navigation system uses the GPS satellite and map data to determine a location. Direction and speed are determined by the navigation computer from inputs from the satellite, plus the yaw sensor and vehicle speed sensor. The following symptoms may occur and be a customer complaint.

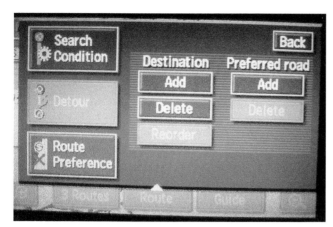

FIGURE 25–24 A typical navigation display showing various options. Some systems do not allow access to these if the vehicle is in gear and/or moving.

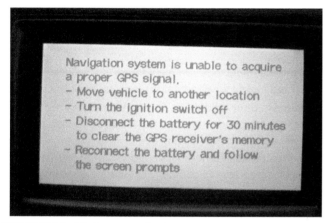

FIGURE 25–25 A screen display of a navigation system that is unable to acquire usable signals from GPS satellites.

Knowing how the system malfunctions helps to determine the most likely cause.

- If the vehicle symbol jumps down the road, a fault with the vehicle speed (VS) sensor input is usually indicated.
- If the symbol rotates on the screen, but the vehicle is not being driven in circles, a fault with the yaw sensor or yaw sensor input to the navigation controller is likely.
- If the symbol goes off course and shows the vehicle on a road that it is not on, a fault with the GPS antenna is the most common reason.
- Most factory-installed navigation systems use a GPS antenna inside the rear back glass or under the rear package shelf. If a metalized window tint is applied to the rear glass, the signal strength from the GPS satellites can be reduced. If the customer concern includes inaccurate or nonfunctioning navigation, check for window tint.

Sometimes the navigation system itself displays a warning that views from the satellite are not being received. Always follow the displayed instructions. ● **SEE FIGURE 25–25.**

TELEMATICS

WHAT IS TELEMATICS? **Telematics** is an interconnected system that combines telecommunications (cellular systems) and GPS navigation satellite system technology. Telematics is a method of monitoring a vehicle by combining a GPS system with on-board diagnostic systems. It is possible to record and map exactly where a vehicle is located and how fast it's traveling.

A typical telematics system includes:

- Telecommunications, such as cell phone communication
- Vehicle technologies, such as self-diagnostics
- Electrical sensors, instrumentation, wireless communications
- Multimedia and Internet

Telematics, such as OnStar, can be a manufacturer-installed system or an aftermarket-installed system. The systems offer a variety of features, including the following:

1. **Vehicle tracking**—Used by the GPS, an onboard telematics system can track the vehicle location.

2. **User-based Insurance (UBI)**—Insurance companies want to control their cost, so many offer a discount if the vehicle owner allows a tracking device to be installed on their vehicle. This unit usually plugs into the data link connector (DLC) under the dash for its power and ground, as well as some of the data that is available on the data stream, such as throttle position and vehicle speed.

Note: This type of add-on tracking devices are sometimes responsible for some false diagnostic trouble codes. The devices should be removed when diagnosing any suspected vehicle network faults.

3. **Security Services**—Services, such as vehicle-collision notification and emergency services, are the core telematics features found on all systems. When an airbag deploys or other sensors are triggered, the vehicle-collision notification sends an alert to a telematics command center. An operator then contacts the vehicle's occupants through the telematics system's built-in cellular modem to assess the situation. Once the occupants confirm there's been an accident—or if the operator doesn't get a response—the command center dispatches emergency-response personnel. A telematics system also pinpoints the vehicle's location using GPS.

4. **Convenience Services**—Telematics systems offer various convenience features to help vehicle owners out of a non-emergency jam, or just make their lives easier. The system can remotely unlock a car's door after you've accidentally left the keys inside, for example. A telematics system can also flash a car's lights and sound the horn in a crowded parking lot to help you find it.

TELEMATICS SYSTEMS

There are many brand names for what is considered to be a telematics system, including:

- Acura Link
- Audi Connect
- Blue Link (Hyundai)
- BMW Assist
- Care Track (Volvo)
- Car-Net (VW)
- CUE (Cadillac)
- Honda Link
- InControl (Jaguar)
- IntelliLink (Buick and GMC)
- Lexus Enform
- Mbrace (Mercedes)
- OnStar (Chevrolet and others)
- Porsche Car Connect
- Starlink (Subaru)
- Sync (Ford)
- T Connect (Toyota)
- UVO (Kia)

PARTS AND OPERATION

One example of a telematics system is OnStar. OnStar was first introduced in 1996 as an option on some Cadillac models. This is a system that includes the following functions.

1. Cellular telephone
2. Global positioning antenna and computer

The cellular telephone is used to communicate with the driver from advisors at service centers. The advisor at the service center is able to see the location of the vehicle as transmitted from the GPS antenna and computer system in the vehicle on a display.

OnStar does not display the location of the vehicle to the driver unless the vehicle is also equipped with a navigation system. Unlike most navigation systems, the OnStar system requires a monthly fee. The driver interface unit is a group of three buttons mounted on the inside rearview mirror and a hands-free cellular telephone. ● **SEE FIGURE 25–26.**

The OnStar system includes the following features, which can vary, depending on the level of service desired and cost per month.

- **Automatic notification of airbag deployment.** If the airbag is deployed, the advisor is notified immediately and attempts to call the vehicle. If there is no reply, or if the occupants report an emergency, the advisor contacts emergency services and gives them the location of the vehicle.
- **Emergency services.** If the red button is pushed, OnStar immediately locates the vehicle and contacts the nearest emergency service agency.

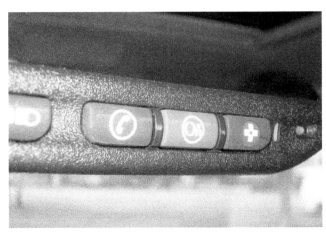

FIGURE 25–26 The three-button OnStar control is located on the inside rearview mirror. The left button (telephone handset icon) is pushed if a hands-free cellular call is to be made. The center button is depressed to contact an OnStar advisor and the right emergency button is used to request that help be sent to the vehicle's location.

- **Stolen vehicle location assistance.** If a vehicle is reported stolen, a call-center advisor can track the vehicle.
- **Remote door unlock.** An OnStar advisor can send a cellular telephone message to the vehicle to unlock the vehicle, if needed.
- **Roadside assistance.** When called, an OnStar advisor can locate a towing company or locate a provider who can bring gasoline or change a flat tire.
- **Accident assistance.** An OnStar advisor is able to help with the best way to handle an accident. The advisor can supply a step-by-step checklist of the things that should be done, plus call the insurance company, if desired.
- **Remote horn and lights.** The OnStar system is tied into the lights and horn circuits, so an advisor can activate them, if requested, to help the owner locate the vehicle in a parking lot or garage.
- **Vehicle diagnosis.** Because the OnStar system is tied to the PCM, an OnStar advisor can help with diagnosis if there is a fault detected. The system works as follows:

  - The malfunction indicator light (MIL) (check engine) comes on to warn the driver that a fault has been detected. The driver can depress the OnStar button to talk to an advisor and ask for a diagnosis.
  - The OnStar advisor sends a signal to the vehicle requesting the status from the powertrain control module, as well as the controller for the antilock brakes and the airbag module.
  - The vehicle then sends any diagnostic trouble codes (DTCs) to the advisor. The advisor can then inform the driver about the importance of the problem and give advice as to how to resolve the problem.

DIAGNOSIS AND SERVICE The OnStar system can fail to meet the needs of the customer if any of the following conditions occur.

1. Lack of cellular telephone service in the area
2. Poor global positioning system (GPS) signals, which can prevent an OnStar advisor from determining the position of the vehicle
3. Transport of the vehicle by truck or ferry so that it is out of contact with the GPS satellite for an advisor to properly track the vehicle

If all of the above are normal and the problem still exists, follow service information diagnostic and repair procedures. If a new vehicle communication interface module (VCIM) is installed in the vehicle, the electronic serial number (ESN) must be tied to the vehicle. Check service information instructions for the exact procedures to follow.

BACKUP CAMERA

PARTS AND OPERATION A backup camera is used to display the area at the rear of the vehicle in a screen display on the dash, or in the inside rear-view mirror when the gear selector is placed in reverse. Backup cameras are also called:

- *Reversing cameras*
- *Rearview cameras*

Backup cameras are different from normal cameras because the image displayed on the dash is flipped, so it is a mirror image of the scene at the rear of the vehicle. This reversing of the image is needed because the driver and the camera are facing in opposite directions. Backup cameras were first used in large vehicles with limited rearward visibility, such as motor homes. Many vehicles equipped with navigation systems today include a backup camera for added safety while reversing. ● **SEE FIGURE 25–27.**

The backup camera contains a wide-angle or fisheye lens to give the largest viewing area. Most backup cameras are pointed downward so that objects on the ground, as well as walls, are displayed. ● **SEE FIGURE 25–28.**

REAR CAMERA IMAGE ISSUES The quality of the image projected on the display may be not be clear if any of the following conditions occur:

- Dark conditions
- Damage to the rear camera or the rear of the vehicle, affecting the aiming of the camera
- Dirt, mud, ice, or snow blocking the camera view
- Excessive high or low temperature that could affect the camera or lens
- Glare caused by the sun or a nearby bright light source, such as headlights of another vehicle.

FIGURE 25–27 A dash display on a Ford F-150 pickup truck showing the backup camera image on the left side of the screen and a bird's eye view on the right side showing the vehicle next to the truck on the right and the handicap parking stop on the left. The bird's eye view is created by combining the images from the front, side mirror, and rear cameras together to create the virtual image.

FIGURE 25–28 A typical fisheye-type backup camera usually located near the center on the rear of the vehicle near the license plate.

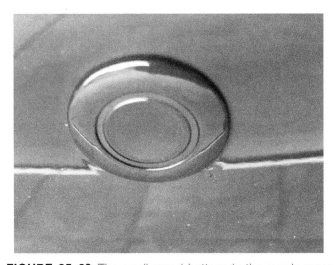

FIGURE 25–29 The small round buttons in the rear bumper are ultrasonic sensors used to sense distance to an object.

DIAGNOSIS AND SERVICE Faults in the backup camera system can be related to the camera itself, the display, or the connecting wiring. The main input to the display unit comes from the transmission range switch, which signals the backup camera when the transmission is shifted into reverse.

To check the transmission range switch, perform the following:

1. Check if the backup (reverse) lights function when the gear selector is placed in reverse with the key on, engine off (KOEO).

2. Check that the transmission/transaxle is fully engaged in reverse when the selector is placed in reverse.

Most of the other diagnosis involves visual inspection:

1. Check the backup camera for damage.
2. Check the screen display for proper operation.
3. Check that the wiring from the rear camera to the body is not cut or damaged.
4. Always follow the vehicle manufacturer's recommended diagnosis and repair procedures.

SUMMARY

1. Most digital and analog (needle-type) dash gauges use variable-resistance sensors.
2. Dash warning lamps are called telltale lamps.
3. Many electronically operated or computer-operated dash indicators require that a service manual be used to perform accurate diagnosis.
4. Permanent magnet (PM) generators produce an AC signal and are used for vehicle speed and wheel speed sensors.
5. Navigation systems and warning systems are part of the driver information system on many vehicles.

REVIEW QUESTIONS

1. How does a stepper motor analog dash gauge work?
2. What do the colors of the dash symbols mean?
3. Night vision is used to detect what type of objects?
4. What is meant by the term telematics?
5. How does a navigation system determine the location of the vehicle?

CHAPTER QUIZ

1. Which color symbol requires immediate attention by the driver?
   a. Red
   b. Amber
   c. Green
   d. White
2. Technician A says that LCDs may be slow to work at low temperatures. Technician B says that an LCD dash display can be damaged if pressure is exerted on the front of the display during cleaning. Which technician is correct?
   a. Technician A only
   b. Technician B only
   c. Both Technicians A and B
   d. Neither Technician A nor B
3. Technician A says that metal-type tinting can affect the navigation system. Technician B says most telematic systems require a monthly payment for full use of their system. Which technician is correct?
   a. Technician A only
   b. Technician B only
   c. Both Technicians A and B
   d. Neither Technician A nor B
4. Technician A says that the data displayed on the dash can come from the powertrain control module (PCM). Technician B says that a virtual display can be set to show what the driver wishes to see displayed.
   a. Technician A only
   b. Technician B only
   c. Both Technicians A and B
   d. Neither Technician A nor B
5. Which of the following is NOT included on a vehicle using a steering wheel control system?
   a. Power window control
   c. Radio controls
   b. Cruise control
   d. HVAC functions
6. What is the minimum oil pressure required to keep the oil pressure warning light turned OFF?
   a. 10 PSI (70 kPa)
   b. 3 to 7 PSI (20 to 50 kPA)
   c. 60 PSI (400 kPa)
   d. None of these
7. Where are the total miles traveled stored in a vehicle equipped with an electronic odometer?
   a. LCD
   c. LED
   b. NVRAM
   d. VTF

8. A backup camera can show a poor quality image on the interior display if what occurs?
   a. Ice or snow on the camera
   b. Bright lights aimed at the camera
   c. Extreme temperatures
   d. Any of the above

9. The vehicle symbol jumps down the road on a vehicle equipped with an on-board navigation. What is the most likely cause?
   a. A defective yaw sensor
   b. A defective vehicle speed (VS) sensor or a fault in the circuits
   c. A fault with the GPS antenna
   d. Metalized window tint

10. What can a telematics system do?
    a. Track a vehicle
    b. Operate the horn and lights
    c. Communicate for convenience services
    d. Any of the above

chapter
26

SECURITY AND ANTI-THEFT SYSTEMS

LEARNING OBJECTIVES:

After studying this chapter, the reader should be able to:

Describe the purpose and function of a security system.

Explain how an immobilizer system works and identify its major components.

Compare immobilizer systems in Chrysler, Ford, and General Motors vehicles.

Explain how to diagnose a fault with an immobilizer system.

This chapter will help prepare for the ASE Electrical/Electronic Systems (A6) certification test content area "G" (Body Electrical Systems Diagnosis and Repair).

KEY TERMS : Key fob 339 • Radio frequency identification (RFID) 339 • Remote keyless entry (RKE) 339 • Transceiver 339 • Transponder 339

VEHICLE SECURITY SYSTEMS

PURPOSE AND FUNCTION The purpose and function of a security system on a vehicle is to prevent the unauthorized use (theft) of the vehicle. This function is accomplished by installing the following locks:

 FREQUENTLY ASKED QUESTION

What Is Content Thief Protection?

Content Thief protection is a security system that includes sensors that detect glass breakage or entry into the vehicle and sounds an alarm when these occur. The purpose of the content theft system is to prevent the theft of objects inside the vehicle and sound an alarm when someone enters the vehicle without using the proper remote or key. Most systems use a motion detector for content theft protection, as well as switches in the doorjambs, trunk, and hood that provide an input signal to the control module. Some antitheft systems are more complex and also have electronic sensors that trigger the alarm if glass is broken or a change in battery current draw occurs. These sensors also provide an input signal to the control module, which may be a separate antitheft unit, or may be incorporated into the PCM or BCM. ● **SEE FIGURE 26–1**.

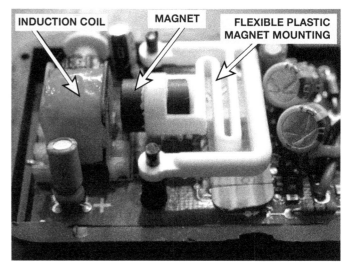

FIGURE 26–1 A shock sensor used in alarm and antitheft systems. If the vehicle is moved, the magnet moves relative to the coil, inducing a small voltage that triggers the alarm.

1. A lock on the doors to help prevent unauthorized entry to the interior of the vehicle.
2. A lock for the ignition so a key is needed to crank and start the engine and unlock the steering wheel, starting in 1970.

While these locks have worked, vehicles can still be easily stolen if access to the interior and the ignition switch is accessible. It is the purpose and function of an immobilizer system to prevent the vehicle from being started if the correct ignition key is not used, even if an intruder gets access to the interior of the vehicle and tries to use a key that fits the lock cylinder.

POSSIBLE IMMOBILIZER CAUSED FAULTS Faults with the immobilizer system can be the cause of one of the following conditions depending on the exact make and model of a vehicle:

- No crank condition (the starter motor does not operate)
- The engine cranks but does not start (fuel disabled in most vehicles)
- The engine starts but then almost immediately stalls.

Therefore, if a customer concern involves any of these situations, a fault in the immobilizer system is a possible cause, rather than a fault with the ignition or fuel system.

IMMOBILIZER SYSTEMS

NORMAL OPERATION A vehicle equipped with an immobilizer system operates normally as follows:

- When a valid key is used, and is rotated to the start position, the engine cranks and starts and the immobilizer symbol on the dash flashes on and off for about two seconds, and then goes off. ● **SEE FIGURE 26–2**.
- If there is a fault with an invalid key, the dash symbol flashes continuously and the engine does not start or, if it does crank and start, the engine does not continue to run.

IMMOBILIZER SYSTEM PARTS Most security systems today use a **Radio Frequency Identification (RFID)** security system, which has two main components:

1. A **key fob** is the object that is a decoration on a key ring and usually contains a transmitter used to unlock a vehicle. While the **remote keyless entry (RKE)** part of the key fob has a battery to power the transmitter, the RFID chip part of the key fob does not require a battery to function. The **transponder** is mounted in the key or the body of

FIGURE 26–2 The security system symbol used on a Ford. The symbol varies by make, model, and year, so check service information to determine what symbol is used on the vehicle being diagnosed.

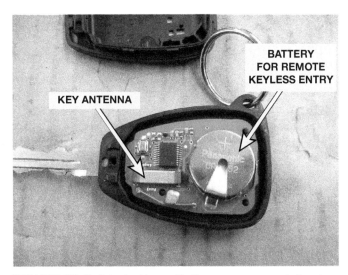

FIGURE 26–3 A typical key with the cover removed showing the battery used to power the door lock and the antenna used for the immobilizer system.

the key fob. A transponder has an antenna, which consists of a coil of wire, as well as a circuit board containing the processing electronics and data memory. ● **SEE FIGURE 26–3**.

2. The transponder key has the transponder electronics integrated in its plastic body. It consists of the following components:

- A microchip contains the unique internal identification (ID) number. To prevent an unauthorized scanning of the ID number, the code changes with each transfer and uses several million different coding possibilities. ● **SEE FIGURE 26–4**.
- The coil antenna in the key consists of a copper coil wound up in a ring case and an integrated circuit to create a high-frequency alternating voltage for the inductive coupling. Through inductive (electromagnetic) coupling, the data from the key is transferred to the immobilizer module.
- Another coil is installed around the lock cylinder and connected to the control module of the immobilizer system. This coil transfers and receives all data signals to and from the immobilizer control module using the coil antenna/transceiver. It does not need to be reprogrammed to the immobilizer system in case of replacement.
- A **transceiver** is inside the vehicle and receives the signal transmitted by the transponder in the key. A "transceiver" functions as both a reviewer and a transmitter. The transceiver is usually mounted on the steering column assembly. The antenna for the transceiver is a coil of wire mounted within the plastic ring that mounts around the lock cylinder. ● **SEE FIGURE 26–5**.

IMMOBILIZER SYSTEM OPERATION When the ignition key in inserted, the transceiver sends out an electromagnetic energy pulse. This energy pulse is received by the coil inside

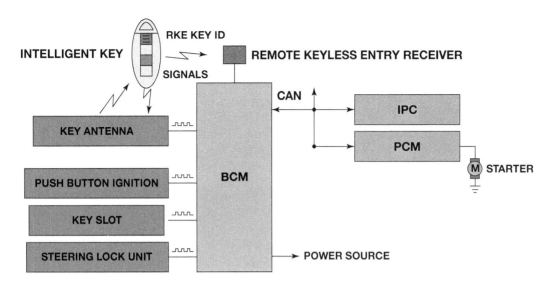

INTELLIGENT KEY

RKE KEY ID

SIGNALS

REMOTE KEYLESS ENTRY RECEIVER

KEY ANTENNA

PUSH BUTTON IGNITION

KEY SLOT

STEERING LOCK UNIT

BCM

CAN

IPC

PCM

M STARTER

POWER SOURCE

FIGURE 26–4 The remote keyless entry is used to unlock the doors as well as create the signals to the powertrain control module (PCM) used to control the starter motor and/or the fuel system and the warning lamp on the instrument panel cluster (IPC).

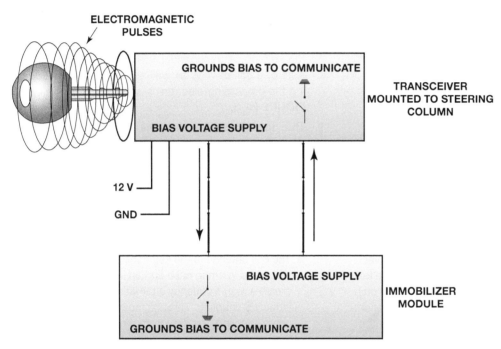

ELECTROMAGNETIC PULSES

GROUNDS BIAS TO COMMUNICATE

BIAS VOLTAGE SUPPLY

TRANSCEIVER MOUNTED TO STEERING COLUMN

12 V

GND

BIAS VOLTAGE SUPPLY

IMMOBILIZER MODULE

GROUNDS BIAS TO COMMUNICATE

FIGURE 26–5 A typical immobilizer circuit showing the communication between the key and the transceiver. The transceiver then communicates with the immobilizer module over data lines.

the key transponder, which creates a voltage. The information or data in the magnetic pulses is in the form of a frequency modulated signal.

A typical immobilizer system consists of transponder key, coil antenna, key reminder switch, separate immobilizer module, PCM, and security light. Most immobilizer systems work as follows:

- The key identification (ID) numbers are stored in a nonvolatile memory of the immobilizer module. At each start, the module compares the ID number of the transponder key used with those stored in the memory.

- If the verification has been successful, the immobilizer module sends a request signal to the PCM to compare the key ID number with the numbers registered in the PCM.

- Each immobilizer module has its unique code word that is stored in the PCM. After the verification of the ID number,

the immobilizer module requests the code word from the PCM.

- The immobilizer module controls the starter circuit and the security light and signals the PCM to activate fuel injection and ignition when the ID number and code word verification have been successful.

- The signals between immobilizer module and PCM are transmitted via a serial data line.

SECURITY LIGHT OPERATION Normal operation of the security light includes a self-test and flashes a few times, then goes out. However, if a fault is detected, the security light continues to flash and the engine may not start. If a fault occurs with the immobilizer system when the engine is running, then the security light comes on, but the engine is not shut off, as this condition is not a theft attempt.

Do Not Have Other Keys Near

Whenever diagnosing an immobilizer system, keep other key fobs away from the area. If another key fob were close, it could be transmitting a signal that is not recognized by the vehicle and the security system could prevent proper vehicle operation. Even having other metal objects near the key can affect the strength of the electromagnetic pulses and could interfere with the immobilizer system and prevent it from working as designed. ● **SEE FIGURE 26–6.**

PRECAUTIONS To avoid damage to the key, do not allow the key to:

- Be dropped onto a hard surface
- Get wet
- Be exposed to any kind of magnetic field
- Be exposed to high temperatures on places, such as the top of the dash under direct sunlight.

A system malfunction may occur if any of the following items are touching the key or are near the key head.

- A metal object
- Spare keys or keys for other vehicles equipped with an immobilizer system
- An electronic device, such as cards with magnetic strips

TYPICAL IMMOBILIZER CIRCUITS The diagnostic process involved with positively identifying the defective security system component can be quick and accurate. At the transceiver, check for power, ground, and proper communication on data transmission lines. ● **SEE FIGURE 26–7.**

CAUTION: Do not leave the key in the ignition, as this often keeps the immobilizer system alive and drains the vehicle battery. If leaving the vehicle, take the key out of the ignition and place it 15 feet (5 meters) away to help avoid possible issues.

CHRYSLER IMMOBILIZER SYSTEM

Beginning in 1998, Chrysler started a security system known as the **Sentry Key Immobilizer System (SKIS)**. When an attempt to start a vehicle arises, the onboard computer sends out a radio-frequency (RF) signal that is read by the electronic transponder chip embedded in the key. The transponder then returns a unique signal back to the SKIM, giving it the okay signal for the vehicle to start and continue to run. This all happens in under a second, and is completely transparent to the vehicle driver. For additional security, two preprogrammed keys are needed in order to register additional keys into the system. In the event of the loss of all keys, special programming equipment is needed to register new keys into the system.

CHRYSLER SELF-PROGRAMMING ADDITIONAL SENTRY KEYS (REQUIRES TWO ORIGINAL KEYS)
Quick steps:

STEP 1 Purchase a blank key and have it cut to fit the lock cylinder.

STEP 2 Insert the original key #1 into the ignition and turn to ON.

STEP 3 Wait five seconds and turn the key to OFF.

STEP 4 Immediately insert the original key #2 into the ignition and turn to ON.

STEP 5 Wait 10 seconds for the SKIS indicator in the dash to start to flash.

STEP 6 Turn the ignition off, insert the new blank key, and turn the ignition back on.

STEP 7 Once the SKIS light stops flashing and turns off, the new key is programmed.

FORD PATS SYSTEM

Ford uses a responder key for their antitheft system, which is called the **Passive Antitheft System (PATS)**.

(a)　　　　(b)　　　　(c)

FIGURE 26–6 (a) Avoid using a key where the key ring is over the top of the key, which can interfere with the operation of the immobilizer system. (b) Do not angle another key upward from the key being used to help prevent interference with the magnetic field used to energize the key. (c) Do not have the keys from another vehicle near the key being used.

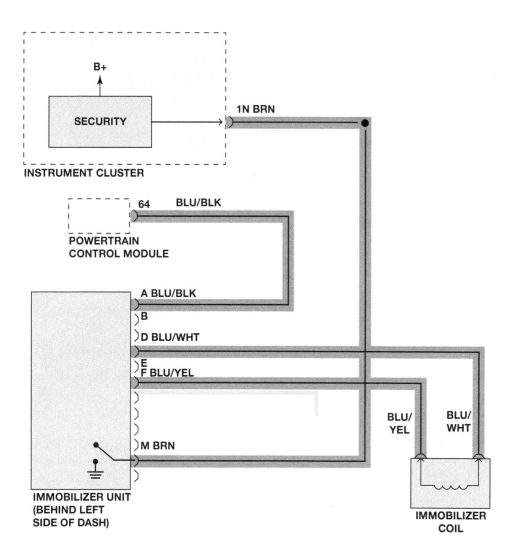

B+

SECURITY

INSTRUMENT CLUSTER

1N BRN

64 BLU/BLK

POWERTRAIN
CONTROL MODULE

A BLU/BLK
B
D BLU/WHT
E
F BLU/YEL

M BRN

IMMOBILIZER UNIT
(BEHIND LEFT
SIDE OF DASH)

BLU/
YEL

BLU/
WHT

IMMOBILIZER
COIL

FIGURE 26–7 Check service information for the exact wiring diagram (schematic) for the vehicle being tested. Highlighting the wires and noting their color helps when following the specified testing procedures.

FORD PROGRAMMING FOR ADDITIONAL (PATS) KEYS

This procedure works only if two or more programmed ignition keys are available. The steps include:

STEP 1 Insert the first programmed ignition key into the ignition lock cylinder. Turn the ignition switch from the LOCK to RUN position (ignition switch must stay in the run position for one second). Turn the ignition switch to the LOCK position and remove the ignition key from the ignition lock cylinder.

STEP 2 Within five seconds of turning the ignition switch to the LOCK position, insert the second programmed ignition key into the ignition lock cylinder. Turn the ignition switch from the LOCK to RUN position (ignition switch must stay in the RUN position for one second). Turn the ignition switch to the LOCK position and remove the second ignition key from the ignition lock cylinder.

STEP 3 Within five seconds of turning the ignition switch to the LOCK position, insert a new unprogrammed ignition key into the ignition lock cylinder. Turn the ignition switch from the LOCK to RUN position (the ignition switch must stay in the RUN position for one second). Turn the ignition switch to the LOCK

position and remove the ignition key from the ignition lock cylinder. The new ignition key should now be programmed. To program additional key(s), repeat the key programming procedure from Step 1.

GENERAL MOTORS ANTITHEFT SYSTEM

The type of antitheft system used on General Motors vehicles has included many different systems, starting with an antitheft system that used a resistor pellet in the ignition key. If the key fit the lock cylinder and the resistance was the correct value, the engine would crank and start. This system was called the **Vehicle Antitheft System** or **(VATS)**. A special tester was required to test this system. ● **SEE FIGURE 26–8**.

Newer systems include the **Passkey I** and **Passkey II**, which also use a resistor pellet in the ignition key. **Passlock I**, **Passlock II**, and **Passlock truck** systems use a Hall-effect sensor and magnets in the lock cylinder with a conventional key. ● **SEE FIGURE 26–9**.

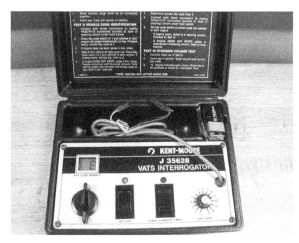

FIGURE 26–8 A special tool is needed to diagnose a General Motors VATS security system and special keys that contain a resistor pellet.

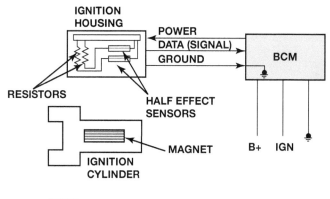

FIGURE 26–9 The Passlock series of General Motors security systems uses a conventional key. The magnet is located in the ignition lock cylinder and triggers the Hall-effect sensors.

Passkey III systems use a transponder embedded into the head of the key, which is stamped "SK3." Most of the systems disable the starter, and the fuel injectors, but Passlock I disables fuel after the engine starts, and the security light then flashes. Due to the various systems, service information must be used and followed to diagnose and repair a fault in these systems.

TESTING IMMOBILIZER SYSTEMS

DIAGNOSTIC STEPS Most vehicle manufacturers recommend a series of steps that a technician should follow when diagnosing a fault with the immobilizer system.

STEP 1 **Verify the Customer Concern**—A fault with the immobilizer system often causes the engine to not start or start, then stall. Faults can also be intermittent because many systems "time out" after 20 minutes if an error occurs, and then works normally after the wait period. A "no-start" condition can also occur that is not associated with the immobilizer system and should be handled using normal diagnostic procedures as specified by the vehicle manufacturer for a no-start condition.

STEP 2 **Visual Inspection**—Most vehicle manufacturers specify that the first step after the customer concern has been verified is that a visual inspection be performed. A visual inspection includes checking the security light status. A typical security light status includes the following:

- **Normal**—The security dash lamp comes on for two to five seconds for a bulb check when the ignition is turned on, then goes out.
- **Tamper mode**—The security lamp flashes about once per second if the system detects a bad key,

lock cylinder, or security-related wiring problem. The engine does not start or, if it does start, does not continue to run.
- **Fail enable mode**—If a fault with the security system occurs when the vehicle is running, the security light remains on, but the immobilizer system is disabled because it is apparently not a theft attempt. Therefore, the engine starts and runs as normal, except that the security warning light on the dash is on all the time.

Check for the presence of aftermarket accessories, such as an add-on remote starter system. These systems require the use of a spare key that is held near the lock cylinder, thereby allowing the engine to start

---

TECH TIP

Look for DTCs in "Body" and "Chassis"

Whenever diagnosing a customer concern with the immobilizer system, check for diagnostic trouble codes (DTCs) under chassis and body systems. A global or generic scan tool that can read only "P" codes is not suitable for diagnosing many faults with the immobilizer system. Engine or emission control-type codes are "P" codes, whereas module communications are "U" codes. These are most often found when looking for DTCs under chassis or body systems. Chassis-related codes are labeled "C" and body system-related codes are labeled "B" codes and these can cause an immobilizer issue if they affect a sensor that is used by the system.
● **SEE FIGURE 26–10.**

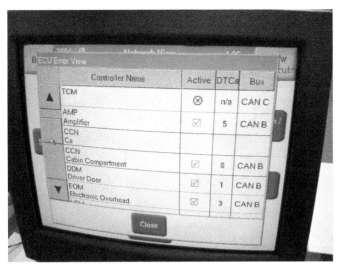

FIGURE 26–10 Scan tools, such as this factory tool being used on a BMW, are capable of many diagnostic functions that can help the technician zero in on the root cause of a problem.

FIGURE 26–11 After checking for stored diagnostic trouble codes (DTCs), the wise technician checks service information for any technical service bulletins (TSBs) that may relate to the vehicle being serviced.

using a remote control. A fault with the aftermarket system could have an effect on the proper operation of the immobilizer system.

STEP 3 **Check for Diagnostic Trouble Codes**—Use a factory or enhanced factory-level aftermarket scan tool and retrieve diagnostic trouble codes. Check service information for the exact codes for the vehicle being checked. ● **SEE CHART 26–1** for some sample DTCs and their meaning.

STEP 4 **Check for Technical Service Bulletins**—Technical service bulletins (TSBs) are issued by vehicle and aftermarket manufacturers to inform technicians of a situation or technical problem and give the corrective steps and a list of parts needed to solve the problem. Any diagnostic trouble codes should be retrieved before looking at the technical service bulletins because many bulletins include what DTCs may or may not be present. ● **SEE FIGURE 26–11**.

While some of these TSBs concern minor problems covering few vehicles, many contain very helpful

solutions to hard-to-find problems that cover many vehicles. TSBs can also be purchased through aftermarket companies that are licensed and available on a website. Visit the National Automotive Service Task Force (NASTF) website (www.NASTF.org) for a list of the Web addresses for all vehicle manufacturers' sites where the full text of TSBs can be purchased directly. Factory TSBs can often save the technician many hours of troubleshooting.

STEP 5 **Perform Pinpoint Tests**—Following the specified diagnostic steps found in service information, check for the system for proper voltage at each of the components.

DTC	DESCRIPTION OF FAULT
P0513	Incorrect immobilizer key
P1570	Fault in antenna detected
P1517	Reference code not compatible with ECM
P1572	Communications failure with ECM
B2957	Security system data circuit low
B2960	Security system data wrong but valid

CHART 26–1

Sample diagnostic trouble codes for an immobilizer system. These codes vary by make, model, and year of manufacture, so check service information for the exact vehicle being diagnosed.

TECH TIP

Use an Antenna Coil Tester to Save Time

The procedure for testing the antenna coil using an antenna tester includes the following:

- Insert the ignition key into the ignition lock cylinder. On some vehicles, inserting the key causes the transceiver to activate. On some vehicles, the key must be rotated to the ON position.
- Use a handheld tester to check that the transceiver is able to transmit a signal. A coil detector is used to check the immobilizer coil that surrounds the lock cylinder. The coil is working normally if the LED lights up as the key is inserted into the lock cylinder. If the coil is defective, this can save the technician a lot of time troubleshooting the system. The coil can be replaced without the need to reprogram the keys. ● **SEE FIGURE 26–12**.

STEP 6 Determine the Root Cause—By following the specified diagnostic routine, the root cause can often be determined. If a module is replaced, it usually must be programmed to accept the ignition key and this can be a huge problem if a used module is chosen instead of a new one. Always check service information for the exact procedure to follow.

STEP 7 Verify the Repair—After the repairs or service procedures have been performed, verify that the system is working as designed. If needed, operate the vehicle under the same conditions that it was when the customer concern was corrected to verify the repair. Document the work order and return the vehicle to the customer in clean condition.

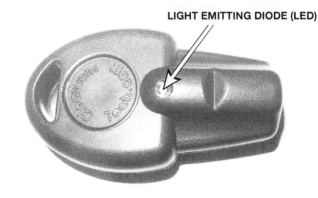

LIGHT EMITTING DIODE (LED)

FIGURE 26–12 Immobilizer coil detectors can be found online by searching for immobilizer transponder coil detector.

SUMMARY

1. Faults with the immobilizer system can cause one of the following conditions:
   - No crank condition (the starter motor does not operate)
   - The engine cranks but does not start
   - The engine starts but then almost immediately stalls.
2. Most security systems today use a Radio Frequency Identification (RFID) security system.
3. The transponder key has the transponder electronic integrated in its plastic handle where it is encapsulated in a glass or plastic body.
4. The transceiver is usually mounted to the steering column assembly. The antenna for the transceiver is a coil of wire mounted within the plastic ring that mounts around the lock cylinder.
5. A typical immobilizer system consists of transponder key, coil antenna, key reminder switch, separate immobilizer module, PCM, and security light.
6. Normal operation of the security light includes a self-test and flashes a few times then goes out. However, if a fault is detected, the security light will continue to flash and the engine may not start.
7. To diagnose an immobilizer system, use a factory or enhanced factory-level aftermarket scan tool and retrieve diagnostic trouble codes, then follow the specified diagnostic procedures.

REVIEW QUESTIONS

1. What faults will an immobilizer system cause?
2. How is the security information transferred from the key to the vehicle?
3. A typical immobilizer system consists of what parts?
4. To avoid damage to the key, what precautions are needed to be performed?
5. An antenna coil tester is used to test what part of the immobilizer system?

CHAPTER QUIZ

1. What is the purpose and function of an immobilizer system?
   a. To prevent entry inside the vehicle
   b. Only allows the use of the ignition key that is properly matched to the lock cylinder
   c. Prevents the vehicle from starting or running if the correct key is not used
   d. Requires that the driver enter a password to start the vehicle

2. What does the battery in the key fob power?
   a. The shock sensor
   b. The remote keyless entry (RKE)
   c. The immobilizer circuit
   d. Both the remote keyless entry and the immobilizer circuit

3. What can occur if the immobilizer system is not working as designed?
   a. No crank condition (the starter motor does not operate)
   b. The engine cranks but does not start
   c. The engine starts but then almost immediately stalls
   d. Any of the above

4. An immobilizer fault may occur if the _____.
   a. the key is dropped onto a hard surface
   b. the key gets wet
   c. the key is exposed to any kind of magnetic field
   d. Any of the above

5. How is data transmitted between the key and the steering column (lock cylinder)?
   a. By inductive coupling
   b. By electrical contacts inside the lock cylinder
   c. Transmitted from the key to the vehicle using the battery inside the key
   d. Transferred from the key to the BCM using a small transmitter in the key

6. A typical Ford immobilizer system is called _____.
   a. VATS
   b. PATS
   c. Passlock
   d. SKIS

7. A typical Chyrsler immobilizer system is called _____.
   a. VATS
   b. PATS
   c. Passlock
   d. SKIS

8. The security dash lamp comes on for two to five seconds and then goes out. This indicates what condition?
   a. A fault has been detected in the key transponder
   b. A fault has been detected in the wiring near the ignition lock cylinder
   c. Normal security light operation
   d. The system has entered tamper mode

9. Immobilizer diagnostic trouble codes are often found under what area?
   a. Engine-related "P" codes
   b. Body-related "B" codes
   c. Chassis-related "C" codes
   d. Any of the above

10. If an immobilizer-related fault occurs, what symbol is likely to be displayed on the dash?
    a. "IM"
    b. A padlock symbol
    c. The "check engine" light
    d. The "service engine soon" light

chapter 27

AIRBAG AND PRETENSIONER CIRCUITS

LEARNING OBJECTIVES:

After studying this chapter, the reader should be able to:

Explain how safety belts and retractors function.

Explain the operation of front airbags.

Describe the procedures to diagnose and repair common faults in airbag systems.

Explain how the passenger presence system works.

Describe how seat and side curtain airbags function.

Describe the data recorded by an event data recorder when an airbag is deployed.

This chapter will help prepare for the ASE Suspension and Steering (A4) certification test content area "B" (Steering Systems Diagnosis and Repair).

KEY TERMS: Airbag 349 • Arming sensor 349 • Clockspring 352 • Deceleration sensors 351 • Dual-stage airbags 351 • EDR 359 • Integral sensors 351 • Occupant detection system (ODS) 357 • Passenger presence system (PPS) 357 • Pretensioners 347 • SAR 349 • SIR 349 • Squib 349 • SRS 349

SAFETY BELTS AND RETRACTORS

SAFETY BELTS Safety belts are used to keep the driver and passengers secured to the vehicle in the event of a collision. Most safety belts include three-point support and are constructed of nylon webbing about 2 inches (5 cm) wide. The three support points include two points on either side of the seat for the belt over the lap and one crossing over the upper torso, which is attached to the "B" pillar or seat back. Every crash consists of three types of collisions.

Collision 1: The vehicle strikes another vehicle or object.

Collision 2: The driver and/or passengers hit objects inside the vehicle if unbelted.

Collision 3: The internal organs of the body hit other organs or bones, which causes internal injuries.

If a safety belt is being worn, the belt stretches, absorbing a lot of the impact, thereby preventing collision with other objects in the vehicle and reducing internal injuries. ● **SEE FIGURE 27–1**.

BELT RETRACTORS Safety belts are also equipped with one of the following types of retractors.

■ Emergency locking retractors, which lock the position of the safety belt in the event of a collision or rollover

■ Emergency and web speed-sensitive retractors, which allow freedom of movement for the driver and passenger,

but lock if the vehicle is accelerating too fast or if the vehicle is decelerating too fast

● **SEE FIGURE 27–2** for an example of an inertia-type seat belt locking mechanism.

SAFETY BELT LIGHTS AND CHIMES All late-model vehicles are equipped with a safety belt warning light on the dash and a chime that sounds if the belt is not fastened. ● **SEE FIGURE 27–3**.

Some vehicles intermittently flash the reminder light and sound a chime until the driver, and sometimes the front passenger, fasten their safety belts.

PRETENSIONERS A **pretensioner** is an explosive (pyrotechnic) device that is part of the seat belt retractor assembly and tightens the seat belt as the airbag is being deployed. The purpose of the pretensioning device is to force the occupant back into position against the seat back and to remove any slack in the seat belt. ● **SEE FIGURE 27–4**.

CAUTION: The seat belt pretensioner assemblies must be replaced in the event of an airbag deployment. Always follow the vehicle manufacturer's recommended service procedure. Pretensioners are explosive devices that could be ignited if voltage is applied to the terminals. Do not use a jumper wire or powered test light around the seat belt latch wiring. Always follow the vehicle manufacturer's recommended test procedures.

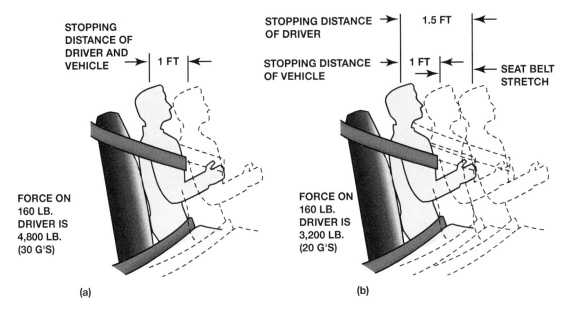

FIGURE 27–1 (a) Safety belts are the primary restraint system. (b) During a collision, the stretching of the safety belt slows the impact to help reduce bodily injury.

STOPPING DISTANCE OF DRIVER AND VEHICLE

1 FT

FORCE ON 160 LB. DRIVER IS 4,800 LB. (30 G'S)

(a)

STOPPING DISTANCE OF DRIVER

1.5 FT

STOPPING DISTANCE OF VEHICLE

1 FT

SEAT BELT STRETCH

FORCE ON 160 LB. DRIVER IS 3,200 LB. (20 G'S)

(b)

CRASH SCENARIO WITH A VEHICLE STOPPING IN ONE FOOT DISTANCE FROM A SPEED OF 30 MPH.

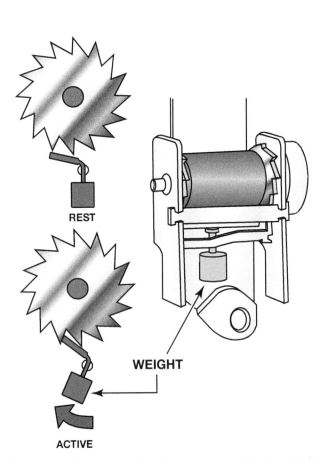

REST

WEIGHT

ACTIVE

FIGURE 27–2 Most safety belts have an inertia-type mechanism that locks the belt in the event of rapid movement.

FIGURE 27–3 A typical safety belt warning light.

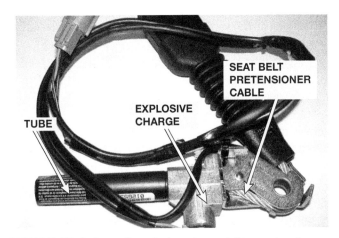

SEAT BELT PRETENSIONER CABLE

EXPLOSIVE CHARGE

TUBE

FIGURE 27–4 A small explosive charge in the pretensioner forces the end of the seat belt down the tube, which removes any slack in the seat belt.

FRONT AIRBAGS

PURPOSE AND FUNCTION **Airbag** passive restraints are designed to cushion the driver (or passenger, if the passenger side is so equipped) during a frontal collision. The system consists of one or more nylon bags folded up in compartments located in the steering wheel, dashboard, interior panels, and/or side pillars of the vehicle. During a crash of sufficient force, pressurized gas instantly fills the airbag and then deploys out of the storage compartment to protect the occupant from serious injury. These airbag systems may be known by many different names, including the following:

1. **Supplemental restraint system (SRS)**
2. **Supplemental inflatable restraints (SIR)**
3. **Supplemental air restraints (SAR)**

Most airbags are designed to supplement the safety belts in the event of a collision, and front airbags are meant to be deployed only in the event of a frontal impact within 30 degrees of center. Front (driver and passenger side) airbag systems are *not* designed to inflate during side or rear impact. The force required to deploy a typical airbag is approximately equal to the force of a vehicle hitting a wall at over 10 MPH (16 km/h).

The force required to trigger the sensors within the system prevents accidental deployment if curbs are hit or the brakes are rapidly applied. The system requires a substantial force to deploy the airbag to help prevent accidental inflation.

PARTS INVOLVED ● **SEE FIGURE 27–5** for an overall view of the parts included in a typical airbag system.

The parts include:

1. Sensors
2. Airbag (inflator) module
3. Clockspring wire coil in the steering column
4. Control module
5. Wiring and connectors

OPERATION To cause inflation, the following events must occur.

■ To cause a deployment of the airbag, two sensors must be triggered at the same time. The **arming sensor** is used to provide electrical power, and a *forward* or *discriminating sensor* is used to provide the ground connection.

■ The arming sensor provides the electrical power to the airbag heating unit, called a **squib**, inside the inflator module.

■ The squib uses electrical power and converts it into heat for ignition of the propellant used to inflate the airbag.

■ Before the airbag can inflate, however, the squib circuit also must have a ground provided by the forward or the discriminating sensor. In other words, two sensors (arming and forward sensors) *must* be triggered *at the same time* before the airbag is deployed. ● **SEE FIGURE 27–6.**

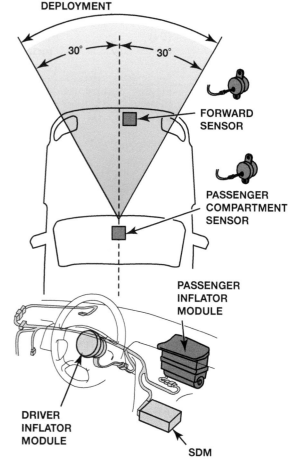

FIGURE 27–5 A typical airbag system showing many of the components. The SDM is the "sensing and diagnostic module" and includes the arming sensor, as well as the electronics that keep checking the circuits for continuity and the capacitors that are discharged to deploy the airbags.

TYPES OF AIRBAG INFLATORS There are two different types of inflators used in airbags.

1. **Solid fuel.** This type uses sodium azide pellets, and when ignited, generates a large quantity of nitrogen gas that quickly inflates the airbag. This was the first type used and is still commonly used in driver and passenger side airbag inflator modules. ● **SEE FIGURE 27–7.** The squib is the electrical heating element used to ignite the gas-generating material, usually sodium azide. It requires about 2 amperes of current to heat the heating element and ignite the inflator.

2. **Compressed gas.** Commonly used in passenger side airbags and roof-mounted systems, the compressed gas system uses a canister filled with argon gas, plus a small percentage of helium at 3,000 PSI (435 kPa). A small igniter ruptures a burst disc to release the gas when energized. The compressed gas inflators are long cylinders that can be installed inside the instrument panel, seat back, door panel, or along any side rail or pillar of the vehicle. ● **SEE FIGURE 27–8.**

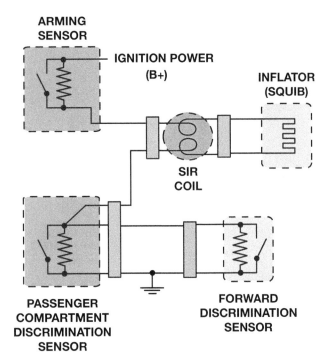

FIGURE 27–6 A simplified airbag deployment circuit. Note that both the arming sensor and at least one of the discriminating sensors must be activated at the same time. The arming sensor provides the power, and either one of the discriminating sensors can provide the ground for the circuit.

FIGURE 27–7 The inflator module is being removed from the airbag housing. The squib, inside the inflator module, is the heating element that ignites the pyrotechnic gas generator that rapidly produces nitrogen gas to fill the airbag.

Once the inflator is ignited, the nylon bag quickly inflates (in about 30 milliseconds or 0.030 second) with nitrogen gas generated by the inflator. During an actual frontal collision accident, the driver is being thrown forward by the driver's own momentum toward the steering wheel. The strong nylon bag inflates at the same time. Personal injury is reduced by the spreading of the stopping force over the entire upper-body region. The normal collapsible steering column remains in operation and collapses in a collision when equipped with an airbag system. The bag is equipped with two large side

FIGURE 27–8 This figure shows a deployed side curtain airbag on a training vehicle.

vents that allow the bag to deflate immediately after inflation, once the bag has cushioned the occupant in a collision.

TIMELINE FOR AIRBAG DEPLOYMENT Following are the times necessary for an airbag deployment in milliseconds (each millisecond is equal to 0.001 second or 1/1,000 of a second).

1. Collision occurs: 0.0 millisecond
2. Sensors detect collision: 16 milliseconds (0.016 second)
3. Airbag is deployed and seam cover rips: 40 milliseconds (0.040 second)
4. Airbag is fully inflated: 100 milliseconds (0.100 second)
5. Airbag deflated: 250 milliseconds (0.250 second)

In other words, an airbag deployment occurs and is over in about a quarter of a second. ● **SEE FIGURE 27–9.**

SENSOR OPERATION All three sensors are basically switches that complete an electrical circuit when activated. The sensors are similar in construction and operation, and the *location* of the sensor determines its name. All airbag sensors are rigidly mounted to the vehicle and *must* be mounted with the arrow pointing toward the front of the vehicle to ensure that the sensor can detect rapid forward deceleration.

There are three basic styles (designs) of airbag sensors.

1. **Magnetically retained gold-plated ball sensor.** This sensor uses a permanent magnet to hold a gold-plated steel ball away from two gold-plated electrical contacts. ● **SEE FIGURE 27–10.**
   If the vehicle (and the sensor) stops rapidly enough, the steel ball is released from the magnet because the inertia force of the crash was sufficient to overcome the magnetic pull on the ball and then makes contact with the two gold-plated electrodes. The steel ball only remains in contact with the electrodes for a relatively short time because the steel ball is drawn back into contact with the magnet.

2. **Rolled up stainless-steel ribbon-type sensor.** This sensor is housed in an airtight package with nitrogen

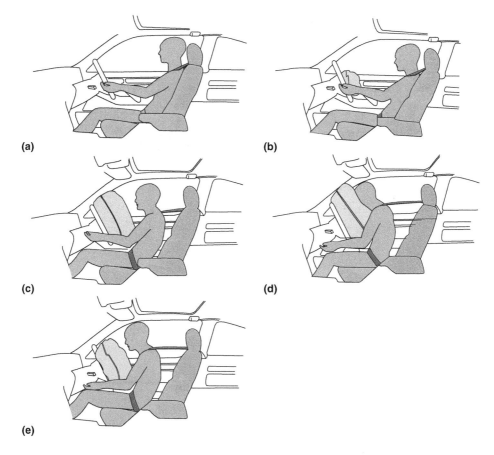

(a)

(b)

(c)

(d)

(e)

FIGURE 27–9 The sequence of deployment of a typical airbag includes the following:

(a). The driver is sitting in a normal driving position.

(b). About 16 milliseconds (0.016 second) after an impact with a solid object that results in a rapid deceleration causing the triggering of the airbag.

(c). About 40 milliseconds after impact, the airbag deploys and the driver's body is moving forward.

(d). At 100 milliseconds after impact, the airbag has fully inflated and the driver's body is being slowed by the airbag and by the seat belt.

(e). Starting at about 120 milliseconds, the driver's body will start to move back toward the seat and the airbag will be deflated by 250 milliseconds after the impact.

gas inside to prevent harmful corrosion of the sensor parts. If the vehicle (and the sensor) stops rapidly, the stainless-steel roll "unrolls" and contacts the two gold-plated contacts. Once the force is stopped, the stainless-steel roll rolls back into its original shape. ● **SEE FIGURE 27–11**.

3. **Integral sensor.** Some vehicles use electronic **deceleration sensors** built into the inflator module, called **integral sensors**. For example, General Motors uses the term *sensingand diagnostic module* (SDM) to describe their integrated sensor/module assembly. These units contain an accelerometer-type sensor that measures the rate of deceleration and, through computer logic, determines if the airbags should be deployed. ● **SEE FIGURE 27–12**.

TWO-STAGE AIRBAGS Two-stage airbags, often called advanced airbags or smart airbags, use an accelerometer-type of sensor to detect force of the impact. This type of sensor

 **SAFETY TIP**

Dual-Stage Airbag Caution

Many vehicles are equipped with **dual-stage airbags** (two-stage airbags) that actually contain two separate inflators, one for less severe crashes and one for higher-speed collisions. These systems are sometimes called smart airbag systems because the accelerometer-type sensor used can detect how severe the impact is and deploy one or both stages. If one stage is deployed, the other stage is still active and could be accidentally deployed. A service technician cannot tell by looking at the airbag whether both stages have deployed. Always handle a deployed airbag as if it has not been deployed, and take all precautions necessary to keep any voltage source from getting close to the inflator module terminals.

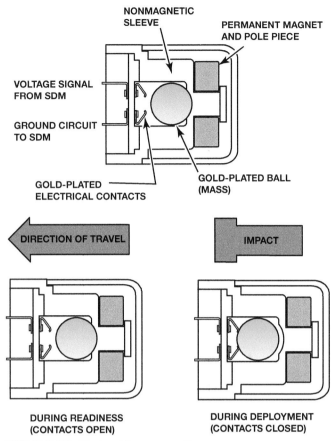

FIGURE 27–10 An airbag magnetic sensor.

VOLTAGE SIGNAL FROM SDM

GROUND CIRCUIT TO SDM

NONMAGNETIC SLEEVE

PERMANENT MAGNET AND POLE PIECE

GOLD-PLATED ELECTRICAL CONTACTS

GOLD-PLATED BALL (MASS)

DIRECTION OF TRAVEL

IMPACT

DURING READINESS (CONTACTS OPEN)

DURING DEPLOYMENT (CONTACTS CLOSED)

measures the actual amount of deceleration rate of the vehicle and is used to determine whether one or both elements of a two-stage airbag should be deployed.

- **Low-stage deployment.** This lower-force deployment is used if the accelerometer detects a low-speed crash.

- **High-stage deployment.** This stage is used if the accelerometer detects a higher-speed crash or a more-rapid deceleration rate.

- **Both low- and high-stage deployment.** Under severe high-speed crashes, both stages can be deployed.

  ● **SEE FIGURE 27–13.**

WIRING Wiring and connectors are very important for proper identification and long life. Airbag-related circuits have the following features.

- All electrical wiring connectors and conduit for airbags are colored yellow.

- To ensure proper electrical connection to the inflator module in the steering wheel, a coil assembly is used in the steering column. This coil is a ribbon of copper wires that operates much like a window shade when the steering wheel is rotated. As the steering wheel is rotated, this coil, usually called a **clockspring**, prevents the lack of continuity between the sensors and the inflator assembly that might result from a horn-ring type of sliding conductor.

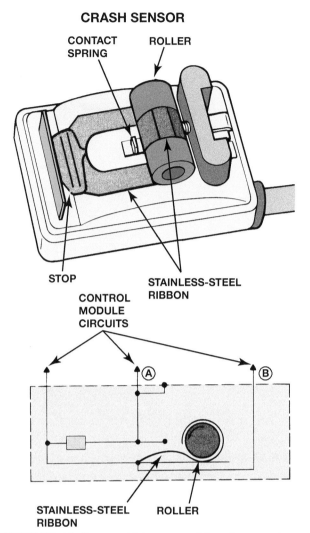

CRASH SENSOR

CONTACT SPRING

ROLLER

STOP

STAINLESS-STEEL RIBBON

CONTROL MODULE CIRCUITS

STAINLESS-STEEL RIBBON

ROLLER

FIGURE 27–11 Some vehicles use a ribbon-type crash sensor.

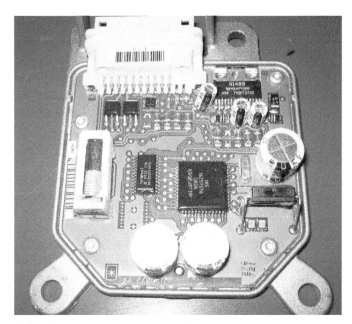

FIGURE 27–12 A sensing and diagnostic module that includes an accelerometer.

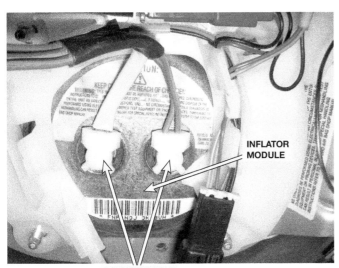

CONNECTORS
TO EACH STAGE

INFLATOR
MODULE

FIGURE 27–13 A driver's side airbag showing two inflator connectors. One is for the lower-force inflator and the other is for the higher-force inflator. Either can be ignited, or both at the same time if the deceleration sensor detects a severe impact.

- Inside the yellow plastic airbag connectors are gold-plated terminals that are used to prevent corrosion.
  - ● **SEE FIGURE 27–14**.

Most airbag systems also contain a diagnostic unit that often includes an auxiliary power supply, which is used to provide the current to inflate the airbag if the battery is disconnected from the vehicle during a collision. This auxiliary power supply normally uses capacitors that are discharged through the squib of the inflation module. When the ignition is turned off, these capacitors are discharged. Therefore, after a few minutes, an airbag system does not deploy if the vehicle is hit while parked.

AIRBAG DIAGNOSIS TOOLS AND EQUIPMENT

SELF-TEST PROCEDURE The electrical portion of airbag systems is constantly checked by the circuits within the airbag-energizing power unit or through the airbag controller. The electrical airbag components are monitored by applying a small-signal voltage from the airbag controller through the various sensors and components. Each component and sensor uses a resistor in parallel with the load or open sensor switch for use by the diagnostic signals. If continuity exists, the testing circuits measure a small voltage drop. If an open or short circuit occurs, a dash warning light is lighted and a possible diagnostic trouble code (DTC) is stored. Follow exact manufacturer's recommended procedures for accessing and erasing airbag DTCs.

Diagnosis and service of airbag systems usually require some or all of the following items.

- Digital multimeter (DMM)
- Airbag simulator, often called a load tool
- Scan tool
- Shorting bar or shorting connector(s)
- Airbag system tester
- Vehicle-specific test harness
- Special wire repair tools or connectors, such as crimp-and-seal weatherproof connectors
  - ● **SEE FIGURE 27–15**.

CAUTION: Most vehicle manufacturers specify that the negative battery terminal be removed when testing or working around airbags. Be aware that a memory saver device used to keep the computer and radio memory alive can supply enough electrical power to deploy an airbag.

PRECAUTIONS Take the following precautions when working with or around airbags.

1. Always follow all precautions and warning stickers on vehicles equipped with airbags.
2. Maintain a safe working distance from all airbags to help prevent the possibility of personal injury in the unlikely event of an unintentional airbag deployment.
   - Side impact airbag: 5 inches (13 cm) distance
   - Driver front airbag: 10 inches (25 cm) distance
   - Passenger front airbag: 20 inches (50 cm) distance
3. In the event of a collision in which the bag(s) is deployed, the inflator module *and* all sensors usually must be replaced to ensure proper future operation of the system.
4. Avoid using a self-powered test light around the yellow airbag wiring. Even though it is highly unlikely, a self-powered test light could provide the necessary current to accidentally set off the inflator module and cause an airbag deployment.

 TECH TIP

Pocket the Ignition Key to Be Safe

When replacing any steering gear, such as a rack-and-pinion steering unit, be sure that no one accidentally turns the steering wheel. If the steering wheel is turned without being connected to the steering gear, the airbag wire coil (clockspring) can become off center. This can cause the wiring to break when the steering wheel is rotated after the steering gear has been replaced. To help prevent this from occurring, simply remove the ignition key from the ignition and keep it in your pocket while servicing the steering gear.

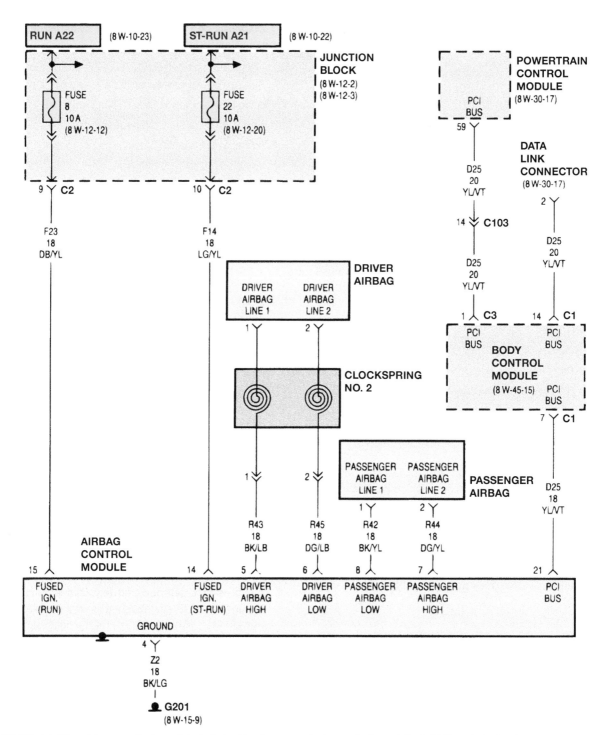

FIGURE 27–14 The airbag control module is linked to the powertrain control module (PCM) and the body control module (BCM) on this Chrysler system. Notice the airbag wire connecting the module to the airbag through the clockspring. Both power, labeled "driver airbag high," and ground, labeled "driver airbag low," are conducted through the clockspring.

5. Use care when handling the inflator module section when it is being removed from the steering wheel. Always hold the inflator away from your body.

6. If handling a deployed inflator module, always wear gloves and safety glasses to avoid the possibility of skin irritation from the sodium hydroxide dust, which is used as a lubricant on the bag(s), that remains after deployment.

7. Never jar or strike a sensor. The contacts inside the sensor may be damaged, preventing the proper operation of the airbag system in the event of a collision.

8. When mounting a sensor in a vehicle, make certain that the arrow on the sensor is pointing toward the front of the vehicle. Also be certain that the sensor is securely mounted.

FIGURE 27–15 An airbag diagnostic tester. Included in the plastic box are electrical connectors and a load tool that substitutes for the inflator module during troubleshooting.

FREQUENTLY ASKED QUESTION

What Are Smart Airbags?

Smart airbags use the information from sensors to determine the level of deployment. Sensors used include the following:

- **Vehicle speed (VS) sensors.** This type of sensor has a major effect on the intensity of a collision. The higher the speed is, the greater is the amount of impact force.
- **Seat belt fastened switch.** If the seat belt is fastened, as determined by the seat belt buckle switch, the airbag system deploys accordingly. If the driver or passenger is not wearing a seat belt, the airbag system deploys with greater force compared to when the seat belt is being worn.
- **Passenger seat sensor.** The sensor in the seat on the passenger's side determines the force of deployment. If there is not a passenger detected, the passenger side airbag does not deploy on the vehicle equipped with a passenger seat sensor system.

AIRBAG SYSTEM SERVICE

DIS-ARMING The airbags should be disarmed (temporarily disconnected) whenever performing service work on any of the following locations.

- Steering wheel
- Dash or instrument panel
- Glove box (instrument panel storage compartment)

Check service information for the exact procedure, which usually includes the following steps.

STEP 1 Disconnect the negative battery cable.

STEP 2 Remove the airbag fuse (has a yellow cover).

STEP 3 Disconnect the yellow electrical connector located at the base of the steering column to disable the driver's-side airbag.

STEP 4 Disconnect the yellow electrical connector for the passenger-side airbag.

This procedure is called "disabling airbags" in most service information. Always follow the vehicle manufacturer's specified procedures.

DIAGNOSTIC AND SERVICE PROCEDURE Airbag system components and their location in the vehicle vary according to system design, but the basic principles of testing are the same as for other electrical circuits. Use service information to determine how the circuit is designed and the correct sequence of tests to be followed.

- Some airbag systems require the use of special testers. The built-in safety circuits of such testers prevent accidental deployment of the airbag.
- If such a tester is not available, follow the recommended alternative test procedures specified by the manufacturer.
- Access the self-diagnostic system and check for DTC records.
- The scan tool is needed to access the data stream on most systems.

SELF-DIAGNOSIS All airbag systems can detect system electrical faults and, if found, disables the system and notifies the driver through an airbag warning lamp in the instrument cluster. Depending on circuit design, a system fault may cause the warning lamp to fail to illuminate, remain lit continuously, or flash. Some systems use a tone generator that produces an audible warning when a system fault occurs, or if the warning lamp is inoperative.

The warning lamp should illuminate with the ignition key on and engine off as a bulb check. If not, the diagnostic module is likely disabling the system. If the airbag warning light remains on, the airbags may or may not be disabled, depending on the specific vehicle and the fault detected. Some warning lamp circuits have a timer that extinguishes the lamp after a few seconds. The airbag system generally does not require service unless there is a failed component. However, a steering wheel–mounted airbag module is routinely removed and replaced in order to service switches and other column-mounted devices.

KNEE AIRBAGS Some vehicles are equipped with knee airbags usually on the driver's side. Use caution if working under the dash and always follow the vehicle manufacturer's specified service procedures.

Why Change Knee Bolsters If Switching to Larger Wheels?

Larger wheels and tires can be installed on vehicles, but the powertrain control module (PCM) needs to be reprogrammed so the speedometer and other systems that are affected by a change in wheel/tire size can work effectively. When 20 inch wheels are installed on General Motors trucks or sport utility vehicles (SUVs), GM specifies that replacement knee bolsters be installed. Knee bolsters are the padded area located on the lower part of the dash where a driver or passenger's knees would hit in the event of a front collision. The reason for the need to replace the knee bolsters is to maintain the crash testing results. The larger 20 inch wheels tend to be forced further into the passenger compartment in the event of a front-end collision. Therefore, to maintain the frontal crash rating standard, the larger knee bolsters are required.

WARNING: Failure to perform the specified changes when changing wheels and tires could result in the vehicle not being able to provide occupant protection as designed by the crash test star rating that the vehicle originally achieved.

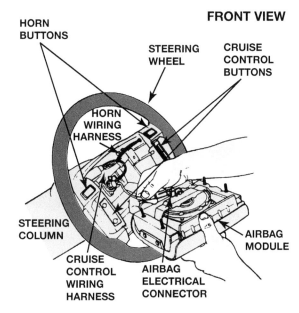

FRONT VIEW

FIGURE 27–16 After disconnecting the battery and the yellow connector at the base of the steering column, the airbag inflator module can be removed from the steering wheel and the yellow airbag electrical connector at the inflator module be disconnected.

DRIVER SIDE AIRBAG MODULE REPLACEMENT

For the specific model being serviced, carefully follow the procedures provided by the vehicle manufacturer to disable and remove the airbag module. Failure to do so may result in serious injury and extensive damage to the vehicle. Replacing a discharged airbag is costly. The following procedure reviews the basic steps for removing an airbag module. Do not substitute these general instructions for the specific procedure recommended by the manufacturer.

1. Turn the steering wheel until the front wheels are positioned straight ahead. Some components on the steering column are removed only when the front wheels are straight.

2. Switch the ignition off and disconnect the negative battery cable, which cuts power to the airbag module.

3. Once the battery is disconnected, wait as long as recommended by the manufacturer before continuing. When in doubt, wait at least 10 minutes to make sure the capacitor is completely discharged.

4. Loosen and remove the nuts or screws that hold the airbag module in place. On some vehicles, these fasteners are located on the back of the steering wheel. On other vehicles, they are located on each side of the steering wheel. The fasteners may be concealed with plastic finishing covers that must be pried off with a small screwdriver to access them.

5. Carefully lift the airbag module from the steering wheel and disconnect the electrical connector. Connector location varies: Some are below the steering wheel behind a plastic trim cover; others are at the top of the column under the module. ● **SEE FIGURES 27–16 AND 27–17**.

6. Store the module pad side up in a safe place where it can not be disturbed or damaged while the vehicle is being serviced. Do not attempt to disassemble the airbag module. If the airbag is defective, replace the entire assembly.

When installing the airbag module, make sure the clockspring is correctly positioned to ensure module-to-steering-column continuity. ● **SEE FIGURE 27–18**.

Always route the wiring exactly as it was before removal. Also, make sure the module seats completely into the steering wheel. Secure the assembly using new fasteners, if specified.

SAFETY WHEN MANUALLY DEPLOYING AIRBAGS

Airbag modules cannot be disposed of unless they are deployed. Do the following to prevent injury when manually deploying an airbag.

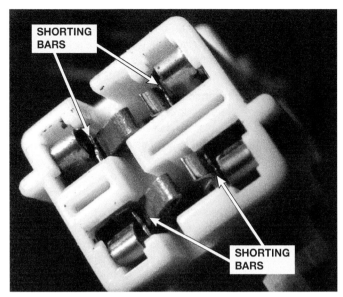

FIGURE 27–17 Shorting bars are used in most airbag connectors. These spring-loaded clips short across both terminals of an airbag connector when it is disconnected to help prevent accidental deployment of the airbag. If electrical power is applied to the terminals, the shorting bars simply provide a low-resistance path to the other terminal and do not allow current to flow past the connector. The mating part of the connector has a tapered piece that spreads apart the shorting bars when the connector is reconnected.

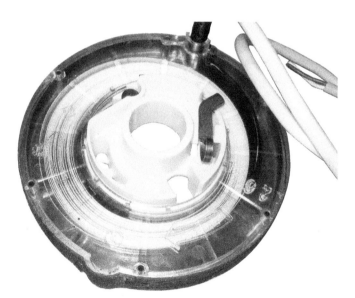

FIGURE 27–18 An airbag clockspring showing the flat conductor wire. It must be properly positioned to ensure proper operation.

- When possible, deploy the airbag outside of the vehicle. Follow the vehicle manufacturer's recommendations.
- Follow the vehicle manufacturer's procedures and equipment recommendations.
- Wear the proper hearing and eye protection.
- Deploy the airbag with the trim cover facing up.

FIGURE 27–19 An airbag being deployed as part of a demonstration in an automotive laboratory.

- Stay at least 20 feet (6 m) from the airbag. (Use long jumper wires attached to the wiring and routed outside the vehicle to a battery.)
- Allow the airbag module to cool.
  - ● **SEE FIGURE 27–19.**

OCCUPANT DETECTION SYSTEMS

PURPOSE AND FUNCTION The U.S. Federal Motor Vehicle Safety Standard 208 (FMVSS) specifies that the passenger side airbag be disabled or deployed with reduced force under the following conditions. This system is referred to as an **occupant detection system (ODS)** or the **passenger presence system (PPS)**.

- When there is no weight on the seat and no seat belt is fastened, the passenger-side airbag does not deploy and the passenger airbag light should be off.
  - ● **SEE FIGURE 27–20.**
- The passenger-side airbag is disabled and the disabled airbag light is "on" only if at least 10 to 37 pounds (4.5 to 17 kg) is on the passenger seat, which generally represents a seated child.

FIGURE 27–20 A dash warning lamp lights if the passenger side airbag is off because no passenger was detected by the seat sensor.

FIGURE 27–21 The passenger side airbag "on" lamp lights if a passenger is detected on the passenger seat.

- If 38 to 99 pounds (17 to 45 kg) is detected on the passenger seat, which represents a child or small adult, the airbag deploys at a decreased force.
- If 99 pounds (45 kg) or more is detected on the passenger seat, the airbag deploys at full force, depending on the severity of the crash, speed of the vehicle, and other factors, which may result in the airbag deploying at a reduced force.
  ● **SEE FIGURE 27–21**.

TYPE OF SEAT SENSOR The passenger presence system uses one of three types of sensors.

- **Gel-filled bladder sensor.** This type of occupant sensor uses a silicone-filled bag that has a pressure sensor attached. The weight of the passenger is measured by the pressure sensor, which sends a voltage signal to the module controlling the airbag deployment. A safety belt

tension sensor is also used with a gel-filled bladder system to monitor the tension on the belt. The module then uses the information from both the bladder and the seat belt sensor to determine if a tightened belt may be used to restrain a child seat. ● **SEE FIGURE 27–22**.

- **Capacitive strip sensors.** This type of occupant sensor uses several flexible conductive metal strips under the seat cushion. These sensor strips transmit and receive a low-level electric field, which changes due to the weight of the front passenger seat occupant. The module determines the weight of the occupant based on the sensor values.
- **Force-sensing resistor sensors.** This type of occupant sensor uses resistors, which change their resistance based on the stress that is applied. These resistors are part of the seat structure, and the module can determine the weight of the occupant based on the change in the resistance of the sensors. ● **SEE FIGURE 27–23**.

CAUTION: Because the resistors are part of the seat structure, it is very important that all seat fasteners be torqued to factory specifications to ensure proper operation of the occupant detection system. A *seat track position* (STP) *sensor* is used by the airbag controller to determine the position of the seat. If the seat is too close to the airbag, the controller may disable the airbag.

FIGURE 27–22 A gel-filled (bladder-type) occupant detection sensor showing the pressure sensor and wiring.

FIGURE 27–23 A resistor-type occupant detection sensor. The weight of the passenger strains these resistors, which are attached to the seat, thereby signaling to the module the weight of the occupant.

DIAGNOSING OCCUPANT DETECTION SYSTEMS

A fault in the system may cause the passenger side airbag light to turn on when there is no weight on the seat. A scan tool is often used to check or calibrate the seat, which must be empty, by commanding the module to rezero the seat sensor. Some systems, such as those on Chrysler vehicles, use a unit that has various weights along with a scan tool to calibrate and diagnose the occupant detection system. ● **SEE FIGURE 27–24.**

SEAT AND SIDE CURTAIN AIRBAGS

SEAT AIRBAGS Side and/or *curtain airbags* use a variety of sensors to determine if they need to be deployed. Side airbags are mounted in one of two general locations.

- In the side bolster of the seat (● **SEE FIGURE 27–25.**)
- In the door panel

Most side airbag sensors use an electronic accelerometer to detect when to deploy the airbags, which are usually mounted to the bottom of the left and right "B" pillars (where the front doors latch) behind a trim panel on the inside of the vehicle.

CAUTION: Avoid using a lockout tool (e.g., a "slim jim") in vehicles equipped with side airbags to help prevent damage to the components and wiring in the system.

SIDE CURTAIN AIRBAGS Side curtain airbags are usually deployed by a module based on input from many different sensors, including a lateral acceleration sensor and wheel speed sensors. For example, in one system used by Ford, the ABS controller commands that the brakes on one side of the vehicle be applied, using down pressure while monitoring the wheel speed sensors. If the wheels slow down with little brake pressure, the controller assumes that the vehicle could roll over, thereby deploying the side curtain airbags.

TECH TIP

Aggressive Driving and OnStar

If a vehicle equipped with the OnStar system is being driven aggressively and the electronic stability control system has to intercede to keep the vehicle under control, OnStar may call the vehicle to see if there has been an accident. The need for a call from OnStar is usually determined if the accelerometer registers slightly over 1 g-force, which could be achieved while driving on a race track.

FIGURE 27–24 A test weight is used to calibrate the occupant detection system on a Chrysler vehicle.

FIGURE 27–25 A typical seat (side) airbag that deploys from the side of the seat.

EVENT DATA RECORDERS

PARTS AND OPERATION As part of the airbag controller on many vehicles, the **event data recorder (EDR)** is used to record parameters just before and slightly after an airbag deployment. The following parameters are recorded.

- Vehicle speed
- Brake on/off
- Seat belt fastened
- G-forces as measured by the accelerometer

Unlike an airplane event data recorder, a vehicle unit is not a separate unit and does not record voice conversations nor include all crash parameters. This means that additional crash data, such as skid marks and physical evidence at the crash site, is needed to fully reconstruct the incident.

The EDR is embedded into the airbag controller and receives data from many sources and at varying sample rates. The data are constantly being stored in a memory buffer and are not recorded into the EPROM unless an airbag deployment has been commanded. The combined data are known as an *event file*. The airbag is commanded on, based on input mainly from the accelerometer sensor. This sensor, usually built into the airbag controller, is located inside the vehicle. The accelerometer calculates the rate of change of the speed of the vehicle. This determines the acceleration rate and is used to predict if that rate is high enough to deploy the frontal airbags. The airbags are deployed if the threshold g-value is exceeded. The passenger side airbag is also deployed unless it is suppressed by either of the following:

- No passenger is detected.
- The passenger side airbag switch is off.

DATA EXTRACTION Data extraction from the event data recorder in the airbag controller can only be achieved using a piece of equipment known as the Crash Data Retrieval System, manufactured by Vetronics Corporation. This is the only authorized method for retrieving event files and only certain organizations are allowed access to the data. These groups or organizations include:

- Original equipment manufacturer's representatives
- National Highway Traffic Safety Administration
- Law enforcement agencies
- Accident reconstruction companies

Crash data retrieval must only be done by a trained crash data retrieval (CDR) technician or analyst. A technician undergoes specialized training and must pass an examination. An analyst must attend additional training beyond that of a technician to achieve CDR analyst certification.

SUMMARY

1. Airbags use a sensor(s) to determine if the rate of deceleration is enough to cause bodily harm.
2. All airbag electrical connectors and conduit are yellow and all electrical terminals are gold plated to protect against corrosion.
3. Always follow the manufacturer's procedure for disabling the airbag system prior to any work performed on the system.
4. Frontal airbags operate only within 30 degrees from center and do not deploy in the event of a rollover, side, or rear collision.
5. Two sensors must be triggered at the same time for an airbag deployment to occur. Many newer systems use an accelerometer-type crash sensor that actually measures the amount of deceleration.
6. Pretensioners are explosive (pyrotechnic) devices that remove the slack from the seat belt and help position the occupant.
7. Occupant detection systems use sensors in the seat to determine whether the airbag will be deployed and with full or reduced force.

REVIEW QUESTIONS

1. What are the safety precautions to follow when working around an airbag?
2. What sensor(s) must be triggered for an airbag deployment?
3. How should deployed inflation modules be handled?
4. What is the purpose of pretensioners?
5. What is the purpose of the event data recorder?

CHAPTER QUIZ

1. A vehicle is being repaired after an airbag deployment. Technician A says that the inflator module should be handled as if it is still live. Technician B says gloves should be worn to prevent skin irritation. Which technician is correct?
   a. Technician A only
   b. Technician B only
   c. Both Technicians A and B
   d. Neither Technician A nor B

2. A seat belt pretensioner is _____.
   a. a device that contains an explosive charge
   b. used to remove slack from the seat belt in the event of a collision
   c. used to force the occupant back into position against the seat back in the event of a collision
   d. All of the above

3. The occupant detection system measures the _____ of the person in the passenger seat.
   a. height
   b. weight
   c. age
   d. distance from the seat belt

4. Two technicians are discussing dual-stage airbags. Technician A says that a deployed airbag is safe to handle, regardless of which stage caused the deployment of the airbag. Technician B says that both stages ignite, but at different speeds, depending on the speed of the vehicle. Which technician is correct?
   a. Technician A only
   b. Technician B only
   c. Both Technicians A and B
   d. Neither Technician A nor B

5. Where are shorting bars used?
   a. In pretensioners
   b. At the connectors for airbags
   c. In the crash sensors
   d. In the airbag controller

6. Technician A says that a deployed airbag can be repacked, reused, and reinstalled in the vehicle. Technician B says that a deployed airbag should be discarded and replaced with an entire new assembly. Which technician is correct?
   a. Technician A only
   b. Technician B only
   c. Both Technicians A and B
   d. Neither Technician A nor B

7. What color are the airbag electrical connectors and conduit?
   a. Blue   c. Yellow
   b. Red   d. Orange

8. On some vehicles, the side curtain airbags use which of the following devices to determine when to deploy?
   a. Wheel speed sensors
   b. Lateral acceleration sensor
   c. Passenger presence system (PPS) seat sensor
   d. Seat belt sensor

9. How many sensors must be triggered at the same time to cause an airbag deployment?
   a. One   c. Three
   b. Two   d. Four

10. Which parameters might be stored in the airbag controller in the event of a deployment?
   a. Voice recordings
   b. A 10-second video of the driver
   c. Whether the windows were open or closed
   d. Seat belt fastened

chapter 28

BODY ELECTRICAL ACCESSORIES

LEARNING OBJECTIVES:

After studying this chapter, the reader should be able to:

Describe how the horn operates and diagnose faulty horn operation.

Explain the testing and diagnosis of windshield wipers and windshield washers.

Describe the operation of cruise control.

Discuss electrically heated rear window defogger systems.

Explain the operation and testing procedures for power windows and locks.

Discuss the operation of power sunroofs, moon roofs, and sun shades.

Describe the operation of power seats and heated/cooled seats, plus heated steering wheels and mirrors.

Explain the operation of adjustable pedals and folding outside mirrors.

Describe the operation and diagnosis of remote keyless entry, garage door openers, and remote start systems.

This chapter will help prepare for the ASE Electrical/Electronic Systems (A6) certification test content area "G" (Repair Body Electrical Systems Diagnosis and Repair).

KEY TERMS: Automatic reversal systems (ARS) 375 • Cruise control 372 • Electric adjustable pedals (EAP) 385 • Heated rear window defogger 373 • Heated seats 383 • Heated steering wheel 384 • Horns 362 • Moon roof 380 • Power windows 375 • Pulse wipers 365 • Rain-sense wipers 369 • Remote start 389 • Sun roof 380 • Sun shades 380 • Variable-delay wipers 365 • Windshield wipers 364

HORNS

PURPOSE AND FUNCTION **Horns** are electric devices that emit a loud sound used to alert other drivers or persons in the area. Horns are manufactured in several different tones, ranging from 1,800 to 3,550 Hz, and must be heard from a minimum distance of 200 feet (60 m). Vehicle manufacturers select from various horn tones for a particular vehicle sound. ● SEE FIGURE 28–1.

When two horns are used, each has a different tone, yet the sound combines when both are operated. Most horns since 2000 have used the body control module (BCM) to control the actual operation.

HORN CIRCUITS

Automotive horns usually operate on full battery voltage wired from the battery, through a fuse, switch, and then to the horns. Most vehicles use a horn relay and the horn button on the steering wheel or column completes a circuit to ground that closes the control side of the relay. The heavy current flow required to operate the horn travels through the load side of the relay to the horn. ● SEE FIGURE 28–2.

FIGURE 28–1 Two horns are used on this vehicle. Many vehicles use only one horn, often hidden underneath the vehicle.

COMPUTER-CONTROLLED HORNS On most recent model vehicles, the horn button is an input to the body control module (BCM) or electronic control unit (ECU). The BCM controls the operation of the horn relay. The horn relay may also be controlled by the BCM, which "beeps" the horn when the vehicle is locked or unlocked, using the key fob remote, and can be sounded by the alarm system. Check service information for the exact details about the horn circuit for the vehicle being checked. ● SEE FIGURE 28–3.

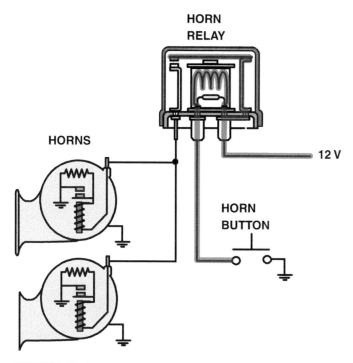

HORN RELAY

HORNS

12 V

HORN BUTTON

FIGURE 28–2 A simplified horn circuit where the horn button completes the ground circuit of the relay coil.

de-energize the armature circuit. As the diaphragm moves down, the contact points close, re-energizing the armature circuit, and the diaphragm moves up again. This rapid opening and closing of the contact points causes the diaphragm to vibrate at an audible frequency. The sound created by the diaphragm is magnified as it travels through a trumpet attached to the diaphragm chamber. Most horn systems typically use one or two horns, but some have up to four. Those with multiple horns use both high- and low-pitch units to achieve a harmonious tone. Only a high-pitched unit is used in single-horn applications. The horn assembly is marked with an "H" or "L" for pitch identification.

HORN DIAGNOSIS

SCAN TOOL TESTING A scan tool can be used to test a horn that is computer controlled by using the bidirectional feature of a factory or factory-level aftermarket scan tool. Because most horn buttons are an input to the BCM or similar module, a scan tool can often be used to command the horn to sound. Check service information for the vehicle being tested for the exact tests and testing procedures to follow.

HORN OPERATION A vehicle horn is an actuator that converts an electrical signal to sound. The horn circuit has an armature (a coil of wire) and contacts that are attached to a diaphragm. When energized, the armature causes the diaphragm to move up, which then opens a set of contact points that

HORN CIRCUIT TESTING Once the cause of an inoperative horn has been reduced to the horn wiring circuit, the wiring needs to be checked. Typically, a digital multimeter (DMM) is used to perform voltage drop and continuity checks to isolate the failure. A momentary contact switch, horn button, is used

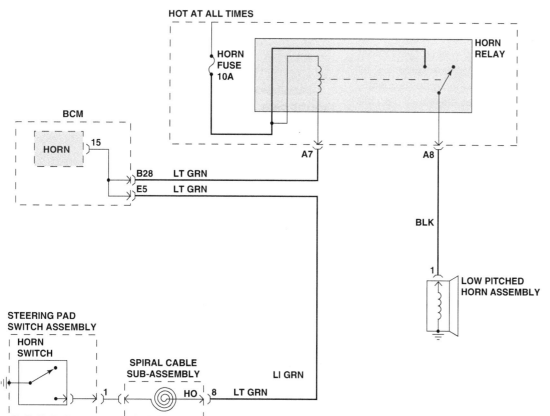

FIGURE 28–3 A typical schematic of a horn circuit. Note that the horn relay can be activated by either the horn switch in the steering wheel or by the body control module (BCM).

to sound the horn. The horn switch is mounted to the steering wheel in or near the center of the steering column.

CAUTION: If the steering wheel needs to be removed for diagnosis or repair of the horn circuit, follow service information procedures for disarming the airbag circuit prior to removing the steering wheel, and for the specified test equipment to use.

On most recent-model vehicles, the horn relay is in a centralized power distribution center along with other relays, circuit breakers, and fuses. Check the relay to determine if the coil is being energized and if current passes through the power circuit when the horn switch is depressed. Check service information for the exact diagnosis and horn replacement procedures to follow.

HORN REPLACEMENT Horns are generally mounted on the radiator core support by bolts and nuts or sheet metal screws. To replace a horn, remove the fasteners and lift the old horn from its mounting bracket. Clean the attachment area on the mounting bracket and chassis before installing the new horn. Some models use a corrosion-resistant mounting bolt to ensure a ground connection.

WINDSHIELD WIPERS

PURPOSE AND FUNCTION Windshield wipers are used to keep the viewing area of the windshield clear of rain. Windshield wiper systems and circuits vary greatly between manufacturers as well as between models. Some vehicles combine the windshield wiper and windshield washer functions into a single system. Many minivans and sport utility vehicles (SUVs) also have a rear window wiper and washer system that works independently of the windshield system. Generally, all windshield and rear window wiper and washer systems operate in a similar fashion. Wiper control switches are installed on the steering column, usually as part of a multifunction switch that controls several other functions.

COMPUTER CONTROLLED WIPERS Most wipers, since the 1990s, have used the BCM to control the actual operation of the wiper. The wiper controls are an input to the control module and may also turn on the headlights whenever the wipers are on, which is the law in some states. ● **SEE FIGURE 28–4.**

WIPER AND WASHER COMPONENTS A typical combination wiper and washer system consists of the following:

- Wiper motor(s)
- Gearbox
- Wiper arms and linkage
- Wiper blades
- Washer pump
- Hoses and jets (nozzles)
- Fluid reservoir

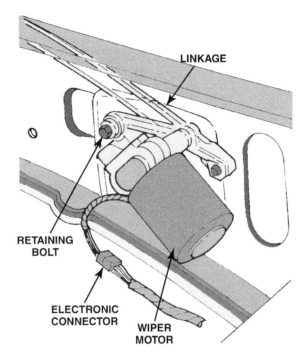

FIGURE 28–4 The motor and linkage bolt to the body and connect to the switch with a wiring harness.

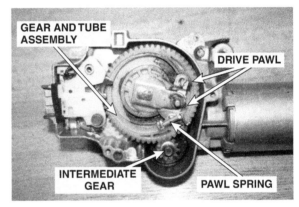

FIGURE 28–5 A typical wiper motor with the housing cover removed. The motor itself has a worm gear on the shaft that turns the small intermediate gear, which then rotates the gear and tube assembly, which rotates the crank arm (not shown) that connects to the wiper linkage.

- Combination switch
- Wiring and electrical connectors
  ● **SEE FIGURE 28–5.**

WINDSHIELD WIPER MOTORS The windshield wipers ordinarily use a special two-speed electric motor. Some are compound-wound motors, a motor type that provides for two different speeds.

- Series-wound field
- Shunt field

One speed is achieved in the series-wound field and the other speed in the shunt-wound field. Other wiper motors are of the permanent magnet type. ● **SEE FIGURE 28–6.**

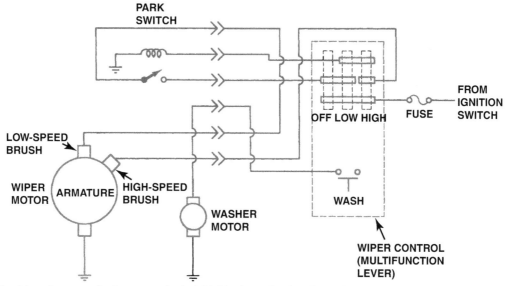

RUN—CLOSED BY RELAY
PARK—OPENED BY MECHANICAL LEVER

PARK SWITCH

LOW-SPEED BRUSH

WIPER MOTOR

ARMATURE

HIGH-SPEED BRUSH

WASHER MOTOR

OFF LOW HIGH

FUSE

FROM IGNITION SWITCH

WASH

WIPER CONTROL (MULTIFUNCTION LEVER)

FIGURE 28–6 A wiring diagram of a two-speed windshield wiper circuit using a three-brush, two-speed motor. The dashed line for the multifunction lever indicates that the circuit shown is only part of the total function of the steering column lever.

WIPER MOTOR OPERATION Wiper motors using a permanent magnet motor have a low-speed positive brush, a high-speed positive brush, and a ground (negative) brush. The brushes connect the battery to the internal windings of the motor, and the two brushes provide for two different motor speeds. The ground brush is directly opposite the low-speed brush. The high-speed brush is off to the side of the low speed brush. When current flows through the high-speed brush, there are fewer turns on the armature between the hot and ground brushes and, therefore, the resistance is less. With less resistance, more current flows and the armature revolves faster.

PARK POSITION Windshield wiper motor park operation is controlled by the wiper motor module using an input from the park switch within the wiper motor assembly. When the windshield wiper/washer switch is turned to the OFF position while the wiper blades are somewhere on the windshield, the wiper motor module continues to operate the wiper motor until the wipers reach the park position. Check service information for the exact operation for the vehicle being serviced.

VARIABLE WIPERS The **variable-delay wipers** (also called **pulse wipers**) is a term used to describe the operation of the wipers that operate on an interval that can be delayed when the rain is light. Older vehicles use an electronic circuit with a variable resistor that controls the time of the charge and discharge of a capacitor. The charging and discharging of the capacitor controls the circuit for the operation of the wiper motor. On newer vehicles, the wipers are controlled by the BCM with input from the driver using a knob or dial to adjust the wiper interval.

WINDSHIELD WIPER DIAGNOSIS If the windshield wipers are not working, use a factory or factory-level scan tool and check for operation using the bidirectional controls.

- If the wipers function when commanded by the scan tool, check service information for the exact procedures to follow when checking the switch input and BCM connections.

- If the wipers do not function when being commanded by the scan tool, perform circuit testing, which usually includes determining if the fault is electrical or mechanical. ● **SEE FIGURE 28–7.**

To determine if there is an electrical or mechanical problem, access the motor assembly and disconnect the wiper arm linkage from the motor and gearbox. If the motor operates, but the wipers do not, check for the following:

- Stripped gears in the gearbox or stripped linkage connection
- Loose or separated motor-to-gearbox connection

? FREQUENTLY ASKED QUESTION

How Do Wipers Park?

Some vehicles have wiper arms that park lower than the normal operating position, so they are hidden below the hood when not in operation. This is called a *depressed park position*. When the wiper motor is turned off, the park switch allows the motor to continue to turn until the wiper arms reach the bottom edge of the windshield. Then the park switch reverses the current flow through the wiper motor, which makes a partial revolution in the opposite direction.

The wiper linkage pulls the wiper arms down below the level of the hood and the park switch is opened, stopping the wiper motor.

Wipers Would Stop Working

The owner of a Ford Focus stated that the wipers would stop working randomly in the middle of a sweep. The technician saw that the wiper blades were aftermarket multiple blade type. The wiper motors have a fail-safe over load protection built in. If the body control module (BCM) detects too much current, it will shut the motors down to protect them. The motors communicate over a LIN network between the two motors.

The technician replaced the wiper blades with factor original equipment (OE) blades. This corrected the customer concern.

Summary:

- **Complaint**—The wipers would stop working randomly in the middle of a sweep.

- **Cause**—The aftermarket wiper blades created too much of a drag on the wiper motor and caused it to stop working.

- **Correction**—The wiper blades were replaced with the factory original type.

- Loose linkage to the motor connection

If the motor does not shut off, check for the following:

- Defective park switch inside the motor
- Defective wiper switch
- Poor ground connection at the wiper switch

WIPER MOTOR REPLACEMENT Wiper motors are replaced if defective. The motor usually mounts on the bulkhead (firewall). Bulkhead-mounted units are accessible from under the hood, while the cowl panel needs to be removed to service a motor mounted in the cowl. ● **SEE FIGURE 28–8.**

REAR WIPERS Rear window wiper motors are generally located inside the rear hatch panel on vehicles with a hatchback or lift gate. After removing the trim panel covering the motor, replacement is essentially the same as replacing the front wiper motor.

WINDSHIELD WASHERS

OPERATION Windshield washers are used to squirt washer fluid onto the surface of the windshield where it can help dissolve debris and clean the viewing area of the windshield when the wipers are used. Most vehicle windshield washers use a positive-displacement or centrifugal-type washer pump located in the washer reservoir. A momentary contact switch, which is often part of a steering column–mounted combination switch assembly, energizes the washer pump. Washer pump switches are installed either on the steering column or on the instrument panel. The nozzles can be located on the bulkhead, in the hood, or mounted as part of the wiper arms, depending on the vehicle.

REAR WASHERS Vehicles equipped with a rear wiper are also equipped with a rear washer. The rear washer may share a fluid reservoir with the front wipers, or it may have its own reservoir. The rear washer switch is located on either the steering column or on the instrument panel.

HEADLIGHT WASHERS Many vehicles are equipped with headlight washers that spray washer fluid into the surface of the headlights when actuated. Some systems even include small wiper blades. Headlight washers are usually operated from the main headlight control switch, if equipped. Most headlight washers use the same windshield washer reservoir as is used for the front windshield washers.

WINDSHIELD WASHER DIAGNOSIS To diagnose the washer system, follow service information procedures that usually include the following steps.

Scan Tool Bidirectional Control

Most vehicles built since 2000 can have the lighting and accessory circuits checked using a scan tool. A technician can use the following:

Factory scan tool, such as:

- Tech 2 or Multiple Diagnostic Interface (MDI) (General Motors vehicle)
- DRB III, Star Scan, Star Mobile, WiTech, or MicroPOD II (Chrysler-Jeep vehicles)
- New Generation Star or IDS (Ford)
- Honda Diagnostic System (HDS)
- TIS Tech Stream (Toyota/Lexus)

An enhanced aftermarket scan tool has body bidirectional control capability, including:

- Snap-on Modis, Solus, or Verus
- OTC Genisys
- AutoEnginuity

Using a bidirectional scan tool allows the technician to command the operation of electrical accessories, such as horns, windows, lights, door locks, and wipers. ● **SEE FIGURE 28–9.**

If the circuit operates correctly when commanded by the scan tool and does not function using the switch(s), follow service information instructions for the exact tests and testing procedures to follow for the vehicle being tested.

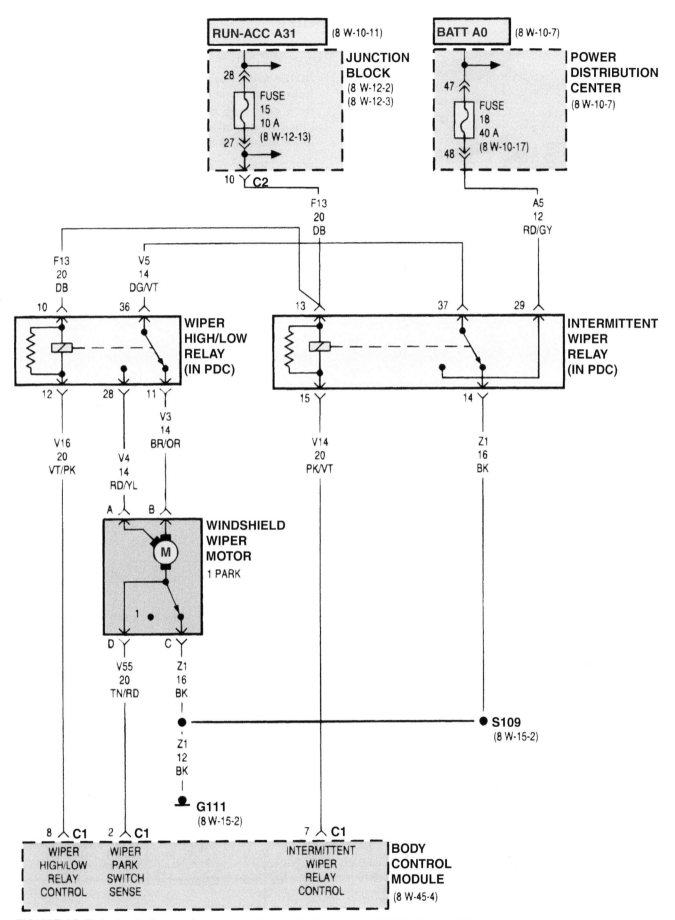

FIGURE 28–7 A circuit diagram is necessary to troubleshoot a windshield wiper problem.

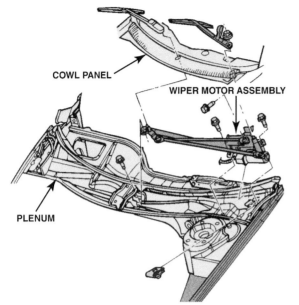

COWL PANEL

WIPER MOTOR ASSEMBLY

PLENUM

STEP 1 To quick check any washer system, make sure the reservoir has fluid and is not frozen. Then, disconnect the pump hose and operate the washer switch.

NOTE: Always use good-quality windshield washer fluid from a closed container to prevent contaminated fluid from damaging the washer pump. Radiator antifreeze (ethylene glycol) should never be used in any windshield wiper system. ● SEE FIGURE 28–10.

STEP 2 If fluid squirts from the pump, the delivery system is at fault, not the motor, switch, or the electrical circuits (switch input, BCM, etc.).

STEP 3 If no fluid squirts from the pump, the problem is most likely a circuit failure, defective pump, or faulty switch.

STEP 4 A clogged reservoir screen also may be preventing fluid from entering the pump.

FIGURE 28–8 The wiper motor and linkage mount under the cowl panel on many vehicles.

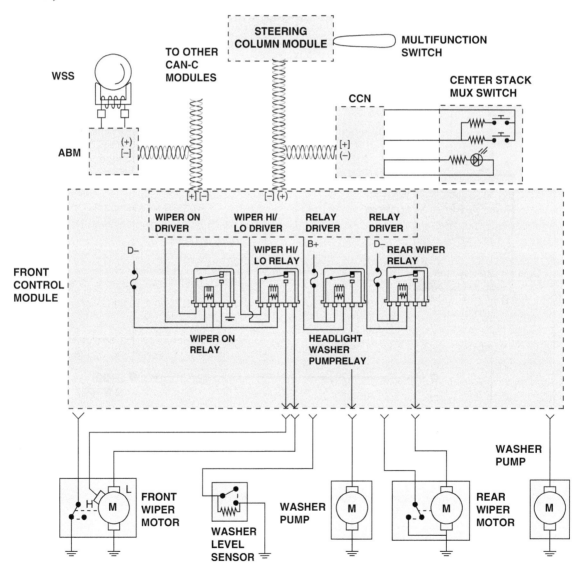

FIGURE 28–9 A typical schematic showing how relays inside the front control module are all tied to other modules on the bus.

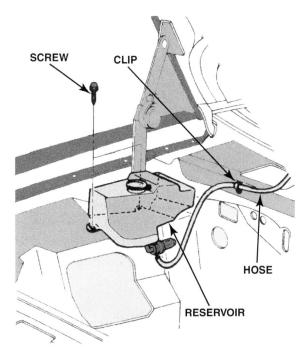

SCREW CLIP

HOSE

RESERVOIR

FIGURE 28–10 A typical windshield washer reservoir and pump assembly.

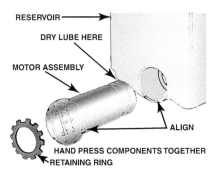

RESERVOIR

DRY LUBE HERE

MOTOR ASSEMBLY

ALIGN

HAND PRESS COMPONENTS TOGETHER
RETAINING RING

FIGURE 28–11 Washer pumps usually install into the reservoir and are held in place with a retaining ring.

WINDSHIELD WASHER SERVICE
When a fluid delivery problem is indicated, check for:

- Blocked, pinched, broken, or disconnected hoses
- Clogged nozzles
- Blocked washer pump outlet

If the pump motor does not operate, check for battery voltage available at the pump while operating the washer switch.

- If voltage is available and the pump does not run, check for continuity on the pump ground circuit.
- If there is no voltage drop on the ground circuit, replace the pump motor. If battery voltage is not available at the motor, check for power through the washer switch.
- If voltage is available at and through the switch, there is a problem in the wiring between the switch and pump. Perform voltage drop tests to locate the fault. Repair the wiring as needed and retest.

Washer motors are not repairable and are replaced if defective. Centrifugal or positive-displacement pumps are located on or inside the washer reservoir tank or cover. ● **SEE FIGURE 28–11.**

RAIN-SENSE WIPERS

Parts and Operation
Rain-sense wiper systems use a sensor located on the inside and at the top of the windshield to detect rain droplets. This sensor is often called the *rain-sense module (RSM)*. It determines and adjusts the time delay of the wiper based on how much moisture it detects on the

  CASE STUDY

Intermittent Wipers Inoperative

The owner of a Chevrolet Tahoe LTZ complained the intermittent wipers did not work. On the initial selection of the wiper switch to one of the pulse positions, the wipers made one swipe and stopped working after that. The wipers would just sit in the park position. The low speed, high speed, and park positions worked fine.

This vehicle was equipped with rain-sense wipers. The wipers are not supposed to work in the pulse mode unless there is water on the windshield. In this case, the rain sensor at the top of the windshield was defective. The wipers would not come on because the body control module (BCM) was not being notified that there was a wipe pulse required. The rain sensor was replaced. After replacement of the sensor, with wipers in pulse mode, the windshield was sprayed with a spray bottle and the wipers operated correctly.

Summary:

- **Complaint**—Intermittent wipers inoperative.
- **Cause**—The rain senor on the inside of the windshield was defective.
- **Correction**—The rain sensor was replaced and normal operation of the windshield wipers was restored.

windshield. The wiper switch can be left on the sense position all the time, and if no rain is sensed, the wipers do not swipe. ● **SEE FIGURE 28–12.**

The control knob is rotated to the desired wiper sensibility level. The microprocessor in the RSM sends a command to the body control module. The rain-sense module is a triangle- or rectangle-shaped black plastic housing. Fine openings on the windshield side of the housing are fitted with eight convex clear plastic lenses. The unit contains four infrared (IR) diodes, two photocells, and a microprocessor.

FIGURE 28–12 A typical rain-sensing module located on the inside of the windshield near the inside rearview mirror.

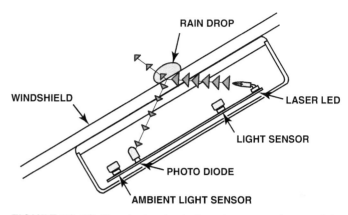

FIGURE 28–13 The electronics in the rain-sense wiper module can detect the presence of rain drops under various lighting conditions.

The IR diodes generate IR beams that are aimed by four of the convex optical lenses near the base of the module through the windshield glass. Four additional convex lenses near the top of the RSM are focused on the IR light beam on the outside of the windshield glass and allow the two photocells to sense changes in the intensity of the IR light beam. When sufficient moisture accumulates, the RSM detects a change in the monitored IR light beam intensity. The RSM processes the rain intensity signal and sends it over the data BUS to the BCM, which then commands a swipe of the wiper. ● **SEE FIGURE 28–13.**

DIAGNOSIS AND SERVICE If there is a complaint about the rain-sense wipers not functioning correctly, check the owner's manual to be sure that they are properly set. Also, verify that the windshield wipers are functioning correctly on all speeds before diagnosing the rain-sensor circuits. Most rain-sensing wiper systems can be tested by misting water on the windshield in the area of the sensor. Always follow the vehicle manufacturer's recommended diagnosis and testing procedures.

 TECH TIP

Rain Sense and Cruise Control

The rain-sense wiper module communicates with the BCM over the data links and, if the rain is heavy, a signal is sent to deactivate the cruise control. A message is then displayed on the instrument panel warning that the cruise control is not available. This is normal operation and is used to help prevent the vehicle from hydroplaning during heavy rain. Normal cruise control operation resumes when the rain intensity is reduced. This is normal operation and not a fault with the cruise control system.

BLOWER MOTOR

PURPOSE AND FUNCTION The same blower motor moves air inside the vehicle for:

1. Air conditioning
2. Heat
3. Defrosting
4. Defogging
5. Venting of the passenger compartment.

The motor turns a squirrel cage-type fan. A squirrel cage-type fan is able to move air without creating a lot of noise. The fan switch controls the path that the current follows to the blower motor. ● **SEE FIGURE 28–14.**

PARTS AND OPERATION The motor is usually a permanent magnet, one-speed motor that operates at its maximum speed with full battery voltage. The switch gets current from the fuse panel with the ignition switch on, and then directs full battery voltage to the blower motor for high speed and to the blower motor through resistors for lower speeds.

VARIABLE SPEED CONTROL The fan switch controls the path of current through a resistor pack to obtain different fan speeds of the blower motor. The electrical path can be:

- Full battery voltage for high-speed operation
- Through one or more resistors to reduce the voltage and the current to the blower motor, which then rotates at a slower speed.

The resistors are located near the blower motor and mounted in the duct where the airflow from the blower can cool the resistors. The current flow through the resistor is controlled by the switch and often uses a relay to carry the heavy current (10 to 12 amperes) needed to power the fan. Normal operation includes:

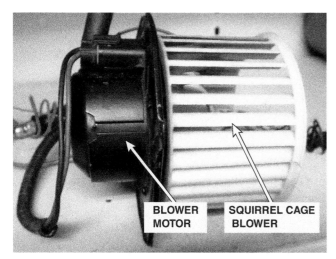

FIGURE 28-14 A squirrel cage blower motor. A replacement blower motor usually does not come equipped with the squirrel cage blower, so it has to be switched from the old motor.

- Low speed. Current flows through three resistors in series to drop the voltage to about 4 volts and 4 amperes
- Medium-low speed. Current is directed through two resistors in series to lower the voltage to about 6 volts and 6 amperes
- Medium-high speed. Current is directed through one resistor resulting in a voltage of about 9 volts and 9 amperes
- High speed. Full battery voltage, usually through a relay, is applied to the blower motor resulting in a current of about 12 amperes. ● SEE FIGURES 28–15 AND 28–16.

Some blower motors are electronically controlled by the body control module and include electronic circuits to achieve a variable speed. ● SEE FIGURE 28–17.

FIGURE 28-16 A blower motor resistor pack used to control blower motor speed. Some blower motor resistors are flat and look like a credit card and are called "credit card resistors."

BLOWER MOTOR DIAGNOSIS If the blower motor does not operate at any speed, the problem could be any of the following.

1. Defective ground wire or ground wire connection.
2. Defective blower motor (not repairable; must be replaced).
3. Open circuit in the power-side circuit, including fuse, wiring, or fan switch. If the blower works on lower speeds, but not on high speed, the problem is usually an in-line fuse or high-speed relay that controls the heavy current flow for high-speed operation.

The high-speed fuse or relay usually fails as a result of internal blower motor bushing wear, which causes excessive resistance to motor rotation. At slow blower speeds, the resistance is not as noticeable and the blower operates normally. The blower motor is a sealed unit and, if defective, must be replaced as a unit. The squirrel-cage fan usually needs to be removed from the old motor and attached to the replacement motor. If the blower motor operates normally at high speed, but not at any of the lower speeds, the problem could be melted wire resistors or a defective switch.

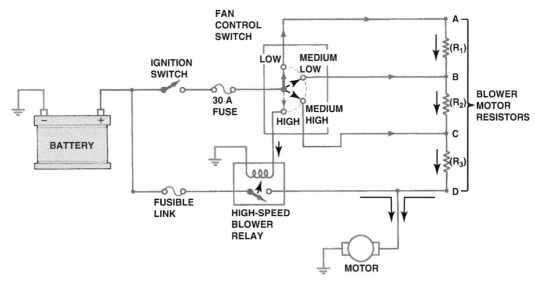

FIGURE 28-15 A blower motor circuit with four speeds controlled ng resistors. The three lowest fan speeds (low, medium-low, and medium-high) use the blower motor resistors to drop the voltage to the motor and reduce current to the motor. On high, the resistors are bypassed. The "high" position on the fan switch energizes a relay, which supplies the current for the blower on high through a fusible link or maxi fuse.

FIGURE 28–17 A brushless DC motor that uses the body computer to control the speed.

FIGURE 28–18 Using a mini AC/DC clamp-on multimeter to measure the current drawn by a blower motor.

The blower motor can be tested using a clamp-on DC ammeter. ● **SEE FIGURE 28–18**.

Most blower motors do not draw more than 15 amperes on high speed. A worn or defective motor usually draws more current than normal and could damage the blower motor resistors or blow a fuse if not replaced.

CRUISE CONTROL

PURPOSE AND FUNCTION **Cruise control**, also called vehicle *speed control*, is used to maintain a preset vehicle speed, even up gentle grades. Some vehicles are programmed to downshift the transmission to maintain the vehicle speed when descending grades if the speed increases more than 5 MPH (7 km/h) faster than the preset speed. Using cruise control avoids the tendency to drive at varying speeds, helps to reduce driver fatigue, and allows for driver position changes when driving for a long period of time. Cruise control should be avoided if driving on curving roads or when it is raining.

TECH TIP

Bump Problems

Cruise control problem diagnosis can involve a complex series of checks and tests. The troubleshooting procedures vary among manufacturers (and year), so a technician should always check service information for the exact vehicle being serviced. However, every cruise control system uses a brake safety switch and, if the vehicle has manual transmission, a clutch safety switch. The purpose of these safety switches is to ensure that the cruise control system is disabled if the brakes or the clutch are applied. Some systems use a redundant brake pedal safety switch. If the cruise control "cuts out" or disengages itself while traveling over bumpy roads, the most common cause is a misadjusted brake (and/or clutch) safety switch(es). Often, a simple readjustment of these safety switches cures the intermittent cruise control disengagement problems.

CAUTION: Always follow the manufacturer's recommended safety switch adjustment procedures. If the brake safety switch(es) is misadjusted, it could keep pressure applied to the master brake cylinder, resulting in severe damage to the braking system.

CRUISE CONTROL OPERATION A typical cruise control system can be set only if the vehicle speed is 25 MPH (40 km/h) or more. Older systems use a throttle actuator to control the throttle opening, control switches for driver control of cruise control functions, and electrical brake and clutch (if equipped) pedal-release switches. The typical actuator uses a stepper motor to move the throttle linkage based on commands from the cruise control module, which is often inside the cruise control assembly. ● **SEE FIGURE 28–19.**

NOTE: Older Toyota-built vehicles do not retain the set speed in memory if the vehicle speed drops below 25 MPH (40 km/h). The driver is required to set the desired speed again. This is normal operation and not a fault with the cruise control system.

Most computer-controlled cruise control systems use the vehicle's speed sensor input to the powertrain control module (PCM) for speed reference. Older cruise control systems also use an actuator to control the throttle opening, as well as control switches for driver control, electrical brake, and clutch (if equipped) pedal release switches. ● **SEE FIGURE 28–20.**

ELECTRONIC THROTTLE CRUISE CONTROL Many vehicles are equipped with an electronic throttle control (ETC) system. Vehicles equipped with such a system do not use throt-

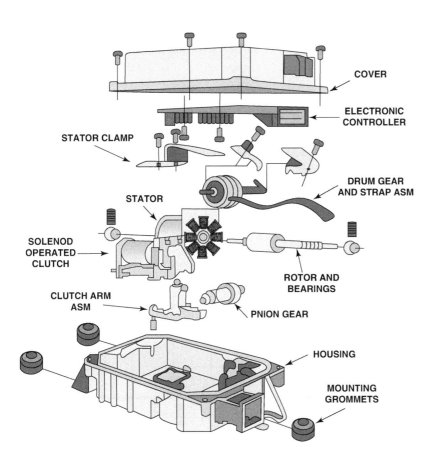

FIGURE 28–19 An exploded view of a cruise control assembly used on a vehicle that does not have an electronic throttle. The motor is connected to the throttle of the engine and is used to increase or decrease engine speed to maintain the set speed.

COVER

ELECTRONIC CONTROLLER

STATOR CLAMP

DRUM GEAR AND STRAP ASM

STATOR

SOLENOD OPERATED CLUTCH

ROTOR AND BEARINGS

CLUTCH ARM ASM

PNION GEAR

HOUSING

MOUNTING GROMMETS

 **TECH TIP**

Check the Brake Lights

On many vehicles, the cruise control does not work if the brake lights are not working. This includes the third brake light, commonly called the center high-mounted stop light (CHMSL). Always check for the proper operation of the brake lights first if the cruise control does not work.

tle actuators for the cruise control, but instead use the electronic throttle to control vehicle speed. ● **SEE FIGURE 28–21.**

The cruise control on a vehicle equipped with an electronic throttle control system consists of a switch to set the desired speed. The PCM receives the vehicle speed information from the vehicle speed (VS) sensor. The PCM then commands the ETC throttle to open or close the throttle valve as needed to maintain desired vehicle speed.

DIAGNOSIS AND SERVICE Any fault in the accelerator pedal position (APP) sensor, brake switch, or ETC system disables the cruise control function. Always follow the specified troubleshooting procedures, which usually include the use of a scan tool to properly diagnose the ETC system.

HEATED REAR WINDOW DEFOGGERS

PARTS AND OPERATION An electrically **heated rear window defogger** system uses an electrical grid baked on the glass that warms the glass to about 85°F (29°C) and clears it of fog or frost. The rear window is also called a *backlight*. The rear window defogger system is controlled by a driver-operated switch and a timer relay. ● **SEE FIGURE 28–22.**

The timer relay is necessary because the window grid can draw up to 30 amperes, and continued operation puts a strain on the battery and the charging system. Generally, the timer relay permits current to flow through the rear window grid for only 10 minutes. If the window is still not clear of fog after 10 minutes, the driver can turn the defogger on again, but after the first 10 minutes, any additional defogger operation is limited to 5 minutes.

The electrical current through the grids depends, in part, on the temperature of the conductor grids. As the temperature decreases, the resistance of the grids decreases and the current flow increases, helping to warm the rear glass. As the temperature of the glass increases, the resistance of the conductor grids increases and the current flow decreases. Therefore, the defogger system tends to self-regulate the electrical current requirements to match the need for defogging.

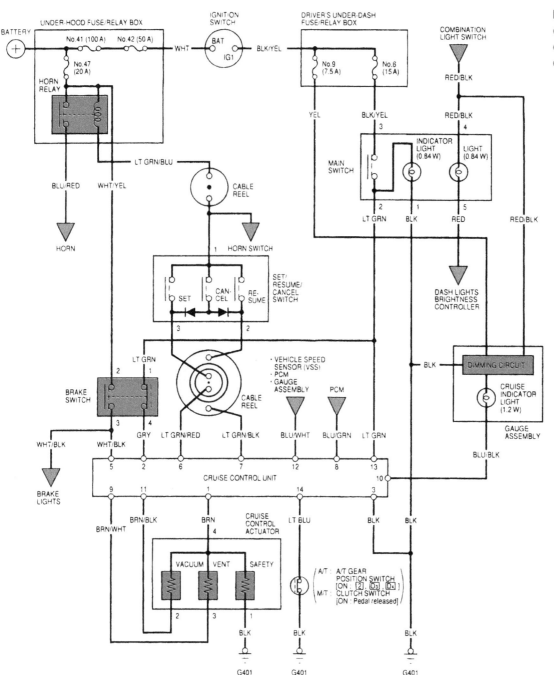

FIGURE 28–20 Circuit diagram of a typical electronic cruise control system.

TECH TIP

The Infrared Camera Test

It is difficult to test for the proper operation of all grids of a rear window defogger unless the rear window happens to be covered with fog. A common trick that works is to turn on the rear defogger and look at the outside of the rear window glass using an infrared camera. The image shows if all sections of the rear grids are working. ● SEE FIGURE 28–23.

NOTE: Some vehicles use the wire grid of the rear window defogger as the radio antenna. Therefore, if the grid is damaged, radio reception can also be affected.

HEATED REAR WINDOW DEFOGGER DIAGNOSIS

Trouble-shooting a nonfunctioning rear window defogger unit involves using a test light or a voltmeter to check for voltage to the grid. If no voltage is present at the rear window, check for voltage at the switch and relay timer assembly. A poor ground connection on the opposite side of the grid from the power side can also cause the rear defogger not to operate. Because most defogger circuits use an indicator light switch and a relay timer,

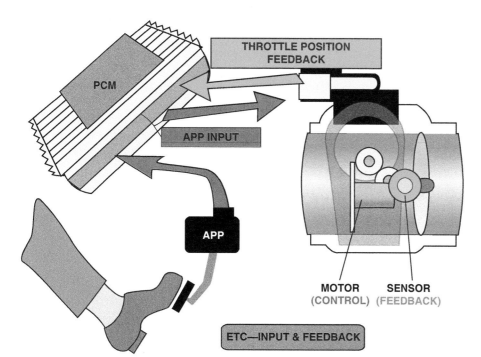

FIGURE 28–21 The electronic throttle control (ETC) system uses a sensor that measures the position and the speed of the driver's foot on the accelerator pedal. A throttle position sensor measures the throttle angle. An electric motor operates the movement of the throttle plate using commands from the PCM.

THROTTLE POSITION FEEDBACK

PCM

APP INPUT

APP

MOTOR (CONTROL)   SENSOR (FEEDBACK)

ETC—INPUT & FEEDBACK

it is possible to have the indicator light on, even if the wires are disconnected at the rear window grid. A voltmeter can be used to test the operation of the rear window defogger grid. ● SEE FIGURE 28–24.

With the negative meter lead attached to a good body ground, carefully touch the positive meter lead to the grid conductors. There should be a decreasing voltage reading as the meter lead is moved from the power ("hot") side of the grid toward the ground side of the grid.

REPAIR OR REPLACEMENT Electric grid-type rear window defoggers can be damaged easily by careless cleaning or scraping of the inside of the rear window glass. If there is a broken grid wire, it can be repaired using an electrically conductive substance available in a repair kit. Most vehicle manufacturers recommend that grid wire less than 2 inches (5 cm) long be repaired. If a bad section is longer than 2 inches, the entire rear window needs to be replaced. ● SEE FIGURE 28–25.

POWER WINDOWS

SWITCHES AND CONTROLS **Power windows** use electric motors to raise and lower door glass. They can be operated by both a master control switch located beside the driver and additional independent switches located at each electric window. Some power window systems use a lockout/child safety switch located on the driver's controls to prevent operation of the power windows from the independent switches. Power windows are designed to operate only with the ignition switch in the on (run) position, although some manufacturers use a time delay for accessory power after the ignition switch is turned off. This feature permits the driver and passengers an opportunity to close all

windows or operate other accessories for about 10 minutes or until a vehicle door is opened after the ignition has been turned off. This feature is often called *retained accessory power (RAP)*.

POWER WINDOW MOTORS Most power window systems use permanent magnet (PM) electric motors. It is possible to run a PM motor in the reverse direction by reversing the polarity of the two wires going to the motor. Most power window motors do not require that the motor be grounded to the body (door) of the vehicle. The ground for all the power windows is most often centralized near the driver's master control switch. The up-and-down motion of the individual window motors is controlled by double-pole, double-throw (DPDT) switches. These DPDT switches have five contacts and permit battery voltage to be applied to the power window motor, as well as reverse the polarity and direction of the motor.

Each motor is protected by a positive temperature coefficient (PTC) electronic circuit breaker. These circuit breakers are built into the motor assembly and are not a separate replaceable part. ● SEE FIGURE 28–26.

The power window motors rotate a mechanism called a *window regulator*. The window regulator is attached to the door glass and controls opening and closing of the glass. Door glass adjustments, such as glass tilt and upper and lower stops, are usually the same for both power and manual windows. ● SEE FIGURE 28–27.

AUTO DOWN/UP FEATURES Many power windows are equipped with an auto down feature that allows windows to be lowered all the way if the control switch is moved to a detent or held down for longer than 0.3 second. The window then moves down all the way to the bottom, and then the motor stops.

Public Law 110-189, also known as the Cameron Gulbransen Kids Transportation Safety Act, mandated the use of power window **automatic reversal systems (ARS)**. The

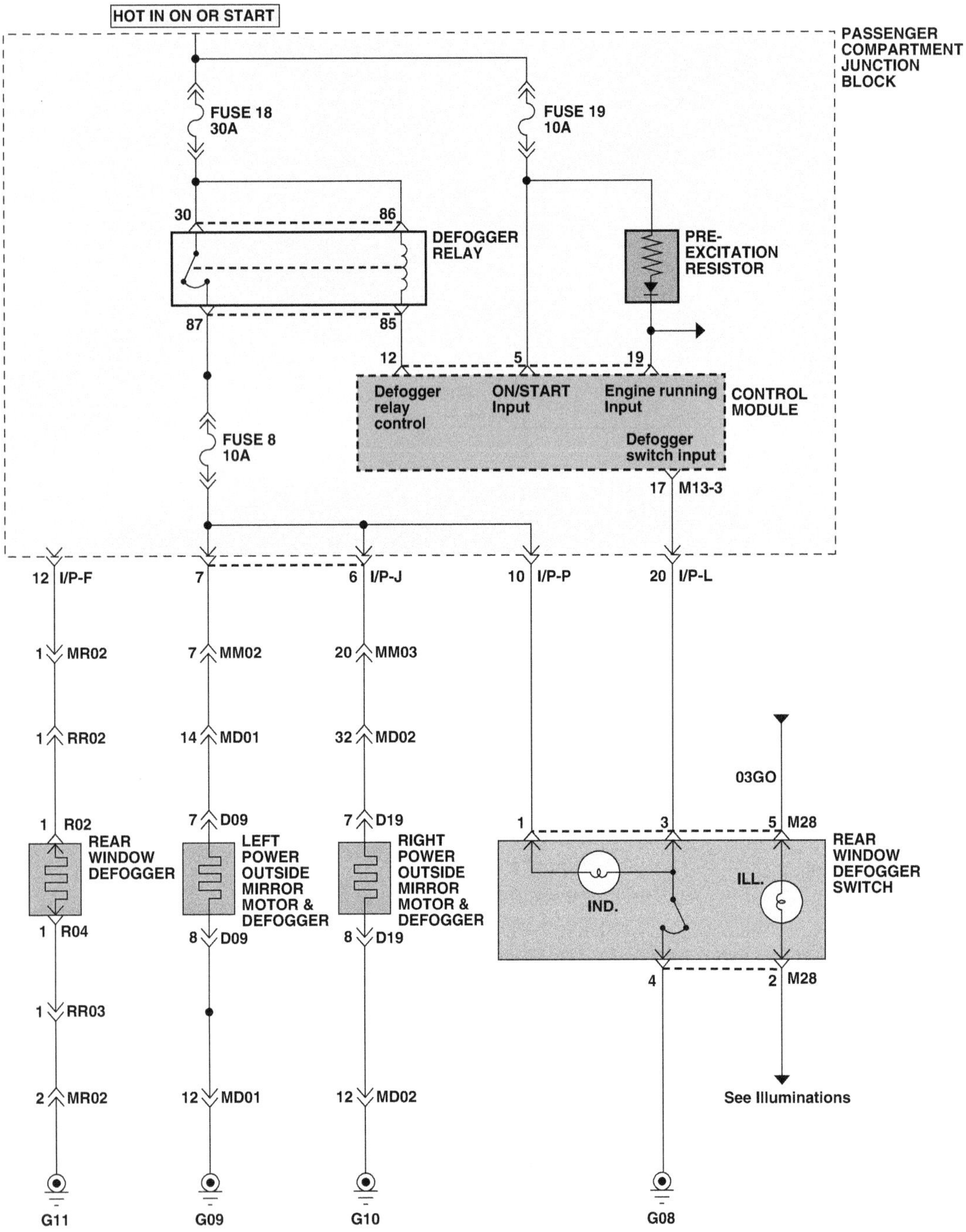

HOT IN ON OR START

PASSENGER COMPARTMENT JUNCTION BLOCK

FUSE 18 30A

FUSE 19 10A

30   86

DEFOGGER RELAY

PRE-EXCITATION RESISTOR

87   85

12   5   19

Defogger relay control

ON/START Input

Engine running Input

CONTROL MODULE

Defogger switch input

17   M13-3

FUSE 8 10A

12 I/P-F   7   6 I/P-J   10 I/P-P   20 I/P-L

1 MR02   7 MM02   20 MM03

1 RR02   14 MD01   32 MD02

1 R02   7 D09   7 D19   1   3   5 M28

REAR WINDOW DEFOGGER

LEFT POWER OUTSIDE MIRROR MOTOR & DEFOGGER

RIGHT POWER OUTSIDE MIRROR MOTOR & DEFOGGER

03GO

REAR WINDOW DEFOGGER SWITCH

IND.   ILL.

1 R04   8 D09   8 D19

1 RR03

2 MR02   12 MD01   12 MD02

4   2 M28

See Illuminations

G11   G09   G10   G08

FIGURE 28–22 A schematic showing that the side view mirrors are heated along with the rear window defogger whenever the rear window switch (lower right) is turned to the on position.

automatic reversal system is designed to prevent windows from causing injury when they are closing, if the vehicle is equipped with power windows. The Department of Transportation (DOT) established a limit of 136 ft-lb (100 NM) of force be exerted by the window before the window retracts. There are two methods used for controlling ARS and auto up and auto down windows, including:

1. An encoder wheel and position sensor are used to monitor the speed and position of the window as it travels up and down.

2. The current (amperes) required is measured by the power window control module.

The window direction reverses if the current draw exceeds a predetermined value. If an object is in the path of the window, the current draw and or slowing of the window causes the control module to reverse. The system is designed to expect increased current flow and slower window movement in cold weather conditions. However, sudden vehicle movement, such as hitting a bump in the road as the window is moving upward or a fault in the window track, can cause the window to reverse.

A factory or factory-level scan tool is used to diagnosis this system, which can monitor switch operation and can be used to control the operation of the windows using bidirectional controls. ● **SEE FIGURE 28–28.**

FIGURE 28–23 A typical image captured using an infrared camera of a rear defogger that is working as designed.

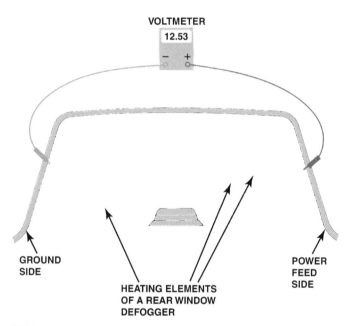

FIGURE 28–24 A rear window defogger electrical grid can be tested using a voltmeter to check for a decreasing voltage as the meter lead is moved from the power side toward the ground side. As the voltmeter positive lead is moved along the grid (on the inside of the vehicle), the voltmeter reading should steadily decrease as the meter approaches the ground side of the grid.

TROUBLESHOOTING POWER WINDOWS Before troubleshooting a power window problem, check for proper operation of all power windows. Also check that the child-proof switch is not in the disable position, which prevents the windows from being operated from any position except the driver's master control. Check service information for the exact procedure to follow. In a newer system, a scan tool can be used to perform the following:

- Check for B (body) or U (network) diagnostic trouble codes (DTCs)

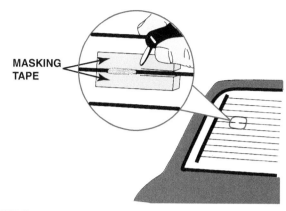

FIGURE 28–25 The typical repair material contains conductive silver-filled polymer, which dries in 10 minutes and is usable in 30 minutes.

🔧 **TECH TIP**

Programming Auto Down/Up Power Windows

Many vehicles are equipped with automatic operation that can cause the window to go all the way down (or up) if the switch is depressed beyond a certain point or held for a fraction of a second. Sometimes this feature is lost if the battery in the vehicle has been disconnected. Although this programming procedure can vary depending on the make and model, many times the window(s) can be reprogrammed without using a scan tool by depressing and holding the down button for 10 seconds. If the vehicle is equipped with an auto up feature, repeat the procedure by holding the button up for 10 seconds. Always check exact service information for the vehicle being serviced.

- Operate the power windows using the bidirectional control feature
- Relearn or program the operation of the power windows after a battery disconnect

Always follow the diagnosis and repair procedures as specified in service information.

ELECTRIC POWER DOOR LOCKS

PARTS AND OPERATION Electric power door locks use a permanent magnet (PM) reversible motor to lock or unlock all vehicle door locks from a control switch or switches. The electric motor uses a built-in circuit breaker and operates the lock-activating rod. PM reversible motors do not require grounding

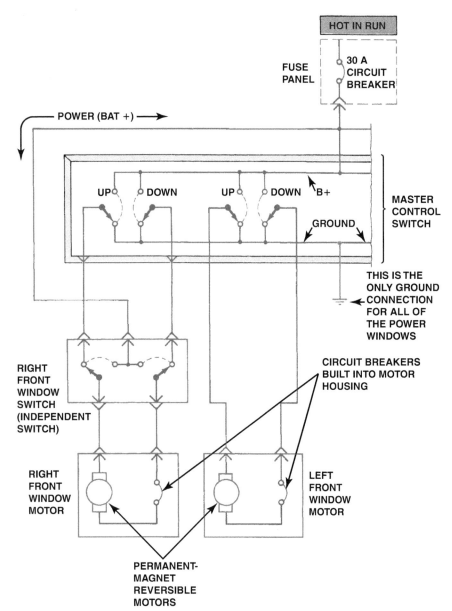

FIGURE 28–26 A typical power window circuit using PM motors. Control of the direction of window operation is achieved by directing the polarity of the current through the non-grounded motors. The only ground for the entire system is located at the master control (driver's side) switch assembly.

HOT IN RUN

FUSE PANEL

30 A CIRCUIT BREAKER

POWER (BAT +)

UP DOWN UP DOWN B+

GROUND

MASTER CONTROL SWITCH

THIS IS THE ONLY GROUND CONNECTION FOR ALL OF THE POWER WINDOWS

RIGHT FRONT WINDOW SWITCH (INDEPENDENT SWITCH)

CIRCUIT BREAKERS BUILT INTO MOTOR HOUSING

RIGHT FRONT WINDOW MOTOR

LEFT FRONT WINDOW MOTOR

PERMANENT-MAGNET REVERSIBLE MOTORS

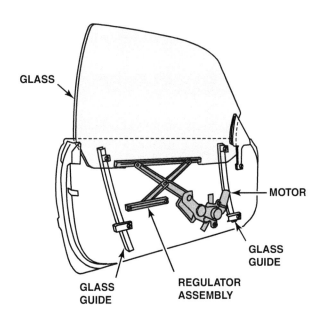

FIGURE 28–27 An electric motor and a regulator assembly raise and lower the glass on a power window.

GLASS

MOTOR

GLASS GUIDE

GLASS GUIDE

REGULATOR ASSEMBLY

FIGURE 28–28 A master power window control panel with the buttons and the cover removed.

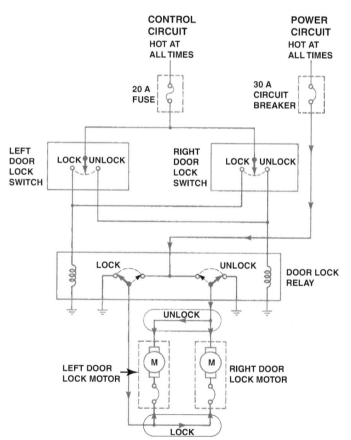

FIGURE 28–29 A typical electric power door lock circuit diagram. Note that the control circuit is protected by a fuse, whereas the power circuit is protected by a circuit breaker. As with the operation of power windows, power door locks typically use reversible permanent magnet (PM) non-grounded electric motors. These motors are geared mechanically to the lock–unlock mechanism.

because, as with power windows, the motor control is determined by the polarity of the current through the two motor wires. ● SEE FIGURES 28–29 AND 29–30.

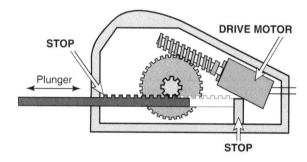

FIGURE 28–30 A typical power door lock mechanism showing a DC drive motor used to move the door lock plunger

Some two-door vehicles do not use a power door lock relay because the current flow for only two PM motors can be handled through the door lock switches. However, most four-door vehicles and vans with power locks on rear and side doors use a relay to control the current flow necessary to operate four or more power door lock motors. The door lock relay is controlled by the door lock switch and is commonly the location of the one and only ground connection for the entire door lock circuit.

🔧 TECH TIP

Check the Glove Box Switch Position

A common customer complaint is that the trunk or lift gate can be opened manually, but it cannot be opened using the remote. Most vehicles are equipped with a lockout switch in the glove compartment (instrument panel compartment) that can be switched off, and the glove box door locked to limit access when the vehicle is parked, and the valet has the key to the ignition. If the switch is in the locked position, the trunk cannot be opened using the remote. Check that first before following the recommended diagnostic procedures found in service information. ● SEE FIGURE 28–31.

FIGURE 28–31 The switch to disable the outside opening of the trunk/lift gate is often in the glove box.

TROUBLESHOOTING POWER LOCKS If all power door locks are inoperative, use a factory or factory-level aftermarket scan tool and try operating the locks using the bidirectional control. If the door locks do not operate using a scan tool, refer to service information for the exact procedure to follow.

If only the power door lock is inoperative, check for the power and ground, as well as possible physical binding of the lock mechanism. Repair or replace as needed.

TRUNK/LIFT GATE LOCKS

CIRCUIT DESCRIPTION The electric power trunk/lift gate lock uses a permanent magnet (PM) reversible motor to lock or unlock the trunk/lift gate lock from a control switch or with the remote. The electric motor uses a built-in circuit breaker and operates the lock-activating rod. PM reversible motors do not require grounding because, as with power windows and door locks, the motor control is determined by the polarity of the current through the two motor wires.

POWER SUN ROOF/ MOON ROOF

DEFINITIONS While they are similar in nature and often used interchangeably, there is a difference between a sun roof and a moon roof.

- **Sun roof**—A sun roof is basically any kind of panel on the roof of a car that permits light, air, or both to come into a vehicle, but only if the panel is opened. A sunroof includes two types of panels:
  1. One panel may be made of either metal or the same material as the ceiling of the car and can be retracted to expose the glass panel above.

2. The other panel is made of glass that can be either tilted open or completely retracted to essentially serve as an open window in the roof.

- **Moon roof**—A moon roof is made of a tinted glass panel that can be either tilted open or completely retracted to operate as an open window in the roof. Most new cars have moon roofs.

OPERATION Most moon or sun roof systems use permanent magnet (PM) electric motors to open and close the moveable glass panel. The open and close, or tilt up or down, motion of the moon roof motors is controlled by double-pole, double-throw (DPDT) switches. These DPDT switches have five contacts and permit battery voltage to be applied to the power moon roof motor, as well as reverse the polarity and direction of the motor. Each motor is protected by an electronic circuit breaker. These circuit breakers are built into the motor assembly and are not a separate replaceable part.

DIAGNOSIS AND SERVICE Always check service information for the exact procedure to use because the moon roofs have many different service items that are likely to need service or repair, including:

- **Water leaks**—Engineers refer to water seals around moon roofs as "controlling the flow of water" and not necessarily trying to provide a water-proof seal. Because the roof of a vehicle flexes when the being driven, no seal can prevent water from leaking around the area around the moon roof. Instead, the water is directed to a tray under the outer seal and then tubes are installed at the four corners of the moon roof to drain the water from the tray to the ground. If water is entering the passenger compartment, make sure the drain tubes are not clogged. The tubes are routed though the two front "A" pillars and the two rear "C" pillars. ● **SEE FIGURE 28–32.**
- **Electrical/Mechanical Issues**—Electrical or mechanical issues can prevent the moon roof from opening or closing. Most vehicle manufacturers include a crank or a way to close the roof if the roof fails to close due to an electrical fault.

Always follow the vehicle manufacturer's recommended service and repair instructions and procedures.

SUN SHADES

DESCRIPTION **Sun shades** are fabric or screen-like material installed on the inside of the vehicle that can be raised, lowered, or moved to block the rays of the sun from entering the interior of the vehicle. Most of the sun shades used on the side windows are operated manually and either can be pulled down from the top of the inside of the door or up from the inner part of the door panel. Sun shades used to block the sun in the rear backlight or moon roof are often electrically powered and

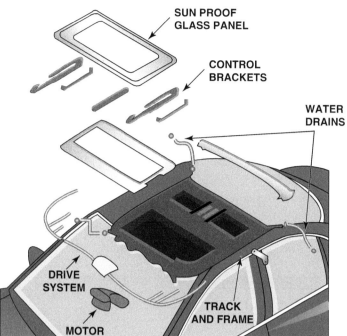

FIGURE 28–32 An exploded view of a typical moveable roof showing the location of the motor and the drain tubes that direct the water to the ground.

use a reversible PM motor to drive the roll holding the fabric.
● **SEE FIGURE 28–33.**

Sun shades are vehicle-specific, so check service information for the exact procedures to follow when servicing or repairing a sun shade.

POWER SEATS

PARTS AND OPERATION A typical power-operated seat includes a reversible electric motor and a transmission assembly that may have three solenoids or motors, and six drive cables that turn the six seat adjusters. A six-way power seat offers seat movement forward and backward, plus seat cushion movement up and down at the front and the rear. The drive cables rotate inside a cable housing and connect the power output of the seat transmission to a gear or screw jack assembly that moves the seat. ● **SEE FIGURE 28–34.**

A *screw jack assembly* is often called a *gear nut*. It is used to move the front or back of the seat cushion up and down. A rubber coupling, usually located between the electric motor and the transmission, prevents electric motor damage in the event of a jammed seat. This coupling is designed to prevent motor damage. Most power seats use a permanent magnet motor that can be reversed by reversing the polarity of the current sent to the motor by the seat switch. ● **SEE FIGURE 28–35.**

POWER SEAT MOTOR(S) Power seats use a PM motor to power the movement of the seat. Most PM motors have a built-in circuit breaker or PTC circuit protector to protect the motor from

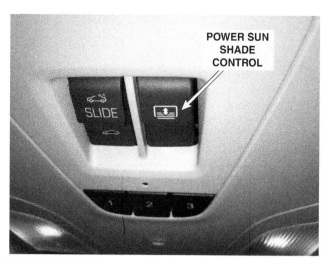

FIGURE 28–33 The control for the operation of the powered inside sun shade on this Chevrolet Impala is in the overhead control panel.

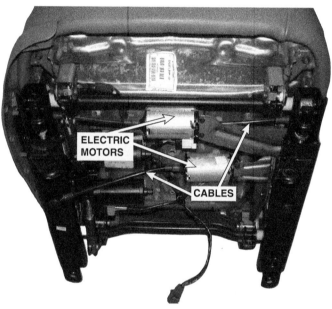

FIGURE 28–34 A power seat uses electric motors under the seat, which drive cables that extend to operate screw jacks (up and down) or gears to move the seat forward and back

overheating. Some older Ford power seat motors use three separate armatures inside one large permanent magnet field housing. Some power seats use a series-wound electric motor with two separate field coils, one field coil for each direction of rotation. This type of power seat motor typically uses a relay to control the direction of current from the seat switch to the corresponding field coil of the seat motor. This type of power seat can be identified by the "click" heard when the seat switch is changed from up to down or front to back, or vice versa. The click is the sound of the relay switching the field coil current. Some power seats use as many as eight separate PM motors that operate all functions of the seat, including headrest height, seat length, and side bolsters, in addition to the usual six-way power seat functions.

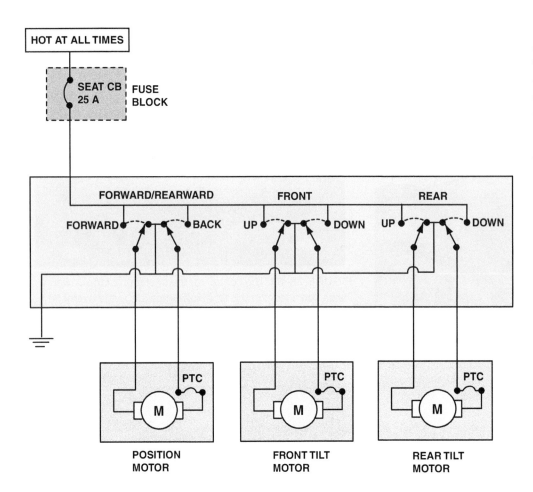

FIGURE 28–35 A typical power seat circuit diagram. Notice that each motor has a built-in electronic (solid-state) PTC circuit protector. The seat control switch can change the direction in which the motor(s) runs by reversing the direction in which the current flows through the motor.

NOTE: Some power seats use a small air pump to inflate a bag (or bags) in the lower part of the back of the seat, called the lumbar, because it supports the lumbar section of the lower back. The lumbar section of the seat can also be changed, using a lever or knob that the driver can move to change the seat section for the lower back.

MEMORY SEAT Memory seats use a potentiometer to sense the position of the seat. The seat position can be programmed into the BCM or memory seat module, and stored by position number 1, 2, or 3. The driver pushes the desired button and the seat moves to the stored position. On some vehicles, the memory seat position is also programmed into the remote keyless entry (RKE) key fob.● **SEE FIGURE 28–36.**

Check service information for the exact procedure to follow when diagnosing power seats.

 TECH TIP

Easy-Exit Seat Programming

Some vehicles are equipped with memory seats that allow the seat to move rearward when the ignition is turned off to allow easy exit from the vehicle. Vehicles equipped with this feature include an *exit/entry* button that is used to program the desired exit/entry position of the seat for each of two drivers. If the vehicle is not equipped with this feature and only one driver primarily uses the vehicle, the second memory position can be programmed for easy exit and entry. Set position 1 to the desired seat position and position 2 to the entry/exit position. When exiting the vehicle, press memory 2 to allow easy exit and easy entry the next time. Press memory 1 to return the seat memory to the desired driving position.

TECH TIP

What Every Driver Should Know About Power Seats

Power seats use an electric motor or motors to move the position of the seat. These electric motors turn small cables, gears, and/or shafts that operate mechanisms that move the seat. Never place rags, newspapers, or any other object under a power seat. Even ice scrapers can get caught between moving parts of the seat and can often cause serious damage or jamming of the power seat. In many cases, after the object is removed that caused the seat jam, the memory function needs to be relearned for proper operation to resume.

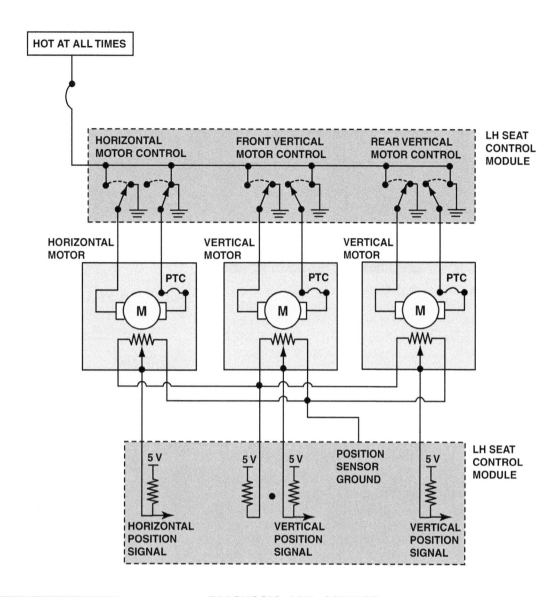

FIGURE 28–36 A typical memory seat module showing the three-wire potentiometer used to determine seat position.

ELECTRICALLY HEATED SEATS

PARTS AND OPERATION **Heated seats** use electric heating elements in the seat bottom, as well as in the seat back, in many vehicles. The heating element is designed to warm the seat and/or back of the seat to about 100°F (38°C) or close to normal body temperature (98.6°F [37°C]). Many heated seats also include a high-position or a variable temperature setting, so the temperature of the seats can, therefore, be as high as 110°F (44°C).

A temperature sensor in the seat cushion is used to regulate the temperature. The sensor is a variable resistor, which changes with temperature and is used as an input signal to a heated seat control module. The heated seat module uses the seat temperature input, as well as the input from the high–low (or variable) temperature control, to turn the current on or off to the heating element in the seat. Some vehicles are equipped with heated seats in both the front and the rear seats.

DIAGNOSIS AND SERVICE When diagnosing a heated seat concern, start by verifying that the switch is in the on position and that the temperature of the seat is below normal body temperature. Using service information, check for power and ground at the control module and to the heating element in the seat. Most vehicle manufacturers recommend replacing the entire heating element if it is defective. ● **SEE FIGURE 28–37.**

HEATED AND COOLED SEATS

PARTS AND OPERATION Most electrically heated and cooled seats use a thermoelectric device (TED) located under the seat cushion and seat back. The thermoelectric device consists of positive and negative connections between two ceramic plates. Each ceramic plate has copper fins to allow the transfer of heat to or from air passing over the device and directed into the seat cushion. The thermoelectric device uses the Peltier effect, named after

FIGURE 28–37 The heating element of a heated seat is a replaceable part, but service requires that the upholstery be removed. The yellow part is the seat foam material and the entire white cover is the replaceable heating element. This is then covered by the seat material.

the inventor Jean C. A. Peltier (1785–1845), a French clockmaker. When electrical current flows through the module, one side is heated, and the other side is cooled. Reversing the polarity of the current changes the side to be heated. ● **SEE FIGURE 28–38.**

Most vehicles equipped with heated and cooled seats use two modules per seat, one for the seat cushion and one for the seat back. When the heated and cooled seats are turned on, air is forced through a filter and then through the thermoelectric modules. The air is then directed through passages in the foam of the seat cushion and seat back. Each thermoelectric device has a temperature sensor called a thermistor. The control module uses sensors to determine the temperature of the fins in the thermoelectric device so the controller can maintain the set temperature. ● **SEE FIGURE 28–39.**

Always follow the vehicle manufacturer's recommended diagnosis and service procedures for the repair of heated and cooled seat systems.

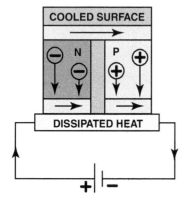

FIGURE 28–38 A Peltier effect device is capable of heating or cooling, depending on the polarity of the applied current.

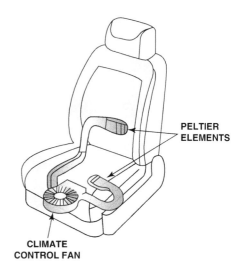

FIGURE 28–39 A fan is used to move the heated or cooled air to heat or cool the bottom or the back of the seat.

TECH TIP

Check the Seat Filter

Heated and cooled seats often use a filter to trap dirt and debris to help keep the air passages clean. If a customer complains of a slow heating or cooling of the seat, check the air filter and replace or clean as necessary. Check service information for the exact location of the seat filter and for instructions on how to remove and/or replace it.

HEATED STEERING WHEEL

PARTS INVOLVED A **heated steering wheel** usually consists of the following components.

- Steering wheel with a built-in heater in the rim
- Heated steering wheel control switch
- Heated steering wheel control module

OPERATION When the steering wheel heater control switch is turned on, a signal is sent to the control module and electrical current flows through the heating element in the rim of the steering wheel. ● **SEE FIGURE 28–40.**

The system remains on until the ignition switch is turned off or the driver turns off the control switch. The temperature of the steering wheel is usually calibrated to stay at about 90°F (32°C), and it requires three to four minutes to reach that temperature, depending on the outside temperature. Most heated steering wheels only heat a part and often not all the steering wheel. Before trying to repair a condition where just some sections of the steering wheel are being warmed, check service information for what parts are normally heated.

FIGURE 28–40 The heated steering wheel is controlled by a switch on the steering wheel in this vehicle.

Always follow the vehicle manufacturer's recommended diagnosis and testing procedures for heated steering wheel diagnosis and repair.

HEATED MIRRORS

PURPOSE AND FUNCTION The purpose and function of heated outside mirrors is to heat the surface of the mirror, which evaporates moisture on the surface. Heated mirrors may be an option for the left-side outside mirror or both the left- and right-side outside mirrors, depending on the vehicle. The heat helps keep ice and fog off the mirrors to allow for better driver visibility.

PARTS AND OPERATION Heated outside mirrors are often tied into the same electrical circuit as the rear window defogger. Therefore, when the rear defogger is turned on, the heating grid on the backside of the mirror is also turned on. On some vehicles, the heated mirrors are activated when the heating, ventilation, and cooling (HVAC) system is placed in the defrost mode. Some vehicles use a switch for each mirror.

DIAGNOSIS The first step in any diagnosis procedure is to verify the customer concern. Check the owner's manual or service information for the proper method to use to turn on the heated mirrors.

NOTE: Heated mirrors are *not* designed to melt snow or a thick layer of ice.

If a fault has been detected, check service information instructions for the exact procedure to follow. If the mirror itself is found to be defective, it is usually replaced as an assembly, instead of being repaired.

ADJUSTABLE PEDALS

PURPOSE AND FUNCTION Adjustable pedals, also called *pedal height* or **electric adjustable pedals (EAP)**, place the brake pedal and the accelerator pedal on movable brackets that are motor operated. The height of the accelerator pedal and the brake pedal are adjusted together and cannot be adjusted individually. A typical adjustable pedal system includes the following components.

- Adjustable pedal position switch: Allows the driver to position the pedals.
- Adjustable pedal assembly: Includes the motor, threaded adjustment rods, and a pedal position sensor. ● **SEE FIGURE 28–41.**

The position of the pedals, as well as the position of the seat system, is usually included as part of the memory seat function and can be set for two or more drivers.

DIAGNOSIS AND SERVICE The first step when there is a customer concern about the functioning of the adjustable pedals is to verify that the unit is not working as designed. Check the owner's manual or service information for the proper operation. Follow the vehicle manufacturer's recommended troubleshooting procedure. Many diagnostic procedures include the use of a factory scan tool with bidirectional control capabilities to test this system.

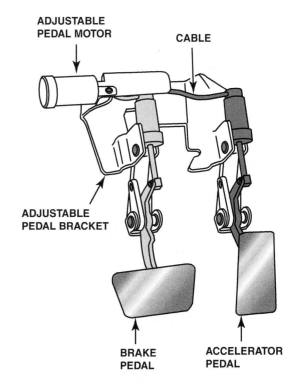

FIGURE 28–41 A typical adjustable pedal assembly. Both the accelerator and the brake pedal can be moved forward and rearward by using the adjustable pedal position switch.

Check the Remote

The memory function may be programmed to a particular key fob remote, which commands the adjustable pedals to move to the position set in memory. Always check the settings of all remotes before attempting to repair a problem, which may not be a problem.

 CASE STUDY

The Case of the Haunted Mirrors

The owner complained that while driving, either one or the other, outside mirror folded in without any button being depressed. Unable to verify the customer concern, the service technician looked at the owner's manual to find out exactly how the mirrors were supposed to work. In the manual, a caution statement said that if the mirror is electrically folded inward and then manually pushed out, the mirror does not lock into position. The power folding mirrors must be electrically cycled outward, using the mirror switches to lock them in position. After cycling both mirrors inward and outward electrically, the problem was solved. ● **SEE FIGURES 28–42 AND 28–43.**

Summary:

* **Complaint**—Customer stated that the outside power folding mirror folded by itself at times.
* **Cause**—The mirrors must be moved electrically, not manually, to work correctly.
* **Correction**—Cycling the mirrors electrically restored proper operation.

FIGURE 28–43 The electric mirror control is located on the driver's side door panel on this Cadillac Escalade.

FOLDING OUTSIDE MIRRORS

Mirrors that can be electrically folded inward are a popular feature, especially on larger sport utility vehicles. A control inside is used to fold both mirrors inward when needed, such as when entering a garage or a tight parking spot. For diagnosis and servicing of outside folding mirrors, check service information for details.

KEYLESS ENTRY

SYSTEM DESCRIPTION   Even though some Ford vehicles use a keypad located on the outside of the door, most keyless entry systems use a wireless transmitter built into the key fob or remote. A key fob is a decorative item on a key chain. ● **SEE FIGURE 28–44.**

FIGURE 28–42 Electrically folded mirror in the folded position.

FIGURE 28–44 A key fob remote.

The transmitter broadcasts a signal that is received by the electronic control module, which is generally mounted in the trunk or under the instrument panel. ● SEE FIGURE 28–45.

The electronic control unit sends a voltage signal to the door lock actuator(s) located in the doors. Generally, if the transmitter unlock button is depressed once, only the driver's door is unlocked. If the unlock button is depressed twice, then all doors unlock.

ROLLING CODE RESET PROCEDURE
Many keyless remote systems use a rolling-code type of transmitter and receiver. In a conventional system, the transmitter emits a certain fixed frequency, which is received by the vehicle control module. This single frequency can be intercepted and rebroadcast to open the vehicle. A rolling-code type of transmitter emits a different frequency every time the transmitter button is depressed and then rolls over to another frequency so that it cannot be intercepted. Both the transmitter and the receiver must be kept in synchronized order so that the remote functions correctly. If the transmitter is depressed when it is out of range from the vehicle, the proper frequency may not be recognized by the receiver, which did not roll over to the new frequency when the transmitter was depressed. If the transmitter does not work, try to resynchronize the transmitter to the receiver by depressing and holding both the lock and the unlock button for 10 seconds when within range of the receiver.

PASSIVE KEYLESS ENTRY SYSTEM
A passive system uses the key fob as a transmitter, which communicates with the vehicle as it comes close. The key is identified using one of several antennas around the body of the vehicle and a radio pulse generator in the key housing. Depending on the system, the vehicle is automatically unlocked when a button or sensor on the door handle or trunk release is depressed. ● SEE FIGURE 28–46.

A passive system can also be used to unlock and open a rear lift gate on an SUV if a foot is moved under the edge of the vehicle, allowing it to open the slider or the rear hatch. Vehicles with a passive (smart) key system can also have a mechanical backup, usually in the form of a key blade built into the key fob. Vehicles with a smart key system can be started without inserting a key in the ignition, provided the driver has the key fob inside the vehicle. On most vehicles, this is done most often by pressing a start button. When leaving a vehicle equipped with a smart key system, the vehicle is locked, depending on the make, model, and year of manufacture of vehicle, by:

- Pressing a button on one of the door handles
- Touching a capacitive area on a door handle
- Walking away from the vehicle and the door locks when the key fob is further away than 15 feet (5 m).

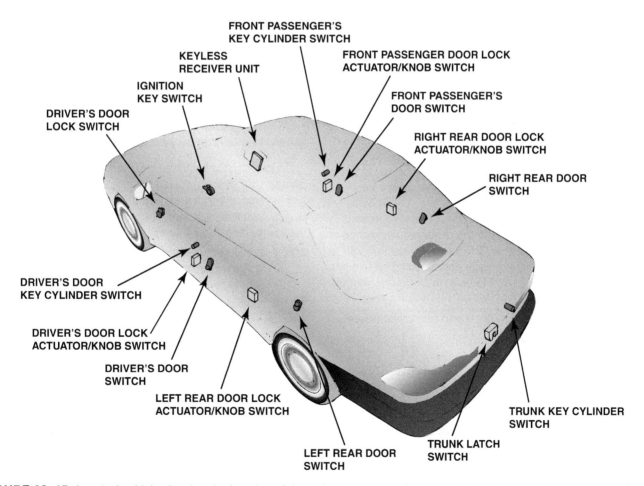

FIGURE 28–45 A typical vehicle showing the location of the various components of the remote keyless entry system.

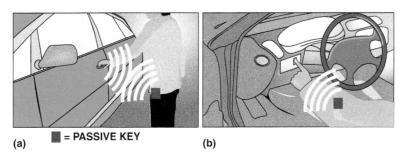

(a)　■ = PASSIVE KEY　　　　(b)

FIGURE 28–46 (a) If the passive key is within about 15 feet (5 m) of the vehicle when the door handle is touched, the door unlocks, allowing access to the interior. (b) The engine starts if the smart key is detected being inside the vehicle. This system is commonly called the passive entry, passive starting (PEPS) system.

KEYLESS ENTRY DIAGNOSIS A small battery powers the transmitter, and a weak battery is a common cause of remote power locks failing to operate. If the keyless entry system fails to operate after the transmitter battery has been replaced, check the following items.

- Mechanical binding in the door lock
- Low vehicle battery voltage
- Blown fuse
- Open circuit to the control module
- Defective control module
- Defective transmitter

PROGRAMMING A NEW REMOTE If a new or additional remote transmitter is to be used, it must be programmed to the vehicle. Generally, all remotes previously programmed to the vehicle must be present during the programming or they no longer work. The programming procedure varies and may require the use of a scan tool. Check service information for the exact procedure to follow.

GARAGE DOOR OPENER

OPERATION HomeLink or Car2U is a device installed in many new vehicles that duplicates the radio-frequency code of the original garage door opener. The frequency range is 288 to 418 MHz. The typical vehicle garage door opening system has three buttons that can be used to operate one or more of the following devices.

- Garage doors equipped with a radio transmitter electric opener
- Gates
- Entry door locks
- Lighting or small appliances

The devices include both fixed-frequency devices, usually in older units, and rolling (encrypted) code devices. ● **SEE FIGURE 28–47.**

PROGRAMMING A VEHICLE GARAGE DOOR OPENER
When a vehicle is purchased, it must be programmed using the transmitter for the garage door opener or other device.

FIGURE 28–47 Typical HomeLink garage door opener buttons. Notice that three different units can be controlled from the vehicle using the HomeLink system.

NOTE: The garage door opening controller can only be programmed by using a transmitter. If an automatic garage door system does not have a remote transmitter, the system cannot be programmed.

Normally, the customer is responsible for programming the garage door opener. However, some customers may find that help is needed from the service department. The steps that are usually involved in programming a garage door opener in the vehicle to the garage door opener are as follows:

STEP 1 Unplug the garage door opener during programming to prevent it from being cycled on and off, which could damage the motor.

STEP 2 Check that the frequency of the handheld transmitter is between 288 and 418 MHz.

STEP 3 Install new batteries in the transmitter to be assured of a strong signal being transmitted to the garage door opener module in the vehicle.

STEP 4 Turn the ignition on, engine off (KOEO).

STEP 5 While holding the transmitter 4 to 6 inches away from the opener button, press and hold the button while pressing and releasing the handheld transmitter every two seconds. Continue pressing and releasing the transmitter until the indicator light near the opener button changes from a slow blink to a rapid flash.

STEP 6 Verify that the vehicle garage door system (HomeLink or Car2U) button has been programmed. Press and hold the garage door button. If the indicator light blinks rapidly for two seconds and then comes on steady, the system has been successfully programmed using a rolling code design. If the indicator light is on steady, then it has been successfully programmed to a fixed frequency device.

DIAGNOSIS AND SERVICE If a fault occurs with the garage door opening system, first verify that the garage door opener is functioning correctly. Also, check if the garage door opener remote control can operate the door. Repair the garage door opener system as needed. If the problem still exists, attempt reprogramming the HomeLink/Car2U vehicle system, being sure that the remote has a newly purchased battery.

REMOTE START

PURPOSE AND FUNCTION A **remote start** is the ability to start the engine of the vehicle from a distance by using a remote control. This a popular option, especially in cold climates, which allows the driver to start the engine when inside the house or office to start the warm-up process before even entering the vehicle. It is also popular in the warm weather areas where the interior can be cooled by the air conditioning before entering the vehicle. Most factory-installed remote start systems use the same key fob that it used to unlock the doors. ● **SEE FIGURE 28–48.**

PARTS AND OPERATION The remote start system uses a signal from the transmitter (usually the key fob on factory systems) to start the engine. The engine runs for about ten

WARNING:

Never use the remote start to start the engine if the vehicle is located inside a garage or an area without proper ventilation, or if a car cover is covering the body of the vehicle.

TECH TIP

Try to Purchase an Aftermarket System That Has a Long Range

Most factory remote start systems have a range of 400 to 600 feet (120–180 m) and may work as far away as 1,500 feet (450 m) in open areas. The distance is affected by buildings and walls, which can greatly reduce the effective range. If purchasing an aftermarket remote start device, look for a high transmitter power rating because this is the value that determines the range of the remote. Many units are advertised as having a 500 foot range or 3,000 foot range, but these numbers are for areas without any obstructions. While few vehicle owners need to start their vehicles from more than 1,000 feet away, most want to start a vehicle from inside a building. A longer range (more transmitter power) is needed if it is used from a mall, sporting events, parking garages, hospitals, or restaurants. If in doubt, pay a little more to get a more powerful unit.

minutes, depending on the system, and then shuts off. The vehicle needs to be setup ahead of time with the HVAC system set to heat or A/C and the transmission gear selector in park,

FIGURE 28–48 A remote start system allows the engine to be started from a distance, usually form inside the house before leaving for the day. Most systems only allow the engine to run for ten minutes.

or in neutral on vehicles equipped with a manual transmission. Always check service information for the conditions that allow remote starting, which often includes the following:

- The keyless remote is not inside the vehicle.
- The gearshift lever is in the "P" (Park) position.
- The security warning system is not activated.
- The brake pedal is not depressed.

- The engine hood is closed.
- All the doors are closed and locked.
- The trunk or tailgate is closed.
- The ignition key is removed from the ignition switch.
- The vehicle battery is not low.

Check service information for the exact procedures to follow when diagnosing a fault with the remote engine start system.

SUMMARY

1. Horn frequency can range from 1,800 to 3,550 Hz.
2. Most horn circuits use a relay, and the current through the relay coil is controlled by the horn switch.
3. Most windshield wipers use a three-brush, two-speed motor.
4. Windshield washer diagnosis includes checking the pump both electrically and mechanically for proper operation.
5. Many blower motors use resistors wired in series to control blower motor speed.
6. A good blower motor should draw less than 20 amperes.
7. Most power windows and power door locks use a permanent magnet motor that has a built-in circuit breaker and is reversible. The control switches and relays direct the current through the motors.
8. The current flowing through a rear window defogger is often self-regulating. As the temperature of the grid increases, its resistance increases, reducing current flow. Some rear window defoggers are also used as radio antennas.
9. Remote keyless entry systems use a wireless transmitter built into the key fob to operate the power door lock.
10. A remote start is the ability to start the engine of the vehicle from a distance by using a remote control.

REVIEW QUESTIONS

1. What are the advantages of using the BCM to able to operate the horns?
2. How do rain-sense wipers work?
3. What is the purpose of a radar cruise control system?
4. How can an infrared camera be used to test a rear window defogger?
5. What is meant by a "rolling code"?

CHAPTER QUIZ

1. In most recent-model vehicles, the horn button is an input to the _____, which then activates the horn circuit.
   a. horn relay
   b. instrument cluster
   c. BCM
   d. fuse controller
2. Technician A says that the cruise control on a vehicle that uses an electronic throttle control (ETC) system uses a servo to move the throttle. Technician B says that the cruise control on a vehicle with ETC uses the accelerator pedal position (APP) sensor to set the speed. Which technician is correct?
   a. Technician A only
   b. Technician B only
   c. Both Technicians A and B
   d. Neither Technician A nor B
3. Most vehicles use _____ to control the actual operation of the wipers?
   a. variable resistors
   b. changing the voltage to the brushes
   c. the BCM
   d. the changing the position of the brushes
4. Technician A says that the automatic reversal system operates by detecting the force needed to close the window. Technician B says that the child-proof lock switch position should be checked if there is a power window operation customer concern. Which technician is correct?
   a. Technician A only
   b. Technician B only
   c. Both Technicians A and B
   d. Neither Technician A nor B

5. A typical radar cruise control system uses _____.
   a. long-range radar (LRR)
   b. short-range radar (SRR)
   c. electronic throttle control system to control vehicle speed
   d. All of the above

6. When checking the operation of a rear window defogger with a voltmeter, _____.
   a. the voltmeter should be set to read AC volts
   b. the voltmeter should read close to battery voltage anywhere along the grid
   c. voltage should be available anytime at the power side of the grid because the control circuit just completes the ground side of the heater grid circuit
   d. the voltmeter should indicate decreasing voltage when the grid is tested across the width of the glass.

7. PM motors used in power windows, mirrors, and seats can be reversed by _____.
   a. sending current to a reversed field coil
   b. reversing the polarity of the current to the motor
   c. using a reverse relay circuit
   d. using a relay and a two-way clutch

8. How is the panel of a sun roof opened and closed?
   a. With a reversable PM motor
   b. By way of vacuum actuators
   c. With a handle and cables
   d. None of these

9. A keyless remote start is not working. Technician A says the trunk of the vehicle may be open. Technician B says that the key fob may be too far away from the vehicle. Which technician is correct?
   a. Technician A only
   b. Technician B only
   c. Both Technicians A and B
   d. Neither Technician A nor B

10. Technician A says that adjustable pedals move both the accelerator pedal and the brake pedal. Technician B says that only the brake pedal moves when adjusting the pedals. Which technician is correct?
    a. Technician A only
    b. Technician B only
    c. Both technicians are correct
    d. Neither technician is correct

Chapter 29

ADVANCED DRIVER ASSIST SYSTEMS (ADAS)

LEARNING OBJECTIVES

After studying this chapter, the reader should be able to:

Describe the purpose and function of advanced driver assist systems.

Discuss blind spot monitors and parking assist, as well as self-parking systems.

Explain lane departure warning and lane keep assist systems.

Describe how adaptive cruise control systems work.

Discuss rear cross-traffic warning system operation.

Explain automatic emergency braking and pre-collision systems.

Describe the operation of hill start assist.

Describe the diagnostic and calibrations procedures for advanced driver assist systems.

This chapter will help prepare for the ASE Electrical/Electronic Systems (A6) certification test content area "G" (Repair Body Electrical)

KEY TERMS: Adaptive cruise control (ACC) 396 • Automatic emergency braking (AEB) 398 • Blind spot monitor (BSM) 393 • Cross-traffic alert 394 • Electromagnetic parking sensors (EPS) 394 • Human–machine interface (HMI) 393 • Intelligent Speed Advice (ISA) 398 • Lane departure warning system (LDWS) 395 • Lane keep assist (LKA) 395 • Rear cross-traffic warning (RCTW) 398 • Self-parking 395 • Ultrasonic object sensors 394

ADVANCED DRIVER ASSIST SYSTEMS

PURPOSE The purpose of advanced driver assist systems (ADAS) is to provide the driver with systems that help the driver by doing the following:

- Alert the driver of a potential issue, such as getting too close to the center line or too far to the right of the roadway.
- Take the responsibility off the driver, such as maintaining an ensured clear distance from the vehicle in front while

at the same time handling the accelerator pedal to maintain a set speed.

- Help the driver avoid a collision if a vehicle in front of the driver stops quickly.
- Make the parking safer through parking assist systems that use ultrasonic sensors to detect when the front or rear bumper is getting close to an object.

CAUTION: The advanced driver assist systems are designed as a driver aid and are not intended to replace the driver. It is the responsibility of the driver to be aware of the surroundings and be able to take control of the vehicle at all times.

What Is Meant by Human–Machine Interface (HMI)?

Human–machine interface (HMI) was very basic in the past because the vehicles were equipped with most of the following to let the driver know what the vehicle (the machine) was doing:

- Speedometers
- Fuel level gauge
- Engine coolant temperature
- Oil pressure (some vehicles)

Vehicles with advanced technology need to communicate to the driver or occupants using the following:

1. Visual displays (eyes)
2. Sounds
3. Tactile (called "haptic" feedback vibrations of the seat or the steering wheel, which are created using a DC motor turning an offset weight to create the vibrations)

The hardware involved includes the following:

1. A display
2. Speakers
3. Input devices, such as a mouse or joystick
4. Microphone for voice commands

Behind the scenes, software is used to sort out the vast amount of information and reduce it to the levels where the driver can understand and react to situations as needed.

FIGURE 29–1 Blind spot monitoring systems usually use a warning system in the side-view mirror or in the "A" pillar near the side-view mirror to warn the driver that there is a vehicle in the potential blind spot.

BLIND SPOT MONITOR

FUNCTION AND TERMINOLOGY The **blind spot monitor (BSM)** is a vehicle-based sensor device that detects other vehicles located to the side and rear of the vehicle. Warnings can be any of the following:

- Visual—Usually a warning light in the outside rearview mirrors. ● **SEE FIGURE 29–1.**
- Audible—Usually a beep or buzzer sound.
- Vibrating (tactile)—A vibration is often created in the steering wheel or the driver's seat.

The term used varies with vehicle manufacturers and includes the following:

Acura—Blind Spot Information (BSI)

Audi—Side Assist

BMW—Active Blind Spot Detection

Buick—Side Blind Zone Alert

Cadillac—Side Blind Zone Alert

Chevrolet—Side Blind Zone Alert

Dodge—Blind Spot Monitoring

Fiat—Blind Spot Monitoring

Ford—Blind Spot Information System (BLIS)

GMC—Side Blind Zone Alert

Honda—Lane Watch System

Hyundai—Blind Spot Detection

Infiniti—Blind Spot Intervention System

Jeep—Blind Spot Monitoring

Land Rover—Blind Spot Monitor

Lexus—Blind Spot Monitor

Mazda—Blind Spot Monitoring (BSM)

Mercedes-Benz—Active Blind Spot Assist

Mitsubishi—Blind Spot Warning (BSW)

Nissan—Blind Spot Warning

Porsche—Lane Change Assist

Subaru—Blind Spot Detection

Toyota—Blind Spot Monitor

Volvo—Blind Spot Information System (BSIS)

PARTS AND OPERATION When the vehicle is first started, the outside mirrors displays will come on briefly indicating that the system is turned on and operating. The typical detection zone includes the following:

- Most systems are designed to detect objects that are as small as a motorcycle with rider.
- The detection zone extends out from the sides and behind the vehicle about 10 feet (3 m).
- It is capable of detecting objects that are about 2 to 6 feet (0.6 to 1.8 m) tall (above the ground).

NOTE: The blind spot monitoring system does not detect objects that are not moving, such as walls, curbs, bridges, or parked vehicles.

If the blind spot monitoring system fails to work as designed, check service information for the specified troubleshooting and repair procedure to follow.

PARKING-ASSIST SYSTEMS

FUNCTION AND COMPONENTS The parking-assist system is used to help drivers avoid contact with another object while moving slowly. When backing up at speed of less than 5 MPH (8 km/h), the system constantly monitors for objects located around the vehicle. The parking-assist system can usually detect objects that are greater than 3 inches (8 cm) wide and 10 inches (25 cm) tall, but the system cannot detect objects below the bumper or underneath the vehicle. As the vehicle gets closer to an object, there is an audible beep out of the speakers, and the time between the beeps becomes shorter, the closer to the object. The parking-assist system usually includes the following components:

■ **Ultrasonic object sensors** are used to measure the distances to nearby objects and are built into the fender, and front and rear bumper assembly. The sensors send out acoustic pulses, and a control unit measures the return interval of each reflected signal, calculating object distances. ● **SEE FIGURE 29–2.**

The system warns the driver with warning tones with the frequency indicating object distance. The faster the tone sounds, the closer is the vehicle to the object. A continuous tone indicates a minimal predefined distance. Systems may also include visual aids, such as LED or LCD readouts, to indicate object distance. A vehicle may include a vehicle pictogram on the infotainment screen. ● **SEE FIGURE 29–3.**

■ **Electromagnetic parking sensors (EPS)** detect when a vehicle is moving slowly and toward an object. Once detected, the sensor continues to give signal of presence of the obstacle. If the vehicle then continues to move toward the object, the alarm signal becomes more and more impressive as the obstacle approaches. Electromagnetic parking sensors do not require any holes in the bumper and cannot be seen from the outside of the vehicle. A BSM is an option that may include more than monitoring the front, rear, and sides of the vehicle. It can include **cross-traffic alert**, which can sound an alarm when backing out of a parking space and traffic is approaching from either side.

OPERATION The system is activated automatically when the vehicle is started. The indicator light on the dash or driver information center indicates the system is on. The parking-assist system is active from the time the engine is started until the vehicle exceeds a speed of approximately 6 MPH (10 km/h). It is also active when the vehicle is backing up. The parking-assist system is automatically reactivated the next time the engine is started, even if the system was turned off by the driver the last time the vehicle was driven.

TECH TIP

Check for Repainted Bumpers
The ultrasonic sensors embedded in the bumper are sensitive to paint thickness because the paint covers the sensors. If the system does not seem to be responding to objects, and if the bumper has been repainted, measure the paint thickness using a nonferrous paint thickness gauge. The maximum allowable paint thickness is 6 mils (0.006 inch or 0.15 millimeter).

FIGURE 29–2 The small round buttons in the rear bumper are ultrasonic sensors used to sense distance to an object.

FIGURE 29–3 The dash display on a Chevrolet pickup truck showing that an object is being detected at the front and left-front of the vehicle.

DIAGNOSIS The parking-assist control module can detect faults and store diagnostic trouble codes. If a fault has been detected by the control module, the red lamp flashes and the system is disabled. Follow service information diagnostic procedures because the parking-assist module cannot usually be accessed using a scan tool.

SELF-PARKING **Self-parking** vehicles, also called *automatic parking vehicles*, use the camera(s) and control the electric power steering to guide the vehicle into a parking space. The driver may or may not have to add anything in many advanced systems, whereas the driver must control the throttle and the brakes in early systems. ● **SEE FIGURE 29–4.**

LANE DEPARTURE WARNING

PARTS AND OPERATION The **lane departure warning system (LDWS)** uses cameras to detect if the vehicle is crossing over lane marking lines on the pavement. Some systems use two cameras, one mounted on each outside rearview mirror. Some systems use infrared sensors located under the front bumper to monitor the lane markings on the road surface. The

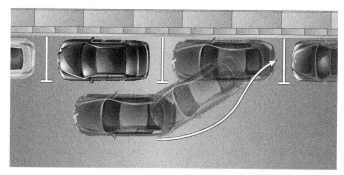

FIGURE 29–4 A self-parking-capable vehicle is able to parallel park or enter into a parking spot with little, or no input from the driver.

system names also vary according to vehicle manufacturers, including the following:

Honda/Acura: Lane Keep Assist System (LKAS)

Toyota/Lexus: Lane Monitoring System (LMS)

General Motors: Lane Departure Warning (LDW)

Ford: Lane Departure Warning (LDW)

Nissan/Infiniti: Lane Departure Prevention (LDP) System

If the cameras detect that the vehicle is starting to cross over a lane dividing line, a warning chime sounds or a vibrating mechanism mounted in the driver's seat cushion is triggered on the side where the departure is being detected. This warning does not occur if the turn signal is on in the same direction as detected. ● **SEE FIGURE 29–5.**

DIAGNOSIS AND SERVICE Before attempting to service or repair an LDWS fault, check service information for an explanation on how the system is supposed to work. If the system is not working as designed, perform a visual inspection of the sensors or cameras, checking for damage from road debris or evidence of body damage, which could affect the sensors. After a visual inspection, follow the vehicle manufacturer's recommended diagnosis procedures to locate and repair the fault in the system.

LANE KEEP ASSIST

PURPOSE AND FUNCTION The purpose of **lane keep assist (LKA)**, also called *lane keep assist system (LKAS)*, is not only to warn the driver if the vehicle is moving out of the lane of traffic, but when no no response, to also automatically use the electric power steering system to steer the vehicle back into the lane. ● **SEE FIGURE 29–6.**

PARTS AND OPERATION Most lane keep assist systems use a camera mounted in front of the inside rearview mirror with a clear view of the road ahead. A typical LKAS is able to monitor the road about 160 feet (50 m) ahead, and at vehicle speeds above 40 MPH (60 km/h) with the camera observing a

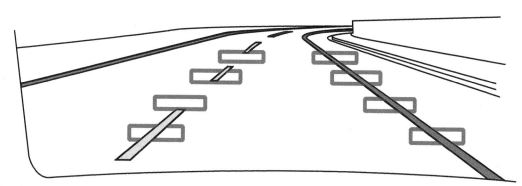

FIGURE 29–5 A lane departure warning system often uses cameras to sense the road lines and warns the driver if the vehicle is not staying within the lane, unless the turn signal is on.

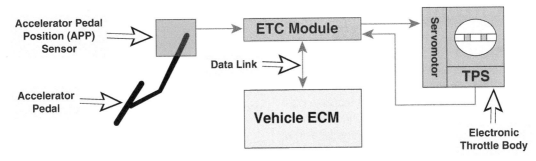

FIGURE 29–7 Adaptive cruise control can use radar to determine the distance of another vehicle in front. The control unit checks the driver's selected speed and sets the distance between the vehicles to determine what action is needed. The PCM then can operate the throttle or the brakes through the antilock brake/electronic stability control system to slow the vehicle, if needed, to maintain the set distance.

40-degree view ahead of the vehicle. The camera can detect the lane marking, which includes the center line and the right-side painted line, often called the fog line because it helps drivers see the right side of the road under poor or in foggy visibility.

When the camera detects that the vehicle is starting to get close to either lane marking, the vehicle performs the following functions:

1. It warns the driver by a warning sound, and/or lights the LKA symbol on the dash. In some vehicles, the warning includes vibrating the steering wheel in an attempt to get the driver's attention.

2. If the warnings do not result in corrective action by the driver, the LKAS uses the electric power steering to steer the vehicle back into the lane between the two lane markings.

ADAPTIVE CRUISE CONTROL

PURPOSE AND FUNCTION Adaptive cruise control (ACC), also called *radar cruise control*, gives the driver more control over the vehicle by keeping an assured clear distance behind the vehicle in front. If the vehicle in front slows, the ACC detects the slowing vehicle and automatically reduces the speed of the vehicle to keep a safe distance. Then, if the vehicle speeds up, the ACC also allows the vehicle to increase to the preset speed. This makes driving in congested areas easier and less tiring.

TERMINOLOGY Depending on the manufacturer, adaptive cruise control is also referred to as the following:

- **Adaptive cruise control** (Audi, Ford, General Motors, and Hyundai)
- **Dynamic cruise control** (BMW, Toyota/Lexus)
- **Active cruise control** (Mini Cooper, BMW)
- **Autonomous cruise control** (Mercedes)

It uses forward-looking radar to sense the distance to the vehicle in front and maintains an assured clear distance. This type of cruise control system works within the following conditions:

- Speeds from 20 to 100 MPH (30 to 161 km/h)
- Designed to detect objects as far away as 500 feet (150 m)

The cruise control system is able to sense both distance and relative speed. ● **SEE FIGURE 29–7.**

PARTS AND OPERATION Radar cruise control systems use long-range radar (LRR) to detect faraway objects in front

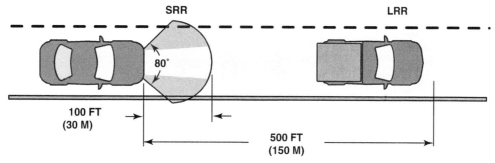

FIGURE 29–8 Most radar cruise control systems use radar, both long and short range. Some systems use optical or infrared cameras to detect objects.

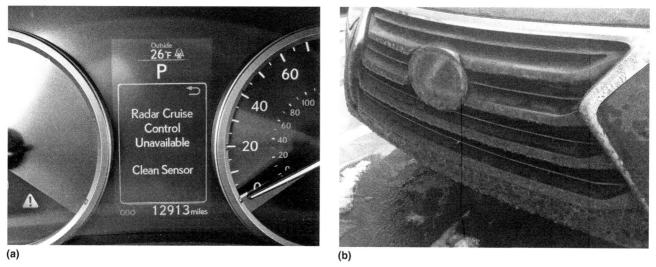

(a)   (b)

FIGURE 29–9 (a) This dash warning message appeared when the cruise control stopped working. (b) The front of a Lexus shows some ice buildup that was enough to block the radar signals needed for the radar cruise control to work.

of the moving vehicle. Some systems use a short-range radar (SRR) and/or infrared (IR) or optical cameras to detect when the distance between the moving vehicle and another vehicle in front is reduced. ● **SEE FIGURE 29–8.**

The radar frequencies include the following:
- 76 to 77 GHz (long-range radar)
- 24 GHz (short-range radar)

 Case Study

The Case of The Inoperative Radar Cruise Control

The driver of a Lexus NX experienced a situation where the radar cruise control stopped working due to ice on the sensor after driving through light snow showers. When the front was checked, it was discovered that ice had accumulated on the front grille. Using an ice scraper brush, the grille was cleaned, which restored the proper operation of the radar cruise control. ● **SEE FIGURE 29–9.**

In automated vehicles, the sensors need to be heated, and maybe cleaned, so that they can operate under all driving conditions.

Summary:

Complaint—Radar cruise stopped working and a message appeared to clean the sensor.

Cause—Ice buildup on the grille.

Correction—Cleaning the front of the grille, using a brush restored the proper operation of the radar cruise control.

What Is Intelligent Speed Advice (ISA)?

Intelligent Speed Advice (ISA) uses a sign recognition camera or a navigation system (GPS) to determine the speed limit, which is used to warn the driver of the posted speed limit. Some ISA systems automatically limit the speed of the vehicle by limiting engine power to prevent the vehicle from accelerating past the current speed limit unless overridden. The European New Car Assessment Program (Euro NCAP) is a European car safety performance assessment program which is awarding vehicle manufacturers if their vehicle is equipped with this system.

RADAR SENSOR

FIGURE 29–10 Rear cross-traffic warning systems use radar sensors at the rear corners of the vehicle which are able to detect a moving vehicle approaching from the sides.

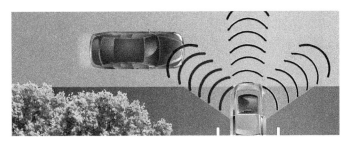

FIGURE 29–11 If a vehicle is approaching from the side when the gear selector is in reverse, a warning is sounded.

DIAGNOSIS AND SERVICE If the radar cruise control is not working properly, begin by making sure the sensor, which is usually behind the grille on most vehicles, is not covered. The system does not operate if the system is covered by heavy mud, ice, or snow. Additionally, some aftermarket vehicle front covers obstruct the sensor view. If the sensor is replaced, some systems require a re-alignment using special tools. Always refer to the manufacturer's service information for specific instructions.

- If a vehicle is detected, the system will sound a warning and often flash the side mirror indicators.
- Rear cross-traffic alert may not work if one of the rear sensors is blocked or during heavy rain or snow.
  ● **SEE FIGURES 29–10 AND 29–11.**

REAR CROSS-TRAFFIC WARNING (RCTW)

PURPOSE AND FUNCTION A **rear cross-traffic warning (RCTW)** system sounds an audible warning when a vehicle is crossing at the rear while backing. Some vehicles are capable of automatically braking to avoid a collision.

PARTS AND OPERATION Rear cross-traffic alert is used to warn the driver when backing from a parking space if there is a vehicle approaching from either side. The system uses radar sensors that are installed on both sides of the vehicle near the rear bumper. These sensors are able to detect vehicles approaching from the left or right side of the vehicle. These sensors activate when the vehicle is placed in reverse and can detect vehicles from up to 65 feet (20 m) on either side. The system is usually designed to function under the following conditions:

- When the vehicle is in reverse and your speed is less than 5 MPH (8 km/h)
- The system is designed to detect other vehicles approaching between 5 and 18 MPH (8 to 29 km/h).

AUTOMATIC EMERGENCY BRAKING

PURPOSE AND FUNCTION An **automatic emergency braking (AEB)** system intervenes and automatically applies the brakes if needed. Automatic braking is often part of a safety package that includes radar cruise control, and will apply the brakes in the event of a possible collision. Sensors such as radar, sonar, and/or cameras are used depending on the system to detect the distance to another object. The controller, usually an antilock braking system (ABS) controller, then issues a warning if a collision is possible.

This warning can include one or more of the following:

1. A buzzer
2. A warning light flashing on the dash
3. A vibration of the driver's seat

If the warnings are ignored, the automatic braking system will intervene and either provide brake assist or apply the brakes autonomously (by itself) to achieve maximum braking in an effort to avoid a collision. ● **SEE FIGURE 29–12.**

PRE-COLLISION SYSTEM

PURPOSE AND FUNCTION The purpose and function of a pre-collision system is to monitor the road ahead and prepare to avoid a collision, and to protect the driver and passengers. A pre-collision or a collision avoidance system uses the following systems:

1. The long-range and short-range radar or detection systems used by a radar cruise control system to detect objects in front of the vehicle
2. Antilock brake system (ABS)
3. Adaptive (radar) cruise control
4. Brake assist system

TERMINOLOGY Pre-collision systems can be called by various names, depending on the make of the vehicle. Some commonly used names for a pre-collision or pre-crash system include the following:

- ■ **Ford/Lincoln:** Collision Warning with Brake Support
- ■ **Honda/Acura:** Collision Mitigation Brake System (CMBS)
- ■ **Mercedes-Benz:** Pre-Safe or Attention Assist
- ■ **Toyota/Lexus:** Pre-Collision System (PCS) or Advanced Pre-Collision System (APCS)
- ■ **General Motors:** Pre-Collision System (PCS)
- ■ **Volvo:** Collision Warning with Brake Support or Collision Warning with Brake Assist Operation

The system functions by monitoring objects in front of the vehicle and can act to avoid a collision by the following actions:

- ■ Sounds an alarm
- ■ Flashes a warning lamp
- ■ Applies the brakes and brings the vehicle to a full stop (if needed), if the driver does not react following actions:

1. Applies the brakes in full force to reduce vehicle speed as much as possible.
2. Closes all windows and the sunroof to prevent the occupants from being ejected from the vehicle.
3. Moves the seats to an upright position.
4. Raises the headrest (if electrically powered).
5. Pretensions the seat belts.
6. Airbags and seat belt tensioners function as designed during the collision.

   ● **SEE FIGURE 29–13.**

HILL START ASSIST

PURPOSE AND FUNCTION The hill start assist feature allows the driver to launch his vehicle without a rollback while moving the foot from the brake pedal to the accelerator pedal. The electronic brake control module calculates the brake pressure that is needed to hold the vehicle on an incline, and locks that pressure for a certain time by commanding the appropriate solenoid valves on and off when the brake pedal is released. Hill

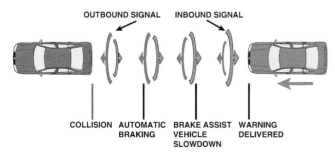

OUTBOUND SIGNAL   INBOUND SIGNAL

COLLISION   AUTOMATIC   BRAKE ASSIST   WARNING
             BRAKING   VEHICLE   DELIVERED
                          SLOWDOWN

FIGURE 29–12 Sensors are used to detect when the distance is closing fast enough that a collision may be possible, and the system intervenes to automatically apply the brakes if needed.

PRECOLLISION
SYSTEM DETECTS
POSSIBLE COLLISION

ALERTS AND
APPLIES BRAKES

FIGURE 29–13 A pre-collision system is designed to prevent a collision first, and interacts to prepare for a collision, if needed.

WITH HILL START ASSIST

WITHOUT HILL START ASSIST

FIGURE 29–14 A hill start assist system applies the brakes when the system detects that the vehicle is stopped on a hill, either down or up. This system keeps the vehicle from rolling down the hill without requiring the driver to keep the brakes applied.

start assist is activated when the electronic brake control module determines that the driver wishes to move his vehicle uphill, either backward or forward. ● **SEE FIGURE 29–14.**

The following inputs are used for the hill start assist feature:

- Brake switch
- Brake pressure sensors
- Longitudinal acceleration sensor
- Engine torque
- Reverse gear information
- Clutch switch
- Accelerator pedal position
- Vehicle speed

Drivers of vehicles equipped with hill start assist systems are often not aware that the vehicle is equipped with this system. As a result, it is often a concern of drivers when the brake pedal is released when starting forward after being stopped on a hill (the brakes seem to be slow to release). This is normal and not a fault with the system.

ADAS DIAGNOSIS

VIN DECODER To identify what ADAS a vehicle is equipped with, use the vehicle identification number (VIN), or the regular production order (RPO) for vehicles built by General Motors.

There are many online VIN decoders available, including one on the National Highways Traffic Safety Administration (NHTSA) website. Visit https://vpic.nhtsa.dot.gov/decoder/

At this site, enter the VIN and select "decode." The results will show all of the ADAS used on that specified vehicle.

DIAGNOSTIC STEPS Similar to troubleshooting any other system or fault, the steps in the diagnostic procedure include the following:

STEP 1 Verify the customer concern. Check the customer concern and determine that it is a true fault, and not a misunderstanding, on how the system is supposed to work.

STEP 2 Perform a visual inspection. Check for any physical faults that could affect the operation of the advanced driver assist system, such as road debris and/or minor collision damage.

STEP 3 Check for any stored or pending diagnostic trouble codes. Check all modules by performing a full module scan to check for faults in all of the modules.

STEP 4 Check service information for the specified procedure to follow to service or repair the verified fault.

STEP 5 Perform the specified procedure and static calibrations of the sensors as needed.

STEP 6 Perform the specified dynamic celebration of the sensors as needed.

STEP 7 Test drive the vehicle under the same operating conditions that were used to verify the fault to verify the repair.

STEP 8 Clear all advanced driver assist system-related diagnostic trouble codes (DTCs) and return the vehicle to the customer.

CAMERA AND RADAR SENSOR CALIBRATION

CAMERA CALIBRATION The operation of the camera can be affected by heavy rain, snow, or an accumulation of ice or mud. Before making any repairs, it is important to verify that the lens of the camera is free of anything that obstructs its view.

Calibration of the camera is required when one or more cameras are replaced on a mounting component, such as a windshield, bumper cover, mirror, or door. The calibration is an in-shop static process. Large patterned mats are placed around the vehicle at specific locations and the scan tool is used to initiate the process. ● **SEE FIGURE 29–15.**

TYPICAL PROCEDURE Some camera systems require a specific target so that the camera can be calibrated. Some vehicles that do not require a special target require a factory or

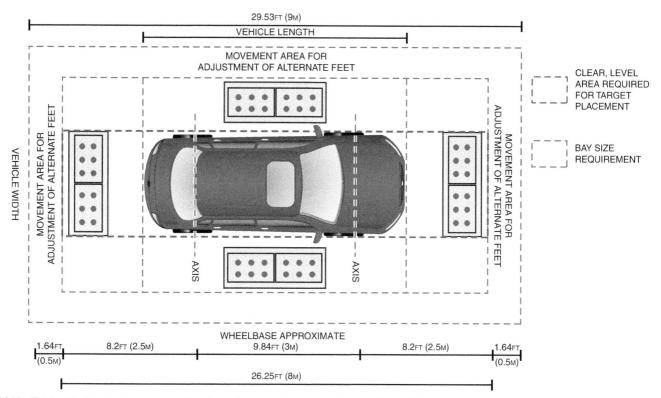

FIGURE 29-15 A typical camera calibration shop requirement to be used to calibrate the cameras on a vehicle equipped with advance driver assist systems. The area around the vehicle must be open and free from objects or windows that could affect the camera calibration.

factory-level scan tool to imitate the learning process. They will often use lines that are taped to the floor around the vehicle to use as a target. ● **SEE FIGURE 29-16.**

Some systems also require that the vehicle be driven at slow speeds under specific operating conditions to complete the learning. This process is used to do the final accurate calibrations.

Refer to service information for specific diagnostic and calibration information for the vehicle being serviced.

RADAR CALIBRATION Calibration of the radar is required anytime the unit is replaced or reinstalled. In many cases, the calibration procedure must be performed anytime a grille or fascia is removed or replaced. The calibration process may be static (in the shop), or dynamic (on the road), or a combination of the two. The static process involves the use of a scan tool and an aiming procedure. The aiming procedure requires manufacturer-specific targets. ● **SEE FIGURES 29-17 AND 29-18.**

Check service information for specific diagnostic and calibration information for the vehicle being serviced.

FIGURE 29-16 A typical target setup required to calibrate the camera on a vehicle equipped with an advanced driver assist system. Always follow the specified calibration procedure for the vehicle being serviced.

FIGURE 29-17 Before the radar sensor can be calibrated, the target must be installed at a very precise location at the front of the vehicle. The measurements involved include finding the exact center of the vehicle often using a special tool as shown.

FIGURE 29-18 A typical radar target being placed in the specified position after careful measurements from the centerline of the vehicle and the exact distance from the front and at the specified height.

SUMMARY

1. The advanced driver assist systems are designed as a driver aid and are not intended to replace the driver.
2. The blind spot monitor (BSM) is a vehicle-based sensor device that detects other vehicles located to the side and rear of the vehicle.
3. The parking-assist system is used to help drivers avoid contact with another object while moving slowly.
4. Self-parking vehicles, also called automatic parking vehicles, use the camera(s) and control the electric power steering to guide the vehicle into a parking space.
5. The lane departure warning system (LDWS) uses cameras to detect if the vehicle is crossing over lane marking lines on the pavement.
6. The purpose of lane keep assist (LKA), also called lane keep assist system (LKAS), is not only to warn the driver if the vehicle is moving out of the lane of traffic, but when no no response, to also automatically use the electric power steering system to steer the vehicle back into the lane.
7. Adaptive cruise control (ACC), also called radar cruise control, gives the driver more control over the vehicle by keeping an assured clear distance behind the vehicle in front.

8. A rear cross-traffic warning (RCTW) system sounds an audible warning when a vehicle is crossing at the rear while backing. Some vehicles are capable of automatically braking to avoid a collision.
9. An automatic emergency braking (AEB) system intervenes and automatically applies the brakes if needed.
10. The purpose and function of a pre-collision system is to monitor the road ahead, prepare to avoid a collision, and to protect the driver and passengers.
11. The hill start assist feature allows the driver to launch his vehicle without a rollback while moving the foot from the brake pedal to the accelerator pedal.
12. To identify what ADAS a vehicle is equipped with, use the vehicle identification number (VIN), or the regular production order (RPO) for vehicles built by General Motors.
13. The ADAS diagnosis includes eight steps to find and correct the root cause of the problem and to be properly calibrate the radar and cameras.

1. Parking-assist systems use what type of sensor?
2. What is the difference between a lane departure warning and a lane keep assist?
3. What type of sensors are used in adaptive cruise control systems?
4. What type of sensors are used in automatic emergency braking and pre-collision control systems?
5. What is the purpose and function of advanced driver assist systems?

1. What is not a function of advanced driver assist systems?
   a. Self-drive capability
   b. Take the load off the driver
   c. Help the driver avoid a collision if a vehicle in front of them stops quickly
   d. Alert the driver of a potential issue

2. Blind spot monitor (BSM) warnings can be_____.
   a. visual
   b. audible
   c. vibrating (tactile)
   d. Any of the above

3. Self-parking vehicles use _____ and control the _____ to control the vehicle into a parking space.
   a. radar; throttle
   b. camera; electric power steering X
   c. sonic sensor; brakes
   d. radar; electric power steering

4. The purpose of lane keep assist (LKA) is _____.
   a. to warn the driver if moving out of a lane
   b. used with adaptive cruise control to self-drive the vehicle without driver input or control
   c. use the electric power steering to keep the vehicle within the lane
   d. Both a and c

5. A driver complains that the brakes seem to release slowly at times, usually when stopped on a hill. This is normal operation of the _____ systems.
   a. hill keep assist
   b. adaptive cruise control
   c. pre-collision systems
   d. automatic emergency braking

6. Adaptive cruise control systems can also be called _____.
   a. dynamic cruise control
   b. active cruise control
   c. radar cruise control
   d. Any of the above

7. Rear cross-traffic alert is used to warn the driver when backing out from a parking space if there is a vehicle approaching from either side. The system uses _____ installed on both sides of the vehicle near the rear bumper.
   a. sonar
   b. ultrasonic
   c. radar
   d. cameras

8. What is needed to identify what ADAS systems a vehicle is equipped with?
   a. Vehicle identification number (VIN)
   b. RPO (if General Motors vehicle)
   c. ADAS number
   d. Either a or b

9. A parking-assist system works to warn the driver if the vehicle is getting close to an object. What type of object *cannot* be detected by most systems?
   a. Objects larger than 3 inches (8 cm) wide
   b. Objects larger than 10 inches (25 cm) high
   c. Objects under the vehicle
   d. Any of the above

10. Calibrating radar and cameras involves all of the following *except* _____.
    a. factory or factory-level scan tool
    b. special targets set at precisely specified location around the vehicle
    c. both static (stationary and dynamic (moving) calibration is required
    d. driving the vehicle in a circle 10 times to calibrate the cameras

chapter 30
AUDIO SYSTEM OPERATION AND DIAGNOSIS

LEARNING OBJECTIVES:

After studying this chapter, the reader should be able to:

Describe how AM, FM, and satellite radio work.

Describe radios, receivers, antennas, and antenna diagnosis.

Discuss the purpose, function, and types of speakers, and explain the decibel scale.

Discuss crossovers, aftermarket sound system upgrades, and voice recognition systems.

Explain how Bluetooth and satellite radio systems work.

List causes and corrections of radio noise and interference.

This chapter will help prepare for the ASE Electrical/Electronic Systems (A6) certification test content area "D" (Body Electrical Systems Diagnosis and Repair).

KEY TERMS: Active crossovers 411 • Alternator whine 415 • AM 405 • Bluetooth 413 • Crossover 411 • Decibel (dB) 410 • Floating ground system 410 • FM 405 • Frequency 405 • Ground plane 407 • Hertz (Hz) 405 • High-pass filter 411 • Impedance 408 • Low-pass filter 411 • Modulation 405 • Powerline capacitor 412 • Radio choke 416 • Radio frequency (RF) 405 • RMS 412 • SDARS 414 • Speakers 408 • Stiffening capacitor 412 • Subwoofer 410 • THD 412 • Tweeter 410 • Voice recognition 413

AUDIO FUNDAMENTALS

INTRODUCTION The audio system of today's vehicles is a complex combination of antenna system, receiver, amplifier, and speakers, all designed to provide living room–type music reproduction while the vehicle is traveling in city traffic or at highway speed.

Audio systems produce audible sounds and include the following:

- Radio (AM, FM, and satellite)
- Antenna systems that are used to capture electronic energy broadcast to radios
- Speaker systems
- Aftermarket enhancement devices that increase the sound energy output of an audio system
- Diagnosis of audio-related problems

Many audio-related problems can be addressed and repaired by a service technician.

TYPES OF ENERGY There are two types of energy that affect audio systems.

- **Electromagnetic energy or radio waves.** Antennas capture the radio waves, which are then sent to the radio or receiver to be amplified.

- **Acoustical energy, usually called sound.** Radios and receivers amplify the radio wave signals and drive speakers, which reproduce the original sound as transmitted by radio waves.

  ● **SEE FIGURE 30–1.**

TERMINOLOGY Radio waves travel at approximately the speed of light (186,282,000 miles per second) and are

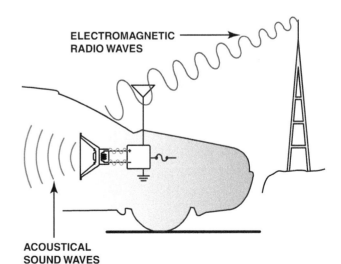

ELECTROMAGNETIC RADIO WAVES

ACOUSTICAL SOUND WAVES

FIGURE 30–1 Audio systems use both electromagnetic radio waves and sound waves to reproduce sound inside the vehicle.

electromagnetic. Radio waves are measured in two ways, wavelength and frequency. A radio wave has a series of high points and low points. A wavelength is the time and distance between two consecutive points, either high or low. Wavelength is measured in meters. **Frequency**, also known as **radio frequency (RF)**, is the number of times a particular waveform repeats itself in a given amount of time and is measured in **hertz (Hz)**. A signal with a frequency of 1 Hz is one radio wavelength per second. Radio frequencies are measured in kilohertz (kHz), thousands of wavelengths per second, and megahertz (MHz), millions of wavelengths per second. ● **SEE FIGURE 30–2**.

- The higher the frequency, the shorter the wavelength.
- The lower the frequency, the longer the wavelength.

A longer wavelength can travel a further distance than a shorter wavelength. Therefore, lower frequencies provide better reception at further distances.

- AM radio frequencies range from 530 to 1,710 kHz.
- FM radio frequencies range from 87.9 to 107.9 MHz.

MODULATION **Modulation** is the term used to describe when information is added to a constant frequency. The base radio frequency used for RF is called the *carrier wave*. A carrier is a radio wave that is changed to carry information. The two types of modulation are:

- **Amplitude modulation (AM)**
- **Frequency modulation (FM)**

AM waves are radio waves that have amplitude that can be varied, transmitted, and detected by a receiver. Amplitude is the height of the wave as graphed on an oscilloscope. ● **SEE FIGURE 30–3**.

FM waves are also radio waves that have a frequency that can be varied, transmitted, and detected by a receiver. This type of modulation changes the number of cycles per second, or frequency, to carry the information. ● **SEE FIGURE 30–4**.

RADIO WAVE TRANSMISSION More than one signal can be carried by a radio wave. This process is called *sideband operation*. Sideband frequencies are measured in kilohertz. The amount of the signal above the assigned frequency is referred to as the upper sideband. The amount of the signal below the assigned frequency is called the lower sideband. This capability allows radio signals to carry stereo broadcasts. Stereo broadcasts use the upper sideband to carry one channel of the stereo signal and the lower sideband to carry the other channel. When the signal is decoded by the radio, these two signals become the right and left channels. ● **SEE FIGURE 30–5**.

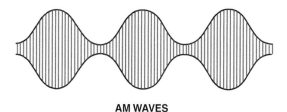

AM WAVES

FIGURE 30–3 The amplitude changes in AM broadcasting.

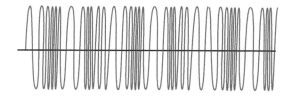

FM WAVES

FIGURE 30–4 The frequency changes in FM broadcasting and the amplitude remains constant.

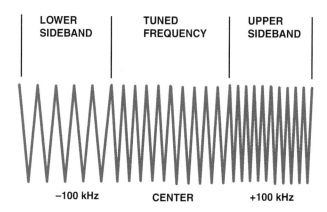

| LOWER SIDEBAND | TUNED FREQUENCY | UPPER SIDEBAND |

−100 kHz   CENTER   +100 kHz

FIGURE 30–5 Using upper and lower sidebands allows stereo to be broadcast. The receiver separates the signals to provide left and right channels.

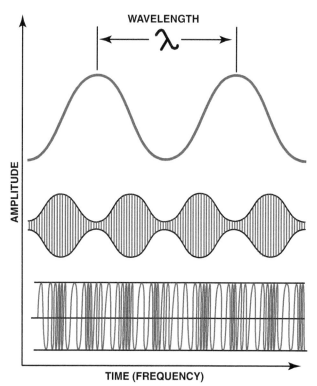

FIGURE 30–2 The relationship among wavelength, frequency, and amplitude.

NOISE Because radio waves are a form of electromagnetic energy, other forms of energy can impact them. For example, a bolt of lightning generates broad radio-frequency bandwidths known as radio-frequency interference (RFI). RFI is one type of electromagnetic interference (EMI) and is the frequency that interferes with radio transmission.

AM CHARACTERISTICS AM radio reception can be achieved over long distances from the transmitter because the waves can bounce off the ionosphere, usually at night. Even during the day, the AM signals can be picked up some distance from the transmitter. AM radio reception depends on a good antenna. If there is a fault in the antenna circuit, AM reception is affected the most.

FM CHARACTERISTICS Because FM waves have a high RF and a short wavelength, they travel only a short distance. The waves cannot follow the shape of the earth but instead travel in a straight line from the transmitter to the receiver. FM waves travel through the ionosphere and into space and do not reflect back to earth like AM waves.

MULTIPATH Multipath is caused by reflected, refracted, or line-sight signals reaching an antenna at different times. Multipath results from the radio receiving two signals to process on the same frequency. This causes an echo effect in the speakers. *Flutter,* or *picket fencing* as it is sometimes called, is caused by the blocking of part of the FM signal. This blocking causes a weakening of the signal resulting in only part of the signal getting to the antenna, causing an on-again off-again radio sound. Flutter also occurs when the transmitter and the receiving antenna are far apart.

RADIOS AND RECEIVERS

The antenna receives the radio wave where it is converted into very weak fluctuating electrical current. This current travels along the antenna lead-in to the radio that amplifies the signal

and sends the new signal to the speakers where it is converted into acoustical energy.

Most late-model radios and receivers use five input/output circuits.

1. **Power.** Usually a constant 12 volt feed to keep the internal clock alive.
2. **Ground.** This is the lowest voltage in the circuit and connects indirectly to the negative terminal of the battery.
3. **Serial data.** Used to turn the unit on and off and provide other functions, such as steering wheel control operation.
4. **Antenna input.** From one or more antennas.
5. **Speaker outputs.** These wires connect the receiver to the speakers or as an input to an amplifier.

ANTENNAS

TYPES OF ANTENNAS The typical radio electromagnetic energy from the broadcast antenna induces a signal in the antenna that is very small, only about 25 microvolts AC (0.000025 volt AC), in strength. The radio contains amplifier circuits that increase the received signal strength into usable information.

For example, the five types of antennas used on vehicles include the following:

- **Slot antenna.** The slot antenna is concealed in the roof of some plastic body vehicles, such as older General Motors plastic body vans. This antenna is surrounded by metal on a Mylar sheet.

- **Rear window defogger grid.** This type of system uses the heating wires to receive the signals and special circuitry to separate the RF from the DC heater circuit.

- **Powered mast.** These antennas are controlled by the radio. When the radio is turned on, the antenna is raised; when the radio is shut off, the antenna is retracted. The antenna system consists of an antenna mast and a drive motor controlled by the radio "on" signal through a relay.

- **Fixed mast antenna.** The mast is simply a vertical rod. Mast antennas are typically located on the fender or rear quarter panel of the vehicle.

- **Integrated antenna.** This type of antenna is sandwiched in the windshield and an appliqué on the rear window glass. The antenna in the rear window is the primary antenna and receives both AM and FM signals. The secondary antenna is located in the front windshield typically on the passenger side of the vehicle. This antenna receives only FM signals. ● **SEE FIGURE 30–6.**

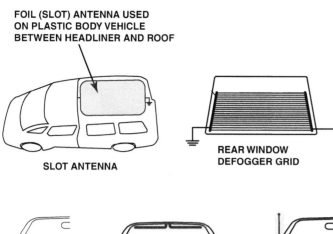

FOIL (SLOT) ANTENNA USED
ON PLASTIC BODY VEHICLE
BETWEEN HEADLINER AND ROOF

SLOT ANTENNA

REAR WINDOW
DEFOGGER GRID

POWER MAST

INTEGRATED ANTENNA

FIXED MAST

FIGURE 30–6 The five types of antennas used on General Motors vehicles include the slot antenna, fixed mast antenna, rear window defogger grid antenna, powered mast antenna, and integrated antenna.

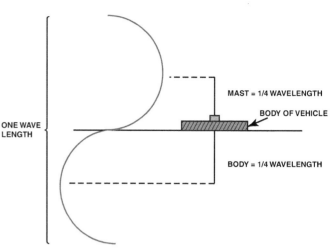

ONE WAVE LENGTH

MAST = 1/4 WAVELENGTH

BODY OF VEHICLE

BODY = 1/4 WAVELENGTH

FIGURE 30–7 The ground plane is actually one-half of the antenna.

FREQUENTLY ASKED QUESTION

What Is a Ground Plane?

Antennas designed to pick up the electromagnetic energy that is broadcast through the air to the transmitting antenna are usually one-half wavelength high, and the other half of the wavelength is the **ground plane**. This one-half wavelength in the ground plane is literally underground.

For ideal reception, the receiving antenna should also be the same as the wavelength of the signal. Because this length is not practical, a design compromise uses the length of the antenna as one-fourth of the wavelength; in addition, the body of the vehicle itself is one-fourth of the wavelength. The body of the vehicle, therefore, becomes the ground plane. ● **SEE FIGURE 30–7**.

Any faulty condition in the ground plane circuit causes the ground plane to lose effectiveness, such as:

• Loose or corroded battery cable terminals
• Acid buildup on battery cables
• Engine grounds with high resistance
• Loss of antenna or audio system grounds
• Defective alternator, causing an AC ripple exceeding 50 millivolts (0.050 volt)

ANTENNA DIAGNOSIS

ANTENNA HEIGHT The antenna collects all radio-frequency signals. An AM radio operates best with as long an antenna as possible, but FM reception is best when the antenna height is exactly 31 inches (79 cm). Most fixed-length antennas are, therefore, exactly this height. Even the horizontal section of a windshield antenna is 31 inches (79 cm) long.

A defective antenna:

■ Greatly affects AM radio reception
■ May affect FM radio reception

ANTENNA TESTING If the antenna or lead-in cable is broken (open), FM reception is heard but may be weak, and there is *no* AM reception. An ohmmeter should read infinity between the center antenna lead and the antenna case. For proper reception and lack of noise, the case of the antenna must be properly grounded to the vehicle body. ● **SEE FIGURE 30–8**.

TECH TIP

The Hole in the Fender Cover Trick

A common repair is to replace the mast of a power antenna. To help prevent the possibility of causing damage to the body or paint of the vehicle, cut a hole in a fender cover and place it over the antenna. ● **SEE FIGURE 30–9**.

If a wrench or tool slips during the removal or installation process, the body of the vehicle is protected.

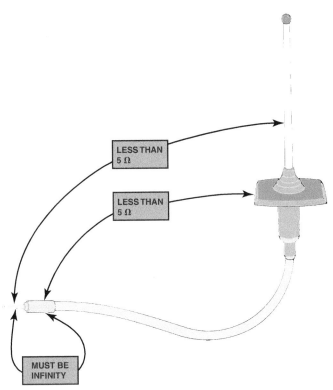

FIGURE 30–8 If all ohmmeter readings are satisfactory, the antenna is good.

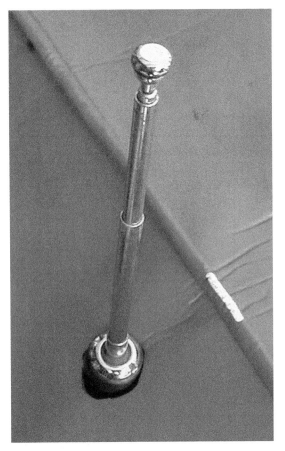

FIGURE 30–9 Cutting a small hole in a fender cover helps to protect the vehicle when replacing or servicing an antenna.

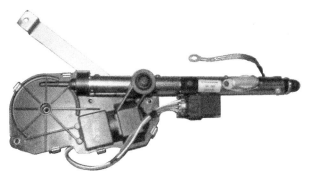

FIGURE 30–10 A typical power antenna assembly. Note the braided ground wire used to ensure that the antenna has a good ground plane.

POWER ANTENNA TESTING AND SERVICE Most power antennas use a circuit breaker and a relay to power a reversible, permanent magnet (PM) electric motor that moves a nylon cord attached to the antenna mast. Some vehicles have a dash-mounted control that can regulate antenna mast height and/or operation, whereas many operate automatically when the radio is turned on and off. The power antenna assembly is usually mounted between the outer and inner front fender or in the rear quarter panel. The unit contains the motor, a spool for the cord, and upper- and lower-limit switches. The power antenna mast is tested in the same way as a fixed-mast antenna. (An infinity reading should be noted on an ohmmeter when the antenna is tested between the center antenna terminal and the housing or ground.) Except in the case of cleaning or mast replacement, most power antennas are either replaced as a unit or repaired by specialty shops. ● **SEE FIGURE 30–10**.

Making certain that the drain holes in the motor housing are not plugged with undercoating, leaves, or dirt can prevent many power antenna problems. All power antennas should be kept clean by wiping the mast with a soft cloth and lightly oiling with light oil, such as WD-40 or a similar-grade oil.

SPEAKERS

PURPOSE AND FUNCTION The purpose of any **speaker** is to reproduce the original sound as accurately as possible. Speakers are also called *loudspeakers*. The human ear is capable of hearing sounds from a very low frequency of 20 Hz (cycles per seconds) to as high as 20,000 Hz. No one speaker is capable of reproducing sound over such a wide frequency range. ● **SEE FIGURE 30–11**.

Good-quality speakers are the key to a proper sounding radio or sound system. Replacement speakers should be securely mounted and wired according to the correct *polarity*. ● **SEE FIGURE 30–12**.

IMPEDANCE MATCHING All speakers used on the same radio or amplifier should have the same internal coil resistance, called **impedance**. If unequal-impedance speakers are used,

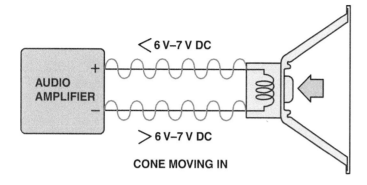

CONE MOVING IN

FIGURE 30–11 Between 6 and 7 volts is applied to each speaker terminal, and the audio amplifier then increases the voltage on one terminal and at the same time decreases the voltage on the other terminal, causing the speaker cone to move. The moving cone then moves the air, causing sound.

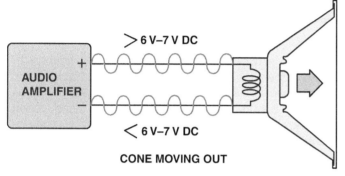

CONE MOVING OUT

FIGURE 30–12 A typical automotive speaker with two terminals. The polarity of the speakers can be identified by looking at the wiring diagram in the service manual or by using a 1.5 volt battery to check. When the battery positive is applied to the positive terminal of the speaker, the cone moves outward. When the battery leads are reversed, the speaker cone moves inward.

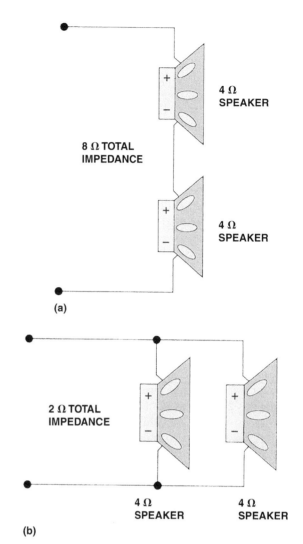

(a)

(b)

FIGURE 30–13 (a) Two 4 ohm speakers connected in series result in total impedance of 8 ohms. (b) Two 4 ohm speakers connected in parallel result in total impedance of 2 ohms.

sound quality may be reduced and serious damage to the radio may result. ● **SEE FIGURE 30–13**.

All speakers should have the same impedance. For example, if two 4 ohm speakers are being used for the rear and they are connected in parallel, the total impedance is 2 ohms.

$$R_T = \frac{4 \; \Omega \; \textbf{(Impedance of each speaker)}}{2 \; \textbf{(number of speakers in parallel)}} = \textbf{2 ohms}$$

The front speakers should also represent a 2 ohm load from the radio or amplifier. See the following example.

Two front speakers: each 2 ohms

Two rear speakers: each 8 ohms

Solution: Connect the front speakers in series (connect the positive [+] of one speaker to the negative [−] of the other) for a total impedance of 4 ohms ($2 \; \Omega + 2 \; \Omega = 4 \; \Omega$). Connect the two rear speakers in parallel (connect the positive [+] of each speaker together and the negative [−] of each speaker together) for a total impedance of 4 ohms ($8 \; \Omega \div 2 = 4 \; \Omega$).

Skin Effect

When a high-frequency signal (AC voltage) is transmitted through a wire, the majority of it travels on the outside surface of the wire. This characteristic is called skin effect. The higher the frequency is, the closer to the outer surface the signal moves. To increase audio system output, most experts recommend the use of wire that has many strands of very fine wire to increase the surface area or the skin area of the conductor. Therefore, most aftermarket speaker wires are stranded with many small-diameter copper strands.

SPEAKER WIRING The wire used for speakers should be as large a wire (as low an AWG number) as is practical in order to be assured that full power is reaching the speakers. Typical "speaker wire" is about 22 gauge (0.35 mm²), yet tests conducted by audio engineers have concluded that increasing the wire gauge—up to 4 gauge (19 mm²) or larger—greatly increases sound quality. All wiring connections should be soldered after making certain that all speaker connections have the correct polarity.

CAUTION: Be careful when installing additional audio equipment on a General Motors vehicle system that uses a two-wire speaker connection called a floating ground system. Other systems run only one power (hot) lead to each speaker and ground the other speaker lead to the body of the vehicle.

This arrangement helps prevent interference and static that could occur if these components were connected to a chassis (vehicle) ground. If the components are chassis grounded, there may be a difference in the voltage potential (voltage); this condition is called a *ground loop*.

CAUTION: Regardless of radio speaker connections used, *never* operate any radio without the speakers connected, or the speaker driver section of the radio may be damaged as a result of the open speaker circuit.

SPEAKER TYPES

INTRODUCTION No one speaker is capable of reproducing sound over such a wide frequency range. Therefore, speakers are available in three basic types.

1. Tweeters are for high-frequency ranges.
2. Midrange are for mid-frequency ranges.
3. Woofers and subwoofers are for low-frequency ranges.

Hearing loss is possible if exposed to loud sounds. According to noise experts (audiologists), hearing protection should be used whenever the following occurs.

1. You must raise your voice to be heard by others next to you.
2. You cannot hear someone else speaking who is less than 3 feet (1 m) away.
3. You are operating power equipment, such as a lawnmower.

TWEETER A **tweeter** is a speaker designed to reproduce high-frequency sounds, usually between 4,000 and 20,000 Hz (4 and 20 kHz). Tweeters are very directional. This means that the human ear is most likely to be able to detect the location of the speaker while listening to music. This also means that a tweeter should be mounted in the vehicle where the sound can be directed in line of sight to the listener. Tweeters are usually mounted on the inside door near the top, windshield "A" pillar or similar locations.

MIDRANGE A midrange speaker is designed and manufactured to be able to best reproduce sounds in the middle of the human hearing range, from 400 to 5,000 Hz. Most people are sensitive to the sound produced by these midrange speakers. These speakers are also directional in that the listener can usually locate the source of the sound.

SUBWOOFER A **subwoofer**, sometimes called a *woofer*, produces the lowest frequency of sounds, usually 125 Hz and lower. A *midbass* speaker may also be used to reproduce those frequencies between 100 and 500 Hz. Low-frequency sounds from these speakers are *not* directional. This means that the listener usually cannot detect the source of the sound from these speakers. The low-frequency sounds seem to be everywhere in the vehicle, so the location of the speakers is not as critical as with the higher frequency speakers.

The subwoofer can be placed almost anywhere in the vehicle. Most subwoofers are mounted in the rear of the vehicle where there is more room for the larger subwoofer speakers.

SPEAKER FREQUENCY RESPONSE Frequency response is how a speaker responds to a range of frequencies. A typical frequency response for a midrange speaker may be 500 to 4,000 Hz.

SOUND LEVELS

DECIBEL SCALE A **decibel (dB)** is a measure of sound power, and it is the faintest sound a human can hear in the midband frequencies. The dB scale is not linear (straight line)

What Is a Bass Blocker?

A bass blocker is a capacitor and coil assembly that effectively blocks low frequencies. A bass blocker is normally used to block low frequencies being sent to the smaller front speakers. Using a bass blocker allows the smaller front speakers to more efficiently reproduce the midrange and high-range frequency sounds.

but logarithmic, meaning that a small change in the dB reading results in a large change in volume of noise. An increase of 10 dB in sound pressure is equal to doubling the perceived volume. Therefore, a small difference in dB rating means a big difference in the sound volume of the speaker.

EXAMPLES Some examples of decibel sound levels include the following:

- Quiet, faint
  - 30 dB: whisper, quiet library
  - 40 dB: quiet room
- Moderate
  - 50 dB: moderate-range sound
  - 60 dB: normal conversation
- Loud
  - 70 dB: vacuum cleaner, city traffic
  - 80 dB: busy noisy traffic, vacuum cleaner
- Extremely loud
  - 90 dB: lawnmower, shop tools
  - 100 dB: chain saw, air drill
- Hearing loss possible
  - 110 dB: loud rock music

CROSSOVERS

DEFINITION A **crossover** is designed to separate the frequency of a sound and send a certain frequency range, such as low-bass sounds, to a woofer designed to reproduce these low-frequency sounds. There are two types of crossovers: passive and active.

PASSIVE CROSSOVER A passive crossover does not use an external power source. Rather, it uses a coil and a capacitor to block certain frequencies that a particular type of speaker cannot handle and allows just those frequencies that it can handle to be applied to the speaker. For example, a 6.6 millihenry coil and a 200 microfarad capacitor can effectively pass 100 Hz frequency sound to a large 10 inch subwoofer. This type of passive crossover is called a **low-pass filter**, because it passes (transfers) only the low-frequency sounds to the speaker and blocks all other frequencies. A **high-pass filter** is used to transfer higher frequency (over 100 Hz) to smaller speakers.

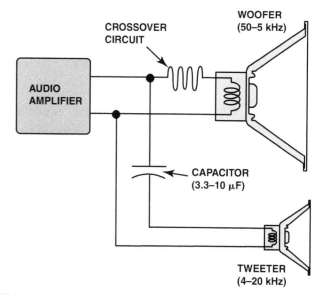

FIGURE 30–14 Crossovers are used in audio systems to send high-frequency sounds to the small (tweeter) speakers and low-frequency sounds to larger (woofer) speakers.

ACTIVE CROSSOVER **Active crossovers** use an external power source and produce superior performance. An active crossover is also called an *electronic crossover* or *crossover network.* These units include many powered filters and are considerably more expensive than passive crossovers. Two amplifiers are necessary to fully benefit from an active crossover. One amplifier is for the higher frequencies and midrange and the other amplifier is for the subwoofers. If you are on a budget and plan to use just one amplifier, then use passive crossover. If you can afford to use two or more amplifiers, then consider using the electronic (active) crossover. ● **SEE FIGURE 30–14** for an example of crossovers used in factory-installed systems.

AFTERMARKET SOUND SYSTEM UPGRADE

POWER AND GROUND UPGRADES If adding an amplifier and additional audio components, be sure to include the needed power and ground connections. These upgrades can include the following:

- A separate battery for the audio system
- An inline fuse near the battery to protect the wiring and the components
- Wiring that is properly sized to the amperage draw of the system and the length of wire (The higher the output wattage, the greater the amperage required and the larger the wire gauge needed. The longer the distance between the battery and the components, the larger the wire gauge needed for best performance.)

■ Ground wires at least the same gauge as the power-side wiring (Some experts recommend using extra ground wires for best performance.)

Read, understand, and follow all instructions that come with audio system components.

POWERLINE CAPACITOR

A **powerline capacitor**, also called a **stiffening capacitor**, refers to a large capacitor (often abbreviated CAP) of 0.25 farad or larger connected to an amplifier power wire. The purpose and function of this capacitor is to provide the electrical reserve energy needed by the amplifier to provide deep bass notes. ● SEE FIGURE 30–15.

Battery power is often slow to respond; and when the amplifier attempts to draw a large amount of current, the capacitor tries to stabilize the voltage level at the amplifier by discharging stored current as needed.

A rule of thumb is to connect a capacitor with a capacity of 1 farad for each 1,000 watts of amplifier power. ● SEE CHART 30–1.

CAPACITOR INSTALLATION

A powerline capacitor connects to the power leads between the inline fuse and the amplifier. ● SEE FIGURE 30–16.

If the capacitor were connected to the circuit as shown without "precharging," the capacitor would draw so much current that it would blow the inline fuse. To safely connect a large capacitor, it must be *precharged*. To precharge the capacitor, follow these steps.

STEP 1 Connect the negative (2) terminal of the capacitor to a good chassis ground.

STEP 2 Insert an automotive 12 volt lightbulb, such as a headlight or parking light, between the positive (1) terminal of the capacitor and the positive terminal of the battery. The light comes on as the capacitor is being charged and then goes out when the capacitor is fully charged.

STEP 3 Disconnect the light from the capacitor, then connect the power lead to the capacitor. The capacitor is now fully charged and ready to provide the extra power necessary to supplement battery power to the amplifier.

FIGURE 30–15 Two capacitors connected in parallel provide the necessary current flow to power large subwoofer speakers.

POWERLINE (STIFFENING) CAPACITORS

? FREQUENTLY ASKED QUESTION

What Do the Amplifier Specifications Mean?

RMS power	**RMS** means root-mean-square and is the rating that indicates how much power the amplifier is capable of producing continuously.
RMS power at 2 ohms	This specification in watts indicates how much power the amplifier delivers into a 2 ohm speaker load. This 2 ohm load is achieved by wiring two 4 ohm speakers in parallel or by using 2 ohm speakers.
Peak power	Peak power is the maximum wattage an amplifier can deliver in a short burst during a musical peak.
THD	**Total harmonic distortion (THD)** represents the amount of change of the signal as it is being amplified. The lower the number, the better the amplifier (e.g., a 0.01% rating is better than a 0.07% rating).
Signal-to-noise ratio	This specification is measured in decibels (dB) and compares the strength of the signal with the level of the background noise (hiss). A higher volume indicates less background noise (e.g., a 105 dB rating is better than a 100 dB rating).

POWERLINE CAPACITOR USAGE GUIDE

WATTS (AMPLIFIER)	RECOMMENDED CAPACITOR IN FARADS (MICROFARADS)
100 W	0.10 farad (100,000 µF)
200 W	0.20 farad (200,000 µF)
250 W	0.25 farad (250,000 µF)
500 W	0.50 farad (500,000 µF)
750 W	0.75 farad (750,000 µF)
1,000 W	1.00 farad (1,000,000 µF)

CHART 30–1

The rating of the capacitor needed to upgrade an audio system is directly related to the wattage of the system.

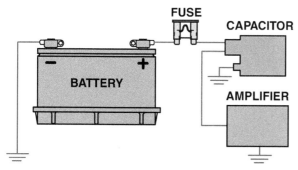

FIGURE 30–16 A powerline capacitor should be connected through the power wire to the amplifier, as shown. When the amplifier requires more electrical power (watts) than the battery can supply, the capacitor discharges into the amplifier and supplies the necessary current for the fraction of a second it is needed by the amplifier. At other times, when the capacitor is not needed, it draws current from the battery to keep it charged.

VOICE RECOGNITION

PARTS AND OPERATION **Voice recognition** is an expanding technology. It allows the driver of a vehicle to perform tasks, such as locate an address in a navigation system by using voice commands rather than buttons. In the past, users had to say the exact words to make it work such as the following examples listed from an owner's manual for a vehicle equipped with a voice-actuated navigation system.

"Go home"

"Repeat guidance"

"Nearest ATM"

The problem with these simple voice commands was that the exact wording had to be spoken. The voice recognition software compares the voice command to a specific list of words or phrases stored in the system in order for a match to occur. Newer systems recognize speech patterns and take action based on learned patterns. Voice recognition can be used for the following functions.

1. Navigation system operation (● **SEE FIGURE 30–17.**)

2. Sound system operation

3. Climate control system operation

4. Telephone dialing and other related functions (● **SEE FIGURE 30–18.**)

A microphone is usually placed in the driver's side sun visor or in the overhead console in the center top portion of the windshield area.

DIAGNOSIS AND SERVICE Voice recognition is usually incorporated into many functions of the vehicle. If a problem occurs with the system, perform the following steps.

1. Verify the customer complaint (concern). Check the owner's manual or service information for the proper voice commands and verify that the system is not functioning correctly.

FIGURE 30–17 Voice commands can be used to control many functions, including navigation systems, climate control, telephone, and radio.

FIGURE 30–18 The voice command icon on the steering wheel of a Cadillac.

2. Check for any aftermarket accessories that may interfere or were converted to components used by the voice recognition system, such as remote start units, MP3 players, or any other electrical component.

3. Check for stored diagnostic trouble codes (DTCs) using a scan tool.

4. Follow the recommended troubleshooting procedures as stated in service information.

BLUETOOTH

OPERATION **Bluetooth** is a (radio frequency) standard for short-range communications. The range of a typical Bluetooth device is 33 feet (10 m) and it operates in the ISM (industrial, scientific, and medical) band between 2.4000 and 2.4835 MHz.

Bluetooth is a wireless standard that works on two levels.

■ It provides physical communication using low power, requiring only about 1 milliwatt (1/1,000 of a watt) of electrical power, making it suitable for use with small handheld or portable devices, such as an ear-mounted speaker/microphone.

■ It provides a standard protocol for how bits of data are sent and received.

The Bluetooth standard is an advantage because it is wireless, low cost, and automatic. The automotive use of Bluetooth technology is in the operation of a cellular telephone being tied into the vehicle. The vehicle allows the use of hands-free telephone usage. A vehicle that is Bluetooth telephone equipped has the following components.

- A Bluetooth receiver can be built into the navigation or existing sound system.
- A microphone allows the driver to use voice commands as well as telephone conversations from the vehicle to the cell via Bluetooth wireless connections.

Many cell phones are equipped with Bluetooth, which may allow the caller to use an ear-mounted microphone and speaker. ● **SEE FIGURE 30–19**.

If the vehicle and the cell phone are equipped with Bluetooth, the speaker and microphone can be used as a hands-free telephone when the phone is in the vehicle. The cell phone can be activated in the vehicle by using voice commands.

SATELLITE RADIO

PARTS AND OPERATION Satellite radio, also called **Satellite Digital Audio Radio Services** or **SDARS**, is a fee-based system that uses satellites to broadcast high-quality radio. SDARS broadcasts on the S-band of 2.1320 to 2.345 GHz.

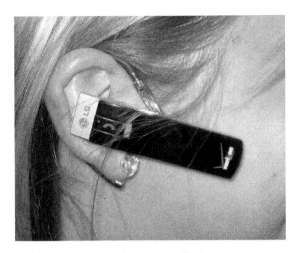

FIGURE 30–19 Bluetooth earpiece that contains a microphone and speaker unit that is paired to a cellular phone. The telephone has to be within 33 feet (10 m) of the earpiece.

SIRIUS/XM RADIO Sirius/XM radio is standard equipment but is optional in most vehicles. XM radio uses two satellites launched in 2001 called Rock (XM-2) and Roll (XM-1) in a geosynchronous orbit above North America. Two replacement satellites, Rhythm (XM-3) and Blues (XM-4), were launched in 2006. Sirius and XM radio combined in 2008 and now share some programming. The two types of satellite radios use different protocols and, therefore, require separate radios, unless a combination unit is purchased.

RECEPTION Reception from satellites can be affected by tall buildings and mountains. To help ensure consistent reception, both SDARS providers do the following:

- Include in the radio itself a buffer circuit that can store several seconds of broadcasts to provide service when traveling out of a service area
- Provide land-based repeater stations in most cities (● **SEE FIGURE 30–20**.)

ANTENNA To be able to receive satellite radio, the antenna needs to be able to receive signals from both the satellite and the repeater stations located in many large cities. There are various types and shapes of antennas, including those shown in ● **FIGURES 30–21 AND 30–22**.

DIAGNOSIS AND SERVICE The first step in any diagnosis is to verify the customer complaint (concern). If no satellite service is being received, first check with the customer to verify that the monthly service fee has been paid and the account is up to date. If poor reception is the cause, carefully check the antenna for damage or faults with the lead-in wire. The antennas must be installed on a metal surface to provide the proper ground plane.

For all other satellite radio fault problems, check service information for the exact tests and procedures. Always follow

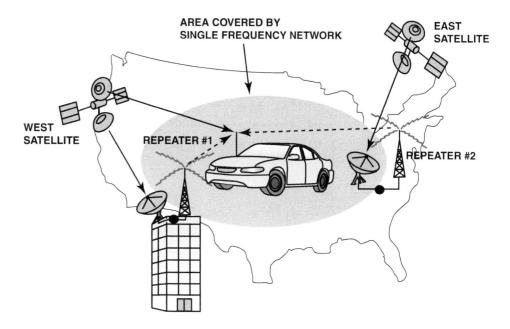

FIGURE 30–20 SDARS uses satellites and repeater stations to broadcast radio.

AREA COVERED BY SINGLE FREQUENCY NETWORK

EAST SATELLITE

WEST SATELLITE

REPEATER #1

REPEATER #2

FIGURE 30–21 An aftermarket XM radio antenna mounted on the rear deck lid. The deck lid acts as the ground plane for the antenna.

FIGURE 30–22 A shark-fin-type factory antenna used for both XM and OnStar.

the factory recommended procedures. Check the following websites for additional information.

■ **www.xmradio.com**

■ **www.sirius.com**

■ **www.siriusxm.com**

RADIO INTERFERENCE

DEFINITION Radio interference is caused by variations in voltage in the powerline or may be picked up by the antenna. A "whine" that increases in frequency with increasing engine speed is usually referred to as an **alternator whine** and is eliminated by installing a radio choke or a filter capacitor in the power feed wire to the radio. ● **SEE FIGURE 30–23**.

CAPACITOR USAGE Ignition noise is usually a raspy sound that varies with the speed of the engine. This noise is usually

FREQUENTLY ASKED QUESTION

What Does ESN Mean?

ESN means electronic serial number. This is necessary information to know when reviewing satellite radio subscriptions. Each radio has its own unique ESN, often found on a label at the back or bottom of the unit. It is also often shown on scan tools or test equipment designed to help diagnose faults in the units.

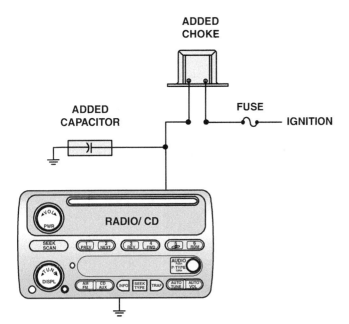

FIGURE 30–23 A radio choke and/or a capacitor can be installed in the power feed lead to any radio, amplifier, or equalizer.

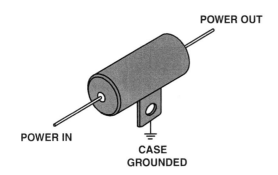

FIGURE 30–24 Many automobile manufacturers install a coaxial capacitor, like this one, in the power feed wire to the blower motor to eliminate interference caused by the blower motor.

eliminated by the installation of a capacitor on the positive side of the ignition coil. The capacitor should be connected to the power feed wire to either the radio or the amplifier, or both. The capacitor *has* to be grounded. A capacitor allows AC interference to pass through to ground while blocking the flow of DC. Use a 470 μF, 50 volt electrolytic capacitor, which is readily available from most radio supply stores. A special coaxial capacitor can also be used in the powerline. ● **SEE FIGURE 30–24**.

RADIO CHOKE A **radio choke**, which is a coil of wire, can also be used to reduce or eliminate radio interference. Again, the radio choke is installed in the power feed wire to the radio equipment. Radio interference being picked up by the antenna can best be eliminated by stopping the source of the interference and making certain that all units containing

a coil, such as electric motors, have a capacitor or diode attached to the power-side wire.

BRAIDED GROUND WIRE Using a braided ground wire is usually specified when electrical noise is a concern. The radio-frequency signals travel on the surface of a conductor, rather than through the core of the wire. A braided ground strap is used because the overlapped wires short out any radio-frequency signals traveling on the surface.

AUDIO NOISE SUMMARY In summary:

- Radio noise can be broadcast or caused by noise (voltage variations) in the power circuit to the radio.
- Most radio interference complaints come when someone installs an amplifier, power booster, equalizer, or other radio accessory.
- *A major cause of this interference is the variation in voltage through the ground circuit wires. To prevent or reduce this interference, make sure all ground connections are clean and tight.*
- Placing a capacitor in the ground circuit also may be beneficial.

CAUTION: Amplifiers sold to boost the range or power of an antenna often increase the level of interference and radio noise to a level that disturbs the driver.

Capacitor and/or radio chokes are the most commonly used components. Two or more capacitors can be connected in parallel to increase the capacity of the original capacitor. A "sniffer" can be used to locate the source of the radio noise. A sniffer is a length of antenna wire with a few inches of insulation removed from the antenna end. The sniffer is attached to the antenna input terminal of the radio, and the radio is turned on and set to a weak station. The other end of the sniffer is then moved around areas of the dash to locate where the source of the interference originates. The radio noise greatly increases if the end of the sniffer comes close to where electromagnetic leakage is occurring. ● **SEE FIGURE 30–25.** ● **SEE CHART 30–2.**

AUDIO NOISE CONTROL SYMPTOM CHART

NOISE SOURCE	WHAT IT SOUNDS LIKE	WHAT TO TRY
Alternator	A whine whose pitch changes with engine speed	Install a capacitor to a ground at the alternator output
Ignition	Ticking that changes with engine speed	Use a sniffer to further localize the source of the problem
Turn signals	Popping in time with the turn signals	Install a capacitor across the turn signal flasher
Brake lights	Popping whenever the brake pedal is depressed	Install a capacitor across the brake light switch contacts
Blower motor	Ticking in time with the blower motor	Install a capacitor to ground at the motor hot lead
Dash lamp dimmer	A buzzy whine whose pitch changes with the dimmer setting	Install a capacitor to ground at the dimmer hot lead
Horn switch	Popping when the horn is sounded	Install a capacitor between the hot lead and horn lead at the horn relay
Horn	Buzzing synchronized with the horn	Install a capacitor to ground at each horn hot lead
Amplifier power supply	A buzz, not affected by engine speed	Ground the amplifier chassis using a braided ground strap

CHART 30–2

Radio noise can have various causes, and knowing where or when the noise occurs helps pin down the location.

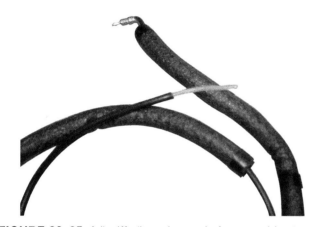

FIGURE 30–25 A "sniffer" can be made from an old antenna lead-in cable by removing about 3 inches of the outer shielding from the end. Plug the lead-in cable into the antenna input of the radio and tune the radio to a weak station. Move the end of the antenna wire around the vehicle dash area. The sniffer is used to locate components that may not be properly shielded or grounded and can cause radio interference through the case (housing) of the radio itself.

 CASE STUDY

Lightning Damage

A radio failed to work in a vehicle that was outside during a thunderstorm. The technician checked the fuses and verified that power was reaching the radio. Then the technician noticed the antenna. It had been struck by lightning. Obviously, the high voltage from the lightning strike traveled to the radio receiver and damaged the circuits. Both the radio and the antenna were replaced to correct the problem. ● **SEE FIGURE 30–26**.

Summary:

- **Complaint**—Customer stated that the radio did not work.
- **Cause**—Visual inspection showed an antenna that had been stuck by lightning.
- **Correction**—Replacing the radio and the antenna restored proper operation.

FIGURE 30–26 The tip of this antenna was struck by lightning.

1. Radios receive AM (amplitude modulation) and FM (frequency modulation) signals that are broadcast through the air.

2. The radio antenna is used to induce a very small voltage signal as an input into the radio from the electromagnetic energy via the broadcast station.

3. AM requires an antenna, whereas FM may be heard from a radio without an antenna.

4. Speakers reproduce the original sound, and the impedance of all speakers should be equally matched.

5. Crossovers are used to block certain frequencies to allow each type of speaker to perform its job better. A low-pass filter is used to block high-frequency sounds being sent to large woofer speakers, and a high-pass filter blocks low-frequency sounds being sent to tweeters.

6. Radio interference can be caused by many different things, such as a defective alternator, a fault in the ignition system, a fault in a relay or solenoid, or a poor electrical ground connection.

REVIEW QUESTIONS

1. Why do AM signals travel farther than FM signals?

2. What are the purpose and function of the ground plane?

3. How do you match the impedance of speakers?

4. What two items may need to be added to the wiring of a vehicle to control or reduce radio noise?

5. What can affect the reception of a satellite radio signal?

CHAPTER QUIZ

1. Technician A says that a radio can receive AM signals, but not FM signals, if the antenna is defective. Technician B says that a good antenna should give a reading of about 500 ohms when tested with an ohmmeter between the center antenna wire and ground. Which technician is correct?
   a. Technician A only
   b. Technician B only
   c. Both Technicians A and B
   d. Neither Technician A nor B

2. An antenna lead-in wire should have how many ohms of resistance between the center terminal and the grounded outer covering?
   a. Less than 5 ohms
   b. 5 to 50 ohms
   c. 300 to 500 ohms
   d. Infinity (OL)

3. Technician A says that a braided ground wire is best to use for audio equipment to help reduce interference. Technician B says to use insulated 14-gauge or larger ground wire to reduce interference. Which technician is correct?
   a. Technician A only
   b. Technician B only
   c. Both Technicians A and B
   d. Neither Technician A nor B

4. What maintenance should be performed to a power antenna to help keep it working correctly?
   a. Remove it from the vehicle and lubricate the gears and cable
   b. Clean the mast with a soft cloth and lubricate with a light oil
   c. Disassemble the mast and pack the mast with silicone grease (or equal)
   d. Loosen and then retighten the retaining nut

5. If two 4 ohm speakers are connected in parallel, meaning positive (+) to positive (+) and negative (−) to negative (−), the total impedance is_____.
   a. 8 ohms
   b. 4 ohms
   c. 2 ohms
   d. 1 ohm

6. If two 4 ohm speakers are connected in series, meaning the positive (+) of one speaker connected to the negative (−) of the other speaker, the total impedance is _____.
   a. 8 ohms
   b. 5 ohms
   c. 4 ohms
   d. 1 ohm

7. An aftermarket satellite radio has poor reception. Technician A says that a lack of a proper ground plane on the antenna could be the cause. Technician B says that mountains or tall buildings can interfere with reception. Which technician is correct?
   a. Technician A only
   b. Technician B only
   c. Both Technicians a and b
   d. Neither Technician a nor b

8. 100,000 µF means _____.
   a. 0.10 farad
   b. 0.01 farad
   c. 0.001 farad
   d. 0.0001 farad

9. XM radio service uses _____ to transmit the audio signal.
   a. satellites
   b. repeater towers
   c. Both A and B
   d. Neither A nor B

10. What device passes AC interference to ground and blocks DC voltage, and is used to control radio interference?
    a. Resistor
    b. Capacitor
    c. Coil (inductor)
    d. Transistor

appendix 1

SAMPLE ELECTRICAL (A6) ASE-TYPE CERTIFICATION TEST WITH ANSWERS

1. Copper wiring resistance _____ as the temperature increases.
   a. Increases
   b. Decreases

2. A voltage spike is created whenever any component containing a coil is shut off.
   a. True
   b. False

3. A corroded light socket could most likely cause _____.
   a. A fuse to blow in the circuit
   b. The light to be dim as a result of reduced current flow
   c. A feedback to occur to another circuit
   d. Damage to occur to the bulb as a result of decreased voltage

4. A fuse keeps blowing. Technician A says that a test light can be used in place of the fuse to help find the problem. Technician B says that a circuit breaker can be used in the place of the fuse. Which technician is correct?
   a. Technician A only
   b. Technician B only
   c. Both Technicians A and B
   d. Neither Technician A nor B

5. Technician A says that a low or zero reading on an ohmmeter indicates continuity. Technician B says that a meter reading indicating infinity means no continuity. Which technician is correct?
   a. Technician A only
   b. Technician B only
   c. Both Technicians A and B
   d. Neither Technician A nor B

6. What makes a meter a high-impedance tester?
   a. The effective resistance of the meter circuit
   b. The amount of current the meter can safely carry
   c. The maximum voltage that can be measured
   d. The maximum resistance that can be measured

7. The wire at the output terminal of a generator (alternator) connects to _____.
   a. The ignition switch input terminal
   b. The starter at the S terminal
   c. The battery positive terminal
   d. The fuse panel

8. When the parking lamps are on and the turn signal is flashing, the side-marker lamp alternates flashes with the turn signal. The reason for this is that _____.
   a. There are opposing voltages at the marker light filament
   b. The marker lamp ground path goes through the turn signal lamp

   c. The marker lamp feed comes from the parking lamp circuit
   d. All of the above

9. The headlamp on the right side is dim and yellow when turned on. The left headlamp is bright and normal in color. Which statement is false?
   a. The left side has more current.
   b. The left side is normal.
   c. The right side has more resistance.
   d. The right side has a bad sealed beam.

10. A meter reads OL. This means that the component or circuit being measured _____.
    a. Is open
    b. Is shorted
    c. Is grounded
    d. Has low resistance

11. A starter motor is drawing too many amperes (current). Technician A says that this could be due to low battery voltage. Technician B says that it could be due to a defective starter motor. Which technician is correct?
    a. Technician A only
    b. Technician B only
    c. Both Technicians A and B
    d. Neither Technician A nor B

12. All of the following could be a cause of excessive starter ampere draw except _____.
    a. A misadjusted starter pinion gear
    b. A loose starter housing
    c. Armature wires separated from the commutator
    d. A bent armature

13. The starter motor armature has been rubbing on the pole shoes. The probable cause is _____.
    a. A bent starter shaft
    b. A worn commutator on the armature
    c. Worn starter bushing(s)
    d. Both a and c

14. A starter cranks for a while, then whines. Technician A says that the starter solenoid may be bad. Technician B says that the starter drive may be bad. Which technician is correct?
    a. Technician A only
    b. Technician B only
    c. Both Technicians A and B
    d. Neither Technician A nor B

15. Airbag wiring connectors are _____.
    a. Red
    b. Orange
    c. Yellow
    d. Blue

16. A blower motor stopped working on all speeds. A technician tested the motor by touching a jumper wire from the battery positive terminal to the motor power terminal, and the motor did run. Technician A says that the motor should be checked using a fused jumper lead or ammeter to test for excessive current draw. Technician B says that the resistor pack and/or relay is likely to be defective. Which technician is correct?
    a. Technician A only
    b. Technician B only
    c. Both Technicians A and B
    d. Neither Technician A nor B

17. A technician is checking the charging system for low output. A voltage drop of 1.67 volts is found between the generator (alternator) output terminal and the battery positive terminal. Technician A says that a corroded connector could be the cause. Technician B says that a defective rectifier diode could be the cause. Which technician is correct?
    a. Technician A only
    b. Technician B only
    c. Both Technicians A and B
    d. Neither Technician A nor B

18. An ohmmeter on the 30-K scale reads 1.93 on a digital face. How many ohms of resistance is being measured?
    a. 193   c. 1930
    b. 19,300   d. 19.30

19. In a parallel 12 volt circuit with three bulbs (each 10 ohms in resistance), which statement below would be correct if one of the bulbs burned out (had an open)?
    a. The total resistance would be the same.
    b. The total resistance would be lower.
    c. The current would increase in the circuit.
    d. The current would decrease in the circuit.

20. Technician A says that high resistance in the cables or connections can cause rapid clicking of the solenoid. Technician B says that a battery must be 75% charged for accurate testing of the starting and charging systems. Which technician is correct?
    a. Technician A only
    b. Technician B only
    c. Both Technicians A and B
    d. Neither Technician A nor B

21. On a negative ground battery system _____.
    a. Disconnect the ground cable first and reconnect the positive cable first
    b. Disconnect the ground cable first and reconnect the positive cable last
    c. Disconnect the positive cable first and reconnect the ground cable first
    d. Disconnect the positive cable first and reconnect the ground cable last

22. A starter motor is drawing too many amperes (current) and the starter motor is not working. Technician A says that this could be due to low battery voltage. Technician B says that it could be due to a defective (grounded) starter motor. Which technician is correct?
    a. Technician A only
    b. Technician B only
    c. Both Technicians A and B
    d. Neither Technician A nor B

23. On a single-headlight system, the right-side high beam does not work. The probable cause is _____.
    a. A bad dimmer switch
    b. A bad headlight
    c. A bad headlight ground
    d. A discharged battery

24. A driver turns the ignition switch to "start" and nothing happens (the dome light remains bright). Technician A says that dirty battery connections or a defective or discharged battery could be the cause. Technician B says that an *open* control circuit such as a defective neutral safety switch could be the cause. Which technician is correct?
    a. Technician A only
    b. Technician B only
    c. Both Technicians A and B
    d. Neither Technician A nor B

25. Normal battery drain (parasitic drain) on a vehicle with many computer and electronic circuits is _____.
    a. 20 to 30 milliamperes
    b. 2 to 3 amperes
    c. 150 to 300 milliamperes
    d. 0.3 to 0.4 ampere

26. Whenever jump-starting, _____.
    a. The last connection should be the positive post of the dead battery
    b. The last connection should be the engine block of the dead vehicle
    c. The generator (alternator) must be disconnected on both vehicles
    d. The bumpers should touch to provide a good ground between the vehicles

27. A charge light is on, but dim. The most likely cause is _____.
    a. A defective rectifier bridge
    b. A defective diode trio
    c. A defective rotor
    d. Worn brushes

28. An electric motor is drawing more current (amperes) than specified. Technician A says that a corroded connector at the motor could be the cause. Technician B says that a corroded ground connection could be the cause. Which technician is correct?
    a. Technician A only
    b. Technician B only
    c. Both Technicians A and B
    d. Neither Technician A nor B

29. Technician A says that many wiper motors use a three-brush, two-speed motor. Technician B says that if the low speed does not work, then the wiper will also not operate on pulse (delay). Which technician is correct?
    a. Technician A only
    b. Technician B only
    c. Both Technicians A and B
    d. Neither Technician A nor B

30. Two technicians are discussing jump-starting a computer-equipped vehicle with another computer-equipped vehicle. Technician A says that the ignition of both vehicles should be in the off position while making the jumper cable connections. Technician B says that the computer-equipped vehicles should not be jump-started. Which technician is correct?
    a. Technician A only
    b. Technician B only
    c. Both Technicians A and B
    d. Neither Technician A nor B

31. Technician A says not to touch a halogen bulb with your fingers. Technician B says to handle a halogen bulb with care because it has high-pressure gas in it. Which technician is correct?
    a. Technician A only
    b. Technician B only
    c. Both Technicians A and B
    d. Neither Technician A nor B

32. Which of the following is the correct range for charging voltage measured across the battery terminals?
    a. 9.5 to 12 volts
    b. 13 to 15 volts
    c. 14 to 16.5 volts
    d. 15.2 to 18.5 volts

33. Battery voltage reads 11.85 volts on a DMM during cranking. Technician A says that the battery could be weak. Technician B says the starter may be defective. Which technician is correct?
    a. Technician A only
    b. Technician B only
    c. Both Technicians A and B
    d. Neither Technician A nor B

34. A technician is checking a headlight door motor with an ammeter. It shows excessive current draw. The most likely cause is a _____.
    a. Bad ground
    b. Binding headlight door
    c. Loose connection
    d. Blown fuse

35. The charge light does not come on when the key is turned to the "run" position. This could be caused by _____.
    a. An open circuit to the sending unit
    b. A burned-out bulb
    c. A bad diode
    d. A short inside the generator (alternator)

36. When the key is turned to the "start" position, the solenoid chatters and the interior lights flicker. The most likely cause is _____.
    a. Low battery voltage
    b. Defective pull-in winding
    c. Defective hold-in winding
    d. Defective starter motor

37. A vehicle being checked for parasitic draw shows a reading of 300 milliampere. The specification for the vehicle is 0.02 ampere. Technician A says this reading is satisfactory. Technician B says this reading needs to be taken with the key on. Which technician is correct?
    a. Technician A only
    b. Technician B only
    c. Both Technicians A and B
    d. Neither Technician A nor B

38. A blower is running slow on all speeds. The most likely cause is _____.
    a. A blown resistor
    b. Worn/dry bearings in the motor
    c. A bad fan switch
    d. Open ignition switch

39. A rebuilt starter turns but will not disengage the flywheel. The most likely cause is _____.
    a. A missing solenoid return spring
    b. A defective starter drive
    c. The shifting fork installed backward
    d. The solenoid contact installed backward

40. Technician A says a high-scale ammeter can be used to test the current draw of a starting circuit. Technician B says a high-scale voltmeter can be used to test the current draw of a starting circuit. Which technician is correct?
    a. Technician A only
    b. Technician B only
    c. Both Technicians A and B
    d. Neither Technician A nor B

41. The left-turn signal indicator on the instrument panel stays on and does not flash. The right-side signal functions properly. What is the most likely cause?
    a. A defective flasher
    b. A bad bulb
    c. A defective turn signal switch
    d. A low battery voltage

42. A fusible link between the battery and generator (alternator) is hot to the touch. The charging system voltage is 9.8 volts. This could indicate _____.
    a. Overcharging
    b. Undercharging
    c. High resistance in the fusible link
    d. A poor connection

43. A vehicle comes in with a nonfunctioning gas gauge. When the sending unit wire is grounded, the gauge reading goes to "full." Technician A says this proves that the gauge is OK. Technician B says this proves that the sending unit is bad. Which technician is correct?
    a. Technician A only
    b. Technician B only
    c. Both Technicians A and B
    d. Neither Technician A nor B

44. A vehicle's reverse lights are always on, even in "drive." The most likely cause is _____.
    a. A misadjusted neutral safety switch
    b. An open neutral safety switch
    c. A bulb installed backward
    d. A wrong bulb installed for the reverse lights

45. A vehicle cannot hold a steady speed in cruise control over bumpy roads. The most likely cause is _____.
    a. A misadjusted brake switch
    b. A vacuum leak to the servo
    c. A loose ground connection at the servo unit
    d. A defective fuse

46. Technician A says that disconnecting a battery can cause driveability problems after the battery has been reconnected. Technician B says that disconnecting a battery can cause radio station presets to be lost. Which technician is correct?
   a. Technician A only
   b. Technician B only
   c. Both Technicians A and B
   d. Neither Technician A nor B

47. When do you remove a battery surface charge?
   a. Before load testing
   b. After load testing
   c. Anytime you are testing the battery, starter, or generator (alternator)
   d. Before starting the engine to avoid damage to the generator (alternator)

48. A customer comes in complaining of radio static. Technician A says to check the antenna. Technician B says to check the speakers and radio ground. Which technician is correct?
   a. Technician A only
   b. Technician B only
   c. Both Technicians A and B
   d. Neither Technician A nor B

49. A customer arrives at a shop and his battery voltage is measured to be 13.6 volts with the engine off. This indicates _____.
   a. Overcharging
   b. Undercharging
   c. Normal surface charge
   d. Sulfated battery

50. When the parking lights are turned on, the left light is dim while the right light is a normal brightness. When the brake is applied, the left light totally goes out, while the right side works properly. What is the problem?
   a. A bad ground at the left bulb
   b. A shorted left bulb
   c. A bad switch
   d. A shorted right bulb

SAMPLE ELECTRICAL (A6) ASE-TYPE CERTIFICATION TEST WITH ANSWERS

1.	a	14.	b	27.	b	40.	a
2.	a	15.	c	28.	d	41.	b
3.	b	16.	c	29.	b	42.	c
4.	c	17.	a	30.	a	43.	a
5.	c	18.	c	31.	c	44.	a
6.	a	19.	d	32.	b	45.	a
7.	c	20.	c	33.	d	46.	c
8.	d	21.	a	34.	b	47.	a
9.	d	22.	b	35.	b	48.	c
10.	a	23.	c	36.	a	49.	c
11.	c	24.	b	37.	d	50.	a
12.	c	25.	a	38.	b		
13.	d	26.	b	39.	c		

MLR- Maintenance & Light Repair
AST- Auto Service Technology (Includes MLR)
MAST- Master Auto Service Technology (Includes MLR and AST)

Electrical/Electronic (A6)

TASK	PRIORITY	MLR	AST	MAST	TEXT PAGE #	TASK PAGE #
A. GENERAL: ELECTRICAL SYSTEMS DIAGNOSIS						
1. Research vehicle service information including vehicle service history, service precautions, and technical service bulletins.	P-1	✔	✔	✔	1-5	1-6
2. Demonstrate knowledge of electrical/electronic series, parallel, and series-parallel circuits using principles of electricity (Ohm's Law).	P-1	✔	✔	✔	53-88	6-24; 32
3. Demonstrate proper use of a digital multimeter (DMM) when measuring source voltage, voltage drop (including grounds), current flow, and resistance.	P-1	✔	✔	✔	95-109	25
4. Demonstrate knowledge of the causes and effects from shorts, grounds, opens, and resistance problems in electrical/electronic circuits.	P-1	✔	✔	✔	64-70	25
5. Demonstrate proper use of a test light on an electrical circuit.	P-1	(P-2)	✔	✔	94	26
6. Use fused jumper wires to check operation of electrical circuits.	P-1	(P-2)	✔	✔	93	27
7. Use wiring diagrams during the diagnosis (troubleshooting) of electrical/ electronic circuit problems.	P-1			✔	134-150	34
8. Diagnose the cause(s) of excessive key-off battery drain (parasitic draw); determine needed action.	P-1	✔	✔	✔	231-235	42
9. Inspect and test fusible links, circuit breakers, and fuses; determine needed action.	P-1	✔	✔	✔	122-127	29
10. Inspect, test, repair, and/or replace components, connectors, terminals, harnesses, and wiring in electrical/electronic systems (including solder repairs).	P-1		✔	✔	128-132	30; 31; 37
11. Check electrical/electronic circuit waveforms; interpret readings and determine needed repairs.	P-2			✔	111-117; 298	28
12. Repair data bus wiring harness.	P-1			✔	129-132	31
B. BATTERY DIAGNOSIS AND SERVICE						
1. Perform battery state-of-charge test; determine needed action.	P-1	✔	✔	✔	225-228	43
2. Confirm proper battery capacity for vehicle application; perform battery capacity and load test; determine needed action.	P-1	✔	✔	✔	226-228	44
3. Maintain or restore electronic memory functions.	P-1	✔	✔	✔	233-235	45
4. Inspect and clean battery; fill battery cells; check battery cables, connectors, clamps, and hold-downs.	P-1	✔	✔	✔	224-225	47
5. Perform slow/fast battery charge according to manufacturer's recommendations.	P-1	✔	✔	✔	228-231	48

TASK	PRIORITY	MLR	AST	MAST	TEXT PAGE #	TASK PAGE #
6. Jump-start vehicle using jumper cables and a booster battery or an auxiliary power supply.	P-1	✔	✔	✔	231	49
7. Identify safety precautions for high voltage systems on hybrid electric, hybrid electric, and diesel vehicles.	P-2	✔	✔	✔	35-37	11; 12
8. Identify electrical/electronic modules, security systems, radios, and other accessories that require reinitialization or code entry after reconnecting vehicle battery.	P-1	✔	✔	✔	233-235	46
9. Identify hybrid vehicle auxiliary (12v) battery service, repair, and test procedures.	P-3	✔	✔	✔	223-231	50

C. STARTING SYSTEM DIAGNOSIS AND REPAIR

TASK	PRIORITY	MLR	AST	MAST	TEXT PAGE #	TASK PAGE #
1. Perform starter current draw tests; determine needed action.	P-1	✔	✔	✔	254-265	53
2. Perform starter circuit voltage drop tests; determine needed action.	P-1	✔	✔	✔	252-254	54
3. Inspect and test starter relays and solenoids; determine needed action.	P-2	✔	✔	✔	254	52
4. Remove and install starter in a vehicle.	P-1	✔	✔	✔	255; 257	55
5. Inspect and test switches, connectors, and wires of starter control circuits; determine needed action.	P-2	✔	✔	✔	254	52
6. Differentiate between electrical and engine mechanical problems that cause a slow-crank or a no-crank condition	P-2		✔	✔	255	53
7. Demonstrate knowledge of an automatic idle-stop/start-stop system.	P-2	✔	✔	✔	248-249	51

D. CHARGING SYSTEM DIAGNOSIS AND REPAIR

TASK	PRIORITY	MLR	AST	MAST	TEXT PAGE #	TASK PAGE #
1. Perform charging system output test; determine needed action.	P-1	✔	✔	✔	286	59
2. Diagnose (troubleshoot) charging system for causes of undercharge, no-charge, or overcharge conditions.	P-1		✔	✔	279-287	58; 60
3. Inspect, adjust, and/or replace generator (alternator) drive belts; check pulleys and tensioners for wear; check pulley and belt alignment.	P-1	✔	✔	✔	281-282	62
4. Remove, inspect, and/or replace generator (alternator).	P-1	(P-2)	✔	✔	287; 291-292	62
5. Perform charging circuit voltage drop tests; determine needed action.	P-1	✔	✔	✔	285-286	61

E. LIGHTING SYSTEMS DIAGNOSIS AND REPAIR

TASK	PRIORITY	MLR	AST	MAST	TEXT PAGE #	TASK PAGE #
1. Diagnose (troubleshoot) the causes of brighter-than-normal, intermittent, dim, or no light operation; determine needed action.	P-1	✔	✔	✔	308-311	68
2. Inspect interior and exterior lamps and sockets including headlights and auxiliary lights (fog lights/driving lights); replace as needed.	P-1		✔	✔	301-305	69
3. Aim headlights.	P-2	✔	✔	✔	314-315	70
4. Identify system voltage and safety precautions associated with high-intensity discharge headlights	P-2	✔	✔	✔	309-312	71

F. INSTRUMENT CLUSTER AND DRIVER INFORMATION SYSTEMS DIAGNOSIS AND REPAIR

TASK	PRIORITY	MLR	AST	MAST	TEXT PAGE #	TASK PAGE #
1. Inspect and test gauges and gauge sending units for causes of abnormal readings; determine needed action.	P-2		✔	✔	323-324; 328-331	72
2. Diagnose (troubleshoot) the causes of incorrect operation of warning devices and other driver information systems; determine needed action.	P-2		✔	✔	321-331	73; 74; 75
3. Reset maintenance indicators as required.	P-2	✔	✔	✔	323	74

TASK	PRIORITY	MLR	AST	MAST	TEXT PAGE #	TASK PAGE #
G. REPAIR BODY ELECTRICAL SYSTEMS DIAGNOSIS AND REPAIR						
1. Diagnose operation of comfort and convenience accessories and related circuits (such as power window, power seats, pedal height, power locks, truck locks, remote start, moon roof, sun roof, sun shade, remote keyless entry, voice activation, steering wheel controls, back-up camera, park assist, cruise control, and auto dimming headlamps); determine needed repairs.	P-2		✔	✔	314; 322; 372-386	9; 80; 81; 82; 85; 86; 87
2. Diagnose operation of security/anti-theft systems and related circuits (such as theft deterrent, door locks, remote keyless entry, remote start, and starter/fuel disable); determine needed repairs.	P-2		✔	✔	338-345; 386-389	76; 84
3. Diagnose operation of entertainment and related circuits (such as radio, DVD, remote CD changer, navigation, amplifiers, speakers, antennas, and voice-activated accessories); determine needed repairs.	P-3		✔	✔	404-417	36; 88
4. Diagnose operation of safety systems and related circuits (such as horn, airbags, seat belt pretensioners, occupancy classification, wipers, washers, speed control/collision avoidance, heads-up display, park assist, and back-up camera); determine needed repairs.	P-1		✔	✔	324-325; 347-360; 362-370; 392-402	10; 81; 83; 85; 86; 87
5. Diagnose body electronic systems circuits using a scan tool; check for module communication errors (data bus systems); determine needed action.	P-2		✔	✔	331	40; 83
6. Describe the process for software transfer, software updates, or reprogramming of electronic modules	P-2		✔	✔	233	39

GLOSSARY

Above-ground storage tank   A type of oil storage.

AC coupling   A signal that passes the AC signal component to the meter, but blocks the DC component. Useful to observe an AC signal that is normally riding on a DC signal—for example, a charging ripple.

AC/DC clamp-on DMM   A type of meter that has a clamp that is placed around the wire to measure current.

AC ripple voltage   An alternating current voltage that rides on top of a DC charging current output from an AC generator (alternator).

Active crossover   A type of crossover that uses electronic components to block certain frequencies.

Actuator   An electromechanical device that performs mechanical movement as commanded by a controller.

Adhesive-lined heat shrink tubing   A type of heat shrink tubing that shrinks to one-third of its original diameter and has glue inside.

Adjustable pedals   Brake and accelerator pedals are mounted on a moveable support that allows them to be moved by the driver.

Adjustable wrench   A wrench that has a moveable jaw to allow it to fit many sizes of fasteners.

Advanced Engagement (AE) Starter   An AE starter works like a typical starter. When energized, the pinion shifts forward by the starter solenoid and engages with the engine's ring gear/ flywheel, and immediately spins. This starter design requires that the engine speed is zero before re-engagement and engine restart can occur.

AFS   Active front headlight system. A name for the system that causes the headlights to turn when cornering.

AGM   Absorbed glass mat. AGM batteries are lead–acid batteries, but use an absorbent material between the plates to hold the electrolyte. AGM batteries are classified as valve-regulated lead–acid (VRLA) batteries.

AGST   Above-ground storage tank used to store oil.

Airbag   An inflatable fabric bag that deploys in the event of a collision that is severe enough to cause personal injury.

Alternator   An electric generator that produces alternating current, also called an *AC generator.*

Alternator whine   A noise made by an alternator with a defective diode(s).

AM   Amplitude modulation.

American wire gauge (AWG)   A method used to measure wire diameter.

Ammeter   An electrical test instrument used to measure amperes (unit of the amount of current flow).

Ampere   The unit of the amount of current flow. Named for André Ampère (1775–1836).

Ampere hours   A method used to rate battery capacity.

Ampere-turns   The unit of measurement for electrical magnetic field strength.

Analog display   An analog display uses a needle to show the values, such as vehicle speed or engine RPM.

Analog-to-digital (AD) converter   An electronic circuit that converts analog signals into digital signals that can then be used by a computer.

Anode   The positive electrode; the electrode toward which electrons flow.

Armature   The rotating unit inside a DC generator or starter, consisting of a series of coils of insulating wire wound around a laminated iron core.

Arming sensor   A sensor used in an airbag circuit that is most sensitive and completes the circuit first of two sensors that are needed to deploy an airbag.

Asbestosis   A health condition where asbestos causes scar tissue to form in the lungs causing shortness of breath.

Auto link   A type of automotive fuse.

Automatic headlights   Automatic headlights automatically turn on the headlights when the light sensor detects low ambient light level. These sensors are usually located on the dash of the vehicle. If the light level is low, the headlights turn on automatically when the engine starts.

Automatic reversal systems (ARS)   The automatic power window reversal system is designed to prevent windows from causing injury when they are closing. The Department of Transportation (DOT) established a limit of 136 ft-lb (100 NM) of force be exerted by the window before the window retracts.

Backlight   Light that illuminates the test tool's display from the back of the LCD. Also the rear window of a vehicle.

Backup camera   A camera that mounts on the rear of the vehicle that is used to display what is behind a vehicle when the gear selector is placed in reverse.

Base   The name for the section of a transistor that controls the current flow through the transistor.

Battery cables   Cables that attach to the positive and negative terminals of the battery.

Battery electrical drain test   A test to determine if a component or circuit is draining the battery.

Baud rate   The speed at which bits of computer information are transmitted on a serial data stream. Measured in bits per second (bps).

BCI   Battery Council International. This organization establishes standards for batteries.

Bench grinder   A type of electric motor–driven grinder that mounts to a bench.

Bench testing A test of a component such as a starter before being installed in the vehicle.

Binary system A computer system that uses a series of zeros and ones to represent the information.

Bipolar transistor A type of transistor that has a base, emitter, and collector.

Blind spot monitor The blind spot monitor (BSM) is a vehicle-based sensor device that detects other vehicles located to the side and rear of the vehicle. Warnings can be audible, visual, or tactile such as vibrating the seat.

Bluetooth A short-range wireless communication standard named after a Danish king who had a bluetooth.

BNC connector Coaxial-type input connector. Named for its inventor, Neil Councilman.

Bolt A threaded fastener with a head at one end used for a wrench or socket to turn to install or remove.

Bound electrons Electrons that are close to the nucleus of the atom.

Braided ground straps Ground wires that are not insulated and braided to help increase flexibility and reduce RFI.

Brake lights Lights at the rear of the vehicle which light whenever the brake pedal is depressed.

Branches Electrical parts of a parallel circuit.

Breaker bar A hand tool used to rotate a socket.

Break-out box (BOB) An electrical tester that connects to a connector or controller and allows access to each terminal so testing can be performed using a meter or scope.

Brush-end housing The end of a starter or generator (alternator) where the brushes are located.

Brushes Carbon or carbon-copper connections used to pass electrical current to a rotating assembly such as an armature in a starter motor or a rotor in a generator (alternator).

Bulb test A bulb test is performed when the ignition is first turned on. All of the warning lights come on as part of a self-test, and to help the driver or technician spot any warning light that may be burned out or not operating.

Bump cap A hat that is made of plastic and is hard to protect the head from bumps.

Burn in A process of operating an electronic device for a period from several hours to several days.

Bus An electrical network which ties several modules together.

CA Cranking amperes. A battery rating.

CAA Clean Air Act. Federal legislation passed in 1970 and updated in 1990 that established national air quality standards.

Calibration codes Codes used on many powertrain control modules.

Campaign A recall where vehicle owners are contacted to return a vehicle to a dealer for corrective action.

CAN Controller area network, a type of serial data transmission.

Candlepower A rating of the amount of light produced by a light source such as a lightbulb.

Capacitance *Electrical capacitance* is a term used to measure or describe how much charge can be stored in a capacitor (condenser) for a given voltage potential difference. Capacitance is measured in farads or smaller increments of farads such as microfarads.

Casting number An identification number cast into an engine block and other large castings.

Cathode The negative electrode.

CCA Cold cranking amps. A rating of a battery tested at 0° F.

Cell A group of negative and positive plates to form a cell capable of producing 2.1 volts.

CFL Cathode fluorescent lighting.

CFR Code of Federal Regulations.

Channel A term used to describe a wheel brake being controlled by the antilock brake system controller.

Charging voltage test An electrical test using a voltmeter and an ammeter to test the condition of the charging circuit.

Cheater bar A pipe or other device used to increase the amount of force applied to a wrench or ratchet. Not recommended to be used because it can cause the wrench or ratchet to break, thus causing possible personal injury.

Check Engine The term used to describe the malfunction indicator light (MIL).

Chisels A sharpened tool used with a hammer to separate two pieces of an assembly.

CHMSL Centrally high mounted stop light; the third brake light.

Circuit A circuit is the path that electrons travel from a power source, through a resistance, and back to the power source.

Circuit breakers A mechanical unit that opens an electrical circuit in the event of excessive current flow.

Clamping diode A diode installed in a circuit with the cathode toward the positive. The diode becomes forward biased when the circuit is turned off thereby reducing the high voltage surge created by the current flowing through a coil.

Class 2 A type of BUS communication used in General Motors vehicles.

Claw poles The magnetic points of a generator (alternator) rotor.

Clock generator A crystal that determines the speed of computer circuits.

Clockspring A flat ribbon of wire used under the steering wire to transfer airbag electrical signals. May also carry horn and steering wheel control circuits depending on make and model of vehicle.

Coil A coil of wire that is used to create a strong electromagnetic field or used to increase voltage such as in an ignition coil, which uses two coils of wire: a primary and a secondary winding. The purpose of an ignition is to produce a high voltage (20,000–40,000 V), low-amperage (about 80 mA) current necessary for spark ignition.

Cold solder joint   A type of solder joint that was not heated to high enough temperature to create a good electrical connection. Often a dull gray appearance rather than shiny for a good solder connection.

Collector   The name of one section of a transistor.

Color shift   A term used to describe the change in the color of an HID arc tube assembly over time.

Combination circuit   Another name for a series–parallel electrical circuit.

Combination valve   A valve used in the brake system that performs more than one function, such as a pressure differential switch, metering valve, and/or proportioning valve.

Commutator segments   The name for the copper segments of the armature of a starter or DC generator.

Commutator-end housing   The end of a starter motor that contains the commutator and brushes. Also called the brush end housing.

Complete circuit   A type of electrical circuit that has continuity and current would flow if connected to power and ground.

Composite headlight   A type of headlight that uses a separate, replaceable bulb.

Compound circuit   Another name for a series–parallel electrical circuit.

Compression spring   A spring which is part of a starter drive that acts on the starter pinion gear.

Condenser   Also called a capacitor; stores an electrical charge.

Conductor   A material that conducts electricity and heat. A metal that contains fewer than four electrons in its atom's outer shell.

Continuity   A test to check wiring, circuits, connectors, or switches for breaks (open circuit) or short circuits (closed circuit).

Continuity light   A test light that has a battery and lights if there is continuity (electrical connection) between the two points that are connected to the tester.

Controller   A term that is usually used to refer to a computer or an electronic control unit (ECU).

Control wires   The wires used in a power window circuit that are used to control the operation of the windows.

Conventional theory   The theory that electricity flows from positive (+) to negative (−).

Core   A part that is returned to a parts store and which will be turned over to a company to be repaired or remanufactured.

Coulomb   A measurement of electrons. A coulomb is 6.28×10^1 (6.28 billion billion) electrons.

Counter electromotive force (cemf)   A voltage produced by a rotating coil such as a starter motor where the armature is being moved through a magnetic field.

Courtesy lights   General term used to describe all interior lights.

CPA   Connector position assurance. A clip used to help hold the two parts of electrical connector together.

CPU   Central processor unit.

Crimp-and-seal connectors   A type of electrical connector that has glue inside which provides a weather-proof seal after it is heated.

Crossover   An electronic circuit that separates frequencies in a sound (audio) system.

CRT   Cathode ray tube. A type of display which is commonly used in TVs.

Cruise control   A system that maintains the desired vehicle speed. Also called speed control.

Darlington pair   Two transistors electrically connected to form an amplifier. This permits a very small current flow to control a large current flow. Named for Sidney Darlington, a physicist at Bell Laboratories from 1929 to 1971.

DC coupling   A signal transmission that passes both AC and DC signal components to the meter.

Deceleration sensor   A sensor mounted to the body frame of a vehicle that detects and measures the deceleration of the vehicle. Used to control the activation of the airbags and vehicle stability systems.

Decibels (dB)   A unit of the magnitude of sound.

Deep cycling   The full discharge and then the full recharge of a battery.

Delta winding   A type of stator winding where all three coils are connected in a triangle shape. Named for the triangle-shape Greek capital letter.

Despiking diode   Another name of clamping diode.

Dielectric   An insulator used between two conductors to form a capacitor.

Digital computer   A computer that uses on and off signals only. Uses an A to D converter to change analog signals to digital before processing.

Digital display   A digital display uses numbers to indicate values, such as vehicle speed.

Diode   An electrical device that allows current to flow in one direction only.

Direction wires   The wires from the control switch to the lift motor on a power window circuit. The direction of current flow through these wires determines which direction the window moves.

Division   A block of time on a scope display.

DMM   Digital multimeter. A digital multimeter is capable of measuring electrical current, resistance, and voltage.

Doping   The adding of impurities to pure silicon or germanium to form either P or N-type material.

DOT   Abbreviation for the Department of Transportation.

DPDT   Double-pole, double-throw switch.

DPST   Double-pole, single-throw switch.

Drive sizes   The size in fractions of an inch of the square drive for sockets.

Drive-end (DE) housing   The end of a starter motor that has the drive pinion gear.

DRL Daytime running lights. Lights that are located in the front of the vehicle and come on whenever the ignition is on. In some vehicles, the vehicle has to be moving before they come on. Used as a safety device on many vehicles and required in many countries such as Canada since 1990.

DSO Digital storage oscilloscope.

Dual inline pins (DIP) A type of electronic chip that has two parallel lines of pins.

Dual-stage airbags Airbags that can deploy either with minimum force or full force or both together based on the information sent to the airbag controller regarding the forces involved in the collision.

Duty cycle The percentage of time a unit is turned on.

DVOM Digital volt-ohm-millimeter.

Dynamic voltage Voltage measured with the circuit energized and current flowing through the circuit.

EAP Electric adjustable pedals.

E & C Entertainment and comfort.

E²PROM Electronically erasable programmable read only memory. A type of memory that can be electronically erased and reprogrammed.

EAP An abbreviation for electrical adjustable pedals.

ECA Electronic control assembly. The name used by Ford to describe the computer used to control spark and fuel on older-model vehicles.

ECM Electronic control module. The name used by Ford to describe the computer used to control spark and fuel on older-model vehicles.

ECU Electronic control unit. A generic term for a vehicle computer.

EDR Event data recorder. The hardware and software used to record vehicle information before, during, and after an airbag deployment.

EEPROM *See* E²PROM.

Electrical load Applying a load to a component such as a battery to measure its performance.

Electrical potential Another term to describe voltage.

Electrical Power Management (EPM) A General Motors term used to describe a charging system control sensor and the control of the generator (alternator) output based on the needs of the vehicle.

Electricity The movement of free electrons from one atom to another.

Electrochemistry The term used to describe the chemical reaction that occurs inside a battery to produce electricity.

Electrolyte Any substance which, in solution, is separated into ions and is made capable of conducting an electric current. The acid solution of a lead–acid battery.

Electromagnetic interference (EMI) An undesirable electronic signal. It is caused by a magnetic field building up and collapsing, creating unwanted electrical interference on a nearby circuit.

Electromagnetic parking sensors Electromagnetic parking sensors (EPS) detect when a vehicle is moving slowly and toward an object. Once detected, the sensor continues to give signal of presence of the obstacle. If the vehicle then continues to move toward the object, the alarm signal becomes more and more impressive as the obstacle approaches. Electromagnetic parking sensors do not require any holes in the bumper and cannot be seen from the outside of the vehicle.

Electromotive force (EMF) The force (pressure) that can move electrons through a conductor.

Electron theory The theory that electricity flows from negative (−) to positive (+).

EMF *See* electromotive force.

Emitter The name of one section of a transistor. The arrow used on a symbol for a transistor is on the emitter and the arrow points toward the negative section of the transistor.

Engine mapping A computer program that uses engine test data to determine the best fuel-air ratio and spark advance to use at each speed of the engine for best performance.

Engine stop/start (ESS) AStop-start systems are designed to stop the engine when the vehicle is stopped and then starts the engine again when the driver releases the brake pedal. Engine stop-start systems are designed to increase fuel economy and reduce exhaust emissions.

Enhanced Flooded Battery (EFB) Enhanced Flooded Battery (EFB) is a flooded battery that is optimized to work with stop-start vehicle systems.

EPA Environmental Protection Agency. A federal government agency that oversees the enforcement of laws related to the environment. Included in these laws are regulations on the amount and content of automotive emissions.

ESD Electrostatic discharge. Another term for ESD is static electricity.

External trigger Occurs when the trace starts when a signal is received from another (external) source.

ETC Electronic throttle control.

External trigger Occurs when the trace starts when a signal is received from another (external) source.

Extensions Steel bars with male and female ends to extend the reach of a ratchet to rotate a socket wrench.

Eye wash station A unit that looks similar to a drinking fountain but used to wash the eyes with a large amount of water at relatively low pressure. To be used in the event that a person gets some chemical in the eyes.

Farad A unit of capacitance named for Michael Faraday (1791–1867), an English physicist. A Farad is the capacity to store 1 coulomb of electrons at 1 volt of potential difference.

Feedback The reverse flow of electrical current through a circuit or electrical unit that should not normally be operating. This feedback current (reverse-bias current flow) is most often caused by a poor ground connection for the same normally operating circuit.

FET Field effect transistor. A type of transistor that is very sensitive and can be harmed by static electricity.

Fiber optics   The transmission of light through special plastic that keeps the light rays parallel even if the plastic is tied in a knot.

Field coils   Coils or wire wound around metal pole shoes to form the electromagnetic field inside an electric motor.

Field housing   The part of a starter that supports the field coils.

Field poles   The magnets used as field coils in a starter motor.

File   A hand tool used to smooth metal.

Fire blanket   A fire-proof wool blanket used to cover a person who is on fire to smother the fire.

Fire extinguisher classes   The types of fires that a fire extinguisher is designed to handle is referred to as fire class.

Floating ground system   An electrical system that uses a ground that is not connected to the chassis of the vehicle.

Flooded cell battery   A type of secondary (rechargeable) battery that uses a liquid electrolyte.

Flooded lead acid (FLA)   Flooded lead acid (FLA) batteries are conventional batteries that use a liquid electrolyte. In this design, vents are used to allow the gases (hydrogen and oxygen) to escape. It is this loss of the hydrogen and oxygen that results in a battery using water during normal use.

Flux density   The density of the magnetic lines of force around a magnet or other object.

Flux lines   Individual magnetic lines of force.

FM   Frequency modulation. A type of radio transmission.

Forward bias   Current flow in normal direction. Used to describe when current is able to flow through a diode.

Free electrons   The outer electrons in an atom that has fewer than four electrons in its outer orbit.

Frequency   The number of times a waveform repeats in one second, measured in Hertz (Hz), frequency band.

Fuse   An electrical safety unit constructed of a fine tin conductor that will melt and open the electrical circuit if excessive current flows through the fuse.

Fuse link   A safety device used on a solvent washer which would melt and cause the lid to close in the event of a fire. A type of fuse used to control the maximum current in a circuit.

Fusible link   A type of fuse that will melt and open the protected circuit in the event of a short circuit, which could cause excessive current flow through the fusible link. Most fusible links are actually wires that are four gauge sizes smaller than the wire of the circuits being protected.

Gassing   The release of hydrogen and oxygen gas from the plates of a battery during charging or discharging.

Gauss gauge   A gauge used to measure the unit of magnetic induction or magnetic intensity named for Karl Friedrich Gauss (1777–1855), a German mathematician.

GAWR   Gross axle weight rating. A rating of the load capacity of a vehicle and included on placards on the vehicle and in the owner's manual.

Gel battery   A lead–acid battery with silica added to the electrolyte to make it leak proof and spill proof. Also called a valve-regulated lead–acid (VRLA) battery.

Germanium   A semiconductor used in early diodes.

GMLAN   General Motors local area network. GM's term for CAN used in GM vehicles.

GMM   Graphing multimeter. A cross between a digital meter and a digital storage oscilloscope.

GPS   Global positioning system. A government program of 24 satellites that transmit signals that are used by receivers to determine their location.

Grade   The measure of the strength or quality of a bolt or fastener.

Graticule   The grid lines on the scope screen.

Grid   A part of a battery onto which the active material is pasted.

Ground brushes   The brushes in a starter motor that carry current to the housing of the starter or ground.

Ground (return) path   The electrical return path that the current flows through in a complete circuit.

Ground plane   A part of antenna that is metal and usually the body of the vehicle.

Grounded   An electrical fault where the current is going to ground rather than through the load and then to ground.

Growler   Electrical tester designed to test starter armatures.

GVWR   Gross vehicle weight rating. The total weight of the vehicle including the maximum cargo.

Hacksaw   A type of saw used to cut metal and uses a replaceable blade.

Hammer   A hand tool used to deliver a force to a concentrated place.

Hazard warning   A sticker or decal warning that a hazard is close.

Hazardous waste material   Chemicals or components that pose a danger to the environment or to people.

Heated rear window defogger   An electrically heated rear window defogger system uses an electrical grid baked on the glass that warms the glass to about 85°F (29°C) and clears it of fog or frost. The rear window defogger system is controlled by a driver-operated switch and a timer relay.

Heated seats   Heated seats use electric heating elements in the seat bottom, as well as in the seat back, in many vehicles. The heating element is designed to warm the seat and/or back of the seat to about 100°F (38°C) or close to normal body temperature (98.6°F [37°C]).

Heat shrink tubing   A type of rubber tubing that shrinks to about half of its original diameter when heated. Used over a splice during a wire repair.

Heat sink   Usually, a metallic-finned unit used to keep electronic components cool.

Heated steering wheel   A heated steering wheel usually consists of a built-in heater in the rim as well as heated steering wheel control switch and heated steering wheel control module.

HEV   Abbreviation for hybrid electric vehicles.

HEPA vacuum   High efficiency particulate air filter vacuum used to clean brake dust.

Hertz   A unit of measurement of frequency. One Hertz is one cycle per second, abbreviated Hz. Named for Heinrich R. Hertz, a 19th-century German physicist.

HID High intensity discharge. A type of headlight that uses high voltage to create an arc inside the arc tube assembly which then produces a blue-white light.

High-impedance meter Measures the total internal resistance of the meter circuit due to internal coils, capacitors, and resistors.

High-pass filter A filter in an audio system that blocks low frequencies and allows only high frequencies to pass through to the speakers.

Hold-in winding One of two electromagnetic windings inside a solenoid; used to hold the movable core into the solenoid.

Hole theory A theory which states that as an electron flows from negative (−) to positive (+), it leaves behind a hole. According to the hole theory, the hole would move from positive (+) to negative (−).

HomeLink A brand name of a system used and included in many new vehicles to operate the automatic garage door opener.

Horn An electromechanical device that creates a loud sound when activated.

HUD Head-up display.

Hybrid electric vehicles (HEVs) A type of vehicle that has two sources of power: an electric motor and an internal combustion engine, to propel the vehicle.

Hybrid flasher A type of flasher unit that can operate two or more bulbs at a constant rate.

Hydrometer An instrument used to measure the specific gravity of a liquid. A battery hydrometer is calibrated to read the expected specific gravity of battery electrolyte.

IEC International Electrotechnical Commission.

Ignition control module (ICM) Controls (turns on and off) the primary ignition current of an electronic ignition system.

Impedance Impedance is a combination of resistance and inductance in a speaker coil measured in ohms.

Impurities Doping elements used in the construction of diodes and transistors.

Inductive ammeter A type of ammeter that is used as a Hall-effect sensor in a clamp that surrounds a conductor carrying a current.

Independent switches Switch located at each door and used to raise or lower the power window for that door only.

Input Information on data from sensors to an electronic controller is called input. Sensors and switches provide the input signals.

Input conditioning What the computer does to the input signals to make them useful; usually includes an analog-to-digital converter and other electronic circuits that eliminate electrical noise.

Instrument panel cluster Vehicle information is displayed on the instrument panel cluster (IPC). The IPC may use analog or digital display or a combination of both.

Insulated brushes Brushes used in a starter motor that connect to battery power through the solenoid.

Insulator A material that does not readily conduct electricity and heat. A nonmetal material that contains more than four electrons in its atom's outer shell.

Integral sensor A term used to describe a crash sensor that is built into the airbag control module.

Integrated circuit (IC) An electronic circuit that contains many circuits all in one chip.

Inverter An electronic device used to convert DC (direct current) into AC (alternating current).

IOD Ignition off draw. A Chrysler term used to describe battery electrical drain or parasitic draw.

Ion An atom with an excess or deficiency of electrons forming either a negative or a positive charged particle.

IP Abbreviation for instrument panel.

Jumper cables Heavy-gauge (4 to 00) electrical cables with large clamps, used to connect a vehicle that has a discharged battery to a vehicle that has a good battery.

Junction The point where two types of materials join.

KAM Keep alive memory.

Kelvin (K) A temperature scale where absolute zero is zero degrees. Nothing is colder than absolute zero.

Key fob A decorative unit attached to keys. Often includes a remote control to unlock/lock vehicles.

Keyword A type of network communications used in many General Motors vehicles.

Kilo Means 1,000; abbreviated k or K.

Kirchhoff's current law A law that states "The current flowing into any junction of an electrical circuit is equal to the current flowing out of that junction."

Kirchhoff's voltage law A law about electrical circuits that states: "The voltage around any closed circuit is equal to the sum (total) of the resistances."

LCD Liquid crystal display.

LDWS Lane departure warning system.

LED Light-emitting diode. A high-efficiency light source that uses very little electricity and produces very little heat.

LED test light Uses an LED instead of a standard automotive bulb for a visual indication of voltage.

Left-hand rule A method of determining the direction of magnetic lines of force around a conductor. The left-hand rule is used with the electron flow theory (- flowing to +).

Legs Another name for the branches of a parallel circuit.

Lenz's law The relative motion between a conductor and a magnetic field is opposed by the magnetic field of the current it has induced.

Leyden jar A device first used to store an electrical charge. The first type of capacitor.

Load A term used to describe a device when an electrical current is flowing through it.

Load test A type of battery test where an electrical load is applied to the battery and the voltage is monitored to determine the condition of a battery.

Lock tang A mechanical tab that is used to secure a terminal into a connector. This lock tang must be depressed to be able to remove the terminal from the connector.

Lockout switch   A lock placed on the circuit breaker box to insure that no one turns on the electrical circuit while repairs are being made.

Logic probe   A type of tester that can detect either power or ground. Most testers can detect voltage but some cannot detect if a ground is present without further testing.

Low-pass filter   A device used in an audio system that blocks high frequencies and allows only low frequencies to pass to the speakers.

Low-water-loss battery   A type of battery that uses little water in normal service. Most batteries used in cars and light trucks use this type of battery.

Lumbar   The lower section of the back.

Magnetic flux   The lines of force produced in a magnetic field.

Magnetic induction   The transfer of the magnetic lines of force to another nearby metal object or coil of wire.

Magnetism   A form of energy that is recognized by the attraction it exerts on other materials.

Maintenance-free battery   A type of battery that does not require routine adding of water to the cells. Most batteries used in cars and light truck are maintenance-free design.

Malfunction indicator lamp (MIL)   *This amber, dashboard warning* light may be labeled check engine or service engine soon.

Master control switch   The control switch for the power windows located near the driver who can operate all of the windows.

MCA   Marine cranking amps. A battery specification.

Mercury   A heavy metal that is liquid at room temperature.

Mesh spring   A spring used behind the starter pinion on a starter drive to force the drive pinion into mesh with the ring gear on the engine.

Mega (M)   Million. Used when writing larger numbers or measuring a large amount of resistance.

Meter accuracy   The accuracy of a meter measured in percent.

Meter resolution   The specification of a meter that indicates how small or fine a measurement the meter can detect and display.

Metric bolts   Bolts manufactured and sized in the metric system of measurement.

Metric wire gauge   The metric method for measuring wire size in the square millimeters. This is the measure of the core of the wire and does not include the insulation.

Milli (m)   One thousandth of a volt or ampere.

Modulation   A combination of a carrier wave frequency with an audio frequency.

Momentary switch   A type of switch that toggles between on and off.

Moon roof   A moon roof is made of a tinted glass panel that can be either tilted open or completely retracted to operate as an open window in the roof.

MOSFET   Metal oxide semiconductor field effect transistor. A type of transistor.

MSDS   Material safety data sheets.

Multiplexing   A process of sending multiple signals of information at the same time over a signal wire.

Mutual induction   The generation of an electric current due to a changing magnetic field of an adjacent coil.

N.C.   Normally closed.

N.O.   Normally open.

Network   A communications system used to link multiple computers or modules.

Neutral charge   An atom that has the same number electrons as protons.

Neutral safety switch   An electrical switch that allows the starter to be energized only if the gear selector is in neutral or park.

Night vision   Night vision systems use a camera that is capable of observing objects in the dark to assist the driver while driving at night. The night vision option uses a HUD to improve the vision of the driver beyond the scope of the headlights.

Node   A module and computer that is part of a communications network.

Nonvolatile RAM   Computer memory capability that is not lost when power is removed.

NPN transistor   A type of transistor that has the P-type material in the base and the N-type material is used for the emitter and collector.

NTC   Negative temperature coefficient. Usually used in reference to a temperature sensor (coolant or air temperature). As the temperature increases, the resistance of the sensor decreases.

N-type material   Silicon or germanium doped with phosphorus, arsenic, or antimony.

Nuts   A female threaded fastener to be used with a bolt or stud.

NVRAM   Nonvolatile random access memory.

Occupant detection systems   An airbag system that includes a sensor in the passenger seat used to detect whether or not a passenger is seated in the passenger side and the weight range of that passenger.

Ohm   The unit of electrical resistance. Named for George Simon Ohm.

Ohm's law   An electrical law that requires 1 volt to push 1 ampere through 1 ohm of resistance.

Ohmmeter   An electrical tester deigned to measure electrical resistance in ohms.

OnStar   An example of a telematics system is OnStar. OnStar was first introduced in 1996 as an option on some Cadillac models. This is a system that includes a cell phone and global positioning antenna and computer.

OP-amps   An abbreviation for operational amplifier. Used in circuits to control and simplify digital signals.

Open circuit   Any circuit that is not complete and in which no current flows.

Open circuit voltage   Voltage measured without the circuit in operation.

Open-end wrench   A type of wrench that allows access to the flats of a bolt or nut from the side.

Oscilloscope (scope)   A tester that displays voltage levels on a screen.

OSHA   Occupational Safety and Health Administration. OSHA is the main federal agency responsible for enforcement of workplace safety and health legislation.

OL   Overload or overlimit.

Output drivers   PCM switches are actually transistors and are often called output drivers.

Overrunning alternator dampener (OAD)   An alternator (generator) drive pulley that has a one-way clutch and a dampener spring used to smooth the operation of the alternator and reduce the stress on the drive belt.

Override alternator pulley (OAP)   An alternator (generator) drive pulley that has a one-way clutch used to smooth the operation of the alternator and reduce the stress on the drive belt.

Overrunning clutch   A part of a starter drive assembly that allows the engine to rotate faster than the starter motor to help protect the starter from harm in the event the ignition switch is held in the crank position after the engine starts.

Pacific fuse element   A type of automotive fuse.

Parallel circuit   An electrical circuit with more than one path from the power side to the ground side. Has more than one branch or leg.

Parasitic load test   An electrical test that measures how much current (amperes) is draining from the battery with the ignition off and all electrical loads off.

Partitions   Separations between the cells of a battery. Partitions are made of the same material as that of the outside case of the battery.

Passenger presence system (PPS)   An airbag system that includes a sensor in the passenger seat used to detect whether or not a passenger is seated in the passenger side and the weight range of that passenger.

Passkey I and II   A type of antitheft system used in General Motors vehicles.

Passlock I, Passlock II, and Passlock III   A type of antitheft system used in General Motors vehicles.

PATS   Passive antitheft system. A type of antitheft system used in Ford, Lincoln, and Mercury vehicles.

PCM   Powertrain control module.

Peltier effect   A French scientist Peltier found that electrons moving through a solid can carry heat from one side of the material to the other side. This effect is called the **Peltier effect.**

Permanently Engaged (PE) Starter   In this system, the starter and flywheel gears are permanently connected. The PE starter eliminates the starter pinion gear shifting mechanism with its slight delay in activating by mounting the starter to the engine permanently engaged with the flywheel.

Permanent magnet electric motors   Electric motors that use permanent magnets for the field instead of electromagnets.

Permeability   The measure of how well a material conducts magnetic lines of force.

Phosphor   A chemical-coated light-emitting element called a phosphor is hit with high-speed electrons which cause it to glow and creates light.

Photodiodes   A type of diode used as a sun-load sensor. Connected in reverse bias, the current flow is proportional to the sun load.

Photoelectricity   When certain metals are exposed to light, some of the light energy is transferred to the free electrons of the metal. This excess energy breaks the electrons loose from the surface of the metal. They can then be collected and made to flow in a conductor, which is called photoelectricity.

Photons   Light is emitted from an LED by the release of energy in the form of photons.

Photoresistor   A semiconductor that changes in resistance with the presence or absence of light. Dark is high resistance and light is low resistance.

Phototransistor   An electronic device that can detect light and turn on or off. Used in some suspension height sensors.

Piezoelectricity   The principle by which certain crystals become electrically charged when pressure is applied.

Pinch weld seam   The area under a unit-body vehicle where two body panels join and are bent together and then welded. A typical location to place a jack if the vehicle needs to be hoisted.

Pitch   The number of threads per inch of a threaded fastener.

PIV   Peak inverse voltage. A rating for a diode.

Pliers   A hand tool with two movable jaws.

PM generator   A sensor that has a permanent magnet and a coil of wire and produces an analog voltage signal if a metal wheel with notches passes close to the sensor.

PNP transistor   A type of transistor that used N-type material for the base and P-type material for the emitter and collector.

Pole   The point where magnetic lines of force enter or leave a magnet.

Pole shoes   The metal part of the field coils in a starter motor.

Porous lead   Lead with many small holes to make a surface porous for use in battery negative plates; the chemical symbol for lead is Pb.

Positive temperature coefficient (PTC)   Usually used in reference to a conductor or electronic circuit breaker. As the temperature increases, the electrical resistance also increases.

Potentiometer   A 3-terminal variable resistor that varies the voltage drop in a circuit.

Powerline capacitor   A capacitor used to boost the output of a sound system to move the speakers especially when reproducing low frequencies.

Power source   In electrical terms, the battery or generator (alternator).

Power windows   Power windows use electric motors to raise and lower door glass. They can be operated by both a master control switch located beside the driver and additional independent switches located at each electric window.

PPE   Personal protective equipment that can include gloves, safety glasses, and other items.

Pressure differential switch   Switch installed between the two separate braking circuits of a dual master to light the dash board "brake" light in the event of a brake system failure, causing a *difference* in brake pressure.

Pretensioners   An explosive device used to remove the slack from a safety belt when an airbag is deployed.

Primary wire   Wire used for low voltage automotive circuits, typically 12 volts.

Programmable Controller Interface (PCI)   A type of network communications protocol used in Chrysler brand vehicles.

PROM   Programmable read-only memory.

PRV   *See* peak reverse voltage.

PTC circuit protection   Usually used in reference to a conductor or electronic circuit breaker. As the temperature increases, the electrical resistance also increases.

P-type material   Silicon or germanium doped with boron or indium.

Pull-in winding   One of two electromagnetic windings inside a solenoid used to move a movable core.

Pulse train   A DC voltage that turns on and off in a series of pulses.

Pulse wipers   Windshield wipers that operate intermittently. Also called delay wipers.

Pulse width   A measure of the actual on-time measured in milliseconds.

Punches   A hand tool used with a hammer to drive out pins and other small objects.

PWM   Pulse width modulation; operation of a device by an on/off digital signal that is controlled by the time duration the device is turned on and off.

Radio choke   A small coil of wire installed in the power lead, leading to a pulsing unit, such as an IVR to prevent radio interference.

Radio frequency   A form of electromagnetic energy that is within the frequency that radios can detect and transmit.

Radio Frequency Identification (RFID)   Most security systems today use a Radio Frequency Identification (RFID) security system.

Rain sense wipers   Windshield wiper that uses an electronic sensor to detect the presence of rain on the windshield and start operating automatically if the wiper switch is in the Auto position.

RAM   Random access memory. A nonpermanent type of computer memory used to store and retrieve information.

Ratchet   A reversible hand tool used to rotate a socket.

RCRA   Resource Conservation and Recovery Act.

Recall   A notification to the owner of a vehicle that a safety issue needs to be corrected.

Recombinant battery   A battery design that does not release gasses during normal operation. AGM batteries are known as recombinant batteries.

Rectifier bridge   A group of six diodes, three positive (+) and three negative (−), commonly used in generators (alternators).

Relay   An electromagnetic switch that uses a movable arm.

Reluctance   The resistance to the movement of magnetic lines of force.

Remote start   A remote start is the ability to start the engine of the vehicle from a distance by using a remote control. Most factory-installed remote start systems use the same key fob that is used to unlock the doors

Reserve capacity   The number of minutes a battery can produce 25 amperes and still maintain a battery voltage of 1.75 volts per cell (10.5 volts for a 12 volts battery).

Residual magnetism   Magnetism remaining after the magnetizing force is removed.

Resistance   The opposition to current flow measured in ohms.

Reverse bias   When the polarity of a battery is connected to a diode backward and no current flows.

RF   *See* radio frequency.

Rheostat   A two-terminal variable resistor.

Right-to-know laws   Laws that state that employees have a right to know when the materials they use at work are hazardous.

RMS   Root mean square. A method of displaying variable voltage signals on a digital meter.

Remote keyless entry (RKE)   The part of the key fob has a battery to power the transmitter, which is used to lock and unlock a vehicle door(s) by remote control.

Residual magnetism   Magnetism remaining after the magnetizing force is removed.

ROM   Read-only memory.

Rotor   The rotating part of a generator where the magnetic field is created.

Rosin-core solder   A type of solder for use in electrical repairs. Inside the center of the solder is a rosin that acts as a flux to clean and help the solder flow.

RPA   Rear park assist. The General Motors term to describe the system used to detect objects and warn the drive when backing.

Rubber coupling   A flexible connection between the power seat motor and the drive cable.

RVS   Remote vehicle start. A General Motors term for the system that allows the driver to start the engine using a remote control.

SAE   Society of Automotive Engineers.

SAR   Supplemental air restraints. Another term used to describe an airbag system.

SCR   Silicon controller rectifier.

Screw jack assembly   A screw jack that is used to raise or lower a power seat.

Screwdrivers A hand tool used to install or remove screws.

SDARS Satellite Digital Audio Radio Services. Another term used to describe satellite radio.

Sediment chamber A space below the cell plates of some batteries to permit the accumulation of sediment deposits flaking from the battery plates. A sediment chamber keeps the sediment from shorting the battery plates.

Semiconductor A material that is neither a conductor nor an insulator; has exactly four electrons in the atom's outer shell.

Serial Communication Interface (SCI) A type of serial data transmission used by Chrysler.

Serial data Data that is transmitted by a series of rapidly changing voltage signals.

Series circuit An electrical circuit that provides only one path for current to flow.

Series circuit laws Laws that were developed by Kirchhoff, which pertain to series circuits.

Series–parallel circuits Any type of circuit containing resistances in both series and parallel in one circuit.

Series-wound field A typical starter motor circuit where the current through the field windings is connected in series with the armature before going to ground. Also called a series-wound starter.

Service Engine Soon (SES) light See Malfunction indicator lamp (MIL)

Shim A thin metal spacer.

Short circuit A circuit in which current flows, but bypasses some or all the resistance in the circuit. A connection that results in a "copper-to-copper" connection.

Shorted A condition of being shorted such as a short circuit.

Short-to-ground A short circuit in which the current bypasses some or all the resistance of the circuit and flows to ground. Because ground is usually steel in automotive electricity, a short-to-ground (grounded) is a "copper-to-steel" connection.

Short-to-voltage A circuit in which current flows, but bypasses some or all the resistance in the circuit. A connection that results in a "copper-to-copper" connection.

Shunt field A field coil used in a starter motor that is not connected to the armature in series but is grounded to the starter case.

Shunt A device used to divert or bypass part of the current from the main circuit.

Silicon A semiconductor material.

SIR Supplemental inflatable restraints. Another term for airbags.

SKIS Sentry Key Immobilizer System. A type of antitheft system used in Chrysler vehicles.

SLA Abbreviation for sealed lead–acid battery.

SLI The battery that is responsible for starting, lighting, and ignition.

Slip-ring-end (SRE) housing The name for the rear housing of an alternator where the slip rings are located.

Snips A hand tool designed to cut sheet metal.

Socket A tool used to grasp the head of a bolt or nut and then rotated by a ratchet or breaker bar.

Socket adapter A tool used to adapt one size of socket drive for use with another size drive unit such as a ratchet or breaker bar.

Solvent Usually colorless liquids that are used to remove grease and oil.

SPDT Single-pole, double-throw switch. A type of electrical switch.

Speakers A device consisting of a magnet, a coil of wire, and a cone that reproduces sounds from the electrical signals sent to the speakers from a radio or amplifier.

Specific gravity The ratio of the weight of a given volume of a liquid divided by the weight of an equal volume of water.

Spike protection resistor A resistor usually between 300 and 500 ohms that is connected in a circuit in parallel with the load to help reduce a voltage spike caused when a current following through a coil is turned off.

Splice pack A term used by General Motors to describe the connection of modules in a network.

Sponge lead Lead with many small holes used to make a surface porous or sponge-like for use in battery negative plates; the symbol for lead is Pb.

Spontaneous combustion A condition that can cause some materials, such as oily rags, to catch fire without a source of ignition.

SPST Single-pole, single-throw switch. A type of electrical switch.

Squib The heating element of an inflator module which starts the chemical reaction to create the gas that inflates an airbag.

SRS Supplemental restraint system. Another term for an airbag system.

SST Special service tools. Tools specified by a vehicle manufacturer needed to service a vehicle or a unit repair component of a vehicle.

Standard Corporate Protocol (SCP) A network communications protocol used by Ford.

Starter drive A term used to describe the starter motor drive pinion gear with overrunning clutch.

Starter solenoid A type of starter motor that uses a solenoid to activate the starter drive.

State-of-health (SOH) A signal sent by modules to all of the other modules in the network indicating that it is well and able to transmit.

Static electricity An electrical charge that builds up in insulators and then discharges to conductors.

Stator A name for three interconnected windings inside an alternator. A rotating rotor provides a moving magnetic field and induces a current in the windings of the stator.

Stepper motor A motor that moves a specified amount of rotation.

Steering wheel controls Steering wheel controls are steering wheels that include buttons to allow the driver to control certain audio, vehicle information, and HVAC functions. The purpose of having steering wheel controls is to allow the driver to keep their hands on the wheel and their eyes on the road at all times.

Stiffening capacitor *See* powerline capacitor.

Stud A short rod with threads on both ends.

Subwoofer A type of speaker that is used to reproduce low frequency sounds.

Sun roof A sun roof is basically any kind of panel on the roof of a car that permits light, air, or both to come into a vehicle, but only if the panel is opened.

Sun shades Sun shades are fabric or screen-like material installed on the inside of the vehicle that can be raised, lowered, or moved to block the rays of the sun from entering the interior of the vehicle.

Suppression diode A diode installed in the reverse-bias direction and used to reduce the voltage spike that is created when a circuit that contains a coil is opened and the coil discharges.

SVR Sealed valve-regulated. A term used to describe a type of battery that is valve-regulated lead–acid or sealed lead–acid.

SWCAN An abbreviation for single wire CAN (controller area network).

Tandem Solenoid (TS) Starter Using a starter that has two solenoids allows the starter to engage the flywheel of the engine when it is still moving, such as when the vehicle is coasting to a stop. The use of a dual solenoid allows the two functions of the starter solenoid to work independently. One solenoid is used to engage the starter drive into the engine ring gear. The other solenoid is used to engage the operation of the starter motor

Telematics Telematics is an interconnected system that combines telecommunications (cellular systems) and GPS navigation satellite system technology. Telematics is a method of monitoring a vehicle by combining a GPS system with on-board diagnostic systems. It is possible to record and map exactly where a vehicle is located and how fast it is traveling.

Tensile strength The strength of a bolt or fastener in the lengthwise direction.

Terminal The metal end of a wire that fits into a plastic connector and is the electrical connection part of a junction.

Terminating resistors Resistors placed at the end of a high-speed serial data circuit to help reduce electromagnetic interference.

Test light A light used to test for voltage. Contains a light bulb with a ground wire at one end and a pointed tip at the other end.

THD Total harmonic distortion. A rating for an amplifier used in sound system.

Thermistor A resistor that changes resistance with temperature. A positive-coefficient thermistor has increased resistance with an increase in temperature. A negative-coefficient thermistor has increased resistance with a decrease in temperature.

Thermocouple Two dissimilar metals when connected and heated creates a voltage. Used for measuring temperature.

Thermoelectricity The production of current flow created by heating the connection of two dissimilar metals.

Thin-film transistor (TFT) Thin-film transistor (TFT) is a type of a liquid-crystal (LCD) display that uses thin-film transistor (TFT) technology.

Three-minute charge test A method used to test batteries. Not valid for all types of batteries.

Threshold voltage Another name for barrier voltage or the voltage difference needed to forward bias a diode.

Through bolts The bolts used to hold the parts of a starter motor together. The long bolts go through field housing and into the drive-end housing.

Throws The term used to describe the number of output circuits in a switch.

Time base Setting how much time will be displayed in each block.

Tone generator tester A type of tester used to find a shorted circuit that uses a tone generator. Headphones are used along with a probe to locate where the tone stops, which indicates where in the circuit the fault is located.

Total circuit resistance (R_T) The total resistance in a circuit.

Trade number The number stamped on an automotive lightbulb. All bulbs of the same trade number have the same candlepower and wattage, regardless of the manufacturer of the bulb.

Transceiver A transceiver functions as both a reviewer and a transmitter. The transceiver is usually mounted on the steering column assembly. The antenna for the transceiver is a coil of wire mounted within the plastic ring that mounts around the lock cylinder.

Transponder The transponder is mounted in the key or the body of the key fob. A transponder has an antenna, which consists of a coil of wire as well as a circuit board containing the processing electronics and data memory.

Transistor A semiconductor device that can operate as an amplifier or an electrical switch.

Trigger level The start of the display.

Trigger slope The voltage direction that a waveform must have in order to start the display.

Trouble light A light used to help a service technician see while performing service work on a vehicle.

Troxler effect The Troxler effect is a visual effect where an image remains on the retina of the eye for a short time after the image has been removed. The effect was discovered in 1804 by Igney Paul Vital Troxler (1780–1866), a Swiss physician. Because of the Troxler effect, headlight glare can remain on the retina of the eye and create a blind spot.

TSB Technical service bulletin.

Turns ratio The ratio between the number of turns used in the primary winding of the coil to the number of turns used in the secondary winding. In a typical ignition coil, the ratio is 100:1.

Tweeter A type of speaker used in an audio system that is designed to transmit high frequency sounds.

Twisted pair   A pair of wires that are twisted together from 9 to 16 turns per foot of length. Most are twisted once every inch (12 per foot) to help reduce electromagnetic interference from being induced in the wires as one wire would tend to cancel out any interference picked up by the other wire.

UART   Universal asynchronous receive/transmit, a type of serial data transmission.

UART-based protocol (UBP)   A type of module communication that uses universal asynchronous receive and transmit (UART) format.

UNC   Unified national coarse.

UNF   Unified national fine.

Universal joint   A joint in a steering or drive shaft that allows torque to be transmitted at an angle.

Used oil   Oil that has been used in an engine and has a chance to absorb metal particles and other contaminants.

UST   Underground storage tank.

Valence ring   The outermost ring or orbit of electrons around a nucleus of an atom.

Variable-delay wipers   Windshield wipers whose speed can be varied.

VATS   Vehicle antitheft system. A system used on some General Motors vehicles.

VECI   Vehicle emission control information. This sticker is located under the hood on all vehicles and includes emission-related information that is important to the service technician.

VIN   Vehicle identification number.

Virtual display   A virtual display is a dash that allows the driver to select what data is being displayed. Many vehicles are equipped with an LCD dash display that can be changed to display various functions based on the driver's preference. This allows the dash display to be totally customized to what the driver wishes to see displayed.

Voice activation   Most recent vehicles include voice commands, commonly called voice activation, that can be used to perform various functions or settings in the vehicle.

Voice recognition   A system that uses a microphone and a speaker connected to an electronic module, which can control the operation of electronic devices in a vehicle.

Voltage drop   Voltage loss across a wire, connector, or any other conductor. Voltage drop equals resistance in ohms times current in amperes (Ohm's law).

Voltmeter   An electrical test instrument used to measure volts (unit of electrical pressure). A voltmeter is connected in parallel with the unit or circuit being tested.

VRLA   Valve-regulated lead–acid battery. A sealed battery that is both spill proof and leakproof. AGM and gelled electrolyte are both examples of VRLA batteries.

VTF   Vacuum tube fluorescence. A type of dash display.

Washers   Flat or shaped pieces of round metal with a hole in the center used between a nut and a part or casting.

Watt   An electrical unit of power; 1 watt equals current (amperes) × voltage (1/746 hp). Named after James Watt, a Scottish inventor.

Watt's law   The formula for Watts is the voltage times the amperes in the circuit that represents the electrical power in the circuit.

WHMIS   Workplace Hazardous Materials Information Systems.

Window regulator   A mechanical device that transfers the rotating motion of the window hand crank or electric motor to a vertical motion to raise and lower a window in a vehicle.

Windshield wipers   The assembly of motor, motor control, operating linkage, plus the wiper arms and blades that are used to remove rain water from the windshield.

Wiring schematic   A drawing showing the wires and the components in a circuit using symbols to represent the components.

WOW display   A dash display when it first comes on and lights all possible segments. Can be used to test the dash display for missing lighted segments.

Wrenches   Hand tools used to rotate bolts or nuts.

Xenon headlights   Headlights that use an arc tube assembly that has a xenon gas inside which produces a bright bluish light.

Zener diode   A specially constructed (heavily doped) diode designed to operate with a reverse-bias current after a certain voltage has been reached. Named for Clarence Melvin Zener.

INDEX

Note: Page numbers followed by f indicate Figures

A

Aboveground storage tank (AGST). See Underground storage tank (UST)
Absorbed glass mat (AGM), 219
ACC. See Adaptive cruise control (ACC)
AC coupling, 113
AC/DC clamp-on digital multimeter (DMM), 100
Acoustical energy, 404
AC ripple
  testing current, 284, 284f
  voltage check, 282–284, 284f
AC ripple voltage, 283
Active crossovers, 411
Active cruise control, 396
Actuator, 190
AC voltage, 113
AC volts (ACV), 95
Adaptive cruise control (ACC), 396–398, 396f, 397f
Adaptive front lighting system (AFS), 312
ADAS. See Advanced driver assist systems (ADAS)
Adhesive-lined heat shrink tubing, 130
Adjustable wrench, 24
Advanced driver assist systems (ADAS), 392–402
  adaptive cruise control (ACC), 396–398
  automatic emergency braking (AEB) system, 398–399
  blind spot monitor (BSM), 393–394
  camera calibration, 400–401
  diagnosis, 400
  hill start assist, 399–400
  lane departure warning system (LDWS), 395
  lane keep assist (LKA), 395–396
  parking-assist system, 394–395
  pre-collision system, 399
  purpose, 392
  radar calibration, 401–402
  rear cross-traffic warning (RCTW) system, 398
Advanced Engagement (AE) Starter, 248
AEB. See Automatic emergency braking (AEB)
Aftermarket sound system upgrade, 411–413
  capacitor installation, 412, 413f
  power and ground upgrades, 411–412
  powerline capacitor, 412, 412f, 412t
Air and electrically operated tools, 36–38
  air ratchet, 36, 38f
  bench or pedestal-mounted grinder, 37, 38f
  die grinder, 36, 38f
  impact wrench, 36
Airbag, 349
  deployed, 356–357, 357f
  diagnosis tools and equipment, 353–355, 355f
  driver module replacement, 356
  front, 349–353
  seat and side curtain, 359
  system service, 355–356

Airbag handling, 8
Airbag system service, 355–356
Air-conditioning refrigerant oil disposal, 9, 9f
Alternator, 266
  components and operation, 269–270, 269–270f
  construction, 266
  cooling, 274–275, 275f
  disassembly, 288–290
  installation, 291–292
  output factors, 272–273
  output, minimum required, 286–287
  output test, 286
  overrunning pulleys, 267–268, 267–268f
  principle, 266
  reassembly, 290–291, 290f
  remanufactured, 291
  removal, 287–288, 287f
  voltage regulation, 273–274, 274f
  works, 271–272
Alternator cooling, 274–275
Alternator whine, 415
American wire gauge (AWG), 119
Ammeter, 57
Ampere, 57, 57f
Ampere hour, 221
Ampere-turns, 162
Amplitude modulation (AM), 405, 405f
  characteristics, 406
Analog and digital displays, 323–324
  network communication, 324
  stepper motor analog gauges, 324
Analog display, 323
Analog-to-digital (AD) converter, 190
Anode, 173
Antenna
  diagnosis, 407–408, 408f
  lightning damage, 417, 417f
  types of, 406–407, 407f
Armature, 243
Arming sensor, 349
Asbestos hazards
  EPA Regulations, 3
  handling guidelines, 3–4
  OSHA standards, 3
Asbestosis, 3
Audio system
  aftermarket sound system upgrade, 411–413
  antenna diagnosis, 407–408
  antennas, 406–407
  bluetooth, 413–414
  crossovers, 411
  fundamentals, 404–406
  operation and diagnosis, 404–417
  radio interference, 415–417
  radios and receivers, 406

satellite radio, 414–415
sound levels, 410–411
speakers, 408–410
speaker type, 410
types of energy, 404, 404f
voice recognition, 413
Auto link. *See* Pacific fuse elements
Automatic emergency braking (AEB), 398–399, 399f
Automatic headlights, 313
Automatic reversal systems (ARS), 375
Automotive wiring, 119–121
american wire gauge (AWG), 119–120, 120t
definition and terminology, 119
metric wire gauge, 120
Autonomous cruise control, 396

B

Backlight, 373
Backup camera, 334–336
Base, 179
Bass blocker, 411
Battery/Batteries
charge time, 230
charging, 228–230, 229f
construction, 214–217, 215f
construction types, 218–219
defective, 223–224, 224f
failure, 219–220
float-type charger, 230–231, 230f
introduction, 214
jump start, 231, 231f
load testing, 226–227, 227f
maintenance, 224–225
ratings, 220–221
safety procedures, 223
sizes, 221
symptom guide, 235
voltage test, 225, 225f
works, 217
Battery cables, 121–122, 122f
Battery charging
AGM batteries, 229–230
procedure, 228–229
Battery Council International (BCI), 7, 221
Battery electrical drain test, 231
exists, 233
finding the source, 233
procedure, 231–232
reserve capacity, 232
Battery load test, 226–227, 227f
Battery maintenance, 224–225
Battery voltage test, 225
Baud rate, 192
Bench grinders, 37
Bench testing, 257
Bendix, 246
Binary system, 192
Bipolar transistor, 179
Blind spot monitor (BSM), 393–394, 393f
Blower motor, 75, 370–372
Bluetooth, 413–414, 414f
BNC connector, 115
Body Control Module (BCM), 301, 302f, 362

Bolts, 20, 242
Bound electrons, 55
Box-end wrench, 24
Braided ground straps, 121
Brake lights, 305
Branches, 79
Breaker bar, 25
Breakout box (BOB), 207–208f
Brush-end housing, 242
Brushes, 243
BSM. *See* Blind spot monitor (BSM)
Bulb number, 304–305, 304–305f
Bulb test, 321
Bump cap, 38
Burn in, 174
BUS, 199

C

Camera calibration, 400–401, 401f
Campaign, 13
CAN. *See* Controller area network (CAN)
Capacitance, 152
factors of, 155
Capacitor
in circuits, 156, 156f
construction and operation, 152–154, 153–154f
uses for, 155–156, 155f
Carrier wave, 405
Cathode, 173
Cathode ray tube (CRT), 111
Cells, 216
Center high-mounted stoplight (CHMSL), 178, 178f, 373
Central processing unit (CPU), 191
Channel, 114
Charging system
computer-controlled, 275–277
testing and service, 279–281, 281f
voltage drop testing, 285–286, 285f
Charging voltage test, 279
Cheater bar, 29
Chisels, 33, 33f
Chrysler Collision Detection (CCD), 203
Chrysler communications protocols, 203–205, 205f
Chrysler immobilizer systems, 341
Circuit, 64, 64f
fault types, 65–67
troubleshooting procedure, 145
Circuit breakers, 124
Circuit fault types
high resistance, 66–67
open circuits, 65
short-to-ground, 66, 67f
short-to-voltage, 65–66
Clamping diode, 174
Class 2 communication, 200
Claw poles, 269
Clean Air Act (CAA), 3
Clock generator, 191
Clockspring, 352
Clutch safety switch, 239
Code of Federal Regulations (CFR), 1
Coil, 140
Cold chisel, 33

Cold-cranking amperes (CCA), 220
Cold solder joint, 129
Collector, 179
Combination circuit, 86
Common power or ground, 144–145
Communication configuration, 199
Communication protocols, general Motors, 200–203
   class 2, 200
   entertainment and comfort (E & C), 200
   GMLAN, 201–203, 202f
   keyword, 200–201
   UART, 200
Communications and networks, 197
Commutator-end housing, 242
Commutator segments, 243
Complete circuit, 64
Composite headlights, 308
Compound circuit, 86
Compression spring, 246
Computer
   digital, 191–192, 191–192f
   functions, 189–190f, 189–191
   fundamentals, 189
   input sensors, 193
   outputs, 193–194f, 193–195
Computer-controlled charging system, 275–277
Computer-controlled starting, 239–240
Computer functions, 189–190f, 189–191
   input, 189–190
   output, 190–191
   processing, 190
   storage, 190
Computer fundamentals, 189
Computer input sensors, 193
Computer outputs, 193–195, 193–195f
   controls, 193–194
   drivers, 194
   pulse-width modulation (PWM), 194–195
Condenser, 152
Conductors, 55
   electrons move, 56–57
Conductors and resistance, 60–61
Connector, 128, 128f
Connector position assurance (CPA), 128
Continuity, 64
Control circuit test, 254
Controller, 189
Controller area network (CAN), 200, 205–206, 206f
Conventional theory, 56, 57f
Converters, 185–186, 185f
Coolant disposal, 6–7, 7f
Cores, 291
Coulomb, 57
Counter electromotive force (CEMF), 165, 241
Country of origin, 17
Courtesy lights, 316
Cranking amperes (CA), 220
Cranking circuit, 238–239
Crest, 20
Crimp-and-seal connectors, 130
Crossover, 411, 411f
Cross-traffic alert, 394
Cruise control, 372–373

D

Darlington pair, 180
Dash gauges, 330–331
Dash lights, 74
Dash warning symbols, 321–322, 322f
Daytime running lights (DRLs), 308
DC coupling, 113
DC volts (DCV), 95
Dead-blow hammer, 29
Deceleration sensors, 351
Decibel (dB), 410
Deep cycling, 221
Delta winding, 272
Department of Transportation (DOT), 376
Despiking diode. *See* Clamping diode
Dielectric, 152
Digital computer, 191–192, 191–192f
Digital display, 323
Digital multimeter (DMM), 95–99, 96–98f, 363
   AC/DC clamp-on, 100
   measuring amperes, 97–99
   measuring resistance, 95–97
   measuring voltage, 95
   steps to read, 102–105
   terminology, 95
Digital storage oscilloscope (DSO), 111
Digital volt-ohm-meter (DVOM), 95
Digit rattle, 104
Diode, 173, 173f
   light-emitting, 176–177
   photo, 177, 177f
   ratings, 176
   testing, 184–185
   zener, 174
Diode check, 100
Diodes, 269
Disabling airbags, 355
Division, 112
Doping, 171
Double cut file, 31
Double-pole, double-throw (DPDT), 139, 380
Double-pole, single-throw (DPST), 139
Drive belt inspection and adjustment, 281–282, 282f
Drive-end (DE) housing, 242, 266
Drive-on ramps, 42–43
Drive sizes, 25
Dual inline pins (DIP), 181
Dual-stage airbags, 351
Duty cycle, 101, 114, 194, 276
Dynamic cruise control, 396
Dynamic random-access, 155
Dynamic voltage, 224

E

EEPROM. *See* Electrically erasable programmable read-only memory (EEPROM)
Electric adjustable pedals (EAP), 385
Electrical conduit, 131–132
Electrical cords safety, 43
Electrical hand tool, 34–36
   digital meter, 35–36
   electrical related work, 35

soldering gun, 35
test light, 34–35
Electrical load, 64
Electrically erasable programmable read-only
    memory (EEPROM), 190
Electrical/Mechanical Issues, 380
Electrical potential, 58
Electrical power management (EPM), 275
Electrical unit prefixes, 101–102
Electricity, 53
    conductors, 55–56, 55f, 56f
    definition, 53–54
    electron shells, 55, 55f
    free and bound electrons, 55
    insulators, 56, 56f
    ions, 54, 54f
    magnets and electrical charges, 54
    positive and negative charges,
        54, 54f
    semiconductors, 56
    sources of, 59–60
    units of, 57–59
Electricity, sources of
    chemical, 60
    friction, 59
    heat, 59
    light, 59
    magnetism, 60
    pressure, 59–60
Electricity, units of
    amperes, 57, 57f
    ohms, 58, 58f
    volts, 57–58
    watt, 59
Electric power door locks, 377–380
Electrochemistry, 60
Electrolyte, 216
Electromagnetic energy, 404
Electromagnetic induction, 165–166
Electromagnetic interference (EMI),
    168–169, 169f
Electromagnetic parking sensors (EPS), 394
Electromagnetism, 160–162, 161f
    uses of, 162–164, 164f
Electromagnets, 162
Electromotive force (EMF), 58
Electronic components, failure cause
    of, 183–184
Electronic conductance test, 227–228, 228f
Electronic control assembly (ECA), 189
Electronic control module (ECM), 189
Electronic control unit (ECU)189. See also Body
    control module (BCM)
Electronic displays, 326–327
    light-emitting diode (LED), 326, 326f
    liquid crystal display (LCD), 327
    vacuum tube fluorescent (VTF),
        326–327
    WOW, 327
Electronic memory functions,
    233–235
    disconnect issues, 233–234
    maintaining memory methods, 234
    reinitialization, 234–235

Electronic serial number (ESN), 415
Electronic throttle control (ETC), 372
Electron theory, 57
Electrostatic discharge (ESD), 186–187
Elements, 53
EMI. See Electromagnetic interference (EMI)
Emitter, 179
Engine mapping, 191
Engine Stop-Start (ESS), 248
Enhanced Flooded Battery (EFB), 218
Entertainment and comfort (E & C), 200
Environmental Protection Agency (EPA), 1
EPS. See Electromagnetic parking
    sensors (EPS)
ESN. See Electronic serial number (ESN)
European BUS communicatuions, 207–208
Event data recorder (EDR), 359–360
Extensions, 25
External trigger, 114
Eye wash station, 46, 46f

F
Farads, 155
Federal and state laws
    clean air act, 3
    environmental protection agency (EPA), 1–2
    lockout/tagout, 3
    Occupational Safety and Health Act (OSHA), 1
    Resource Conservation and Recovery
        Act (RCRA), 2
    right-to-know laws, 2, 2f
Field coils, 242–243
Field-effect transistors (FETs),
    180–181, 180f
Field housing, 242
Field poles, 243
Files, 31
Fire blankets, 45
Fire extinguisher classes, 44–45, 45f
First aid kit, 46, 46f
Flat rate, 14
Floating ground system, 410
Flooded cell batteries, 219
Flooded lead acid (FLA), 218
Flux density, 159
Flux lines. See Magnetic lines of force
Fog line, 396
Ford network communications
    protocols, 203
Ford pats system, 341–342
Forward bias, 173
Four wheel drive (4WD). See Front-wheel
    drive (FWD)
Free electrons, 55
Frequency, 101, 114, 405
Frequency modulation (FM), 405, 405f
    characteristics, 406
Front-wheel drive (FWD), 16
Front-wheel drive vs rear-wheel drive, 16
Fuel safety and storage, 7–8
Fused jumper wire, 93, 93f
    uses of, 93
Fuse link. See Pacific fuse elements
Fuses, 122

Fuses and circuit protection devices,
    122–127
  blade fuses, 122
  checking fusible links and mega
    fuses, 126–127
  circuit breakers, 124–125
  construction, 122
  fuse ratings, 122
  fusible link, 125–126, 126f
  maxi fuses, 122–123, 127f
  mega fuses, 126
  mini fuses, 122
  pacific fuse element, 123
  PTC circuit protectors, 125, 126f
  replacing a fusible link, 127
Fusible link, 125–126
FWD. See Front-wheel drive (FWD)

G

Garage door opener, 388–389
Gassing, 215, 216
Gauss gauge, 147, 147f
Gear nut, 381
Gel battery, 219
General Motors antitheft system, 342–343
Germanium, 171
Glitches, 111
Global positioning system (GPS),
    331–333, 332f
Gloves, 38–39
GM local area network (GMLAN), 201
GMM. See Graphing multimeter (GMM)
Grade, 21
Graphing multimeter (GMM), 117
Graphing scan tools, 117
Graticule, 111
Grid, 215
Gross axle weight rating (GAWR), 18
Gross vehicle weight rating (GVWR), 18
Ground brushes, 244
Grounded, 66
Ground loop, 410
Ground plane, 407
Ground wires, 121
Growler, 256

H

Hacksaw, 33, 33f
Hammers, 28–29, 29f
Hand tools, 24–27
  basic list, 33–34
  electrical, 34–36
  maintenance, 36
  ratchets, sockets, and extensions,
    25–26, 26f
  safety precautions, 39–40
  safe use of sockets and ratchets,
    26–27
  safe use of wrenches, 25
  torque wrenches, 26, 27f
  wrenches, 24–25, 25f
Haptic response system, 328
Hazardous waste, 1, 6
  definition of, 1
  personal protective equipment (PPE), 1

Hazardous waste material, 1
Hazard warning, 308
Headlights, 308–309, 309f
  aiming, 314, 315f
  auto dimming, 314
  automatic, 313
  automatic dimming mirrors,
    314–316
  bulb faults, 308
  cloudy restoration, 308–309
  composite, 308
  courtesy, 316
  fog and driving, 314
  high/low beam switch, 314
  illuminated entry, 316
  LED, 312, 312f
  switches, 308
  system diagnosis, 316
Head-up display (HUD),
    324–325, 325f
Heated mirrors, 385
Heated rear window defogger,
    373–375
Heated seats, 383
  and cooled seats, 383–384
Heated steering wheel, 384
Heat shrink tubing, 129
Heat sink, 181
Hertz (Hz), 114, 405
High-efficiency particulate air (HEPA)
    vacuum, 3
High-impedance test meters, 95
High-intensity discharge (HID), 309–312, 311f
High-pass filter, 411
High resistance, 66
High-voltage spike protection, 174–176,
    175–176f
Hill start assist, 399–400, 400f
HMI. See Human-machine interface (HMI)
Hold-in winding, 247
Hole theory, 172
Honda/Toyota communicatuions, 206–207, 207f
Horns, 362–363
  diagnosis, 363–364
Hot restrike, 312
Human–machine interface (HMI), 393
Hybrid electric vehicles (HEVs), 46
  safety issues, 46–48, 47f, 48f
Hydrometer, 226

I

Ignition coils, 166–168, 168f
Ignition control module (ICM), 167
Ignition off draw (IOD), 231
Immobilizer systems, 339–341, 339f
  chrysler, 341
  testing, 343–345
Impact screwdrivers, 28
Impedance, 408–409, 409f
Impurities, 171
Induced voltage, 165, 165f
Induction, 165
Inductive ammeters, 99–100, 99f
  AC/DC clamp-on digital multimeter (DMM), 100
  operation, 99–100

Input, 189
Input conditioning, 190
Instrument panel (IP), 321
Instrument panel cluster (IPC), 323
Insulated brushes, 244
Insulators, 56
Integral sensors, 351
Integrated circuit (IC), 181
Intelligent Speed Advice (ISA), 398
International Electrotechnical Commission (IEC), 105
International Standards Organization (ISO), 140
Inverter, 186, 186f
Ion, 54
ISA. See Intelligent Speed Advice (ISA)

J

Jacks and safety stands, 42
Jumper cables, 122
Jump starting and battery safety, 43–44, 44f
Junction, 173

K

Keep-alive memory (KAM), 190
Kelvin (K), 311
Key fob, 339
Keyless entry, 386–388
Keyword communication, 200
Kilo (k), 101
Kirchhoff's current law, 79–80
Kirchhoff's voltage law, 73–74

L

Lane departure warning system (LDWS), 395, 395f
Lane keep assist (LKA), 395–396, 396f
LDWS. See Lane departure warning system (LDWS)
Lead-acid battery waste, 7
LED. See Light-emitting diode (LED)
LED headlights, 312, 312f
LED lightning, 302–304, 303–304f
LED test light, 94
Left-hand rule, 161
Legs, 79
Lenz's law, 165
Leyden jar, 152
Light-emitting diode (LED), 36, 37f, 176, 326
Lightning systems, 301–302, 302f
    diagnosis, 317–318
    symptom guide, 318
Line wrenches, 25
Liquid crystal display (LCD), 327
LKA. See Lane keep assist (LKA)
LKAS. See Lane keep assist system (LKAS)
Load, 64
Load test, 226
Lock tang, 128
Lodestone, 158
Logic probe, 95, 95f
Long-range radar (LRR), 396
Loudspeakers, 408
Lower sideband, 405
Low-pass filter, 411
Low-water-loss batteries, 215
LRR. See Long-range radar (LRR)

M

Magnetic flux. See Magnetic lines of force
Magnetic induction, 159
Magnetic lines of force, 159
Magnetism, 158
    fundamentals of, 158–160
Maintenance-free battery, 215
Maintenance indicators, 323
Mallets, 29, 29f
Marine cranking amperes (MCA), 220
Material safety data sheets (MSDS), 2
Mega (M), 101
Mercury, 10
Mesh spring, 246
Meter accuracy, 104
Meter resolution, 103
Metric bolts, 21, 23f
Metric wire gauge, 120
Milli (m), 101
Model year (MY), 17
Modulation, 405
Momentary switch, 139–140
Moon roof, 380
MOSFETs, 181
Multi-function steering wheels, 322
Multipath, 406
Multiplexing, 198
Mushroomed, 33
Mutual induction, 165

N

National Highways Traffic Safety Administration (NHTSA), 13, 400
Negative slope, 114
Negative temperature coefficient (NTC), 178
Network, 198
Network communications classifications, 199–200
Network communications diagnosis, 208–211
Network fundamentals, 197–199, 198–199f
Neutral charge, 54
Neutral safety switch, 239
NHTSA. See National Highways Traffic Safety Administration (NHTSA)
Night vision, 325–326, 326f
Node, 197
Noise, 406
Nonvolatile RAM, 190
Nonvolatile random access memory (NVRAM), 328
Normally closed (N.C.), 139
Normally open (N.O.), 139
NPN transistor, 179
N-type material, 171
Number of channels
    four, 114
    single, 114
    two, 114
Nuts, 22, 23f

O

OBD-II data link connector, 211–212, 211f
Occupant detection system (ODS), 357–359, 358f
Occupational Safety and Health Act (OSHA), 1
Offset screwdrivers, 28
Ohmmeter, 58
Ohms, 58

Ohm's law, 67–68, 68f
  applied to simple circuits, 68
  formulas, 68
OnStar, 334
Open circuit, 65, 143–144
Open circuit battery voltage test, 225
Open circuit voltage, 224
Open-end wrench, 24
Operational amplifiers (op-amps), 182, 182f
Oscilloscope, 111
Oscilloscope, types of
  display grid, 111–112, 112f
  terminology, 111
OSHA. See Occupational Safety and
    Health Act (OSHA)
Output drivers, 194
Over limit (OL), 97
Overrunning alternator dampener (OAD), 268
Overrunning alternator pulley (OAP), 267
Overrunning clutch, 246
Owner's manual, 12, 12f

P

Pacific fuse elements, 123
Parallel circuit, 79, 79f
  examples, 83–84, 83f, 84f
  Kirchhoff's current law, 79–80, 80f
  laws, 80, 80f
  total resistance, determining, 80–83,
    81f, 82f, 83f
Parallel circuit laws, 80, 80f
Parasitic load test, 231
Parking-assist system, 394–395, 394f
Partitions, 216
Passenger presence system (PPS), 357
Passive crossover, 411
Pasting, 215
Peak inverse voltage (PIV), 176
Peak reverse voltage (PRV), 176
Peltier effect, 59
Permanently Engaged (PE) Starter, 249
Permanent magnet (PM), 328, 380
Permeability, 159
Personal protective equipment (PPE),
    38–39
Phillips screwdriver, 27–28, 28f
Phosphor, 326
Photodiodes, 177, 177f
Photoelectricity, 59
Photons, 177
Photoresistor, 177, 177f
Phototransistor, 181
Piezoelectricity, 60
Pinch weld seam, 41
Pin punch, 33
Pitch, 20, 21f
Pliers, 30–33
  diagonal, 30, 31f
  linesman, 30, 30f
  locking, 31, 31f
  multigroove adjustable, 30, 30f
  needle-nose, 31, 31f
  safe use of, 31
  slip-joint, 30, 30f
  snap-ring, 31, 32f

PNP transistor, 179
Polarity, 165
Poles, 139, 159
Pole shoes, 243
Porous lead, 215
Positive slope, 114
Positive temperature coefficient (PTC), 61
Positive temperature coefficient (PTC) circuit
    protectors, 125
Potentiometer, 62
Powerline capacitor, 412, 412f, 412t, 413f
Power path, 64
Power seat, 381–383
Power source, 64
Powertrain control module (PCM),
    189, 372
Power windows, 375–377
Pre-collision system, 399, 399f
Pretensioner, 347
Primary winding, 166
Primary wire, 120
Programmable controller interface (PCI), 205
Programmable read-only memory (PROM), 190
Protection, 64
Protocol, 199
P-type material, 172
Puddle lights, 316
Pull-in winding, 247
Pulse train, 114
  definition, 114
  duty cycle, 114
  frequency, 114
  pulse width, 114
Pulse width, 114
Pulse-width modulated (PWM), 114,
    184, 194
Pulse wipers, 365. See also Variable-delay wipers
Punches, 33, 33f
PWM. See Pulse-width modulation (PWM)

R

Radar calibration, 401–402, 402f
Radar cruise control, 396, 397, 397f
Radio choke, 416
Radio frequency (RF), 405
Radio Frequency Identification (RFID), 339
Radio-frequency interference (RFI), 168
Radio interference, 415, 416f
  audio noise, 416–417, 417f, 417t
  braided ground wire, 416
  capacitor usage, 415–416, 416f
  radio choke, 416
Radio waves, 404, 405f
Radio wave transmission, 405, 405f
Rainsense module (RSM), 369
Rain-sense wipers, 369–370
RAM. See Random-access memory (RAM)
Random-access memory (RAM), 190
Range, 95
Ratchet, 25
RCTW. See Rear cross-traffic warning (RCTW)
Read-only memory (ROM), 190
Rear cross-traffic warning (RCTW),
    398, 398f
Rear-wheel drive (RWD), 16

Recall, 13
Recombinant battery, 219
Rectifier, 270
Rectifier bridge, 178–179, 179f
Rectifier, testing, 290
Regular production order (RPO), 400
Relative motion, 165
Relay, 140, 162
Relay terminal identification, 140–143,
    141–143f
Reluctance, 160
Remote keyless entry (RKE), 339
Remote start, 389
Remote vehicle start (RVS), 240
Repair order (RO). See Work order
Reserve capacity, 220
Residual magnetism, 159
Resistance, 58
Resistors, 61–62, 62f
    fixed, 61
    variable, 62
Resource Conservation and Recovery
    Act (RCRA), 2
Retained accessory power (RAP), 375
Return path (ground), 64
Reverse bias, 173
Rheostat, 62
Right-to-know laws, 2
Ring link networks, 199
RMS, 412
ROM. See Read-only memory (ROM)
Rootmean-square (RMS), 103
Rosin-core solder, 129, 129f
RPO. See Regular production order (RPO)
RWD. See Rear-wheel drive (RWD)

S

SAE. See Society of Automotive Engineers (SAE)
Safety
    electrical cord, 43
    jump starting and battery, 43–44, 44f
Safety belts and retractors, 347–348, 348f
Safety data sheets (SDS), 2
Safety lifting (hoisting) a vehicle, 40–42, 41f, 42f
Satellite Digital Audio Radio Services (SDARS), 414, 415f
Schematic symbols, 135–140
    battery, 135
    boxed components, 138
    capacitors, 138
    electrical components, 137
    electric heated unit, 138
    electric motors, 137
    momentary switch, 139–140
    resistors, 137–138
    separate replaceable part, 139
    switches, 139
    wiring, 135–137
Scope setup and adjustments, 112–113
Screwdriver, 27
    hammers and mallets, 28–29, 29f
    impact, 28
    offset, 28
    phillips, 27–28, 28f
    safe use of, 28
    straight blade, 27, 28f

SDARS. See Satellite Digital Audio Radio
    Services (SDARS)
Sealed lead-acid (SLA). See Sealed
    valve-regulated (SVR)
Sealed valve-regulated (SVR), 219
Secondary winding, 166
Sediment chamber, 214
Self-parking, 395, 395f
Semiconductor, 56
    summary, 172
Semiconductors, 171
Sentry Key Immobilizer System (SKIS), 341
Serial communications interface (SCI), 205
Serial data, 198
Series circuit, 72
    examples, 76–77, 76f
    Kirchhoff's voltage law, 73–74
    laws, 75–76
    Ohm's law and, 72–73, 73f
    voltage drops, 74–75
Series circuit laws, 75–76
Series–parallel circuits, 86–87, 86f
    calculation problems, solving, 87
    definition, 86
    examples, 87–88, 87f, 88f
    faults, 86–87
    types, 86
Service information, 13
    aftermarket, 13
    factory, 13
    purpose of, 13
Service manuals, 13
Service records, 14–15
Shims, 257
Short circuit, 145–148, 148f
Shorted. See Short-to-voltage
Short-to-ground, 66, 67f
Short-to-voltage, 65
Shunts, 79
Sideband operation, 405
Silicon, 171
Silicon-controlled rectifier (SCR),
    178, 178f
Single cut file, 31
Single-pole, double-throw (SPDT), 139
Single-pole, single-throw (SPST), 139
Singlewire CAN (SWCAN), 201
Sirius/XM radio, 414
Slip-joint pliers, 30
Slip-ring-end (SRE) housing, 266
Snips, 31
Society of Automotive Engineers (SAE),
    189, 199, 266
Socket, 25
    extensions, 25
    universal joints, 25
Socket adapter, 29
Solvent(s), 4, 5–6
    effects of chemical poisoning, 5–6
    hazardous solvents and regulatory
        status, 6
    used, 6
Sound. See Acoustical energy
Speakers, 408–410, 409f
    types, 410

Special service tools (SSTs), 16, 36
Specific gravity, 217
Speedometers/odometers, 328–330, 329f
Spike protection resistor, 175
Splice pack, 199
Sponge lead, 215
Spontaneous combustion, 40
Sport utility vehicles (SUVs), 364
Squib, 349
Standard corporate protocol (SCP), 203
Star link networks, 199
Starter amperage test, 254–255, 254f
Starter drive, 245
Starter motor
    drives, 245–247, 246f
    drive-to-flywheel clearance, 257–258, 258f
    gear-reduction, 245, 245f
    installation, 257
    operation, 240–242
    removal, 255
    service, 255–257, 256f
    solenoids, 247–248, 247f
    symptom guide, 259
    works, 242–245
Starter motor operation, 240–242
    compound, 242
    permanent magnet, 242
    series, 241
    shunt, 241–242
Starter solenoid, 247
Starting, lighting, and ignition (SLI), 214
Starting system troubleshooting procedure, 251–252
State of health (SOH), 209
Static electricity, 59
Stator, 269
Steering wheel controls, 322, 323f
Stepper motor, 324, 328
Step-up transformer, 166
Stiffening capacitor, 412
Stop-start systems, 248–249
Straight blade screwdriver, 27, 28f
Stud, 20
Subwoofer, 410
Sulfated battery, 219
Sun roof, 380
Sun shades, 380–381
Supplemental air restraints (SAR), 349
Supplemental inflatable restraints (SIR), 349
Supplemental restraint system (SRS), 349
Suppression diode. See Clamping diode

T
Tandem Solenoid (TS) Starter, 248
Technical service bulletin (TSB), 13
Telematics, 333–334
Telltale lights, 321
Tensile strength, 22
Terminal, 128, 128f, 135
Terminating resistors, 209
Terminology, 134
Testing AC ripple current, 284, 284f
Test light, 94, 94f
    high-impedance, 94
    nonpowered, 94
    uses of A 12 volt, 94

Thermistor, 178, 178f, 274, 384
Thermocouple, 59
Thermoelectric device (TED), 383
Thermoelectricity, 59
Thin-film-transistor (TFT), 327
Threaded fasteners, 20–24
    bolts and threads, 20
    fractional bolts, 20
    grades of bolts, 21–22
    metric bolts, 21, 23f
    nuts, 22–23, 23f
    tensile strength, 22
    washers, 23–24, 23f
Three-minute charge test, 226
Threshold voltage, 180
Throws, 139
Time base, 112, 112t
Tone generator tester, 148
Tool sets and accessories, 34
Torx, 29–30
Total circuit resistance (RT), 81
Total harmonic distortion (THD), 412
Touch screen, 327–328
Trade number, 304
Transceiver, 339
Transistor, 179
    testing, 184–185
Transistor gate, 182, 182f
Transponder, 339
Trigger level, 114
Trigger slope, 114–115
Trouble light, 36
    fluorescent, 36
    incandescent, 36
    LED, 36, 37f
Troubleshooting
    circuit procedure, 145
    electrical guide, 148–149
    step-by-step procedure, 149–150
Troxler effect, 316
Turn signals, 305–308, 307f
    BCM-controlled, 306
    bulb outage warning, 306–308
    hazard warning lights, 308
    mechanical system operation, 305–306
Turns ratio, 167
Tweeter, 410
Twisted pair, 121, 197, 202

U
UART-based protocol (UBP), 203
Ultrasonic object sensors, 394
Underground storage tank (UST), 5
Unified national coarse (UNC), 20
Unified national fine (UNF), 20
Universal asynchronous receive and transmit (UART), 200
Universal joints, 25
Used brake fluid, 4, 4f
Used Oil, 4–5
Used tire disposal, 8
Utility knife, 32, 32f

V
Vacuum tube fluorescent (VTF), 326–327
Valence ring, 55

Valve-regulated lead–acid (VRLA), 219
Variable-delay wipers, 365
VECI. *See* Vehicle emissions control information (VECI)
Vehicle
  identification, 16–17, 17f
  parts, 16, 16f
  protection, 40
  safety certification label, 18
  safety lifting (hoisting), 40–42, 41f, 42f
  VECI label, 18, 18f
Vehicle Antitheft System (VATS), 342
Vehicle emissions control information (VECI), 18, 18f
Vehicle identification number (VIN), 14, 17, 400
Vehicle protection, 40
  fender covers, 40
  interior, 40
Vehicle security systems, 338–339, 338f
VIN. *See* Vehicle identification number (VIN);
  Vehicle identification number (VIN)
Virtual display, 327
Voice activation, 322–323
Voice recognition, 413, 413f
Voltage drops, 74, 252
  circuits, used in, 74–75
  testing method, 75, 252–254, 253–254f
Voltage drops testing method, 252–254, 253–254f
Voltmeter, 58

W

Washers, 23
Waste chart, 9

Water leaks, 380
Watt, 59
Watt's law, 69–70
  background, 69
  formulas, 69
  magic circle, 69–70, 70f
Window regulator, 375
Windshield washers, 366–369
Windshield wipers, 364–366
Wire repair, 129–131
Wire size, 134–135
Wiring schematic, 134
Wiring schematic symbols,
  134–135
  circuit information, 134
Woofer. *See* Subwoofer
Work order, 14
  labor time documentation, 14
  parts documentation, 14
  service advisor documentation, 14
  service technician documentation, 14
Workplace Hazardous Materials Information
  Systems (WHMIS)., 2
WOW display, 327
Wrenches, 23

X

Xenon headlights, 309

Z

Zener diode, 174